CSR and Socially Responsible Investing Strategies in Transitioning and Emerging Economies

Anetta Kuna-Marszałek
University of Łódź, Poland

Agnieszka Kłysik-Uryszek
University of Łódź, Poland

A volume in the Advances in Business Strategy and Competitive Advantage (ABSCA) Book Series

IGI Global
DISSEMINATOR OF KNOWLEDGE

Published in the United States of America by
IGI Global
Business Science Reference (an imprint of IGI Global)
701 E. Chocolate Avenue
Hershey PA, USA 17033
Tel: 717-533-8845
Fax: 717-533-8661
E-mail: cust@igi-global.com
Web site: http://www.igi-global.com

Copyright © 2020 by IGI Global. All rights reserved. No part of this publication may be reproduced, stored or distributed in any form or by any means, electronic or mechanical, including photocopying, without written permission from the publisher. Product or company names used in this set are for identification purposes only. Inclusion of the names of the products or companies does not indicate a claim of ownership by IGI Global of the trademark or registered trademark.

Library of Congress Cataloging-in-Publication Data

Names: Kuna-Marszałek, Anetta, editor. | Kłysik-Uryszek, Agnieszka, 1978- editor.
Title: CSR and socially responsible investing strategies in transitioning and emerging economies / Anetta Kuna-Marszałek and Agnieszka Kłysik-Uryszek, editors.
Description: Hershey : Business Science Reference, 2020. | Includes bibliographical references and index. | Summary: “”This book identifies the scale and scope of implementation of CSR and socially responsible investing strategies and standards in companies operating in different transition and emerging economies as well as assessing the global effects of these activities”--Provided by publisher”-- Provided by publisher.
Identifiers: LCCN 2019037798 (print) | LCCN 2019037799 (ebook) | ISBN 9781799821939 (hardcover) | ISBN 9781799821946 (paperback) | ISBN 9781799821953 (ebook)
Subjects: LCSH: Social responsibility of business--Developing countries. | Investments--Moral and ethical aspects--Developing countries. | Business ethics.
Classification: LCC HD60.5.D44 .C35 2020 (print) | LCC HD60.5.D44 (ebook) | DDC 658.4/08--dc23
LC record available at https://lccn.loc.gov/2019037798
LC ebook record available at https://lccn.loc.gov/2019037799

This book is published in the IGI Global book series Advances in Business Strategy and Competitive Advantage (ABSCA) (ISSN: 2327-3429; eISSN: 2327-3437)

British Cataloguing in Publication Data
A Cataloguing in Publication record for this book is available from the British Library.

All work contributed to this book is new, previously-unpublished material. The views expressed in this book are those of the authors, but not necessarily of the publisher.

For electronic access to this publication, please contact: eresources@igi-global.com.

Advances in Business Strategy and Competitive Advantage (ABSCA) Book Series

Patricia Ordóñez de Pablos
Universidad de Oviedo, Spain

ISSN:2327-3429
EISSN:2327-3437

Mission

Business entities are constantly seeking new ways through which to gain advantage over their competitors and strengthen their position within the business environment. With competition at an all-time high due to technological advancements allowing for competition on a global scale, firms continue to seek new ways through which to improve and strengthen their business processes, procedures, and profitability.

The **Advances in Business Strategy and Competitive Advantage (ABSCA) Book Series** is a timely series responding to the high demand for state-of-the-art research on how business strategies are created, implemented and re-designed to meet the demands of globalized competitive markets. With a focus on local and global challenges, business opportunities and the needs of society, the **ABSCA** encourages scientific discourse on doing business and managing information technologies for the creation of sustainable competitive advantage.

Coverage

- Foreign Investment Decision Process
- Economies of Scale
- Differentiation Strategy
- Adaptive Enterprise
- Value Chain
- Balanced Scorecard
- Strategy Performance Management
- Value Creation
- Small and Medium Enterprises
- Strategic alliances

IGI Global is currently accepting manuscripts for publication within this series. To submit a proposal for a volume in this series, please contact our Acquisition Editors at Acquisitions@igi-global.com or visit: http://www.igi-global.com/publish/.

The Advances in Business Strategy and Competitive Advantage (ABSCA) Book Series (ISSN 2327-3429) is published by IGI Global, 701 E. Chocolate Avenue, Hershey, PA 17033-1240, USA, www.igi-global.com. This series is composed of titles available for purchase individually; each title is edited to be contextually exclusive from any other title within the series. For pricing and ordering information please visit http://www.igi-global.com/book-series/advances-business-strategy-competitive-advantage/73672. Postmaster: Send all address changes to above address. Copyright © 2020 IGI Global. All rights, including translation in other languages reserved by the publisher. No part of this series may be reproduced or used in any form or by any means – graphics, electronic, or mechanical, including photocopying, recording, taping, or information and retrieval systems – without written permission from the publisher, except for non commercial, educational use, including classroom teaching purposes. The views expressed in this series are those of the authors, but not necessarily of IGI Global.

Titles in this Series

For a list of additional titles in this series, please visit: www.igi-global.com/book-series

Handbook of Research on the Strategic Management of Family Businesses
Jesús Manuel Palma-Ruiz (Autonomous University of Chihuahua, Mexico) Ismael Barros-Contreras (Austral University of Chile, Chile) and Luca Gnan (Tor Vergata University, Italy)
Business Science Reference • ©2020 • 350pp • H/C (ISBN: 9781799822691) • US $275.00

Utilizing Gamification in Servicescapes for Improved Consumer Engagement
Miralem Helmefalk (Linnaeus University, Sweden) and Leif Marcusson (Linnaeus University, Sweden)
Business Science Reference • ©2020 • 300pp • H/C (ISBN: 9781799819707) • US $225.00

Cases on Strategic Management Issues in Contemporary Organizations
Mona Rashidirad (University of Brighton, UK)
Business Science Reference • ©2020 • 300pp • H/C (ISBN: 9781799816300) • US $195.00

Competitive Drivers for Improving Future Business Performance
Carlos Martins (Lusiada University - North, Portugal) and Paula Rodrigues (Lusiada University - North, Portugal)
Business Science Reference • ©2020 • 360pp • H/C (ISBN: 9781799818434) • US $225.00

Handbook of Research on Approaches to Alternative Entrepreneurship Opportunities
José Guilherme Leitão Dantas (CARME, School of Technology and Management, Polytechnic of Leiria, Portugal) and Luísa Cagica Carvalho (University of Évora, Portugal)
Business Science Reference • ©2020 • 450pp • H/C (ISBN: 9781799819813) • US $295.00

Challenges and Opportunities of Corporate Governance Transformation in the Digital Era
Mikhail Yevgenievich Kuznetsov (Moscow State University, Russia) and Maria Igorevna Nikishova (Financial University Under the Government of the Russian Federation, Russia)
Business Science Reference • ©2020 • 230pp • H/C (ISBN: 9781799820116) • US $235.00

Senior Entrepreneurship and Aging in Modern Business
José Manuel Saiz-Álvarez (EGADE Business School, Tecnologico de Monterrey, Mexico & Mexican Academy of Sciences, Mexico) and Jorge Alberto Gámez-Gutiérrez (Uniagustiniana, Colombia)
Business Science Reference • ©2020 • 372pp • H/C (ISBN: 9781799820192) • US $235.00

IGI Global
DISSEMINATOR OF KNOWLEDGE

701 East Chocolate Avenue, Hershey, PA 17033, USA
Tel: 717-533-8845 x100 • Fax: 717-533-8661
E-Mail: cust@igi-global.com • www.igi-global.com

EDITORIAL ADVISORY BOARD

Hamit Can, *Technical University of Sofia, Bulgaria*
Raluca Clipa, *Alexandru Ioan Cuza University of Iasi, Romania*
Dan-Cristian Dabija, *Babeş-Bolyai University, Cluj-Napoca, Romania*
Tomasz Dorożyński, *University of Łódź, Poland*
Magdalena Godek-Brunel, *ESTRI School for International Careers of UCLY, France*
Szabolcs Nagy, *University of Miscolc, Hungary*
Agata Rudnicka-Reichel, *University of Łódź, Poland*

LIST OF REVIEWERS

George K. Amoako, *Central University, Ghana*
Ekaterina Arabska, *University of Agribusiness and Rural Development, Bulgaria*
Hristina Vilhelm Blagoycheva, *University of Economics, Varna, Bulgaria*
Dmitry Burakov, *Moscow State Institute of International Relations, Russia*
Mark Anthony Camilleri, *University of Malta, Malta*
Hamit Can, *Technical University of Sofia, Bulgaria*
Burak Çapraz, *Ege University, Turkey*
Raluca Clipa, *Alexandru Ioan Cuza University of Iaşi, Romania*
Dan Cristian Dabija, *Babeş-Bolyai University, Romania*
Pavlina Dimitrova, *University of Agribusiness and Rural Development, Bulgaria*
Nikolay Todorov Dolchinkov, *National Military University, Bulgaria & National Research University MPEI, Russia*
Tomasz Dorożyński, *University of Łódź, Poland*
Vilma Kazlauskiene, *Vytautas Magnus University, Lithuania*
Ayesha Khatun, *Lovely Professional University, India*
Özge Korkmaz, *Bayburt University, Turkey*
Remya Lathabhavan, *VIT University, India*
Olga Melitonyan, *National Research University Higher School of Economics, Russia*
Szabolcs Nagy, *University of Miscolc, Hungary*
Cornelia Philipova, *University of Economics, Varna, Bulgaria*
Agata Rudnicka-Reichel, *University of Łódź, Poland*
Tomasz Uryszek, *University of Łódź, Poland*

Table of Contents

Detailed Table of Contents

The processes accompanying state social policy over recent decades as well as their contradictory impact on the sustainable development of the society are one of the fundamental problems of our time. Nowadays, there are still no clear solutions to the debate how to alleviate some of the fundamental problems like environmental pollution, poverty, aged population, income inequality, social exclusion, etc. This chapter aims to show how multinational corporations (MNCs) take the role to solve these issues following some corporate social responsibility (CSR) policies. In this way, they offer a means by which the current CSR model can be used more effectively to achieve these sustainable development targets. The structure of the chapter is organized as follows: Section 2 presents an evolution while Section 3 provides a summary of some contemporary views of CSR. Section 4 describes the way in which CSR is used as a sustainable development tool.

Corporate social responsibility (CSR) attributes economic, legal, social, and philanthropic responsibilities within the corporate sector. Sustainable financial social responsibility is primarily addressed by socially responsible investment (SRI). This chapter addresses the concepts of CSR and SRI in emerging markets and the developing world with special attention to top-down and bottom-up approaches. Theoretical descriptions discuss the human constituents of responsibility and the international emergence of CSR, with special attention to multi-stakeholder partnerships. The rise of SRI in the international arena in the wake of stakeholder activism and intrinsic socio-psychological motives are outlined. Recommendations target ingraining social responsibility in economic systems by global governance, multi-stakeholder management, and governmental assistance of the implementation and administration of corporate and financial social responsibility.

It has already been proven that digitization creates economic growth. But a key factor for the future of society is its perception from the social point of view. Digitization leads to changes that will inevitably affect aggregate demand, employment, and labor costs. Therefore, the purpose of this chapter is to investigate how the digitization interacts with the corporate social responsibility to increase the positive effects over the society. Corporate social responsibility is the sphere that implements the non-economic aspects of the digitization. But before its full deployment, there are still a number of obstacles. Numerous studies have shown that digitization can provide tools to facilitate the socially responsible activities. At the same time, it can also serve as a push for corporate social responsibility, as the formation of a socially conscious market leads to socially committed employees and to increasing their demands on the social responsibility of the business.

This chapter examines the extent to which corporate social responsibility (CSR) could generate and boost better brand perceptions and improve competitive advantage within some selected banks in Ghana. The concept of CSR, brand perception, and competitive advantage are discussed in relation to findings from a study that was conducted at the national headquarters of GCB Bank and Barclays Bank Limited in Accra. The results showed a good understanding of the concept of CSR from both customers and employees of both banks. There was a significant and positive connection between effective implementation of CSR initiatives, brand perception, and competitive advantage. CSR was discovered as a tool for business success in the banking sector in Ghana. This chapter explains the benefits of CSR activities to the development of impalpable organizational assets, and as a result, generating better results for banking institutions in Ghana. The authors make a case for the inclusion and active involvement of customers and employees in the CSR initiatives of banks in order to boost brand perception.

The purpose of the chapter is to present results of case studies of socially responsible initiatives and their communication inside and outside the organizations through the official websites impacting their performance and image, as well as to make recommendations for improvements. Investigations focus on forms and goals of initiatives taken by companies in Bulgaria, including examples of the influence of foreign corporate practice and experience. Theoretical and practical basis and trends, international framework, and national institutional positions and support to corporate social responsibility are discussed. Socially responsible activities are analyzed through the official websites in their short- and long-term aspects and links to sustainable development initiatives. Main CSR principles are defined, and a model is proposed containing the main steps of incorporating CSR strategies in companies and linking all that to business communications and public relations. A special focus is put on capacity building and CSR teams.

The economy ecologization process should take into account the development needs of each nation by developing effective systems of production and consumption. That is why in the system of measures ensuring the transition to a "green" economy, overcoming poverty and expanding the livelihoods of the most vulnerable sections of society should be a priority. At the same time, the convergence of economic and environmental policies, where prospects for economic growth are at the forefront, avoiding stress on nature resulting in unpredictable and qualitative implications for natural resources is important. Today, with resource constraints and harmful emissions, the main problem lies in the complete elimination of reliance on economic growth materials and energy resource use, which involves the identification of opportunities to increase the efficiency of the material sectors of the economy.

Energy is considered the main input for economic and industrial development. In this context, it is important that countries develop sustainable energy policies in order to meet economic growth and energy demand. Government policies play a critical role in economic growth and incentives for innovation. This chapter summarizes Bulgaria's energy policies as an increasingly important energy transit country due to its strategic location. These policies were presented in line with the European Union energy policies and the solutions of the characteristics of the country. Some of the targets to be implemented are as follows: ensuring energy supply security, achieving RES share targets, energy efficiency improvements, development of a competitive energy market, safe energy needs and protection of consumers, establishment of the necessary infrastructure and diversification of energy resources, strengthening the external relations and solidarity coordinated in the field of energy.

This chapter focuses on identifying motivation for socially responsible behavior in small and medium enterprises (SMEs) in Russia. It also investigates the attitudes of owners and executives of Russian SMEs toward the concepts of business ethics and social responsibility of business. A research set the background of this chapter, including the gathering of primary data through 57 focused interviews. Results of a critical analysis conclude that top managers and owners of Russian SMEs do not thoroughly understand these concepts. However, it also shows that they do not neglect them. Research findings point

Preface

Responsible entrepreneurship has become one of the most important enterprises' activities. Corporate social responsibility (CSR) and socially responsible investing (SRI) treated as a voluntary inclusion of the needs of stakeholders in the company's strategy are more and more recognizable concepts in the modern economy. They are usually believed to concern the biggest transnational companies, which have already grown their business to the point where they can give back to society. But recently they started to refer also to the small and medium firms. Often enterprises from the very beginning start to take into account environmental protection or local community activities in their strategies, assuming that it will help them to boost the brand and build good relations with stakeholders.

The idea of responsible entrepreneurship refers to issues raised in many different fields of science, e.g., economics, management, law or ethics, and philosophy. It had a significant impact on the development of theories such as Social Responsiveness, or Corporate Social Performance, which emphasize the appropriate behavior patterns, mechanisms, structures, and procedures to respond to the expectations of stakeholders in the right way. In addition, other acronyms more and more often highlight the areas of interest of researchers related to the concept of responding business, such as CSI (*corporate social investment, corporate social integration, corporate social innovation*), CSD (*corporate social development*), CSO (*corporate social opportunity*), CSE (*corporate social entrepreneurship*) etc. In other words, the concept of responsible entrepreneurship can be treated in an interdisciplinary and multidimensional way.

In today's world, an active commitment to, e.g., social responsibility, has been becoming more common for a company. Carefully planned responsible entrepreneurship behaviors (like CSR, SRI, etc.) are equally valuable for a company and the community. It entails, on the one hand, that investors must bear the consequences of their decisions and actions and, on the other, that they should take into account the specific needs of people, social organizations, and economic entities operating in their environment and on the local market. Implementation of the CSR and SRI concepts can also help to forge a stronger bond between employees and the corporation; they can boost morale and can help both employees and employers feel more connected with the world around them. Moreover, the growing importance of this concept results from the fact that it is perceived as an effective tool for increasing competitiveness, improving the image of the company or contributing to the generation of higher profits.

The main research goal of the book is to identify the scale and scope of implementation of CSR and SRI strategies and standards in companies operating in different transition and emerging economies as well as assessing the global effects of these activities. It is essential to know how MNEs behave in the area of social responsibility on host markets as well as to assess how local companies respond to these strategies and all in all – how local clients and stakeholders perceive the social duties and responsibilities of enterprises.

The research cope of the book are focused on, but not limited to, the following key subjects: responsible entrepreneurship, responsible investing, social investment from the perspective of transition and emerging economies. The book provides an in-depth insight into socially responsible business strategies, their impact on the company's performance as well as global wellbeing of the society. Apart from that, it will also deliver a set of "best practices", ready to use in companies.

Until now, CSR and SRI concepts have been widely discussed in the literature and the debate among scholars of different disciplines. This discussion has produced a rich set of contributions, especially in highly developed countries, but much less in developing and emerging countries. It is also worth stressing that in the last decade, studies of responsible entrepreneurship have merged with those on sustainable development of the company what other authors sometimes forget. This book will be able to fill this gap, because it will contribute to debates over "holistic development" of a firm, paying particular attention to the importance of implementing CSR or/and SRI ideas into business philosophy.

Our book consists of 2 sections and 14 chapters. The first section (Chapters 1-7) is dedicated to "Corporate Social Responsibility and Socially Responsible Investing Strategies: Practices in the Context of Sustainable Development," the second section (Chapters 8-14) analysis the processes and mechanisms of "Value Creation Through Responsible Business and Socially Responsible Investing Strategies."

In the first chapter, Cornelia Philipova from University of Economics – Varna (Bulgaria) underlines that the processes accompanying state social policy over recent decades as well as their contradictory impact on the sustainable development of the society are one of the fundamental contemporary problems. Nowadays, there are still no clear solutions to the debate on how to alleviate some of the significant problems like environmental pollution, poverty, aged population, income inequality, social exclusion, etc. Her chapter, "Corporate Social Responsibility: Business Contribution to Sustainable Development", aims to show how multinational corporations take the role to solve these issues following some CSR policies. She argues that the current CSR model can be used more effectively to achieve these sustainable development targets.

Next chapter, "Corporate and Financial Social Leadership in Emerging Markets and the Developing World", by Julia M. Puaschunder from The New School, The Schwartz Center for Economic Policy Analysis, Columbia University and Graduate School of Arts and Sciences, (USA) addresses the concepts of CSR and SRI in emerging markets and the developing world with special attention to top-down and bottom-up approaches. Theoretical descriptions discuss the human constituents of responsibility and the international emergence of CSR, with special attention to multi-stakeholder partnerships. The rise of SRI in the international arena in the wake of stakeholder activism and intrinsic socio-psychological motives are outlined. Recommendations target ingraining social responsibility in economic systems by global governance, multi-stakeholder management, and governmental assistance of the implementation and administration of corporate and financial social responsibility. She argues that future research must attribute the newly defined role of social responsibility in the interplay of public and private actors, given concurrent anti-globalization trends.

Third Author, Hristina Blagoycheva from University of Economics – Varna (Bulgaria) focuses on a slightly different perspective. In the chapter entitled "The Digitization as a Stimulus for Corporate Social Responsibility", she starts with the statement that it has already been proved that the digitization creates economic growth. But she points out that a key factor for the future of society is its perception from the social point of view. Digitization leads to changes that will inevitably affect aggregate demand, employment, and labor costs. Therefore, the purpose of the chapter is to investigate how the digitization interacts with the corporate social responsibility to increase the positive effects over the society.

The author argues that CSR is the sphere that implements the non-economic aspects of the digitization. But before its full deployment, there are still a number of obstacles. Numerous studies have shown that digitization can provide tools to facilitate socially responsible activities. At the same time, it can also serve as a push for CSR, as the formation of a socially conscious market leads to socially committed employees and to increasing their demands on the social responsibility of the business.

Ayesha Khatun and Sajad Nabi Dar from Lovely Professional University (India) in "Corporate Social Responsibility in Emerging Economies: A Study With Special Reference to India" bring us closer to the Indian perspective. India, a developing and the second largest populated country in the world, is characterized by many burning issues like unemployment, low literacy, lack of modern medical facilities mainly in rural areas, lack of connectivity of the rural areas with the mainland cities and the like. Authors highlight that although the government has been working on all these issues and has been very much successful, the government alone can not solve all these problems in such a vast populated country. Amidst such situation it is the business sector that can play a more significant role in the all-round development of the society through its CSR initiatives. This chapter attempts to study corporate social responsibility, its role and issues in a developing country with special reference to India. The findings show that lack of understanding, inadequately trained personnel, lack of proper policy making, lack of participation of the local people and so on affects the reach and effectiveness of CSR programs in India.

The purpose of the fifth chapter entitled "Communicating Socially Responsible Initiatives: New Incentives to Sustainable Development" by Ekaterina Arabska from University of Agribusiness and Rural Development (Bulgaria) is to present results of case studies of socially responsible initiatives and their communication inside and outside the organizations through the official websites as well as to make recommendations for improvements. Investigations are directed towards forms and goals of initiatives taken by companies in Bulgaria, including examples of the influence of international corporates' practice and experience. Theoretical and practical basis and trends, international framework, and national institutional positions and support to corporate social responsibility are discussed. The author finds out and defines the main CSR principles of companies operating on the Bulgarian market as well as proposes a model explaining and enumerating the main steps of incorporating CSR strategies in companies and linking all that to business communications and public relations.

In the sixth chapter, "The Challenges of Green Growth in Armenia", Susanna Aghajanyan and Gagik Aghajanyan from Armenian State University of Economics, highlight that the process of economy ecologization should take into account the development needs of each nation by developing effective systems of production and consumption. That is why – in their opinion – in the system of measures ensuring the transition to a green economy, overcoming poverty and expanding the livelihoods of the most vulnerable sections of society should be a priority. At the same time, the convergence of economic and environmental policies, where prospects for economic growth are at the forefront, avoiding stress on nature resulting in unpredictable and qualitative implications for natural resources is important. Today, with resource constraints and harmful emissions, the main problem lies in the complete elimination of reliance on economic growth materials and energy resource use, which involves the identification of opportunities to increase the efficiency of the material sectors of the economy.

Hamit Can and Daniela Minkovska representing Technical University of Sofia (Bulgaria) in their chapter "The Energy Policy of Bulgaria" focus on the fact that energy is considered to be the main input for economic and industrial development, and in this context, countries (and governments) must develop sustainable energy policies in order to meet economic growth and energy demand. Their chapter summarizes Bulgaria's energy policies in the context of the country's strategic location. Due to the specific location advantages, Bulgaria may become an important energy transit country. Therefore an appropriate energy policies relevant to characteristics of the country and corresponding with the European Union energy policies play a crucial role. Authors outline that targets to be implemented are as follows: ensuring energy supply security, developing a competitive energy market, satisfying energy needs and protection of consumers, developing the necessary infrastructure and diversifying energy resources, strengthening the external relations and solidarity coordinated in the field of energy.

Chapter 8, starting the second section of a book, by Olga Melitonyan from National Research University Higher School of Economics (Russia), Bela Bataeva from Finance University under the Government of Russian Federation, and Liudmila Cheglakova from National Research University Higher School of Economics (Russia), focuses on identifying motivation for socially responsible behavior in small and medium enterprises (SMEs) in Russia. It also investigates the attitudes of owners and executives of Russian SMEs toward the concepts of business ethics and social responsibility of business. A research is set on 57 focused interviews. Results of a critical analysis conclude that top managers and owners of Russian SMEs do not thoroughly understand these concepts. However, it also shows that they do not neglect them. Research findings point to a growing level of adherence to the principles of business ethics and responsible behavior. There is strong evidence showing motivation for following principles of ethical and responsible behavior. In addition to an understanding of legal requirements, company owners and top managers are finding that positive relationships between firms and stakeholders are crucial for sustainable performance.

The next chapter, entitled "The Market for Socially Responsible Investments: A Review and Evaluation" by Mark Anthony Camilleri from University of Malta (Malta) explains how SRI concept has evolved in the last few decades and sheds light on its latest developments. It describes different forms of SRI in the financial markets; and deliberates on the rationale for the utilization of positive and negative screenings of listed businesses and public organizations. It also presents a key theoretical underpinnings on the subject, and reports that the market for the responsible investments has recently led to an increase in contractors, non-governmental organizations and research firms who are involved in the scrutinization of the enterprises' environmental, social and governance credentials. This contribution raises awareness on the screenings of positive impact and sustainable investments. It puts forward future research avenues in this promising field of study.

The chapter "Green Investment Financing Instruments" by Vilma Kazlauskiene from Vytautas Magnus University (Lithuania) and Aura Draksaite from Kaunas University of Technology (Lithuania), is aimed to analyze the peculiarities of modern green financing instruments. The authors spot that rapid development of these instruments markets prompts the need to comprehend the main factors behind it, and thus the necessity to recognize opportunities to profit by the occasion. Therefore, in the chapter, such green financial instruments as green bonds, green equities, and green loans are discussed. Also, private green investment promotion instruments are overviewed. Moreover, the authors present and discuss current green financial instrument market development trends and the main contributing factors, as well as the main challenges of investing and the development of environmentally sustainable business practices. Based on the analysis and discussion results, insight regarding further development of green financial markets is offered.

The concept of creating company value is constantly evolving due to globalization, changing business realities, and the widely expanded idea of corporate social responsibility. The purpose of the chapter "Value Creation via Corporate Social Responsibility: The Case of Emerging Countries" by Małgorzata Macuda and Justyna Fijałkowska (from respectively Poznań University of Economics and Business, and University of Łódź, Poland) is three-fold. Firstly, it describes CSR involvement and CSR reporting practices in emerging countries. Secondly, it presents different theories related to value creation. Thirdly, it investigates CSR value creation measurement and disclosure in emerging economies (Brazil, Chile, China, Colombia, Indonesia, Korea, Malaysia, Peru, Russia, and Taiwan). The authors conducted a content analysis of all publications concerning CSR issues and value creation in emerging countries over the years 1984-2019 included in the Scopus database. Among publications over the years 2014-2019, several concerned CSR implications to value creation in emerging economies strictly.

In the twelfth chapter, Burak Çapraz from Ege University (Turkey) underlines that for many years, companies have tried to keep the public as close partners. In this bilateral relationship, the financial gains of the companies have raised public views on the distribution of these gains. Likewise, regulations and standards determined by supranational institutions such as the United Nations forced companies to give higher priority on CSR activities. The primary purpose of his chapter entitled "'It Fits My Business': Corporate Social Responsibility Activities of Companies on the Route to Gain Competitive Advantage" is to explain the relation between CSR activities and the preferability of these activities among companies. Summative content analysis is conducted on data collected from the websites of the top 100 companies in the Turkish BIST 100 Stock Index. Findings show that CSR activity choices differ among industries, and these choices unveil related and unrelated differentiation in CSR activities.

The chapter proposed by George K. Amoako (from Central University in Ghana), Kwasi Dartey-Baah (from University of Ghana Business School) examines the extent to which corporate social responsibility could generate and boost better brand perceptions and improve competitive advantage within some selected banks in Ghana. The concept of CSR, brand perception and competitive advantage are discussed in relation to findings from a study that was conducted at the national headquarters of GCB Bank and Barclays Bank Limited in Accra. The findings indicated a good understanding of the concept of corporate social responsibility from both customers and employees of both banks. There is a significant and positive connection between effective implementation of CSR initiatives, brand perception, and competitive advantage. Furthermore, CSR is discovered as a tool for business success in the banking sector in Ghana. This chapter, entitled "Corporate Social Responsibility: Strategy for Boosting Brand Perception and Competitive Advantage" explains the benefits of CSR activities to the development of impalpable organizational assets, and as a result, generating better results for banking institutions in Ghana. The authors make a case for the inclusion and active involvement of customers and employees in the CSR initiatives of banks in order to boost brand perception.

And last but not least, it should be outlined that India became the first country in the world to have a mandatory CSR contribution legislation in 2014. This mandate every qualifying company must spend at least 2% of its average net profit on CSR activities. "Mandatory Corporate Social Responsibility and After That? An Analysis from India" by Remya Lathabhavan from VIT University (India) analyses these following aspects of CSR. First, it describes Sustainable Development, CSR, and its relevance across the world. Second, it explores the prevailing CSR models and models used in India. Third, it discusses the importance of CSR in India, mandatory CSR, and its provisions. Fourth, it analyses existing SRI strategies in India and their scope. Finally, it shows the current scenario after mandatory CSR, considering the CSR contributions from different corporates. Such discussion is essential for a country like India, an emerging economy with diverse groups with non-aligned social, cultural, economic, and environmental backgrounds.

We wish you a pleasant reading

Agnieszka Kłysik-Uryszek
University of Łódź, Poland

Anetta Kuna-Marszałek
University of Łódź, Poland

Section 1

Corporate Social Responsibility and Socially Responsible Investing Strategies: Practices in the Context of Sustainable Development

Chapter 1
Corporate Social Responsibility: A Business Contribution to Sustainable Development

Cornelia Philipova
https://orcid.org/0000-0002-6484-9922
University of Economics – Varna, Bulgaria

ABSTRACT

The processes accompanying state social policy over recent decades as well as their contradictory impact on the sustainable development of the society are one of the fundamental problems of our time. Nowadays, there are still no clear solutions to the debate how to alleviate some of the fundamental problems like environmental pollution, poverty, aged population, income inequality, social exclusion, etc. This chapter aims to show how multinational corporations (MNCs) take the role to solve these issues following some corporate social responsibility (CSR) policies. In this way, they offer a means by which the current CSR model can be used more effectively to achieve these sustainable development targets. The structure of the chapter is organized as follows: Section 2 presents an evolution while Section 3 provides a summary of some contemporary views of CSR. Section 4 describes the way in which CSR is used as a sustainable development tool.

INTRODUCTION

The topic of companies' social responsibility is becoming increasingly relevant nowadays. However, its evolutionary beginning is still embedded in the ideas of Charles Robert Darwin (1809-1882). The British scientist and naturalist was the first to launch the concept of the evolution of all species over time from a common ancestor through a process called *"biological evolution of natural selection". In the 19th century, he pondered over the survival and extinction of biological species. He said "Survival of the Fittest" alone inducts any species to grow and continue to survive in any given geographical and environmental infrastructure in the world. (Note: He did not say "Survival of the Biggest, Fastest, Healthiest, Mightiest, Smartest or Toughest", etc..!!). He inferred that the organism that best adjusts and*

DOI: 10.4018/978-1-7998-2193-9.ch001

Copyright © 2020, IGI Global. Copying or distributing in print or electronic forms without written permission of IGI Global is prohibited.

"fits" into the changing environment, puts up with sufferings and adjust with what is available alone continues to live and progresses... All human beings, hence try to fit into a three dimensional survival concept namely (a) The geography and environment (b) The social influences and (c) The Economic infrastructure (Subramaniam, 2013, p. 6). Nowadays, it is easy to conclude that the words of Charles Darwin are still applicable especially concerning social survival and social responsibility.

The responsibility for dealing with social problems is a major priority of the public sector and the governments in particular. In the backdrop of rising social problems and still emerging economies since the global financial and economic crisis of recent years, the question arises as to the extent of voluntary entrepreneurial engagement that could contribute to the potential counteracting against social challenges. Regardless of all growth forecasts, there is a trend towards the polarization of incomes, which brings with it an increased level of poverty. More and more people living with less money (below the poverty line) increase their income through state social transfers. This trend has put the societal consensus for reduction of social inequality to a serious test. And here comes one alternative named Corporate Social Responsibility (CSR). It could be said that this alternative can play an important role and act as a major pillar of the prosperous society. The emerging interest in corporate responsibility as a means to alleviate social challenges can be treated as a potential solution in the battle against social polarization.

CSR is backed by the idea that companies may take responsibility for social processes through and in addition to their economic activities. CSR refers to the measures that companies use to influence social processes positively. Thus, the enterprise's policies are not focused exclusively on the interests of shareholders but on the entire business environment. In this relation the stakeholders may be the workers, clients, directors, suppliers, residents, NGOs, investors, politicians, the media, research and educational institutions, as well as supranational organizations involved in the development of guidelines on Corporate Social Responsibility.

This publication aims to review and evaluate the potential of CSR and relevant corporate policies. For this purpose, the following objectives have been set:

- To timeline the chronological evolution of CSR;
- To review and perform a critical analysis of the main theoretical formulations of CSR;
- To consider the importance of CSR as sustainable development (SD) tool.

BACKGROUND OF THE THEORETICAL VIEWS ON CSR TO SOCIETY

The current business model is facing the mega-trends of exhausted natural resources, climate change, urbanization and migrating population, increasing efficiency and artificial intelligence, cyber reality, crypto technologies, blockchain-distributed registers, etc. As a result of global changes, new market opportunities, regulatory, and governance regimes are emerging. Thus, at the end of the twentieth century, and with the global discussion on CSR, the role of business in society was reviewed. Economies took a direction towards sustainable development. Because of the demographic, market and high-tech trends, it is necessary to predict the needs of present and future generations.

In the theoretical views of different authors CSR is used alongside the synonyms like social responsibility (SR) or socially conscious (SC) activities. There is still the unresolved problem of the terminological ambiguity of the concept of CSR. It can only be used for the activities of corporations, while for individuals the term "Corporate Responsibility" should apply. However, in recent years, the two concepts have been used as synonyms, encompassing business activities in general. Investors using this strategy encourage corporate practices that promote environmental management, consumer protection and human rights. Some of them are incorporated only in ethical projects and investments. Therefore, they exclude businesses involved in areas such as military weapons, alcohol, tobacco, junk food, animal testing, gambling, fossil fuel production, nuclear energy, pesticides, greenhouse gas emitters, etc. (Camilleri, 2017; Ghoul & Karam, 2007, and Statman 2000). The areas that investors are concerned about are corporate governance, social justice, and environmental care. They are trying to impact their business portfolio positively. Also Terziev and Can (2018a; 2018b) theoretically analyzed the relationship between demographic change and the economic growth of the aging population, involving areas such as education, ecology, the environment, renewable energy, medical research and inventions, CO_2 emissions, etc. Under the heading of CSR, companies point to their social responsibility and a supposedly new form of social commitment is gaining public and political visibility.

The debate on modern ideas of CSR grew in the second half of the 20th century. Despite its relevance in recent decades, in global economic literature there is still no consensus on the explicit definition of corporate social responsibility, the understanding of which is not unambiguous. Arriving at an adequate comprehension of the phenomenon requires tracing the historical logic of the emergence of a socially responsible business idea with regard to society.

The idea that companies should be responsible has its roots in the work of some American managers from the 1950s. Their concept is that if companies do not focus only on profits but also on the impact they have on society, they will gain more benefits. If a company has a positive impact on the environment, it will save money in the long run by avoiding having to deal with natural disasters. *Naturally, any business is initially created with the idea of profit and forming added value for its owners. It cannot therefore be expected that a business operating for profit will itself decide to restrict these opportunities at the expense of society* (Blagoycheva, 2016, p. 271).

Historically, the first conception for CSR was launched in Howard Bowen's book "Social responsibilities of the businessman". He explains why companies have an interest in being more responsible and gives the first "recognized" definition of CSR. The view in Bowen's book is defined like *set forth an initial definition of the social responsibilities of businessmen: It refers to the obligations of businessmen to pursue those policies, to make those decisions, or to follow those lines of action which are desirable in terms of the objectives and values of our society* (Bowen, 1953, p. 6). He quoted Fortune magazine's survey (1946, as cited in Bowen, 1953, p. 44), wherein the magazine's editors thought that CSR, or the "social consciousness", of managers meant that businessmen were responsible for the consequences of their actions in a sphere somewhat wider than that covered by their profit-and-loss statements (Bowen, 1953, p. 6). All of this is briefly described in the article "The Pyramid of Corporate Social Responsibility: Toward the Moral Management of Organizational Stakeholders" of Prof. Archie Carroll. *In this Pyramid, a corporation has four types of responsibilities. The first and most obvious is the economic responsibility to be profitable. The second is the legal responsibility to obey the laws set forth by society. The third, which is closely linked to the second, is the ethical responsibility. That is to do what is right even when business is not compelled to do so by law. The fourth is the philanthropic responsibility. Also called the discretionary responsibility, it is best described by the resources contributed by corporations toward social, educational, recreational and/or cultural purposes* (Greater Kansas City Community Foundation, 2010). It is fascinating to note that *93.5% of the business-men responding agreed with the statement* (Carroll, 1999, p. 270).

A feature of the concept of CSR at the end of the 20th century is the understanding that it derives the power and social influence they have in society. Such understanding provides the definition of Keith Davis: *Social responsibility is a nebulous idea and, hence, is defined in various ways. It is used here within a management context to refer to businessmen's decisions and actions taken for reasons at least partially beyond the firm's direct economic or technical interest* (Davis, 1960, p. 70). In addition, *whoever does not use his social power responsibly will lose it. In the long run those who do not use power in a manner which society considers responsible will tend to lose it because other groups eventually will step in to assume those responsibilities* (Davis, 1960, p. 70). In the same way, Keith Davis and Robert Blomstrom present the definition of SR in their book "Business and its environment". So it is *social responsibility, therefore, refers to a person's obligation to consider the effects of his decisions and actions on the whole social system. Businessmen apply social responsibility when they consider the needs and interest of others who may be affected by business actions. In so doing, they look beyond their firm's narrow economic and technical interests* (Davis & Blomstrom, 1966, p. 12). Similarly, the definition in Clarence Cyril Walton's book "Corporate Social Responsibilities" shows the role of the business firm and business person and their actions in society and the whole social system. In particular, *the new concept of social responsibility recognizes the intimacy of the relationships between the corporation and society and realizes that such relationships must be kept in mind by top managers as the corporation and the related groups pursue their respective goals* (Walton, 1967), as cited in (Low, 2016, p. 58).

In Keith Davis' article "The Case for and against Business Assumption of Social Responsibilities" he described the Iron Law of Responsibility (the Law of Long-Run Self-Interest) Davis (1973). It is theorized by Keith Davis, supporting the idea that great social power calls for great responsibilities at the enterprise level. The powerful managers, who cannot use their power responsibly, ultimately lose their power. This law provides an explanation as to why CSR has become an imperative of the corporate economy. In Keith Davis and Robert Blomstrom's book "Business and Society: Environment and Responsibility" (1975) the authors also argue that when the organization is growing that means that its SR is also growing in size. An even more prominent social impact of socially responsible businesses is argued in the opinion: *Social responsibility usually refers to the objectives or motives that should be given weight by business in addition to those dealing with economic performance (e.g., profits). Employment of minority groups, reduction in pollution, greater participation in programs to improve the community, improved medical care, improved industrial health and safety-these and other programs designed to improve the quality of life are covered by the broad umbrella of social responsibility* (Backman, 1975, p. 2). In the same year three more definitions were articulated. *Social responsibility implies bringing corporate behavior up to a level where it is congruent with the prevailing social norms, values, and expectation of performance* (Sethi, 1975, p. 62). The same meaning is inferred in Bowman and Haire's quote: *it is becoming increasingly clear that, just at the time when the art of internal control is reaching its highest stage, firms are pressed by the need for an external information system, for the organization structure to utilize it, and for decision rules to guide their interpretation of the signals* (Bowman & Haire, 1975, p. 57). According to Preston and Post, they *preferred the term "public responsibility", which is intended to define the functions of organizational management within the specific context of public life* (Preston & Post, 1975, pp. 9-10), as cited in: (Carroll, 1999, p. 280). Additionally, Gordon Fitch's view is connected with the following definition: *Corporate social responsibility is defined as the serious attempt to solve social problems caused wholly or in part by the corporation. The problem concept is operationally defined, and social problems are distinguished from non-social problems. A method of social problem solution, based on the principles of applied behavior analysis, is demonstrated using an industrial accident reduction example* (Fitch, 1976, p. 38). According to Carroll, *the social responsibility of business encompasses the economic, legal, ethical, and discretionary expectations that society has of organizations at a given point in time* (Carroll, 1979, p. 499). In brief *before anything else, the business institution is the basic economic unit in our society. As such it has a responsibility to produce goods and services that society wants and to sell them at a profit. All other business roles are predicated on this fundamental assumption* (Carroll, 1979, p. 500). A good example of the growing interest of operational CSR is to ensure that it has a positive relationship with financial results.

From everything mentioned above, it becomes clear that the majority of authors consider CSR as adopting and demonstrating behavior and actions beyond the initial pursuit of profit, aiming to improve conditions for the community and individuals in society. So generally this publication can define the concept as an ongoing commitment to ethical conduct of businesses, combined with responsibility for economic development and at the same time - improving people's quality of life and that of the labor force in particular.

CSR is a concept that companies voluntarily incorporate into their business strategies to show their long-term commitment to the sustainable development of their businesses, the society and the environment. According to the government, it is part of a social and ecological market economy. It is *a concept whereby companies integrate social and environmental concerns in their business operations and in their interaction with their stakeholders on a voluntary basis* (Commission of the European Communities, 2002). According to the Commission of the European Communities, CSR means not only fully satisfying the applicable legal obligations, but also going beyond and investing more in human capital, the environment and the relations with stakeholders. However, the concept of social responsibility is not unambiguous. While the so-called "reformers" consider this societal demand to be a must, and argue that it can help to protect the company's markets, their more "conservative" opponents believe that businesses should stick to their legal obligations.

The central and most important element of the CSR concept is its voluntary nature. It is based on principles that are fundamental to business, most notably in the International Labor Organization (ILO) Tripartite Declaration of Principles on Multinational Enterprises and Social Policy (2017) and the United Nations Global Compact (2018). Two objectives are central to CSR activities. Firstly, companies aim to strengthen their competitiveness. On the other hand, they want to help to find answers to social problems. However, the debate about CSR approaches was controversial. The liberal American Nobel prize winner Milton Friedman (1912-2006), for example, argued that it was not an entrepreneur's responsibility to reduce poverty and social exclusion through voluntary action. Rather, the responsibility lies with politics, since the legal framework, which must be observed by the companies in the implementation of their entrepreneurial goals (1970) have to be defined. The same meaning with arguments about the central place of corporate businesses and their contribution to society was expressed by Henderson (2001, 2005). In his book "Misguided Virtue: False Notions of Corporate Social Responsibility" David Henderson mentions that *the system effects of CSR, as well as the enterprise effects, will tend to make people, in general, worse off* (Henderson, 2001). As a result, both Milton Friedman and David Henderson argue that social temptations inevitably erode corporate profits and should therefore be considered a lack of competence on the part of directors. In their 2001 report Shell International Petroleum Company Ltd. also take the following position concerning their business principles: *To conduct business as responsible corporate members of society, to observe the laws of the countries in which they operate, to express support for fundamental human rights in line with the legitimate role of business and to give proper regard to health, safety and the environment consistent with their commitment to contribute to sustainable development* (Shell International Petroleum Company Ltd., 2001, p. 49). Indeed, from the point of view of multinational corporations, it is claimed that market forces, competition, regulatory frameworks, and scarce resources exert considerable pressure on multinational corporations to survive and contribute to the welfare of society in the form of economic growth (Rodriguez, Siegel, Hillman, & Eden 2006; Galbreath 2011), as cited in: (Pimpa, 2013, p. 62). The number of accompanying circumstances may cause complications in the management and in particular for decisions concerning corporate social responsibility. These complications arise due to factors such as competition for resources, unfair competition, and environmental impact. All of these can influence the role of transnational corporations in international markets (Spence et al., 2003; Pimpa et al., 2012).

The focus of the positive impact of CSR on society is described by UK's Department for International Development (DIFD) as follows: *poverty reduction is not the starting point either for many donors nor for many governments in* (Department for International Development, 2004a) middle-income countries (MICs). It raises the problem of *how DFID can ensure that in its relationships with MICs it does not simply become the default provider of poverty reduction programmes. DFID's strategy is to ensure that its programmes in MICs are part of a co-ordinated and focused international effort, and to increase the effectiveness of the international system as a whole at dealing with the MICs* (Department for International Development, 2004, p. 18). In addition, Antonio Vives define *CSR, by its very nature, is development done by the private sector, and it perfectly complements the development efforts of governments and multilateral development institutions. This is not to say that all MDIs*[1] *have to play some role, the suggestions that this article makes will apply to some MDIs but not others* (Vives, 2004, p. 46).

Some authors highlight the necessity of an alternative and critical research agenda derived from the practice and history of international business. Every CSR initiative should benefit not only companies financially, but also their workers and communities socially and environmentally (Prieto-Carrón et al., 2006, p. 979). *Most of the companies in their growth phase consider CSR activities as mere regulatory pressures. In practice, the element of collaboration with society is completely lacking in CSR which does not address the ever growing gap between the society and business thereby making it hard to justify and sustain in the long run. In contrast, creating shared value represents a transition and expansion of the concept of CSR by virtue of its bi directional flow – the benefits are derived by both the company and society* (Sanjeev & Sharma, 2019, p. 40). Contributing to society is not just a charitable gesture, but it can be actionable. The public should also acknowledge that corporations are organizations that create value in their work and not simply offer some of their profits to the public (Moon & Parc, 2019: 115). When both corporations and the public realize this mutually beneficial role, we can develop a virtuous cycle to grow and develop both corporations and society.

In recent years, initiatives to engage business organizations with socially responsible activities stem from a rapidly changing "business-society" relationship. Historically, the prerequisites for the emergence of business behavior are varied. At the same time, they are not accepted unequivocally today. The point of view of this publication is related to the ability to point the way towards sustainable development.

CONTEMPORARY VIEWS ON SOME CONCEPTS OF CSR

There are different theoretical views about the scope of CSR. Some contemporary views covering areas of CSR are in the context of humanity. One example is from the authors Elisabet Garriga and Domènec Melé. They map the territory of main CSR theories in four groups. Their approaches are defined as is mentioned: *(1) instrumental theories, in which the corporation is seen as only an instrument for wealth creation, and its social activities are only a means to achieve economic results; (2) political theories, which concern themselves with the power of corporations in society and a responsible use of this power in the political arena; (3) integrative theories, in which the corporation is focused on the satisfaction of social demands; and (4) ethical theories, based on ethical responsibilities of corporations to society* (Garriga & Melé, 2004, p. 51).

Three groups have been defined in the article as basic concepts: human rights, corporate philanthropy and socially responsible investment (SRI). The first group is "human rights". "Every human being, as such and regardless of his social condition, has rights "inherent in his person, inalienable and sacred" and therefore opposing in all circumstances of society and states" (Lahrich, 2018, p. 1). Thus, the concept of human rights is by definition universalized and incompatible with systems and regimes based on the superiority of the dignity of caste, race, country, class or of any social group or individual in relation to another; equally incompatible with the idea that building a better society justifies the elimination or suppression of those who should hinder this construction. Some of the authors that are involved in the first group are Cassel (2001), Welford & Frost (2006), Debrah & Ofori (2006) and Crook et al. (2011). In their publications, these authors find out that human capital is positively related to the company's performance. For example, Douglass Cassel explains that companies like Gap, Reebok, Levi's, *Nike and countless others have found that it is usually cheaper and safer not to build their own plants or employ their own work forces in low-wage developing nations, but simply to contract with local producers. Then, if local wages rise or labor troubles start, or there is a civil war, Levi's assets are not at risk, and it is not directly involved in sticky matters like firing workers or closing plants. Levi's can terminate its contract on short notice, and swiftly move production elsewhere by simply contracting with a low-wage producer in another country* (Cassel, 2001, p. 266). Richard Welford and Stephen Frost (2006) revealed that *in most cases, codes of conduct designed for workplaces in low wage locations stick to legal standards such as minimum wages, hours of work, health and safety, forced and child labour and so on. CSR via codes of conduct has often become an exercise in seeking compliance with local law rather than moving beyond it* (Welford & Frost, 2006, p. 168). Similary, Yaw Debrah and George Ofori *shed light on an important but hidden (or overlooked) aspect of training financing in developing countries. In spite of assertions in the literature that the state can play a useful leading or activist role in developing training programmes and linking training to national economic development strategies* (Ashton & Green, 1996; Ashton & Sung, 1994) *the findings suggest that the majority of the interviewees would like the training problems and the financing of training to be tackled by the industry itself rather than the government. This is contrary to what prevails in most developing countries where training and skills development are financed from general government revenue* (Debrah & Ofori, 2006, p. 457). The human capital is an organization's most valuable asset for Russell Crook, Samuel Todd, James Combs, David Woehr and David Ketchen, Jr. The implications for *the human capital–performance relationship indicates that, on average, human capital relates to performance at* $\bar{r}_c = .21$. *We interpret this to mean that increasing human capital by one standard deviation increases performance by .21 of a standard deviation. Applying this result to an individual study demonstrates how human capital shapes performance* (Crook, Todd, Combs, Woehr, & Ketchen, 2011, p. 451). Moreover, they also find out that for researchers, the results of *received theory has correctly pointed to the importance of human capital, and, in particular, specific human capital, as key determinants of firm success, but that not all human capital is equal and not all benefits go to owners* (Crook, Todd, Combs, Woehr, & Ketchen, 2011, p. 453).

Publications of the authors Jörg Andriof, Sandra Waddock, Brian Husted and Sandra Sutherland Rahman (2002), Sandra Waddock, Charles Bodwell, Samuel Graves (2002), Michael Porter and Mark Kramer (2003), Archie Carroll (2004), Dirk Matten and Andrew Crane (2005), Heli Wang and Cuili Qian (2011) are typical for the second group, namely "corporate philanthropy". The authors mentioned above are just some of the economists dealing with this scientific topic. It is appropriate to note that corporate philanthropy is a partnership that clearly differs from sponsorship. The difference is that philanthropy is like a donation, while sponsorship is a public operation that is usually taxed on commercial taxes but can benefit from exceptions. Stakeholders' management is presented like stakeholder communication, conflict resolution and firm performance in the book "Unfolding Stakeholder Thinking: Relationships, Communication, Reporting and Performance". This two-way relationship between stakeholders and corporations is based on the principles of reciprocity, interdependence and power (Andriof et al., 2002, p. 19). Companies can no longer exist outside their business environment. Stakeholder analysis of an ethically-based approach is based on respect for and consideration of the constituencies of a firm. *Managing stakeholders' relationships and natural resources is becoming the new business imperative* (Waddock et al., 2002), as cited in: (de Leaniz & Gómez-López, 2019, p. 232). Michael Porter and Mark Kramer point out companies that achieve both economic and social gains. For example, such entrepreneurs are Cisco System (Cisco Networking Academy) (Porter & Kramer, 2003), Gilead (Gilead Sciences Inc.), Wells Fargo & Company, Walmart Inc., ExxonMobil (STEM education programs), JPMorgan Chase & Company (Phillpott, 2018), Goldman Sachs Group Inc., Google Inc. (Google.org, Alphabet Inc.), etc. *CSR is a broad concept that deals directly with the relationship between a firm and its effects on society Carroll (2004), Carroll & Shabana (2010), Hack., Kenyon, & Wood (2014), and Kraus & Brtitzelmaier (2012). The scope of such initiatives tends to vary considerably. In some instances, firms may seek to improve the labor conditions across their supply chains as demonstrated by the fair-trade coffee industry. In other cases, manufacturing firms may take on efforts to reduce their environmental impacts through waste minimization and pollution reduction programs*, as cited in: (Massoud, Daily, & Willi, 2019). It is clear that with the assistance of CSR there is a two-way relationship between companies and society Carroll (2000) and Snider, Hill, & Martin (2003).

There is also an explanation of the social role of business offered by Dirk Matten and Andrew Crane. They focus on the human rights of citizens (for example access to basic needs and service) as an important part of a corporation's role in the society (Matten & Crane, 2005). The authors identify three methods by which the governmental and corporate role in administering individual civil rights are changing. These are (1) responding to internal pressure whereby the government withdraws from the administration of civil rights through mechanisms such as privatization or social security reform; (2) with regard to internal pressure where governments of economically developed countries have never applied civil rights, as in developing or underdeveloped countries where health, education and other rights are not yet secured; and (3) with regard to the external challenges that have had the implications that the administration of civil rights is beyond the scope of the national state, such as tackling the effects of globalization on markets and global environmental issues. *Corporate philanthropy is expected to positively affect firm financial performance because it helps firms gain sociopolitical legitimacy, which enables them to elicit positive stakeholder responses and to gain political access. The positive philanthropy-performance relationship is stronger for firms with greater public visibility and for those with better past performance, as philanthropy by these firms gains more positive stakeholder responses. Firms that are not government-owned or politically well-connected were shown to benefit more from philanthropy, as gaining political resources is more critical for such firms* (Wang & Qian, 2011, p. 1159).

The third group related to socially responsible investing, or also known as responsible investment, sustainable, socially conscious, "green" or ethical investing. SRI is the application of the principles of sustainable development to financial investments. In July 2013, the French Association of Financial Management (AFG) and the Forum for Responsible Investment (FIR) published a definition to clarify the role of SRI (Socially Responsible Investment): *SRI is an investment that aims to reconcile economic performance and social and environmental impact by financing companies and public entities that contribute to sustainable development regardless of their sector of activity. By influencing the governance and behavior of actors, SRI promotes a responsible economy* (Boursorama, 2013). Some of the authors that are publishing in this area are Alyson Warhurst, Michael Ross Jayne, Glynn Skerratt, Duncan McLaren, etc. According to Warhurst, *a growing 'voice of society' is demanding that corporations, particularly those that have benefited from privatisation, address past inequalities and broaden the distribution of business benefits. Society also calls for these corporations to mitigate the more far-reaching and indirect effects of their activities on the quality of life of local communities, including environmental damage and health liabilities resulting from previously unregulated pollution, as well as past social exclusion*" (Warhurst, 2001). In addition to and following empirical tests Jayne and Skerratt remarked that the financial aspect is the most important and the ethical aspect is the least important for every corporation. *In the light of the fact that the majority of respondents specialized in ethical investment, this is perhaps surprising. ... The main outcome here is that ethical investments are considered to be the most important for good business in the long run. ... Although ethical considerations were ranked ahead of societal considerations, their main use was when considered with societal factors* (Jayne & Skerratt, 2003, p. 9). McLaren expressed same meaning, namely that: *From the perspective of stakeholders, new forms of corporate accountability are today more vital than ever: public interest constraints are being removed or relaxed in the course of removing non-tariff barriers to trade; the growth of truly global companies makes it more difficult for citizens and communities to seek redress, while consolidating the power and influence of those companies; corporations are increasingly taking control of industries and services previously run by governments, without taking on the associated public interest responsibilities; and the scale of corporate impacts is both growing and increasingly remote from both the owners and the customers of the companies* (McLaren, 2004, p. 199). Information on financial results is also often communicated by companies to increase the trust of foreign firms and stakeholders. Based on this, good corporate performance, namely optimal income, and effective and controlled spending can also increase investor interest in allocating funds to the company or other initiatives with a positive impact on society.

The conclusions of this part of the chapter of the nature and dimensions of CSR provide a basis for generalizing the following trends in its interpretation. The authors mentioned above accept that social responsibility is part of the contemporary strategic management of business organizations. It is part of their corporate culture and understanding of ethics in business. Voluntary adherence to socially responsible business behavior is the path to long-term growth and sustainable development of organizations. It is important to note that modern concepts of social responsibility are its purpose. It is essential to create opportunities to meet the interests of all stakeholders, as well as to achieve sustainability and balance between different decile groups in society.

CSR AND SUSTAINABLE DEVELOPMENT DEFINED BY MULTINATIONAL CORPORATIONS AND INITIATIVES

Although there is no single definition of the term "Corporate Social Responsibility", it can generally be defined as a business practice that contributes to achieving sustainable development worldwide (SDW). The definition of SD is unambiguous: It is the development whereby each generation satisfies its needs so that it does not compromise the ability of future generations to meet their needs. SDW includes three components - a stable economy, a stable society and a stable environment. It means that companies and corporations in general, in which the greatest power and resources are usually concentrated, impact the economy, society and the environment to achieve sustainable development worldwide - that is, they have to show CSR (to work responsibly) to ensure SDW. In this connection, it is important to make a clear distinction between CSR, which is a strategic and systematic management model and charity, sponsorship and philanthropy. CSR is much, much more than donating money for various causes. It is the contribution of each company to the socio-economic development and environmental sustainability at a local, regional and global level and is part of a comprehensive management approach that aims to create added value not only for the company but also for all stakeholders - inside and outside a company. Under CSR, the company has to take care of workers' health and safety (Blagoycheva, Andreeva & Yolova, 2019) to increase their welfare and moral satisfaction with their work.

To define or demonstrate the extent to which a company is socially responsible in its activities and contributes to the sustainable development worldwide, it is necessary to use commonly accepted criteria. This cannot be done on any subjective external features or initiatives of the company itself. For this purpose, a specific standard for accounting for CSR has been developed or is also known as the Sustainability Development Report. *The current version of the standard is G3.1 and is being developed by the Global Reporting Initiative (GRI), a UN co-operation center. The first version of the standard dates back to 2000, and then it has been reported by some 50 leading global companies, and to date, tens of thousands of companies of varying sizes and industries have been competing in the race for which company is more transparent and more responsible in its activity and contributes more to the Sustainable Development Worldwide* (Popov, 2013). In fact, 250 (G250) of the largest companies by revenue based on the 2016Fortune 500 ranking, announce their CSR in their annual financial reports. Reference made to the GRI from G250 is 78% in 2016. Around 43% of G250 link Corporate Responsibility activities to the UN Sustainable Development Goals, while 98% of them acknowledge human rights as a business issue, 67% link carbon targets to global climate goals and 48% to climate change (KPMG, 2019).

GRI's G3.1 standard is comprised of over 80 measurement metrics divided into over 30 aspects and 6 categories, which are: economic indicators; environmental indicators; labor practices and decent working conditions; human rights; community; and responsibility for the products. All metrics have a clear definition of feasibility, measurement, and disclosure in the report. A key point in the development of the CSR Sustainable Development Report is identifying and involving stakeholders - these are individuals, groups or organizations that are substantially affected by the company's activities or can materially impact on the realization of its strategic and business goals (Popov, 2013). The most common stakeholders are: Employees, clients, suppliers, shareholders, families of employees, the community, human rights NGOs, trade associations, regulators, local authorities, government, etc. *Actually, the opposition between the economic and social goals is unacceptable because companies do not function in isolation from the society they work in. Moreover, the unilateral focus on maximizing profits for owners neglects the in-depth identification of all people involved in forming values in the company: workers, suppliers, customers, government regulations and the environment. Disregarding this fact and non-compliance with the social status of the population may lead to distortions in consumption and on a subsequent stage – to pressure on the general economic development in the form of insufficient demand, which will also harm the owners themselves. Therefore, the use of company resources for socially responsible activities, and hence for the general social well-being, does not necessarily harm the benefit of shareholders* (Blagoycheva, 2018, p. 121). The company needs to engage with stakeholders and, together with them, decide which G3.1 benchmarks should account for their performance because they are the most important for stakeholders. Unlike financial statements, where companies report their financial results for the past year and compare them with the results for the previous year, CSR reports on Sustainable Development under the G3.1 standard, apart from showing the company's performance for the past year, are compared with the company's presentation for two previous periods, declaring the development targets for the following year, and reporting on the objectives of the previous year. Here the accountability is more complex and engaging, because the more important of a company's financial performance is its contribution and the trend in the development of its contribution to achieving Sustainable Development Worldwide. As in the financial statements, also in CSR, the Sustainability Reports are intended to be audited by independent auditors to verify and substantiate what is written in them. For the purpose of the CSR Sustainable Development Reports audit, a special auditing standard AA1000 AS has been developed (Popov, 2013). Contemporary views on CSR and SDW are present in a Table 1 (Appendix).

Transparency in a company developed under G3.1 is the fastest-accelerating and influential organizational change that makes the company more competitive. Generally, in the future corporate world, opaque wholly-oriented companies have no future, they will remain isolated, lose authority among their customers and employees, and will quickly be pushed out of the market by transparent, responsible and constantly improving their responsible performance.

Many of the multinational corporations (MNCs) are trying to improve local conditions of some countries. For example, they bring about education improvement, enhanced health care and nutrition, poverty alleviation, environment excellence, etc. The main focus in this publication is on social problems in society. The proof of this statement is that poverty and social exclusion continue to be epidemic problems even in the modern society. The public sector cannot be the only alleviation tool. Therefore, the role of the private sector in helping governments' socially responsible activities has to be reconsidered. Some authors and publications in this scientific field are Frynas (2000), Jenkins (2005), Kolk & van Tulder (2006), Reggiani (2008), Curtis & Bradly (2012), Pimpa, Fry & Gekara (2012), Pimpa (2013), Subramaniam (2013), Anggraini, Kriyantono, & Wulandari (2018), López-Morales & Ortega-Ridaura (2019), DiGabriele (2019), etc. *The debate about the need for international business organizations to go beyond their profit motive has been ongoing. Most MNCs identify CSR as a business tool to promote a positive image to business stakeholders and as a way to improve the quality of life among citizens of the host countries* (Pimpa, 2013, p. 61). As a business strategy CSR *placed in the context of other MNCs' behavior, a sector-coordinated morality seems important, which means that a meso approach to poverty alleviation needs to complement the current global (macro) and individual company (micro) focus* (Kolk & van Tulder, 2006). Actually, there is less critical analysis related to the private sector and its role in the social development of the society by the authors Scheyvens, Banks, & Hughes (2016). It is a well-known fact that on 25-27 September 2015, world leaders had an appointment in New York (United Nations, 2015) to set up Sustainable Development Goals (SDGs). *Many assert that the private sector has particular strengths to bring to bear in delivering on the Sustainable Development Goals (SDGs), including innovation, responsiveness, efficiency and provision of specific skills and resources*

(Scheyvens, Banks, & Hughes, 2016, p. 372). SDGs are known as a global partnership for "successful sustainable development" (United Nations, 2019). And here comes the private sector option as a sustainable development tool – CSR. It *has come to be considered a worthwhile endeavor of the private sector in its efforts to deliver sustainable development projects, particularly for those communities adjacent to extraction and production sites* (Spencer, 2018, p. 75). "*The SDGs emphasize that governments and multilateral development agencies cannot achieve the 2030 development agenda alone and that the private sector has the capital, resources and power to take on a central role in poverty reduction*" (Spencer, 2018, p. 73). "*For CSR to produce social outcomes that are not necessarily constrained by corporate rationality there needs to be a change in the normative framework of public decision making at the institutional level*" (Banerjee, 2014, p. 84). The application of new financial ethics is aimed at preventing the most important trap in CSR - to spread CSR policy to the outside world only because of reputation (Soppe, 2016). Even CSR can be a driver for successful sustainable development worldwide, due to the differences in the forms of government, as well as the foreign and domestic policies of the individual states, a single regulatory framework concerning international law between the individual states and their corporations operating in them could not be applied.

FUTURE RESEARCH DIRECTIONS

The future expectations of human society directed toward the government and multinational organizations shift the interest of business to sustainable development. The unsuccessful attempts of the public sector to solve some of the still existing social problems require the intervention of business organizations. In the age of innovations and digitalization this relation will become more and more urgent. This publication outlines the logic for future research opportunities. An example of such a study could be the development of a complete economic model for integration of multinational organizations into governmental sustainable development projects. Another option is to research the drivers of sustainable development and the influence of multinational organizations on them.

CONCLUSION

The study of CSR and its perception and evaluation shows that there is a wide variety of views among scientists, researchers and business representatives. The reasons for their existence can be found in the various historical prerequisites, the usage of different approaches for their interpretation and the presence of different terminology for the problems under consideration.

There is a wide variety of concepts for business social responsibility as well as methods used for its evaluation. Although the fact that some of them are oriented towards social investment, there is still no uniform criteria under which organizations can be classified as socially responsible for the development of both the society and the corporate values. Nevertheless, Corporate Social Responsibility has the potential to be one of the pillars of today's society. Every business could contribute to a different sphere of public life. One of the main goals of both the government and the corporations is to help build a stable socially responsible business environment. In the context of the rapidly changing markets their striving must be directed towards creating a lasting link between the needs and the resources of the business on the one hand and the society on the other, aiming to deliver benefits to both parties.

REFERENCES

Andriof, J., Waddock, S., Husted, B., & Rahman, S. (2002). Unfolding Stakeholder Thinking: Theory, Responsibility and Engagement. (S. Andriof, J., Waddock, Eds.). Abingdon, UK: Routledge.

Anggraini, C., Kriyantono, R., & Wulandari, M. P. (2018). Corporate Social Responsibility (CSR): An Opportunity for the Poverty Alleviation. *Advanced Science Letters*, *24*(12), 9341–9344. doi:10.1166/asl.2018.12269

Ashton, D., & Green, F. (1996). *Education, Training and the Global Economy* (1st ed.). Cheltenham, UK: Edward Elgar.

Ashton, D., & Sung, J. (1994). *The State, Economic Development and Skill Formation: A New Asian Model?* CLMS Working Paper No 3. Retrieved from https://www.researchgate.net/publication/242641461_The_State_Economic_Development_and_Skill_Formation_A_New_East_Asian_Model

Backman, J. (1975). *Social responsibility and accountability* (1st ed.). New York: New York University Press.

Banerjee, S. (2014). A Critical Perspective on Corporate Social Responsibility. *Critical Perspectives on International Business*, *10*(1/2), 84–95. doi:10.1108/cpoib-06-2013-0021

Blagoycheva, H. (2016). *Corporate Social Responsibility Between the Profit and Social Welfare. International scientific and practical conference "Economics, management, law: realities and perspectives", April 29, 2016*. Retrieved from http://conferencii.com/files/archive/2016-04.pdf

Blagoycheva, H., Andreeva, A., & Yolova, G. (2019). Obligation and Responsibility of Employers to Provide Health and Safety at Work – Principles, Current Regulation and Prospects. *Economic Studies*, *28*(2), 115–137.

Boursorama. (2013). *L'AFG et le FIR donnent une nouvelle définition à l'ISR*. Retrieved from https://www.boursorama.com/bourse/actualites/l-afg-et-le-fir-donnent-une-nouvelle-definition-a-l-isr-7b9a4fd7c8cf2466c003dfc0e21a1d46

Bowen, H. R. (1953). *The Social Responsibility of the Businessman* (1st ed.). New York: Harper.

Bowman, E. H., & Haire, M. (1975). A Strategic Posture toward Corporate Social Responsibility. *California Management Review*, *18*(2), 49–58. doi:10.2307/41164638

Camilleri, M. A. (2017). Socially Responsible and Sustainable Investing. In *Corporate Sustainability, Social Responsibility and Environmental Management* (pp. 61–77). Cham: Springer International Publishing. doi:10.1007/978-3-319-46849-5_4

Carroll, A. B. (1979). A Three-Dimensional Conceptual Model of Corporate Performance. *Academy of Management Review*, *4*(4), 497–505. doi:10.5465/amr.1979.4498296

Carroll, A. B. (1999). Corporate Social Responsibility: Evolution of a definitional construct. *Business & Society*, *38*(3), 268–295. doi:10.1177/000765039903800303

Carroll, A. B. (2000). Ethical Challenges for Business in the New Millennium: Corporate Social Responsibility and Models of Management Morality. *Business Ethics Quarterly*, *10*(1), 33–42. doi:10.2307/3857692

Carroll, A. B. (2004). Managing ethically with global stakeholders: A present and future challenge. *The Academy of Management Perspectives*, *18*(2), 114–120. doi:10.5465/ame.2004.13836269

Carroll, A. B., & Shabana, K. M. (2010). The Business Case for Corporate Social Responsibility: A Review of Concepts, Research and Practice. *International Journal of Management Reviews*, *12*(1), 85–105. doi:10.1111/j.1468-2370.2009.00275.x

Cassel, D. (2001). Human Rights and Business Responsibilities in the Global Marketplace. *Business Ethics Quarterly*, *11*(2), 261–274. doi:10.2307/3857749

Commission of the European Communities. (2002). *Corporate Social Responsibility: A business contribution to Sustainable Development*. Retrieved from https://ec.europa.eu/europeaid/sites/devco/files/communication-corporate-social-responsibility-sustainable-development-com2002347-20020702_en.pdf

Crook, T. R., Todd, S. Y., Combs, J. G., Woehr, D. J., & Ketchen, D. J. (2011). Does human capital matter? A meta-analysis of the relationship between human capital and firm performance. *The Journal of Applied Psychology*, *96*(3), 443–456. doi:10.1037/a0022147 PMID:21244126

Curtis, S., & Bradly, A. P. (2012). Corporate Social Responsibility and Poverty Alleviation: A Conceptual Framework. Academy of Management Proceedings, 2012(1), 10406. doi:10.5465/AMBPP.2012.10406abstract

Davis, K. (1960). Can Business Afford to Ignore Social Responsibilities? *California Management Review*, *2*(3), 70–76. doi:10.2307/41166246

Davis, K. (1973). The Case for and Against Business Assumption of Social Responsibilities. *Academy of Management Journal*, *16*(2), 312–322. doi:10.2307/255331

Davis, K., & Blomstrom, R. (1966). *Business and its environment* (1st ed.). New York: McGraw-Hill Book Company.

Davis, K., & Blomstrom, R. (1975). *Business and society: Environment and responsibility* (3rd ed.). New York: McGraw-Hill Book Company.

Debrah, Y. A., & Ofori, G. (2006). Human resource development of professionals in an emerging economy: The case of the Tanzanian construction industry. *International Journal of Human Resource Management*, *17*(3), 440–463. doi:10.1080/09585190500521425

Department for International Development. (2004a). Achieving the Millennium Development Goals: The Middle-Income Countries. London: Academic Press.

Department for International Development. (2004b). *Department for International Development: Departmental Report 2004*. Retrieved from https://publications.parliament.uk/pa/cm200304/cmselect/cmintdev/749/749.pdf

DiGabriele, M. (2019). Corporate Social Responsibility as a Tool for Poverty Reduction. In J. DiGabriele, J., Goyal, A., Joshi, M., Miguez, J., Neumann, & N., Ojo (Eds.), Corporate Social Responsibility (pp. 1463–1470). IGI Global. doi:10.4018/978-1-5225-6192-7.ch077

Fitch, H. G. (1976). Achieving Corporate Social Responsibility. *Academy of Management Review*, *1*(1), 38–46. doi:10.5465/amr.1976.4408754

Friedman, M. (1970). The Social Responsibility of Business is to Increase its Profits. *The New York Times Magazine, 13*(9), 6. Retrieved from http://umich.edu/~thecore/doc/Friedman.pdf

Frynas, J. (2000). *Oil in Nigeria: Conflict and Litigation between Oil Companies and Village Communities* (1st ed.). Hamburg, Germany: LIT Verlag Münster.

Galbreath, J. (2011). Sustainable development in business: a strategic view. In Theory and Practice of Corporate Social Responsibility (pp. 89–105). London: Springer-Verlag Berlin Heidelberg. doi:10.1007/978-3-642-16461-3_6

García de Leaniz, P. M., & Gómez-López, R. (2019). Responsible Management in the CSR 2.0 Era. In Corporate Social Responsibility (pp. 231–248). IGI Global. doi:10.4018/978-1-5225-6192-7.ch013

Garriga, E., & Melé, D. (2004). Corporate Social Responsibility Theories: Mapping the Territory. *Journal of Business Ethics*, *53*(1/2), 51–71. doi:10.1023/B:BUSI.0000039399.90587.34

Ghoul, W., & Karam, P. (2007). MRI and SRI Mutual Funds. *Journal of Investing*, *16*(2), 96–102. doi:10.3905/joi.2007.686416

Greater Kansas City Community Foundation. (2010). *Pyramid of Corporate Social Responsibility*. Retrieved from https://www.growyourgiving.org/giving-blog/pyramid-corporate-social-responsibility

Hack, L., Kenyon, A. J., & Wood, E. (2014). A critical Corporate Social Responsibility (CSR) timeline: How should it be understood now? *International Journal of Management Cases*, *16*(4), 46–55. Retrieved from http://connection.ebscohost.com/c/articles/97489531/critical-corporate-social-responsibility-csr-timeline-how-should-be-understood-now

Henderson, D. (2001). *Misguided Virtue: False Notions of Corporate Social Responsibility* (1st ed.). Oxford, UK: New Zealand Business Roundtable. Retrieved from http://www.iea.org.uk/sites/default/files/publications/files/upldbook126pdf.pdf

ILO. (2017). *Tripartite Declaration of Principles concerning Multinational Enterprises and Social Policy*. Retrieved from https://www.ilo.org/wcmsp5/groups/public/---ed_emp/---emp_ent/---multi/documents/publication/wcms_094386.pdf

Jayne, M. R., & Skerratt, G. (2003). Socially responsible investment in the UK? Criteria that are used to evaluate suitability. *Corporate Social Responsibility and Environmental Management*, *10*(1), 1–11. doi:10.1002/csr.25

Jenkins, R. (2005). Globalization, Corporate Social Responsibility and poverty. *International Affairs*, *81*(3), 525–540. doi:10.1111/j.1468-2346.2005.00467.x

Kolk, A., & van Tulder, R. (2006). Poverty alleviation as business strategy? Evaluating commitments of frontrunner Multinational Corporations. *World Development*, *34*(5), 789–801. doi:10.1016/j.worlddev.2005.10.005

Kraus, P., & Brtitzelmaier, B. (2012). A literature review on corporate social responsibility: Definitions, theories and recent empirical research. *International Journal of Management Cases*, *14*(4), 273–287. doi:10.5848/APBJ.2012.00105

Lahrich, I. (2018). *Human Rights: Yesterday and today*. Retrieved from https://www.academia.edu/19694864/Human_Rights_General_overview

López-Morales, J. S., & Ortega-Ridaura, I. (2019). Internationalization, Corporate Social Responsibility, and Poverty Alleviation. In Corporate Social Responsibility: Concepts, Methodologies, Tools, and Applications (pp. 1276–1298). IGI Global. doi:10.4018/978-1-5225-6192-7.ch067

Low, M. P. (2016). Corporate Social Responsibility and the Evolution of Internal Corporate Social Responsibility in 21st Century. *Asian Journal of Social Sciences and Management Studies*, *3*(1), 56–74. doi:10.20448/journal.500/2016.3.1/500.1.56.74

Massoud, J. A., Daily, B. F., & Willi, A. (2019). How do Argentine SMEs define CSR? Cases in educational social development. *World Journal of Entrepreneurship, Management and Sustainable Development*. doi:10.1108/WJEMSD-10-2018-0090

Matten, D., & Crane, A. (2005). Corporate Citizenship: Toward an Extended Theoretical Conceptualization. *Academy of Management Review*, *30*(1), 166–179. doi:10.5465/amr.2005.15281448

McLaren, D. (2004). Global Stakeholders: Corporate accountability and investor engagement. *Corporate Governance*, *12*(2), 191–201. doi:10.1111/j.1467-8683.2004.00360.x

Moon, H., & Parc, J. (2019). Shifting Corporate Social Responsibility to Corporate Social Opportunity through Creating Shared Value. *Strategic Change*, *28*(2), 115–122. doi:10.1002/jsc.2252

Orsato, R. J., Garcia, A., Mendes-Da-Silva, W., Simonetti, R., & Monzoni, M. (2015). Sustainability indexes: Why join in? A study of the 'Corporate Sustainability Index (ISE)' in Brazil. *Journal of Cleaner Production*, *96*, 161–170. doi:10.1016/j.jclepro.2014.10.071

Phillpott, S. (2018). The 13 Most Philanthropic Companies in the World. Dublin: Academic Press.

Pimpa, N. (2013). Poverty Alleviation: Corporate Social Responsibility Approaches by Multinational Corporations in Lao PDR and Thailand. *Journal of Business and Policy Research*, *8*(1), 60–77. Retrieved from https://www.researchgate.net/publication/231537882_Poverty_Alleviation_CSR_Approaches_by_Multinational_Corporations_in_Lao_PDR_and_Thailand

Pimpa, N., Fry, S., & Gekara, V. (2012). MNCs and poverty alleviation: Approaches and challenges in Lao PDR and Thailand. In *Proceedings of the Academy of Management Annual Meeting 2012* (pp. 1–37). Boston: Academy of Management. doi:10.5465/AMBPP.2012.11068abstract

Porter, M., & Kramer, M. (2003). The Competitive Advantage of Corporate Philanthropy. *Harvard Business Review*, *80*(12), 1–16. Retrieved from https://www.sharedvalue.org/sites/default/files/resource-files/Competitive_Advantage.pdf PMID:12510538

Preston, L. E., & Post, J. E. (1975). Private management and public policy: The principle of public responsibility (1st ed.). Englewood Cliffs, NJ: Prentice- Hall.

Prieto-Carrón, M., Lund-Thomsen, P., Chan, A., Muro, A., & Bhushan, C. (2006). Critical perspectives on CSR and development: What we know, what we don't know, and what we need to know. *International Affairs*, *82*(5), 977–987. doi:10.1111/j.1468-2346.2006.00581.x

Reggiani, T. (2008). *Recensione a Muhammad Yunus - "Un mondo senza povertà."* Retrieved from https://mpra.ub.uni-muenchen.de/14974/1/MPRA_paper_14974.pdf

Rodriguez, P., Siegel, D., Hillman, A., & Eden, L. (2006). Three lenses on the multinational enterprise: Politics, corruption, and corporate social responsibi. *Journal of International Business Studies*, *37*(6), 733–746. doi:10.1057/palgrave.jibs.8400229

Scheyvens, R., Banks, G., & Hughes, E. (2016). The Private Sector and the SDGs: The Need to Move Beyond 'Business as Usual.'. *Sustainable Development*, *24*(6), 371–382. doi:10.1002d.1623

Serafimova, D. (2017). CSR and Sustainable Development – Two Concepts with Different Beginnings and a Common Future. *Journal of Emerging Trends in Marketing and Management*, *I*(1), 77–87. Retrieved from https://ideas.repec.org/a/aes/jetimm/v1y2017i1p77-87.html

Sethi, S. P. (1975). Dimensions of Corporate Social Performance: An Analytical Framework. *California Management Review*, *17*(3), 58–64. doi:10.2307/41162149

Sharma, A., & Sanjeev, M. A. (2019). Can Creating Shared Value Supersede Corporate Social Responsibility. In *International Conference on Creating a Sustainable Business: Managerial Implications and Challenges (ICSBMC-12)* (pp. 37–41). Jaipur, India: Academic Press.

Shell International Petroleum Company. (2001). *People, planet and profits. The Shell Report 2001.* Retrieved from http://www.bcsd.org.tw/2010/images/doc/301/002/002_3/SHELL REPORT_2001.PDF

Snider, J., Hill, R. P., & Martin, D. (2003). Corporate Social Responsibility in the 21st Century: A View from the World's Most Successful Firms. *Journal of Business Ethics*, *48*(2), 175–187. doi:10.1023/B:BUSI.0000004606.29523.db

Soppe, A. (2016). New Financial Ethics A Normative Approach. New York: Routledge. doi:10.4324/9781315462578

Spence, L., Schmidpeter, R., & Habisch, A. (2003). Assessing social capital: Small and medium sized enterprises in Germany. *Journal of Business Ethics*, *47*(1), 17–29. doi:10.1023/A:1026284727037

Spencer, R. (2018). CSR for Sustainable Development and Poverty Reduction? Critical Perspectives from the Anthropology of Development. In Disciplining the Undisciplined? Perspectives from Business, Society and Politics on Responsible Citizenship, Corporate Social Responsibility and Sustainability (pp. 73–87). Springer International Publishing. doi:10.1007/978-3-319-71449-3_5

Statman, M. (2000). Socially Responsible Mutual Funds (corrected). *Financial Analysts Journal*, *56*(3), 30–39. doi:10.2469/faj.v56.n3.2358

Subramaniam, V. (2013). *Poverty : A Corporate Creation and Ratio Controls for Eradication*. Retrieved from https://mpra.ub.uni-muenchen.de/75234/1/MPRA_paper_75234.pdf

United Nations. (2015). *United Nations Sustainable Development Summit 2015*. Retrieved from https://sustainabledevelopment.un.org/post2015/summit

United Nations. (2018). *United Nations Global Compact*. Retrieved from https://www.unglobalcompact.org/

United Nations. (2019). *Goal 17: Revitalize the global partnership for sustainable development*. Retrieved from https://www.un.org/sustainabledevelopment/globalpartnerships/

Vives, A. (2004). The Role of Multilateral Development Institutions in Fostering Corporate Social Responsibility. *Development*, *47*(3), 45–52. doi:10.1057/palgrave.development.1100065

Waddock, S. A., Bodwell, C., & Graves, S. B. (2002). Responsibility: The new business imperative. *The Academy of Management Perspectives*, *16*(2), 132–148. doi:10.5465/ame.2002.7173581

Walton, C. (1967). *Corporate Social Responsibilities* (1st ed.). Belmont, CA: Wadsworth Publishing Company.

Wang, H., & Qian, C. (2011). Corporate Philanthropy and Corporate Financial Performance: The Roles of Stakeholder Response and Political Access. *Academy of Management Journal*, *54*(6), 1159–1181. doi:10.5465/amj.2009.0548

Warhurst, A. (2001). Corporate Citizenship and Corporate Social Investment. *Journal of Corporate Citizenship*, *2001*(1), 57–73. doi:10.9774/GLEAF.4700.2001.sp.00008

Welford, R., & Frost, S. (2006). Corporate social responsibility in Asian supply chains. *Corporate Social Responsibility and Environmental Management*, *13*(3), 166–176. doi:10.1002/csr.121

ADDITIONAL READING

Ashrafi, M., Adams, M., Walker, T. R., & Magnan, G. (2018). How Corporate Social Responsibility can be Integrated into Corporate Sustainability: A Theoretical Review of their Relationships. *International Journal of Sustainable Development and World Ecology*, *25*(8), 672–682. doi:10.1080/13504509.2018.1471628

Cramer, J. (2017). *Corporate Social Responsibility and Globalisation: an Action Plan for Business*. Routledge. doi:10.4324/9781351282642

Crane, A., Matten, D., & Spence, L. (Eds.). (2019). *Corporate Social Responsibility: Readings and Cases in a Global Context*. Routledge. doi:10.4324/9780429294273

Forcadell, F. J., & Aracil, E. (2019). Can Multinational Companies Foster Institutional Change and Sustainable Development in Emerging Countries? A Case Study. *Business Strategy & Development*, *2*(2), 91–105. doi:10.1002/bsd2.45

Foss, N. J., & Klein, P. G. (2018). Sustainability, Stakeholder Governance, and Corporate Social Responsibility. *Advances in Strategic Management,* 38, 17À35.

Hahn, T., Figge, F., Pinkse, J., & Preuss, L. (2018). A Paradox Perspective on Corporate Sustainability: Descriptive, Instrumental, and Normative Aspects. *Journal of Business Ethics*, *148*(2), 235–248. doi:10.100710551-017-3587-2

Idowu, S. O., Schmidpeter, R., & Zu, L. (2020). *The Future of the UN Sustainable Development Goals.* Springer; doi:10.1007/978-3-030-21154-7

Preuss, L. (2020). Tracing the Global Diffusion of Corporate Social Responsibility: The Example of Business in the Community's CSR Framework. In V. Shirodkar, R. Strange, & S. McGuire (Eds.), *Non-market Strategies in International Business. The Academy of International Business.* Cham: Palgrave Macmillan; doi:10.1007/978-3-030-35074-1_6

Saeidi, S. P., Sofian, S., Saeidi, P., Saeidi, S. P., & Saaeidi, S. A. (2015). How does Corporate Social Responsibility Contribute to Firm Financial Performance? The Mediating Role of Competitive Advantage, Reputation, and Customer Satisfaction. *Journal of Business Research*, *68*(2), 341–350. doi:10.1016/j.jbusres.2014.06.024

Sharma, E. (2019). A Review of Corporate Social Responsibility in Developed and Developing Nations. *Corporate Social Responsibility and Environmental Management*, csr.1739. doi:10.1002/csr.1739

KEY TERMS AND DEFINITIONS

Business Portfolio: These are all sectors of activity in which the company is present. These models are tools that are designed to help managers choose which business areas to retain. The purpose is to know whether the portfolio is balanced and which activity should be maintained or sold.

Corporate Philanthropy: With sponsorship, companies participate in the financing of associations and charities. Corporate philanthropy is defined as financial support or material, without direct compensation, brought by a company in favor of a cause of general interest. It can concern various fields such as education, research, humanitarian, culture, art, environmental protection.

Corporate Social Responsibility: A concept according to which organizations take into account the interests of society, taking responsibility for the impact of their activities on companies and other public stakeholders. This commitment goes beyond the legal obligation to comply with legislation and suggests that organizations voluntarily taking further steps to improve the quality of life of workers and their families, as well as the whole local community and society.

Human Rights: According to this concept, every human being—as such, and regardless of his social status—has rights inherent in his personality, irrevocable and sacred, and therefore contradictory in all circumstances of society and authority.

Multilateral Development Institutions: They share a common mission to promote economic and social progress in developing countries by financing projects, supporting investments and generating financial resources for the benefit of the world population.

Multinational Corporation: When the company makes progress on internationalization to the extent that leads to foreign direct investment (FDI), it acquires a multinational character.

Organization and Effective Management of a Company: The concept of a business organization should ideally be integrated with the operational management of the company from the very beginning of the business and should continue until the end. Business management that is flexible and responsive is a management that will be effective. The dynamism of employees and their adaptability is also a problem that is becoming increasingly important with globalization.

Socially Conscious Activities: They promote social change, resolve human relationships and develop people's capabilities to enhance well-being.

Socially Responsible Investments: They represent the application of the principles for the sustainable development of financial investments.

Sustainable Development: It is the use of resources that addresses human needs while preserving the environment, so that these needs are met not only for the present, but also for future generations.

ENDNOTE

1 MDIs is an abbreviation of multilateral development institutions.

APPENDIX

Table 1. Selected definitions, main terms of use and dimensions for CSR and SDW<Tbl_Large></ Tbl_Large>

Organization/ Year of establishment	Mission/ main objectives	Main terms used	Main dimensions
Organizations and business partner networks			
International Business Leaders Forum (IBLF) 1990 in London, with the Prince of Wales and International Business Leaders	To engage in development activities… contributing to sustainable economic growth,… to encourage responsible business in the markets in which companies are operating	*Corporate Social Responsibility* – Dissemination of the practices of responsible business which benefit the society and facilitate social, economic and environmental sustainable development by means of maximizing the positive impact of business on society and minimizing the negative one.	- Economic - Social - Environmental
United Nations Global Compact (GC) 1999, in Davos, during the World Economic Forum	To encourage the private sector, civil society, trade unions, UN agencies and other stakeholders to apply ten principles for social and environmental responsibility in their daily practices	*Corporate citizenship* – defined by a company's contribution to society through its business activity, social investments and charity campaigns, including events for the public welfare.	- Human Rights - Labour standards - Environment - Anti-corruption
Business Social Compliance Initiative (BSCI) 2003, the Foreign Trade Association	To provide companies with the best system to improve working conditions in the global supply chain	The standard of *social responsibility* SA 8000 is considered a benchmark for "best practice" and BSCI members are required to be certified according to this standard.	- Human Rights - Labour standards - Discrimination - Environment
CSR Certification Standards			
SA 8000 – CSR certification standard 1997, USA, Social Accountability International (SAI) More about *SA 8000*: http://www.sa-intl.org/index.cfm?fuseaction=Page.ViewPage&PageID=1689	To encourage organizations to develop, maintain, and apply socially acceptable practices in the workplace	*SA8000* is a *sustainable standard* for ensuring the empowerment and protection of the health and welfare of all personnel throughout a worksite and a company's supply chain, while providing a management system for employers to demonstrate and verify their compliance with the Standard.	- Labour standards - Health and Safety - Freedom of Association - Discrimination - Remuneration
ISO 26000-CSR certification Standard 2010, by ISO More about *ISO 26000*: https://www.iso.org/iso-26000-social-responsibility.html	To provide guidance on how businesses and organizations can operate in a socially responsible way. It means acting in an ethical and transparent way that contributes to the health and welfare of society.	*Social Responsibility* is the responsibility of an organization for the impacts of its decisions and activities on society and the environment through transparent and ethical behavior that: (1) contributes to *sustainable development*, including the health and welfare of society; (2) takes into account the expectations of *stakeholders*; (3) is in compliance with applicable law and consistent with international norms of behavior, and (4) is integrated throughout the organization and practiced in its relationships.	- Human rights - Labour practices - Environment - Fair operating practices - Consumer issues - Community involvement and development
CSR and Corporate Sustainability Stock Exchange Indexes			
Dow Jones Sustainability Index (DJSI) 1999, The Dow Jones Group More about DJSI: http://www.sustainability-index.com/	To evaluate the sustainability performance of the top 2500 companies worldwide (largest companies, based on the size and price of their stocks)	*Corporate Sustainability – a business approach that creates long-term shareholder value by embracing opportunities and managing risks deriving from economic, environmental and social developments*	- Economic - Environmental - Social
Calvert Responsible Large Cap Core Index (formerly named the Calvert Social Index; CSI) 2000, Calvert Research and Management	To measure the economic situation of American companies defined as socially responsible	The Calvert Responsible Indexes include companies with strong sustainability profiles that, collectively, may have the potential to meet or exceed the performance of the common broad-market benchmarks.	- Environmental - Social

continued on following page

Table 1. Continued

Organization/ Year of establishment	Mission/ main objectives	Main terms used	Main dimensions
FTSE4 Good Indexes 2001, Financial Times & London Stock Exchange More about FTSE4GOOD indices: http://www.ftse.com/Indices/FTSE4Good_Index_Series/index.jsp	To measure the performance of companies that meet globally recognized corporate responsibility standards	FTSE4 Good Indexes serve as a benchmark index to track the performance of *responsible investment* portfolios.	- Environmental - Social - Governance
FTSE Johannesburg Stock Exchange Socially Responsible Index (JSE SRI) 2004, the Johannesburg Stock Exchange in collaboration with EIRIS, FTSE4GOOD – FTSE International Ltd. and KPMG More about JSE SRI: http://www.jse.co.za/About-Us/SRI/Introduction_to_SRI_Index.aspx	The Index philosophy is founded on the principles of the three pillars of the triple bottom line, namely environmental, social and economic sustainability, with good corporate governance underpinning each one. These principles are encapsulated in the Index indicators, which are structured along with the categories of Environment, Society and Governance and related sustainability concerns (ESG), with company response to climate change being assessed as a focus area.	The SRI Index Criteria continuously evolves to align more closely with global benchmarks, while remaining reflective of local developments.	- Environmental - Social - Governance
Sao Paolo Stock Exchange Corporate Sustainability Index (ISE) 2008, BM&FBovespa, Sao Paulo Stock Exchange in collaboration with Centre for Sustainability Studies of Fundaçao Getulio Vargas and International Finance Corporation More about ISE: http://www.b3.com.br/pt_br/	To implement a benchmark for investors interested in responsible investment and to promote CSR amongst Brazilian companies.	Originally funded by the International Finance Corporation (IFC), the private sector arm of the World Bank. Developed by the Center for Sustainability Studies of the Getúlio Vargas Foundation (GVces).	
KLD Global Sustainability Index Series (GSI) 2007, KLD Research & Analytics More about KLD GSI: http://www.kld.com/indexes/gsindex/index.html	Currently MSCI constructs MSCI Global Sustainability Indexes for: - Standard size-segment in all Developed and Emerging Markets; - Small Cap size-segment in the USA.	The FTSE KLD Global Sustainability Index is a broadly diversified global benchmark based on environmental, social, and governance (ESG) rankings.	- Environmental - Sustainable impact - Governance

Source: International organizations official web-sites, (Orsato, Garcia, Mendes-Da-Silva, Simonetti, & Monzoni, 2015) and (Serafimova, 2017, pp. 80-81)

Chapter 2
Corporate and Financial Social Leadership in Emerging Markets and the Developing World

Julia M. Puaschunder
The Schwartz Center for Economic Policy Analysis,The New School, USA & Graduate School of Arts and Sciences, Columbia University, USA

ABSTRACT

Corporate social responsibility (CSR) attributes economic, legal, social, and philanthropic responsibilities within the corporate sector. Sustainable financial social responsibility is primarily addressed by socially responsible investment (SRI). This chapter addresses the concepts of CSR and SRI in emerging markets and the developing world with special attention to top-down and bottom-up approaches. Theoretical descriptions discuss the human constituents of responsibility and the international emergence of CSR, with special attention to multi-stakeholder partnerships. The rise of SRI in the international arena in the wake of stakeholder activism and intrinsic socio-psychological motives are outlined. Recommendations target ingraining social responsibility in economic systems by global governance, multi-stakeholder management, and governmental assistance of the implementation and administration of corporate and financial social responsibility.

INTRODUCTION

The 2008/09 World Financial Recession heralded the 'Age of Responsibility', as the societal call for responsible market behavior reached unprecedented momentum. Responsibility is part of human nature, and complements corporate activities and financial considerations. The economic, legal, social, and philanthropic responsibilities within the corporate sector are attributed in Corporate Social Responsibility (CSR). Sustainable Financial Social Responsibility is primarily addressed by Socially Responsible Investment (SRI). Globalization, political changes and societal trends, but also the current state of the world economy, have leveraged a societal demand for ingraining responsibility into market systems.

DOI: 10.4018/978-1-7998-2193-9.ch002

Copyright © 2020, IGI Global. Copying or distributing in print or electronic forms without written permission of IGI Global is prohibited.

Corporate and Financial Intergenerational Leadership explores corporate and financial social responsibility by the cases of Corporate Social Responsibility (CSR) and Socially Responsible Investment (SRI) in order to draw attention to contemporary and prospective future opportunities for intergenerational equity (Puaschunder 2011, 2015a, b, 2016b, c, f). Theoretical descriptions discuss the human constituents of responsibility and the international emergence of CSR, with special attention to multi-stakeholder partnerships. The rise of SRI in the international arena in the wake of stakeholder activism and intrinsic socio-psychological motives are outlined.

Recommendations target ingraining social responsibility in economic systems by global governance, multi-stakeholder management, and governmental assistance of the implementation and administration of corporate and financial social responsibility. Transparency and accountability are key for monitoring corporate and financial social responsibility. As for the ongoing adaptation and adoption of CSR and SRI in the wake of the 2008 financial crisis, future research must attribute the newly-defined role of social responsibility in the interplay of public and private actors, given concurrent anti-globalization trends.

BACKGROUND

Corporate Social Responsibility and Socially Responsible Investment

Issues in Emerging Markets and Developing Economies

As of today, social responsibility has emerged as an *en vogue* topic for corporate executives, government officials, international public servants, and stakeholder representatives. Due to globalization, worldwide business mergers, and also for international deficiencies beyond the scope of nation states, the call for CSR and SRI has reached unprecedented momentum (Ahmad 2008, Beck 1998, Levitt 1983, Livesey 2002, Scholte 2000). In the wake of the 2008/09 World Financial Recession, corporate social misconduct and financial fraud have steered consumers and investors to pay increasing attention to democracy and social responsibility within market systems (Roberts 2012). Current stakeholder pressure addresses social responsibility of market actors and information disclosure of corporate and financial conduct. Legislative reforms enhance the accountability of financial market operations. With the era of liberalization being halted by the 2008/09 World Financial Recession, the reinterpretation of the public-private sector roles in providing social services has leveraged social responsibility into a pressing topic of debate. The renaissance of attention to responsibility as a prerequisite for the functioning of economic systems portrays CSR and SRI as windows of opportunity to re-establish trust in fallible market systems (Little 2008, Livesey 2002, Matten & Crane 2005, Trevino & Nelson 2004). The research explores up-to-date issues of concern for all these trends.

As a multi-stakeholder phenomenon, various actors impact on the management of financial social responsibility (Cuesta & Valor 2007, Little 2008, Rosen, Sandler & Shani 1991, Williams 2005). As a novel topic under debate, multiple SRI constituents may lack a standardized SRI notion, which limits their understanding of social responsibility within financial market systems, and hinders the overall communication on SRI (Bruyn 1987). As investors differ in their social concerns, priorities and tactics to address financial social responsibility, SRI features a plethora of forms of expression (Cooper & Schlegelmilch 1993, Frankel 1984, Pandey & Wright 2006). In order to promote the successful rise of

SRI, an understanding of the essential stakeholders' perception of SRI, and their attribution of success factors for financial social responsibility, is key (Puaschunder, 2016a, e, f, Puaschunder 2017d).

Overall, the research may delineate the dynamics and implementation of social responsibility within markets in the interplay of the public and private sectors, as well as financial markets within emerging markets and the developing world. In summary, the proposed research may serve as a first step towards resolving conflicts embedded in the ambiguity of relatively newly emerging CSR and SRI phenomena. The research is targeted at the successful rise of social responsibility within modern market economies to become a mainstream economic trend. Implications for corporate management and global governance, as well as financial decision-making theory and practice, may foster financial stability and sustainable market economies as future guarantors of sustainable societal progress.

Corporate Social Responsibility

In recent decades, CSR has emerged as several trends. International organizations have strengthened CSR by providing guidelines and oversight on corporate social conduct. Concurrently, governments have fostered social responsibility by legislative reforms and governmental regulations that raised corporate actors' awareness of social deficiencies. With the rise of CSR, governmental entities have started to count in corporate resources and expertise in social welfare provision. At the same time, stakeholder pressure for information disclosure of corporate conduct has propelled CSR and let consumers increasingly pay attention to the social impact of corporate activities. As a consequence, corporations have integrated total responsibility management as an innovative corporate success factor. Public-private partnerships have created win-win situations in addressing societal challenges by the combined forces of the public and private sectors. Given these trends, corporate social conduct is an en vogue phenomenon with the potential to steer entire market systems into a more socially conscientious direction.

International attention: The UN, World Bank, and the Organization for Economic Cooperation and Development, but also the European Commission and the US Congress play key roles in advancing social responsibility. International regulatory regimes must set CSR standards that harmonize corporate social endeavors, in accordance with global responsibility legislations such as the UNGC, the International Labour Organization (ILO)'s labor regulations, or the International Organization for Standardization (ISO) guidelines. At the same time, international initiatives must create supporting environments for the adoption of socially responsible business practices and assist public policy makers in crafting CSR frameworks.

Governmental assistance: In a plethora of legislative requirements, best practice principles, and implementation guidelines; governments must strive for stakeholder consensus on corporate social conduct. By raising awareness for social deficiencies, CSR stakeholders must be encouraged to administer corporate social conduct. Governmental networking forums must engage corporate actors, the media, and NGOs, to discuss societal concerns and find common ground on social solution strategies. The invitation to social solution finding will convince corporations to contribute to social goals beyond legal requirements. Based on a universal understanding of CSR, long-term focused governmental regulations and legislation must set social responsibility standards. In a continuing dialogue on CSR standards, governments must promote an authentic adoption of social responsibility practices by outlining the economic, social, and environmental impact corporations can have on society. The link between CSR, productivity, and innovation, will serve as an additional motivating factor for the consideration of social responsibility.

Research focused on tangible and intangible CSR assets will portray CSR as a competitive advantage that mitigates social risks for corporations.

To close the gap between the theoretical planning and actual application of CSR, governments must administer the implementation of CSR. Governmental managerial guidelines that pay attention to international legal requirements, national laws and corporate constraints will set best-practice standards. The corporate adoption of responsibility codes must be monitored by governmental control. In the implementation assistance of CSR, governments need to move from the qualitative expression of policy objectives to the quantitative measurement of results. Governments must also set up multi-stakeholder collaborative CSR networks as centres of expertise that constantly advance the social responsibility idea.

Governments should incentivize CSR. By steering capital and aid towards social and environmental attention, economic incentives encourage corporations to take on responsibilities. International export opportunities, credits, and insurances, based on social performance, must be coupled with internationally-renowned accreditations, licenses to operate, and CSR certifications. Positive governmental incentives feature tax and fee exemptions, credits, subsidies, and loans. Public entities may also fall back on negative sanctions of taxation, penalties, litigations, and charges, to avert socially irresponsible corporate conduct. Implicit incentives comprise trade controls and outsourcing contracts for corporations that commit to social and environmental standards.

Corporate social engagement: Paying attention to strategic opportunities and risks of societal challenges, CSR departments must assign leaders to adopt social responsibility policies, integrate social responsibility in corporate mission plans, and assist the implementation of ethical codes of conduct. Corporate leaders must promote a shared CSR vision and provide responsible leadership throughout the corporation and supply chain. At the operational level, the integration of CSR must be guided by action plans on day-to-day corporate social practices.

Accountability: Accountability refers to the expectation of having to justify actions to others (Lerner & Tetlock 1994). Accountability provides an external quality control feedback by public and private actors periodically monitoring corporate social contributions. Civil society must maintain a watch-dog function on corporate social impacts and thereby implicitly supervise the CSR implementation.

Transparency: Transparent corporate conduct is ensured by governmental legal obligations (e.g., freedom of information legislation), the removal of industrial information transfer barriers, economic incentives, stakeholder campaigns and CSR reporting. Information disclosure will help verify the quality and accuracy of CSR conduct. As the basis for monitoring and benchmarking, transparent CSR information will help identify areas for improvement, grow the confidence of the stakeholder community, and therefore secure investment capital.

Capacity building: Corporations and governments must educate socially responsible leaders. Academic institutions must ingrain CSR in educational curricular to bestow future leaders with the ability to manifest and implement CSR codes of conduct at all hierarchical levels. CSR capacity building must be supported by trade unions and NGOs.

The United Nations

International CSR standards are the basis for the worldwide spread of corporate social conduct. Universal CSR standards leverage CSR from legal compliance and voluntary philanthropy to a state-of-the-art mainstream corporate practice. Corporate social standards guideline corporate social conduct, and are essential for a harmonious CSR implementation. The United Nations Global Compact (UNGC) offers a framework that sets corporate social standards as an industrial 'level playing field'. The UNGC must be fortified by stakeholder management, implementation assistance, and quality control.

Stakeholder management: As CSR is not only a demand on the current agenda of multinational organizations operating in industrialized countries, but also a concern for the developing world, the UNGC must approach global players entering international markets and embrace corporate professionals along the supply chain. In the international arena, inconsistent standards must be harmonized, based on the international law. The UNGC framework must extend its range from legal constituents to offering coherent CSR codes of conduct and standardized best practices that are based on internationally agreed principles, formal requirements and contractual agreements. At the same time, the UNGC must remain applicable to national specificities and multi-stakeholder formations. A continued stakeholder dialogue on CSR must ensure that the UNGC implementation remains in accordance with societal demands and meets civic expectations.

The formulation of universal UNGC standards is hindered by differing missions, goal accomplishment time frames, and expectations of the constituents who may have diverse motivations to engage in the UNGC. The UNGC global network must mediate conflicts between the UNGC partners by a variety of means. By fostering a mutual understanding of common societal goals, the UNGC should work towards a universal consensus on CSR. Intercultural research projects must target finding harmonization strategies that strengthen the UNGC's cooperation. To foster the common understanding of CSR, the UNGC initiative must encourage participants to share information within the network and consult responsibility predicaments for the sake of a harmonious CSR conduct. Additional value campaigns must decrease divergences among international constituents. Networking events should engage the corporate world, the public sector, and civil society in expertise exchange on CSR. Internet platforms may store data on CSR information to create a common sense and best practice learning platform on corporate social conduct.

Implementation assistance: The UNGC must be integrated into corporate practices at the operational level. The UNGC participants are advised to change corporate policies in sync with the Ten Principles. By the year 2007, approximately 50 percent of the UNGC members had adopted CSR standards in accordance with the Ten Principles. The principles must further be ingrained in corporate conduct throughout all hierarchical levels. The UNGC and industrial CSR departments must coordinate and oversee the principles' implementation. Corporate executives' adoption of CSR must be assisted by respective action plans in accordance with the Ten Principles. The Ten Principles implementation must be advanced by concrete activities.

In the light of international corporate conduct, the enforcement of international human rights standards is challenged by differing national legal frameworks and public policy settings. As some countries have not codified international human rights, these governments are advised to comply with international standards. Transnational legal agreements and contractual CSR requirements must ensure the codification of human rights. The implementation of basic human rights must be supported and monitored by international and national governance. Gaps in the legal codification and the actual application of human rights must be addressed by the UN and NGOs. International councils and national governments must be encouraged to exchange information and work closely on a joint human rights strategy before multinational corporations.

The improvement of labor standards and working conditions contributes to the efficiency of markets, socio-political stability and societal welfare. Governments must, therefore, promote compliance with labor standards, and empower unions. The removal of legal, political, and developmental barriers to the exercise of freedom of association will back up labor unions and protect workers' rights. Freedom of association and the right to collective bargaining have to be monitored by the UN – with a special focus on politically unstable countries. Forced and compulsory labor must be detected to overcome human exploitation and discrimination. Citizens must be educated on their rights by governmental and NGO information campaigns. Equal opportunities must be ensured by legal frameworks, quota systems, and structural empowerment featuring educational scholarships. In the domain of CSR, interdisciplinary research must attribute the skills needed, and motivational factors for socially responsible corporate conduct. UNGC education campaigns must foster CSR learning plans and training facilities advocating the integration of CSR practices in daily operations. The UNGC's principles must be ingrained in university curricula and business management programs that train employees to consider externalities of corporate conduct.

In terms of social responsibility towards the environment, corporate innovations are key. Environmental responsibility must be promoted as an innovative corporate conduct that attracts financial investment. Corporations and investors must be incentivized for aligning corporate conduct with sustainability goals. The UNGC should create a database on environmental responsibility best practices, to allow benchmarking and quality control.

The UNGC must engage private and public stakeholders in the set-up of a global governance framework on anti-corruption. In the international arena, anti-corruption standards must bundle multi-stakeholder efforts. Backed up by regulatory reforms and legal codifications, anti-corruption codes of conduct must be established. Anti-corruption topics should be addressed by conferences, publications, newsletters and blogs that stress accountability, oversight and public scrutiny on corporate and financial social conduct as prerequisites of economic stability.

Quality control: A more sophisticated UNGC partner identification and selection based on the real commitment to the UN endeavors will foster the UNGC's credibility. As self-imposed goals and self-reporting on accomplishments give partners leeway to lower the bar of performance, the compliance with the UNGC standards must be enhanced by transparent goal setting and quality control. The UNGC must provide outcome, output, and performance indicators that help monitor the participants' engagement and the overall effectiveness of the UNGC initiative. CSR auditing will serve as a benchmark for the improvement of CSR practices and a basis for international legislative reforms. Accountability control will nurture credibility and trust in the UNGC, and therefore attract investments. In the international arena, successful UNGC goal accomplishments must be rewarded by governmental and national incentives, as well as internationally renowned accreditations and certifications for CSR best practice. Failed CSR goals must be made transparent to provide learning examples and allow assistance for improvement. Goal accomplishment deficiencies should be sanctioned. Up until now, no immediate actions have been instigated against corporations joining the UNGC and not meeting self-imposed goals. Current failures to provide an annual report on progress results solely in mild consequences. Corporations that do not meet self-set targets remain in the UNGC community, which negatively impacts on the overall UNGC's credibility. Transparent and stringent warnings and sanction procedures will counterwork the partners' non-compliance with the UNGC.

Public-Private-Partnerships (PPPs)

In the wake of the 2008/09 World Financial Recession, corporate scandals and the recapitalization of the finance sector have raised the demand for restoring public trust and credibility in corporate and financial markets. In the aftermath of the crisis, governmental and corporate actors bear unknown risks, and face growing societal expectations of disciplined corporate conduct and responsible financial investments, under conditions of heightened levels of public scrutiny. The recent trends have rebalanced social responsibility contributions in partnership models. Currently, PPPs feature responsibility restructuring between governance entities, the corporate world, and the finance sector. In these challenging times of change, PPPs must meet social responsibility demands by attention to global governance, governmental assistance, stakeholder management and local networks.

Global governance: In the international arena, PPP-administered CSR should be backed up by international organizations. Global governance entities must create a partnership-enhancing institutional, political, and judicial infrastructure. Legislative frameworks which aim at corporate social value creation must be established. International public policy makers must ratify social responsibility declarations that are in sync with societal goals and advocate for the adoption of social responsibility policies.

The UN plays a key role in advancing PPPs. The UNGC initiative must become an entry point for corporations to engage in social partnership projects featuring operational flexibility and focus on pragmatic solutions. In addition, the UNGC secretariat should promote CSR to the corporate world as a competitive advantage, and PPP-administered social responsibility as a corporate success factor beyond the boundaries of legal compliance and philanthropy. Pro-active CSR reporting should be awarded by UN rewards that gain public recognition.

In networking events, public and private partners must be brought together to find a consensus on social responsibility. A fruitful dialogue of UNGC partners and stakeholders will guideline a successful implementation of CSR partnerships. International conferences must serve as CSR vision councils in which governmental representatives, business executives, financial professionals, NGO representatives and academics share insights on CSR success factors to advance PPPs. Summits will produce a constant stream of literature on PPP best practices that must be made accessible on the internet to further CSR in PPPs.

Governmental assistance: Apart from the social value created, PPPs engage multiple stakeholders in the policy dialogue and mobilize resources for societal welfare. Governments must create a CSR-fostering environment and assist the coordination of multi-stakeholder CSR partnerships. Based on international regulations, governments must build PPPs frameworks to mitigate social, environmental and political risks in the implementation of CSR. Governmental officials must advocate the adoption of socially responsible corporate practices and encourage responsible leadership. Thereby governmental initiatives must inform corporate leaders about societal challenges and nurture an understanding of governmental priorities throughout the stakeholder community. Corporate executives' motivation must be enhanced by information on the positive, economic, social, and environmental advantages of CSR.

Stakeholder management: Partnerships are networking forums in which multiple stakeholders discuss topics of social concern in an atmosphere of trust and confidentiality. Mutual understanding of public and private partners is challenged by differing goals and time perspectives. Frictions may also stem from industry-specific expectations and individual motivations of the partners. As for these challenges, partners must focus on common goals and determine their roles and responsibilities in their accomplishment. By raising awareness for shared endeavors, the confidence in the UNGC network will be strengthened. Actionable work agendas must feature transparent timetables that pinpoint goal accomplishment strategies. Constant communication on the work in progress will allow monitoring the partners' contributions. Transparency on local goal accomplishment strategies will identify and disseminate best practices for the UNGC implementation. Evaluations must assess the impact of partners and benchmark the partners' CSR practices. As a quality control, external audits will boost the overall efficiency of partnerships.

Local networks: To manage the UNGC's expansion, networks must facilitate the local progress. As the impact of partnerships depends on coordinated action, local initiatives must foster the implementation of the UNGC principles. Local stakeholder events will bring together CSR administrators to find a common solution and create multi-stakeholder engagement opportunities. Local ownership of UNGC targets will help to root CSR in national and cultural contexts. National campaigns in local languages should also comprise seminars and workshops as for providing local learning possibilities. In addition, local meetings will give grass-root feedback opportunities to the UNGC leadership board and allow reflection about future strategies and challenges for the development of partnerships.

Regional Leadership

Sustainable development: Regional leadership and long-term financial sustainability must be ensured by securing multi-year donations. By outlining the progress that has already been accomplished, but also drawing attention to future needs, current donors must be motivated to contribute more extensively. In order to tap into new sources of funding, regional efforts have to build additional alliances with international organizations – foremost the UN and the World Bank – as well as corporate professionals, trade unions, NGOs, and academic communities. These entities must be asked for capital, in-kind contributions, and collaborative support, to develop the initiative. Increasing the visibility of the initiative will help regional development to reach out for novel donors. Providing access to information on regional advancements by the use of innovative interaction tools – e.g., e-newsletters, blogs, and Facebook – will engage a broad audience. Internet information portals must position regional leadership as a network hub for information exchange that attracts stakeholders' attention and raises the participants' commitment.

Stakeholder management: In its 'think tank' function, the regional secretariats must play an active role in the coordination of the partners' endeavors and fortify the networks' connectivity by launching stakeholder events. As UN-led networking forums, conferences will bring together executives from international organizations and corporations, government officials, and the civil society, to discuss ICT for development interests. The agreement on common goals will implicitly coordinate the partners' activities and fortify the impact of the entire GAID network. Social gatherings will build a mutual understanding about ICT for development, and promote a trust-based, supportive environment throughout the network. For the longer-term planning of the network, stakeholder meetings will also help identify emerging issues of concern and foster information exchange on future endeavors.

Regional goal accomplishment strategies: The partners must agree on implementation strategies and align activities accordingly. By committing themselves to specific goal accomplishment strategies, the partners must specify how their activities will contribute to regional goals. Transparency on goal accomplishment plans will help monitoring the partners' contributions and work in progress. The degree to which partners feature standardized or local ownership of goals must be outlined to all stakeholders at early stages of the partnering process. The regional constituents must work closely on implementing collectively-shared goals. Corporate partners must incorporate regional goals into business plans that become the basis for respective training programs. Local meetings must gather participants to coordinate and govern the implementation of ICT for development. Regional campaigns will root ICT for development in the cultural context and thereby support the network extension. Regional seminars and workshops must create learning experiences to foster the overall effectiveness of regional leadership in local networks. Regional dialogues will foster the transfer of knowledge of local success patterns, and generate applicable problem-solving capabilities. Information sharing on ICT best-practice standards will lead to contemporary ICT solutions and prepare for future challenges.

Accountability control: Accountability of the partners' commitments will counterbalance a lack of clarity about the purpose of the initiative. Based on transparent activities and monitoring, benchmarking of impact assessments will derive best practice learning models for future PPPs. Accountability control must also feature external goal accomplishment measurement. External audits should become the basis for rewarding positive results and providing assistance in case of defaults. Non-compliance with the goal accomplishment and communication deficiencies of the partners must be sanctioned – e.g., by warnings, de-linking partners from the regional internet portal or exclusion from the network. As for a long-term development, a reintegration into regional development must be made possible to steer partner behavior into a favorable direction.

SOLUTIONS AND RECOMMENDATIONS

Identified inconsistencies and gaps in available statistical data make us approach all results of studies with caution and require good knowledge about the basis on which conclusions have been drawn. The scope of data and potential exclusions may considerably impact the picture. Hence, the attention is to be paid to the methodology of data collecting used in particular studies and avoid direct comparisons.

Dynamically changing international business relations, expanded activities of international corporations, and globalisation favour new organisational and financial solutions between economic operators. Many of them are close to internationalisation, which forces out changes in the approach to definition and classification of FDI, as well as notions used to describe firms involved in direct investment. Theoretical achievements connected with the analysis of the phenomenon should be the closest possible to what actually happens in economy.

Besides, it seems justified to collect data for the same time, i.e. data on business activities in different countries should reflect the situation as at the end of calendar year. Data collected either for the beginning or for the end of fiscal year (which may be different for each country) may impact their comparability at international level. Besides, for many enterprises, information on reinvested earnings is available only after a very long delay and thus early estimates are subject to considerable change when more complete data become available. Uniform time, for which data are collected facilitates comparisons not only at international but also at national level.

It is also important to collect data for the same degree of consolidation of accounts in multinational enterprises (e.g., if in a given country data on the number of dependent entities are collected based on consolidated accounts while other data are taken from non-consolidated accounts we are not able to compare the variable which is subject to analysis) and to distinguish between direct and indirect control. Some countries do not treat all investments on an equal footing that is why we need to harmonise the rules.

It is also worth mentioning that statistical data must be allocated to places where investor's business actually takes place, not to his headquarters (Domański 2002) – but this postulate seems the most difficult to comply with. In most cases it is impossible to unequivocally identify the location where business takes place, especially when we deal with investment in the financial sector.

Financial Social Leadership

In the course of the 2008/09 World Financial Recession, stakeholder pressure on financial social responsibility has reached unprecedented momentum. Corporate social misconduct and fiduciary breaches have geared consumers and investors to increasingly pay attention to social responsibility within the financial market. Citizens' attention to social responsibility has fostered information disclosure of financial market conduct. As a consequence, legislative reforms and governmental regulations currently promote transparent social responsibility in financial markets. In the light of these occurrences, SRI appears as a window of opportunity for implementing financial social responsibility whilst re-establishing trust in financial markets. Interviews with financial experts and practitioners on financial social responsibility were targeted at gaining insight into the perception of SRI in order to derive recommendations on how to integrate social responsibility in financial markets. The respondents were found to be ambiguous about SRI. Whilst being optimistic about the innovative potential of financial social responsibility, they lack information on SRI. To leverage SRI from a niche market solution to a state-of-the-art financial practice, global governance on financial social responsibility, coupled with governmental assistance in providing access to information on SRI are recommended. The interplay of heightened SRI supply of the financial community and demand for SRI options will innovate the financial social responsibility idea.

Global governance: International organizations must support long-term financial social responsibility. The UN must continue to promote SRI as a means of environmental and social governance. The World Bank Group, the International Monetary Fund, the European Commission, and bilateral donors, must introduce social responsibility criteria as innovative financial practices. Transnational financial institutions must oversee the implementation of SRI in a systemic way.

Access to information: The expert interviews on SRI revealed a lack of information about socially conscientious financial practices. Information on SRI builds a shared understanding on social investment within the financial community. In line with the mere exposure effect, access to information on SRI fosters the integration of environmental and social governance in financial decision-making and heightens consumer confidence in markets (Frey & Irle 2002). Information disclosure about the stability and effectiveness of SRI will promote financial social responsibility in times of crisis. Information on SRI has the potential to concurrently stimulate the demand for SRI, and vitalize the financial industry's efforts to further advance SRI innovations. The combined supply and demand increase will result in a quantitative and qualitative extension of SRI, and advance the financial market social responsibility idea. In this light, transparency and accountability of financial social market operations will sophisticate SRI into a mainstream feature of financial decision-making. With the rising importance of transparent financial social responsibility and financial institutions integrating social, environmental and governance issues into investment analysis; social investment criteria will become part of the fiduciary duty of trustees, financial advisers, asset managers, and intermediary institutions.

International financial institutions and governmental policy makers must therefore provide market actors information on CSR for SRI screenings. International governance bodies must regulate financial social responsibility information disclosure to ensure the widespread availability of accurate, timely and comparable information about SRI. International organizations and governments must launch freedom of information acts that set minimum disclosure standards on environmental and social financial practices. Governance entities must also subsidize media industries and information service providers. New media tools should be used to disseminate material on financial social performance in an easily accessible and standardized form. Web-portals will help promoting social responsibility as a state-of-the-art financial practice and provide internet-based SRI best practice standards.

Governmental assistance: SRI must be backed up by governmental support. Governmental policy-makers must incentivize the integration of social responsibility into the agenda of financial institutions. Governmental control must ensure that financial regulations are balanced with current societal needs, governmental obligations and market demands. Governmental regulatory frameworks must set SRI standards for governmental agencies, financial institutions, self-regulatory bodies, accounting entities, rating agencies, index providers, and NGOs. Governments must encourage the integration of social responsibility in financial analyses by regulating fiduciary responsibilities. Concurrently governmental regulations must foster accountability of socially responsible financial conduct by transparency guidelines for the retail of SRI funds. Governmental assistance must provide information on how to adopt SRI-attentive regulations in order to achieve social responsibility goals. As a basis for improvements, governments must reward CSR reporting, based on monitoring and benchmarking financial institutions' social performance.

Financial market actors: Financial institutions and experts are encouraged to consider environmental and social responsibility in a variety of ways. Information on CSR and SRI must become part of financial market operations. Media reports must inform asset managers and financial analysts about the link between CSR and SRI. Supervisory bodies must promote the inclusion of SRI criteria in financial management. Accounting entities, rating agencies, and index providers, must adopt environmental and social governance standards as a basis for evaluation criteria that guarantee the concurrent financial and ethical performance. Stock exchange advisors must communicate the importance of environmental and social responsibility governance to listed corporations. Asset managers must encourage brokers to conduct SRI screenings. Investors are advised to request information on SRI and develop SRI proxy voting strategies. Pension fund trustees must consider environmental and social criteria in the formulation of investment mandates. Consultants and financial advisers must incorporate environmental and social corporate governance in their portfolio allocation strategies and accept social responsibility as a state-of-the-art of fiduciary obligations. Financial analysts must assess market opportunities with respect for social contributions and actively participate in ongoing voluntary responsibility initiatives.

Innovations: The SRI community must ensure that financial social responsibility is constantly innovated. Analysts must assist policy makers in setting up an SRI framework that reflects practitioners' needs. Financial experts must sophisticate financial social responsibility measurement models and contribute to research on environmental and social investments. Novel SRI options that fulfil unmet responsibility needs will open up the market for socially responsible economic growth, whilst bringing societal change. Academic institutions must nurture the financial community's ethical sense. Business schools and think tanks must support SRI research and offer financial ethics education. Financial economists must integrate socio-economic factors into standard economic profit maximization models. Concurrently, behavioral economists should delve into human decision-making fallibility in responsibility considerations and ethicality perceptions. Profound research findings are the basis for stimulating SRI innovations that lead to the concurrent economic prosperity and societal advancement.

SOLUTIONS AND RECOMMENDATIONS

The implementation of intergenerational equity ensures that future generations enjoy at least the same choices, if not better opportunities, as prevail today. Global challenges, like demographic aging, climate change and sustainable development, that cannot be solved on the national level, demand international leadership which facilitates and structures public engagement on common concerns. In top-down approaches, global consortia concertedly solve internationally-interconnected common goods problems and work towards a common vision of global justice throughout the world (Puaschunder 2017f, g, i, 2018a, c). Sustainability councils – such as the UN 'Ombudsman for Future Generations', address intergenerational considerations and define intergenerationally-equitable goals based on normative ethics and procedural justice. Transnational democracy coordinates and sets solidarity standards of common goods preservation, based on notions of fairness, on equal opportunities and merit-based allocation of resources.

Legal writings inspire vision councils' understanding of intergenerational equity as a human right to development. Connecting intergenerational equity to human rights of life, liberty and freedom grants sustainability for future generations and equal access to common goods for humankind over time. At the Rio Conference in 1992 – the first global conference on sustainability providing the Rio Agenda 21 – first inferences were drawn between sustainability and human rights in the realization that responsibility for the future is a prerequisite of well-being for humankind. The following year in Vienna, human rights were referred to environmental sustainability. At the 10th anniversary of the 1992 Rio conference on sustainable development in Johannesburg, there was a clear coming together of sustainability and human rights.

The legal enforcement of intergenerational fairness is limited, as the future unborn are not able to sue their grandfathers for debts, request pensions today, or avert environmental lock-ins. Top-down approaches may not give voice to future needs, since constitutional experts do not even agree on the rights of the unborn embryo, are not present in courtrooms and lobbies, do not advocate future concerns. Legal frameworks and structural reforms must be accompanied by behavioral changes – such as education to efficiently use scarce resources, invest for the future and be conscientious of energy consumption – in order to overcome current intergenerational constraints. Societal frameworks featuring responsibility, as respect for future generations, and decisions at an early stage, will lead to new forms of institutional governance determining the living conditions of following generations.

The intergenerational equity implementation requires a multi-stakeholder approach in which public and private sector forces concertedly increase productivity through technological advantages and social innovations. Equality of merit-based access to opportunity accelerates economic growth attuned to sustainability goals and social integration. Intergenerational justice on the operative level, features foresight and socially responsible policies. Age-diversified juries, well-tempered investigation panels, and generation-partnerships foster information exchange between young and old. Through voting, the young partake in societal decision-making. Youth coalitions advocate for long-term decision-making in parliamentary circles – such as in the case of the German debt break constitutionalized in 2011. In participatory democracy, in which decisions are made publicly and discussed openly with people having a say in their solution, citizens decide with greater consciousness of their children's needs. The political communication on intergenerational equity implementation strategies may focus on easily understandable, personal examples, that help to bring the present into the future, to encourage people to think in terms of their own children and imagine the sustainability of their welfare; it will be your children, who will get a house, because you used to earn more than they will, they cannot afford that extra education, they will face higher levels of taxation and a longer working life ahead, while suffering from climate change, and so in the end, your children are not going to enjoy the same future as you had. Accompanied with peaceful democracy-in-action protests, this will lead people to think and give beyond their personal lives (Puaschunder, forthcoming a).

Bottom-up discussion platforms ingrain intergenerational perspectives in current decision-making. Generations coming together will allow the discussion of problems in the social compound. Open debates about commonly-shared values and goals will clarify what public debt, pension welfare, and environmental responsibility mean for future generations, and leverage intergenerational equity into a uniting, politically-driven, issue. General discussions nurture consensus on societal problems of all age groups. Combining the old and young's perspectives in dialogues between generations helps in paying attention to future generations' needs and balances, between the young, who strive for novel change, and the old, who pass on their wisdom of experience. New media technologies help bridging the young and old, by granting access to information about the needs of all age groups. The current interconnectedness of the world becomes a tool to embrace older people and include them in society, so that they are more willing to save for their children, invest in the youth, and pass on wealth, rather than spending it on their current consumption. A harmonious representation of diversified viewpoints is gained in a dialogue between generations that integrates young and old viewpoints, and represents all societal groups. Beyond legal and regulatory boundaries, partnerships between young and old encourage a culture of voluntary intergenerational fairness. Transfers of wisdom from the old to the young raises solidarity in the social compound and grants stability for the community, whilst fostering positive social development and societal welfare.

Intergenerational equity, as a natural behavioral law, serves as an ethical anchor to steer behavior towards future-orientation and societal responsibility. Beyond legal contracts, family bonds and responsible education form pro-social, intergenerationally conscientious norms, as a basis for a favorable societal climate. Education will lead people to feel obliged to invest in the upcoming young and see future-allocations as societal progress. While the young should be brought up with intergenerational values, their elders should be taught to understand the needs of the young. Benefitting from crystallized intelligence of the old, the young must drive technological and social innovations to change societal patterns. Change laboratories should focus on how to embrace moral codes of wealth distribution between generations. The family compounds should support the upcoming generations – for example with credits for long-term investments like housing and education, in times when it has become more difficult to borrow from the banks, as first time house purchase and education have become more expensive.

Regarding overindebtedness, the public good of a stabilized economy depends on merit-based, fair, asset allocation and risk management. Macro-economic policy frameworks reduce risks in the interplay of financial markets and the real economy. Regulation must alleviate 'boom and bust'-related market downfalls, and work towards a fair resource (re)distribution in accordance with societal values. After a pendulum swing from liberal to state interventionism, a well-tempered policy balance may feature anti-cyclical politics of credits, controlled inflation, debt breaks, and debt cancellation. Creating economically-favorable locations that attract international capital, and sustainable projects that fortify future potentials, vitalize the economy. Capital institutions' focus on core activities, away from value-at-risk seeking, will establish lasting and sustainable relations with customers.

Social welfare provision constraints related to demographic changes can be solved by market productivity growth, wealth redistribution, pension reform and adjusted pension expectations. Increase in the efficiency of pension schemes, targets raising tax revenues, cutting social benefits, and merit-based pension distribution. Inheritance tax redistributes wealth from the old to the young on the individual level, yet problematically, it appears that inheritance tax breeds inequality, and has been ceased in most EU countries. People should be incentivized to belong to a certain tax group, and remunerated according to their work productivity for society. A pay-as-you-go pension insurance could be considered as a market approach to solve the social welfare problems of an aging population. Direct governmental transfers to the underprivileged, and tax breaks, grant access to health and education. Structural reforms may ensure that the young have an at least as favorable standard as the old today, by raising the pension age in accord with life expectancy. Increased pension ages, however, crowd out opportunities for the young to enter the workforce. Requiring pensioners not to work, by law, opens the market, but puts productivity pressure on the young and strips crystallized expertise off the labor force. Pensioners should thus be encouraged to use their potential for society away from the labor market. Based on their expertise and former affiliations, healthy civilians may contribute to labor charity – similar to Norwegian welfare models or Kibbutz systems – to aid the sustainability of the pension scheme, alongside providing engagement opportunities for the elderly. Solidarity in supporting pensioners, based on social responsibility, is a strong social welfare safety net. Aging population-related social welfare crunches can also be curbed by migration overcoming reproduction gaps. Immigration, however, requires integration, education, and policies on harmonization expenditure – especially throughout territories with differing languages and cultures, such as Europe. Migration should be pegged to merit-based performance of immigrants.

Ecologically, we must not live at the expense of future generations regarding natural resource consumption and climate change. As the market is not future-oriented by itself, ecological problems demand a political frame to implement foresight and governmental will to find a well-balanced resource distribution over time. Climate conscientiousness will require a modern, multi-cultural, multi-factual, and urgent response, to ensure climate stabilization in the future. International consensus must ensure that large, emerging economies, such as China and India, incept systems of monitoring, reporting, and verification, of emission reduction. Legislation backing intergenerational equity will leverage climate justice as a human right, in order to alleviate the global emergent risks of resource scarcity. Legal frameworks, such as international contracts, define generational justice. Injustices and inequalities created by present world inhabitants must be treated as human rights abuses and addressed by international institutions – like The United National Environmental Program. International cooperation and regional collaborations on the preservation of global common goods comprise coordinated action to ensure fair usage of global common goods, in accordance with international laws, as a prerequisite of security and a basis for socio-economic development of a sustainable humankind. Contracts with precautionary principle attribute common, but differentiated, responsibilities to ensure sustainable development and common goods preservation for posterity. Political leadership addresses climate change mediating discussions on a fair share of the global commons in the long run. Open discussions will advance mechanisms for a fair common goods distribution in the international interest.

FUTURE RESEARCH DIRECTIONS

The humanitarian dimension of climate change has to become central. Climate negotiations, UN Framework discussions, and UN agencies, must address the impact of climate change on the most vulnerable, who have done the least to cause climate change, but who are most severely affected. Climate justice links human rights and development to safeguard those who carry a disproportionally large burden of climate change, and it amplifies the voices of future world inhabitants to ensure fairness to the future unborn. Low carbon growth and access to energy for all, using non-fossil fuel sources, will ensure sustainable development. Developing countries must build resilience to the effects of climate change. Global partnerships and international alliances lead on the human rights of climate change aversion. Sustainable welfare education bestows long-term foci to foresightedly strive towards climate justice for the sake of eternal equity. Philosophically intergenerational equity must become a moral obligation when considering the consequences of climate justice.

Climate justice incorporates a strong gender perspective. Women are powerful change agents; as environmentally-conscientious, energetic mothers, with interest in their children's well-being, they innovatively decide and implement climate adaptation solutions in local communities. On the global political stage, Connie Hedegaard, former Danish Minister for the Environment and Danish Minister for Climate and Energy, hosted the UN Climate Change Conference in Copenhagen in 2009, subsequently took up a position with the European Commissioner for Climate Action. Cancun, Copenhagen, and South Africa conferences had female chairs, and the Secretary-General of climate negotiations, and the Climate Change Commissioner in Europe, were women. We need a platform of female leadership on climate change aversion to be developed for the Cup 17 in Durban, as we had in the Rio+20 meetings.

While international actors craft international laws on intergenerational equity, nation states implement intergenerational fairness by finding access to affordable renewable energy in innovative ways, using new technologies and green retrofits. Energy efficiency can also be created by changes to the infrastructure of public transportation to reduce energy consumption. City designs can make streets more secure and arrange public transport for pedestrians. Education can trigger fundamental change processes in individuals' lifestyles, so they can become more consumption-conscientious and energy efficient.

CONCLUSIONS

External shocks of economic depressions and wars of the past have impacted on the quality of life of the young ever since they took place, and steered attention towards social responsibility (Puaschunder 2010). But the future risks and opportunities which will arise for the future perspectives of the youth of today in the aftermath of the 2008/09 World Financial Crisis, given unprecedented governmental overindebtedness, an aging Western world population, and irreversible environmental damage, is unknown. How to face these unfamiliar challenges should become the focus of future research on intergenerational equity.

Investigating intergenerational equity is a formidable task, touching on unprecedented predicaments comprising manifold stakeholders. An engagement of various stakeholders on differing intergenerational predicaments results in a disparity of intergenerational equity notions. As a first step towards resolving the societal losses imbued in the complexity of this novel phenomenon, but also to innovatively explore new opportunities to ingrain intergenerational responsibility within globalizing economies, future research may study intergenerational equity paying special attention to expert opinions and stakeholder facets, in the interplay of public and private sector approaches. Holistically describing intergenerational equity with attention to stakeholders' perspectives will help overcoming socio-economic losses implied by various societal notions. Averting multi-stakeholder conflicts in the implementation of intergenerational equity will aid in harmonizing intergenerational equity on a grand scale.

When investigating the natural human intergenerational conscientiousness, behavioral economics insights on human decision-making may, innovatively, be considered. Behavioral economics depict human rationality, bounded by mental limitations and heuristic decision short-cuts (Tversky & Kahneman 1974) in an overly complex governmental architecture over which political leaders have limited control

(Roberts 2012). These errors are crucial in ethical considerations which have an irreversible impact on society. The emerging field of bounded ethicality describes predictable psychological processes that let people engage in ethically questionable behavior inconsistent with their preferred ethics (Bazerman & Tenbrunsel 2011). Bounded ethicality occurs when ethical individuals are unaware of indirect unethical consequences which erode over time (Bazerman & Chugh 2005, Bazerman & Moore 2009, Gino & Margolis 2011, Gino, Schweitzer, Mead & Ariely 2011, Tenbrunsel & Messick 2004). While bounded ethicality research offers a way to realistically capture intergenerational conscientiousness, we miss a whole-rounded intergenerational equity decision-making frame to test the applicability of the bounded ethicality paradigm onto intergenerational concerns, and explore motives for sacrificing to future generations within the social compound (Shu & Bazerman 2011, Tsay, Shu & Bazerman 2011).

Intergenerational conscientiousness requires social responsibility and intertemporal foresight to discount future lives. In the search to alleviate human-bounded ethicality on intertemporal dilemmas, emotions were recently found to influence time perspectives and social responsibility (Bazerman, Gino, Shu & Tsay 2011, Horberg, Oveis & Keltner 2011). Emotionally-laden intergenerational values appear as windows of opportunity to steer intergenerational ethicality in human decision-making. Trust – as a concept related to emotionality – could be an additional intergenerational ethicality nudge to overcome the lack of identification with future beneficiaries (Ostrom 2009).

Investigating intergenerational constraints from a global governance perspective helps in understanding the impact of public and private sector contributions on intergenerational fairness. Studying public welfare problems concurrently with financial market predicaments and environmental constraints elucidates the similarities and differences of public and private sector approaches to ensuring intergenerational equity. Mapping intergenerational equity throughout the world allows international comparisons of public and private sector intergenerational responsibility approaches, in order to derive multi-faceted success factors for a concerted implementation of intergenerational responsibility. Paying attention to the 2008/09 World Financial Crisis provides a unique snapshot of socio-economic changes implied by a financial turmoil, and helps to portray crises as opportunities for ingraining ethicality throughout society. In sum, understanding the socio-dynamics of intergenerational equity will serve as a prerequisite for an intergenerationally harmonious, and future-sustainable humankind.

REFERENCES

Ahmad, M. (2008, Jan. 24). Global CEOs at World Economic Forum cite sovereign wealth funds as the new power broker. *BI-ME*.

Bazerman, M. H., & Chugh, D. (2005). Bounded awareness: Focusing failures in negotiation. In L. Thompson (Ed.), *Frontiers of Social Psychology: Negotiation* (pp. 7–26). New York, NY: Psychological Press.

Bazerman, M. H., Gino, F., Shu, L. L., & Tsay, C.-J. (2011). Joint evaluation as a real-world tool for managing emotional assessment of morality. *Emotion Review*, *3*(3), 290–292. doi:10.1177/1754073911402370

Bazerman, M. H., & Moore, D. (2009). *Judgment in managerial decision making*. Hoboken: Wiley.

Bazerman, M. H., & Tenbrunsel, A. E. (2011). *Blind spots: Why we fail to do what's right and what to do about it*. Princeton, NJ: Princeton University Press. doi:10.1515/9781400837991

Beck, U. (1998). Wie wird Demokratie im Zeitalter der Globalisierung möglich? In U. Beck (Ed.), *Politik der Globalisierung* (pp. 7–67). Frankfurt am Main: Suhrkamp.

Bekefi, T. (2006). *Business as a partner in tackling micronutrient deficiency: Lessons in multisector partnership. Report of the Corporate Responsibility Initiative*. Cambridge, MA: Harvard University Press.

Bruyn, S. T. (1987). *The field of social investment*. Cambridge, MA: Cambridge University Press. doi:10.1017/CBO9780511570872

Carroll, A. B. (1979). A three-dimensional model of corporate social performance. *Academy of Management Review*, *4*, 497–505. doi:10.5465/amr.1979.4498296

Chua, A. (2003). *World on fire: How exporting free market democracy breeds ethnic hatred and global instability*. New York: Anchor.

Cooper, C., & Schlegelmilch, B. (1993). Key issues in ethical investment: Business ethics: A European approach. Prentice Hall, NJ: Hemel Hempstead.

Crane, A., Matten, D., & Moon, D. (2004). Stakeholder as citizens? Rethinking rights, participation and democracy. *Journal of Business Ethics*, *53*(1/2), 107–122. doi:10.1023/B:BUSI.0000039403.96150.b6

Cuesta de la, G. M. & Valor, C. (2007). Fostering corporate social responsibility through public initiative: From the EU to the Spanish case. *Journal of Business Ethics*, *55*(3), 275–293.

De Silva, S., & Amerasinghe, F. (2004). *Corporate social responsibility: Issues, problems and challenges*. Colombo: Lake House.

Detomasi, D. A. (2007). The political roots of corporate social responsibility. *Journal of Business Ethics*, *82*(4), 807–819. doi:10.100710551-007-9594-y

Elkington, J. (1998). *Cannibals with forks: The triple bottom line of 21st century business*. New Society.

Fitzgerald, N., & Cormack, M. (2007). *The role of business in society: An agenda for action*. Retrieved from the internet at Frankel, T. (1984). Decision making for social investing. In D. M. McGill (Ed.), *Social Investing* (pp. 131–162). Homewood, IL: Irwin.

Gino, F., & Margolis, J. (2011). Bringing ethics into focus: How regulatory focus and risk preferences influence (un)ethical behavior. *Organizational Behavior and Human Decision Processes*, *115*(2), 145–156. doi:10.1016/j.obhdp.2011.01.006

Gino, F., Schweitzer, M., Mead, N., & Ariely, D. (2011). Unable to resist temptation: How self-control depletion promotes unethical behavior. *Organizational Behavior and Human Decision Processes*, *115*(2), 191–203. doi:10.1016/j.obhdp.2011.03.001

Greenspan, A. (2007). *The age of turbulence: Adventures in a new world*. New York, NY: Penguin.

Horberg, E. J., Oveis, C., & Keltner, D. (2011). Emotions as moral amplifiers: An appraisal tendency approach to the influences of distinct emotions upon moral judgment. *Emotion Review*, *3*(3), 237–244. doi:10.1177/1754073911402384

Jones, I., & Pollitt, M. (1998). *The role of business ethics in economic performance*. London: Macmillan. doi:10.1057/9780230379794

Kettl, D. F. (2006). *The global public management revolution*. Washington, DC: The Brookings Institution.

Lea, R. (2002). Corporate social responsibility: Institute of Directors (IoD) member opinion survey. IoD.

Levitt, T. (1983). The globalization of markets. *Harvard Business Review*, *61*, 2–11.

Little, K. (2008). *Socially responsible investing: Put your money where your values are*. New York, NY: Penguin.

Livesey, S. (2002). The discourse of the middle ground: Citizen Shell commits to sustainable development. *Management Communication Quarterly*, *15*(3), 313–349. doi:10.1177/0893318902153001

Matten, D., & Crane, A. (2005). Corporate citizenship: Toward an extended theoretical conceptualization. *Academy of Management Review*, *30*(1), 166–179. doi:10.5465/amr.2005.15281448

Micklethwait, J., & Wooldridge, A. (2003). *A future perfect: The challenge and promise of globalization*. New York, NY: Crown Business Press.

Mohr, L. A., Webb, D. J., & Harris, K. E. (2001). Do consumers expect companies to be socially responsible? The impact of corporate social responsibility on buying behavior. *The Journal of Consumer Affairs*, *35*(1), 45–72. doi:10.1111/j.1745-6606.2001.tb00102.x

Moon, J., Crane, A., & Matten, D. (2003). Can corporations be citizens? Corporate citizenship as a metaphor for business participation in society. *Research Paper Series of ICCSR, 4*, 2-17.

Nelson, J. (2004). *Leadership, accountability and partnership: Critical trends and issues in corporate social responsibility. Report of the Corporate Responsibility Initiative*. Cambridge, MA: Harvard University.

Ostrom, E. (2009). The Sveriges Riksbank Prize in Economic Sciences in Memory of Alfred Nobel Laureate 2009 speech.

Pandey, S. K., & Wright, B. E. (2006). Connecting the dots in public management: Political environment, organizational goal ambiguity and public manager's role ambiguity. *Journal of Public Administration: Research and Theory*, *16*(4), 511–532. doi:10.1093/jopart/muj006

Prahalad, C. K., & Hammond, A. (2003). *Serving the world's poor profitably. Harvard Business Review on Corporate Responsibility*. Cambridge, MA: Harvard Business School.

Puaschunder, J. M. (2010). *On Corporate and Financial Social Responsibility* (Unpublished Dissertation). Faculty of Psychology, Department of General and Basic Psychology, University of Vienna.

Puaschunder, J.M. (2011). *Intergenerational equity as a natural behavioral law*. Library of Congress United States of America Copyright Office Copyright Catalogue TXu001743422/2011-03-08.

Puaschunder, J. M. (2015a). On the social representations of intergenerational equity. *Oxford Journal of Finance and Risk Perspectives*, *4*(4), 78–99.

Puaschunder, J. M. (2015b). The call for global responsible intergenerational leadership in the corporate world: The quest of an integration of intergenerational equity in contemporary Corporate Social Responsibility (CSR) models. In *Proceedings of the 2015 6th International Conference of the Association of Global Management Studies at* Alfred Lerner Hall of Columbia University. New York: The Association of Global Management Studies. 10.2139srn.2591032

Puaschunder, J. M. (2015c). Trust and reciprocity drive common goods allocation norms. In *Proceedings of the Cambridge Business & Economics Conference*. Cambridge, UK: Cambridge University.

Puaschunder, J. M. (2016a). Global responsible intergenerational leadership: The quest of an integration of intergenerational equity in Corporate Social Responsibility (CSR) models. *Annals in Social Responsibility*, *2*(1), 1–12. doi:10.1108/ASR-10-2015-0016

Puaschunder, J. M. (2016b). On eternal equity in the fin-de-millénaire. *Journal of Leadership, Accountability and Ethics*, *13*(2), 11–24.

Puaschunder, J. M. (2016c). On eternal equity in the fin-de-millénaire: Rethinking capitalism for intergenerational justice. *Journal of Leadership, Accountability and Ethics*, *13*(2), 11–24.

Puaschunder, J. M. (2016d). On the emergence, current state and future perspectives of Socially Responsible Investment (SRI). *Consilience: The Columbia University Journal of Sustainable Development*, *16*(1), 38–63.

Puaschunder, J. M. (2016e). The call for global responsible inter-generational leadership: The quest of an integration of inter-generational equity in Corporate Social Responsibility (CSR) models. In D. Jamali (Ed.), *Comparative Perspectives on Global Corporate Social Responsibility* (pp. 276–289). Hershey, PA: IGI Global Advances in Business Strategy and Competitive Advantage Book Series.

Puaschunder, J. M. (2016f). The call for global responsible inter-generational leadership: The quest of an integration of inter-generational equity in Corporate Social Responsibility (CSR) models. In *Natural Resources Management: Concepts, Methodologies, Tools, and Applications. Information Resource Management Association*. Hershey, PA: IGI Publishing.

Puaschunder, J. M. (2017a). Ethical decision making under social uncertainty: An introduction to Überethicality. *Sustainable Production and Consumption*, *12*, 78–89. doi:10.1016/j.spc.2017.05.005

Puaschunder, J.M. (2017b). Ethical, environmental, social and governance-oriented investments. *Archives of Business Research, 5*(8), 151-159.

Puaschunder, J. M. (2017c). Financing climate justice through climate change bonds. *Oxford Journal of Finance and Risk Perspectives*, *6*(3), 1–10.

Puaschunder, J. M. (2017d). Intergenerational leadership: Coordinating common goods and economic stability. *Journal of Applied Business and Economics*, *19*(11/12), 65–78.

Puaschunder, J. M. (2017e). Krisenrobuste Alternativen. *Global Investor*, *3*(5), 69.

Puaschunder, J. M. (2017f). Mapping Climate Justice in the 21st Century. *Agriculture Research and Technology*, *10*(5), 1–3.

Puaschunder, J. M. (2017g). Mapping Climate in the 21st Century. *Development*, *59*(3), 211–216.

Puaschunder, J. M. (2017h). Socio-psychological motives of socially responsible investors. *Global Corporate Governance: Advances in Financial Economics*, *19*, 209–247.

Puaschunder, J. M. (2017i). The climatorial imperative. *Agriculture Research and Technology*, *7*(4), 1–2.

Puaschunder, J. M. (2017j). We – today's and tomorrow's – people of the United World: Rethinking capitalism for intergenerational justice in the fin-de-millénaire. *Corporate Governance and Sustainability Review*, *1*(2), 30–35. doi:10.22495/cgsrv1i2p4

Puaschunder, J. M. (2018a). Climate Wealth of Nations. In *Proceedings of the 11th International Research Association for Interdisciplinary Studies (RAIS) Conference on Social Sciences*. Academic Press.

Puaschunder, J. M. (2018b). *Corporate Social Responsibility and Opportunities for Sustainable Financial Success*. Hershey, PA: IGI Publishing.

Puaschunder, J. M. (2018c). Intergenerational leadership: An extension of contemporary corporate social responsibility models. *Corporate Governance & Organizational Behavior Review*, *2*(1), 7–17. doi:10.22495/cgobr_v2_i1_p1

Puaschunder, J. M. (2018d). *Intergenerational responsibility in the 21st century*. Wilmington, DE: Vernon Art and Science.

Puaschunder, J. M. (2018e). Nachhaltigkeit und Investment: Psychologische Aspekte von nachhaltigkeitsorientiertem Investitionsverhalten. In C. T. Schmitt & E. Bamberg (Eds.), *Psychologie und Nachhaltigkeit: Konzeptionelle Grundlagen, Anwendungsbeispiele und Zukunftsperspektiven* (pp. 127–134). Wiesbaden: Springer. doi:10.1007/978-3-658-19965-4_11

Puaschunder, J. M. (2018f). Socio-psychological motives of Socially Responsible Investments (SRI). In S. Boubaker, D. Cumming, & D. K. Nguyen (Eds.), *Research Handbook of Investing in the Triple Bottom Line: Finance, Society and the Environment* (pp. 447–472). London: Edward Elgar. doi:10.4337/9781788110006.00029

Puaschunder, J. M. (2018g). The history of ethical, environmental, social and governance-oriented investments as a key to sustainable prosperity in the finance world. In Corporate Social Responsibility, Ethics and Sustainable Prosperity, (pp. 359-388), Heidelberg: Springer.

Puaschunder, J.M. (forthcoming a). *Governance and Climate Justice: Global South and Developing Nations*. Cham: Switzerland: Springer International & Nature, New York, New York: Palgrave Macmillan.

Puaschunder, J. M. (Ed.). (forthcoming b). Intergenerational Governance and Leadership in the Corporate World. Idea Group, Inc.

Puaschunder, J.M. (forthcoming c). Long-term investments. *Encyclopedia of the UN Sustainable Development Goals: Partnerships for the Goals*.

Puaschunder, J.M. (forthcoming d). When investors care about causes: Learning from political divestiture during Apartheid and the Sudan crisis for the transition to renewable energy via green bonds. Academic Press.

Puaschunder, J.M. (forthcoming e). On Corporate and Financial Social Responsibility. Cambridge, UK: Cambridge Scholars Publishing.

Puaschunder, J. M., & Schwarz, G. (2012). *The future is now: How joint decision making curbs hyperbolic discounting but blurs social responsibility in the intergenerational equity public policy domain.* Harvard University Situationist Law and Mind Sciences Working Paper.

Roberts, A. S. (2010). *Disciplined democracies: Global capitalism and the new architecture of government.* Oxford, UK: Oxford University Press. doi:10.1093/acprof:oso/9780195374988.001.0001

Rosen, B. N., Sandler, D. M., & Shani, D. (1991). Social issues and socially responsibility investment behavior: Preliminary empirical investigation. *The Journal of Consumer Affairs*, *25*(2), 221–234. doi:10.1111/j.1745-6606.1991.tb00003.x

Rothkopf, D. (2008). *Superclass: The global power elite and the world they are making.* New York, NY: Farrar, Straus & Giroux.

Scholte, J. A. (2000). *Globalization: A critical introduction.* Basingstoke, UK: Palgrave.

Shu, L. L., & Bazerman, M. H. (2011). *Cognitive barriers to environmental action: Problems and solutions. In Oxford Handbook of Business and the Environment.* Oxford, UK: Oxford University Press. doi:10.1093/oxfordhb/9780199584451.003.0009

Sichler, R. (2006). *Autonomie in der Arbeitswelt: Psychologie und Beruf.* Göttingen: Vandenhoeck & Ruprecht.

Smith, A. (1976). *An inquiry into the nature and causes of the wealth of nations.* Oxford, UK: Clarendon. (Original work published 1776)

Sparkes, R. (2002). *Socially responsible investment: A global revolution.* Wiley.

Tenbrunsel, A. E., & Messick, D. M. (2004). Ethical fading: The role of self-deception in unethical behavior. *Social Justice Research*, *17*(2), 223–236. doi:10.1023/B:SORE.0000027411.35832.53

Trevino, L. K., & Nelson, K. A. (2004). *Managing business ethics: Straight talk about how to do right.* Hoboken, NJ: Wiley.

Tsay, Ch.-J., Shu, L. L., & Bazerman, M. (2011). Naiveté and cynicism in negotiations and other competitive contexts. *The Academy of Management Annals*, *5*(1), 495–518. doi:10.5465/19416520.2011.587283

Tversky, A., & Kahneman, D. (1974). Judgment under uncertainty: Heuristics and biases. *Science*, *185*(4157), 1124–1131. doi:10.1126cience.185.4157.1124 PMID:17835457

Werther, W. B., & Chandler, D. (2006). *Strategic corporate social responsibility: Stakeholders in a global environment.* Thousand Oaks, CA: Sage.

Williams, G. (2005). *Are socially responsible investors different from conventional investors? A comparison across six countries.* Unpublished working paper, University of Bath.

Wolff, M. (2002). Response to "Confronting the critics.". *New Academy Review*, *1*, 230–237.

ADDITIONAL READINGS

Puaschunder, J. M. (2010). *On corporate and financial social responsibility*. Unpublished Doctoral Thesis. Vienna: University of Vienna, Faculty of Psychology.

Puaschunder, J. M. (2015). On the social representations of intergenerational equity. *Oxford Journal of Finance and Risk Perspectives*, *4*(4), 78–99.

Puaschunder, J. M. (2016a). Intergenerational climate change burden sharing: An economics of climate stability research agenda proposal. *Global Journal of Management and Business Research: Economics and Commerce*, *16*(3), 31–38.

Puaschunder, J. M. (2016b). *Mapping Climate Justice*. Proceedings of the 2016 Young Scientists Summer Program Conference, International Institute for Applied Systems Analysis (IIASA), Laxenburg, Austria. 10.2139srn.2819947

Puaschunder, J. M. (2016c). On eternal equity in the fin-de-millénaire: Rethinking capitalism for intergenerational justice. *Journal of Leadership, Accountability and Ethics*, *13*(2), 11–24.

Puaschunder, J. M. (2016d). The call for global responsible intergenerational leadership in the corporate world: The quest for an integration of intergenerational equity in contemporary Corporate Social Responsibility (CSR) models. In D. Jamali (Ed.), *Comparative Perspectives in Global Corporate Social Responsibility* (pp. 275–288). Hershey, PA: IGI Global Advances in Business Strategy and Competitive Advantage Book Series.

Puaschunder, J. M. (2017a). *Climate in the 21st century: A macroeconomic model of fair global warming benefits distribution to grant climate justice around the world and over time. Proceedings of the 8th International RAIS Conference on Social Sciences and Humanities organized by Research Association for Interdisciplinary Studies (RAIS) at Georgetown University, Washington, D.C., United States*, March 26-27, pp. 205-243.

Puaschunder, J. M. (2017b). Mapping Climate in the 21st Century. *Development*, *59*(3), 211–216.

Puaschunder, J. M. (2017f). The climatorial imperative. *Agriculture Research and Technology*, *7*(4), 1–2.

Puaschunder, J. M. (2018c). *Intergenerational responsibility in the 21st century*. Wilmington, DE: Vernon.

Puaschunder, J. M. (2019e). *Intergenerational equity: Corporate and Financial Social Responsibility*. New York, NY: Edward Elgar. doi:10.4337/9781788978835

Puaschunder, J. M. (forthcoming). *Governance and climate justice: Global South and developing nations*. Cham, Switzerland. *Springer Nature, Palgrave Macmillan.*

Puaschunder, J. M., & Schwarz, G. (2012). *The future is now: How joint decision making curbs hyperbolic discounting but blurs social responsibility in the intergenerational equity public policy domain.* Cambridge, MA: Harvard University Situationist Law and Mind Sciences Working Paper.

KEY TERMS AND DEFINITIONS

Accountability: Accountability refers to the expectation of having to justify actions to others (Lerner & Tetlock, 1994). Accountability provides an external quality control feedback by public and private actors periodically monitoring corporate social contributions. Civil society must maintain a watch-dog function on corporate social impacts and thereby implicitly supervise the CSR implementation.

Corporate Social Engagement: Paying attention to strategic opportunities and risks of societal challenges, CSR departments must assign leaders to adopt social responsibility policies, integrate social responsibility in corporate mission plans, and assist the implementation of ethical codes of conduct. Corporate leaders must promote a shared CSR vision and provide responsible leadership throughout the corporation and supply chain. At the operational level, the integration of CSR must be guided by action plans on day-to-day corporate social practices.

Corporate Social Responsibility (CSR): Attributes economic, legal, social, and philanthropic responsibilities within the corporate sector.

Financial Social Leadership: SRI appears as a window of opportunity for implementing financial social responsibility whilst re-establishing trust in financial markets.

Financial Social Responsibility: Is primarily addressed by socially responsible investment (SRI), which embraces the social, ethical and economic dimensions of financial allocation strategies.

Public-Private-Partnerships (PPPs): Involve collaboration between a government agency and a private-sector company that can be used to finance, build, and operate public projects. In the international arena, PPP-administered CSR should be backed up by international organizations.

Transparency: Transparent corporate conduct is ensured by governmental legal obligations (e.g., freedom of information legislation), the removal of industrial information transfer barriers, economic incentives, stakeholder campaigns and CSR reporting. Information disclosure will help verify the quality and accuracy of CSR conduct. As the basis for monitoring and benchmarking, transparent CSR information will help identify areas for improvement, grow the confidence of the stakeholder community, and therefore secure investment capital.

United Nations Global Compact (UNGC): The United Nations Global Compact is a non-binding United Nations pact to encourage businesses worldwide to adopt sustainable and socially responsible policies, and to report on their implementation.

Chapter 3
Digitization as a Stimulus for Corporate Social Responsibility

Hristina Vilhelm Blagoycheva
https://orcid.org/0000-0003-2267-1641
University of Economics - Varna, Bulgaria

ABSTRACT

It has already been proven that digitization creates economic growth. But a key factor for the future of society is its perception from the social point of view. Digitization leads to changes that will inevitably affect aggregate demand, employment, and labor costs. Therefore, the purpose of this chapter is to investigate how the digitization interacts with the corporate social responsibility to increase the positive effects over the society. Corporate social responsibility is the sphere that implements the non-economic aspects of the digitization. But before its full deployment, there are still a number of obstacles. Numerous studies have shown that digitization can provide tools to facilitate the socially responsible activities. At the same time, it can also serve as a push for corporate social responsibility, as the formation of a socially conscious market leads to socially committed employees and to increasing their demands on the social responsibility of the business.

INTRODUCTION

On 24 November 2012, a fire broke out in Tazreen Fashion Factory on the outskirts of Dhaka, Bangladesh. There were 117 dead and 200 injured (Ahmed, 2012). Tazreen factory had been producing clothing items for some of the biggest companies in the USA and Europe (Bergman & Rashid, 2012) among which Walmart, Dutch chain C&A and the Hong Kong-based Li & Fung company (Khan, 2012). Following investigation revealed that factory workers were forced to endure extremely bad working conditions, with negligible pay and that the building had outdated electrical installation and insufficient exits. (Bajaj, 2012). Five months later, on April 24th 2013, the eight-story building Rana Plaza in Savar Upazila in Bangladesh collapsed. The building was designed for offices and shops only but it also housed some clothing factories although that its construction wasn't robust enough to withstand machine vibrations (Blair & Bergman, 2013). The clothing factories work for some of the top fashion brands such as

DOI: 10.4018/978-1-7998-2193-9.ch003

Copyright © 2020, IGI Global. Copying or distributing in print or electronic forms without written permission of IGI Global is prohibited.

Benetton, Bonmarché, The Children's Place, El Corte Ingles, Joe Fresh, Monsoon Accessorize, Mango, Matalan, Primark and Walmart (Palidda, 2016, p. 47) A day earlier, a TV channel showed cracks in the building and the people were evacuated. However, on the next day, factory workers were made to return to work with Ether Tex managers even threatening to withhold monthly staff payments if they refused to go back to work (Devnath & Srivastava, 2013). The reckoning - 1134 dead (Hopkins, 2015), and 2 500 injured (Smithers, 2013).

Longhua Science and Technology Park, a branch of the Taiwan Foxconn Technology Group has been notorious for the many suicide incidents among their workers. For the period 2009 – 2017 more than 21 workers committed suicide, unable to bear the physical and psychological burden they were forced to endure in the factory. (Fullerton, 2018). The Group was involved in assembling iPhone, iPod and iPads for Apple Company and electronic components for Hewlett-Packard, Dell, Sony, Nokia and Nintendo (Guo, Hsu, Holton & Jeong, 2012).

It is only a small part of the many examples that can be given for the illegal exploitation of human labor, especially in developing countries. After the collapse of the building in Savar, all fashion brands were quick to claim they had no relationships with the clothing factories in question but documents and clothes, found with their logos, seem to prove the opposite (Palidda, 2016, p. 47). Benetton Group even stated publicly, that none of the participating companies served as a supplier for the Benetton Group or its brands (Allchin & Kazmin, 2013). In response to public criticism, Walmart initiated an investigation of its global supply chain to find out whether some of the factories in the building had been making clothing items for Walmart. It turned out that the items produced there were subcontracted (Allchin & Kazmin, 2013). Of course, Walmart immediately ends its relationship with this subcontractor.

However the question of whether large companies claiming to be socially responsible can afford to outsource part of their production to companies that exploit human life in this way remains on the agenda. This question is also raised by the considerable criticism that society makes of large companies after each tragedy.

This chapter is a case-study. It aims to present how the entry of digital technologies may to some extent encourage the business to implement a broader range of corporate social responsibility (CSR) initiatives. In the 21 century we live in a digital world, saturated with considerable computing power and fast communication. The civil society places more demands on the business towards higher social responsibility and ethical policies. The main objective includes several sub-goals:

1. To look into the discussions on the need to implement CSR and substantiate its benefits to the society and the business;
2. Review specific definitions of CSR and justify the need for a single framework;
3. To study the impact digitization has on the business today and its possible side effects;
4. Explain the positive impact of digitization and its role in expanding the socially responsible initiatives/activities of the business.

The approach chosen is to research the scientific literature and the real-life events related to the topic under consideration. The author wants to show the digital technologies create preconditions for socially responsible employers to provide better working conditions and quality employment for their workers.

The material is organized as follows: section 2 provides a literary overview of the concepts of corporate social responsibility and the attempts to define it. Examples are also provided to prove that the informed workforce is demanding that its future employer be socially responsible. Section 3 presents both some of the benefits of integrating CSR into the business and examples of the power that digital technologies provide to stakeholders to counteract socially irresponsible companies. Section 4 addresses situations where digitization can be used for unethical purposes. Section 5 provides guidance for future research. The last section presents the conclusions drawn.

CORPORATE SOCIAL RESPONSIBILITY IN THE WORLD TODAY

Since the 1950s when the concept of CSR emerged, in the USA the idea was raised that business owes the society something more than the pursuit of a profit (Frederick, 2006). Words such as fairness, honesty and striving to increase social welfare are beginning to be heard. It is believed that any businessman should follow such policies, make such decisions and follow such directions of action which are deemed necessary in terms of the goals and values of the whole society (Bowen, 1953, p. 6).

Then how to assess corporate conduct and its goals? This is an issue which originates in the bipolar division between the theories of protecting the interests of the shareholders and the stakeholders. According to the theory of owners' benefits, the company's theory is built upon socially defined property rights (Locke, 1988; Greenspan, 2003). Therefore, the main goal of company management should be to maximize the profit (Friedman, 1970), and policies in favor of society must be left to the public sector (Levitt, 1958). In fact, these ideas seem to be in line with Adam Smith's theory of the 'invisible hand' according to which rational actions in favour of personal interest maximize the benefits for society (Smit, 1776).

The traditional interpretation of the 'invisible hand' theory is that it gives shareholders the right to dominate the scene under corporate governance. However, the new situation of today's global community deems necessary to review the applicability of classical mechanisms. Proponents of the stakeholders' theory emphasize the importance of company independence from its shareholders and claim that this is the only social institution which must be detached from the idea to be managed only in the interests of shareholders (Evan & Freeman, 1988, p. 103). A survey shows that only 6% of the world population believes that a business should be focused on generating profit only (Cisco, 2015, p. 8). According to Freeman (1984, p. 52) *'Organizations have stakeholders. That is, there are groups and individuals who can affect, or are affected by the achievement of an organization's mission.'* It is therefore necessary to take into account the ethical dimension of economic activity (Carroll, 2000, p. 35). A broader interpretation of the 'invisible hand' and its effect may even cover the ability and aptitude of people to think about the others. (Stovall, Neill & Perkins, 2004). This point of view now is more akin to the concept of CSR and stresses a more extensive corporate governance approach linked to the interests of stakeholders.

Although at first glance these two theories may seem completely contradictory, they should not be interpreted one-sidedly. For example, Friedman does not deny the possibility for the shareholders to use their profit for charitable activities. It explains why Microsoft is often blamed for anti-competitive behavior. At the same time, Bill and Melina Gates Foundation alone, donates more money for malaria vaccine research than EU as a whole, investing much of Microsoft's profits (Ganuza, 2012). On the other hand, the stakeholder theory does not deny the benefit to owners but suggests that managers can create it *through products and services that customers are willing to buy, offering more job vacancies to be filled, building good relationships with suppliers and being good citizens in the community* (Freeman, Wicks & Parmar, 2004, p. 366).

The reason why these two theories are opposed can be seen in the shift of stress from economic to ethical or moral values. But today, such opposition is unacceptable as the economic performance of the business is strongly dependent, along with many other factors, on the way the public perceives it. CSR is seen as a type of ethical behavior on the part of the company to the community. It means, that the company management should operate with responsibility not only to its shareholders but to other stakeholders that have a vested interest in the business. A problem however arises from the fact that stakeholders represent different groups and different interests within the social welfare system. Now, we arrive at defining the principle of "*Who or what really counts?*" (Freeman, 1994) and "*To who or what do managers pay attention?*" Broad stakeholder theories do not specifically propose as to how they compete in their relationships with other companies and how they could balance potential conflicts of interest? The stakeholder theory, reviewed in this paper, offers a *maddening variety* of signals on how questions of stakeholder identification might be answered (Mitchell, Agle & Wood, 1997, p. 854). As a result, a certain likelihood arises that at a particular time some of the groups may be more favoured than others.

Numerous authors attempt to seek answers to the question of identification and preference of stakeholders (Mitchell, Agle & Wood, 1997; Donaldson & Preston, 1995). The final conclusion is that the extent to which managers prioritize the competitive claims of stakeholders goes beyond the question of identifying them because the dynamics inherent in each link include complex considerations that are not easily explained by the theory framework (Mitchell, Agle & Wood, 1997, p. 854). It remains to be concluded that the classic view is of purely economic and is a distinction between economic and social aspects, whereas, according to the stakeholder theory, governance combines the economic aspects of business with the social aspects of society.

Although CSR activities are increasingly undertaken (Garriga & Domènec, 2004), and the CSR concept is widely popular in the media, academia and business, the term still has no uniform definition. Moreover, CSR is being described as a contested concept (Visser, 2007) or a term which is *so vague and ambiguous that it can be interpreted in almost any way to accomplish anything* (Idowu, 2012, p. 242). The problem with definitions is that CSR relates to other categories, hence the entry of terms such as corporate governance, corporate conscience, corporate citizenship, sustainable development, inter alia. The lack of such a unified base impedes current research due to overlapping terminology and the inexplicable conceptual model (Göbbels, 2002).

An attempt to understand its heterogeneity is the statement that *CSR is a supportive term which overlaps with some concepts or manifests itself as synonymous to other concepts of the business - society* relationship (Matten & Moon, 2008, p. 405).

Some of the benchmarks for defining CSR are presented in Table 1. It can be inferred that companies apply corporate social responsibility by implementing voluntary (not imposed by law) actions so that the result is to achieve social goals or limit the negative externalities of their production activity. Social goals can include improving staff living standards, limiting greenhouse emissions, preventing over-exploitation of human labor by subcontractors (cases such as Tazreen Fashion Factory, Rana Plaza or Foxconn), etc. The pursuit of social goals may indeed cost additional expenses for companies, but the ultimate positive effects and favorable response from different stakeholders may ultimately provide them with better financial stability over the long term. Moreover, by taking socially responsible actions, businesses also contribute to the general social well-being, which in turn will also influence the ultimate benefit for shareholders.

Table 1. Definitions of corporate social responsibility (Nyborg, 2014, p. 3)

Name of the organization	Type of organization	Definition	Source
International Labour Organization	Non-governmental organization (international)	Corporate social responsibility is a way in which enterprises give consideration to the impact of their operations on society and affirm their principles and values both in their own internal methods and processes and in their interaction with other actors.	International Labour Organization (ILO). Online at: http://www.ilo.org/wcmsp5/groups/public/ed_emp/emp_ent/multi/documents/publication/wcms_116336.pdf.
Foreign Affairs and International Trade	Governmental organization (Canada)	Corporate social responsibility is defined as the voluntary activities undertaken by a company to operate in an economic, social and environmentally sustainable manner.	Foreign Affairs, Trade and Development Canada. Online at: http://www.international.gc.ca/tradeagreementsaccords-commerciaux/topics-domaines/otherautre/csr-rse.aspx?lang=eng.
European Commission	Governmental organization (EU)	The responsibility of enterprises for their impact on society. Corporate social responsibility concerns actions by companies over and above their legal obligations towards society and the environment. Certain regulatory measures create an environment more conducive to enterprises voluntarily meeting their social responsibilities.	Commission of the European Communities. Communication from the Commission to the European Parliament, the Council, the European Economic and Social Committee of the Regions: A Renewed EU Strategy 2011–14 for Corporate Social Responsibility. 2011.
World Bank	International organization (International)	CSR is the commitment of business to contribute to sustainable economic development, working with employees, their families, the local community and society at large to improve quality of life, in ways that are both good for business and good for development.	World Bank. Public Policy for Corporate Social Responsibility. 2011. Online at: http://info.worldbank.org/etools/docs/library/57434/publicpolicy_econference.pdf.

Based on these definitions and taking into account the multilateral aspects of CSR, it can be defined as a long-term commitment to ethical business conduct, in which economic objectives are combined with measures to improve the quality of life of the workforce and of society as a whole.

CSR practices often adopt the format of company events aimed at employees' welfare or other outside stakeholders. Thus, CSR can be seen as an extra form of prosperity that is made by non-state producers (Blagoycheva, 2018). In this respect, Internet challenges companies to prove that their production methods do not harm stakeholders but create a favorable environment for work and staff career development.

The established reputation of a socially responsible company and the maintenance of competitiveness and organizational growth are good prerequisites for a company to be sought as an employer by better and more responsible employees. As early as the 1960s, a study of motivation factors for work indicated that the salary was just one of them. The rest are achievement, recognition, responsibility, progress, personal growth and the work itself (Herzberg, Mausner & Snyderman, 1959). In more recent times, a study involving around 180,000 students in 28 countries has shown that for 22% of US respondents and 20% of European respondents, among the most important factors determining the choice of the ideal employer is whether this employer applies the principles of CSR (Brekke & Nyborg, 2008).

One of the drivers to enhance corporate social responsibility are millennials, who determine themselves as responsible citizens. In the US, they already account for USD 1 trillion worth of consumer spending (Miles, 2019). Concerning to the recruitment of highly efficient staff, another study (Cognizant, 2015) reveals the most important considerations of recruiting and retaining millennials. Among the main factors for choosing an employer are: business impact capability (23%), a clear path to progress (20%) and personal development (16%). The choice of a company to apply to depends on: buy-in to the mission/vision of the organization (38%) and, again, a clear path for advancement (28%).An interesting fact is that the best way to attract millennials is through social media (42%) or networking (28%).

It can be concluded that millennials are beginning to require their employers to be responsible for corporate structures as they emphasize the concepts of trust and loyalty. Another study shows that more than half of children aged 13 to 25 would refuse to work for a socially irresponsible company (Miles, 2019). And since that part of the population is already starting to form the bulk of the workforce, it is obvious that meeting their requirements is no longer just an option – it is a necessity.

Employer's social responsibility interacts with the attitudes of already recruited staff. A survey among 11,600 employees in 7,700 French firms finds that employees of companies with adopted voluntary environmental standards feel significantly more useful at their workplace and are inclined to become more involved with the company's final results (Lanfranchi & Pekovic, 2012). The survey of the impact of corporate social responsibility on employee loyalty and morale shows that 55% of enterprises with strong sustainability programs have a higher employee morale, 43% have a stronger public image and more efficient business processes, and 38% are more loyal to their staff (Miles, 2019). Other studies concluded that many employees prefer to work for socially responsible employers and if offered the same salary by two employers, they would choose the socially responsible company (Nyborg, 2014). In this situation, the other company to be competitive, must offer higher remuneration. In this line of thought, it appears that socially responsible companies can attract employees with lower labor costs, which gives them a competitive edge on the market. Moreover, as already mentioned, socially responsible workers are more productive than others. The ultimate conclusion is that corporate social responsibility brings serious economic benefits to employers. It is evident that the workplace of the future is changing conventional standards. Companies that fail to adapt to the new requirements are at risk of losing their best talent.

INTEGRATION OF DIGITAL TECHNOLOGIES INTO CSR

For the past 30 years, the advent of digital technologies has brought about considerable changes in the world of business, society and individuals. Not only have conditions of work and production changed but new jobs and sectors emerged, and new products and services have been offered. In some cases, the entire organization of work has been rebooted.

Digital technologies are applicable in all sectors of the economy. What is more, their scale can be adapted to any size or number. *And anything that is incorporated in the software, can be duplicated millions of times at zero costs at night* (European Commission, 2017a, p. 4). It results in lower production costs, lower prices, cutting down on resources and increasing competitiveness. Digitalization, intelligent machine interface, automated production systems and new forms of integrated management lead to a significant increase in labor productivity. It has been found for example, that companies which have data-based decision making, exhibited 5-6% higher performance (Brynjolfsson, Hitt & Kim, 2011). Studies show that nearly 100 000 new data-related jobs will be created in Europe by 2020 (European Commission. 2014) whereas the introduction of Big Data even for the top 100 of EU producers could result in savings of 425 billion euro for the period mentioned. It equals an increase in the EU GDP of 206 billion euro (European Commission, 2017b).

The fourth industrial revolution entailed a number of benefits too – opportunities to use digital logic circuits and their derivative technologies in the economic and social life, including computers, the cell phone and Internet. The mobile digital devices became accessible for a large part of the population, and access to Internet alongside information and communication capabilities allows for expansion of the so far stationary workplace. New forms and patterns of work are emerging characterized by lack of geographic location, digital labor platforms, use of network effects and large data bases (Valenduc & Vendramin, 2016).

Opportunities for flexible working offered by digital technologies have reached new dimensions in both qualitative and quantitative terms. Working hours for employers and workers can be made more flexible to suit both parties. In practice, there are already examples of socially responsible employers who have reaped the benefits of change.

Since 2004, working time at Netflix (US company for on-line streaming services on demand) has not been strictly regulated. The company's employees have the right to decide how many days they need for their annual leave, when to start work and how many hours a day to clock (Pink, 2010). The management decision is based on the fact, that technological advancement has shifted the focus of working hours, no more fixed 8 a.m. to 5 p.m. working hours. Flexible working hours help to manage your time between your private and professional life better. Mobile devices help workers to perform their tasks no matter where they are.

The company policy of unlimited paid leave appears to be extremely profitable. In 2005, Netflix annual revenue reached 682 million USD. Since then, its earnings are constantly on the rise. For the financial year 2018, Netflix reported an annual revenue of 15,8 billion dollars and thus ranked 261 on the list of the biggest US companies in 2018 by revenue (Netflix).

Netflix policy is not an isolated case. In 2016, its Melbourne based consultancy firm Inventium introduced unlimited paid leave, called 'rebalance leave'. Employment contracts for the consulting industry in Australia are generally based on 38 hrs working week. However, its owners realized that it is not unusual for consultants to work more than 50 hrs a week. The above measure was also introduced as a kind of compensation for such a workload. As a result, with a standard 4-week annual leave, leisure time has increased to an average of five and a half weeks. At the same time, paid sick leave (which is one of the qualitative factors for corporate social responsibility) dropped twice. The year 2017 was extremely productive for the company and its managers felt confident that employees who had enjoyed a good rest had a better chance to be happy and perform better at work (Pash, 2018). In November 2015, LinkedIn introduced a new approach called "Discretionary Time Off" (DTO). With it, they gave their employees more flexibility and a sense of empowerment as the workers were able to set their own time for work and rest. In the opinion of the management, this will help them handle stress at work and make them more responsible and more efficient in performing their tasks. The STW Communications Group also offers its employees unlimited paid annual leave. The only condition is the workers to coordinate with their superiors to make sure the work will be done (Cosic, 2016). These are just some of the examples but they are already attracting the attention of other socially responsible employers.

The conclusion is that, thanks to digitization, voluntary application of social responsibility in companies can improve the social welfare of employees and lead to higher productivity for the company. CSR is further associated with various actions towards a better working environment, ensuring healthier and safer working conditions (Blagoycheva, Andreeva & Yolowa, 2019), provision of career opportunities and skills upgrade as well as a range of policies to stimulate commitment of employees to the company they work for. A socially responsible behavior of the employer is perceived to be one that translates into a job satisfaction on the part of the workers and positive feedback from their families, friends and social groups (Riordan, Gatewood & Bill, 1997). A worker who is convinced that his present working environment is better than that of other companies in the sector, has more motivation to be loyal and contribute to the company's success on a long-term basis.

Increased labor productivity, reduced production costs and a higher competitive edge give companies more room to invest in socially responsible initiatives. The Internet itself creates myriad of opportunities and economic incentives to promote corporate social responsibility and build positive attitudes towards it in the public mind.

The three pillars of sustainable development linked to corporate social responsibility are economic growth (including business owners' profit), people and environmental responsibility for future generations. Given the increasing impact of digitization, we can fully accept Knaut's (2017) proposal to include the latter as the fourth pillar. Digital technologies are more and more integrated into all aspects of the business and can be aligned with corporate social responsibility, respectively. Digitalization provides channels for communication and coordination with the stakeholders, transparency of decisions and messages to the general public.

These processes decentralize the corporate power and orientate it towards interested parties, giving them the opportunity to have a greater influence on corporate decisions or to counteract them. The Ethical Consumer website, for example, calls for boycotting companies whose operations are deemed harmful to society from an economic, social or environmental point of view. Currently, the boycott list contains 40 companies from different countries around the world. Proof for the power of society is that for many companies, public boycotting has had serious repercussions. A good case in point is Nestlé company, which has been the subject of boycott calls around the world since the 1970s for its aggressive marketing practices promoting baby milk formula as a superior option to breastfeeding. In developing countries, the use of said milk led to the death of many babies due to water-borne diseases in regions where the parents had no access to clean drinking water. As a result of the boycott, the World Health Assembly drafted a strict International Code of Marketing of Breast Milk Substitutes (Ethical Consumer, 2018).

Amazon also faced a boycott for incurring losses to the UK state budget through the export of capital and tax avoidance or unfair tax policies. Thus the UK government was severely restricted in its ability to finance social initiatives. Furthermore, Amazon exerted competitive pressure on smaller UK companies which dutifully filed in their tax returns and paid their taxes. Even though Amazon's offices are UK based, the company transferred its profits to its subsidiary Amazon EU Sarl. In 2017 about 75% of Amazon's UK revenue (GBP 6.88bn) was diverted through the tax haven in Luxemburg. The annual tax paid by Amazon in the UK is only GBP 4.6 million, but in the opinion of certain experts, it must be above GBP 50 million (Ethical Consumer, 2018).

Another means of boycotting is the initiative launched against the application of Amazon Mechanical Turk (AMT) of Amazon. It is a crowdsourcing marketplace that makes it easier for individuals and businesses (mostly underqualified) to post jobs and routine tasks that fall outside existing software systems. The application enables workers to complete simple tasks at zero operating costs (rent, social insurance or tax payment) and get paid. However there has been plenty of evidence where the contractors failed to pay for the commissioned job or the pay was negligible. Amazon though offers no guarantees in case of irregularities - how much the worker is getting paid or whether it is cash, gift or voucher (Irani, 2015). In response to the unfair practices of unregulated sites, in 2009 on-line users created Turkopticon, a site which allows workers to evaluate their relationships with employers and report unfair practices. In this way, each new worker visiting the AMT site can download an extension to the web browser and see the reviews of previous workers of a certain employer (Degryse, 2016).

In addition to supervision, digital technologies enable support for CSR, mainly to address certain challenges it is faced with. Let's return to the examples given in the introduction - Tazreen Fashion Factory, Rana Plaza and Longhua Science and Technology Park. When working with chains of subcontractors, in some cases large companies may be unable to monitor all stages in the production, transportation and delivery of goods to their door, as well as the social or environmental conditions of the various units in the chain. But when a tragic incident happens, it inevitably reflects on their reputation. By claiming to be socially responsible, they must be able to assure their customers that no child labor or over-exploitation of workers have been used in the production of their goods and no damage has been done to the environment, etc. In this relation, it could help for example, to create an Internet data base, in which each supplier can report who was in the chain before that and the origin of the goods. Access to this information will undoubtedly allow the main company to cut down on costs and unnecessary suppliers, and to manage the risk in a better way, in order to improve the working conditions in its factories located in poor countries. Transparency on the other hand, will enable auditors to uncover more efficiently any violations in the production ethics.

In the context of globalization, business development is geared towards penetrating ever wider markets, most of which can be found in developing countries. In contrast to previous expansion strategies, this expansion now should be done responsibly. By entering new markets which are often in poor countries, the companies need to be aware that they are to a certain degree responsible for their development. In these parts of the world, where the majority of the population live in poverty, local population is mainly preoccupied with their daily necessities and need to address social issues such as low income, poor living conditions, lack of clean drinking water, pollution, education, health care, corruption, to name but a few. On the other hand, the limited resources of these countries do not allow them to resolve their problems effectively. The socially responsible behavior of wealthy companies can be directed at implementing measures to help protect the environment and set more environmentally friendly policies. It is where digital technologies come into play. Companies can invest in solar systems or other alternative energy sources, land surveyor drones and exploration of pure water sources (Miles, 2019), equipment for medical diagnostics, communication systems, computerization of some processes, etc. The benefits of these measures can be manifested in several ways. First of all, big companies will engage in social missions, which will help them build a more positive image among the stakeholders. Secondly, these measures will also enhance the development of local communities and allow them to pass over several stages in their social development quickly. Similarly, some emerging world societies were made to frogjump the landline and switch directly to mobile communication devices.

The social perspective of sustainable development requires companies to be responsible to society (Marrewijk, 2003). And if the ambition of digital technologies is to make the world a better place to live in, then from the point of view of ethical business objectives this suggests not only economic growth but also cooperation in building a better society.

THE REVERSE SIDE – DIGITIZATION AND SOCIAL IRRESPONSIBILITY

Digitization offers a number of incentives to implement corporate social responsibility. But the medal has two sides. If placed in the hands of socially irresponsible companies, digitization will be seen as a tool to accumulate huge profits at the expense of labor exploitation or circumvention of rules. Here, we can include practices directed at tax avoidance, abuse of personal or public data, evasion of regulatory and self-regulatory communication, etc. The VW "Dieselgate" scandal broke in 2015 with Volkswagen company being accused of cheating for low carbon emissions of VW cars sold worldwide, using a defeat device or software to dupe regulatory bodies. Despite the company's socially responsible behavior and policies towards environmental protection, in September-October 2015, it was found that on 11 million VW cars fraud software was fitted that could detect when they were being tested, changing the performance accordingly, to improve results. The Environmental Protection Agency (EPA) in the USA found that the actual emission levels in the atmosphere are about 40 times higher than the levels measured during tests (Plumer, 2015).

Companies like Google, Facebook, LinkedIn, Amazon, Apple or Microsoft have relatively few employees on permanent contracts, but offer jobs to workers from low-cost countries with potentially weaker labour protection standards and lower operating costs (PES, 2017, p. 16). The term 'cybertariat' (Huws, 2014), which emerged earlier, was used for crowds of workers made to compete at the lowest standards possible with counterparts from other countries, under insecure working conditions and performing multiple simple tasks for which no special qualification was required but necessary for the smooth running of the company's operations.

For instance, a search into US Upwork platform in December 2015 for the positions of virtual assistant for administrative support, secretarial position, data handling or professional consulting, submitted a total of 9088 applicants, offering their services on-line, from 40 different countries – developed countries (the USA, Canada, France, Belgium, UK, Holland, Spain, etc.), developing countries (Brazil, China, South Africa, Russia, India) and under-developed (the Philippines, Bangladesh, Vietnam, Pakistan, Algeria, Kenya, etc.) (Degryse, 2016, p. 31). The pay rates cited by applicants for their services ranged from USD 60 to USD 3,3 per hour. The total number of workers registered on the platform and waiting for a call was around 10 million. Apparently, on this huge virtual market where competition is fierce, workers from developed countries are induced to adjust their rates according to the lower rates of other candidates. The concentration of labor on offer to a single buyer will inevitably result in lower wages or distribution at the discretion of the employer.

What are the options to deal with this problem? Some analysts believe that the only way to resist to digital divide is to harmonize legislature internationally. But whether this approach will succeed depends to a large extent on political decisions about the rights to manage and impose cyberspace conditions and the amount of pressure exerted by the civil society. The creation of a democratic platform with transparent regulatory framework is deemed necessary, in order to overcome the discriminatory effects, and focus on the needs of less developed countries.

Digital technologies, robotics, computerization and communications are bound to change the agenda. Alignment of the human society with the new conditions on the path to global prosperity is impossible without placing knowledge in the focus of attention. However, a significant part of the population of poor countries is denied the perspective of knowledge and communications thus becoming a prerequisite for continued exploitation by some large companies.

In fact, problems do exist in developed countries too. As stated earlier, one of the benefits of digitization for CSR is mobile work. It is convenient and gives more flexibility to workers who wish to manage their working hours by themselves. But for many people who are looking for security and balance, mobile work may be unacceptable. That's why, the scientific community warns that: "Recent developments in employment practices have increased the prevalence of non-standard work schedules—non-daytime shifts in which most hours do not fall between 8 a.m. and 4 p.m., when shifts rotate, or when schedules vary weekly or otherwise." (Morsy & Rothstein, 2015, p. 1). Apart from being able to influence family relationships, this 'unwanted' flexibility leads to health problems such as stress and burnout. In this regard, in 2017 the European Social Policy Network came out with a report which specifies the problems associated with non-standard employment, (including digital employment issues). The report found that a significant part of existing problems can be explained with lack of reliable and well-defined statutory measures requiring transparency, and norms on income, status, working hours and provision for this type of employment (ESPN, 2017). In view of said report findings, the European Commission introduced the European Pillar of Social Rights, proposing some principles and rights in support of fair labor markets. And in 2018, the European Foundation for the improvement of living and working conditions published its report calling for attention to social protection, income, working time and the unclear status of people working on non-standard contracts (Eurofound, 2018).

Problems are found even in the actions of companies claiming to be socially responsible. Corporate social responsibility is a moral category. As such, it should be aimed at benefits for society even above the norms of the law. Information about the social engagement of the business, actions taken or norms of conduct is fed to the society through a variety of channels for on-line communication. Social media allow for a wide-ranging virtual dialogue with and between stakeholders. These virtual dialogues are capable of generating value and two factors can determine this value. Firstly, it is the extent to which stakeholders identify themselves with the group of participants in the dialogue and secondly, the increased expectations that stakeholders are developing as a result of that dialogue (Korschun & Du, 2013). The Social Platform Network is open to the participation of people or individuals who are not directly related to business activities but feel engaged with the social issues and development of society. As users are actively involved in communication with the company and with each other through social media, companies are beginning to use this form of active interaction with their stakeholders, collecting useful information through feedback, at the same time (Berthon et al., 2012).

Socially responsible companies are required to publish their annual report on corporate social responsibility. A survey established, that only a quarter of people worldwide are reading these reports (Cone, 2015, p. 4), but it is namely social media that are seen as a means of passing information, opinion exchange or resentment if companies fail to adhere to their social responsibility policies. However, Stohl et al. (2015) questions the use of social media communication as an appropriate way to present CSR initiatives, hinting at the possibility of manipulating the information. According to other opinions, the corporation has a motive to use social networks in order to project a good reputation of the business but circumventing a potentially more critical reporting of its activities (Grigore, Molesworth & Watkins, 2017). It leads to the assumption that despite the obvious benefits of using social media, the latter do not always serve as neutral platforms for communication. And this conclusion raises more questions about social responsibility.

FUTURE RESEARCH DIRECTIONS

In terms of organizational structure and corporate culture, digitization is able to offer plenty of opportunities. *Digital technologies have the potential of humanizing jobs in terms of ergonomics* (Walwei, 2016). Some of the hazardous or heavy-duty jobs can be done by robots thus reducing the number of accidents and possible occupational illnesses. Skills and abilities of disabled people can be put to practice using smart machines which can play the role of their assistants. Women on maternity leave will have more time for their kids. Possibilities to reduce standard working time are also at hand. Digital technologies offer opportunities to work flexi time for both workers and their employers.

But some authors are drawing a worrying picture, suggesting that the future is a high-productivity, huge-profits economy, requiring fewer workers (Ford, 2015). Others argue that the capabilities of computers to handle long runs of cognitive tasks will eventually oust human labor (Brynjolfsson & McAfee, 2011). Robots and digital algorithms will increasingly take over human activities and deprive low-qualified workers of their jobs. The question is *how to formulate new ethical principles and rules when computer algorithms replace the human factor?* (Petrov, 2018, p. 508).

In spite of technological advancement, there comes a time when the workers will feel insecure in their new, digitalized work environment. Implementation and use of new technologies calls for workers with special skills who can manage these processes. And the need for specific qualification comes to the fore. In this connection the unemployment in the USA in 2018 presents an interesting paradox. According to official statistics, since April 2018, 6,3 million people in the USA have been jobless (U.S. Bureau of Labor Statistics, 2018a). At the same time, 6,6 million job vacancies remained unfilled for lack of qualified workers (U.S. Bureau of Labor Statistics, 2018b). Many people are unable to participate in the digital economy because they have no access to proper training programs. 39% of employers say that the skills gap is the main reason for unfilled job positions (CISCO, 2015, p. 2). It is indeed in the power of employers to give equal access to vocational training which will be to the mutual benefit of both sides. Together with traditional training, online forms of training have also been on offer, made possible through digitization of education.

In this regard, the future research may focus on employee social security and employers' incentives to provide education for their workers.

CONCLUSION

Due to the broad scope of corporate social responsibility, the study focuses primarily on its social aspects. The economic and environmental implications of CSR remain outside the scope of the study.

This study examines the link between the development of digital technology and the social behavior of businesses. The study complements the available literature on the social effects of the corporate social responsibility, and in particular in the relationship between employers and employees in terms of combining theoretical statements and real facts.

Digital transformation of the economy is an irreversible process happening at an even quicker pace. The business and society have no other choice but to accept this new reality and adapt to it. Digitization creates opportunities to discover new areas for business expansion or offer new forms of business. If these processes are managed properly and responsibly, they may foster sustainability and raise the standard of living for people.

In the era of innovation and digitization, the relationships between employers and company stakeholders will surely become more intensive. Companies being responsible for the social well-being of a large group of people employed by them, seem to be in the best position to manage their workers welfare and society as a whole.

Furthermore, applying the principles of corporate social responsibility entails economic benefits for the employers too. They can rely on more socially aware, efficient and productive workers. And companies unable to adapt to the new requirements are at risk of losing their best talents. In this respect, digital technologies serve companies to be seen as more attractive in the labor markets and remain competitive.

Transformations of the digital environment place knowledge and information as the top items on the agenda. The Internet, data access and knowledge sharing, provide opportunities for transformational dynamics of education which is the key element in building sustainability.

In a globalized world, digital technologies can successfully blend with the corporate social responsibility and bring its benefits to the business, its stakeholders and society as a whole. However, digitization can be used for the wrong reasons, namely to pile up huge profits but be negligent to the environment. Indeed, digital information platforms and social media tend to decentralize corporate power and direct it towards company stakeholders as a way of exerting influence. And if the ambition of digital technologies is to make the world a better one, then for a business that is ethical, these technologies mean higher economic growth and building a better society.

REFERENCES

Ahmed, F. (2012, November 25). At least 117 killed in fire at Bangladeshi clothing factory. *CNN*. Retrieved April 8, 2019, from: https://edition.cnn.com/2012/11/25/world/asia/bangladesh-factory-fire/

Allchin, J., & Kazmin, A. (2013, April 25). Scores dead in Bangladeshi garment factory collapse. *Financial Times*. Retrieved April 9, 2019, from: https://www.ft.com/content/bf534db4-acbe-11e2-b27f-00144feabdc0

Bajaj, V. (2012, November 25). Fatal Fire in Bangladesh Highlights the Dangers Facing Garment Workers. *The New York Times*. Retrieved April 8, 2019, from: https://www.nytimes.com/2012/11/26/world/asia/bangladesh-fire-kills-more-than-100-and-injures-many.html?_r=0

Bergman, D., & Rashid, M. (2012, November 25). Bangladesh factory fire kills 111 garment workers. *The Telegraph*. Retrieved April 8, 2019, from: https://www.telegraph.co.uk/news/worldnews/asia/bangladesh/9701826/Bangladesh-factory-fire-kills-111-garment-workers.html

Berthon, P., Pitt, L., Plangger, K., & Shapiro, D. (2012). Marketing meets Web 2.0, social media, and creative consumers: Implications for international marketing strategy. *Business Horizons*, *55*(3), 261–271. doi:10.1016/j.bushor.2012.01.007

Blagoycheva, H. (2018). The Involvement of the Public Sector in Corporate Social Responsibility – the Changing Reality. *International Journal of Economic Research*, *15*(1), 119–131.

Blagoycheva, H., Andreeva, A., & Yolova, G. (2019). Obligation and Responsibility of Employers to Provide Health and Safety at Work – Principles, Current Regulation and Prospects. *Economic Studies*, *28*(2), 115–137.

Blair, D., & Bergman, D. (2013, May 3). Bangladesh: Rana Plaza architect says building was never meant for factories. *The Telegraph*. Retrieved April 8, 2019, from: https://www.telegraph.co.uk/news/worldnews/asia/bangladesh/10036546/Bangladesh-Rana-Plaza-architect-says-building-was-never-meant-for-factories.html

Bowen, H. (1953). *Social Responsibilities of the Businessman*. New York: Harper.

Brekke, K., & Nyborg, K. (2008). Attracting responsible employees: Green production as labor market screening. *Resource and Energy Economics*, *30*(4), 509–526. doi:10.1016/j.reseneeco.2008.05.001

Brynjolfsson, E., Hitt, L. M., & Kim, H. H. (2011). Strength in numbers: How does data-driven decision making affect firm performance? *SSRN Electronic Journal*, *1*. doi:10.2139srn.1819486

Brynjolfsson, E., & Mcafee, A. (2011). *Race against the machine: how the digital revolution is accelerating innovation, driving productivity, and irreversibly transforming employment and the economy*. Lexington: Digital Frontier Press.

Carroll, A. (2000). Ethical Challenges for Business in the New Millennium: Corporate Social Responsibility and Models of Management Morality. *Business Ethics Quarterly*, *10*(1), 33–42. doi:10.2307/3857692

CISCO. (2015). *White Paper: Launching a Generation of Global Problem Solvers*. Retrieved May 28, 2019, from: https://www.cisco.com/c/dam/assets/csr/pdf/Global-Problem-Solver-whitepaper.pdf

Cognizant. (2015). *Elevating the Digital Employee Experience*. Retrieved May 19, 2019, from: https://www.cognizant.com/whitepapers/Elevating-the-Digital-Employee-Experience.pdf

Cosic, M. (2016, January 25). Unlimited annual leave: is it good HR or good PR? *The Guardian*. Retrieved May 9, 2019, from: https://www.theguardian.com/sustainable-business/2016/jan/25/unlimited-annual-leave-is-it-good-hr-or-good-pr

Degryse, C. (2016). *Digitalisation of the economy and its impact on labour markets*. Working Paper 2016.02, European Trade Union Institute. Retrieved May 27, 2019, from:https://www.etui.org/Publications2/Working-Papers/Digitalisation-of-the-economy-and-its-impact-on-labour-markets

Devnath, A., & Srivastava, M. (2013, April 25). 'Suddenly the Floor Wasn't There,' Factory Survivor Says. *Bloomberg Business.* Retrieved April 8, 2019, from: https://www.bloomberg.com/news/articles/2013-04-25/-suddenly-the-floor-wasn-t-there-factory-survivor-says

Donaldson, T., & Preston, L. (1995). The Stakeholder Theory of the Corporation: Concepts, Evidence and Implications. *Academy of Management Review, 20*(1), 65–91. doi:10.5465/amr.1995.9503271992

ESPN. (2017). *Access to social protection for people working on non-standard contracts and as self-employed in Europe: A study of national policies.* Brussels: European Commission.

Ethical Consumer. (2015, May 29). *Boycott Amazon.* Retrieved May 14, 2019, from: https://www.ethicalconsumer.org/ethicalcampaigns/boycott-amazon

EUROFOUND. (2018). *Non-standard forms of employment: Recent trends and future prospects.* Dublin: Eurofound.

European Commission. (2014). *Fact Sheet Data cPPP.* Retrieved June 22, 2019, from: https://ec.europa.eu/research/industrial_technologies/pdf/factsheet-cppp_en.pdf

European Commission. (2017a). *A concept paper on digitisation, employability and inclusiveness. The role of Europe, DG Communications Networks, Content &Technology (CONNECT).* The Publications Office of the European Union.

European Commission. (2017b). *Enter the Data Economy. EU Policies for a Thriving Data Ecosystem. EPSC Strategic Notes 21.* European Political Strategy Centre.

Evan, W., & Freeman, R. (1988). A stakeholder theory of the modern corporation: Kantian capitalism. In T. Beauchamp & N. Bowie (Eds.), *Ethical theory and business* (pp. 75–93). Englewood Cliffs, NJ: Prentice Hall.

Ford, M. (2015). *Rise of the robots: technology and the threat of a jobless future.* New York: Basic Books.

Frederick, W. C. (2006). *Corporation, Be Good! The story of Corporate Social Responsibility.* Indianapolis, IN: Dog Ear Publishing.

Freeman, R., Wicks, A., & Parmar, B. (2004). Stakeholder Theory and "The Corporate Objective Revisited". *Organization Science, 15*(3), 364–369. doi:10.1287/orsc.1040.0066

Freeman, R. E. (1984). *Strategic Management. A Stakeholder Approach.* Boston: Pitman.

Freeman, R. E. (1994). The politics of stakeholder theory: Some future directions. *Business Ethics Quarterly, 4*(4), 409–421. doi:10.2307/3857340

Friedman, M. (1970, September 13), The Social Responsibility of Business is to Increase its Profits. *The New York Times Magazine.* Retrieved April 21, 2019, from: http://umich.edu/~thecore/doc/Friedman.pdf

Fullerton, J. (2018, January 7). Suicide at Chinese iPhone factory reignites concern over working conditions, *The Telegraph.* Retrieved April 9, 2019, from: https://www.telegraph.co.uk/news/2018/01/07/suicide-chinese-iphone-factory-reignites-concern-working-conditions/

Ganuza, J.-J. (2012). *Corporate Social Responsibility and Social Welfare. How to Promote Socially Responsible Business Strategies*. Barcelona: Centre de Recerca en Economia Internacional. Retrieved May 14, 2019, from: http://www.crei.cat/wp-content/uploads/opuscles/120321092822_ENG_30_ANG.pdf

Garriga, E., & Domènec, M. (2004). Corporate social responsibility theories: Mapping the territory. *Journal of Business Ethics*, *53*(1-2), 51–71. doi:10.1023/B:BUSI.0000039399.90587.34

Göbbels, M. (2002). Reframing Corporate Social Responsibility: The contemporary conception of a fuzzy notion. Journal of Business Ethics, 44, 95-105.

Grigore, G., Molesworth, M., & Watkins, R. D. (2017). Responsibility in the Digital Economy. In *Corporate Social Responsibility Post-Financial Crisis* (pp. 41-62). London: Palgrave MacMillan. Retrieved April 5, 2019, from: http://link.springer.com/chapter/10.1007%2F978-3-319-40096-9_3

Guo, L., Hsu, S.-H., Holton, A., & Jeong, S. H. (2012). A case study of the Foxconn suicides: An international perspective to framing the sweatshop issue. *The International Communication Gazette*, *74*(5), 484–503. doi:10.1177/1748048512445155

Herzberg, F., Mausner, B., & Snyderman, B. (1959). *The Motivation to Work* (2nd ed.). John Wiley and Sons.

Hopkins, T. (2015, April 23). Reliving the Rana Plaza factory collapse: a history of cities in 50 buildings, day 22. *The Guardian*. Retrieved April 8, 2019, from: https://www.theguardian.com/cities/2015/apr/23/rana-plaza-factory-collapse-history-cities-50-buildings

Huws, U. (2014). *Labor in the Digital Economy: The Cybertariat Comes of Age*. NYU Press.

Idowu, S. O. (2012). Corporate social responsibility: A capitalist ideology? *International Journal of Social Entrepreneurship and Innovation*, *1*(3), 239–254. doi:10.1504/IJSEI.2012.047628

Irani, L. (2015). *Justice for 'data janitors', Public Books, 15 January 2015*. Retrieved April 28, 2019, from: http://www.publicbooks.org/nonfiction/justice-for-data-janitors

Khan, K. (2012, November 25). Garment factory blaze kills 109 in Bangladesh. *JakartaGlobe*. Retrieved August 28, 2019, from: https://www.webcitation.org/6CRR29lSi?url=http://www.thejakartaglobe.com/afp/garment-factory-blaze-kills-109-in-bangladesh/558153

Knaut, A. (2017). How CSR Should Understand Digitalization. In T. Osburg & C. Lohrmann (Eds.), *Sustainability in a Digital World. New Opportunities Through New Technologies* (pp. 249–256). Springer International Publishing AG. doi:10.1007/978-3-319-54603-2_21

Korschun, D., & Du, S. (2013). How virtual corporate social responsibility dialogs generate value: A framework and propositions. *Journal of Business Research*, *66*(9), 1494–1504. doi:10.1016/j.jbusres.2012.09.011

Lanfranchi, L. & Pekovic. S. (2012). *How Green is My Firm? Workers' Attitudes towards Job, Job Involvement and Effort in Environmentally-Related Firms*. Document du Travail 160, Centre d'Etudes de L'Emploi.

Levitt, T. (1958, Sept.). The dangers of Social Responsibility. *Harvard Business Review*, 41-50.

Locke, J. (1988). *Two Treatises of Government* (P. Laslett, Ed.). Cambridge, UK: Cambridge University Press. doi:10.1017/CBO9780511810268

Marrewijk, M. (2003). Concepts and Definitions of CSR and Corporate Sustainability. *Journal of Business Ethics*, *44*(2), 95–105. doi:10.1023/A:1023331212247

Matten, D., & Moon, J. (2008). "Implicit" and "explicit" CSR: A conceptual framework for a comparative understanding of Corporate Social Responsibility. *Academy of Management Review*, *33*(2), 402–424. doi:10.5465/amr.2008.31193458

Miles, J. R. (2019, February 27). Corporate social responsibility 2.0, The Bold plan to transform society. *BOLD Business*. Retrieved June 18, 2019, from: https://www.boldbusiness.com/digital/corporate-social-responsibility-2-0-bold-plan-transform-society/

Mitchell, R., Agle, B., & Wood, D. (1997). Toward a Theory of Stakeholders Identification and Salience: Defining the Principle of who and what Really Counts. *Academy of Management Review*, *22*(4), 853–886. doi:10.5465/amr.1997.9711022105

Morsy, L., & Rothstein, R. (2015). *Parents' non-standard work schedules make adequate childrearing difficult, Issue Brief 400*. Washington, DC: Economic Policy Institute. Retrieved June 30, 2019, from: http://www.epi.org/files/pdf/88777.pdf

Netflix. Fortune 500. (n.d.). Retrieved June 3, 2019, from: https://fortune.com/fortune500/netflix/

Nyborg, K. (2014). Do responsible employers attract responsible employees? *IZA World of Labor*, *17*. doi:10.15185/izawol.17

Palidda, S. (Ed.). (2016). *Governance of Security and Ignored Insecurities in Contemporary Europe*. New York: Routledge. doi:10.4324/9781315585482

Pash, C. (2018, August 28). Unlimited leave is working so well, some companies are offering it fully paid. *The Sidney Morning Herald*. Retrieved May 14, 2019, from: https://www.smh.com.au/business/companies/unlimited-leave-is-working-so-well-some-companies-are-offering-it-fully-paid-20180828-p500ah.html

PES. (2017). *Workers' rights and social progress in the digital economy*. Retrieved May 30, 2019, from: http://www.pervencheberes.fr/wp-content/uploads/2017/09/digital-economy-brochure-web-version-002.pdf

Petrov, D. (2018). Blockchain Technology - A Bank Lending (R)evolution: The Case of Syndicated Loans. In *New Challenges of Economic and Business Development. Productivity and Economic Growth: Proceedings*. University of Latvia. Retrieved June 14, 2019, from: https://www.bvef.lu.lv/fileadmin/user_upload/lu_portal/projekti/bvef/konferences/evf_conf2018/Proceedings_2018.pdf

Pink, D. (2010, Aug 14). Netflix lets its staff take as much holiday as they want, whenever they want – and it works. *The Telegraph*. Retrieved June 12, 2019, from: https://www.telegraph.co.uk/finance/newsbysector/mediatechnologyandtelecoms/7945719/Netflix-lets-its-staff-take-as-much-holiday-as-they-want-whenever-they-want-and-it-works.html

Plumer, B. (2015, September 23). Volkswagen's appalling clean diesel scandal, explained. *Vox*. Retrieved June 18, 2019, from: http://www.vox.com/2015/9/21/9365667/volkswagen-clean-diesel-recallpassenger-cars

Riordan, C., Gatewood, R., & Bill, J. (1997). Corporate image: Employee reactions and implications for managing corporate social performance. *Journal of Business Ethics*, *16*(4), 401–412. doi:10.1023/A:1017989205184

Roscoe, A. (2015, July 8). The Digital Future of Corporate Responsibility. *Stanford Social Innovation Review*. Retrieved June 10, 2019, from: https://ssir.org/articles/entry/the_digital_future_of_corporate_responsibility

Smith, A. (1776). *The wealth of nations* (5th ed.). New York: Bantam Dell.

Smithers, R. (2013, April 29). Benetton admits link with firm in collapsed Bangladesh building. *The Guardian*. Retrieved June 3, 2019, from: https://www.theguardian.com/world/2013/apr/29/benetton-link-collapsed-building-bangladesh

Stohl, C., Michael, E., Scott, B., & Woo, D. (2015). Social Media Policies: Implications for Contemporary Notions of Corporate Social Responsibility. *Journal of Business Ethics*, *14*(3), 413–436. doi:10.100710551-015-2743-9

Stovall, O. S., Neill, J. D., & Perkins, D. (2004). Corporate governance, internal decision making, and the invisible hand. *Journal of Business Ethics*, *51*(2), 221–227. doi:10.1023/B:BUSI.0000033615.22269.e3

U.S. Bureau of Labor Statistics. (2018a). *Employment Situation Summary*. United States Department of Labor. Retrieved January 27, 2019, from: https://www.bls.gov/news.release/empsit.nr0.htm

U.S. Bureau of Labor Statistics. (2018b). *Job Openings and Labor Turnover Survey Highlights*. Retrieved January 27, 2019, from: https://www.bls.gov/web/jolts/jlt_labstatgraphs.pdf

Valenduc, G., & Vendramin, P. (2016). *Work in the digital economy: sorting the old from the new*. Working Paper 2016.03 Brussels: ETUI. Retrieved June 17, 2019, from: http://ftu-namur.org/fichiers/Work_in_the_digital_economy-ETUI2016-3-EN.pdf

Visser, W. (2007). Revisiting Carroll's CSR pyramid. In A. Crane & D. Matten (Eds.), *An African Perspective*. Nottingham, UK: The University of Nottingham.

Walwei, U. (2016). *Digitalization and structural labour market problems: The case of Germany*. ILO Research Paper No. 17. Retrieved May 12, 2019, from: https://www.ilo.org/wcmsp5/groups/public/---dgreports/---inst/documents/publication/wcms_522355.pdf

ADDITIONAL READING

Del Baldo, M. (2013). Corporate social responsibility, human resource management and corporate family responsibility. When a company is "The best place to work" *Elica group, the hi-fi company. Ekonomska istraživanja –. Economic Research Journal, 26*(Special Issue), 201–224.

Newell, P., & Frynas, J. (2007). Beyond CSR? Business, poverty and social justice: An introduction. *Third World Quarterly, 28*(4), 669–681. doi:10.1080/01436590701336507

Osburg, T., & Lohrmann, C. (Eds.). (2017). *Sustainability in a Digital World. New Opportunities Through New Technologies*. Springer International Publishing; doi:10.1007/978-3-319-54603-2

Prieto-Carrón, M., Lund-Thomsen, P., Chan, A., Muro, A., & Bhushan, C. (2006). Critical Perspectives on CSR and Development: What we Know, What We Don't Know and What We Need to Know. *International Affairs, 82*(5), 977–987. doi:10.1111/j.1468-2346.2006.00581.x

Schallmo, D., Williams, C., & Boardman, L. (2017). Digital Transformation Of Business Models— Best Practice, Enablers, and Roadmap. *International Journal of Innovation Management, 21*(8), 1740014. doi:10.1142/S136391961740014X

Şerban, R.-A. (2017). The Impact of Big Data, Sustainability, and Digitalization on Company Performance. *Studies in Business and Economics, 12*(3), 181–189. doi:10.1515be-2017-0045

KEY TERMS AND DEFINITIONS

Corporate Social Responsibility: Long-term commitment to ethical business conduct, in which economic objectives are combined with measures to improve the quality of life of the workforce and of society as a whole.

Digital Technologies: Technologies using computer and telecommunications equipment to collect, process, store, and disseminate data.

Employee: A person who, on the basis of a formal employment contract, provides his workforce for temporary use against a remuneration for the work done.

Employer: Institution employing a person on the basis of a formal employment contract for the implementation of certain tasks against remuneration for the work done.

Labor Conditions: Conditions, location, and time of performing a work activity.

Platform Worker: A person who performs specific tasks against remuneration through an online platform without a fixed location and without a standard employment contract.

Shareholders: The owners of the capital of a company that are entitled to a share of its profits.

Social Development: The level of well-being achieved due to historical prerequisites and economic, cultural and political measures.

Stakeholders: Organizations or individuals who are involved in some form with the activities or policies of a given institution and may influence or be affected by its goals and actions. The stakeholders include employees, customers, creditors, suppliers, government, and sometimes individual members of the society.

Chapter 4
Corporate Social Responsibility:
Strategy for Boosting Brand Perception and Competitive Advantage

George Kofi Amoako
Central University, Accra, Ghana

Kwasi Dartey-Baah
Business School, University of Ghana, Ghana

ABSTRACT

This chapter examines the extent to which corporate social responsibility (CSR) could generate and boost better brand perceptions and improve competitive advantage within some selected banks in Ghana. The concept of CSR, brand perception, and competitive advantage are discussed in relation to findings from a study that was conducted at the national headquarters of GCB Bank and Barclays Bank Limited in Accra. The results showed a good understanding of the concept of CSR from both customers and employees of both banks. There was a significant and positive connection between effective implementation of CSR initiatives, brand perception, and competitive advantage. CSR was discovered as a tool for business success in the banking sector in Ghana. This chapter explains the benefits of CSR activities to the development of impalpable organizational assets, and as a result, generating better results for banking institutions in Ghana. The authors make a case for the inclusion and active involvement of customers and employees in the CSR initiatives of banks in order to boost brand perception.

INTRODUCTION

The perception that large corporations, trans-national and global companies make huge amounts of money by exploiting some of the world's most impoverished communities only to turn around and offer them a pittance to assuage their conscience by way of CSR is rife. Various arguments have been made both for and against the practice of CSR. Followers of the growth of the firm theory believe that the sole goal of a firm ought to be to make profits for its owners (Penrose, 1959). Likewise, Friedman (1970) supports this theory as he indicates that it is illogical for firms to spend money on social projects as they decrease

DOI: 10.4018/978-1-7998-2193-9.ch004

Copyright © 2020, IGI Global. Copying or distributing in print or electronic forms without written permission of IGI Global is prohibited.

the funds available for running the firm. He posits that the sole responsibility of a firm is to make high profits for its stakeholders.

On the other hand, proponents of CSR assert that organizations have an obligation to act responsibly. Several people are becoming progressively aware of the environmental and ethical effects of the activities of corporations. Issues like environmental protection, employee protection, and customer convenience have become major highlights in the media in this era and are shaping and influencing the relationships between organizations and their stakeholders. Universally, governments have tightened laws and standards to regulate social and environmental challenges. Some shareholders also now consider the CSR of businesses in making decisions concerning investments. Consequently, corporations are now compelled to operate in ways that can sustain them economically, socially and environmentally.

In the light of these pressures, organizations are saddled with the burden of incorporating CSR programs into their core business strategy. The importance of integrating CSR with business strategy has become virtually impossible to ignore as it is becoming very complex for business stakeholders to keep up with future business development (Saeed & Arshad, 2012). CSR is a central aspect of managing the costs and benefits of business activities both internally (i.e., employees, stockholders, investors, etc.) and externally (regulators, inhabitants of the community a firm operates in, civil society organizations and other corporations).

In the face of growing interests in CSR, the main literature available on CSR concentrates mainly on activities that are geared towards the fulfillment of laws, government concerns, stakeholder management and satisfaction, and fulfilling community concerns of the triple bottom line. Although some researchers have tried to link CSR with competitive advantage from a strategic management perspective, most of the emphases have been on the financial return to be realized from these activities. The study of CSR in relation to gaining strategic competitive advantage has not been explored in-depth.

This chapter, therefore, seeks to achieve the following objectives:

1. To assess the CSR initiatives and competitive advantage of some banks in Ghana.
2. To investigate the relationship between CSR initiatives and Brand Perceptions of some banks in Ghana.
3. To measure the connection between Competitive Advantage and Brand Perceptions of some banks in Ghana.

BACKGROUND

The Concept of Corporate Social Responsibility

CSR is perceived as situations where organizations undertake social initiatives in support of the communities within which they operate, which goes beyond their interests as well as the requirements of law (McWilliams & Siegel, 2000). The term CSR was first propounded in the 1950s and received much attention in management studies in the 1970s. Principally, CSR initiatives are categorized into three groups: economic growth, ecological balance, and social progress (Saeed & Arshad, 2012). In the estimation of Saeed and Arshad (2012), the accepted influence of CSR includes its effect on a firm's Financial Performance (FP) and social performance. In underdeveloped nations, charitable CSR practices are being considered by several businesses; for instance, humanitarian acts in the society as well as issues pertaining to CSR's benefit to human capital, and human resource management and fulfillment, are receiving much attention (Jamali & Mirshak, 2007).

The World Business Council for Sustainable Development's (WBCSD) report "Making Good Business Sense" (2000) indicate that Ghanaians perceive CSR to be enhancing the capacity of people for sustainable livelihoods, respecting cultural differences, identifying prospects to enhance employees' skills, and helping the community and government. Likewise, the report posits that the Philippines perceive CSR as "giving back to society". This stance is similar to the conventional definition given the term in the USA, which sees CSR in relation to a humanitarian model.

Dartey-Baah and Amponsah-Tawiah (2015) posit that over the last decade, some African countries such as South Africa and Kenya have progressed significantly as regards issues of human rights and CSR. Nevertheless, this progress is not as much as it could be as there are still many countries in Africa that have abundant natural resources that are neglected and abused even though their resources continue to be looted by various multinational firms. Dartey-Baah and Amponsah-Tawiah (2015) further state that much attention has been given to environmental issues and philanthropy compared with legal and ethical organizational practices. Their assertion illustrates CSR perceptions in Ghana because mostly, it is the activities of mining and oil and gas firms that have greatly affected the environment even though they do very little to take responsibility. It is, therefore, only natural that these companies, which are multinationals, are compelled by international and local EPA regulations and other applicable laws to operate and transact business in a socially responsible way.

The Concept of Competitive Advantage

According to Kotler and Keller (2013), competitive advantage (CA) is "the ability to perform in one or more ways that competitors cannot or will not match" A competitive advantage is what differentiates one firm from other firms in the thoughts of customers. Employees, firms, or nations must have a distinct competitive advantage, which is communicated to their clients. Passemard and Calantone (2000) refer to competitive advantage as "Successfully implemented strategies that lift a firm to superior performance by facilitating the firm with a competitive advantage to outperform current or potential players".

Basically, a competitive advantage could be defined as the distinctive feature of any organization that enables it to cater for or serve customers better than other organizations and, therefore, generate better customer value and attain higher performance (Ma, 1999). For example, these features include a better location, control of shelf-space in retail shops, sole or advantageous access to supply, a popular brand name, employee expertise, and effective business operations. In addition to any of these features, the better an organization does than its competitors, the superior its competitive advantage.

The two main viewpoints of competitive advantage are the positioning approach (Porter, 1980) and the Resource-Based View (RBV) (Barney, 1991). There are several means of making profits in a business, but all these aids to place it in a superior position that could be maintained for a period of time (sustainable competitive advantage) (Porter & Kramer, 2006). This study focuses on how the scope of CSR enables firms in the Ghanaian Banking Sector to gain competitive advantage.

Brand Perception

Brand refers to the total experiences associated with a company, its product, and services. Aaker (1991) defines a brand as the perceptions that distinguish products or companies. Brand perceptions are generally formed by practical experiences (that is speed, quality, dependability, ease of use) and through the emotional experiences, customers link to a product and a firm. (i.e. in terms of feelings, improved performance or making one's life easier). Brand can serve as a major influencing factor in a user's choice of a product or service and not others. Due to the fact that CSR-related issues could directly destroy the organization's legitimacy as well as its brand, which serves as the foundation for building market value. It is suggested that CSR of companies must move from being a minimum commitment to become a strategic necessity (Werther & Chandler, 2005). Brand perception controls the expectations consumers or employees have of a company's brand (Yaniv & Farkas, 2005). Such expectations represent the customer's feelings towards the company (Herman, 2001). Generally, a firm's staff look out firm values and firm brand values to match. (Yaniv & Farkas, 2005). According to Harris and de Chernatony (2001) and Key (2002), the fact that corporate values and corporate brand values must correspond cannot be overemphasized.

EMPIRICAL STUDIES ON CSR, BRAND PERCEPTION AND COMPETITIVE ADVANTAGE

CSR and Brand Perception

CSR can contribute to a firm's creation of exceptional resources, including reputation, better brand perceptions, build the capacity of their staff, knowledge and a network of relationships. Hence, Branco and Rodingues (2006) define CSR as a vital asset for firms from a resource-based point of view. Barney (1991) postulates that firms could take advantage of their exceptional resources for sustainability when their resources are valuable, inimitable, rare, and immobile. CSR and corporate reputation positively impact industrial brand equity and brand performance (Lai et al., 2010). Assessments of brand perception indicate that costumers do not solely care about a brand's features and its advantages, but they likewise care about the connection between the company and the society (Kervyn, Fiske & Malone, 2012).

Furthermore, Porter and Kramer (2006) contend that when organizations engage in strategic CSR activities (such as environmentally sustainable initiatives), they could aid the organization to attain cost management or differentiation (or both). Likewise, engaging in strategic CSR can contribute to branding an organization as socially, ethically, and environmentally sensitive (Porter & Kramer, 2006). This aids an organization to distinguish its products and services from others that do not utilize CSR. Consequently, buyers are always ready to pay a premium for the organization's product or reward it through other mediums (McWilliams et al., 2006). In this regard, the brand perception of the company would be improved.

In certain advanced countries, buyers or users may decide to be customers of organizations that engage in significant and meaningful CSR activities (Kotler & Lee 2005). Hence, strategic CSR projects could result in product distinction and better brand perception; therefore, they aid an organization to pursue the general strategy of "Product Differentiation" (McWilliams et al., 2006). When a firm is a great corporate citizen, it could strengthen customer loyalty and transform them to become organization/brand ambassadors who advocate for the company (for example, good testimonials, readiness to pay premium rates and resilience in dealing with bad news from the firm) (Du et al., 2007; Walsh & Bartikowski, 2013; Homburg, Stierl & Bornemann, 2013).

CSR and Competitive Advantage

Husted and Allen (2001) opine that CSR strategies could generate competitive advantages when utilized correctly; they indicate a positive connection between strategic social responsibility initiatives and competitive advantage. Zadek (2005) groups companies into three major categories based on their responsible competitiveness. Firms under the first group (first-generation organizations) employ a short-term pain mitigation approach. The second group (second-generation organizations) implement strategic planning and risk management strategies. Finally, third-generation organizations integrate CSR into their plan. However, to some researchers with opposing views, reputation is an internal resource that ought to be properly managed because it is a significant distinguishing factor and a possible creator of competitive advantage (Mahon, 2002; Hanzaee & Sadeghian, 2014).

Ashley (2002) posits that firms should consider adopting CSR as it is at present a source of competitive advantage, which firms should utilize in their pursuit of superior competitiveness and improved outcomes. Barney (1991) postulates that competitive advantage is built by the adoption of strategies that enhance value and create benefits for a firm when other firms fail to do so.

However, it is vital to indicate that competitive advantage could be gained through CSR activities if these activities benefit society as implied in the philosophy of social strategies (Husted & Allen, 2001; Chege, 2013). For CSR to be a source of competitive advantage, it must be real and consistently benefit the society. A higher focus on external factors just as internal value to strategic social decisions causes organizations to reflect on their actions or decisions and helps them to analyze and anticipate the consequences of the organization's behavior while it forecasts the probable positive or negative outcomes of its actions (Alessio, 2003). Zadek (2005) opines that in firms where CSR is entrenched, it is easy to handle new market expectations including handling corruption, human rights issues, environmental management in the supply chain, and others.

Based on the empirical studies reviewed, the following hypotheses were formulated:

Hypothesis One: There will be a positive and significant connection between CSR activities and better brand perceptions.

Hypothesis Two: There is a positive and significant connection between CSR initiatives and Competitive Advantage.

Hypothesis Three: There is a positive and significant connection between Brand perception and competitive advantage.

PARALLELS AND DIVERGENCE OF CSR BETWEEN AFRICA AND THE WORLD

Carroll (1991) specifies that firms are responsible for producing goods and services to meet society's needs as well as make profits. Though CSR is discussed in an international context, not much research has been conducted on CSR in the context of developing nations Despite its extensive acceptance in the CSR literature, Carroll's conceptualization has been criticized and categorized as not a suitable model for assessing CSR internationally (Lindgreen et al., 2009) particularly in Africa (Visser, 2006).

However, Baskin (2006) study the corporate responsibility behavior of 127 top firms in 21 emerging markets within Asia, Africa, Latin America, and Central and Eastern Europe. He compares these organizations with over 1,700 top firms in high-income OECD (Organization for Economic Cooperation and Development) nations. It was found that, though CSR activities were more widespread than thought to be, they are less incorporated in strategies, less persistent and less embedded politically than in most developed nations. Additionally, it was discovered that firms in developing markets have a good representation in the Dow Jones Sustainability Index and demonstrate increasing levels of reception of the Global Reporting Initiative and ISO 14001 (Visser, 2008). More precisely, more than two-thirds of the firms in developing markets that were studied either had written a sustainability report or had dedicated a section of their website to CSR or in recorded their CSR initiatives in their yearly reports.

Nature of CSR in Africa

CSR in Africa, as well as in other emerging nations, differs from the western point of view as it is perceived philanthropic initiatives that attempt to cater for the lapses of government; poverty alleviation and cater for other kinds of socio-economic needs such as sponsorship of community development projects; provision of educational and health, facilities, and the development of sports, etc. (Hamidu et al., 2016). In Africa, CSR initiatives are usually made up of projects that contribute to infrastructural or economic advancement of communities through job creation, taxation, etc. On the other hand, CSR activities in the West are focus on ethical issues and these activities are carefully regulated by both formal and informal legislation.

Application of CSR Theory in Africa

In Africa, Western CSR theory is limited by Africa's CSR drivers as well as its cultural and managerial behaviors (Hamidu et al., 2016). Traditional African methods of community leadership and business vary from western principles. Contemporary issues for CSR in Africa comprise health (HIV/AIDS and Malaria), sanitation, sports, and education (Dartey-Baah, & Amponsah-Tawiah, 2011). Also, CSR initiatives are usually influenced by traditional values Such as Ubuntu (African Humanism) in South Africa, African Renaissance (African solutions for Africa by Africans) started by ex-South African president Thabo Mbeki, and Omoluwabi (Yoruba tradition of Southwestern Nigeria) have significant influences on CSR initiatives in Africa.

METHODOLOGY

Method and Approach

The study utilized the quantitative research method. Consequently, the paper adopted a survey design involving two banks (a multinational bank and Ghanaian Bank). The purposive sampling method was used in the selection of the banks. Two prestigious banks (Barclays Bank and GCB) out of a total of about twenty-five registered banks in Ghana were chosen for the survey. This is because they share similar characteristics with the population under study. Also, these two banks are the largest networked banks in Ghana and have branches in each of almost all the sixteen regions of Ghana. With such contextual background to the criteria for selection, the selection of these two banks is considered as an appropriate sample that is representative of the views of both bankers and customers along across the nation.

The primary data was collected through the administration of a designed questionnaire. A research questionnaire was developed based on the research questions and objectives of the study. Utilizing the mathematical equation propounded by Krejcie and Morgan (1970) determining the sample size for a study, 166 respondents (customers) were randomly chosen for the study. This was to ensure that the sample size selected represented the population (banks) under study. The researcher administered 170 questionnaires to customers of the two banks selected for the study. In all, 150 questionnaires were retrieved from respondents. Out of this number, customers of Barclays bank returned 120 valid questionnaires (80% response rate) while GCB customers returned 83 valid ones (55.3% response rate). The study again sampled 25 respondents each from both banks. Out of the 25 questionnaires administered to employees of each bank, 17 valid questionnaires from Barclays bank were retrieved (68% response rate) while 24 from GCB were valid (96% response rate).

Measures

The paper adopted Maigan & Ferrell's (2000) 18 item CSR questionnaire scale. The scale measures the four dimensions of CSR: economic CSR, legal CSR, ethical CSR, and discretionary CSR. The four dimensions were combined into a single Corporate Social Responsibility composite. The scale has a reliability coefficient of α=.92. Again, Zhang's (2001) 16 item organizational competitiveness scale was adopted to measure competitive advantage. It measures five dimensions of competitiveness namely cost, quality, delivery dependability, time to market and product innovation. The instrument was reported to have a Cronbach's alpha coefficient ranging between 0.89 in a study conducted by Bratic (2011). Brand reputation was measured using Chen-Yu et al. (2016) brand reputation scale. The scale recorded a Cronbach alpha coefficient of 0.82.

Analysis

The data was analyzed using simple linear regressions. This rationale was to know how the variables were related. The age, gender and educational level of respondents were used as control variables because of their perceived effects on the variables. Initial tests for normality were done to ensure that the data was evenly distributed and standard. The skewness and kurtosis values were within -1 and +1, which demonstrate a standard distribution of scores.

Results

H1: *There will be a positive and significant connection between CSR activities and better brand perceptions.*

The result indicates a positive significant connection between CSR activities and better brand perceptions (R^2=.41, F(1,163)=112.53, p<.000). This implies that CSR activities explained almost 41% variance in the dependent variable (brand perception). There was a positive and significant connection between the two variables (β= .64, p<.000); hence, the hypothesis was supported. Table 1 displays the correlation matrix of the two variables as well as all study variables. As a result, it supports hypothesis 1.

Table 1. Correlation matrix between the variables of study

Variables	Mean	SD					
Control variables			1	2	3	4	5
Age	1.54	.50	-				
Gender	2.68	.97	.09	-			
Level of education	2.83	.52	.08	-.15	-		
Study variables							
Corporate Social Responsibility	188.33	31.73	.03	.01	-.06	-	
Competitive Advantage	22.63	6.01	-.12	.12	-.04	.58**	-
Brand Perception	22.57	6.13	-.07	.12	-.07	.64**	.64**

Note: p**=.000, CSR=Corporate Social Responsibility, CA=Competitive Advantage, BP=Brand Perception

H2: There is a positive and significant connection between CSR activities and Competitive Advantage.

Table 2 also presents a summary of the regression analyses of hypotheses 2 and 3. With regard to hypothesis 2, the result demonstrated a positive and significant connection between CSR activities and competitive advantage (R^2=.33, F (1,162) =80.71, p<.000). This implies that CSR activities explained almost 33% variance in the dependent variable (competitive advantage). There was a positive and significant connection between the two variables (β= .57, p<.000); hence, the hypothesis was supported.

H3: There is a positive and significant connection between brand perception and Competitive Advantage.

The result indicated a positive and significant connection between brand perception and competitive advantage (R^2=.41, F (1,163) =114.66, p<.000). This implies that brand perception explained almost 41% variance in the dependent variable (competitive advantage). There was a positive and significant connection between the two variables (β= .64, p<.000); hence, the hypothesis was supported.

Table 2. Summary of regression analyses for CSR, CA and brand perception

	B	*SE*	**Β**	**T**	*p*	*F*	R^2
CSR	.12	.01	.64	10.61	.000	112.53**	.41
CA	.11	.01	.57	8.98	.000	80.71**	.33
BP	.65	.06	.64	10.71	.000	114.66**	.41

Note: p**=.000, CSR=Corporate Social Responsibility, CA=Competitive Advantage, BP=Brand Perception

CONCLUSION

The study's results have demonstrated significant positive relationships among the variables of study (CSR, brand perception and competitive advantage). This, therefore, highlights how pertinent these variables are in promoting sustainable growth in these companies. CSR should be encouraged in order to boost brand perception and give a competitive advantage to the company. Government should also provide an enabling environment for businesses to thrive so that they can push some of their profits into CSR initiatives.

SOLUTION AND RECOMMENDATIONS

The study revealed a significant positive connection between CSR and brand perceptions. This indicates that consumers cared about the brand's features and benefits as well as the relationship between the company and the society (Kervyn, Fiske & Malone, 2012). This is congruent with the study of Lai et al. (2010), who found that CSR and corporate reputation have a positive influence on industrial brand equity and brand performance. Engaging in CSR also projects the image of as company as a socially responsible and environmentally sensitive (Porter & Kramer, 2006). Consequently, the company's products are differentiated and held in high esteem as 'good'. This makes consumers ready to even pay premium rates for the company's products and services (McWilliams et al., 2006). Furthermore, Kotler and Lee (2005) posit that buyers may decide to become loyal customers of businesses that undertake extensive and meaningful CSR activities. This leads to product differentiation and better brand perception. When a firm is a great corporate citizen, it could strengthen customer loyalty and transform them to become organization/brand ambassadors who advocate for the company (Du et al., 2007; Walsh & Bartikowski, 2013).

It was also found that CSR was positively related to competitive advantage. This finding supports the studies of Husted and Allen (2000) and Mahon (2002), who found that CSR creates competitive advantage when properly used and implemented.

Brand perception and CSR were positively related in that, CSR-related issues can directly destroy the organization's legitimacy as well as its brand, which serves as the foundation for building market value. Due to this, the CSR of companies must move from being a minimal commitment to become a strategic requirement because of the impact it could have on brand perception (Werther & Chandler, 2005). Brand perception brings in profit from various avenues, which ultimately aid a company to have a competitive advantage that could be maintained for some time (sustainable competitive advantage) (Porter & Kramer, 2006).

Per the findings of this study, it is recommended that companies make CSR part of their major projects because CSR is now an avenue for boosting competitive advantage. Companies must adopt it strategically as they pursue superior competitiveness and improved outcomes (Ashley, 2002). It should, however, be noted that Competitive Advantage is created when strategies are implemented that add value for the business (Barney, 1991). In order for CSR to be a source of competitive advantage, CSR initiatives ought to create real and constant results for society. Moreover, many multinational corporations are transferring their indigenous notions of corporate responsibility to Africa. For instance, India's Tata Corporation has transferred its long tradition of philanthropic corporate responsibility to its operations in nine African countries. However, managers in Africa must develop CSR strategies based on the cultural needs in order to make CSR initiatives relevant to the African society (China Daily, 2010).

FUTURE RESEARCH DIRECTIONS

The issue of the culture of an individual customer, employee as well as the company in question is a pertinent one as CSR and brand perception are discussed. In this study, corporate culture was not among the variables studied. The connection between corporate company culture and societal cultural practices in the implementation of CSR should be studied so as to identify their probable influence and relations with competitive advantage and brand perception.

REFERENCES

Aaker, D. (1991). Brand equity. *La gestione de lvalore della marca.*

Alessio, R. (2003). Responsabilidade social dasempresas no Brasil: Reprodução de posturas ou novosrumos? *Revista Virtual Textos&Contextos*, *2*(2), 1–10.

Amadeo, K. (2014). *World's largest economy*. Academic Press.

Ashley, P. A. (2002). *Ética e responsabilidade social nosnegócios*. São Paulo: Saraiva.

Barney, J. (1991). Firm resources and sustained competitive advantage. *Journal of Management*, *17*(1), 99–120. doi:10.1177/014920639101700108

Baskin, J. (2006). Corporate Responsibility in Emerging Markets. *Journal of Corporate Citizenship, 24,* 29–47.

Boon, E. K., & Ababio, F. (2009, May). Corporate social responsibility in Ghana: Lessons from the mining sector. *IAIIA09 Conference Proceedings, Impact Assessment and Human Well-Being*.

Branco, M. C., & Rodrigues, L. L. (2006). Corporate social responsibility and resource-based perspectives. *Journal of Business Ethics*, *69*(2), 111–132. doi:10.100710551-006-9071-z

Burns, N., & Grove, S. K. (1997). Selecting a research design. *The Practice of Nursing Research: Conduct, Critique, &. Utilization*, *3*, 249–291.

Carroll, A. B. (1991). The Pyramid of Corporate Social Responsibility: Toward the Moral Management of Organizational Stakeholders. *Business Horizons*, *34*(4), 39–48. doi:10.1016/0007-6813(91)90005-G

Chege, E. S. (2013). *Corporate Social Responsibility and Competitive Advantage of Commercial Banks in Kenya. A Research Project.* School of Business University of Nairobi-Kenya.

Chen-Yu, J., Cho, S., & Kincade, D. (2016). Brand perception and brand repurchase intent in online apparel shopping: An examination of brand experience, image congruence, brand affect, and brand trust. *Journal of Global Fashion Marketing*, *7*(1), 30–44. doi:10.1080/20932685.2015.1110042

China Daily. (2010). *China-Africa trade volume set to hit new record high.* Retrieved from: http://www.chinadaily.com.cn/china/2010–10/14/content_11412120.htm

Dartey-Baah, K., & Amponsah-Tawiah, K. (2011). Exploring the limits of western corporate social responsibility theories in Africa. *International Journal of Business and Social Science*, *2*(18), 126–137.

Dartey-Baah, K., Amponsah-Tawiah, K., & Agbeibor, V. (2015). Corporate social responsibility in Ghana's national development. *Africa Today*, *62*(2), 71–92. doi:10.2979/africatoday.62.2.71

Du, S., Bhattacharya, C. B., & Sen, S. (2007). Reaping relational rewards from corporate social responsibility: The role of competitive positioning. *International Journal of Research in Marketing*, *24*(3), 224–241. doi:10.1016/j.ijresmar.2007.01.001

Hamidu, A. A., Haron, M., & Amran, A. (2016). Exploring the Drivers and Nature of Corporate Social Responsibility Practice from an African Perspective. *International Review of Management and Marketing*, *6*(4), 696–703.

Hanzaee, K. H., & Sadeghian, M. (2014). The impact of corporate social responsibility on customer satisfaction and corporate reputation in automotive industry: Evidence from Iran. *Journal of Islamic Marketing*, *5*(1), 125–143. doi:10.1108/JIMA-05-2013-0033

Harris, F., & de Chernatony, L. (2001). Corporate branding and corporate brand performance. *European Journal of Marketing*, *35*(3/4), 441–456. doi:10.1108/03090560110382101

Homburg, C., Stierl, M., & Bornemann, T. (2013). Corporate social responsibility in business-to-business markets: How organizational customers account for supplier corporate social responsibility engagement. *Journal of Marketing*, *77*(6), 54–72. doi:10.1509/jm.12.0089

Husted, B. W., & Allen, D. B. (2001, August). Toward a model of corporate social strategy formulation. *Proceedings of the Social Issues in Management Division at Academy of Management Conference*, 1-35.

Jamali, D., & Mirshak, R. (2007). Corporate social responsibility (CSR): Theory and practice in a developing country context. *Journal of Business Ethics*, *72*(3), 243–262. doi:10.100710551-006-9168-4

Kervyn, N., Fiske, S. T., & Malone, C. (2012). Brands as intentional agents framework: How perceived intentions and ability can map brand perception. *Journal of Consumer Psychology: The Official Journal of the Society for Consumer Psychology*, *22*(2), 166–176. doi:10.1016/j.jcps.2011.09.006 PMID:24403815

Kotler, P., & Lee, N. (2005). Best of breed: When it comes to gaining a market edge while supporting a social cause, "corporate social marketing" leads the pack. *Social Marketing Quarterly*, *11*(3-4), 91–103. doi:10.1080/15245000500414480

Kotler, P. K., Keller, K. L., & Jha, A. M. (2013). *Marketing Management A South Asian Perspective. Creating Brand Equity* (14th ed.). Pearson.

Krejcie, R. V., & Morgan, D. W. (1970). Determining sample size for research activities. *Educational and Psychological Measurement*, *30*(3), 607–610. doi:10.1177/001316447003000308

Krejcie, R. V., & Morgan, D. W. (1970). Determining sample size for research activities. *Educational and Psychological Measurement*, *30*(3), 607–610. doi:10.1177/001316447003000308

Lai, C. S., Chiu, C. J., Yang, C. F., & Pai, D. C. (2010). The Effects of Corporate Social Responsibility on Brand Performance: The Mediating Effect of Industrial Brand Equity and Corporate Reputation. *Journal of Business Ethics*, *95*(3), 457–469. doi:10.100710551-010-0433-1

Lindgreen, A., Swaen, V., & Campbell, T. T. (2009). Corporate social responsibility practices in developing and transitional countries: Botswana and Malawi. *Journal of Business Ethics*, *90*(S3), 429–440. doi:10.100710551-010-0415-3

Ma, F., & Hanna, M. A. (1999). Biodiesel production: A review. *Bioresource Technology*, *70*(1), 1–15. doi:10.1016/S0960-8524(99)00025-5

Mahon, J. F. (2002). Corporate reputation: Research agenda using strategy and stakeholder literature. *Business & Society*, *41*(4), 415–445. doi:10.1177/0007650302238776

Maignan, I., & Ferrell, O. C. (2000). Measuring corporate citizenship in two countries: The case of the United States and France. *Journal of Business Ethics*, *23*(3), 283–297. doi:10.1023/A:1006262325211

McWilliams, A. (2000). *Corporate social responsibility*. Wiley Encyclopedia of Management.

Meridian Group International. (2006). *CSR in Africa: Internet Research Study*. Extending Service Delivery Project. Retrieved from: http://www.esdproj.org/site/DocServer/CSR_in_Africa_06_FINAL.pdf

Ofori, D. F., & Hinson, R. E. (2007). Corporate social responsibility (CSR) perspectives of leading firms in Ghana. *Corporate Governance: The International Journal Of Business In Society*, *7*(2), 178–193. doi:10.1108/14720700710739813

Passemard, M., & Calantone, K. (2000). *Competitive Advantage: Creating and Sustaining Superior Performance by Michael E.* Academic Press.

Porter, M. E., & Kramer, M. R. (2006). Strategy and society: The link between corporate social responsibility and competitive advantage. *Harvard Business Review*, *84*(12), 78–92. PMID:17183795

Porter, M. F. (1980). An algorithm for suffix stripping. *Program*, *14*(3), 130–137. doi:10.1108/eb046814

Saeed, M. M., & Arshad, F. (2012). Corporate social responsibility as a source of competitive advantage: The mediating role of social capital and reputational capital. *Journal of Database Marketing & Customer Strategy Management*, *19*(4), 219–232. doi:10.1057/dbm.2012.19

Tang, Z., Hull, C. E., & Rothenberg, S. (2012). How corporate social responsibility engagement strategy moderates the CSR–financial performance relationship. *Journal of Management Studies*, *49*(7), 1274–1303. doi:10.1111/j.1467-6486.2012.01068.x

Visser, W. (2006). Revisiting Carroll's CSR pyramid: An African perspective. In M. Huniche & E. R. Pedersen (Eds.), *Corporate citizenship in developing countries: New partnership perspectives* (pp. 29–56). Gylling, Denmark: Narayana Press.

Visser, W. (2008). Corporate social responsibility in developing countries. In *The Oxford Handbook of Corporate Social Responsibility*. Oxford University Press.

Walsh, G., & Bartikowski, B. (2013). Exploring corporate ability and social responsibility associations as antecedents of customer satisfaction cross-culturally. *Journal of Business Research*, *66*(8), 989–995. doi:10.1016/j.jbusres.2011.12.022

Werther, W. B. Jr, & Chandler, D. (2005). Strategic corporate social responsibility as global brand insurance. *Business Horizons*, *48*(4), 317–324. doi:10.1016/j.bushor.2004.11.009

Yaniv, E., & Farkas, F. (2005). The impact of person-organization fit on the corporate brand perception of employees and of customers. *Journal of Change Management*, *5*(4), 447–461. doi:10.1080/14697010500372600

ADDITIONAL READING

Ganescu, M. C. (2012). Corporate social responsibility, a strategy to create and consolidate sustainable businesses. *Theoretical & Applied Economics*, *19*(11), 91–106.

Hsu, K. T. (2012). The advertising effects of corporate social responsibility on corporate reputation and brand equity: Evidence from the life insurance industry in Taiwan. *Journal of Business Ethics*, *109*(2), 189–201. doi:10.100710551-011-1118-0

McWilliams, A., & Siegel, D. S. (2011). Creating and capturing value: Strategic corporate social responsibility, resource-based theory, and sustainable competitive advantage. *Journal of Management*, *37*(5), 1480–1495. doi:10.1177/0149206310385696

Rim, H., Yang, S. U., & Lee, J. (2016). Strategic partnerships with nonprofits in corporate social responsibility (CSR): The mediating role of perceived altruism and organizational identification. *Journal of Business Research*, *69*(9), 3213–3219. doi:10.1016/j.jbusres.2016.02.035

Saeidi, S. P., Sofian, S., Saeidi, P., Saeidi, S. P., & Saaeidi, S. A. (2015). How does corporate social responsibility contribute to firm financial performance? The mediating role of competitive advantage, reputation, and customer satisfaction. *Journal of Business Research*, *68*(2), 341–350. doi:10.1016/j.jbusres.2014.06.024

KEY WORDS AND DEFINITIONS

Brand: It is a name, term, design, symbol, or any other feature that identifies one seller's good or service as distinct from those of other sellers.

Brand Perception: It is what customers believe a product or service represents. It is what stakeholders think about the brand.

Competitive Advantage: It refers to a company's ability to outperform competitors as a result of unique and superior quality products or services delivery. It can also be said to be that which makes a firm's goods or services superior compared to of other choices.

Corporate Social Responsibility: It is a business model that helps a firm be socially accountable to itself and all its stakeholders. It is giving back to the society that firms operate in.

Strategy: A plan of action designed to achieve a long-term or overall aim. A method or plan chosen to bring about a desired future, such as achievement of a goal or solution to a problem.

Chapter 5
Communicating Socially Responsible Initiatives:
New Incentives to Sustainable Development

Ekaterina Arabska
https://orcid.org/0000-0001-6992-4867
University of Agribusiness and Rural Development, Bulgaria

ABSTRACT

The purpose of the chapter is to present results of case studies of socially responsible initiatives and their communication inside and outside the organizations through the official websites impacting their performance and image, as well as to make recommendations for improvements. Investigations focus on forms and goals of initiatives taken by companies in Bulgaria, including examples of the influence of foreign corporate practice and experience. Theoretical and practical basis and trends, international framework, and national institutional positions and support to corporate social responsibility are discussed. Socially responsible activities are analyzed through the official websites in their short- and long-term aspects and links to sustainable development initiatives. Main CSR principles are defined, and a model is proposed containing the main steps of incorporating CSR strategies in companies and linking all that to business communications and public relations. A special focus is put on capacity building and CSR teams.

INTRODUCTION

Corporate social responsibility (CSR) is a modern notion and part of the activities of companies functioning in the contemporary globalized world of economic and social relations. Socially responsible behavior is accepted as the behavior taking responsibilities of societal and environmental impacts. It applies social responsible practices in response to global economic and environmental threats based on the new business culture and in relation to sustainable development. The fact that today there are

DOI: 10.4018/978-1-7998-2193-9.ch005

Copyright © 2020, IGI Global. Copying or distributing in print or electronic forms without written permission of IGI Global is prohibited.

many global threats requires quick reactions towards the adoption of more extended look in terms of risk management options that include environmental social and governance factors; a focus on creating long-term value in companies and markets; displaying responsibility and ethics to the forefront, to reinforce confidence. Socially responsible behavior by businesses in social and environmental terms is necessary because of immediate adverse consequences of globalization (as stated in the Corporate social responsibility strategy of the Republic of Bulgaria 2009-2013).

The question of corporate social responsibility introduces the basic positions and limitations from the point of view of modern organizations and their roles in the balancing of the three pillars of sustainable development – economic growth, social development and environmental protection (Zahariev, 2013, p. 232). Corporate social responsibility, also called *corporate conscience, citizenship, social performance, sustainable responsible business*, is a form of *corporate self-regulation integrated into a business model*. CSR policy functions as a built-in mechanism of self-regulation by which the business controls and provides its active compliance with the law, ethical standards, and international norms (Pop et al., 2011). Corporate social responsibility is accepted as the responsibility and accountability of the organizations for the impacts of their decisions and activities on society and environment implemented in conditions of transparency and ethical behavior and contributing to sustainable development, human health, and social welfare. Being integrated into the organizations at all the levels and expressed by their inner and outer interactions and relations, it considers the expectations of all the parties and is in correspondence to the legislation concerning social and ecological issues and relevant international norms in the implementation of socially responsible initiatives (Nikolova & Yordanova, 2014). CSR is an activity which is not of a single performance but a sustainable process. The concept is developing into a successful business strategy for sustainable development supporting organizations in the raise of their influence on the market and also in establishing a positive public image (Bakardjieva, 2016; Nikolova et al., 2014; Bakardjieva, 2009).

Sustainable development pillars and their balancing are closely connected to the concept of corporate social responsibility. Usually, corporate social responsibility is considered as voluntary concerns, actions, and relations in contemporary business (responsible behavior) concerning employment, environment, and consumers. Social responsibility is the responsibility of companies (decisions and activities, interactions) of their impacts on society and the environment. Its implementation should be in conditions of transparency and ethical behavior concerning legislation and universal values, society needs, etc. The fields of CSR include society, environment, human capital, and labor conditions, knowledge and education, etc. Socially responsible programs should be planned, implemented, and assessed in a long-term scope.

The concept of corporate social responsibility lies in the bases of sustainable development. Studies on its manifestations would reveal innovative approaches in strategic management in contemporary organizations in a direct relation to their competitiveness in conditions of globalization. In the chapter, socially responsible initiatives are discussed in the context of the priorities of sustainable development and the needed orientation of each organization towards consumers' demand and choice on informed decision making and concern about nature and future generations' wellbeing. The ways of communication with stakeholders are discussed through the example of professional teams in the USA (Walker et al., 2010), especially the communication via Internet and its opportunities for distribution of CSR-related content. CSR communication is determined as a vital issue in "building and sustaining the legitimacy of a company in the eyes of stakeholders" (Türkel & Akan, 2015). CSR communication is described as a process in which CSR policy is articulated, and communication tools are designed so that to provide correct information about the integration of companies' operations with social and environmental issues, as well as relations with stakeholders. An exploratory study on how organizations can integrate their stakeholders in online CSR communication and why that is so important poses a number of valuable questions: *Do companies take full advantage of the opportunities provided by the internet for integrating stakeholders in their online CSR communication? If yes, how? And why is it important to create an online CSR dialogue?* (Engsig, 2011). Thus communication is defined as "a process by which meaning is assigned and conveyed between parties in an attempt to create a shared understanding". On the basis of the development of theories on stakeholder management and public relations three CSR communication strategies are presented by Morsing & Schultz (2006) as follows: stakeholder information strategy (one-way communication strategy), stakeholder response strategy (two-way asymmetric communication strategy) and stakeholder involvement strategy (two-way symmetric communication strategy) each of which related to "sense giving" and "sense making". CSR is considered as "a worldwide phenomenon" and CSR communication as a marketing tool contributing to the improvement of corporate image and revenues, but cross-cultural CSR studies on countries at different economic stages are relatively few (Gramser, 2016)

The main purpose of the study presented in the chapter is to examine how companies' websites show the responsibility for the company's actions and encouragement of the positive impact in Bulgaria through activities on the protection and care of the environment, consumers, employees, communities, stakeholders and all other members of the public sphere. It is done in relation to sustainable development goals and priorities, as well as to present some examples of their communication in inner and outer environment and based on those analyses to provide some recommendations on improvement and modeling.

BACKGROUND

Contemporary global threats in relation to climate change, limitations in natural resources, challenges in quality and distribution of human resources, crises in financial and economic sphere, etc. require integrated approaches towards managerial, social and ecological factors in the creation of a long-term value in organizations and markets based on the ethical norms and responsible behavior. The corporate social responsibility is accepted as the responsibility and accountability of the organizations for the impacts of their decisions and activities on society and environment implemented in conditions of transparency and ethical behavior and contributing to sustainable development, human health, and social welfare. Being integrated into the organizations at all levels and expressed by their inner and outer interactions and relations, it considers the expectations of all the parties and is in correspondence to the legislation concerning social and ecological issues and relevant international norms.

In the last few decades, CSR has been developing form a narrow and often marginalized notion into a complex and multilateral concept (Cochran, 2007). Corporate social responsibility (CSR) and corporate social irresponsibility (CSI) are determined as key tasks that could lead to the development of many international policies encouraging CSR and discouraging CSI (Windsor, 2013). CSR is a policy that organizations voluntarily accept and implement in their business strategies in a way showing their long-term engagement in the sustainable development of their business, society, and environment (Pop et al., 2011). Social responsibility is an element of the corporate culture considering the flexibility and security (flexicurity) and management of multiformity in several spheres and business practices.

In the EU Green book, the CSR is the main instrument for creation of new places of work and the sustainable, economic development and encouragement of a more effective regarding use of resources, greener and more competitive economy is one of the main priorities of Europe 2020 (Pop et al., 2011). Discussing the concept from the point of view of the EC's definition from 2001 as a voluntary integration of social and ecological concerns in the activities and interactions of the organizations, the CSR could be scrutinized as based on three fundamental concepts: voluntary nature of initiatives, consciousness and attention on the relations to markets and hence consumers, and inclusion of all stakeholders (Viola et al. 2013). It means that socially responsible business is paying more attention to the environment, employment, and consumers. Considering the significance of natural environmental orientation, it is accepted as comprising of three components: entrepreneurship, corporate social responsibility, and environment commitment (Menguc & Ozanne, 2005).

Corporate social responsibility consists of the obligations of businesses to society. Its directions are connected to community, environment, human capital and work conditions, knowledge, and education. The varieties of CSR open many disputes of the levels of involvement, forms, etc. and turn the concept into the fundamental element of corporate culture in modern organizations. The uniting vector is in the specific attributes of CSR in different spheres (Zahariev & Arabska, 2015).

Corporate social responsibility is not a new concept, but often, it is viewed as such and misinterpreted (Isaksson et al., 2014). Over the past several decades, corporate social responsibility has grown from *"a narrow and often marginalized notion into a complex and multifaceted concept"* (Cochran, 2007) developed into *"a successful managerial tool to build a company's reputation in the global market arena"* (Isaksson et al., 2014). The concept of corporate social responsibility is part of the debate about competitiveness and sustainability in the globalization context (Vasilescu et al. 2010). Defining and delimiting corporate social responsibility and irresponsibility are essential interdependent tasks (Windsor, 2013). The varieties of CSR open many disputes of the levels of involvement, forms, etc. and turn the concept into the necessary element of corporate culture in modern organizations. Among the common characteristics of CSR are environmentally friendly and social policies in organizations, as well as their inner and outer character. Today CSR policies are part of the strategies in many organizations as a means of integrating permanently increasing requirements of society towards business processes and products. Since the mid-1990s, an increasing number of organizations around the world started to disclose nonfinancial information related to social issues, such as environmental preservation, human rights protection, employees' welfare improvement, and contributions to their communities and societies (Dhaliwal et al., 2014).

The issues surrounding the concept of corporate sustainability are complex and far-reaching (Aminia and Bienstock, 2014). Although the pressure to sustainability incorporation into actions of all kinds of organizations, achieving success is a long-term process, and *"most current research is based on a short time horizon and shows mixed results in linking CSR to profitability and aspects of good governance"* (Porter and Miles, 2013). Maas and Reniers (2014) conclude that the current overload of sustainability standards, as well as the oversimplification of traditional management systems, are two factors that often prevent organizations from translating their sustainable aspirations into their core strategy. Jeong et al. (2013) investigate *"how marketers could maximize favorable consumer responses to brand pages on social network sites (SNSs) through the strategic use of corporate social responsibility"*. Addressing the key challenges: climate change and clean energy, sustainable transport, sustainable consumption and production, conservation and management of natural resources, public health, social inclusion, demography and migration, global poverty, Pop et al. (2011) state that *"the goal of sustainable development is not only to conserve the natural environment for successive generations"*. The authors further underline the importance of social dimensions, governance, and business accountability not only through transition to *"energy efficient"* economies but through establishment of social systems *"that are based on justice and equity, and that are built upon democratically controlled political structures, which give people a voice and a stake in their own future"*.

Besides, it is difficult to define all CSR manifestations, it can be concluded that the responsible way of functioning of all kinds of organizations on different levels is imposed by the increasing requirements towards accountability and transparency. This impacts the image and performance of organizations in local and global scope considering globalization processes, innovations and knowledge society.

Vasilescu et al. (2010) write that *"social responsibility goes far beyond the "philanthropy" of the past, it is about the business contribution to sustainable development and about proactive solutions to societal and environmental challenges"* and underline the notion of the ISO Strategic Advisory Group on Social Responsibility (2004) which says that most definitions consider the interrelationship between economic, environmental and social aspects and impacts of an organization's activities and that social responsibility means *"a balanced approach for organizations to address economic, social and environmental issues in a way that aims to benefit people, communities and society"*. Blodgett et al. (2014) examine the association between corporate social responsibility (CSR) and firm value considering that the business case for CSR or *"doing good while making a profit"* appears to be advancing within the business ethics literature as a preferred conception of CSR and state that *"the greater unification and refinement of both profit maximization and stakeholder interests through corporate acts, not statements alone, will sustain the financial value of CSR in a less regulated global business environment"*. Skare and Golja (2014) conclude that CSR is vital for the economic growth in a country: *"countries without an organized and supportive CSR environment and guidelines can hardly expect to increase economic performance through the new growth channels generated by CSR companies (new markets and customers)"*.

Bocken et al. (2014) propose a categorization of *"sustainable business model archetypes"* aiming at categorizing and explaining business model innovations for sustainability; providing mechanisms to assist the innovation process for embedding sustainability in business models (e.g. through case studies and workshops); defining a more precise research agenda for business models for sustainability; and providing exemplars for businesses to de-risk the SBM innovation process. The sustainable business model archetypes are viewed as a starting point to broaden and unify the research agenda for sustainable business models.

Asifa et al. (2013) develop an original framework for the integration of CSR into business processes stating that while many organizations utilize management systems to address their stakeholder requirements, their research *"elaborates on how organizations can capitalize on their existing management systems to more successfully introduce CSR practices"*. Abdirahman et al. (2014) propose an analytical framework of the implementation of CSR in food SMEs aiming at identifying the main network effects considering that innovation networks and networking activities, as in any innovation process, are primary means to enhance and foster CSR in SMEs. They provide a better understanding of how organizational and individual variables fit together and explain the implementation of CSR principles in a particular SME context. Additionally, this framework is also *"an analytical tool useful to identify and to characterize the functions of different groups of actors: indeed, it reveals synergies and complementarities at different levels"*.

The study of Kemper et al. (2013) *"sheds new light on the intersection of the competitive environment, marketing, and corporate sustainability"* examining interactions of competitive intensity, marketing capabilities and CSR, as well as their influence on the performance of organizations and underlining that CSR is *"a significant moderator of the link between marketing capabilities and performance only in industries of high competitive intensity"*. A model of CSR specifies relationships among four categories of CSR initiatives as independent variables, three types of consumer trust as mediating variables, and corporate reputation as the dependent variable (Park et al., 2014) showing that *"that the firm's fulfillment of economic and legal CSR initiatives had a direct positive effect on corporate reputation, whereas neither ethical nor philanthropic CSR initiatives did"*.

Coles et al. (2013), examining CSR in tourism management, emphasize three macro-level topic areas: implementation, the economic rationale for acting more responsibly, and the social relations of CSR. Font et al. (2014), analyzing the pro-sustainability behavior of tourism small and medium enterprises (SME) through different profiles of motivation against the implementation of sustainable measures and generic business variables, made a survey showing that *"small firms are more involved in taking responsibility for being sustainable than previously expected, including eco savings related operational practices but also reporting a wide range of social and economic responsibility actions"*. The study contributes to the understanding of the reasons, practices, and impacts of sustainability management. Concerning that CSR provides principles and guidelines for food risk management, a study finding driving factors for both identifies the following drivers: implementation of international standards, corporate value, trainings received, status of early warning systems, the cost, financial performance of the company, management support, CSR recognition (whether or not CSR being part of the company strategy), and management attitude to CSR (Zhang et al., 2014).

Corporate social responsibility management is one of the main levers for monitoring, assessing, and overcoming non-financial risks, and it has been established that corporate social responsibility is an integral part of corporate governance and requires the observance of principles, standards, and norms analogous to corporate governance (Bakardjieva, 2019).

The main potential benefits of corporate social initiatives for the company are expressed in: building a strong reputation, achieving key business objectives, attracting and retaining motivated employees, reducing operating costs, reducing inspections by regulators, achieving marketing goals, creating a sustainable relationship with society, increasing the impact of existing corporate social initiatives (Zahariev, 2014).

Throughout next parts of the current chapter the results from a study on CSR framework and state in Bulgaria and on the CSR web-pages / websites of different types of companies in Bulgaria (most of them part of foreign groups) – media companies, mobile operators, banks, industrial companies, logistics companies, pharmaceutical companies, sales companies, energy providers, and consulting companies – three of each examined. The selection was based on the results of a search in google.com.

CSR IN BULGARIA: STATE-OF-ART AND MAIN TRENDS

Development Framework and The Importance of Communicating Socially Responsible Initiatives

The term "corporate social responsibility" or "corporate responsibility" is not yet found in the acts of the domestic law of the Republic of Bulgaria. Based on the fact that CSR is actively promoting sustainable development and significantly contributes to the competitiveness of companies and regions, notions, and measures related to CSR can be made in the national strategic documents.

In 2009 a National Strategy for Corporate Social Responsibility (CSR) was adopted, which reflects the state's attitude to CSR issues and aims to create and strengthen a favorable environment for socially responsible practices. The Strategy covered the period 2009-2013 and was structured in three parts: situation analysis, vision, objectives, and principles, and implementation of CSR strategy. The main focus was on achieving the following goals:

- Raising awareness of stakeholders on the nature and implementation of CSR;
- Creating and strengthening the capacity of CSR stakeholders' expertise;
- Promoting the creation of a legal and institutional environment supporting the implementation of CSR;
- Promoting transparency in the implementation of socially responsible initiatives;
- Enhancing the responsibility of businesses to protect the environment.

Thus corporate social responsibility was becoming more and more popular among Bulgarian business circles, and more and more companies declared their social and environmental commitment. However, it is noteworthy that in the majority of cases it is rather a matter of charity and donation or limited scope of activities in this area rather than the application of comprehensive, internationally recognized corporate models and standards that are part of from a long-term strategy to achieve sustainable growth and which includes commitments to: respect for human rights, achieving favorable working conditions, protection of the environment, using of green technologies, reducing resource use, fighting corruption and consumer protection.

The Corporate social responsibility strategy 2009-2013 was an attempt to strengthen the enabling environment for socially responsible practices in Bulgaria. It is an expression of intention and firm determination of the state to promote awareness of CSR and CSR business culture in the country. The vision of the concept is determined as follows: dynamically developing socially responsible behavior of business organizations, leading to their sustainable development based on a balance between corporate interests and the interests of society, as well as mutual trust and ethics among stakeholders, transparency, anti-corruption commitment and combination of economic success, jobs and other social and environmental aspects.

CSR principles are aimed at promoting values of respect for the rights and respect for the individual, support for favorable development of public spaces, and environmental protection. They specify and complement the principles of good governance - legality, reliability and predictability, openness and transparency, accountability, effectiveness, efficiency, partnership, coherence. Other guiding principles are:

- Protection of generally accepted values - the term is associated with business ethics, which is perceived as behavior appropriate to the valuable principles that are generally accepted and shared.
- Principle of responsibility - businesses should assume responsibility for all the consequences and effects of their actions.
- Continuous improvement - a commitment to constant improvement of operations and technology that, to the greatest extent, meet the basic ideas for sustainable development.

Setting objectives targeted at achieving results in this strategy is a direct expression of ensuring sustainability in development - through an integrated approach, mainly related to the implementation of CSR initiatives. It achieves the development of policies and their application with the active and broad participation of stakeholders. Unfortunately, the implementation of the concept in Bulgaria was obscured and unclear, even there is not a new concept till now.

The standards of CSR in Bulgaria are discussed by Bakardjieva (2012). Some directions and positive practices are shown regarding socially responsible initiatives in Bulgarian organizations (Bakardjieva, 2009). The dynamics in CSR development in the economic literature is considered in a study in Bulgaria, which underlies the pressing necessity of social responsibility of organizations (Dimitrov et al., 2014, 66-73). The application of CSR standards in Bulgaria is presented in an analysis revealing interesting trends and responsible practices in Bulgaria showing that Bulgarian organizations have passed the basic stage of conforming basic requirements, and norms and they apply systematically socially responsible initiatives laid down in their business strategies and assuring corporate sustainability (Dimitrov et al., 2014, 197-221).

According to the Bulgarian business leaders forum, the concept of corporate social responsibility, namely the responsibility of companies for the economic, social and environmental impacts of their activities, is relatively new to Bulgaria. Its emergence is mainly related to the processes of integration and acceptance of the country as a full member of the EU and the advent of international companies with established traditions and experience in this field. Despite the slower adoption of CSR principles and policies, compared to global trends, Bulgarian businesses are beginning to pay more attention to these models because, in addition to the benefits they provide for the companies themselves, they are also a prerequisite for survival and competitiveness in a global economy. The state should also play an active role and encourages the introduction of CSR in the country by creating an appropriate regulatory environment and conditions for effective partnerships between all stakeholders.

The first specialized survey on the state of corporate social responsibility in Bulgaria was presented during February 2019 (as given on the Bulgarian NGO's information portal). It was conducted by CSR Advice Box and Junction Bulgaria in the period 1 October – 31 December 2018 among TOP 300 employers in Bulgaria, determined by a number of insured persons. The choice of TOP 300 employers was substantiated by the fact that they are pacing; they are at the forefront of the economy and can invest more than to be successful on the market. They can set the direction of the development of the business culture and the way the modern business should look like – shared Dr. Marina Stefanova, the initiator, and the author of the survey.

The study "State of CSR in Bulgaria" (2018) includes five main areas:

- The impact of the external environment on CSR implementation;
- Corporate CSR practices;
- Non-financial reporting of companies;

- The goals of sustainable development of the United Nations and its application in business;
- Profile of CSO specialist in Bulgaria.

The main findings of the study indicate that:

- Priority areas for business are responsible consumption and smart use of resources;
- Owners and senior managers of companies have a leading role as leaders and inspirators for CSR, both for their own companies and for the industries they work in;
- A large part of the business expects that the state must also be a responsible owner and apply the principles of CSR in enterprises with state and municipal participation, as well as to publicly report the implementation of this activity;
- CSO specialist is an agent of change in companies, but his/her potential is still not being used enough;
- The biggest obstacle to CSR implementation, according to business, is the lack of human resources and knowledge on the subject.

Twenty percent of companies say they have at least one full-time person responsible for corporate social responsibility, and leading companies have a team of at least four employees and a separate CSR budget, which in half of the cases is over 50 000 EUR.

The main corporate CSR priorities for 2019 are:

- Building a stakeholder relationship, integrating into their business and implementing joint initiatives;
- Sharing the values and engaging the CSR team with the goals that companies put in.
- Complete relationships with local communities.

According to the authors, this study will serve their colleagues from the state institutions that are currently preparing the new National Corporate Social Responsibility Strategy because for companies, it is crucial to create an environment in which sectoral policies and good practices are encouraged. "Our companies have said yes to corporate social responsibility, but they still do not know and are looking for ways to make it a daily practice" – says Dr. Marina Stefanova. Justin Toms, communications specialist and part of the study team adds that the difference of ten years ago is that "we have created a CSR ecosystem - there are already master programs, several books have been published, and since the end of last year we have a Bulgarian association of CSR specialists. We are now at a different level because CSR was an exotic topic ten years ago, only seen as donations to homes for children and adults during the holidays. Now, the level is radically different, and the study proves it".

The Bulgarian Association of CSR specialists is expected to work in the following fields:

1. Recognition of the profession and creation of high professional standards for work;
2. Development of new competencies and professional skills in CSR practitioners (corporate sustainability and public responsibility);
3. Validation of the authority and the importance of the profession and the academic institutions in which it is taught.

According to CSR Bulgaria (the first specialized CSR network in the country), CSR is a concept through which companies integrate social engagements and environmental concerns into their business operations and relationships with their partners voluntarily. The social responsibility of the business is accepted as multi-layered. On the first level, the compliance with the principles of corporate social responsibility is predisposed by the compliance with the following obligations: timely payment of taxes, wages, opening new jobs. On the second level, CSR presupposes the provision of adequate working and living conditions for workers by enhancing their qualification, prophylactic treatment, housing construction, social sphere development. The highest third level of responsibility is the performance of charity activities, including improving local infrastructure.

Thus, CSR is addressed in the following areas:

- Community: improvement of the urban environment; PR activities with social impact; voluntary Labor; assistance and social integration of orphans, children and elderly people into homes; preservation of the cultural and historical heritage; product quality and safety; donations; sponsorship;
- Environment: pollution control; restoring or protecting the environment; conservation of natural resources; recycling; costs of energy efficiency and reduction of environmental pollution; managing the impact of the environment and natural resources;
- Human capital and working conditions: development of healthy and safe working conditions; training and staff development; fostering career development; volunteer employee programs; programs for objective and fair payments; employees' satisfaction and commitment;
- Knowledge and education: scholarships to help disadvantaged people; provision of tools, materials for school hours; paid internships; encouraging young, intelligent people;
- Marketing related to a cause: product donations, etc.

CSR Bulgaria aims to promote CSR as a successful investment, to offer a choice of causes and advice on ways of support and participation in social programs and policy.

Stefanova & Toms (2014) present some prejudices and delusions about CSR and communications, as CSR is for big companies having separate budget for advertisements; CSR activities should be obligatory in order to be successful; experts in PR and CSR are the same; in CSR you survive by yourself; only bad news is news; only good news is news; CSR could exist without communication; communication is CSR. In their book, the authors disprove all these statements by examining the essence and the development of the CSR concept as a modern trend in management and its relationship to business ethics and by presenting a good example from world and Bulgaria. Additionally, special attention is paid to the CSR teams and related occupations in modern organizations, as well as communication aspects, channels, and practices. There is also an attractive section about the hypocrisy in CSR. Not the last are the implications on the development of the concept into CSR 2.0 reinventing CSR in the XXI century and the entrance of the concept of Creating Shared Value (CSV). The book also presents experts' opinions and thus consolidates its main thesis that CSR and communications are mutually related but not interchangeable.

Companies' Websites: The First and The Last Step In Communicating Socially Responsible Initiatives

Bearing in mind that communication is a two-direction process, current study does not pretend to embrace all the aspects but it limits to the most important step in contemporary digitalized world – provision of information of official websites about the start, the implementation and the results of CSR initiatives of a company through some specialized web-page/s. Below subsequently are shown the main ideas and messages of different types of companies operating in Bulgaria. Their names are not presented in the text, and their addresses are shown as endnotes intentionally so that the reader to have the opportunity to stay beyond the brands and to choose if he/she wants to know much. The websites are last accessed and checked on 30/06/2019.

Media company #1

Common rules for social and eco-campaigns regulate the relations between the media and its partners concerning their cooperation on social, charity, or eco-calls, campaigns and/or causes organized by the partners. Out of these rules stay social events, initiatives, etc. which generate money for the organizer, as well as individual actions and/or campaigns to raise funds for individuals[1].

Within a partnership, the media can provide time in TV programs and/or publish on websites newsletters (materials) to promote their partner's campaigns. Promotion of a campaign in the television programs of the media shall be carried out by broadcasting a commercial television message (video). Besides, if possible and at the discretion of the media, the campaign may also be announced in media broadcasts, such as duration, content, format, etc. of the message are at the discretion of the media and depending on the possibilities of the program scheme. „Contributing to the development of education and leadership" is the title of a web-page of the media, which states that "People are the most valuable asset". "Think green" aims to present an environmentally responsible company not only realizing some energy-saving solutions in its facilities but also communicating initiatives and activities of its staff, providing good examples for society, e.g., combating climate change or environmental pollution. There are extensive lists on the media website of campaigns supported. One of the most popular is "Let's clean Bulgaria in one day!" which is part of the global campaign "Let's Do It World" launched in 2007 in Estonia.

The media says that its goal is that every major cause of society should receive the widest publicity and the support of millions of viewers, listeners, and Internet users.

Media company #2

„Awareness and long-term commitment to support" is the motto driving its activities among which are: a competition for social entrepreneurs, the social initiative "Mission Education" and others. The media has uploaded on its site some information about the CSR concept and its main definitions[2].

Media company #3

There is no special web-page on the website. Videos broadcasted on the topic of CSR and the opinion of the experts. There is a position of "expert", sector "Corporate Social Responsibility", "Public Communications"[3].

Mobile operator #1

There is a special section "Corporate responsibility" on the website[4].

Corporate responsibility is at the core of the company's philosophy to develop its business sustainably and transparently, and the goal is to maximize the benefits of telecommunication technologies by striving to create added value to both businesses and the public. The company believes that the mobile phone can transform human life by making information, social, health, and financial services much more accessible to every person. It is one of the company's main goals - to provide the benefits of mobile communications to the widest possible range of people. In this way, society's growth and development capabilities are increasing.

The company aims at creating sustainable initiatives that bring added value in the long run and are based on the core competencies of the company - communications. Besides, it strives to contribute to the development of society through targeted investments and long-term partnerships that lead to sustainable social change.

The following priority fields are described:

- Environment:

To be green is the responsible behavior of the company and its employees to the environment. Through its long-term environmental sustainability strategy, it strives to continually reduce our footprint on the environment and make sustained efforts to protect it.

The environmental strategy focuses on the implementation of practical solutions to environmental issues in four main areas:

- offering sustainable products and services;
- recycling mobile phones, batteries, and accessories for mobile phones;
- responsible use of energy and other resources and materials;
- support for public environmental projects.

The company is aware of its role in informing society about responsible behavior and encouraging employees and clients, as well as partners and suppliers.

- Society:

The company realizes that the use of its services is related to some challenges - electromagnetic radiation, Internet security, safe driving, and equal access. These are among the priorities in its work for the benefit of society.

- Market:

The company accepts that ethical attitude is at the core of its long-term success. Ethical competition and marketing are as important as the satisfaction of customers. The company believes that with its actions and investments, it contributes to improving the quality of services, limiting unfair practices and protecting the principles of the market economy. Among the activities are: responsible services to clients, sustainable products and services, responsible supply, and others.

- Staff:

In the company, they believe that each company's successful social strategy begins with responsibility for people who build its success and its good name. Care and recognition for people working is a significant factor in the growth of the company. It is why the company strives to provide them with excellent working and recreational conditions, develop their potential, and motivate their better performance through:

- equal opportunities for employee selection and engagement;
- employee training and qualification program;
- system of objective evaluation and promotion of achievement
- active internal communication;
- team building and development policy;
- permanent health care;
- wide range of social benefits;
- open-door policy.

The company has annual Corporate Responsibility Reports published on the website for the period 2010-2017.

Mobile operator #2

The company has a specialized platform for CSR projects[5]. It says that every year the company supports and invests millions in many projects in the fields of education, sports, professional realization, charity, art, and culture. Established in 2009, the platform is an expression of the company's attitude towards issues and problems affecting Bulgarian society. Its main messages are: "With care and attention ... With will and desire for change ... With faith in the better tomorrow ...".

Mobile operator #3

A web-page containing information about the following fields[6]:

- Network and clients: the main goal of the company is to ensure network quality, make technology accessible, easy and useful for more people and ensure loyal attitude, serenity, and convenience for its customers;
- Environment: in the construction of the base stations the company adheres to the legal requirements and norms for electromagnetic radiation; building solar power stations to reduce emissions and fuel consumption; investing in its recycling center for end-user devices.
- Staff: the company constantly invests effort and resources in the development and comfort of its employees; it provides its employees with additional health insurance, a medical cabinet, a psychologist, a sports and recreation center - a fitness and massage studio, a kindergarten, an office bus, a parking lot, service mobile phones and discounts, annual prophylactic examinations and

others; employees are actively involved in CSR initiatives and twice a year they are included in actions of corporate volunteering.

- Society: there are own initiatives and others supporting major causes and organizations striving to make benefit to society and make life better for people in Bulgaria.

Bank #1

As stated on its website[7], the bank actively participates in overcoming the challenges faced by society, defining one of the institution's main missions - maintaining a distinctive and sustainable corporate culture that responds to changes in the environment and at the same time contributes to creating long-term relationships with clients, partners, employees, shareholders and civil society in the country. The bank has made corporate social responsibility one of the focus of its business by strictly adhering to the corporate interests and spreading the principles and approaches of corporate social responsibility among broad social groups.

The bank accepts that practice and corporate experience have proven that long-term success can't be achieved without introducing the highest standards of corporate governance, control, and an established system of values. Its high corporate responsibility is a guarantee of the serious and honest relationship of mutual respect to partners, clients, and shareholders, amongst which the practices of responsible business that benefit the business and society and support social, economic and environmentally sustainable development are promoted. As a socially responsible institution, the bank supports projects that maximize the positive impact of business on society which are described on the website.

Bank #2

The bank states on its website that it is a socially committed institution supporting projects in the social sphere, programs, and activities in support of young people and education, significant sports initiatives and projects in the field of ecology[8].

Together with a corporate foundation, the bank is actively working to develop social entrepreneurship as a form of sustainable social model development. The bank is committed to discovering, supporting, and promoting good talents - especially among young people - in the sphere of music, fine arts, and sports.

In line with its mission, the bank aims to be a responsible member of society and encourages initiatives aimed at building sustainable practices and successful examples. It is committed to the support of the development of local communities.

The following fields of activities are pointed: innovation and entrepreneurship, education, sports, art and culture, society and environment, sponsorship, and donations.

Bank #3

Extended information uploaded on the website about the principles of the bank as a socially responsible company strictly observing the policy of legality and loyalty and ensuring the correct application of legal and supervisory regulations[9].

In its relations with clients, partners and the public the bank believes that it has built and follows principles of social responsibility - a pledge for transparent relationships in all spheres of business and public life and the basis of its consistency that promotes its corporate reputation by building a clear public image, high ethical standards in managing the bank and investing in meaningful and sustainable projects:

- Principle of non-division according to which the bank does not support initiatives that lead to a division of society on a religious, faith, ethnic or social basis;
- Principle of transparency according to which the information for all projects supported by the bank is public;
- Principle of institutionality which means that the bank supports initiatives, events or projects of organizations, associations, civic associations, companies and institutions, not private individuals;
- Principle of reinvestment in the local society, i.e., projects are supported in regions where the bank has a presence.

The bank implements its CSR mainly through a charity campaign called „Choose to help" started in 2009, which has its own platform[10]. The campaign includes publicly-funded projects of non-profit organizations, hospitals and others in the fields of health, social services, culture, education, and environmental protection. The importance of the donor initiative is proven by the number of awards it has received, including the "The Best Donorship Program", the "Most Transparent Campaign", and the "Investor in Society".

Industrial company #1

On a special web-page, the company states that it has implemented the principles of sustainability in its activities, thus realizing that its long-term development can only be achieved through sustainable development[11]. Concerns about employee health and safety, protection of the environment, satisfaction of customers' needs, and harmonious co existence with local communities are the main issues of the company.

Sustainability policy is in line with corporate values: responsibility, honesty, transparency, efficiency, and innovation, and it is defined by its management which is committed to the following:

- Implementation of the sustainability policy at all levels of the company;
- Strict compliance with the legislation along with the application of standards, policies, internal rules and procedures applied by the company, as well as other commitments stemming from the voluntary agreements signed and accepted;
- Two-way and open communication with all stakeholders to identify and record their needs and expectations;
- Ensuring a safe and healthy environment for employees, partners and third parties;
- Protecting human rights and providing a working environment of equal opportunities without discrimination;
- Continuing efforts to reduce environmental impact by implementing responsible responses and preventive measures following the best possible techniques;
- Collaboration and support to society to contribute to the sustainable development of local communities;

- Continuous striving to create added value for stakeholders.

To implement the commitments above, the company has voluntarily and responsibly planned the implementation of the respective programs, while at the same time defining strategic priorities that focus on the following areas of company sustainability:

1. Economic growth and corporate governance

The company strives to achieve positive financial results, implement a system of good corporate governance, assess and manage business risks in order to protect shareholder interests. It develops procedures and takes measures both to improve transparency and to fight corruption.

2. Markets

The company aims at delivering the best and most complete customer satisfaction and invests in R & D to offer new products and services with high quality and added value, thus improving its position in an increasingly fast developing business environment. Besides, the company also requires responsible business behavior from its suppliers and partners.

3. Human resources - safe and healthy working conditions

The company respects and supports internationally recognized human rights and implements policies for fair remuneration and equal opportunities for all its employees without any discrimination and concerning the differences of their employees. The company also provides opportunities for the continuous development of human resources through regular training and evaluation. A safe and healthy work environment is a matter of paramount importance for the company.

4. Environment

The company applies the precautionary principle and takes systematic steps to minimize the impact of its activities on the environment. The company follows the principles of the circular economy, ensuring optimal management of natural resources, encouraging metal recycling, and the use of secondary materials, also giving priority to waste management based on the degree of circularity of the treatment method.

5. Local communities

The company stands on the side of local communities and addresses their issues by building a close relationship based on dialogue and mutual cooperation. The company develops and implements actions that meet the basic needs of society in terms of employment, development, education, healthcare, social care, and culture. It promotes the voluntary principle and supports initiatives to develop local communities.

Concerning all of these key issues the company sets sustainability targets which are assessed annually for their effectiveness, and reviewed if necessary.

Company policy and performance related to sustainability issues, as well as program and goals set implementation, have been monitored by the company's sustainability team and are announced annually so that all stakeholders are informed.

Industrial company #2

The company has published on its website general information about CSR, its definition, and spheres[12]. The environmental policy is targeted towards social ecology, the relationship man - nature. The company strives to protect and improve both natural and social environments creating conditions that meet biological and social requirements, which are described in the following main components: air, water, soil and earth, protected areas and biodiversity, waste, noise, and vibrations. The company has a policy on safety and health at work and the environment.

Industrial company #3

The company's website states that since its foundation, the company has been guided by the principles of corporate social responsibility and sustainability. Social responsibility is accepted as a springboard for continuous self-improvement, improvement of efficiency and materialization of corporate vision of improving the quality of life of human capital and society as a whole.

The employees are treated as a key asset in which the company is continuously investing and developing. The main concern of the company is the retention of highly qualified personnel, ensuring safe and healthy working conditions, and continuous training. Besides, employees apply corporate social responsibility practices in their relations with customers, understanding their ever-changing needs, and providing safe and quality services.

Regarding the environment, the company conducts a policy of ensuring sustainable development and preservation of the natural environment. The priority for management and staff is the recycling of used resources, which is an important part of the corporate policy.

The company also encompasses education and culture through participation in university-funded research programs and enables students from universities and high schools to participate in the company's educational activities and to visit production facilities.

For the company, CSR activities are an important part not only to improve the quality of products and services but also the level of its contribution to society. Social responsibility is determined not as a passive concept, but a path leading to a better and more sustainable future.

Logistics company #1

„We live responsibly" is the headnote on the site of the company[13], which states that its mission is to connect people and to improve their lives, and it takes the responsibility towards employees, society, and the environment. CSR plays a crucial role in the company strategy till 2020, and this is called "the real responsibility". The goal is to turn into a benchmark for responsible business practices that is expressed in three main pillars: transport of climate-neutral items, technologies to increase efficiency, electricity from renewable energy sources. The following responsible programs are described: GoGreen – about the environmental protection; GoTeach – about the partnerships for improvement of education of children and youth; GoHelp – supporting UN efforts in combating disasters through comprehensive preventive measures; GARD – assisting airports in the preparation for natural disasters and offering fast and effective logistic support in case of an emergency.

Logistics company #2

"Corporate social responsibility is an integral part of our business strategy" says the web-page of this company[14] which offers some information about the policies in the following main directions: health and safety-focused on "the safety culture"; a safe and healthy workplace; road safety and the environment. The last one is oriented into three directions: the company's activity in the improvement of CO_2 effectiveness and air quality, information for customers on how to decrease CO_2 emissions, and information and training for employees in environmental management.

Logistics company #3

"Supporting knowledge" is the motto of the company's web-page of social projects[15]. Unfortunately, the information for the projects is inaccessible or missing.

Pharmaceutical company #1

The company is engaged in the creation of corporate value by developing innovative pharmaceutical products and conducting corporate citizenship activities realizing socially significant projects. Its CSR web-page says: "Our vision is of a world with accessible healthcare for all, where prevention measures are exponentially advanced and billions are freed of disease. We are committed to achieving this goal together with the global community"[16]. The CSR philosophy is oriented towards disease prevention, capacity building, and long-term commitment.

Pharmaceutical company #2

The company is presented as a socially committed company that develops jointly with the WHO initiatives to fight some important diseases[17]. It determines itself as a responsible member of society doing its best to work in a way that is economically sustainable, socially responsible and committed to the environment, in the interests of the long-term success of the company and its shareholders. The company prefers business partners, suppliers, and subcontractors who share its values about society and the environment and support the efforts to disseminate these values in business.

Pharmaceutical company #3

The company views itself as a member of today's dynamically changing world community striving to adapt to the growing needs of society and to contribute to health and well-being in the world[18]. It creates partnerships in different communities around the world through which it seeks to support health systems, expand access to medicines, and find sustainable solutions to current and future health challenges.

Sales company #1

The web-page about CSR includes links to the company's initiatives and campaigns (e.g., in partnership with Bulgarian Red Cross, other foundations, associations, municipalities, etc. There are two CSE reports uploaded – for 2010-2014 and 2015-2016, as well as a special brochure[19].

Sales company #2

An important part of its corporate policy is taking responsibility for the environment - something more important than ever in the face of climate change, the scarcity of natural resources and the loss of biodiversity, as stated on the website[20]. "Assortment with a vision" is the motto showing that the company pays particular attention to the sustainable formation of its assortment. That is why it insists on the conditions of production, the way of animal husbandry, and the preservation of the natural habitat of fish. Three main spheres are pointed out: human and nature, human attitude, and protection of seas.

Sales company #3

The company states that it invests in causes and policies that leave a positive trace and make our lives better[21]. Thus, with all the actions, it declares its commitment to the better tomorrow. It strives to continually improve the quality, efficiency, and sustainability of every process at every level. Its goal is not to invest profits in sustainable and social projects, but to generate profits in a sustainable and socially responsible way, in harmony with nature and people. The socially responsible policy includes five key areas: environment, society, products, employees, and business partners, and for each of these groups, specific measures at a regional and global level are applied.

Energy provider #1

For this company, the social responsibility of a company demonstrates its aspirations to achieve social, economic, and environmental practices that go beyond regulatory requirements and are being conducted in dialogue with all stakeholders. It is expressed both in the care of the employees and in the engagement with the ecology and community issues in which the company operates[22]. The company organizes exciting initiatives with attracting messages targeted to society and the environment.

Energy provider #2

Corporate social responsibility of the company is bound to the values of sustainable development. It is the way to do business. The company makes commitments, striving to improve standards of work, social development, environmental protection, the standard of living of employees and society[23]. The initiatives include projects related to healthcare, art, sports, cultural and historical heritage, etc.

Energy provider #3

The company designs, develops, and implements solutions that have a beneficial impact on the environment, individual well-being and economic prosperity. It achieves these goals by actively supporting its employees and developing the regions where it works, in line with its commitment to sustainable development[24]. Three main targets are pointed on the CSR web-page: employees, local communities and more sustainable world.

Consulting company #1

As part of its corporate vision of being the highest standard of professionalism, this company states that it has a long-term commitment to corporate responsibility, providing quality and reliable services to businesses, communities, and governments around the world[25]. Commitment to social responsibility is an integral part of the company's business. That is why we actively support many charity activities and socially important causes in Bulgaria. The CSR strategy focuses on the opportunities for investment in a society where a company's contribution can bring about real change. Its affiliates and employees demonstrate their solidarity with the many causes with dedication and consistency. CSR projects which are supported cover the following areas: disadvantaged children, schools and young talents, art, socially responsible companies, volunteer activities.

Consulting company #2

The company determines itself as part of society, and it supports social campaigns aimed at positive change. Social campaigns promote initiatives to raise money for needy children, responsible driving and social events[26]. The company's website includes detailed information about the initiatives supported.

The company presents its business model as a responsible, sustainable and continuous source of innovation: "we continually offer innovation to meet the needs of cities and their citizens and to provide smart and responsible mobility solutions".

Consulting company #3

The company states on its website that it is aware of the public and social role which it plays in society. As an international recruitment agency, it applies commonly used good practices and influences the establishment of new, better conditions for market development. The task is to provide people with job opportunities and an adequate future that meets their needs and expectations.

In this sense, the inspirational principle of business is built on the idea of a strong company and human orientation. On the one hand, they put human value first, which can not be reduced or underestimated, and the great importance that it brings with it. On the other hand, the goals are bound with a deep respect for the constancy - a major development tool for the company[27]. There are links directed to the information about the social commitment, code of ethics, and CSR report, which is provided in the English language.

SOLUTIONS AND RECOMMENDATIONS

The companies' experience in CSR initiatives and their communication through websites presented above show that although not big in scope, there is a will to be socially responsible. This is mainly the case under the influence of the current trends in management and the policies and strategies of companies set abroad, which have branches in Bulgaria. Sometimes the information is simply scarce and shows little engagement, which reapproves the statement that very often CSR is misunderstood by companies in Bulgaria (Stefanova & Toms, 2014).

In order to be useful some recommendations could be proposed as follows:

- Developing and implementing transparent and open policy;
- Having business relations based on universal moral values;
- Building a new image in business and society in the aspects of competence and professionalism;
- Establishing honest partnerships inside and outside the organization;
- Defending and encouraging competition and fair trade;
- Engaging in regional and local development.

Main CSR principles in the light of the ways of understanding, application, and perception of responsible activities could be formulated as follows: honesty, competency, engagement, openness, and respect to universal values.

The application of CSR principles should be followed at every step of the following model:

1. Identification and analyses of interested parties;
2. Polices and strategies;
3. Implementation;
4. Monitoring and assessment;
5. Dissemination.

The model considers the first place the engagement aspects concerning employees, clients, partners, competitors, and other stakeholders (e.g., government and different types of organizations), as well as work with local communities. It underlines the importance of strategic planning, incorporation of CSR into and implementation of corporate policies and strategies. The model also includes the phases of monitoring and assessment putting special attention on the feedback, corrective, and preventive actions. Not the last is the dissemination practices and channels, part of which is the focus of the current study.

For all that to be put into practice, companies should rely on CSR teams consisting of competent and motivated persons knowing how to avoid the falsity practices and mastering the instruments of efficient communication for overcoming the mistrust in society. The position of the CSR expert should be consolidated and linked to other areas in organizations as marketing, PR, and HR managers, etc.

FUTURE RESEARCH DIRECTIONS

Next steps in work on the research topic of CSR could be oriented towards the transition to the concept of Creating Shared Value and the guided application of its principles in some companies. Studies could be organized to define some criteria for evaluation of activities in CSR promotion.

Future research on the issues discussed above could be directed towards the creation of a questionnaire as an instrument of collecting additional information from companies examined, its analyses, and elaboration of concrete recommendations and solutions to specific problems. It could be designed to study the relationship between CSR and the economic performance of the companies.

Furthermore, studies could be expanded to other companies outside Bulgaria and aiming at comparisons and common conclusions and recommendations.

CONCLUSION

Corporate social responsibility is addressed as a concept showing companies' long-term engagement in sustainable business, society, and environment development and as an element of corporate culture in conditions when new corporate values are adopted in connection to social and ecological goals.

The social responsibility of business is multi-layered. Aimed at the internal environment of the company, it can be realized in the following areas - safe and healthy working conditions, maintaining adequate remuneration, development of human resources through training programs and programs for training and qualification, and others. Corporate social responsibility aimed at the outside of the company assumes implementation in the following areas - transparency in the activity of enterprises interaction with local communities and local authorities and others. Actions will be specified in initiatives and projects of national, regional, and local importance with a long-term sustainable impact on the economy and social sphere.

Among the common characteristics of CSR are environmentally friendly and social policies in organizations, as well as their inner and outer character. The notion that economic and social goals in organizations are separate and competitive (economic being connected to profit-making and social to profit spending) is not the case anymore considering the fact that the organizations are part of the environment and society. The voluntary applications of CSR in modern organizations aiming at ecological and social effects are scrutinized as closely connected to raise in competitiveness and flexicurity. Today CSR policies are part of the strategies in many organizations as a means of integrating constantly increasing requirements of society towards business and of increase in added value in business. Besides it is difficult to define all CSR manifestations, it can be concluded that the responsible way of functioning of all kind of organizations on different levels imposed by the increasing requirements towards accountability and transparency impacts image and performance of organizations in local and global scope considering globalization processes, innovations and knowledge society.

The results of the current study show that in Bulgaria, the CSR concept is developing but still needing much improvement in understanding, state support, engagement of stakeholders, and communication issues. Socially responsible activities are next analyzed in the context of and their relation to business communications and public relations through the official web-sites in their short and long-term aspects underlining their targeting to the impacts on thinking and behavior both of companies, their owners, managers and employees on the one side, and their partners, suppliers, competitors and clients on the other. The understandings, nature, and dimensions of socially responsive initiatives differ much, but the orientation to sustainable development is unchangeable and clearly stated in all, although very often misunderstood and misapplied. Besides, the concept of corporate social responsibility is widely famous, but there are still some misbeliefs and misconducts in a society based on important communications issues that should be carefully addressed.

ACKNOWLEDGMENT

This research was supported by University of Agribusiness and Rural Development, Plovdiv, Bulgaria according to its Plan of scientific and research activities 2018-2020.

REFERENCES

Abdirahman, Z. Z., Sauvée, L., & Shiri, G. (2014). Analyzing network effects of Corporate Social Responsibility implementation in food small and medium enterprises. *Journal on Chain and Network Science*, *14*(2), 103–115. doi:10.3920/JCNS2014.x005

Aminia, M., & Bienstock, C. C. (2014). Corporate sustainability: An integrative definition and framework to evaluate corporate practice and guide academic research. *Journal of Cleaner Production*, *76*, 12–19. doi:10.1016/j.jclepro.2014.02.016

Asifa, M., Searcy, C., Zutshi, A., & Fisscher, O. A. M. (2013). An integrated management systems approach to corporate social responsibility. *Journal of Cleaner Production*, *56*, 7–17. doi:10.1016/j.jclepro.2011.10.034

Bakardjieva, R. (2009). Corporate social responsibility of the firms in Bulgaria. *Economic Studies, 2*, 33-63.

Bakardjieva, R. (2012). Corporate social responsibility standards. *Economic Studies*, *2*, 149–160.

Bakardjieva, R. (2016). Sustainable development and corporate social responsibility: Linking goals to standards. *Journal of Innovations and Sustainability*, *2*(4), 23–35.

Bakardjieva, R. (2019). *Corporate responsibility through application of international social standards - challenges and European dimensions*. Plovdiv, Bulgaria: Talent Academic Publishing House at the University of agribusiness and rural development.

Blodgett, M. S., Hoitash, R. I., & Markelevich, A. (2014). Sustaining the financial value of global CSR: Reconciling corporate and stakeholder interests in a less regulated environment. *Business and Society Review*, *119*(1), 195–124. doi:10.1111/basr.12026

Bocken, N. M. P., Short, S. W., Rana, P., & Evans, S. (2014). A literature and practice review to develop sustainable business model archetypes. *Journal of Cleaner Production*, *65*, 42–56. doi:10.1016/j.jclepro.2013.11.039

Bulgarian NGO's Information Portal. (2019, February 20). *The first specialized survey on the state of corporate social responsibility in Bulgaria*. Retrieved from https://www.ngobg.info

Bulgarian association of CSR specialists. (2018, December 7). *Corporate responsibility experts have set up their own professional organization*. Retrieved from http://www.bcause.bg/razvitie-na-sredata/news-sredata/449-ekspertite-po-korporativna-otgovornost-s%C5%ADzdadokha-svoyata-profesionalna organizatsiya.html

Bulgarian business leaders forum. (2019). *CSR in Bulgaria*. Retrieved from http://www.bblf.bg/content/30/CSR+in+Bulgaria

Cochran, P. L. (2007). The evolution of corporate social responsibility. *Business Horizons*, *50*(6), 449–454. doi:10.1016/j.bushor.2007.06.004

Coles, T., Fenclova, E., & Dinan, C. (2013). Tourism and corporate social responsibility: A critical review and research agenda. *Tourism Management Perspectives*, *6*, 122–141. doi:10.1016/j.tmp.2013.02.001

Council of Ministers Portal for public consultations (2009, November 25). *Corporate social responsibility strategy of the Republic of Bulgaria 2009-2013*. Retrieved from https://www.strategy.bg/StrategicDocuments/View.aspx?lang=bg-BG&Id=600

CSR advice box. (2018). *State of CSR in Bulgaria. Annual Review, 2018*. Retrieved from https://www.csrab.com/en/products/state-of-csr-in-bulgaria-2018.html

CSR Bulgaria. (2019). *Social responsibility*. Retrieved from https://csr.bg/social-responsibility?start=20

Dhaliwal, D., Zhen Li, O., Tsang, A., & Yang, Y. G. (2014). Corporate social responsibility disclosure and the cost of equity capital: The roles of stakeholder orientation and financial transparency. *Journal of Accounting and Public Policy*, *33*(4), 328–355. doi:10.1016/j.jaccpubpol.2014.04.006

Dimitrov, M., Keremedchiev, S., Chipev, P., Bakardjieva, R., Daskalov, V., & Ivanova, N. (2014). *Corporate governance for XXI century: consolidation of standards for good corporate governance in Bulgaria*. Sofia: Academic Press.

Engsig, H. (2011). *CSR communication – stakeholder information, response or involvement?* (Master thesis). Aarhus School of Business, Aarhus University.

Font, X., Garay, L., & Jones, S. (2014). Sustainability motivations and practices in small tourism enterprises in European protected areas. *Journal of Cleaner Production*, *137*, 1439–1448. doi:10.1016/j.jclepro.2014.01.071

Gramser, S. (2016). *Developing CSR and CSR communication: Brazilian and Dutch consumers' attitude towards CSR (communication) through different communication channels*. Radboud University.

Isaksson, L., Kiessling, T., & Harvey, M. (2014). Corporate social responsibility: Why bother? *Organizational Dynamics*, *43*(1), 64–72. doi:10.1016/j.orgdyn.2013.10.008

Jeong, H. J., Paek, H.-J., & Lee, M. (2013). Corporate social responsibility effects on social network sites. *Journal of Business Research*, *66*(10), 1889–1895. doi:10.1016/j.jbusres.2013.02.010

Kemper, J., Schilke, O., Reimann, M., Wang, X., & Brettel, M. (2013). Competition-motivated corporate social responsibility. *Journal of Business Research*, *66*(10), 1954–1963. doi:10.1016/j.jbusres.2013.02.018

Kotler, Ph., & Lee, N. (2005). *Corporate social responsibility: doing the most good for your company and your cause*. Hoboken, NJ: John Wiley & Sons, Inc.

Maas, S., & Reniers, G. (2014). Development of a CSR model for practice: Connecting five inherent areas of sustainable business. *Journal of Cleaner Production*, *64*, 104–114. doi:10.1016/j.jclepro.2013.07.039

Menguc, B., & Ozanne, L. K. (2005). Challenges of the "green imperative": A natural resource-based approach to the environmental orientation–business performance relationship. *Journal of Business Research*, *58*(4), 430–438. doi:10.1016/j.jbusres.2003.09.002

Morsing, M., & Schultz, M. (2006). Corporate social responsibility communication: Stakeholder information, response and involvement strategies. *Business Ethics a European Review*, *15*(4), 324–338. doi:10.1111/j.1467-8608.2006.00460.x

Nikolova, N., Todorova, I., & Nenova, N. (2014). Corporate social responsibility as a strategic priority in the competitive behavior of the company. Scientific works "MathTech 2014", Bishop Konstantin Preslavski University of Shumen, 1, 333-340.

Nikolova, N., & Yordanova, I. (2014). Corporate social responsibility as a mechanism for the integration of economic, social and ecological goals of the organization. *Proceedings of the Closing conference under the project "System of qualification and career development of the university teachers", Vasil Levski National Military University – Veliko Tarnovo, Bulgaria*, 219-229.

Park, J., Lee, H., & Kim, C. (2014). Corporate social responsibilities, consumer trust and corporate reputation: South Korean consumers' perspectives. *Journal of Business Research*, *67*(3), 295–302. doi:10.1016/j.jbusres.2013.05.016

Pop, O., Dina, G. C., & Martin, C. (2011). Promoting the corporate social responsibility for a green economy and innovative jobs. *Procedia: Social and Behavioral Sciences*, *15*, 1020–1023. doi:10.1016/j.sbspro.2011.03.232

Porter, T., & Miles, P. (2013). CSR Longevity: Evidence from long-term practices in large corporations. *Corporate Reputation Review*, *16*(4), 313–340. doi:10.1057/crr.2013.17

Skare, M., & Golja, T. (2014). The impact of government CSR supporting policies on economic growth. *Journal of Policy Modeling*, *36*(3), 562–577. doi:10.1016/j.jpolmod.2014.01.008

Stefanova, M., & Toms, J. (2014). *Corporate social responsibility and communications for sustainable development of business*. Sofia, Bulgaria: Siela.

Türkel, S., & Akan, A. (2015). Corporate Social Responsibility (CSR) Communication: A Turkish Industry Example. In *Integrated Communications in the Postmodern Era* (pp. 151–174). Palgrave Macmillan. doi:10.1057/9781137388551_7

Vasilescu, R., Barna, C., Epure, M., & Baicu, C. (2010). Developing university social responsibility: A model for the challenges of the new civil society. *Procedia: Social and Behavioral Sciences*, *2*(2), 4177–4182. doi:10.1016/j.sbspro.2010.03.660

Viola, I., Ruggeri, F, & Rotondo, G. (2013) Corporate social responsibility and green economy in the agri-food business. *Quality - Access to Success, 14*(1), 151-156.

Walker, M., Aubrey, K., & Vincent, J. (2010). Communicating Socially Responsible Initiatives: An Analysis of U.S. Professional Teams. *Sport Marketing Quarterly, 19*(4), 187–195.

Windsor, D. (2013). Corporate social responsibility and irresponsibility: A positive theory approach. *Journal of Business Research, 66*(10), 1937–1944. doi:10.1016/j.jbusres.2013.02.016

Zahariev, E. (2013). *Challenges before the industrial management: priorities and solutions*. Plovdiv, Bulgaria: Talent Academic Publishing House at the University of Agribusiness and Rural Development.

Zahariev, E. (2014). *Corporate social responsibility*. Plovdiv, Bulgaria: Talent Academic Publishing House at the University of Agribusiness and Rural Development.

Zahariev, E., & Arabska, E. (2015). Corporate social responsibility and organic production business model – sustainability performance, consumer trust and motivation. *Proceedings of IV International scientific conference Climate Change, Economic Development, Environment and People Conference (CCEDEP) under the subtopic Regional development of Central and Eastern European countries, 7-9 October 2014, UARD – Plovdiv, 2*, 285-296.

Zhang, D., Jiang, Q., Ma, X., & Li, B. (2014). Drivers for food risk management and corporate social responsibility; a case of Chinese food companies. *Journal of Cleaner Production, 66*, 520–527. doi:10.1016/j.jclepro.2013.11.075

ADDITIONAL READING

Arabska, E. (2017). Corporate Social Responsibility in Bulgaria. In *Proceedings of IV IBANESS Congress*, 8-9 April 2017, Ruse, Bulgaria, 114-122.

Arabska, E., & Terziev, V. (2016). Organic production business model and the concept of corporate social responsibility. *Journal of Economic Development. Environment and People, 5*(2), 23–30. doi:10.26458/jedep.v5i2.496

Daood, A., & Menghwar, P. S. (2017). Understanding "Creating Shared Value". In *Proceedings of the 10th Annual Conference of the EuroMed Academy of Business*, 513-525.

Govindan, K., Kannan, D., & Shankar, K. M. (2014). Evaluating the drivers of corporate social responsibility in the mining industry with multi-criteria approach: Multi-stakeholder perspective. *Journal of Cleaner Production, 84*, 214–232. doi:10.1016/j.jclepro.2013.12.065

Hopkins, M. (2006). What is corporate social responsibility all about? *Journal of Public Affairs, 6*(3-4), 298–306. doi:10.1002/pa.238

Ismail, M. (2009). Corporate social responsibility and its role in community development: An international perspective. *The Journal of International Social Research, 2*(9), 199–209.

Karagülle, A. Ö. (2012). Green business for sustainable development and competitiveness: An overview of Turkish logistics industry. *Procedia: Social and Behavioral Sciences*, *41*, 456–460. doi:10.1016/j.sbspro.2012.04.055

Sun, W., & Cui, K. (2014). Linking corporate social responsibility to firm default risk. *European Management Journal*, *32*(2), 275–287. doi:10.1016/j.emj.2013.04.003

Wan Jan, W. S. (2006). Defining corporate social responsibility. *Journal of Public Affairs*, *6*(3-4), 176–184. doi:10.1002/pa.227

Zhou, M., Pan, Y., Chen, Z., & Yang, W. (2013). Optimizing green production strategies: An integrated approach. *Computers & Industrial Engineering*, *65*(3), 517–528. doi:10.1016/j.cie.2013.02.020

KEY TERMS AND DEFINITIONS

Communication: Two-way process of reaching mutual understanding, in which participants not only exchange (encode-decode) information, news, ideas, and feelings but also create and share meaning. In general, communication is a means of connecting people or places. In business, it is a key function of management--an organization cannot operate without communication between levels, departments, and employees (Business Dictionary: http://www.businessdictionary.com/).

Corporate Identity: Combination of color schemes, designs, words, etc., that a firm employs to make a visual statement about itself and to communicate its business philosophy. It is an enduring symbol of how a firm views itself, how it wishes to be seen by others, and how others recognize and remember it. Unlike corporate image (which is 'in there' changeable mental impression), corporate identity is 'out there' sensory-experience conveyed by things such as buildings, décor, logo, name, slogan, stationery, uniforms, and is largely unaffected by its financial performance and ups and downs in its fortunes. Corporate-identity is either strong or weak (not positive, negative, or neutral like a corporate image) and is more or less permanent unless changed deliberately (http://www.businessdictionary.com/).

Corporate Image: The perception of a corporation held by the public, based on how it is portrayed through branding, public relations efforts, news media, stakeholders, employees, labor unions and consumer advocacy organizations. Companies invest a substantial portion of marketing and advertising dollars to build and maintain a positive corporate image, which is critical to their competitive standing (http://www.investorwords.com/).

Corporate Social Responsibility (CSR): the responsibility of enterprises for their impact on society and, therefore, it should be company led. Companies can become socially responsible by: integrating social, environmental, ethical, consumer, and human rights concerns into their business strategy and operations following the law. Public authorities play a supporting role through voluntary policy measures and, where necessary, complementary regulation (https://ec.europa.eu/growth/industry/corporate-social-responsibility_bg).

Corporate/Organizational Culture: Corporate culture refers to the shared values, attitudes, standards, and beliefs that characterize members of an organization and define its nature. Corporate culture is rooted in an organization's goals, strategies, structure, and approaches to labor, customers, investors, and the greater community. As such, it is an essential component of any business's ultimate success or failure (Encyclopedia - Business Terms: https://www.inc.com/encyclopedia/).

Responsibility: A duty or obligation to satisfactorily perform or complete a task (assigned by someone, or created by one's own promise or circumstances) that one must fulfill, and which has a consequent penalty for failure (Business Dictionary: http://www.businessdictionary.com/).

Responsible Business Conduct (RBC): This is an alternative term introduced by the OECD in close cooperation with business, trade unions and non-governmental organizations. The OECD has defined RBC as "making a positive contribution to economic, environmental and social progress with a view to achieving sustainable development and avoiding and addressing adverse impacts related to an enterprise's direct and indirect operations, products or services" (https://ec.europa.eu/growth/industry/corporate-social-responsibility_bg).

ENDNOTES

1 https://www.btv.bg/otgovornost
2 https://nova.bg/csr/social_responsibility
3 https://www.bnt.bg/
4 https://www.telenor.bg/bg/corporate-responsibility
5 https://vivacomfund.bg/#projects
6 https://www.a1.bg/otgovornost
7 https://dskbank.bg/
8 https://www.unicreditbulbank.bg/bg/za-nas/korporativna-sotsialna-otgovornost/
9 https://www.rbb.bg/bg/za-bankata/korporativna-socialna-otgovornost/
10 https://izberi.rbb.bg/
11 http://www.sofiamed.bg/bg/capability/korporativna-socialna-otgovornost
12 http://www.polaris8.bg/bg/korporativna-i-sotzialna-otgovornost.html
13 https://www.logistics.dhl/bg-bg/home/za-nas/korporativna-otgovornost.html
14 https://www.tnt.com/express/bg_bg/site/company/corporate-responsibility.html
15 https://www.econt.com/econt-express/social-projects
16 https://www.takeda.com/bg-bg/corporate-responsibility/
17 https://www.novartis.bg/about-us/corporate-responsibility
18 https://www.pfizer.bg/en/corporate-responsibility
19 https://www.billa.bg/za-billa/korporativna-socialna-otgovornost
20 https://zanas.kaufland.bg/otgovornost/ustoichivo-formirane-na-asortimenta.html
21 https://www.lidl.bg/bg/CSR.htm
22 https://www.evn.bg/Otgovornost.aspx
23 http://www.marica-iztok.com/page/korporativna-otgovornost-4-1.html
24 https://www.veolia.bg/bg/za-nas/korporativna-otgovornost
25 https://www2.deloitte.com/bg/bg/pages/about-deloitte/articles/corporate-social-responsibility.html
26 https://www.jcdimage.com/bg/korporativna-socialna-otgovornost
27 https://bg.gigroup.com/kso/

Chapter 6 Challenges of Green Economy in Armenia

Susanna Aghajanyan
Armenian State University of Economics, Armenia

Gagik Aghajanyan
Armenian State University of Economics, Armenia

ABSTRACT

The economy ecologization process should take into account the development needs of each nation by developing effective systems of production and consumption. That is why in the system of measures ensuring the transition to a "green" economy, overcoming poverty and expanding the livelihoods of the most vulnerable sections of society should be a priority. At the same time, the convergence of economic and environmental policies, where prospects for economic growth are at the forefront, avoiding stress on nature resulting in unpredictable and qualitative implications for natural resources is important. Today, with resource constraints and harmful emissions, the main problem lies in the complete elimination of reliance on economic growth materials and energy resource use, which involves the identification of opportunities to increase the efficiency of the material sectors of the economy.

INTRODUCTION

The term ecologization has become more relevant in the context of sustainable development and poverty reduction and can be considered as a method for understanding and addressing incentives for achieving economic and environmental objectives at the same time. For this reason, production and consumption greening is a key component of the ecologization process and is intended to address the ecological and economic contradictions between human needs and the environment and to ensure the prevention of environmental disturbances. International practice of developing countries shows that the mechanism of stimulating the green economy needs complex instruments, favorable conditions for long-term realization of creating stable economic growth, as well as rationalization of natural resources use. It is,

DOI: 10.4018/978-1-7998-2193-9.ch006

Copyright © 2020, IGI Global. Copying or distributing in print or electronic forms without written permission of IGI Global is prohibited.

therefore, necessary to find out priority directions, the preliminary feasibility and practical measures of the transition to a green economy in the relevant areas in Armenia.

The main methodological difficulties are concerned with the fact that changing the path of development includes empirical evidence that resonates with both environmental and non-environmental communities. That is why it is necessary to reconsider the array of variables they are currently used. Though there is a lot of statistical data, the data collected are often patchy, low in quality, and poorly used in decision-making. The main difficulties are concerned with the necessity of developing and enforcing specific measures, including legislative, financial, administrative, which will support the accelerated process of greening economic activity in Armenia.

Based on the current literature, only several typical questions are taken into consideration, which limits our conclusions. The lack of literature on green economy in Armenia is also a big problem. The literature review shows that the main studies performed in Armenia are carried out by international organizations and there is a lack of scientific literature on green economy.

The goal of the chapter is to shape the theory of sustainable environmental and economic growth at the country level, including theoretical and methodological foundations and practical suggestions to promote the transformation of the country to an eco-oriented or "green" economy.

The chapter is composed of the following parts: the Background gives a general outlook at selected methodological problems connected with ecologization process analysis. It identifies the main theoretical frameworks of economy ecologization, content and main directions of economy greening. The chapter is intended to trigger greening of Armenia economy sectors such as energy, organic agriculture, to summarize the scientific and theoretical basis for the nature of sustainable development and to explain the role of the environmental factor in the process.

This study addresses several further questions on green economy in the context of renewable energy and organic agriculture development. This chapter addresses of researching the main areas so far lacking in the scientific literature. Our chapter is unique as there is no direct scientific literature addressing this issue.

BACKGROUND

The special attention in this chapter has been given to identify the potential synergies of economy greening in Armenia. A green economy is not geared towards economic growth; on the contrary, it is a new growth flywheel which is "inclusive and green". Obviously, the aim is to find favorable conditions for the transition to a green economy, and much can be done in this field, mainly through the development of suitable environment and realistic policies, which are prioritized in this chapter. The decades in which new ideas and wealth are produced on the basis of traditional economic models have failed to counter social marginalization and reform ever-increasing unsustainable resource consumption.

There are not enough publications in Armenian scientific literature concerning the assessment focused on the green economy. The scope of understanding at the national level of the green economy theory and the fact that it covers a variety of industries and goals is reflected in the diversity of organizations involved in promoting it. Some of these are responsible for various aspects of the priority areas, while others are responsible for coordinating the production of selected evaluations.

Environment ministries typically take the lead, have an overview of green economy and resource efficiency, and are charged with bringing different priorities within these concepts together. However, the scope and areas of responsibility of these ministries alone vary enormously and reflect broader national priorities and political boundaries. For example, an environment ministry may be largely responsible for nature protection (Armenia). A variety of organizations produce a range of green economy-related reports and assessments that contain information on Armenia. These are generally based on secondary, evidence-based information from international or national institutions and cover many topics of relevance to the green economy. Some of these are responsible for various aspects of the priority areas, while others are responsible for coordinating the production of selected evaluations.

Therefore, ensuring that economic growth benefits society and the environment as a whole is important. Sustainability remains a primary long-term priority, but additional efforts must be made to incorporate the green economy definition if this goal is to be accomplished.

There is no one-size-fits-all solution to making a transition to a sustainable economy in terms of policy combinations. These must be adapted to the characteristics of each country, the natural resource endowment, the level of development and the strength of its institutions, as well as the nature and size of the prevailing market failures, the industries, goals, and priorities that it wants to prioritize and other contextual factors.

CURRENT ISSUES OF GREEN ECONOMY TRANSITION IN THE PROSPECTS OF ECONOMY ECOLOGIZATION IN ARMENIA

The concept of the green economy was first coined by a team of leading environmental economists (Markandya & Barbier, 1989). UNEP launched its Green Economy Initiative in 2008 to provide analysis and policy support for green sector investment and greening of resource and/or pollution-intensive sectors (UNEP, 2008). In UN Green Economy Initiative the United Nations Environment Programme (UNEP) defines the term as part of the broad economic, social and environmental agenda: a green economy is "one that results in improved human well-being and social equity, while significantly reducing environmental risks and ecological scarcities" (UNEP, 2011). The green economy proposes to fully leverage public sector expenditure to support private sector investment, including through targeted policy and regulatory reforms necessary to support the desired results. The concept of the green economy, in the context of poverty eradication and sustainable development, was discussed at the United Nations Conference on Sustainable Development held in Rio in 2012.

OECD has developed and introduced the concept of "green growth", defined as maximizing economic growth and development while avoiding unsustainable pressure on the quantity and quality of natural assets and harnessing the growth potential that arises from transiting towards a green economy (OECD, 2011). Ultimately, it is intended to provide indicators that can help track progress and calculate performance (OECD, 2011).

UNEMG published a system-wide view of the green economy in 2011. The UN outlined a set of expected characteristics of a green economy (UNEMG, 2011).

A collection of 10 criteria for the transition to a green economy was prepared and published by the Green Economy Task Force of the International Chamber of Commerce at the end of 2011 (ICC, 2011). Ten conditions for a green economy are as follows: awareness, education and skills, employment, resource efficiency and decoupling, life cycle approach, open and competitive markets, metrics, accounting, and reporting – beyond GDP, integrated environmental, social and economic policy and decision-making, governance and partnerships (ICC, 2011).

Green economy may refer to sectors (such as energy), topics (such as pollution), values (such as polluter countries), or policies (such as economic instruments). It can also define a fundamental strategy, such as environmental policy mainstreaming or a supportive economic structure.

The countries committed themselves to the goal of a transition towards the green economy. At the national level, green economy and sustainable development have been recognized as "guiding principles" in several national development strategies (EaPGreen, 2017). Armenia's economy has undergone a profound transformation during the past years: sustained growth, ambitious reforms, as well as inflows of capital and remittances have created a market-oriented environment. By accelerating economic growth and job creation, Armenia still needs to boost shared prosperity and reduce poverty. Nevertheless, environmental issues and the rapid growth of some economic sectors, in addition to the lack of effective management, weigh heavily on economic growth prospects (EaP GREEN, 2015).

The Armenian government has attempted to link economic growth, poverty reduction, and environmental sustainability over the past decade. Several international programs are implemented in Armenia to help government to develop an integrated policy framework for the transition to a green economy by updating policy instruments, adopting new analytical tools, enhancing access to finance for the environment, promoting capacity building and implementing pilot projects in the public and private sectors.

A variety of opportunities are provided by the green economy. Firstly, it aims to increase green investment in various sectors of the economy, foreseeing a specific role for public and private sector actions. Today, policymakers seeking effective ways to lead their nations out of these associated crises while also taking these environmental constraints into account, green economy (in its various forms) has been suggested as a means to catalyze renewed national policy creation and international cooperation and support for sustainable development.

Nowadays, it is obvious that there must be a sustainable, balanced that includes the use of smart ecosystems, an efficient economy, and a fair society. The tasks of each region's economic and social development should be defined following the environmental imperative. The environmental factor is one of the main elements of influence when making political and economic decisions today, and the green economy is a way of capturing economic systems.

The engine of the globalization process is the modernization and transition of the world economy into a new technological structure designed to provide an improvement in the quality of life and living environment, along with a qualitative update of the technological base, increased production efficiency, and competitiveness.

The transition to a green economy is a key driver in ensuring the sustainable development process in all countries, especially in developing ones. In the green economy, the climate is seen not as a place to consume pollution, but as a decisive factor throughout economic growth, leading to an increase in the value chain and long-term sustainability. In other words, environmental factors play a "catalyst" role in implementing innovations in the green economy. The environmental factor in the green economy has a strong impact on economic growth and social security.

Generally speaking, the transition to a green economy has two main paths: developed countries with good financing conditions, high-quality human resources, and advanced technology can transite to a green economy through investment, by developing new economic areas leading to social development and environmental sustainability. The second path is for developing countries which should gradually turn conventional economies into eco-friendly economies.

Compared to developed countries, developing countries have a low level of technology. Such countries also use inexpensive obsolete technology, using natural resources wastefully, which pollute the environment and cause significant losses to the ecosystem. Based on domestic resource development, developing countries are moving independently towards "green growth" and sustainable development, and may even take a step forward in other areas, such as farming, forestry, or limited natural resource production, to restore biodiversity.

Maximizing the value of natural resource use and reducing emissions is a criterion of the economy ecologization, sustainable development of all sectors, and economic growth. In the background of many crises and lack of resources, the economic paradigm of greening is a priority in the global and local processes of sustainable development. Despite the progress made since the Rio de Janeiro meeting, it is clear that the global economy, based on established trends of consumption and production, has a significant impact on a number of key ecosystems and livelihoods.

The concept of ecologization depends on political and institutional factors as well as on resource endowment. The adoption of long-term development strategy, strengthening state control and monitoring of environmental quality, international and regional cooperation on environment protection will lead to economic transformation by increasing the efficiency of natural resource use and environmental impact by decreasing the resource intensity of the economy and reducing of pollution level.

At present, mainly technical and technological capabilities are used to solve the problem of greening production. With these means, in a particular region, you can achieve some improvement environment, but not enough to solve the entire country's pollution problem.

The concept of green growth underlines the importance of integrating environmental and economic policies in a way that will identify new potential sources of economic growth without creating an unstable load on the quantity and quality of natural resources. Green economy is a promising direction for greening the economy, with evidence that greening the economy is a driver of growth. To implement long-term goals of economy "greening", it is necessary to move from raw materials export to the newest type of economy.

The following characteristics characterize green growth:

- modernization of technology that leads to a reduction in environmental pollution and the consumption of natural resources;
- rapid increase in energy efficiency of the economy;
- transition to a low carbon economy;
- reduction of carbon dependency, which will help to reduce greenhouse gas emissions and positive response to global climate change.

PROMOTING THE TRANSITION TO AN INCLUSIVE GREEN ECONOMY IN ARMENIA

Armenia's economic development was followed by an imbalance in the exploitation of natural resources for a long time. The effects of such economic activities tend to have a negative impact on the environment, contributing to the loss of resource resources.

The following areas of "green" economy are promising in Armenia: energy, organic agriculture, specially protected nature areas, secondary resource utilization, environmental protection, etc.

The sectors mentioned above are priorities for integration into the national economy's strategic development planning process. The need for rapid growth of these industries, other specific areas of research and technological development, including environmentally friendly clean energy, new technologies in agriculture and green technologies in industry, require an immediate solution and serve as the first stages of the transition to sustainable development.

The prospects for green industry development and the Armenian economy as a whole are largely associated with energy sector progress, primarily with alternative energy development.

The green economy replaces fossil fuels with renewable energy sources and low-carbon technologies. Increasing the supply of energy from renewable resources reduces the risk of rising fuel prices by reducing their environmental impact. According to the International Energy Agency, every dollar spent on energy-saving measures gives progressively "clean" energy than the dollar spent on creating other sources of energy. At the same time, the energy saved in the field of consumption is ecologically clean, as it has no emissions; moreover, it decreases the amount of it. As a result, increasing the efficiency of fuel economy utilization will contribute to environmental protection as well will lead to sustainable energy sources.

Armenia's power sector has made significant progress in the last two decades. The sector has moved from severe crisis – characterized by crippling supply shortages and near financial bankruptcy of the sector to stability, which is more characteristic of developed countries than emerging markets. The expansion of solutions for energy efficiency reduces GHG emissions and helps improve energy security. It is estimated that more than 2USD in supply-side investments will be avoided for every 1USD invested in energy efficiency (World Bank, 2010).

Armenia, with its domestic supplies, can meet just 35 percent of total energy demand, making it highly dependent on imported energy resources. Therefore, in the Armenian economy, energy efficiency is much lower than that of the region's developed countries. Thus, the development of domestic energy resources and the widespread implementation of energy efficiency throughout the economy must be given priority to ensure Armenia's sustainable development. To achieve sustainable economic growth, Armenians need to increase efficiency in all sectors of energy consumption and build renewable energy resources (USAID, 2007).

The present energy system in Armenia is mainly based on nuclear energy. However, nuclear energy is the energy of the past, and at the same time quite expensive. In some years, we will need more money to modernize the nuclear power plant. The use and development of renewable energy has been an essential part of the transition from crisis to stability and will remain relevant in the coming years as demand increases and the retirement of aging thermal plants.

In Armenia, where there are no industrial fossil fuels, the solution is to increase the energy efficiency of the economy by developing local renewable energy sources. Renewable energy resources in Armenia are as follows: solar energy, wind power, biopotential. In Armenia, solar energy is quickly developing. The private sector introduces solar water-heating technologies, which provide energy savings as well as becoming cost-effective.

Wind power is a high priority energy sector in Armenia, taking into account the average altitude and air density of our country from the sea surface. Armenia can double the production of hydro energy and use our water resources more efficiently instead of operating a nuclear power plant.

As a land-locked country with no significant crude oil deposits, Armenia is mainly dependent on fuel imports to meet the growing demand for petrol in the motor industry.

Energy-saving is not just a matter of one business, so it is necessary to carry out integrated and mutually supportive practices in a variety of areas at the same time. In general, energy efficiency improvement programs in industry will concentrate, in particular, on energy demand, the monitoring, and management of individual technical processes, the implementation of innovative methods aimed at reducing the energy output of industrial products and investment in energy saving in industrial sectors.

Energy development using only natural non-renewable resources is uncertain in terms of their irreversibility and usage in the near future and rising costs so that there is no sustainable development of the economy using renewable resources (sun, wind, etc.) in this case. Renewable technologies will be more economical when considering the cost of using fossil fuel extraction and partial storage technologies.

The basis of green growth is the transformation of the economy's power base for the following reasons:

- the energy sector's enduring significance, which plays a strategic role in economic development and ensures security at all levels (national, regional and international);
- the growing trend of technological aging of Armenia' nuclear power plant;
- the global climate change, arising from a rise in greenhouse gas concentration in the atmosphere.

Therefore, the policy in this sector should tackle the many obstacles to energy efficiency investment to unlock capacity by: providing more data on suitable technologies; enabling more contractors and service firms to enter the market; and alleviating funding constraints.

Organic farming is considered an agricultural production system that ensures the protection of soils, habitats, and humans focused on the development of sustainable, healthy agroforestry systems, the reduction of the use of polluting technology, severe restrictions on the use of pesticides, the increase in soil fertility and organic fertility.

Clean, sustainable methods of agriculture are characterized by water quality, extensive use of organic and natural soil nutrients, and integrated pest control, which helps to reduce the costs of industrial farming resulting from harm to habitats and human health.

There is ample opportunity for Armenia to claim part of the CIS organic food market. Active support from the state is particularly important in solving market development problems and producing organic agricultural products. But, at the same time, problems have accumulated in agriculture; however, which impede growth. In basic food types, Armenia does not have sufficient self-sufficiency. There is a growing area of degraded agricultural land, including arable land and pastures. There is no productive use of water resources, unnecessary depletion of water. Access to financial resources by rural producers remains a major problem, despite government support. The collateral problem of accessing loans was limited access to bank loans. Farmers find it difficult to sell their products (IFAD, 2018). One of the reasons why the agricultural market lacks predictive information to determine crop patterns. The agricultural sector is expanding beyond green growth standards with low capacity of production, low efficiency and poor adaptability to changing climate.

Agriculture is part of a green economy. There are two main reasons for considering agriculture as a priority market. Next, agriculture is the main link in the value chain of the food industry, which is one of the export potential sub-branches. Secondly, agricultural development is essential in order to increase productivity and create non-agricultural jobs in rural areas, thereby contributing to balanced regional development.

"Greening" the economy by rural economic development means improving food security while reducing natural resource consumption through increasing efficiency through all stages of the food chain. This can be achieved by applying the ecosystem approach to agricultural management in a manner that will satisfy society's diverse needs without compromising future generations' ability to use land and marine ecosystem products and services.

The Strategy for Sustainable Rural and Agricultural Development specifies the key directions for agrarian policy. It includes consolidating farms and developing agricultural cooperatives, improving credit, mitigating risk, developing organic farming, reducing vulnerability to climate change in agriculture, and developing social infrastructure in rural communities. The biggest challenge facing the agricultural sector is an inclusive transition – how to move from a fragmented and subsistence-based agricultural sector to a sustainable, productive and export-oriented one while addressing social needs such as poverty reduction, food, and nutrition security and unemployment (IFAD, 2018).

Organic farming is a method of farming that is environmentally and economically sustainable. The shift to more intensive and mechanized farming and the widespread use of genetically modified organisms are serious environmental threats, leading to a decrease in soil fertility, the emergence of new pathogens, and a reduction in biological diversity. Organic farming is a method of farming that is environmentally and economically sustainable.

This is a new sector in the countryside. Farmers and households needed to ensure food safety under current demographic, environmental, and economic conditions, both in terms of quantity and quality of food. Farmers and households needed to ensure food safety under current demographic, environmental, and economic conditions, both in terms of quantity and quality of food.

Organic farming is an intensive form of farming focused on using the full range of local conditions and resources efficiently. This form of organizing agricultural production can be extremely conducive to sustainable socio-economic and environmental development, as it is characterized by low cost and high economic efficiency. In Armenia, the organic farming market is very promising and underdeveloped, so it opens up broad horizons for farmers and exporters. There is land, pastures, water resources, but most importantly-cheap labor to increase the export potential of organic agricultural products. Nevertheless, Armenia needs modern technologies for cultivation and the development of agrarian culture.

First of all, to stimulate innovation in organic farming and the development of environmentally friendly green goods, it will be essential to encourage the creation of eco-innovations that provide a positive effect on the environment and greening and biologization of agricultural production by using new technologies to conserve natural resources and enhance the security of food products. Greening the agrarian sector can also require substantial investment in farmers ' skills development as well as the development of infrastructure.

To develop the organic agriculture sector, the Armenian government should work with most of the tools at its disposal: institutional development, subsidies, investments, and capacity-building regulations.

At present, the economic and social advantages of the green economy change are not properly measured in terms of environmental sustainability and social justice. In addition, acknowledging the need to implement green technologies as an important and necessary precondition for the creation of a green economy, it should be noted that no such conditions are provided for the funding of such developments, with the aid of financial and banking resources, and that there are no adequate mechanisms in place.

Armenia's involvement in the adoption of such technologies is constrained by the lack of scientific studies and green proposals. Thus there are opportunities for ecologically oriented economic growth in the Republic of Armenia, especially in the areas of energy-saving, energy reproduction, agriculture (ecologically clean farms), processing (introduction of green technologies) and tourism (ecotourism, agro-tourism, agro-tourism). Economy should take advantage of these opportunities.

Proceeding from the concept of ecology of economy, it is necessary to solve economic and ecological problems at the same time by subjecting them to a common strategy of ecology of economy, focusing the main attention and resources on improvement of the objects, which are actual or potential sources of environmental pollution.

Analyzing the initial steps of Armenia in the process of transition to a green economy, it should be noted that while there are some positive results in the state, the lack of legislative and methodological foundations is still problematic in almost all problems and, in some cases, the lack of them in general.

Although some initiatives have been taken in the field of green economy, such as organic farming, the construction of small solar plants, closed-cycle and waste generation to the maximum extent possible, there are few examples and restricted in the number of new technologies available to the state.

At the present stage of society's economic development, when there are almost no habitats not impacted by anthropogenic impact on the planet, it should be emphasized with biodiversity positions that one important area of green technology advancement is industrial and domestic waste recycling.

From the point of view of economy ecologization, the question of weak integration of environmental issues in a number of sectors of the economy (transport, electricity, housing, agriculture) in the RA, low ecological and environmental charges, existing obsolete standards and technical regulations, green technology, should be coordinated in different policies.

Today, with resource constraints and harmful emissions, the main problem lies in the complete elimination of dependence on materials of economic growth and the consumption of energy resources, the solution of which requires the identification of opportunities to increase the efficiency of the material sectors of the economy.

It is necessary to develop an effective structural policy, a system designed to implement and maintain the effective use of all types of resources in the economy, in order to make positive structural technological changes. Such a structural change would decrease the feasibility of the end product by increasing environmental demand and consequently decreasing natural resource consumption. At the same time, nature's decline is meant to link the two economic processes organically: natural resource utilization, pollution reduction or stabilization on the one hand, and macroeconomic growth on the other, at the expense of technological upgrades, scarce and resource-saving investment, and resource savings. These two paths suggest a radical structural economic change in favor of energy-saving and knowledge-based practices.

The innovative and anti-crisis multiplicative effects of the green economy play an important role. In terms of the multiplier effect, it is important to highlight the connecting and stimulating role of environmental innovation. Special attention is given to the development of modern infrastructure in the transition to a green economy.

To build up the green economy, the emphasis should be done:

- on the economic sector, which has comparative advantages for each country (ecological agriculture, diversification, and production of environmentally friendly energy sources; development of recreational tourism, a high-quality environmentally friendly resort, including a cultural tourism industry);
  -on investing in the production of high-quality human resources;
- applying technological innovation to manufacturing; addressing environmental problems (e.g. water pollution, waste dumps, etc.).

Therefore, the following forms of encouragement can be considered: receiving financial and technical support for a green economy from the international community; implementation of resource mobilization for green growth investment and socio-economic development planning; Strengthening public administration, efficient operation, development of the state target plan for climate change response; analysis of the funding system; political incentives for the creation of environmental protection credit and financial operations.

The world must, therefore, find a new economic development model that not only stimulates economic growth after the crisis but also protects the environment, reduces the risk of damage to the environment, ensures a fair use of natural resources, weakens social inequality, and creates conditions for sustainable development.

Armenia's move to a sustainable development path requires careful, coordinated action in all areas of economic and industrial potential, such an institutional and economic system model that would transition to a green economy, reorient political, environmental, and social structures to priority areas. There is an immediate need to shift towards an economic model that will improve human well-being while protecting resources and not exposing future generations to significant environmental risks – this is a transition to a green economy. Changes that should occur in Armenia's economic structure in connection with the reorientation of political, social and environmental sustainability In terms of the growth model, they will entail the incorporation of green economy concepts into the country's economic structure.

Current management methods such as the principle of eco-efficiency, "clean growth" method, international standards of eco-management and audit, conceptual methods for increasing resource productivity, a new systemic environmental design and special product labeling, providing a high level of environmental safety of production, products and services while strengthening the competitive position of the business can be used in Armenia for purposeful and systematic implementation of environmental technology into a green economy.

CONCLUSION

The economy ecologization process requires a significant shift in the goals and priorities of the economy as a whole, as well as of its industries and markets and the structural and development policies, by creating adequate market regulatory mechanisms for such changes. This process implies an increase of economic position in the state policy. At the same time, a number of key areas, such as the adoption of an ecologically sustainable long-term development strategy, enhanced state control and monitoring of environmental quality, international and regional environmental cooperation, etc., can directly or indirectly lead to economic transformation by increasing the efficiency of natural resource use and reducing the impact on the environment. Therefore, the effective solution and transition to sustainable development can only be achieved on a whole-scale basis through a holistic approach. That is to say, only a complex study of the economic structure and the peculiarities of the functioning of the spheres will enable to solve the environmental problems effectively.

SOLUTIONS AND RECOMMENDATIONS

Any policy chosen will aim at optimizing the economic and social benefits of moving to a green economy, maintaining environmental sustainability, and social equity. In practice, it is necessary to select the most cost-effective tools to achieve the objectives and targets set. Because of interests and distributional considerations, hereditary policy mixes that do not meet these criteria can be difficult to change. A significant portion of the economy's shift to greening includes policies and investments that decouple growth from real intensive product use and energy consumption.

Armenia should carry out macroeconomic assessments and identify key sectors where opportunities exist. Capacity building is an important area for this process. Armenia has opportunities for green growth, particularly in energy savings (including housing), renewable energy, agriculture (organic farming), mining and manufacturing (by introducing environmentally friendly technologies). Several policies, initiatives, and projects are built at the strategic level. There is scope for the implementation of standardized licensing (including technology-based standards and best available techniques) and enhanced application of economic and business measures, in particular air and water emissions charges or import/production charges for environmentally harmful goods.

Increasing resource efficiency can achieve reductions in economic and social costs and reduce the environmental impact of industrial activities as a result of increased use of resources and energy. These are increasingly needed to deliver sustainable and inclusive growth and to gain competitive advantage in the face of increased global competition for resources and environmental constraints

The implementation of sustainable agricultural practices and technology helps to tackle environmental degradation and inequality at the same time as providing incentives for access to growing international markets. Organic agriculture will give to Armenia the opportunity to access European markets; to create new and more fulfilling jobs; to develop new businesses; to address climate change; to construct natural capital – on which sustainable economic development and wealth creation rely.

The basic recommendation are as follows:

- Integration of green growth concept into national strategies, policies, and plans.
- Additional capacity building with regard to green economy needs (especially concerning environmental economics, eco-innovation and environmental technology assessment, R&D).
- Improvement of national environmental monitoring and statistics systems
- One of the most important factors in developing the green economy is the adoption of environmentally friendly technologies. Environmental licensing is the primary legislative tool in this regard. In all countries, the permitting procedure is more or less fully based on the ad hoc approach developed in the former Soviet Union.
- Establishing free economic zones with a focus on the green economy.

FUTURE RESEARCH DIRECTIONS

The chapter has proved the necessity of the adoption of green growth policies, but the instruments used to evaluate growth often have a narrow economic focus. In the further researches will be applied macroeconomic models, which will indicate the effects that environmental factors can have on the economy and vice versa. Green growth strategies must be based on a good understanding of green growth determinants and must be provided with sufficient indicators to monitor progress. In the future researches, we will discuss how to ensure food security in the green economy.

REFERENCES

Barbier, E. B., & Markandya, A. (1989). *A Blueprint for a Green Economy*. London: Routledge.

EaP GREEN. (2015). *Greening Economies in the EU's Eastern Partnership Countries*. EaP GREEN.

EaP GREEN. (2015). *Promoting better environmental performance of SMEs*. EaP GREEN.

EaP GREEN. (2016). *Measuring the Green Transformation of the Economy: A Guide for EU Eastern Partnership Countries*. Paris: EaP GREEN.

EaP GREEN. (2017). *Greening Economies in the EU Eastern Neighbourhood. From Commitment to Results*. EaP GREEN.

Environment EuropeAid. (2009). Opportunities and options for promoting a green economy in the eastern partnership countries. *Beneficiaries 2009 – LOT 6: Environment EuropeAid.*

European Union. External Action. (2014) *Armenia Development Strategy for 2014-2025*. Annex To RA Government Decree # 442 - N on 27th of March, 2014. European Union. External Action.

ICC. (2011). *10 Conditions for a Transition toward a Green Economy*. ICC.

IFAD. (2018). *Investing in Rural People. Republic of Armenia Country Strategic Opportunities Programme 2018-2024*. IFAD.

IFC. (2010). *Energy Efficiency: A New Resource for Sustainable Growth (Researching energy efficiency practices in Armenia, Azerbaijan, Belarus, Georgia, Russia and Ukraine)*. IFC.

OECD. (2011). *Environmental Governance in Context of Green Growth in EECCA: Main Policy Conclusions. ENV/EPOC/EAP (2011)3*. OECD.

OECD. (2011). *Green Growth Strategy Synthesis Report (Note by the Secretary General). C (2011)29/Rev1*. OECD.

OECD. (2011). *Monitoring Progress towards Green Growth OECD Indicators, OECD working document C (2011)30*. OECD.

OECD. (2015). *Creating Incentives for Greener Products: A Policy Manual for Eastern Partnership Countries*. OECD.

UNEMG. (2011). *Working towards a Balanced and Inclusive Green Economy*. UNEMG.

UNEP. (2008). *Green Jobs: Towards decent work in a sustainable, low carbon world*. UNEP.

UNEP. (2011). *Towards a Green Economy: Pathways to Sustainable Development and Poverty Eradication – Synthesis for Policy Makers*. UNEP.

UNEP. (2015). *Sustainable Consumption and Production Policies and Initiatives in Eastern Europe and the Caucasus: Review of Progress and Way Forward*. Geneva: UNEP.

United Nations Armenia Office. (2012). *"RIO+20" National Assessment Report.* United Nations Armenia Office.

USAID. (2007). *National Program on Energy Saving and Renewable Energy of Republic of Armenia.* USAID.

ADDITIONAL READING

EaP GREEN. (2015). *The Status and Potential of Organic Agriculture in Armenia.* EaP GREEN.

European Environment Agency. (2011). *Summary for Europe's Environment - An Assessment of Assessments.* EEA.

FAO. (2017). *Gender, agriculture and rural development in Armenia.* FAO.

UNDESA. (2012). *A Guidebook to the Green Economy.* UNDESA.

UNEP. (2011). *Organic Agriculture a step towards the Green Economy in the Eastern Europe, Caucasus and Central Asia region Case studies from Armenia, Moldova and Ukraine.* UNEP.

KEY TERMS AND DEFINITIONS

Eco-Friendly: Earth-friendly or not harmful to the environment.

Ecologization: Process of the state control perfection over preservation of environment and natural usage.

Self-Sufficiency: The quality or state of being able to provide everything you need, especially food, without the help of other people or countries.

Sustainable Development: Development that meets the needs of the present without compromising the ability of future generations to meet their own needs.

Chapter 7
The Energy Policy of Bulgaria

Hamit Can
https://orcid.org/0000-0002-6918-3234
Technical University of Sofia, Bulgaria

Daniela Minkovska
Technical University of Sofia, Bulgaria

ABSTRACT

Energy is considered the main input for economic and industrial development. In this context, it is important that countries develop sustainable energy policies in order to meet economic growth and energy demand. Government policies play a critical role in economic growth and incentives for innovation. This chapter summarizes Bulgaria's energy policies as an increasingly important energy transit country due to its strategic location. These policies were presented in line with the European Union energy policies and the solutions of the characteristics of the country. Some of the targets to be implemented are as follows: ensuring energy supply security, achieving RES share targets, energy efficiency improvements, development of a competitive energy market, safe energy needs and protection of consumers, establishment of the necessary infrastructure and diversification of energy resources, strengthening the external relations and solidarity coordinated in the field of energy.

INTRODUCTION

Renewable energy for foreign dependent countries in energy is important in terms of encouraging the use of local resources of countries, improving balance of payments deficits by reducing energy imports, and reducing energy input costs in the production process. In addition, the promotion of environmentally friendly production techniques is among the issues to be addressed. In addition to the necessity of renewable energy production by environmental pollution, the increasing energy demand due to the rapid increase in the world population made it necessary to both maintain the balance of environment and natural life and increase the energy supply to meet the current demand.

DOI: 10.4018/978-1-7998-2193-9.ch007

Copyright © 2020, IGI Global. Copying or distributing in print or electronic forms without written permission of IGI Global is prohibited.

Bulgaria has an important strategic position between the Eastern and Western countries. While it had a centrally planned economy in the period between 1945 and 1989, it can be said that after that, it witnessed to market-based economy. In 2004, the country joined the North Atlantic Treaty Organization (NATO) and has been a member of the European Union since 1 January 2007. All these developments have a great impact on the economic and political development of Bulgaria and energy policy. The main priority of the strategy, which forms the basis of Bulgarian energy reform, is to develop a competitive energy market. In addition to this strategy in the long term, it is aimed to secure energy resources, to position Bulgaria as a regional center for the transition of oil, natural gas, and electricity, to provide more conditions for energy production from renewable energy sources (RES) and to ensure environmentally friendly energy production.

In this study, the connection between Corporate Social Responsibility (CSR) and Socially Responsible Investments (SRI) is presented by the sustainable corporate finance concept. Responsible investment is a phenomenon that is growing rapidly. And according to recent research, it now affects all generations. The mentality is changing in work, consumption, and even investment. Increasingly, consumers, citizens, and workers are seeking to integrate and take into account the dimensions of sustainable development to promote a healthier, greener and more positive society.

It is known, this is especially among young people. For years, many studies have shown that young people are changing paradigms. More and more young people are turning to the professions for sustainable development, they are putting sustainability at the heart of their career concerns, and would even be willing to pay less to work for a greener company. Responsible consumption is developing and with it the desire to invest in more responsible projects.

The different and strengths of our study from other studies examining a similar subject, and the objectives to be achieved can be listed as follows:

- Determining the effects of renewable energy consumption and nuclear power generation on economic growth;
- Environmental impacts of renewable energy and nuclear power generation;
- Discussion of the impact of renewable energy and green business on the national economy and employment;
- The effects of nuclear power generation and renewable energy consumption for the country on sustainable energy supply.

LITERATURE REVIEW

Empirically, the direction of the causality between energy consumption and economic activities has been tried to be put forward to a great extent by using the granger technique in both developed and developing countries. Since Granger (1969)'s new horizons, the literature on granger causality has developed considerably. A significant amount of work in practical studies is dedicated to addressing the aforementioned causality problem between energy consumption and economic development.

Some studies have found unidirectional granger causality from energy consumption to economic growth or from economic growth to energy consumption, while others have identified the 'neutrality hypothesis (no causality in any direction) and others have found a two-way causality. Some results vary depending on the estimation methods applied (univariate or multivariate models using different causal techniques), although similar data sets are used for the same countries and sample periods.

However, since the direction of causality has important policy inferences, economists often proceed by deriving energy policy inferences based on granger causality tests. If there is a unidirectional causality from energy to economy, a general conclusion, limiting energy use (e.g., through energy conservation) will hinder economic growth. It is said that a result showing that there is a continuous causality from the economy to energy states that energy-saving measures can be carried out without leaving economic development at risk. Two-way causality shows the mutual solidarity of energy and economy, and thus two variables must be considered internally in a foresight model. Finally, when the analysis concludes that there is a "neutrality hypothesis", the general explanation is that the economy will develop regardless of energy consumption models. In such a case, economic growth will not affect energy use (probably due to the emancipatory effect), and policies aimed at saving energy will not be detrimental to economic development.

The Literature on Green Economy

Some authors (Apollo Alliance, 2008) state that local governments are a key political factor in green business growth and legislation in greening traditional business. It also states that local policy-makers and economic actors play an important role in preventing the emergence of green economies (Workplace Research Centre, 2007). Hannam (2008) considers that the need for government policies, subsidies, and laws is a crucial political factor for the creation and development of green jobs. It is stated that green sectors (Renewable Energy) will be difficult to develop before they happen. OECD/Martinez-Fernandez, Hinojosa, Miranda (2010) states that labor markets are an important element to consider when analyzing the effects of a green economic restructuring. Bowen, Kuralbayeva (2015) states that financial resources are a very important economic factor for the development of the green economy because without finance, business will not be created.

Cecere, Mazzanti (2015) predicts that technological factors as innovation between political and economic factors can have positive or negative effects on the creation of green employment. According to the study of the International Chamber of Commerce (2012), innovation leads to overcoming economic, environmental and social challenges and creating new opportunities for the creation of green jobs. Social innovation enables awareness rising; ecological increases the efficiency of resources and innovation in the economic field leads to the creation of open and competitive markets. Technological progress is a positive factor in creating new green jobs and new industries (Miteva et al., 2014). OECD/Martinez-Fernandez, Hinojosa, Miranda (2010) states that green skills in the workforce are a key social factor in creating a sustainable green business sector. OECD/Martinez-Fernandezet al. (2010) restructure local economies around environmental activities, and sustainable practices are an important ecological factor to manage the transition to green growth, and wider measures should be taken. Local branding at the same time, eco-innovation networks, and reporting on the state of the environment and economic development are important factors for the development of the green business sector (Potts, 2010).

The Studies Examining the Relationship Between Renewable Energy and Economic Growth

Apergis and Payne (2010a), using the data from 1985 to 2005 for 20 OECD countries, examined the relationship between RNW, GDP, L, Fixed Capital Formation. According to the Panel Cointegration, Panel Causality results, there was a two-way relationship between renewable energy consumption and economic growth.

Apergis and Payne (2010b), using the data from 1992 to 2007 for Eurasian Countries, examined the relationship between RNW, GDP, L, Fixed Capital Formation. According to the Panel Cointegration, Panel Causality results, there was a two-way relationship between renewable energy consumption and economic growth.

Apergis and Payne (2011a), using the data from 1990 to 2007 for 16 developing countries, examined the relationship between RNW, GDP, L, Fixed Capital Formation. According to the Panel Cointegration, Panel Causality results, there was a two-way relationship between renewable energy consumption and economic growth.

Apergis and Payne (2011b), using the data from 1980 to 2006 for 6 Central American countries, examined the relationship between RNW, GDP, L, Fixed Capital Formation. According to the Panel Cointegration, Panel Causality results, there was a two-way relationship between renewable energy consumption and economic growth.

Fang (2011), using the data from 1978 to 2008 for China, examined the relationship between RNW, GDP, L, R & D Expenditures, Capital variables. According to the OLS method results, there was a one-way relationship from renewable energy consumption to economic growth.

Apergis and Payne (2012), using the data from 1990 to 2007 for 80 countries, examined the relationship between RNW, GDP, L, Fixed Capital Formation. According to the Panel Cointegration, Panel Causality results, there was a two-way relationship between renewable energy consumption and economic growth.

Al-mulali, Fereidouni, Lee, & Sab (2013), using the data from 1980 to 2009 for 108 countries, examined the relationship between RNW and GDP. According to the FMOLS method results, there was a two-way relationship between renewable energy consumption and economic growth for 85 countries. There was a one-way relationship from economic growth to renewable energy consumption for two countries. There was no relationship between economic growth and renewable energy consumption for 21 countries.

Pao and Fu (2013), using the data from 1980 to 2010 for Brazil, examined the relationship between RNW, GDP, L, Fixed Capital Formation. According to the Johansen Cointegration, Granger Causality results, there was a two-way relationship between renewable energy consumption and economic growth.

Lin & Moubarak (2014), using the data from 1977 to 2011 for China, examined the relationship between RNW, GDP, L, CO_2. According to the ARDL, Johansen Cointegration, Granger Causality results, there was two-way relationship between renewable energy consumption and economic growth.

Al-mulali, Fereidouni, and Lee (2014), using the data from 1980 to 2010 for 18 Latin American countries, examined the relationship between RNW, GDP, L, Fixed Capital Formation, Foreign trade. According to the Pedroni Panel Cointegration, Panel DOLS, Panel Granger Causality results, there was a two-way relationship between renewable energy consumption and economic growth.

Sebri and Ben-Salha (2014), using the data from 1971 to 2010 for BRICS countries, examined the relationship between RNW, GDP, L, K, CO_2, Foreign trade. According to the ARDL, VECM Granger

Causality results, there was a two-way relationship between renewable energy consumption and economic growth.

Ben Jebli and Ben Youssef (2015), using the data from 1980 to 2010 for 69 countries, examined the relationship between RNW, GDP, NRNW, L, K, and Foreign trade. According to the Pedroni Panel Cointegration, Panel DOLS, Panel Granger Causality results, there was no relationship between renewable energy consumption and economic growth.

Shahbaz et al. (2015), using the data from 1972 Q1 to 2011 Q4 for Pakistan, examined the relationship between RNW, GDP, NRNW, L, Capital. According to the ARDL, VECM Granger Causality results, there was a two-way relationship between renewable energy consumption and economic growth.

Amri (2016), using the data from 1990 to 2010 for 75 countries, examined the relationship between RNW, GDP, NRNW, L, Foreign Direct Investments. According to the Panel GMM test results, there was two-way relationship between renewable energy consumption and economic growth.

Saidi & Ben Mbarek (2016), using the data from 1990 to 2013 for nine developed countries, examined the relationship between RNW, GDP, Nuclear Energy, L, K, CO_2 variables. According to the Panel Cointegration and Panel Granger Causality Tests results, there was a two-way relationship between renewable energy consumption and economic growth.

Kahia et al. (2016), using the data from 1980 to 2012 for 13 Middle East-North Africa Net Oil Exporter Countries, examined the relationship between RNW, GDP, NRNW, K, L, Fixed Capital Formation. According to the Panel FMOLS, Panel Granger causality results, there was a two-way relationship between renewable energy consumption and economic growth for five countries.

Naseri et al. (2016), using the data from 1990 to 2012 for OECD Countries, examined the relationship between RNW and GDP. According to the ARDL, Johansen Cointegration results, there was a one-way relationship from renewable energy consumption to economic growth.

Bélaïd and Youssef (2017), using the data from 1980 to 2012 for Algeria, examined the relationship between RNW, GDP, NRNW, K, L, CO_2. According to the ARDL and VECM Granger causality results, there was no relationship between renewable energy consumption and economic growth.

Paramati, Mo, and Gupta (2017), using the data from 1991 to 2012 for G20 countries, examined the relationship between RNW, GDP, NRNW, CO_2, Fixed Capital Formation, Foreign Direct Investments, Energy Efficiency, Market Capitalization. According to the Panel Cointegration, Dumitrescu-Hurlin Causality results, there was a two-way relationship between renewable energy consumption and economic growth.

Bhattacharya et al. (2017), using the data from 1991 to 2012 for 85 countries, examined the relationship between RNW, GDP, NRNW, CO_2, Index of Economic Freedom, K, L. According to the Panel GMM, FMOLS test results. There was a one-way relationship from renewable energy consumption to economic growth.

Ito et al. (2017), using the data from 2002 to 2011for 42 developed countries, examined the relationship between RNW, GDP, NRNW, CO_2. According to the Panel GMM results, there was a one-way relationship from renewable energy consumption to economic growth.

Brini et al. (2017), using the data from 1980 to 2011for Tunisia, examined the relationship between GDP, Oil Prices, Foreign Trade. According to the ARDL, Johansen Cointegration and Granger Causality results, there was a one-way relationship from renewable energy consumption to economic growth.

Can and Korkmaz (2019), using the data from 1990 to 2016 annual data for Bulgaria, examined the relationship between renewable energy consumption, renewable electricity output, and economic growth. According to Toda-Yamamoto analysis and Autoregressive Distributed Lag (ARDL) bound tests three different results were obtained. One showed that renewable energy consumption and renewable electricity output are the causes of economic growth. Another result of this study is that economic growth and renewable electricity output are the causes of renewable energy consumption. The last result is that economic growth and renewable energy consumption are not causes of renewable electricity output. There was no long-term relationship between variables.

Yoo and Ku (2009) investigated the causality between nuclear consumption and economic growth for six countries (Argentina, France, Germany, Korea, Pakistan, and Switzerland) using time-series analysis covering a time period of more than 20 years until 2005. Inconsistent results were obtained for the six countries. Bi-Directional causality between nuclear energy consumption and economic growth was estimated for Switzerland. For Pakistan and France, economic growth affected nuclear energy consumption whereas reverse causality from nuclear energy consumption to economic growth was found in the case of Korea. Argentina did not show any signs of causality evidence between the two variables.

Wolde-Rufael (2010) examined the relationship between economic growth and nuclear energy consumption for India for 1969-2006 applying the bounds test co-integration approach, Toda and Yamamoto approach to Granger causality and variance decomposition approach. It was concluded that economic growth in India is dependent on nuclear energy consumption. Similar results were found by Yoo and Jung (2005), who investigated causality existing between nuclear energy consumption and economic growth for a Korean sample over the period 1977-2002 using co-integration and error correction modeling and found uni-directional causality running from nuclear energy consumption to economic growth.

Wolde-Rufael and Menyah (2010) tested the causal relationship between nuclear energy consumption and economic growth for nine developed countries over the time period 1971-2005 using Toda And Yamamoto's modified version of the Granger Causality test. Uni-directional causality running from nuclear energy consumption to economic growth was estimated for Japan, The Netherlands, and Switzerland. Reverse causality running from economic growth to nuclear energy consumption was found for Canada and Sweden, whereas bi-directional causality evidence was collected for France, Spain, the UK, and the USA.

Lee and Chiu (2011), in their panel data analysis for developed countries over the period 1971-2006, found evidence of long-run causality running from economic growth to nuclear energy consumption whereas no evidence for short-run causality was estimated between the two variables.

METHODOLOGY AND DATA

This study investigates the relationship between renewable energy consumption (% of total final energy consumption), electricity production from nuclear sources (% of total), CO_2 emissions (kt) and GDP (constant 2010 USD) for the Bulgarian economy. Annual data from 1990 to 2016 were obtained from the website of the World Bank. Only the natural logarithm of the GDP in constant prices in US Dollars is considered in this study.

Descriptive Statistics

Quantitative properties of a group of values are presented in Table 1. The average value of variables is applied by the mean. The mean values of all variables are positive. LN_GDP, REC, NEP and LN_CO_2 have values 24.39, 8.25, 38.41 and 10.82. All variables are positively skewed Kurtosis of the normal

Table 1. Descriptive statistics

	LN_GDP	REC	NEP	LN_CO_2
Mean	24.38718	8.253592	38.40766	10.81588
Median	24.31488	8.733319	40.21451	10.79939
Maximum	24.68983	18.15702	47.95466	11.21829
Minimum	24.13623	1.916849	32.26470	10.58658
Std. Dev.	0.213572	4.869815	4.693500	0.147737
Skewness	0.292026	0.397846	0.176278	0.993400
Kurtosis	1.384309	2.203148	1.785655	3.812009
Jarque-Bera	3.074557	1.320937	1.665552	4.798676
Probability	0.214965	0.516609	0.434840	0.090778
Sum	609.6796	206.3398	960.1915	270.3971
Sum Sq. Dev.	1.094708	569.1624	528.6947	0.523829
Observations	25	25	25	25

Table 2. ADF unit root test

Variables	At level		At first difference	
	ADF Statistics	Critical values	ADF Statistics	Critical values
LN_GDP	-3.506770 (0.0613)	1% -4.532598 5% -3.673616 10% -3.277364	-3.719020 (0.0414)	1% -4.440739 5% -3.632896 10% -3.254671
REC	-2.512828 (0.3195)		-5.394989 (0.0012)	
NEP	-1.766063 (0.6892)		-5.338102 (0.0014)	
LN_CO_2	-3.829468 (0.0376)		-6.513283 (0.0001)	

distribution is between 1.38 and 3.81. *If the kurtosis = 3 means it mesokurtic when kurtosis value > 3 called leptokurtic and if kurtosis <3 means Platykurtic* (Sabir, Sajid 2015: 78). The kurtosis value of LN_GDP, REC and NEP is kurtosis, while the other LN_CO_2 has leptokurtic. This empirical analysis consists of 25 numbers of observations. Table 1 show the descriptive statistics values of all chosen variables.

Unit Root Test (Augmented Dickey-Fuller test; ADF Test)

Stationarity indicates statistical lines that do not depend on the moment they are measured, and all their characteristics are constant over time. Non-stationary rows are difficult to model because they can overestimate the real relationship between the variables or the significance of the coefficients. Mostly used stationarity tests are Dickey-Fuller (DF) and Augmented Dickey-Fuller. ADF test is applied for each variable. The results in Table 2 show that all variables (LN_GDP, REC, NEP and LN_CO_2) are non-stationarity at level. They become stationary after first difference when is used trend and intercept.

Table 3. Phillips-Perron unit root test

Variables	At level		At first difference	
	Adj. t-Statistics	Critical values	Adj. t-Statistics	Critical values
LN_GDP	-3.270490 (0.0952)	1% -4.394309 5% -3.612199 10% -3.243079	-3.675407 (0.0451)	1% -4.416345 5% -3.622033 10% -3.248592
REC	-2.508336 (0.3214)		-5.473319 (0.0010)	
NEP	-1.548309 (0.7831)		-6.275832 (0.0002)	
LN_CO_2	-4.004160 (0.0227)		-10.47440 (0.0000)	

Unit Root Test (Phillips-Perron Test; PP Test)

An alternative unit root test is Phillips–Perron. All the variables (LN_GDP, REC, NEP, and LN_CO_2) are non-stationarity at level and stationary after first difference. The outcomes are in Table 3.

Johansen Co-Integration Test

To evaluate the dynamic relationship between two or more variables, if they are non-stationary, it is desirable to integrate them in the same order. However, if there are more than two variables, not all variables may be integrated in the same order, but the order of integration must be in the right direction. If the dependent variable is stationary, it cannot be explained by integrated variables. However, if the dependent variable is integrated, some of the explanatory variables may be stationary, but there must be at least several integrated explanatory variables.

To test the chosen variables for co-integration is used original data (Table 4). There are four variables and lagged are only two LnGDP and $LnCO_2$. It is applicable only when all variables are stationarity after first difference. The outcome shows two tests. One is Trance, and the other one is Max-Eigen Statistics. There will be checked both. The null hypothesis (H_0) is to trance the number of co-integrated vectors. The guideline is when the *P*-value is less than 5% (*P*-value<α) then the null hypothesis is rejected. And when it is more than 5%, it is accepted.

The first test is Trance Statistics. Level "None" means there is no co-integration. At this level, the *P*-value is equal to 0.09% that is less than 5%, so the null hypothesis cannot be rejected. To check if there is one co-integrated equation is tested the level "At most 1". There the *P*-value (12.9%)>5%=α. The H_0 cannot be rejected. It means that there is one co-integrated equation, or there is co-integration among four variables. In Bulgaria, the variables LN_GDP, REC, NEP and LN_CO_2 are in the long-run association ship for the period 1995-2014.

The second test is Max-Eigen Statistics. As before the number of co-integrated equations is equal to H_0. Again first is checked level "None" *P*-value>α (0.0018>0.05). It means that the null hypothesis cannot be rejected. At level "At most 1" *P*-value>α (0.181>0.05). It indicates one co-integrating equation at the 0.05 level. So it is proved that there is long-run relationship between the variables in the investigated period in Bulgaria.

Table 4. Johansen Co-integration Test

Sample (adjusted): 1992 2014				
Included observations: 23 after adjustments				
Trend assumption: Linear deterministic trend				
Series: LN_GDP REC NEP LN_CO_2				
Lags interval (in first differences): 1 to 1				
Unrestricted Co-integration Rank Test (Trace)				
Hypothesized		Trace	0.05	
No. of CE(s)	Eigenvalue	Statistic	Critical Value	Prob.**
None *	0.805399	63.63512	47.85613	0.0009
At most 1	0.518569	25.98868	29.79707	0.1290
At most 2	0.309238	9.175854	15.49471	0.3494
At most 3	0.028573	0.666761	3.841466	0.4142
Trace test indicates 1 cointegrating eqn(s) at the 0.05 level				
* denotes rejection of the hypothesis at the 0.05 level				
**MacKinnon-Haug-Michelis (1999) p-values				
Unrestricted Co-integration Rank Test (Maximum Eigenvalue)				
Hypothesized		Max-Eigen	0.05	
No. of CE(s)	Eigenvalue	Statistic	Critical Value	Prob.**
None *	0.805399	37.64643	27.58434	0.0018
At most 1	0.518569	16.81283	21.13162	0.1810
At most 2	0.309238	8.509093	14.26460	0.3293
At most 3	0.028573	0.666761	3.841466	0.4142
Max-eigenvalue test indicates 1 cointegrating eqn(s) at the 0.05 level				
* denotes rejection of the hypothesis at the 0.05 level				
**MacKinnon-Haug-Michelis (1999) p-values				

Table 5. Pairwise Granger causality tests

Pairwise Granger Causality Tests			
Sample: 1990 2014			
Lags: 2			
Null Hypothesis:	Obs	F-Statistic	Prob.
REC does not Granger Cause LN_GDP	23	5.49150	0.0137
LN_GDP does not Granger Cause REC		1.10601	0.3523
NEP does not Granger Cause LN_GDP	23	3.59424	0.0486
LN_GDP does not Granger Cause NEP		5.05957	0.0180
LN_CO_2 does not Granger Cause LN_GDP	23	2.44385	0.1151
LN_GDP does not Granger Cause LN_CO_2		0.66472	0.5266
NEP does not Granger Cause REC	23	0.17607	0.8400
REC does not Granger Cause NEP		1.96045	0.1697
LN_CO_2 does not Granger Cause REC	23	0.90040	0.4239
REC does not Granger Cause LN_CO_2		1.02771	0.3779
LN_CO_2 does not Granger Cause NEP	23	0.78598	0.4707
NEP does not Granger Cause LN_CO_2		0.08379	0.9200

Table 6. Correlation matrix

	Ln(GDP)	REC	NEC	$LN(CO_2)$
Ln(GDP)	1			
REC	0.871593	1		
NEC	-0.50821	-0.28513	1	
$LN(CO_2)$	-0.47625	-0.77478	-0.12765	1

Pairwise Granger Causality Test

The outcomes of Table 5 shows no causality link exists among chosen variables (LN_GDP, REC, NEP and CO_2) for the period 1990-2014 in Bulgaria.

Correlation Matrix

A correlation matrix is used to assess the dependence between several variables simultaneously. The result is in Table 6. It is containing the correlation coefficients between each variable and the others. The only positive relationship is between LN_GDP and REC. They are highly correlated. The other variables are negatively correlated. They are REC-NEC (low correlation), REC-LN_CO_2 (significant correlation), NEC-LN_CO_2 NEC (low correlation), LN_GDP-NEC (significant correlation) and LN_GDP- LN_CO_2 (moderate correlation).

The effects of renewable energy consumption have the potential to influence the size of GDP in Bulgaria over the investigated period.

This study shows that the variables under consideration are stationary at first difference. However, they are cointegrated on trace, which makes it possible to assess long-term dependence between them. Based on the analysis can make a selection of an appropriate regression model and evaluation method.

SOLUTIONS AND RECOMMENDATIONS

Increasing renewable energy investments in order to prevent economic crises may be beneficial for the national economy. Besides, the dependence on fossil resources should be reduced by reducing the dependence on fossil resources. In addition, investments in environmentally friendly energy sources are very important for human health. Therefore, it is predicted that there will be benefits in the direction of low-cost energy resources whose negative effects on human health are minimized.

FUTURE RESEARCH DIRECTIONS

Considering the depletion of fossil resources in the coming years, it is necessary to seek solutions to increase investments in renewable energy resources. But in the transition from fossil energy consumption to renewable energy consumption, economic impacts and other impact factors should be considered.

CONSLUSION

The study focuses on the causal relationship between renewable energy consumption, nuclear energy production, CO_2 emissions, and economic growth in Bulgaria for the period between 1990 and 2016 using annual data. Accordingly, it can be said that there was no long-term relationship between variables for Bulgaria during the respective periods. This finding supports the findings of prior study Can and Korkmaz (2019) on renewable energy consumption, renewable electricity output and economic growth in the literature.

According to Granger test results, economic growth will not affect energy use (probably due to the emancipatory effect), and policies aimed at saving energy will not be detrimental to economic development.

The following policies can be foreseen:

1. Sustainable development policies include social policies such as fighting poverty, technological development based on resource efficiency and highly competitive growth, environment, economy, and social components. For example, reducing greenhouse gas emissions that cause climate change can contribute to the economy by increasing the competitiveness and achieving efficiency by triggering technological development in the sector that causes these emissions beyond being an environmental sustainable development objective. The most concrete and obvious example of this is the developments in the energy sector, which has the highest share in greenhouse gas emissions. While energy efficiency and renewable energy applications allow reducing the environmental problems caused by dependence on fossil fuels, on the other hand, they can meet the energy supply security and diversity needs of countries. Renewable energy policies are of more critical importance in countries that depend on imports in energy supply and where energy expenditures have a significant impact on the foreign trade balance. Essentially, renewable energy applications are one of the areas where economic, social and environmental components of sustainable development are integrated with economic contribution, environmentally friendly production structure, and job opportunities.
2. Socially Responsible Investments aim to reconcile the economic performance of an organization with its social and environmental impact. It is possible by financing companies and institutions that contribute to sustainable development. The SRI is based on the conviction that taking into account social and environmental factors, ethics and governance ensures the financial results of the sums invested in the medium and long term, given a better understanding of the risks and better management. So as it seems the connection among them is possible among sustainable development.

REFERENCES

Al-mulali, U., Fereidouni, H. G., & Lee, J. Y. (2014). Electricity Consumption from Renewable and Non-renewable Sources and Economic Growth: Evidence from Latin American countries. *Renewable & Sustainable Energy Reviews*, *30*, 290–298. doi:10.1016/j.rser.2013.10.006

Al-mulali, U., Fereidouni, H. G., Lee, J. Y., & Sab, C. N. B. C. (2013). Examining the Bi-directional Long Run Relationship between Renewable Energy Consumption and GDP Growth. *Renewable & Sustainable Energy Reviews*, *22*, 209–222. doi:10.1016/j.rser.2013.02.005

Amri, F. (2016). The Relationship amongst Energy Consumption, Foreign Direct Investment and Output in Developed and Developing Countries. *Renewable & Sustainable Energy Reviews*, *64*, 694–702. doi:10.1016/j.rser.2016.06.065

Apergis, N., & Payne, J. E. (2010a). Renewable Energy Consumption and Economic Growth: Evidence from a Panel of OECD Countries. *Energy Policy*, *38*(1), 656–660. doi:10.1016/j.enpol.2009.09.002

Apergis, N., & Payne, J. E. (2010b). Renewable Energy Consumption and Growth in Eurasia. *Energy Economics*, *32*(6), 1392–1397. doi:10.1016/j.eneco.2010.06.001

Apergis, N., & Payne, J. E. (2011a). Renewable and Non-renewable Electricity Consumption–growth Nexus: Evidence from Emerging Market Economies. *Applied Energy*, *88*(12), 5226–5230. doi:10.1016/j.apenergy.2011.06.041

Apergis, N., & Payne, J. E. (2011b). The Renewable Energy Consumption–Growth nexus in Central America. *Applied Energy*, *88*(1), 343–347. doi:10.1016/j.apenergy.2010.07.013

Apergis, N., & Payne, J. E. (2012). Renewable and Non-renewable Energy Consumption-Growth Nexus: Evidence from a Panel Error Correction Model. *Energy Economics*, *34*(3), 733–738. doi:10.1016/j.eneco.2011.04.007

Apollo Alliance. (2008). *Green-Collar Jobs in America's Cities, United States*. Retrieved October 23, 2019, from: https://www.cows.org/_data/documents/1165.pdf

Bélaïd, F., & Youssef, M. (2017). Environmental Degradation, Renewable and Non-renewable Electricity Consumption, and Economic Growth: Assessing the evidence from Algeria. *Energy Policy*, *102*, 277–287. doi:10.1016/j.enpol.2016.12.012

Bhattacharya, M., Churchill, S. A., & Paramati, S. R. (2017). The Dynamic Impact of Renewable Energy and Institutions on Economic Output and CO_2 Eemissions across Regions. *Renewable Energy*, *111*, 157–167. doi:10.1016/j.renene.2017.03.102

Bowen, A., & Kuralbayeva, K. (2015). Looking for Green Jobs: the Impact of Green Growth on Employment. *Global Green Growth Institute*. Retrieved October 23, 2019, from: http://www.lse.ac.uk/GranthamInstitute/wp-content/uploads/2015/03/Looking-for-green-jobs_the-impact-of-green-growth-on-employment.pdf

Brini, R., Amara, M., & Jemmali, H. (2017). Renewable energy consumption, International trade, oil price and economic growth inter-linkages: The case of Tunisia. *Renewable & Sustainable Energy Reviews*, *76*, 620–627. doi:10.1016/j.rser.2017.03.067

Can, H., & Korkmaz, Ö. (2019). The Relationship between Renewable Energy Consumption and Economic Growth: The Case of Bulgaria. *International Journal of Energy Sector Management.*, *13*(3), 573–589. doi:10.1108/IJESM-11-2017-0005

Cecere, G., & Mazzanti, M. (2015). *Green Jobs, Innovation and Environmentally Oriented Strategies in European SMEs* (No. 2115). SEEDS, Sustainability Environmental Economics and Dynamics Studies. Retrieved October 23, 2019, https://ideas.repec.org/p/srt/wpaper/2115.html

Fang, Y. (2011). Economic Welfare Impacts from Renewable Energy Consumption: The China Experience. *Renewable & Sustainable Energy Reviews*, *15*(9), 5120–5128. doi:10.1016/j.rser.2011.07.044

Granger, C. (1969). Investigating Causal Relations by Econometric Models and Cross-spectral Methods. *Econometrica*, *37*(3), 424–438. doi:10.2307/1912791

Hannam, P. (2008). *The Challenges Facing Green Job Growth*. Retrieved October 23, 2019, from https://www.greenbiz.com/news/2008/09/21/challenges-facing-green-job-growth

International Chamber of Commerce. (2012). *Green Economy Roadmap – a Guide for Business, Policymakers and Society*. Retrieved October 23, 2019, from https://iccwbo.org/content/uploads/sites/3/2012/08/Green-Economy-Roadmap-a-guide-for-business_-policy-makers-and-society.pdf

Ito, K. (2017). CO_2 Emissions, Renewable and Non-renewable Energy Consumption, and Economic Growth: Evidence from Panel Data for Developing Countries. *International Economics, 151*, 1-6. Retrieved October 23, 2019, from: https://ideas.repec.org/a/eee/inteco/v151y2017icp1-6.html

Jebli, M. B., & Youssef, S. B. (2015). Output, Renewable and Non-renewable Energy Consumption and International Trade: Evidence from a Panel of 69 Countries. *Renewable Energy*, *83*, 799–808. doi:10.1016/j.renene.2015.04.061

Kahia, M., Aïssa, M. S. B., & Charfeddine, L. (2016). Impact of renewable and non-renewable energy consumption on economic growth: New evidence from the MENA Net Oil Exporting Countries (NOECs). *Energy*, *116*, 102–115. doi:10.1016/j.energy.2016.07.126

Lee, C. C., & Chiu, Y. B. (2011). Oil prices, nuclear energy consumption, and economic growth: New evidence using a heterogeneous panel analysis. *Energy Policy*, *39*(4), 2111–2120. doi:10.1016/j.enpol.2011.02.002

Lin, B., & Moubarak, M. (2014). Renewable energy consumption–economic growth nexus for China. *Renewable & Sustainable Energy Reviews*, *40*, 111–117. doi:10.1016/j.rser.2014.07.128

Martinez-Fernandez, C., Hinojosa, C., & Miranda, G. (2010). *Greening Jobs and Skills: Labour Market Implications of Addressing Climate Change*. OECD. Retrieved October 23, 2019, from: www.oecd.org/dataoecd/54/43/44683169.pdf?contentId=44683170

Miteva, A., Stoyanova, Z., Harizanova, H., Peicheva, M., Doichinova, J., & Kanchev, I. (2014). Green Jobs-tool of Ecologisation of Bulgarian Economy. . doi:10.5937/ekoPolj1502369S

Naseri, S. F., Motamedi, S., & Ahmadian, M. (2016). Study of mediated consumption effect of renewable energy on economic growth of OECD countries. *Procedia Economics and Finance*, *36*, 502–509. doi:10.1016/S2212-5671(16)30068-5

Pao, H. T., & Fu, H. C. (2013). Renewable energy, non-renewable energy and economic growth in Brazil. *Renewable & Sustainable Energy Reviews*, *25*, 381–392. doi:10.1016/j.rser.2013.05.004

Paramati, S. R., Mo, D., & Gupta, R. (2017). The effects of stock market growth and renewable energy use on CO_2 emissions: Evidence from G20 countries. *Energy Economics*, *66*, 360–371. doi:10.1016/j.eneco.2017.06.025

Potts, T. (2010). The Natural Advantage of Regions: Linking Sustainability, Innovation, and Regional Development in Australia. *Journal of Cleaner Production*, *18*(8), 713–725. doi:10.1016/j.jclepro.2010.01.008

Sabir, S., Hamza, S. M., Arshad, M. U., Sajid, M., & Tahir, S. (2015). Causality Relationship among Foreign Direct Investment, Gross Domestic Product and Exports for Pakistan. *European Journal of Business and Management*, *7*(13), 76–82. Retrieved from http://citeseerx.ist.psu.edu/viewdoc/download?doi=10.1.1.734.8343&rep=rep1&type=pdf

Saidi, K., & Mbarek, M. B. (2016). Nuclear energy, renewable energy, CO_2 emissions, and economic growth for nine developed countries: Evidence from panel Granger causality tests. *Progress in Nuclear Energy*, *88*, 364–374. doi:10.1016/j.pnucene.2016.01.018

Sebri, M., & Ben-Salha, O. (2014). On the causal dynamics between economic growth, renewable energy consumption, CO_2 emissions and trade openness: Fresh evidence from BRICS countries. *Renewable & Sustainable Energy Reviews*, *39*, 14–23. doi:10.1016/j.rser.2014.07.033

Shahbaz, M., Loganathan, N., Zeshan, M., & Zaman, K. (2015). Does renewable energy consumption add in economic growth? An application of auto-regressive distributed lag model in Pakistan. *Renewable & Sustainable Energy Reviews*, *44*, 576–585. doi:10.1016/j.rser.2015.01.017

Wolde-Rufael, Y. (2010). Bounds test approach to cointegration and causality between nuclear energy consumption and economic growth in India. *Energy Policy*, *38*(1), 52–58. doi:10.1016/j.enpol.2009.08.053

Wolde-Rufael, Y., & Menyah, K. (2010). Nuclear energy consumption and economic growth in nine developed countries. *Energy Economics*, *32*(3), 550–556. doi:10.1016/j.eneco.2010.01.004

Workplace Research Centre. (2007). *Skills and Sustainable Business Development*. A report to the NSW Board of Vocational Education and Training, University of Sydney.

Yoo, S. H., & Ku, S. J. (2009). Causal relationship between nuclear energy consumption and economic growth: A multi-country analysis. *Energy Policy*, *37*(5), 1905–1913. doi:10.1016/j.enpol.2009.01.012

ADDITIONAL READING

Apergis, N., Payne, J. E., Menyah, K., & Wolde-Rufael, Y. (2010). On the causal dynamics between emissions, nuclear energy, renewable energy, and economic growth. *Ecological Economics*, *69*(11), 2255–2260. doi:10.1016/j.ecolecon.2010.06.014

Bhattacharya, M., Paramati, S. R., Ozturk, I., & Bhattacharya, S. (2016). The effect of renewable energy consumption on economic growth: Evidence from top 38 countries. *Applied Energy*, *162*, 733–741. doi:10.1016/j.apenergy.2015.10.104

Fotourehchi, Z. (2017). Clean Energy Consumption and Economic Growth: A Case Study for Developing Countries. *International Journal of Energy Economics and Policy*. *7*(2), 61-64. October 23, 2019, from: https://pdfs.semanticscholar.org/e7e3/2b206960290c4c69fb9ba7303ecf93c6860f.pdf

Kamoun, M., Abdelkafi, I., & Ghorbel, A. (2019). The impact of renewable energy on sustainable growth: Evidence from a panel of OECD countries. *Journal of the Knowledge Economy.*, *10*(1), 221–237. doi:10.100713132-016-0440-2

Mathiesen, B. V., Lund, H., & Karlsson, K. (2011). 100% Renewable energy systems, climate mitigation and economic growth. *Applied Energy*, *88*(2), 488–501. doi:10.1016/j.apenergy.2010.03.001

Menyah, K., & Wolde-Rufael, Y. (2010). CO_2 emissions, nuclear energy, renewable energy and economic growth in the US. *Energy Policy*, *38*(6), 2911–2915. doi:10.1016/j.enpol.2010.01.024

Ozcan, B., & Ozturk, I. (2019). Renewable energy consumption-economic growth nexus in emerging countries: A bootstrap panel causality test. *Renewable & Sustainable Energy Reviews*, *104*, 30–37. doi:10.1016/j.rser.2019.01.020

Tahvonen, O., & Salo, S. (2001). Economic growth and transitions between renewable and nonrenewable energy resources. *European Economic Review*, *45*(8), 1379–1398. doi:10.1016/S0014-2921(00)00062-3

Tiba, S., & Omri, A. (2017). Literature survey on the relationships between energy, environment and economic growth. *Renewable & Sustainable Energy Reviews*, *69*, 1129–1146. doi:10.1016/j.rser.2016.09.113

Zhou, A., & Li, J. (2019). Heterogeneous role of renewable energy consumption in economic growth and emissions reduction: Evidence from a panel quantile regression. *Environmental Science and Pollution Research International*, *26*(22), 22575–22595. doi:10.100711356-019-05447-w PMID:31165449

KEY TERMS AND DEFINITIONS

Autoregressive Distributed Lag (ARDL): The ARDL model is an ordinary least square (OLS) based model, which is applicable for both non-stationary time series as well as for times series with mixed order of integration.

Foreign Trade: It provides opportunity for import and export firms to get the product demands and the information that they may need currently or when they penetrate new markets.

Fully Modified Ordinary Least Square (FMOLS): The FMOLS method produces reliable estimates for small sample size and provides a check for robustness of the results.

Gross Domestic Products (GDP): The GDP is a monetary measure of the market value of all the final goods and services produced in a specific period, often annually.

Gross Fixed Capital Formation: The gross fixed capital formation consists of resident producers' investments, deducting disposals, in fixed assets during a given period. It also includes certain additions to the value of non-produced assets realized by producers or institutional units. Fixed assets are tangible or intangible assets produced as outputs from production processes that are used repeatedly, or continuously, for more than one year.

Johansen Test: The Johansen test, named after Søren Johansen, is a procedure for testing cointegration of several, say k, I(1) time series.

Labor Force (L): The labor force, or currently active population, comprises all persons who fulfill the requirements for inclusion among the employed (civilian employment plus the armed forces) or the unemployed. The employed are defined as those who work for pay or profit for at least one hour a week, or who have a job but are temporarily not at work due to illness, leave or industrial action.

Section 2

Value Creation Through Responsible Business and Socially Responsible Investing Strategies

Chapter 8
Motivation for Responsible Behavior Among Russian SMEs

Bela Bataeva
https://orcid.org/0000-0002-5700-1667
Finance University Under the Government of Russian Federation, Russia

Liudmila Cheglakova
https://orcid.org/0000-0002-7692-4918
National Research University Higher School of Economics, Russia

Olga Melitonyan
https://orcid.org/0000-0002-4654-7103
National Research University Higher School of Economics, Russia

ABSTRACT

This chapter focuses on identifying motivation for socially responsible behavior in small and medium enterprises (SMEs) in Russia. It also investigates the attitudes of owners and executives of Russian SMEs toward the concepts of business ethics and social responsibility of business. A research set the background of this chapter, including the gathering of primary data through 57 focused interviews. Results of a critical analysis conclude that top managers and owners of Russian SMEs do not thoroughly understand these concepts. However, it also shows that they do not neglect them. Research findings point to a growing level of adherence to the principles of business ethics and responsible behavior. There is strong evidence showing motivation for following principles of ethical and responsible behavior. In addition to an understanding of legal requirements, company owners and top managers are finding that positive relationships between firms and stakeholders are crucial for sustainable performance.

DOI: 10.4018/978-1-7998-2193-9.ch008

Copyright © 2020, IGI Global. Copying or distributing in print or electronic forms without written permission of IGI Global is prohibited.

INTRODUCTION

In research and publications dedicated to business ethics and corporate social responsibility (CSR) or social responsibility of business, the discussion of related practice of small and medium enterprises (SMEs) is usually considered apart from the rest of the corporate world. In the late 1990s, (Vyakarnam, Bailey, Myers & Burnett, 1997, p. 1625) expressed a point of view that business ethics of SMEs "remains a largely uncharted area of ethics". This statement remains true for many countries. However, the role of SMEs in economic development continues to grow. Surveys on specifics of business ethics and CSR in SMEs are rare compared to the number of research papers dedicated to CSR and business ethics of large corporations (Chan, Fung & Yau, 2010).

Authors from developed countries pay some attention to this topic. SMEs constitute a dominant form of starting and doing business in many economies within the Organization for Economic Cooperation and Development (OECD, 2002), providing over 50% of jobs in the private sector. In Russia, the economic role played by those enterprises is still much weaker – the contribution of Russian SMEs to the country's GDP in 2019 according to the statistical data from the Russian Ministry of Economics and Development is 21,9%, while in developed economies this indicator reaches 50-60% (RBC, 05.02.2019).

A limited volume of publications by Russian researchers exists on aspects of social responsibility and responsible behavior among SMEs. This situation may be explained by an opinion spread among researchers that social responsibility and business ethics are not essential for SMEs in Russia. This view was based on economic and business situations, including complications related to surviving and breaking even (Savicheva, 2010). Another reason may be an absence of traditions among new Russian entrepreneurs. In fact, most of these entrepreneurs represent SMEs. It can be explained by the relatively young age and early stage of these companies, which is common with private businesses in Russia (the oldest companies "born" as start-ups are no more than 25 years old).

Nevertheless, practical examples and cases show that Russian SMEs follow certain ethical principles in their behavior. They are, in fact, involved in responsible practices, including charity initiatives or assistance programs to employees and families in need (Dzhindzholiia, 2011; Ivashina, 2016; Nikitina, 2015; Pletnev & Nicolaeva, 2016).

Features of social responsibility of business in Russian SMEs include several aspects within the business environment, corporate governance practice, and labor conditions. Savicheva (2010) felt that business practices of Russian SMEs are characterized by a shadow approach to conducting business, constant attempts to circumvent the law, lack of systematic approach to regulating socially responsible behavior, narrow scope of stakeholders, poor labor conditions, and insecurity in the process of dealing with local authorities. The process of assessing the development dynamics of social responsibility in Russia consider the historical background, including the perception of issues that were typical for Soviet plants and almost complete negation of ethical behavior and socially responsible performance in the 1990s (or years of transition). In addition, it considers the transformation of the economic model during the same period.

The goal of this research is to identify features of socially responsible behavior and business ethics in Russian SMEs. The following research questions were set in the course of the study:

1. How do representatives of Russian SMEs (i.e., top managers, owners) perceive the terms "social responsibility," "business ethics," and "corporate social responsibility"?
2. What shapes the motivation of Russian SMEs to follow certain patterns of socially responsible behavior and principles of business ethics?
3. What are the priorities of SMEs with regard to seven most common practices of responsible behavior according to the Russian National Standard, Guidance for Social Responsibility GOST R ISO 26000-2012?

SOCIAL RESPONSIBILITY AND SMES

Approaches to Defining CSR for SMEs

According to the Russian National Standard GOST R ISO 26000-2012 (based on ISO 26000) (Russian National Standard), social responsibility of business is an organization's responsibility for the consequences of its decisions and activities for the society and environment expressed through following high standards of transparent and ethical behavior. This document contains seven areas to assess business responsibility: (1) responsible management practices; (2) human rights; (3) labor relations; (4) environmental issues; (5) compliance practices; (6) consumer relations; and (7) participation in the life and development of local communities.

Some experts believe that the responsible behavior of SMEs from CIS[1] countries can be evaluated using five criteria from those mentioned: (1) labor relations; (2) consumer relations; (3) environmental issues; (4) participation in life and development of local communities; and (5) relations with partners (Maciek, 2013). According to Maciek, five to seven criteria will be considered while analyzing practices of responsible behavior among Russian SMEs. The author recognizes that each company has individual preferences and motivation in prioritizing responsible behavior.

Jenkins (2004) defined socially responsible behavior of SMEs as an intention to reach commercial success by following ethical principles and respecting stakeholders' interests. This research paper outlines traditional approaches to CSR of large corporations. It recognizes that these may not apply to practices of SMEs. In turn, (Van Marrewijk, 2003, p. 102) indicated that socially responsible behavior is "voluntary demonstration of social and ecological issues' inclusion into business operations of a company and its interaction with stakeholders".

This research paper uses the terms "socially responsible business" and "socially responsible behavior" rather than the abbreviation CSR because many aspects of large corporations' CSR agendas do not apply to cases of SMEs (Fox, 2005). In Russia, CSR is often applied to a corresponding practice of large firms and public corporations (Bataeva, 2010; Blagov, 2010; Peregudov & Semenenko, 2008). Some scholars suggested an alternative term, "social responsibility of business," which refers to the market economy as a whole and particularly to the activities of SMEs (Turkin, 2007). Blagov (2010) distinguished CSR of SMEs as a case of CSR.

A need to distinguish the terms "corporate social responsibility" and "social responsibility of business" comes from several limitations of the term "corporation". Corporate social responsibility is a corporation's responsibility for the consequences of its decisions and activities for the society and environment expressed through following high standards of transparent and ethical behavior. In Russia the phenomena "corporation" was legally defined only in 2014 when a few amendments were made to

Table 1. The number of SMEs in the Central Federal Count of Russia and in the Russian Federation as of May 10, 2019

Total	Legal Personalities			Individual Entrepreneurs		
	Micro	Small	Medium	Micro	Small	Medium
Russian Federation	6,184,204	2,535,614	220,245	18,302	3,382,840	26,888
Central Federal Count	1,927,918	897,735	79,705	7,238	936,998	6,162

Source: Web resource of the Federal Tax Authority of the Russian Federation https://ofd.nalog.ru/statistics.html.

the Civil Code of the Russian Federation: according to the article 65.1, all legal personalities in Russia (both for-profit and non-profit ones) are divided into corporations and unitary enterprises (Civil Code of the Russian Federation, 29.12.2017). According to the new edition of the Civil Code, "corporations are those for-profit and non-profit organizations that were founded following the principle of participation, so that their participants (or founders) form their supreme governing bodies according to the point 1 of the article 65.3 of the Civil Code of the Russian Federation" (Civil Code of the Russian Federation, 29.12.2017). Large businesses, especially public limited companies, in most cases, meet the features of a corporation defined above. Meanwhile, small and medium businesses in numerous cases are presented by individual entrepreneurs (or sole traders) and partnerships (see Table 1), which do not go through the process of incorporation and, thus, cannot be considered corporations. In other words, an application of the term "corporate social responsibility" to SMEs is not justified, and the term "social responsibility of business" seems to be more appropriate in this case.

In this paper, the concept of business ethics is applied following the paper by (Kalnitskaya, Gentile & Rohen, 2012) where it is considered as a special set of norms and rules of behavior that influence business decisions. When following principles of business ethics, the term "ethical" characterizes morally good and morally right activities as opposed to those that do not contradict legal standards (Kanungo & Mendonca, 2001). Therefore, this research paper does not include cases of producing goods or providing services of due quality or in due time into the scope of consideration.

As to the correlation of concepts reviewed in this publication, an interesting approach is demonstrated by Storchevoy (2018), who argues that corporate social responsibility is a concept that emerged in the 1960s in the United States of America in the framework of business ethics as a "parent" scientific area. In this regard, Storchevoy distinguishes normative, positive, and practical areas in the concept of business ethics (Storchevoy, 2018).

It is also important to correlate the terms "business ethics", "morality", and "social responsibility of business". Morality includes an individual moral consciousness (feelings, the rational basis, and the purpose), as well as an individual moral practice (i.e., behavior based on individual values) (Petrunin & Borisov, 2010). Business ethics presents a result of an individual's or an organization's critical thinking about a particular attitude and constructing arguments "in favor" or "against" a certain pattern of behavior. Social responsibility of business presumes that an organization voluntarily demonstrates ethical approach embodied in activities. Social responsibility of an organization cannot be perceived as a combination of individual social responsibilities of its employees. Moreover, social responsibility is dynamic: if a company or an individual does not perform actions that can be related to social responsibility, it is not possible to conclude if they are responsible or not. That is why the term "socially responsible behavior" is often used by the authors.

Values and Motivation Of Various Stakeholders In Shaping Responsible Behavior Of SMES

Baumback (1988), Hammann, Habisch, & Pechlaner (2009), Jenkins (2004), and Vives (2006) in their works investigated how personal values of top managers and owners influence business operations and the process of strategic decision making in SMEs.

Vyakarnam et al. (1997) argued that while resolving ethical dilemmas, it is important to consider personal features of a company's executives, values demonstrated and articulated by owners and managers, and specifics of internal relationships between company owners and other stakeholders. According to (Kanungo & Mendonca, 2001), behavior strategies of company owners influence an internal social environment of the business.

Ma (2012) viewed altruism and philanthropic motivation of owners and executives as an intention of SMEs to follow principles of responsible behavior. For large corporations, Ma (2012) argued that social responsibility was a part of corporate strategy and processes in maintaining and developing nonmaterial assets.

According to Spence and Lozano who researched responsible practices of SMEs and behavior models of owners and executives from small and medium enterprises in Great Britain and Spain (Spence & Lozano, 2000), along with legal requirements personal and religion-related values of owners and executives act as powerful moral regulators in the process of decision-making. On the contrary, industrial norms have little influence in this regard (Spence & Lozano, 2000).

Waldman et al. (2006) also focused on evaluating how values of top-managers influence the decision-making process, the data was collected from 561 firms located in 15 countries from 5 continents. The conclusion stated that values of shareholders/owners, top-managers and other stakeholder groups, indeed, play an important role in this process (Waldman et al., 2006). An attitude of the CEO shapes the way of how employees prioritize particular activities and decisions. In turn, executives are more concerned about the values of owners and priority groups of stakeholders (customers, employees, etc.) rather than about the values of local communities. Top-managers from developed economies (wealthy countries) pay more attention to overall social welfare and the overall social impact of their decisions than their counterparts from developing economies. The latter are focused mostly on the interests of shareholders and owners (Waldman et al., 2006).

Among Russian researchers, Mikhailenko studied the influence of owners/shareholders' and executives' interests and values on SMEs' business practices (Mihailenko, 2007). Since in case of small and medium enterprises, one or several owners are directly involved in day-to-day management of a firm, most business decisions are based on informal norms and ethical values of those owners. The researcher argues that paternalistic or autocratic leadership styles are quite common for SMEs. Autocratic approach reflects a situation when major business functions in many SMEs – product development and promotion, production, sales, accounting, and finance, etc. – are monopolized by a few people whose management and leadership style is determined by their personal experience, standards, and judgments (Mihailenko, 2007).

Recent publications (e.g., Jamali, Lund-Thomsen & Jeppesen, 2017) confirm the importance of personal values and attitudes of company owners and shareholders in shaping responsible behavior and decisions to use informal instruments for regulating socially responsible behavior as an attribute in SMEs (Jamali et al., 2017).

There is a representative group of research papers focused on investigating factors and motivators for patterns of responsible behavior among SMEs in different countries. Research by Chrisman and Archer, Spence, and Lozano, Vitell et al. emphasize that attitudes of consumers as stakeholders are equally important for SMEs regardless of their geographic position (Chrisman & Archer, 1984; Spence & Lozano, 2000; Vitell, Dickerson & Festervand, 2000).

McCarthy, Puffer, Dunlap, & Jaeger (2012) have studied evidence of influential stakeholder groups like local communities, informal groups of interest, and relatives in Russia, Brazil, and Spain). According to Vitell et al., other countries, like the United States and Great Britain, have "direct" stakeholders, including employees and shareholders, who play a significant role in shaping patterns of responsible behavior (Vitell et al., 2000).

Clarkson (1995) analyzed social responsibility of business through its interaction with stakeholders. Depending on external response, a company may use a spectrum of strategies, including defense strategies (based on neglecting responsibility) and preventive strategies (based on predicting responsibility under certain circumstances). Moreover, this research distinguishes three levels of company responsibility: (1) social responsibility; (2) organizational responsibility; and (3) individual responsibility (a level of an individual manager) (Clarkson, 1995).

Practices and Mechanisms of Regulation In Case Of SMES' Responsible Behavior

Responsible practices of SMEs form the focus of research in numerous publications. Pohludka & Stverkova (2019) analyze responsible practices of SMEs in the Czech Republic and outline a growing trend according to which small and medium-enterprises focus their attention on customers and their needs. Authors analyze an application of the Customer Relationship Management system (CRM) to business practices of SMEs, and conclude that this system may contribute to achieving competitive advantages not only in cases of large corporations (Pohludka & Stverkova, 2019).

Differences in the practice of responsible behavior in Russian SMEs are carefully examined in many papers (Bobrova & Kovaleva, 2015a, 2015b; Bugai, Akishina & Fannenshtil, 2015; Bugai, Akishina & Fannenshtil, 2014; Dzhindzholiia, 2011; Ivashina, 2016; Neverov & Davydenkova, 2016; Pletnev & Nicolaeva, 2016; Savicheva, 2010; Sizova & Chilipenok, 2017).

Bobrova & Kovaleva (2015a, p. 2603; 2015b) conducted a survey (based on formalized interviews) among representatives of small and medium enterprises in Saint Petersburg to clarify the goals and motives of their responsible behavior as well as their practices in this field. Along with "compliance with the law", respondents mentioned three "classic" types of responsible behavior such as "charity", "protection of employees' rights", "ecological safety in the process of doing business".

Bugai et al. (2015) and Bugai et al. (2014) researched responsible practices of SMEs in a rural area of the Altay region, their survey indicated the following most common practices – SMEs support activities of maintaining and cleaning the territory where they are located; they support employees' transportation needs; cover employees' expenses for mobile communication; provide material assistance to employees; support employees' qualification improvement; participate in charity actions; support activities of constructing and maintaining local roads etc.

Neverov & Davydenkova (2016) surveyed SMEs' owners from Moscow, Moscow region, and Nizhny Novgorod and concluded that the focus of their responsible behavior is rather internal than external. Most common practices of responsible behavior that the researchers registered include ensuring workplace technical safety, supporting employees' qualification improvement, supporting charity actions (helping children with disabilities, orphans, etc.)

Sizova & Chilipenok (2017) researched responsible practices of SMEs from Nizhny Novgorod and Nizhny Novgorod Region of Russian Federation, they outline that employers include employees into their list of priorities in the field of responsible behavior, but their effort in this regard is minimal and explained by a need to keep employees neutral (rather than dissatisfied) to labor conditions. Each employer has a specific attitude towards employees' position in his/her set of values or a list of strategically important stakeholders.

Ivashina (2016) argues that SMEs use responsible practices for building effective communication with various stakeholders and enhancing ways of interacting with them. According to this research, representatives of SMEs consider employees as the most important stakeholder group for their businesses (Ivashina, 2016).

To sum up, the above mentioned authors indicate that social responsibility in small enterprises is largely determined by cultural and organizational factors like business environment, labor conditions, and management specifics.

Some researchers concluded that Russian SMEs continue to find difficulties in doing and developing their business and are preoccupied with survival rather than social responsibility. Moreover, entrepreneurs do not register requests for responsible behavior from consumers and society. Their expectations toward the role of state authorities are much higher than their intent to regulate business relationships following principles of business ethics and standards of responsible behavior (Balashova, 2009; Savicheva, 2010). Other researchers have drawn attention to facts proving that certain patterns of responsible behavior are spread among Russian SMEs. They conclude that an interest of this segment of Russian businesses to social responsibility is growing despite all difficulties that those businesses meet (Bugai et al., 2015; Bugai et al., 2014; Dzhindzholiia, 2011; Ivashina, 2016; Neverov & Davydenkova, 2016; Pletnev & Nicolaeva, 2016).

Informal mechanisms of regulating ethical behavior (i.e., social networks, family relations, etc.) and lack of trust and effective implementation of formal instruments (i.e., code of ethics, standards of ethical behavior) are mentioned as distinctive features of SMEs (Jenkins, 2004; Spence & Lozano, 2000). Jenkins (2004) argued that CSR instruments and methods that are built as elements into corporate strategies of large firms, as in most cases of SMEs, prove to be inefficient. It is because small- and medium-sized businesses tend to have less formalized organizational structures and strategies. Often, these depend on both the owner's involvement in the strategic process and their shifting attitude (Jenkins, 2004). Although SMEs are diverse, issues related to establishing sustainable long-term relationships with target groups of clients are crucial, considered by many as the best way to demonstrate socially responsible behavior (Chrisman & Archer, 1984; Spence & Lozano, 2000).

DATA SET AND SAMPLE

The research sample included micro-, small-, and medium-sized enterprises in Russia. Individual entrepreneurs (or sole traders) constituted a large part of the SMEs (see Table 1). They are accounted in the Unified State Register of Individual Entrepreneurs (USRIE). The criteria for micro- small- and medium-enterprises were amended in 2019 in the article 4 of the Federal Law of the Russian Federation #209-FZ "About the development of small and medium entrepreneurship in the Russian Federation" of July 24th,

2007. According to the Russian statistical classification (Federal Tax Service, 07.03.2019), microenterprises have less than 15 employees. The annual revenue does not exceed 120 mln rubles (USD1,919,386[2]). Small enterprises average no more than 100 employees (between 15 and 100 people). Their annual revenue without value-added tax (VAT) from selling goods and services does not exceed 800 mln rubles (USD12,795,906/400 mln rubles/USD6,397,953 before 2015). Medium enterprises, according to the same classification, average between 101 and 250 employees. Their annual revenue is between 800 mln rubles (USD12,795,906) and 2 bln rubles (USD31,989,762) (1 bln rubles/USD15,994,881 before 2015).

As of January 1, 2019, per the Russian Federal Tax Authority (Federal Tax Service, 07.03.2019), Russian SMEs employed 19 million people. SMEs' contribution to the country's gross domestic product (GDP) was approximately 20%.

In the framework of the survey, 156 interviews were conducted with entrepreneurs (2015-2016). SMEs' representatives participated in 57 interviews (out of 156); thus a sample of 57 interviews was formed, their businesses function in 15 industries of the national economy of Central Federal Count. Of the sample, 27.6% of the SMEs employed less than 15 workers; 72.4% had between 15 and 100 employees. Table 2 presents a detailed description of the sample and includes information on the industries and services that selected SMEs represent, positions of respondents, to what kind of clients SMEs from the sample target their products/ services (b2b, b2c), it also contains information about the participation of foreign investors or shareholders in owning and managing SMEs from the sample. The authors found it possible to spread research conclusions for medium-sized enterprises from the Central Federal Count of Russian Federation, although, as one may see from Table 3, most of the businesses covered by the sample employ 15-100 people. This is due to the fact that some small firms (or microfirms) from the sample are parts of larger financial/industrial groups conducting coordinated market policy and strategy, moreover, revenues of some firms with 15-100 employees fell outside earlier quoted limits of 800 mln rubles (USD12,795,906). The proportion of men-to-women in the sample was almost equal (53.4% and 46.6%, respectively). The average age of the respondent was 36.

In the course of this study, a comfortable sample was selected using the snowball method. While selecting respondents, the authors considered status (i.e., business owner, chief executive officer, department head, deputy CEO, manager, client manager, head of the executive board, sales manager, etc.) and willingness to participate in the survey. In designing the questionnaire for semistructured interviews, the authors considered parameters like companies represented, industry, size of the firm, and form of ownership.

Data was collected using a focused face-to-face interview, a qualitative method of gathering primary research data. Interview guide covered 10 topics[3], in this paper 3 of them are analyzed in detail (since they address 3 research questions set): perception (interpretation) of terms and concepts and/or motivation for responsible and ethical behavior; regulation of ethical behavior within a company; firm's initiatives in business ethics and social responsibility. Authors also took into account information about a respondent and a company that he/she represents.

Editors of the special issue of the "Academy of Management Journal" outline that qualitative research draw attention to under-explored aspects of theory and contribute to its development (Bansal & Corley, 2011). This approach is valuable in the process of studying SMEs' practices of responsible behavior, which are not largely demonstrated to the public through non-financial reporting as in the case of large public corporations. Interviewing as a method of data gathering proved its efficiency in numerous researches related to social responsibility of business (Andreini, Pedeliento & Signori, 2014; Chirikova, 2006, 2007; Hammann et al., 2009; Öberseder, Schlegelmilch & Murphy, 2013; Treviño, den Nieuwenboer, Kreiner & Bishop, 2014; Vyakarnam et al., 1997). According to the literature dedicated to the methodology, methods and techniques of social research (Denzin & Lincoln, 2000; Iadov, 2003; Locke, 2001; Shteinberg, 2009), interviewing allows to realize researcher's plans in minor details and explain attitudes, relations and behavior patterns of people in real life and organizational reality.

Unlike the quantitative surveys where researchers form particular scales, open questions in interviews allow respondents to express their attitudes towards the topic of discussion and state arguments supporting those attitudes, as well as illustrate those attitudes with cases and examples from business practice. The number of papers based on qualitative research in management journals in the last two decades showed an exponential increase (Bass & Milosevic, 2016). The most popular research topics included organizational conditions for various forms of CSR (Andreini et al., 2014), stakeholder approach (Bagire, Tusiime, Nalweyiso & Kakooza, 2011). Remarkable papers focused on issues of CSR and business ethics were published by many authors (Treviño, den Nieuwenboer & Kish-Gephart, 2014; Treviño, den Nieuwenboer, Kreiner, et al., 2014; Treviño, Hartman, & Brown, 2000; Treviño, Weaver, Gibson & Toffler, 1999), they included ones based on the interview method and the methodology of grounded theory. In this case, the reliability of the data obtained is achieved by a detailed description of the transition process from quantitative data to theory enrichment (Bansal & Corley, 2011, p. 236).

Questions that presumed evaluation and sharing of an opinion or a point of view were open and allowed for detailed answers. Only one section of the questionnaire (set of data about a respondent and his/her company) was composed of closed questions of a social and demographic nature. The average duration of an interview was 58 minutes. The minimal duration was 45 minutes. The maximum was 2 hours and 5 minutes.

Interviews were audio-recorded and transcribed following transcription conventions for qualitative research. Analysis was conducted using the original Russian transcripts. An average volume of an interview transcript was 20 pages, single-line spacing. According to Denzin and Lincoln (2000, pp. 273-285), authors of this study consistently realized research procedures. Besides, Denzin and Lincoln (2000) argued that researchers should approach their work with a bundle of skills, assumptions, and practices that are used in the transition from paradigm into the empirical world.

At the first stage, the authors carried out open coding on the data to identify general groups of responsible business practices and make a general list of codes. Interviews were analyzed until knowledge saturation was reached. The authors discussed preliminary assumptions through several rounds until the meanings of codes and assumptions were unambiguously clarified. Categories were identified inductively from the data set. However, the authors used theoretical concepts to label the categories (e.g., individual, organizational, and social levels of responsible business practices). The authors defined categories by separate text fragments in which respondents discuss various types of responsible practices, offering examples or cases to illustrate their practices.

During the next stage of the iterative analysis, the authors repeatedly checked the categories, added data, and updated when necessary. In the final stage, the authors checked and coded all data by applying the resulting coding scheme. As a result, the authors categorized all perceptions and topical nuances from the data set, producing a structural chart illustrating key ideas and perceptions of Russian SMEs toward responsible behavior.

Table 2. Detailed description of the research sample (industries of national economy presented by 57 respondents, types of their business (b2b, b2c), participation of foreign investors or shareholders etc.)

Industry according to state classification	Description of the business	Number of employees	Respondent's position	Foreign investors or share-holders	Type of business
Retail and Catering Total: 8	Internet-trade in paints	1-15	Manager	No	B2C
	Beauty supplies	16-100	Manager	Yes	B2C
	Used-car dealership	1-15	Manager	No	B2C
	Sale of fish and other seafood	1-15	Manager	No	B2C
	Public catering, restaurant	16-100	CEO	No	B2C
	Production and delivery of bathroom equipment	16-100	Deputy CEO	Yes	B2C
	Public catering, restaurant	16-100	Manager	No	B2C
	Public catering, restaurant	16-100	Manager	No	B2C
Domestic trade Total: 7	Distribution of Apple products	1-15	CEO	No	B2C
	Sale of consumer goods and construction materials	16-100	CEO	No	B2C
	Sale of perfumes and cosmetics	16-100	Department Head	No	B2C
	Sale of children's clothes	1-15	Owner	No	B2C
	Distribution of consumer goods	16-100	Department Head	No	B2C
	Sale of construction materials	1-15	Manager	No	B2B
	Sale of construction materials	1-15	Manager	No	B2B
Finance, credit, insurance, pension Total: 7	Banking services	16-100	Chair of the Executive Board	No	B2B
	Auditing services	16-100	Manager	No	B2B
	Auditing services	16-100	Manager	No	B2B
	Mobile acquiring	16-100	Department Head	Yes	B2B
	Mobile acquiring	16-100	Department Head	Yes	B2B
	Consulting and financial services	1-15	CEO	No	B2B
	Collection services	1-15	Manager	No	B2B
IT Total: 5	Development and maintenance of software	1-15	Manager	No	B2B
	IT-services and data processing	1-15	Manager	No	B2B
	Development and maintenance of software	16-100	Manager	No	B2B
	Development and maintenance of software	16-100	Deputy CEO	No	B2B
	Video game development	16-100	Manager	No	B2C
General commercial activity for sustainable market functioning Total: 4	PR-agency in fashion industry	16-100	Client Manager	Yes	B2B
	Personnel recruitment and development	16-100	Manager	Yes	B2B
	HR-branding	16-100	Sales Manager	No	B2B
	Training and consulting services	16-100	Manager	No	B2B
Transportation Total: 4	Taxi services and road transportation	16-100	CEO	No	B2C
	Freight logistics services	16-100	Department Head	Yes	B2B
	Freight logistics services	16-100	Deputy CEO	No	B2B
	Freight logistics services	16-100	Manager	No	B2B
Other types of activities in the material production sector Total: 3	Repair of equipment	1-15	Owner	No	B2B
	Electrical maintenance	16-100	CEO	No	B2B
	-	16-100	Manager	No	B2B

continued on following page

Table 2. Continued

Industry according to state classification	Description of the business	Number of employees	Respondent's position	Foreign investors or share-holders	Type of business
Chemical and petrochemical industry (without chemical and pharmaceutical sector) Total: 3	Styrofoam processing	16-100	Department Head	No	B2B
	Production of natural insulation	1-15	Manager	No	B2B
	Chemical manufacturing	16-100	Manager	Yes	B2B
Culture and Art Total: 2	Advertising agency	16-100	Head of the Group	Yes	B2B
	Theatre classes and drama training	1-15	Manager	No	B2C
Civil engineering, general construction and specialized organizations involved in construction, installation or similar works on a contractual basis Total: 2	Architectural and engineering design of buildings and installations	16-100	CEO	No	B2B
	Architectural and engineering design of buildings and installations	16-100	Manager	No	B2B
Construction Total: 2	Construction works	1-15	Manager	No	B2B
	Construction works	16-100	Manager	No	B2B
Healthcare, physical culture and social care Total: 1	Touristic services	16-100	Sales manager	No	B2C
Public associations Total: 1	Ecological expertise and activities	1-15	Deputy CEO	No	B2B
Geology and mineral exploration, land survey, hydrometeorological service Total: 1	Land management and geodesy	16-100	Deputy CEO	No	B2B
Forestry, timber, wood processing, pulp and paper industry Total: 1	Saw miling, sale of timber	16-100	CEO	No	B2B
Public education Total: 1	Foreign Language training	16-100	CEO	Yes	B2C
Real estate Total: 1	Real estate agency	16-100	Manager	No	B2C
Industrial production Total: 1	Coal mining	16-100	Manager	Yes	B2B
Telecommunications Total: 1	Maintenance and repair of satellite communications equipment	16-100	CEO	No	B2B
Information cannot be disclosed[4] **Total: 2**	-	16-100	Manager		
	-	16-100	Manager		
Total	**57**				

Source: Created by authors from research results

ANTICIPATED RESULTS

Perception of Terms "Business Ethics", "Corporate Social Responsibility" and "Social Responsibility of Business" by SMEs

The first research question focused on how managers and business owners of Russian SMEs perceive the terms "business ethics," "corporate social responsibility," and "social responsibility of business." In the beginning of the interview, respondents were asked to explain their understanding of these concepts. They were asked to finalize the following phrases:

Figure 1. Summarized answers of respondents regarding "social responsibility" and "business ethics"

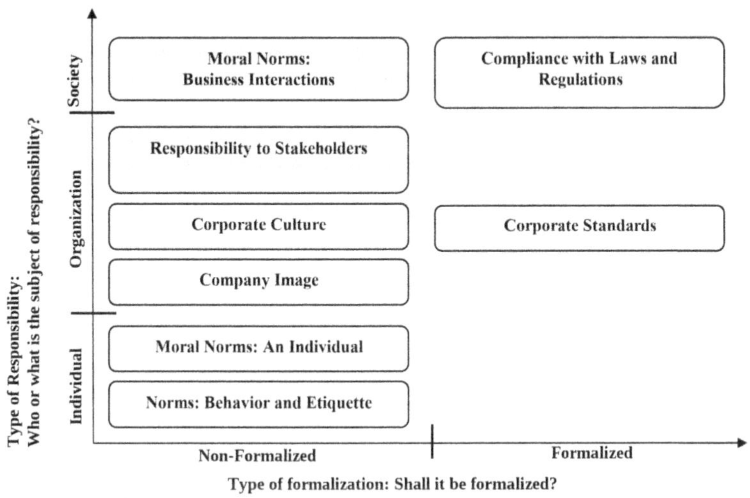

- "In my mind, socially responsible business means ..."
- "Business ethics is ..."
- "Corporate social responsibility means ..."

Research results indicated that respondents had a vague understanding of the concept of corporate social responsibility and social responsibility of business. Most respondents admitted that they did not understand the terms. In the wording of those questions, the authors used the term "corporate social responsibility." This caused a reaction from some interviewees, which indirectly supported the authors' initial intention to differentiate the terms "corporate social responsibility" (believing this term was more applicable to activities of large corporations) and "social responsibility of business" (more appropriate for describing practices of responsible behavior in the case of SMEs).

...it (CSR — authors) is more relevant to large companies, while our firm is quite small, so we do not develop this function, this specific direction of activity. We just do not spend our time on this. (Manager – here and further we indicate the position of a respondent)

In one way or another, most entrepreneurs admitted that they do not completely understand the meaning of corporate social responsibility and social responsibility of business. Some related CSR to companies' social or ecological projects. Few people defined a firm as socially responsible when it cares about its social sphere or employee solidarity. Some interpreted CSR as a legal responsibility of a firm. The discussion around social responsibility of business created the following rhetorical questions and reflections:

- Can a business be socially responsible?
- Who is responsible: a firm or a businessman?
- To whom are we responsible?

In general, these questions are not settled in the minds of entrepreneurs. Meanwhile, ninety percent of executives and owners of SMEs noted "voluntary nature" as a common feature of social responsibility.

Following the respondents' interpretations, the authors made conclusions on the interviewees' perception of the terms and the ratio of interpretations. The authors then found the criteria for those differences (see Figure 1). These are grouped using two criteria, one of which is taken from the approach of Clarkson (1995). First, the type of social responsibility by subject includes an individual, an organization, or a society. It looks at individual responsibility, organizational responsibility, and institutional responsibility. Second, the type of formalizing responsibility includes both formalized and non-formalized responsibility.

The authors described the meanings of business ethics, as expressed by respondents. Meanings ranged by frequency of mentions in the interviews. After some generalization of perceptions expressed by respondents, the authors identified eight angles of interpretation.

According to angles 1-2, respondents perceived business ethics mostly in two ways (gray color in the Figure 1): first, it is viewed as an organization's responsibility toward its stakeholders (organizational level, non-formalized responsibility) and second, business ethics is seen as a system of moral norms (institutional level, non-formalized responsibility). These two angles are most representative among the answers of respondents, and opinions divided almost equally.

In the first case, 31.5% of respondents perceived business ethics as an instrument to regulate relations of a firm with its internal and external environment: *It presumes certain rules of interaction inside the company and between the company and its external shareholders* (Deputy CEO); *It is a set of rules, both articulated and unspoken, that we follow in our business practice when dealing with clients, employees, and bosses* (Department Head).

In the second case, 24.5% of respondents emphasized an importance of business ethics as a system of moral norms (i.e., honesty, respect, openness, fidelity to one's word, civilized interaction) to regulate business relations and major rules of "a business on a particular market": *There are certain rules of behavior, traditions, and patterns that businessmen, as well as employees, are not obliged (but are recommended) to follow* (Manager). In this context, business ethics is perceived as a norm of a right, honest practice of doing business as opposed to a wrong, dishonest practice.

Angles 3-6 are related to the perception of business ethics (they are less numerous and include 7% to 8% of respondents).

According to the 3rd angle, business ethics means following legal requirements (institutional level, formalized responsibility). The company must follow industrial regulations and local and federal legal norms. This view is spread among representatives of companies that provide financial, consulting, tourist, and advertisement services. Legal regulation is high in these industries, which is expressed by a quote: *Business ethics is expressed in legislation* (Manager). It is remarkable that respondents share this view from medium enterprises in public-private partnerships. These respondents also act as suppliers or direct stakeholders in large corporations, participating in social or ecological activities: *The company's compliance to all necessary requirements and state regulations, in a sense, is what makes it ethical ... at least from the legal point of view* (Deputy CEO).

As to the 4th angle, business ethics means "corporate culture" (organizational level, non-formalized responsibility). In this case, business ethics is seen as a set of unspoken regulations related to employee behavior: *Business ethics refers to interactions inside the company ... it is largely defined by its corporate culture* (Deputy CEO). *I do not often talk about business ethics throughout my professional career. I rather believe that this is something people just know ... discussions here are redundant* (Manager).

Followers of the 5th angle see business ethics as a set of "corporate standards" (organizational level, formalized responsibility). In the fifth case, respondents emphasized the codified nature of norms expressed in standards and regulations. Corporate rules and standards are used in decisions on ethical dilemmas, conflict resolution, and professional communication.

Both the 4th and the 5th angles consider business ethics as attributes of an organization. However, they hold different views on the nature of formalization.

The 6th angle in this group is the view of business ethics as a set of individual moral norms (individual level, non-formalized type of responsibility). In this context, the focus is on moral norms inherent to a particular businessman (i.e., honesty, decency, respect).

The final two angles (7th and 8th) of perception of business ethics are presented by only two to three people per case. As for the 7th angle, business ethics is viewed as the company's image on the market (organizational level, non-formalized responsibility). As for the 8th angle, business ethics is the etiquette or good manners of behavior (individual level, non-formalized responsibility): *Business ethics refers to the way employees interact with each other at work or the way a company treats its employees, customers, partners, etc* (Manager). These respondents neglected the role of business ethics as a social institution and a regulator of a company's business interactions.

In general, while talking about the subject of responsible and ethical behavior, respondents often referred to an organizational level. Entrepreneurs and managers in SMEs perceived social responsibility and business ethics as attributes of organizational behavior.

In rare cases, business ethics and social responsibility were considered as individual or institutional features. Those respondents perceived business ethics and social responsibility as norms, including ideal goals and values (i.e., market reputation of the company, responsibility to stakeholders, dignity, respect). These are, in fact, barely formalized.

There was also a small portion of respondents who pointed at an instrumental role of business ethics, mentioning instruments and tools to manage ethical behavior (i.e., corporate standards, rules, channels of communication, sets of values, standards of behavior).

Most respondents found it difficult to distinguish between ethical and responsible behavior. Therefore, this research paper will use these notions as synonyms.

Motivation of Ethical and Responsible Behavior Among Russian SMEs

Research outcomes outline rational motivators and a conscious approach to following principles and patterns of responsible behavior among representatives of Russian SMEs. An overall result of the survey proved the weakness of an earlier quoted belief stating that Russian SMEs are not interested in aspects of ethical and socially responsible behavior (Balashova, 2009; Savicheva, 2010).

In this study, three groups of respondents were identified following criteria related to their emotional attitude toward the concept of social responsibility. 60% were termed "followers" because they followed ethical and responsible behaviors. 14% were termed "skeptics" because they did not believe that principles of business ethics and practices of responsible behavior were relevant to operations of for-profit organizations in general. 25% of respondents did not perceive business ethics and social responsibility as essential concepts for SMEs (as opposed to large corporations). This final group argued that both concepts were irrelevant for Russian SMEs due to specifics of the economic and business environment.

Table 3. Content analysis results of motivation for ethical and responsible behavior

Motives for Socially Responsible/ Ethical Behavior	Directed to	Indicators of Ethical and Responsible Behavior	Frequency of Mentions	
			Frequency of mentions	% of mentions in the group
Caring For Stakeholders	Customers	**Total, including:**	**108**	**100,0**
		Polite treatment of customers	32	29,6
		Maintaining high quality of goods/services	31	28,7
		Providing information additional to technical characteristics of goods/services	12	11,1
		Careful work with customer complaints	12	11,1
		Attention to feedback from the customer	11	10,2
		Provision of fair information about the quality of a goods/service	7	6,5
		Conflict resolution	3	2,8
	Employees	**Total, including:**	**71**	**100,0**
		Benefits additional to ones prescribed by labor regulation, assistance in critical situations	15	21,1
		Maintaining productive atmosphere at work	11	15,5
		Support to new and young employees	11	15,5
		Atmosphere of respect among employees at work	9	12,7
		Friendly treatment of employees by managers and owners	9	12,7
		Supportive teamwork	9	12,7
		Support knowledge transfer and exchange	7	9,8
	Local Communities	**Total, including:**	**31**	**100,0**
		Care about ecological situation	22	71,0
		Participation in community initiatives	9	29,0
Meeting State Requirements	Employees, clients	**Total, including:**	**60**	**100,0**
		Tax payments and privileges	27	45,0
		Investments in ecological issues	22	36,7
		Fulfillment of warranties	11	18,3
Search of Competitive Advantages	Company Strengths	**Total, including:**	**42**	**100,0**
		Stimulation of employees' productive behavior and engagement	12	28,6
		Stable, positive relations with employees	10	23,8
		High internal standards of doing business	7	16,7
		Customer focus	6	14,3
		Reputation improvement	5	11,9
		Attractive image of an employer	2	4,7

Source: Created by authors from research results

After analyzing respondents' attitudes and answers, this study found 25 motives of socially responsible and ethical behavior. These motives were then presented in three major groups: (1) building a sustainable relationship with stakeholders; (2) meeting state requirements; and (3) searching for competitive advantage. All interviews counted the number of phrases and expressions that characterize a certain motive (see Table 3).

According to the authors' definition, socially responsible behavior goes beyond the norms and requirements set by authorities and/or the community. It is voluntary (voluntary contribution and/or initiatives).

The first group of motives for responsible behavior related to a firm's need to interact and maintain sustainable relationships with stakeholders. One of the most frequently mentioned stakeholder group was "customer." Respondents were aware that principles of business ethics and responsible behavior are essential for establishing a sustainable relationship of trust between a business and its customer. Among the characteristics of ethical and responsible behavior, respondents mentioned the following (listed in descending order of the number of mentions – see Table 3):

1. Polite treatment of customers.
2. Maintaining high quality of goods/services.
3. Providing information additional to technical characteristics of goods/services.
4. Careful work with customer complaints.
5. Attention to feedback from customer.
6. Provision of fair information about the quality of a good/service.
7. Conflict resolution.

Most respondents outlined that customer relations in their organization are regulated informally. A few admitted that their organizations had formalized ethical standards in this field. This group of motives is more common for respondents from companies representing the tertiary sector of the national economy (services). Respondents, in this case, are chief executives and business owners. In rare cases, respondents, in this case, are linear managers. There were representatives from service companies who did not mention the importance of responsible behavior in relation to customers. It may be possible to conclude that this motive is related to the respondent's position in a company and scope of obligations (i.e., interaction with clients, focus on clients, or attitude toward a firm) or the industry and their status in the company.

"Employee" was the second group listed in the section "Caring for Stakeholders". An intention to attract and retain strategic employees, as well as gain an attractive image of an employer, motivates entrepreneurs to act responsibly. In some answers, respondents identified employees as the main stakeholders of their businesses.

Many respondents considered business ethics as a vital tool for managing human resources. According to this study's data set, indicators of responsible behavior include (in descending order of the number of mentions – see Table 3):

1. Benefits additional to ones prescribed by labor regulation.
2. Assistance in critical situations.
3. Maintaining a productive atmosphere at work.
4. Support for new and young employees.
5. Atmosphere of respect among employees at work.

6. Friendly treatment of employees by managers and owners.
7. Supportive teamwork.
8. Support of knowledge transfer and exchange.

Socially responsible behavior of an employer to employees is reflected in both interpersonal relations and strict adherence to labor contracts and legislation. Meanwhile, interpersonal relations are often used for compensating an absence of formal mechanisms for regulating labor relations (or even *instead* of those mechanisms).

We have a certain charter ... but we almost do not use it [for resolving problematic situations]. We try to understand what is reasonable and what is unreasonable ... we treat each other as good friends who can provide valuable advice in case of need (Manager).

Other groups of stakeholders listed by respondents included local communities and socially vulnerable groups like older people, veterans, young people, disabled people, and orphans. Socially responsible behavior directed to those stakeholders include arrangements to improve regional ecological situations and participation in initiatives important to local citizens and activist organizations.

In rare cases, respondents mentioned business partners as crucial addressers of their ethical and responsible behavior. In some answers, partners were seen these addressers.

We also care about our dealers and partners ... this refers not only to the fact that we help each other to earn money, but also that we treat each other with due level of respect and honesty. If we promised something to one partner, it is inappropriate to play games and try to negotiate the same thing behind his back with someone else. Our corporate promise is not just a set of words. I can say the same about business ethics. For years, we've built the company's reputation. Believe me, it means a lot. You can lose it in one day. At the same time, you'll lose your customers and partners (CEO).

Some respondents offered examples related to their firm's refusal to partner with certain businesses due to ethical concerns: *We do not work with companies that produce and sell alcohol or tobacco. The aim of our business activity is to help clients develop their ideas, achieve better results, grow further ... the growth of those companies [the ones dealing with alcohol and tobacco products] only creates harmful consequences for the health of the population in our country* (Manager).

Respondents did not often list competitors as market agents that influence their firms' financial sustainability and reputation. However, in some interviews, respondents named competitors as a stakeholder group of concern.

The second group of motives impacting responsible behavior, is related to meeting state requirements and regulations. Indicators of responsible behavior in this group include paying taxes and privileges, investing in ecological sustainability, and fulfilling warranties. This motivation is common for managers and company owners from mining businesses, manufacturing and production plants, catering companies, advertising agencies, firms providing logistics services, and rare (at least in this data set) social enterprises:

State authorities form a major institution that maintains certain order and requires honest behavior from market players in different industries. In our country, company activities that may be considered dishonest, corrupt, or infringing upon other parties are clearly set in the Federal Anti-Corruption Law

... creating and conducting an illegal business (production and dissemination of drugs, cases of extortion, etc.) are prohibited by law and presumed criminal liability. State authorities pay considerable attention to anti-monopoly and anti-trust regulation, creating conditions for a healthy and competitive market environment (Deputy CEO).

According to the respondent, his organization carefully follows industrial regulations. State controlling bodies closely monitor the process of executing obligations.

Respondents also focused on the nature of voluntary or "voluntarily forced" choice made by their companies in favor of socially responsible behavior. They emphasized that the controlling function of state authorities does not cover the sphere of relations between companies. Therefore, it is a "blind area" of ethical regulation.

... for state authorities it does not that much matter how firms interact with each other as long as they keep within legal boundaries ... but they demand certain reverence toward themselves ... (Manager)

The third group of motives to ethical and responsible behavior among Russian SMEs is rather rationale and based on firms' search for competitive advantage. Those advantages, according to some respondents, emerge in response to the responsible behavior of the company directed at customers and/or employees. In the long run, practices of ethical and responsible behavior contribute to the improvement of a firm's reputation, its positive perception as an employer, and faster adaptation of new employees to corporate rules. It also results in a stronger corporate culture, employee loyalty, and effective implementation of customer-oriented techniques in sales. Lastly, responsible behavior results in improved labor productivity and overall efficiency of the firm's performance.

Business ethics improves efficiency and effectiveness of both the team of employees and a business as a whole. If employees follow rules of ethical and responsible behavior, they interact with each other with higher efficiency ... their output and motivation to work are constantly growing. As a consequence, it results in improved productivity (Manager).

Analysis of the ethical and responsible approaches of the "followers" and "skeptics" to business shows that the last group consists of most owners of the SMEs. The authors assume that their skepticism is related to their strong belief that the goal of profit drives a business. This group of respondents doubts that an honest business can survive:

It is quite difficult to run a business at the moment, at least in our country ... being an honest person with high moral values ... you have to forget those values if you wish to succeed. (Owner)

It is important to mention that a skeptical attitude was often expressed by respondents who demonstrated a narrow understanding of business ethics, perceiving it as a behavior or etiquette. They did not believe the sincerity of counterparts who emphasized the importance of social responsibility and business ethics. According to skeptics, those "good" businesses are trying to follow practices from developed countries or "fashion trends."

Table 4. Social responsibility practices of Russian SMEs

Category	Frequency of mentions	
	Frequency of mentions	% of mentions in the group
Initiator of an Initiative	**32**	**100,0**
From top to bottom (from top manager or owner to employees)	24	75,0
From bottom to top (from employees)	8	25,0
Target Groups of Initiatives	**45**	**100,0**
Young people	9	20,0
Veterans (WWII, etc.)	14	31,1
Vulnerable social groups	19	42,2
Local communities	3	6,7
Areas of Social Responsible Practices According to the Russian National Standard (Guidance for Social Responsibility) GOST R ISO 26000-2012	**125**	**100,0**
Responsible management practices	6	4,8
Human rights	3	2,4
Labor relation	34	27,2
Environmental issues	22	17,6
Compliance practices	14	11,2
Consumer relations	37	29,6
Participation in the life and development of local communities	9	7,2
Internal Orientation of Responsible Behavior	**110**	**100,0**
Creation of attractive jobs	13	11,8
Stable payment of wages	31	28,2
Keeping wages at a socially meaningful level	6	5,5
Security and safety of labor	11	10,0
Additional medical and social insurance for employees	15	13,6
Professional development of human resources through educational programs, trainings, and programs of qualification improvement	9	8,2
Assistance in critical situations (complicated diseases requiring expensive treatment, long-term absence of employees, sudden death or accidents with employees' family members, etc.)	7	6,4
Doing business effectively, creation of added value, and contributing to the growth of shareholders' welfare	18	16,3
External Orientation of Responsible Behavior	**106**	**100,0**
Rigorous execution of state requirements related to taxation, employee-employer relations, ecological sustainability, etc.	27	25,5
Sponsorship and charity	19	17,9
Ecological initiatives	22	20,8
Building fair relations with all stakeholders	5	4,7
Considering public expectations and accepted ethical norms in the practice of business	9	8,5
Building dialogue with state and municipal authorities, local activist groups, and communities	6	5,6
Maintaining high-quality standards for goods/services produced	18	17,0

Source: Created by authors from research results

In most cases this [following principles of ethical and responsible behavior] is just a fashion trend. We all know that Russians like to follow ideas that come from western countries ... and as we can see, adopting principles of business ethics is one of those popular fashion trends. (Manager)

Others argued that practices of ethical and responsible behavior represent a marketing tool to manage a firm's reputation and image:

Most important is how it looks in the eyes of an external environment. It is actually the company's image (Deputy CEO).

In this particular study, the authors did not investigate respondents' motives for neglecting the importance and topicality of business ethics and social responsibility. However, studying those motives could become a challenging direction for further research. Additional research could study the connection between SMEs' motivation to ethical and responsible behavior and existing practices of such behavior.

Priorities in Choosing Patterns of Ethical and Responsible Behavior In Case of Russian SMEs

Open sources rarely publish SMEs' information regarding their initiatives in the field of social responsibility. Portions of information on their activities can be found in the news section of Websites of the Russian Chamber of Commerce & Industry, All-Russian Public Organization "Business Russia" (promoting ideas and initiatives of social entrepreneurship), All-Russian Non-Governmental Organization of Small and Medium Businesses "OPORA ROSSII", Small and Medium Enterprise Development Association, regional foundations aimed at the development and support of SMEs, etc. Particular information may be taken from a newly established web-page of the Russian Business Ethics Network RBEN. The segments of Russian SMEs, in general, is hardly available for surveys. Therefore, the authors tried to find information from respondents on company arrangements and initiatives in the field of social responsibility.

Table 4 contains the quantitative results of this research related to SMEs' practices of responsible behavior. The authors took one respondent's reference to a practice of responsible behavior, initiative, or arrangement in this field as an account unit. Detailed qualitative analysis of respondents' answers to the questions from an interview guide allowed the authors to exclude multiple references to the same practices (initiatives or arrangements) in one interview, even if they were different descriptions.

When referring to responsible behavior according to the Russian National Standard (Guidance for Social Responsibility) GOST R ISO 26000-2012 (Russian National Standard), respondents mentioned those aimed at building sustainable relations with consumers (37 times – 29,6% of responses), labor relations or building sustainable relations with employees (34 times – 27,2% of responses), and practices to protect and preserve the environment and ecosystem (22 times – 17,6% of responses). The authors also considered that three cases of practice mentioned by respondents could be related to human rights, which is a group of responsible behavior practices traditionally unpopular in the Russian business community. Representatives of three companies with practices in this group noted that such activities are prescribed by strict industrial regulation, including debt collection firms, advertising agencies as members of powerful international associations, etc. Some practices mentioned by respondents were conditionally classified as referring to "compliance practices" and "responsible management practices" (according to the Russian National Standard [Guidance for Social Responsibility] GOST R ISO 26000-2012) (Russian National Standard).

Approximately one-third of respondents neglected organizational practices of responsible behavior, social initiatives, or projects aimed at external shareholders. SMEs' representatives explained that companies within their segment must focus on internal issues, operations management, and effective and efficient performance. Larger businesses may increase their social investments and projects, taking resources from the company's core business processes. At the same time, respondents from this group (along with others) found importance in internally-oriented responsible practices aimed at maintaining stable wages (31 references – 28,2% of responses); professional development of human resources through educational programs, trainings, and programs of qualification improvement (9 references – 8,2% of responses); doing business effectively, creation of added value, and contributing to the growth of shareholders' welfare (18 references – 16,3% of responses).

There are cases when companies decide to provide additional[5] payments (fringe benefits) and privileges to employees as part of their social responsibility:

We cannot spend a lot of money on charity. We invest some modest funds that we have in our employees, their health, and productivity. We provide them with corporate cards for fitness centers, every week we all play football (we rent a comfortable space for this), and we always pay salaries and bonuses on time and according to promises that were made to employees. We never save money on social payments to state funds ... and in many cases cover the cost of vocation for employees if they are on a payroll. I believe our company is extremely good in this sense and can be considered an attractive employer (CEO);

Our company attempts to improve working conditions for its employees so they feel comfortable here. We invest in their health care, they all have medical insurance, and we regularly deliver professional training to improve employees' qualification. Of course, we arrange corporate holidays and parties, which are usually very well-accepted by everyone in our professional team (Manager)/

In the section "Internal Orientation of Responsible Behavior" in Table 4, the authors registered 13 respondents (11,8% of responses) references regarding companies creating attractive jobs for their employees. Nevertheless, their perception of an attractive job is different from definitions published by international organizations (for instance, an international labor organization). Entrepreneurs and managers from Russian SMEs often evaluate job attractiveness by looking at comfortable work conditions and stability or rate of salary. However, they classified those features as attributes of job attractiveness. Therefore, the authors found it possible to include those references into the table's results.

In some cases, respondents outlined two reasons for the unpopularity of externally oriented responsible practice. These include the individual nature of social responsibility and cases of corruption in the process of implementing those projects.

Russia faced a difficult economic situation during the interview period. This fact adds to the discussion of the revealed position. The authors found a series of publications focused on the shift of companies' opinions related to social responsibility caused by economic and/or financial crisis or a downturn in the economic cycle (Chan et al., 2010; Linsley & Slack, 2013; Rodionova, 2011).

However, a prevailing number of respondents confirmed that their companies follow "externally oriented" practices of social responsibility, support various social initiatives (in most cases they bear an unsystematic order), and are related to the core business of an SME. These include free haircuts for low-income individuals, free restaurant meals for vulnerable social groups, and recycling of foam plastics.

The section titled "External Orientation of Responsible Behavior" shows that it is possible to identify key directions of SMEs' external social efforts and arrangements. "Rigorous execution of state requirements related to taxation, employee-employer relations, ecological sustainability, etc." was mentioned by 27 respondents (25,5% of responses) from the sample. Twenty-two respondents (20,8%) referenced "ecological initiatives." These arrangements are popular among medium-sized businesses, covering the regulation of harmful emissions or investing in production equipment to minimize harmful ecological effects in the region surrounding the plant's location:

... our company uses modern equipment to decrease emissions and avoid any harmful impact that a chemical plant can make to the nature (Manager).

Respondents who represented medium-sized construction organizations noted that their firms invest in ecological improvements like sewage treatment plants, roads for transportation, and the regulation of waste treatment in their regions.

Special activities included organizational participation in ecological programs like "Rivers Flow to the Seas," the transfer of funds to national ecological foundations, and participation in environmental movements like the Green Movement. SMEs also participate in environmental protection.

We do not throw storage batteries into regular waste baskets. We put them into a separate box and then into special containers ... we bring them to a battery-processing plant that we build for recycling and processing used storage batteries from our production equipment (CEO).

Nineteen respondents (17,9%) referenced "Sponsorship and Charity" as social initiatives directed to external environments. This practice is common in SMEs. Aid from SMEs is usually directed to representatives of vulnerable social groups:

We offer free meals for older people with low incomes ... especially during big holidays like Victory Day. We invite all veterans of World War II and other military conflicts ... we serve holiday dinners (Manager);

We prefer to help each case individually (to a particular child or an older person). We arrange celebrations or concerts for retired people ... we think that it is more effective to trace where our aid is going. We do not trust much to charity foundations where you just transfer the money and they decide where those money go (CEO);

We provide help to families with many children. At some point we just decided that those are children that need opportunities and options for better futures, education, etc. (Deputy CEO).

A few managers mentioned that their companies had initiated special social projects:

We've helped a few animal shelters in the Moscow region. We all like animals and care about their well-being (Manager);

We invest in making social videos. These attract the attention of society to pressing issues: homeless children, orphans, disabled people, older people with low income, safety of pedestrians and drivers, etc. We are involved in various charity initiatives. We sponsor the participation of children with disabilities, orphans in various cultural programs, concerts, master classes ... they enjoy the same opportunities as other children and we try to make their lives better (Department Head).

Some respondents mentioned organizational participation in charitable initiatives:

... any employee is free to cooperate with an orphanage or a charity foundation or help a person in need. We believe that this is an individual's choice. We do not have any special department in our company to deal with those issues ... I am involved in social activities (Manager).

Eighteen respondents (17,0%) noted "Maintaining High-Quality Standards for Goods/Services Produced" in the section titled "External Orientation of Responsible Behavior. Nine representatives (8,5%) valued considering public expectations and accepted ethical norms in the practice of doing business.

The authors outlined two trends when connecting the companies' social projects with their industries. Ecological initiatives and concerns were more common with manufacturing and production plants, information technology companies, advertising agencies, and organizations specializing in ecological issues. Charity and sponsorship initiatives were popular among firms that work with large flows of clients (first of all, b2c but in some cases b2b as well). These include construction, catering, and cosmetology/beauty.

CONCLUSION

The first research question of this study is based on conclusions from a review of previous research by Neverov & Davydenkova (2016). Outcomes of the research and analysis show that representatives of Russian SMEs demonstrate a fragmented perception of the concept of social responsibility.

Empirical outcomes show that some respondents, including executives and owners of SMEs from the Central Federal Count of the Russian Federation, lack a complex understanding of business ethics and socially responsible behavior, as well as their relevance to their day-to-day operations. Meanwhile, respondents who expressed their opinion toward those concepts maintained the ethical context while also discussing responsible behavior. In general, survey outcomes are consonant with conclusions expressed in publications of (Ivashina, 2016; Neverov & Davydenkova, 2016).

This research paper also studied the motives and practices of socially responsible and ethical behavior of SMEs which was reflected in the second research question of the study. These motives and practices are mostly rational and were explained by each respondent's intent to achieve strategic competitive advantages for their business in the long run.

The survey questioned attitudes expressed by researchers in the field, particularly the belief that Russian SMEs are uninterested in business ethics and social responsibility because they are preoccupied with survival in uncertain economic conditions. Research outcomes showed that owners and executives of Russian SMEs demonstrated a growing consciousness and adherence to ethical and responsible behaviors. In fact, it is gaining popularity in this community of entrepreneurs. Companies do not only strive for economic profits, also, they are interested in long-term benefits resulting from their involvement in social and environmental issues.

Meanwhile, it is possible to conclude that representatives of Russian SMEs follow a client-oriented approach regarded as a social and cultural attribute of the CSR model. It corresponds to outcomes of research conducted by Hammann et al. (2009), which focused on responsible behavior of German SMEs, and survey results from the Czech Republic published by Pohludka & Stverkova (2019). It also corresponds to conclusions by Ivashina (2016), stating that SMEs in Russia and Italy lack a clear understanding of social responsibility and are not motivated for responsible behavior but in some cases, regard responsible behavior as a tool for creating effective, sustainable relations with strategic external stakeholder groups.

As opposed to conclusions of Ma (2012) who viewed altruism and philanthropic motivation of SMEs' owners as a reason for their businesses to follow principles of responsible behavior, Russian entrepreneurs are quite pragmatic: they have a long-term strategy of becoming sustainable and stable through exploring the benefits of being socially responsible. Outcomes of this study echo the conclusions of many authors (Chrisman & Archer, 1984; Spence & Lozano, 2000; Vitell et al., 2000) who outline that sustainable long-term relationship of SMEs with target groups of clients are crucial and considered by many of them as the best way to demonstrate socially responsible behavior. Chrisman & Archer (1984) argue that while small and medium enterprises are quite diverse, relationship with clients are regarded as important by all of them and act as the major driver for responsible behavior.

Conclusions of this study correspond to the points expressed by (Spence & Lozano, 2000), stating that owners and top-managers of small and medium firms in the UK are very much influenced by social and ethical issues related to their employees. These conclusions point at similar ethical context for responsible behavior in the case of Russian and British SMEs. Representatives of Russian SMEs, as well as their counterparts from Spain and Great Britain, tend to respect legal norms and requirements. Moreover, in many cases, this instrument regulates their relationship with the society in a more effective way than self-regulatory norms created to promote interests of the business community. However, it is important to keep in mind that similarities in commitment to legal norms and regulations does not mean that the numbers of law-abiding entrepreneurs in those countries are proportional. Results of this study do not state that 100% of Russian entrepreneurs completely follow the law.

Vitell et al. (2000) argues that in the case of North American SMEs, it is possible to say that their responsible behavior is mostly aimed at building sustainable relations with clients rather than with employees – authors of this study believe that Russian SMEs focus their practices of responsible behavior on both their clients and employees. At the same time, authors agree with the statement of Vitell et al. (2000) that SMEs see low expectations from society as the major factor contributing to ethical standards' reduction and that SMEs pay attention to the social sphere mostly because they can derive additional profit from this activity.

The Russian National Standard GOST R ISO 26000-2012 (Russian National Standard) listed seven common practices of socially responsible behavior. Representatives of Russian SMEs distinguished the following three as highest priority: (1) consumer relations; (2) labor relations; and (3) environmental issues. Therefore, it is possible to conclude that SMEs in Russia demonstrate responsible behavior to stakeholder groups that are involved in their operations. General results of analysis within the survey show that consumers and employees are considered strategic stakeholders by SMEs' representatives.

Developing sustainable relations with employees based on mutual trust and ethical principles allows SMEs to reduce the number of conflicts at work and enjoy employee loyalty and satisfaction within the organizational atmosphere. Many respondents indicated labor relations as a priority of responsible behavior. In the end, this results in higher productivity, lower costs, and lower labor turnover. This situation illustrates both paternalistic and pragmatic features common for executives and owners of SMEs in Russia. However, in this survey, consumer relations was a prioritized practice of responsible behavior mentioned by respondents.

These outcomes correspond to many conclusions (Bobrova & Kovaleva, 2015b; Ivashina, 2016; Pletnev & Nicolaeva, 2016). Bobrova & Kovaleva (2015a), who argue that owners and executives of Russian SMEs perceive employees and customers as the most important business stakeholders. They noted that responsible behavior contributes positively to building stable and loyal relationships with clients. In the long run, it strengthens the company's reputation, increases brand value, and contributes to revenue and profit growth. A contrasting conclusion is presented in the study by Sizova & Chilipenok (2017) who state that employers tend to minimize their responsibility with regard to employees, however, it was not possible to test this conclusion in the framework of the present research study, so it requires additional examination and shall be checked in separate interviews with representatives of Russian SMEs.

Results of this study match closely with conclusions by Hammann et al. (2009), and Vitell et al. (2000). These authors outline an important role of employees as an object and subject of SMEs' practices of responsible behavior. However, their conclusions reflect the fact that motivators like good business reputation, meeting social expectations, and reaching additional advantages and profit are crucial for shaping the responsible behavior of SMEs in developed countries.

Therefore, it is possible to conclude that the practice of responsible behavior is developing in Russia. Its paternalistic features include informal relationships, personal initiatives of entrepreneurs and employees, and pragmatic motives. The situation is generally positive, illustrating positive dynamics and continuous improvements of the quality of the business environment.

Research Limitations

This research has some limitations, which are related to the composition of the sample, the choice of a region for research, the choice of research indicators, and specific features of an interview as a method of gathering data. In fact, Central Federal Count is one of the most economically affluent regions of the Russian Federation, and this mean that outcomes gained from surveying SMEs located in this region can hardly be extended to a broader community of SMEs within the country and open up avenues of reflections related to particular groups of entrepreneurs.

This study does not focus on organizational and legal forms of SMEs under consideration, peculiarities related to SMEs being located in specific sub-regions within the Central Federal Count were not regarded as well. Therefore, this research does not allow to make any conclusions about differences in responsible practices and values of social responsibility that are relevant to SMEs from urban and rural areas.

Authors did not go into detailed discussions with respondents about possible business cooperation of their companies with large corporations. In fact, many large firms impose their values, codes of conduct and approaches to responsible behavior on the network of their suppliers and partners. In this regard, it is difficult to make any assumptions whether practices mentioned by respondents are specific for particular SMEs, or they are products of propagation and form part of a particular SMEs' relationship with major contractors.

Likewise, the research left aside the respondents' age groups. Although, the study found that representatives of senior generation in many cases are bound by values of paternalism, in contrast to their younger counterparts.

It should be pointed out that the volume of data and the region where a study was conducted can make an important difference to its overall outcomes and their further analysis. Thus, a careful attention shall be paid to the methodology of gathering data for particular research projects.

SOLUTIONS AND RECOMMENDATIONS

This study disclosed specific features inherent to the behavior of Russian entrepreneurs and characterizing Russian SMEs' motivation to responsible behavior. Strengthening of SMEs is an important target of Russia's macroeconomic development. According to the Strategy of Development for Small and Medium Enterprises published by the Russian Ministry of Economics and Development, the goal is to create 25 million jobs in SMEs by 2024. Its contribution to the Russian GDP is expected to increase up to 32.5% (The Russian Government, 09.06.2016).

Stimulating governmental activities and intervention may not be enough in the process of implementing these goals in practice, awareness creation and involvement may add effectiveness to this process. Outcomes of this study may provide food for further analysis and formulation of the growth points contrary to popular belief that small and medium enterprises are completely passive and uninterested in the matter of voluntary contribution to social initiatives. Russian Union of Entrepreneurs and Industrialists, representatives of large corporations, may be motivated by the outcomes of this research to include SMEs' representatives and activists into open dialogues and discussions dedicated to sustainable development, voluntary contribution to social initiatives, and responsible interaction with stakeholders.

A prospective way to promote values of responsible behavior and involve Russian SMEs into responsible practices can be an active promotion and dissemination of positive examples in this field. Important and popular business leaders may become ambassadors of ethical marketing practices and responsible behavior. Russian Business Ethics Network (RBEN) (Russian Business Ethics Network 2019) may also largely contribute to this process.

At the same time, citizens and communities shall also become aware and better informed about SMEs' responsible practices. The potential demand for this kind of activities on behalf of different groups of stakeholders shall be formed. For this purpose the Chamber of Commerce of Moscow suggests to introduce a Register of Responsible SMEs in Moscow and Moscow region. SMEs may be included in this Register if they voluntarily publish their non-financial reports which presume 12 parts. Moreover, this Register can provide the basis for larger companies in choosing providers and suppliers of intermediate goods and services for their businesses among SMEs. At the moment, 12 parts of the non-financial report for SMEs are discussed by experts and SMEs' representatives.

The practice of large corporations in developed economies where so-called "responsible supply networks" are created, may be relevant for the Russian business practice as well. Nowadays a growing number of Russian corporations start to spread their principles of responsible behavior on the network of their suppliers and partners, in this case SMEs have to meet certain requirements and standards that come from their major and strategically important partner. Interviews with representatives of this group of SMEs shall be designed differently than the ones for the general SMEs' community.

FUTURE RESEARCH DIRECTIONS

For further research in the field of business ethics, social responsibility of business and responsible practices among SMEs in Russia, the following issues may be relevant:

- social responsibility of business in case of SMEs: the latest fashion or a necessity?
- social, professional and status profiles of supporters and critics of SMEs' responsible behavior;
- best practices of SMEs' responsible behavior in particular economic sectors;
- instruments of governmental intervention that stimulate and motivate SMEs' responsible behavior;
- influence of cultural values on patterns of responsible behavior of SMEs.

Quantitative and qualitative research in this field may stimulate further scientific discussion and contribute to the institutionalization of social responsibility of business in the case of SMEs. In order to further develop the current research topic, it is essential to survey and interview representatives of Russian SMEs from various federal counts, outcomes from different locations can be then compared. This may produce interesting results since Russian federal counts vary considerably in the level of their economic development, an extent of SMEs' prevalence and in cultural specifics.

Following the logic of Bugai et al. (2014, 2015) it may be interesting to compare answers from SMEs representing different industries and locations (rural locations as opposed to the urban ones). Preliminary conclusions of the authors of this study show that in rural areas cases of responsible behavior on the part of SMEs are registered more frequently than in urban areas, since the social capital of SMEs in rural areas is more developed and is based on stronger and more sustainable relations with relatives and neighbors.

REFERENCES

Andreini, D., Pedeliento, G., & Signori, S. (2014). CSR and service quality in nonprofit organizations: The case of a performing arts association. *International Journal of Nonprofit and Voluntary Sector Marketing*, *19*(2), 127–142. doi:10.1002/nvsm.1488

Bagire, V. A., Tusiime, I., Nalweyiso, G., & Kakooza, J. B. (2011). Contextual environment and stakeholder perception of corporate social responsibility practices in Uganda. *Corporate Social Responsibility and Environmental Management*, *18*(2), 102–109. doi:10.1002/csr.252

Balashova, E. (2009). Problems and prospects of small business development in Russia. *Siberian Trade and Economic Journal,* (9), 3-5.

Bansal, P., & Corley, K. (2011). From the editors: The coming of age for qualitative research: Embracing the diversity of qualitative methods. The Academy of Management Journal, 54(2), 233-237.

Bass, A. E., & Milosevic, I. (2018). The ethnographic method in CSR research: The role and importance of methodological fit. *Business & Society*, *57*(1), 174–215. doi:10.1177/0007650316648666

Bataeva, B. S. (2010). Directions of formation of the Russian model of corporate responsibility. News of St. Petersburg State University, (5), 67-72.

Baumback, C. M. (1988). *How to organize and operate a small business*. Prentice Hall.

Blagov, Y. E. (2010). *Corporate social responsibility: the evolution of the concept. Graduate School of Management.-SPb*. Publishing House of the Graduate School of Management.

Bobrova, O. S., & Kovaleva, A. S. (2015a). How to do it? Russian businessmen about business: happiness and responsibility, innovative activity. *Russian Business, 16*(16), 2313-2498

Bobrova, O. S., & Kovaleva, A. S. (2015b). How to do it? Russian businessmen on business (according to the results of the survey of 2014): goals and motives. *Russian Business, 16*(15)б 2599-2618

Bugai, I. A., Akishina, M. L., & Fannenshtil', A. A. (2014). The level of social responsibility of the rural business and its impact on the development of rural areas. *Journal of the Altai State Agrarian University, 12*(122), 143–148.

Bugai, I. A., Akishina, M. L., & Fannenshtil', A. A. (2015). Impact of corporate social responsibility of rural business on rural employment and development of rural areas. *Journal of the Altai State Agrarian University*, *6*(128), 156–161.

Chan, K. C., Fung, H.-G., & Yau, J. (2010). Business ethics research: A global perspective. *Journal of Business Ethics*, *95*(1), 39–53. doi:10.100710551-009-0346-z

Chirikova, A. (2006). Business as a subject of social policy in modern Russia. *Society and Economy*, (9): 100–119.

Chirikova, A. (2007). Interaction of Government and business in the implementation of social policy: Regional projection. *Independent Institute for Social Policy*, *152*, 90.

Chrisman, J. J., & Archer, R. W. (1984). Small business social responsibility: Some perceptions and insights. *American Journal of Small Business*, *9*(2), 46–58. doi:10.1177/104225878400900206

Civil Code of the Russian Federation. (2017). Retrieved from http://www.consultant.ru/document/cons_doc_LAW_5142/

Clarkson, M. E. (1995). A stakeholder frameswork for analyzing and evaluating corporate social performance. *Academy of Management Review*, *20*(1), 92–117. doi:10.5465/amr.1995.9503271994

Denzin, N. K., & Lincoln, Y. (2000). *Qualitative research* (2nd ed.). Sage.

Dzhindzholiia, O. (2011). Social responsibility of small business (Sotsial'naia otvetstvennost' malogo predprinimatel'stva). *News of Volgograd State Technical University*, *4*(11), 99–103.

Federal Law of Russian Federation #209-FZ of July 24th, 2007. (n.d.). *About the Development of small and medium entrepreneurship in the Russian Federation.* ConsultantPlus. Retrieved from http://www.consultant.ru/cons/cgi/online.cgi?from=329368-0&rnd=B886EF15343A8F61310B2D8B220AD267&req=doc&base=LAW&n=330792&REFDOC=329368&REFBASE=LAW#1xnmj9vjs0q

Federal Tax Service. (2019). *The unified register of subjects of small and medium business*. ConsultantPlus. Retrieved from http://www.consultant.ru/document/cons_doc_LAW_34447/

Fox, T. (2005). *Small and medium-sized enterprises (SMEs) and corporate social responsibility: a discussion paper. International Institute for Environment and Development*. London: IIED.

Hammann, E. M., Habisch, A., & Pechlaner, H. (2009). Values that create value: Socially responsible business practices in SMEs–empirical evidence from German companies. *Business Ethics (Oxford, England)*, *18*(1), 37–51. doi:10.1111/j.1467-8608.2009.01547.x

Iadov, V. A. (2003). *Strategy of sociological research*. Moscow: Akademkniga, Dobrosvet.

Ivashina, M. M. (2016). Peculiarities of realization of corporate social activity in small and medium business of Russia. *Journal of Saratov State Social and Economic University*, *4*(63), 32–34.

Jamali, D., Lund-Thomsen, P., & Jeppesen, S. (2017). SMEs and CSR in developing countries. *Business & Society*, *56*(1), 11–22. doi:10.1177/0007650315571258

Jenkins, H. (2004). A critique of conventional CSR theory: An SME perspective. *Journal of General Management*, *29*(4), 37–57. doi:10.1177/030630700402900403

Kalnitskaya, P., Gentile, M., & Rohen, D. (2012). Peculiarities of realization of corporate social activity in small and medium business of Russia. *International Business Leaders Forum*.

Kanungo, R. N., & Mendonca, M. (2001). Ethical leadership and governance in organizations: A preamble. *Canadian Journal of Administrative Sciences*, *18*(4), 241–243. doi:10.1111/j.1936-4490.2001.tb00259.x

Linsley, P. M., & Slack, R. E. (2013). Crisis management and an ethic of care: The case of Northern Rock Bank. *Journal of Business Ethics*, *113*(2), 285–295. doi:10.100710551-012-1304-8

Locke, K. (2001). Grounded theory in management research. *Sage (Atlanta, Ga.)*.

Ma, J. (2012). A study on the models for corporate social responsibility of small and medium enterprises. *Physics Procedia*, *25*, 435–442. doi:10.1016/j.phpro.2012.03.108

Maciek, E. (2013). Principles of social responsibility in small and medium business. *Skhid,* (5), 65-70.

McCarthy, D. J., Puffer, S. M., Dunlap, D. R., & Jaeger, A. M. (2012). A Stakeholder Approach to the Ethicality of BRIC-firm Managers' Use of Favors. *Journal of Business Ethics*, *109*(1), 27–38. doi:10.100710551-012-1377-4

Mihailenko, O. (2007). Social responsibility as corporate value of the company. *Journal of Saratov State Social and Economic University,* (18), 13-15.

Neverov, A. V., & Davydenkova, E. S. (2016). Social responsibility of small and medium business organizations in Russia. *Journal of the Voronezh University of Friendship of Peoples. Series. Sociology*, (1), 130–140.

Nikitina, Y. (2015). Innovative Behavioral Models as a Method for a Social System Adaptation in the Unstable External Environment. *Procedia: Social and Behavioral Sciences*, *166*, 135–141. doi:10.1016/j.sbspro.2014.12.498

Öberseder, M., Schlegelmilch, B. B., & Murphy, P. E. (2013). CSR practices and consumer perceptions. *Journal of Business Research*, *66*(10), 1839–1851. doi:10.1016/j.jbusres.2013.02.005

OECD. (2002). *OECD For Economic Small and Medium Sized Enterprise Outlook*. Paris: OECD.

Peregudov, S., & Semenenko, I. S. (2008). *Corporate Citizenship: Concepts, world practice and Russian realities*. Moscow: Progress Tradition.

Petrunin, I. I., & Borisov, V. K. (2010). *Business ethics*. Moscow: Prospekt.

Pletnev, D. A., & Nicolaeva, E. V. (2016). The success of small and medium-sized businesses in Russia and the social responsibility of its leaders. *Journal of Chelyabinsk State University*, *6*(388), 128-138.

Pohludka, M., & Stverkova, H. (2019). The Best Practice of CRM Implementation for Small- and Medium-Sized Enterprises. *Administrative Sciences*, *9*(22). doi:10.3390/admsci9010022

RBC. (2019). *Rosstat for the first time revealed the share of small and medium-sized businesses in the economy*. Retrieved from https://www.rbc.ru/economics/05/02/2019/5c5948c59a794758389cfdf7

Rodionova, M. E. (2011). Corporate behavior in business community views. *Higher Education in Russia,* (6), 140-143.

Russian Association of Business Ethics. (2019). *RBEN*. Retrieved from https://rben.ru/

Russian National Standard. (n.d.). *GOST R ISO 26000-2012 Guidance for Social Responsibility*. URL: http://protect.gost.ru/v.aspx

Savicheva, E. Y. (2010). Models of social responsibility of small business in Russia. *Problems of Modern Economy*, *36*(4), 164–167.

Shteinberg, I. E. (2009). *Quality methods. Field Sociological Research*. St. Petersburg: Aleteia.

Sizova, I. L., & Chilipenok, Y. Y. (2017). Social responsibility within labour relations among the employers in small and medium businesses. *Zhurnal Issledovanii Sotsial'noi Politiki*, *15*(1), 67–80. doi:10.17323/1727-0634-2017-15-1-67-80

Spence, L. J., & Lozano, J. F. (2000). Communicating about ethics with small firms: Experiences from the UK and Spain. *Journal of Business Ethics*, *27*(1), 43–53. doi:10.1023/A:1006417425446

Storchevoy, M. (2018). Business Ethics: Normative, Positive, and Practical. In *Business Ethics as a Science: Methodology and Implications* (pp. 71–95). Cham: Springer International Publishing. doi:10.1007/978-3-319-68861-9_3

The Russian Government. (2016). *Approval of the Strategy for the Development of Small and Medium-sized Enterprises until 2030*. Retrieved from http://government.ru/docs/23354/

Treviño, L. K., den Nieuwenboer, N. A., & Kish-Gephart, J. J. (2014). (Un) ethical behavior in organizations. *Annual Review of Psychology*, *65*(1), 635–660. doi:10.1146/annurev-psych-113011-143745 PMID:23834354

Treviño, L. K., den Nieuwenboer, N. A., Kreiner, G. E., & Bishop, D. G. (2014). Legitimating the legitimate: A grounded theory study of legitimacy work among Ethics and Compliance Officers. *Organizational Behavior and Human Decision Processes*, *123*(2), 186–205. doi:10.1016/j.obhdp.2013.10.009

Treviño, L. K., Hartman, L. P., & Brown, M. (2000). Moral Person and Moral Manager: How Executives Develop a Reputation for Ethical Leadership. *California Management Review*, *42*(4), 128–142. doi:10.2307/41166057

Treviño, L. K., Weaver, G. R., Gibson, D. G., & Toffler, B. L. (1999). Managing ethics and legal compliance: What works and what hurts. *California Management Review*, *41*(2), 131–151. doi:10.2307/41165990

Turkin, S. (2007). *How to be good: make your business socially responsible*. Moscow: Alpina Pablisher.

Van Marrewijk, M. (2003). Concepts and definitions of CSR and corporate sustainability: Between agency and communion. *Journal of Business Ethics*, *44*(2-3), 95–105. doi:10.1023/A:1023331212247

Vitell, S. J., Dickerson, E. B., & Festervand, T. A. (2000). Ethical problems, conflicts and beliefs of small business professionals. *Journal of Business Ethics*, *28*(1), 15–24. doi:10.1023/A:1006217129077

Vives, A. (2006). Social and environmental responsibility in small and medium enterprises in Latin America. *Journal of Corporate Citizenship*, *2006*(21), 39–50. doi:10.9774/GLEAF.4700.2006.sp.00006

Vyakarnam, S., Bailey, A., Myers, A., & Burnett, D. (1997). Towards an understanding of ethical behaviour in small firms. *Journal of Business Ethics*, *16*(15), 1625–1636. doi:10.1023/A:1022452502299

Waldman, D. A., De Luque, M. S., Washburn, N., House, R. J., Adetoun, B., Barrasa, A., ... Debbarma, S. (2006). Cultural and leadership predictors of corporate social responsibility values of top management: A GLOBE study of 15 countries. *Journal of International Business Studies*, *37*(6), 823–837. doi:10.1057/palgrave.jibs.8400230

ADDITIONAL READING

Crotty, J. (2016). Corporate social responsibility in the Russian federation: A contextualized approach. *Business & Society*, *55*(6), 825–853. doi:10.1177/0007650314561965

Jamali, D., Zanhour, M., & Keshishian, T. (2009). Peculiar strengths and relational attributes of SMEs in the context of CSR. *Journal of Business Ethics*, *87*(3), 355–377. doi:10.100710551-008-9925-7

Jenkins, H. (2006). Small business champions for corporate social responsibility. *Journal of Business Ethics*, *67*(3), 241–256. doi:10.100710551-006-9182-6

Jondle, D., Ardichvili, A., & Mitchell, J. (2014). Modeling ethical business culture: Development of the ethical business culture survey and its use to validate the CEBC model of ethical business culture. *Journal of Business Ethics*, *119*(1), 29–43. doi:10.100710551-012-1601-2

McCarthy, D. J., & Puffer, S. M. (2013). Regularly Submitted Papers Business and management in Russia: A review of the post-Soviet literature and future research directions. *European Journal of International Management*, *7*(1), 74–111. doi:10.1504/EJIM.2013.052089

Mousiolis, D. T., Zaridis, A. D., Karamanis, K., & Rontogianni, A. (2015). Corporate social responsibility in smes and mnes. The different strategic decision making. *Procedia: Social and Behavioral Sciences*, *175*, 579–583. doi:10.1016/j.sbspro.2015.01.1240

Ortiz-Avram, D., Domnanovich, J., Kronenberg, C., & Scholz, M. (2018). Exploring the integration of corporate social responsibility into the strategies of small-and medium-sized enterprises: A systematic literature review. *Journal of Cleaner Production*, *201*, 254–271. doi:10.1016/j.jclepro.2018.08.011

Perrini, F. (2006). SMEs and CSR theory: Evidence and implications from an Italian perspective. *Journal of Business Ethics*, *67*(3), 305–316. doi:10.100710551-006-9186-2

Rees, C. J., & Miazhevich, G. (2009). Socio-cultural change and business ethics in post-Soviet countries: The cases of Belarus and Estonia. *Journal of Business Ethics*, *86*(1), 51–63. doi:10.100710551-008-9817-x

Spence, L. J. (2016). Small business social responsibility: Expanding core CSR theory. *Business & Society*, *55*(1), 23–55. doi:10.1177/0007650314523256

Worthington, I., Ram, M., & Jones, T. (2006). Exploring corporate social responsibility in the UK Asian small business community. *Journal of Business Ethics*, *67*(2), 201–217. doi:10.100710551-006-9024-6

KEY TERMS AND DEFINITIONS

Business Ethics: As a special set of norms and rules of behavior that influence business decisions. Business ethics presents a result of an individual's or an organization's critical thinking about a particular attitude and constructing arguments "in favor" or "against" a certain pattern of behavior.

CIS Countries: Community of Independent States (CIS) is established by former Republics of the Soviet Union which became independent in 1991.

CSR: Corporate social responsibility is a corporation's responsibility for the consequences of its decisions and activities for the society and environment expressed through following high standards of transparent and ethical behavior. According to the Civil Code of the Russian Federation, large businesses, especially public limited companies, meet the features of a corporation. Meanwhile, small and medium businesses cannot be considered corporations, thus an application of the term "corporate social responsibility" to SMEs is not justified, and the term "social responsibility of business" seems to be more appropriate in this case. Social responsibility of business presumes that an organization voluntarily demonstrates ethical approach embodied in activities.

Ethical Behavior: Characterizes morally good and morally right activities of a company as opposed to those that do not contradict the legal standards. This behavior means going beyond the production and provision of goods and services of due quality.

GDP: The country's gross domestic product.

Guidance for Social Responsibility GOST R ISO 26000-2012: Russian National Standard based on ISO 26000. This document contains seven areas to assess business responsibility: (1) responsible management practices; (2) human rights; (3) labor relations; (4) environmental issues; (5) compliance practices; (6) consumer relations; and (7) participation in the life and development of local communities.

Morality: A set of rules and attitudes (what is considered good or bad) passed on from generation to generation within a particular culture. It includes an individual moral consciousness (feelings, the rational basis, and the purpose), as well as an individual moral practice (i.e., behavior based on individual values).

Motivation of Russian SMEs to Follow Socially Responsible Behavior and Principles of Business Ethics: Altruistic or rational reasons of Russian businessmen from SMEs to participate in activities related to solving social or ecological problems by offering solutions that are built into their operations or presume direct interaction with stakeholders in order to meet their interests.

OECD: Organization for Economic Cooperation and Development.

SMEs: Small and medium enterprises, criteria for categorizing particular enterprises as the ones belonging to the group of small and medium businesses in most countries include the number of personnel and an annual turnover.

Socially Responsible Behavior: Voluntary demonstration of social and ecological issues' inclusion into business operations of a company and its interaction with stakeholders. It presumes both systematic and episodic activities and projects. In the study it is used as a synonym for "social responsibility of business", since authors take into account the dynamic nature of both. Socially responsible behavior goes beyond the norms and requirements set by authorities and/or the community. Its voluntary nature is important (voluntary contribution and/or initiatives).

ENDNOTES

1. Community of Independent States (CIS) is established by former Republics of the Soviet Union which became independent in 1991.
2. Here and further, Russian currency is converted according to the exchange rate of the Russian Central Bank on June 25, 2019: $1 = 62,52 rubles.
3. Survey questionnaire covered 10 topics: perception (interpretation) of terms and concepts and/or motivation for responsible and ethical behavior (1); awareness of areas of state regulation focused on business ethics and social responsibility, as well as sanctions for unethical or irresponsible behavior (2); regulation of ethical behavior within a company (3); awareness and use of regulating internal documents on business ethics and social responsibility within a company (4); availability and evaluation of usefulness of management structures focused on business ethics and social responsibility within a company (5); firm's initiatives in business ethics and social responsibility (6); firm's practice of social reporting (7); existence of a special position or functional area to control ethical and responsible behavior within a company (8); image of a responsible company (9); information about a respondent and a company that he/she represents (10).
4. In the research process some respondents who have obligations related to confidentiality of their status, refused to disclose details related to their organizations, their industry and their position.
5. Payments beyond those officially prescribed by labor legislation (i.e., wages, social payments [medical and social insurance], retirement payments, etc.

Chapter 9
The Market for Socially Responsible Investments:
A Review and Evaluation

Mark Anthony Camilleri
https://orcid.org/0000-0003-1288-4256
University of Malta, Malta

ABSTRACT

This chapter explains how socially responsible investing (SRI) has evolved in the last few decades and sheds light on its latest developments. It describes different forms of SRI in the financial markets and deliberates on the rationale for the utilisation of positive and negative screenings of listed businesses and public organisations. It also presents key theoretical underpinnings on the subject and reports that the market for the responsible investments has recently led to an increase in contractors, non-governmental organisations (NGOs), and research firms who are involved in the scrutinisation of the enterprises' environmental, social, and governance (ESG) credentials. This contribution raises awareness on the screenings of positive impact and sustainable investments. It puts forward future research avenues in this promising field of study.

INTRODUCTION

The investors are attracted to the businesses that yield a return on their investments. Yet, a growing segment of the population, including entrepreneurs, are increasingly integrating their personal values into all aspects of their life, including financial investing (Sparkes, 2017; Schueth, 2003). Many individuals are intrigued to incorporate social and environmental goals into their investment decisions (Epstein, 2018; Humphrey, Warren and Boon, 2016; Sparkes and Cowton, 2004; Schueth, 2003). Therefore, they decide to invest their funds in businesses that promote social responsibility and stakeholder engagement (Majoch, Hoepner, and Hebb, 2017; Mair and Milligan, 2012; Guay, Doh and Sinclair, 2004). The rationale behind socially responsible investing (SRI) is that such investments address societal and community deficits (Camilleri, 2015a; Martí-Ballester, 2015; Nilsson, 2009; Ogrizek, 2002). Therefore,

DOI: 10.4018/978-1-7998-2193-9.ch009

Copyright © 2020, IGI Global. Copying or distributing in print or electronic forms without written permission of IGI Global is prohibited.

some forms of SRI, including; impact investing, sustainability investing and community investing, among other nomenclatures, support the environmental issues, human rights, fair labour practices, sustainable consumption and community involvement (Ooi and Lajbcygier 2013; Capelle-Blancard and Monjon, 2012; Sparkes, 2017; Aras and Crowther, 2009; Friedman and Miles, 2001).

Several investors may usually be interested in allocating their financial capital toward laudable projects, as they try to avoid negative externalities, for the benefit of society and the environment (Renneboog, Ter Horst and Zhang, 2008). Hence, SRI portfolios are regularly screened by specialized contractors in order to evaluate their environmental, social, and governance (ESG) credentials (Camilleri, 2015a, 2015b; Renneboog et al., 2008). Many stakeholders, including investors, are well aware that there are numerous instances where big businesses were accused and found guilty of accounting fraud, bribery, money laundering and/or where they were involved in some corporate scandals, like environmental disasters. Therefore, financial investors should be cautious with their portfolios. Notwithstanding, the SRI investors are looking for more than just decent returns on their investments, as they may be genuinely interested in making a positive impact in their society and/or in the natural environment (Nilsson, 2009). They may be concerned about social justice, human rights, anti-corruption, bribery issues, and diversity in the corporations' boards (Camilleri, 2015a, 2017b).

In this light, this descriptive contribution reviews the foundations of SRI and provides a factual summary of its evolution. It adds value to our academic knowledge as it explains the contemporary developments in the SRI market. Moreover, it reveals how the financial services industry is setting responsible investment screens on all types of businesses hailing from diverse sectors. Afterward, it presents the opportunities and challenges that are affecting the growth or demise of SRI. In conclusion, this contribution suggests future research avenues in this promising field of study.

BACKGROUND

The roots of the SRI notion can be traced back to various religious movements. The original 'ethical investors' were church investment bodies. Hence, the best-known applications of socially responsible investing were initially motivated by religion (Sparkes, 2001). This may well reflect the fact that the first investors to set ethical parameters on SRI were church investors in the U.K., U.S., and Australia (Sparkes and Cowton, 2004). These churches also played a prominent role in the development of 'ethical' investment products (Benijts, 2010; McCann, Solomon and Solomon, 2003; Lydenberg, 2002). Back in 1758, the Religious Society of Friends (Quakers) prohibited members from participating in the slave trade. At the same time, one of the founders of Methodism, John Wesley outlined his basic tenets of social investing. He preached about responsible and irresponsible business practices that could harm the health and safety of workers. Eventually, Miller (1992) argued that individuals or groups who truly care about ethical, moral, religious or political principles should invest their money in accordance with their values and principles.

Sparkes (2001) defined the ethical investments as the exercise of ethical and social criteria in the selection and management of investment portfolios, generally consisting of company shares. However, he argued that ethical investing could have been more appropriate to describe non-profitmaking bodies such as charities and environmental groups (rather than companies). Sparkes (2001) went on to suggest that value-based organizations applied internal ethical principles in their investment strategies. The 'ethical investment' notion mirrored other terms, including; social investing, socially responsible investing, socially aware investing, socially conscious investing, green investing, value-based investing, and mission-based or mission-related investing (Humphrey et al., 2016; Schueth, 2003). Very often, these notions are used interchangeably in the academic literature (Hellsten and Mallin, 2006).

SRI has evolved during the political climate of the 1960s as socially concerned investors were increasingly addressing equality issues amongst women and minority groups (Schueth, 2003). This time was characterized by activism through boycotts and direct actions that were targeting specific corporations (Rojas, M'zali, Turcotte and Merrigan, 2009; Carroll, 1999). Yet, there were also interesting developments, particularly when some trade unions had introduced multiemployer pension fund monies in their targeted investments. During the 70s, a series of themes ranged from the anti-Vietnam war movement to the agenda on the individuals' civil rights, to matters relating to the women's equality rights; these issues have served to escalate the general public's sensitivity on social justice. These movements and pressure groups had broadened to include other topics, including the social responsibility and accountability of businesses, labor relations, and environmental protection (Camilleri, 2015a). Trade unions also sought to leverage pension stocks. This time was characterized by shareholder activism on proxy fights and shareholder resolutions (Guay et al., 2004; Gillan and Starks, 2000; Smith, 1996). By 1980 presidential candidates Jimmy Carter, Ronald Reagan and Jerry Brown advocated some type of social orientation toward investments in pension funds (Barber, 1982). Afterward in the mid to late 1990s, there were health awareness campaigns that effected the tobacco stocks in the US (Krumsiek, 1997). For instance, the California State Teachers' Retirement System (CalSTRS) removed more than USD237 million in tobacco holdings from its investment portfolio after six months of financial analysis and deliberations (Reynolds, Goldberg and Hurley, 2004). Arguably, such a divestment strategy may have satisfied the ethical principle of safeguarding the citizens' health. However, this development but did not necessarily create a huge impact on society(Dumas and Louche, 2016; Lane, 2015).

During the late 1990s, SRI had also focused on the sustainable development of the environment (Richardson, 2008; Brundtland, 1989). Many investors started to consider their environmental responsibility following the Bhopal, Chernobyl, and Exxon Valdez incidents. The international media began to raise an increased awareness of global warming and the ozone depletion (Pienitz and Vincent, 2000). It may appear that the environmental protection and climate change issues were becoming important issues for many responsible investors. However, some businesses have failed to become sustainable in terms of their ecological dimension. The human footprint on the environment had exceeded the Earth's capacity to sustain life (Global Footprint Network, 2019). The consumption of global resources and land degradation in various parts of the globe, including the Amazon forest, is affecting our natural environment (Camilleri, 2019). Evidently, the world's growing populations and their increased wealth is inevitably leading to greater demands for limited and scarce resources. These are some of the contentious issues that have become important rallying points for many institutional investors around the world.

Eventually, SRI has matured to a point where financial investments and portfolios were integrating social and environmental priorities in their institutional mission statements. As a result, impact investing has become one of the fastest growing and promising areas of innovative development finance (Thornley, Wood, Grace and Sullivant, 2011; Freireich and Fulton, 2009). This form of investing had originated from the venture capital community as responsible investments were unlocked from private and public capital into profit and non-profit organizations, with the underlying intention to generate social and environmental impact alongside a financial return.

Positive Impact Investments

The stakeholders or actors in the financial services industry can be divided into four broad categories: (i) asset owners who actually own capital; (ii) asset managers who deploy capital; (iii) demand-side actors who receive and utilise the capital; and (iv) service providers who help make this market work. Recently, several financial services markets have included socially responsible and sustainable investments in both emerging as well as developed jurisdictions. Such positive impact portfolios may usually offer low risk, return investment prospects, ranging from below market to market rate; depending on the individual investors' strategic goals. Bugg-Levine and Emerson (2011) argued that impact investing aligns the individuals' investments and purchase decisions with their personal values. The definition of what is (and what is not) an impact investment has become an increasingly important strand in the SRI agenda, as this term is very popular among academia and practitioners within the financial services industry.

The proliferation of the impact investments is usually characterized by market organizations that are driven by a core group of proponents including: foundations, high-net-worth individuals, family offices, investment banks, and development finance institutions. Many of these financial service providers are increasingly mobilizing capital for investments that are intended to create a meaningful societal impact in addition to significant rates of return (Epstein, 2018). Specific examples of impact investments include micro-finance; community development finance; sustainable agriculture; renewable, clean energy and the provision of affordable and accessible housing, healthcare and education, among other areas (Jackson, 2013). According to the European Forum for Sustainable and Responsible Investment, this form of responsible investing has grown to almost a EUR 23 trillion market (EUROSIF, 2019). Currently, the Netherlands and Switzerland are key markets for impact investment strategies; together, they represented an estimated two-thirds of these assets. These markets are followed by Italy, the United Kingdom, and Germany.

The impact investors expect positive, tangible results from their capital injections in society and the natural environment. Arguably, their impact investing could possibly improve their organization's legitimacy among stakeholders (Camilleri, 2018; Rendtorff, 2009). Therefore, there is scope for the responsible investors to engage with stakeholders, including academia and regulatory organizations (Paul, 2017). Such stakeholder relationships could be facilitated through the organization of conferences, workshops and via regular ongoing communications in online networks (Camilleri, 2015a; McLaren, 2004). The institutions, as well as the financial service providers, need to be equipped with the best knowledge about audit and assurance mechanisms that evaluate the financial and non-financial performance of the receivers of capital investments (Camilleri, 2018). Hence, it is imperative that adequate and sufficient resources are mobilized toward research and analytics. Customized courses in higher education, as well as the provision of professional training and development among practitioners, ought to be designed, tested and refined, in order to improve the screenings on responsible investments (Trinks and Scholtens, 2017; Willis, 2003).

The majority of financial service providers are based in countries that have an appropriate legal framework for regulation and supervision of investment portfolios and target sectors. At the industry-wide level, the work of the Global Impact Investing Network (GIIN) and IRIS (a catalog of generally accepted Environmental, Social and Governance - ESG performance metrics) is generating large datasets as well as a series of case studies on collaborative impact investments. Similarly, the Global Impact Investing Rating System (GIIRS) also issues quarterly analytics reports involving industry metrics on the companies' credentials and their respective funds. For the most part, many responsible businesses are converting impact-investment outcomes into tangible benefits for the poor and the marginalized people in advanced as well as in emerging economies (Garriga and Melé, 2004). Such positive outcomes are meant to focus on precarious issues like the provision of food security, improved housing, the availability of quality jobs, fair labor practices, environmental protection, and the like (Camilleri, 2017; Jackson, 2013). The financial institutions' and venture capitalists' responsible investments could help many governments to support and /or alleviate the position of some of the most vulnerable groups in society. However, their financial injections' in poor countries, and/or in specific geographic regions does not necessarily qualify them as impact investors.

For instance, a clean energy investment will probably involve negative externalities, including emissions, that will invariably have an adverse impact on the flora and fauna in the surrounding areas of the proposed development. It would inadvertently bring long term consequences on the natural environment. Therefore, in this case, such an investment does not qualify as an impact investment. Impact investors make distinctions among sustainability projects as they allocate their capital where it can generate integrated value for the business as well as for society. Notwithstanding, there is an opportunity for the impact investors to outperform other investors over the long-term, both in terms of stock market and accounting performance (Eccles, Ioannou and Serafeim, 2012). This out-performance is stronger in sectors where the customers are individual consumers, rather than companies (Eccles et al., 2012). In many cases, they may be the ultimate beneficiaries of the impact investments at the micro-level. Therefore, they may be intrigued to dedicate a portion of their portfolio toward impact-oriented public equity funds. Very often, capital is placed directly into social enterprises and sustainable projects, as responsible investors advance their private equity and provide direct lending to generate a positive impact for small businesses.

Sustainable Investing

Recently, there has been a shift toward 'sustainability' acronym among stakeholders in the financial services industry. In 2009, the *UK Social Investment Forum* paved the way by changing its name to *UK Sustainable Investment and Finance*. Likewise, in 2011, the *US Social Investment Forum* became the *Forum for Sustainable and Responsible Investment (SIF)* (Capelle-Blancard and Monjon, 2012). The sustainable investments contributed toward sustainable development by integrating long-term ESG criteria into investment decisions for listed businesses and large undertakings (Busch, Bauer and Orlitzky, 2016; Camilleri, 2015b). The financial objectives of sustainable investments are combined with non-financial goals. The investors' objectives and their attention to ESG criteria depends on and varies by asset class (Busch et al., 2016). Perhaps, some of the financial investors' motivations to incorporate ESG information is to improve their returns and to lower their risk, whilst others may have an additional motive to genuinely contribute to sustainable development. Nilsson and Biel's (2008) study indicated that when trade and industry executives were addressed as private citizens; they were willing to accept the sustainability strategies to reduce the effects of climate change. Evidently, they demonstrated that they held positive attitudes toward environmental issues. However, their personal attitudes and values had no impact on their professional capacity within their organization. Traditionally, the managements' fiduciary duties are to administer the financial interests of their principal (that include the beneficiaries) (Juravle and Lewis, 2008; Friedman, 2007). However, there are different opinions on what these duties are or what they should be (UNEP FI, 2016). To date, there is still an emphasis on increasing the financial interests of the institutional investor communities, whereas the beneficiaries seem to take a much broader stance on sustainable and responsible investments (Sandberg, 2011; 2013).

Some investors are devoting their attention on the impact of the ESG criteria in the real estate industry. For instance, Eichholtz, Kok and Quigley (2010) revealed that the buildings' green labels have significantly affected the values of the commercial spaces and has resulted in an increase in market rents. Arguably, the financial capital that is allocated for real estate investment can mutually support the human, social, and ecological systems (Jackson, 2009). This means that relevant systems could be designed in such a way where they are self-sustaining over the long term. For self-sustaining systems, the economic dimension cannot be omitted; as the profit motive is central for the efficient allocation of resources, in order to add value to business and to society.

Currently, corporate disclosures of non-financial performance can also affect the pricing of credit risk of corporate bonds and bank loans (Scholtens and Sievänen, 2016). Notwithstanding, the investors' reliance on ESG information (of any kind, including untrustworthy data) typically leads to more noise in financial markets, which in turn will increase stock market volatility (Camilleri, 2017a; Aras and Crowther, 2007). This argument implies that ESG data can have an effect on market noise and could also distort stock prices (Busch et al., 2016).

THE SCREENING OF SOCIALLY RESPONSIBLE INVESTMENTS

Currently, there are no theoretical models or frameworks that delineate the optimal trade-off between social responsibility or environmental sustainability with the attractiveness of returns on investments (Oikonomou, Platanakis and Sutcliffe, 2018; Berry and Junkus, 2013; Scholtens and Sievänen, 2013; Bilbao-Terol, Arenas-Parra, Cañal-Fernández and Bilbao-Terol, 2013). Hence, the disclosures of SRI present both challenges and opportunities for companies, investors, and fund managers.

During the past decades, the financial investors have clearly distinguished between ethical and unethical companies (Logue, 2009; Ronneborg et al., 2008; Ghoul and Karam, 2007; Schepers and Sethi, 2003). As a result, the compositions of financial portfolios are scrutinized by ethical screens (Rhodes, 2010). It may appear that there is a high degree of subjectivity in such evaluations (Schepers and Sethi, 2003). As screens are applied on funding opportunities, there is a possibility that they can alter the required rate of return on capital. This may result in a change in the corporate behaviors of particular firms.

Arguably, there may be socially and environmentally conscious investors who seek to own profitable companies that make positive contributions to society. For this reason, investors will require professional advice from financial services organizations to help them analyze corporate policies, practices, attitudes that will inevitably affect their profit potential. Notwithstanding, corporate reputations are affected by their CSR credentials as well as by their stakeholder relationships, with employees, customers, suppliers, creditors and investors (Majoch et al., 2017). Therefore, creditors and investors will monitor and evaluate the receivers of capital. They will appraise their financial performance as well as their corporate social performance before investing their money in them. Investors will resort to heuristics and quantitative measures to rate their financial portfolios before making investment decisions (Berry and Junkus, 2013; Rhodes, 2010). Hence, the SRI stock market relies on exclusionary or inclusionary filters that distinguish between values-driven or profit-seeking segments (Derwall et al., 2011). Given the difficulty in observing organizational behaviors and in quantifying corporate actions; the product exclusion approach is often used to examine the composition of SRI portfolios (Berry and Junkus, 2013).

Negative Screening

An exclusionary approach will require investors to avoid certain products from funds. For example, the US Forum for Sustainable and Responsible Investment (SIF) has listed twelve factors in its analysis of screening criteria for its members' mutual funds, including; alcohol, tobacco, gambling, defence weapons, animal testing, products/services, environment, human rights, labour relations, employment/equality, community investment and proxy voting. SIF maintains charts describing the socially responsible mutual funds that are offered by its member firms. Such an exclusionary approach filters out the companies according to their products or corporate behaviors, when selecting possible investments for a portfolio. For example, businesses may be excluded because they are accused of providing inappropriate conditions of employment or for using child labor. Corporations may be sourcing their materials or products from sweatshop factories. Alternatively, they may be collaborating with repressive regimes or in countries where there is no respect for human rights (Emmelhainz and Adams, 1999).

Exclusions criteria grew by 91% between 2011 and 2013. Negative screenings cover an estimated 41% (EUR 6.9 trillion) of European professionally managed assets (EUROSIF, 2019). For instance, in Northern Europe exclusions were aimed at safeguarding the reputation of major institutional investors, and at avoiding them from being linked with controversial issues that affect the companies they invest in. These exclusions may usually involve certain violations of major international human rights or environmental protection norms. They are often called norm-based exclusions and are commonly referred to as "sin stocks", as they are banned from portfolios on moral or ethical grounds (Entine, 2003).

The idea of excluding companies in order to avoid black sheep is gradually gaining ground among SRI sponsors (EUROSIF, 2019). Moreover, an increasing number of investors outside the SRI community are also considering the norm-based exclusions to scrutinize their assets (Bengtsson, 2008). The exclusions of irresponsible businesses from SRI funds enables financial service providers to avoid criticisms over their legitimacy and social usefulness. This way, they adopt strong and sometimes political positions to safeguard their reputation; by implementing norm-based exclusions on the grounds of specific issues, such as the respect for human rights.

This is especially the case for the exclusion of the so-called controversial weapons, which have now been banned through international conventions. Voluntary exclusions related to Cluster Munitions and Anti-Personnel Landmines (CMandAPL) are also among the most common. They cover about 30% (EUR 5.0 trillion) of the European investment market. Other exclusion assets cover about 23% (EUR 4.0 trillion) of the market (Becchetti, Ciciretti, Dalò and Herzel, 2015). The exclusion of these industries may have a dramatic effect on the countries' national economies, their competitiveness, and on their respective labor markets. A relevant review of the academic research reported different findings on 'sinful' investing (Trinks and Scholtens, 2017; Hong and Kacperczyk, 2009; Kempf and Osthoff, 2007; Guay et al., 2004). While some find positive abnormal returns for sin stocks (e.g. Hong and Kacperczyk 2009), others do not find them at all (Lobe and Walkshäuslm 2011).

The exclusion of sin stocks from SRI may not have an effect on the profitability of the financial service providers (Humphrey and Tan 2014) as they will find a market for non-SRI products. However, policy makers and pressure group activity may impose legal and regulatory constraints on the financial service providers' investment decisions (Rhodes, 2010).

Positive Screening

The investors know very well that there are no perfect companies. Nevertheless, a thorough evaluation process (which is also known as social screening) generally seeks to identify better-managed companies. Such an inclusionary approach is more difficult as it involves adjusting the weights of investments according to their degree of corporate responsibility and accountability (Trinks and Scholtens, 2017; Humphrey and Tan, 2014; Salaber 2013; Lobe and Walkshäusl, 2011). Therefore, the positively screened investments are considered as socially responsible and sustainable. Under the positive screening approach, the investors would allocate "points" to firms for acting responsibly. Hence, positive screening provides an opportunity for investors to align their values with their personal financial goals, while earning competitive returns (Schueth, 2003). Firms which are sensitive to worker and human rights, who are concerned about the environment, and who avoid profiting from a few products would seem to have a stronger SRI profile. For instance, in France, investments are positively screened according to best-in-class criteria, rather than basing their selections on the so-called ethical exclusions (Giamporcaro and Gond, 2016; Crifo and Mottis, 2016). Berry and Junkus (2013) suggested that investors reward those firms who display overall positive social behaviors. At the same time, they exclude others on the basis of e irresponsible corporate practices.

Yet, the regular screening of the businesses' operations may not always have a significant effect on their modus operandi (Fabozzi, Ma and Oliphant, 2008; Hong and Kacperczyk, 2009; Durand, Koh and Limkriangkrai, 2013; Salaber, 2013; Humphrey and Tan, 2014). While specific metrics are useful to evaluate corporate responsible and irresponsible behaviors, investors require a more nuanced synthesis of the corporations' actions, both positive and negative (Berry and Junkus, 2013).

It may appear, that there are different shades of opinions about environmental, social, and governance (ESG) metrics as to whether they should be mandatory or not. With such heterogeneous beliefs, it is unlikely that any metrics will adequately address all aspects of the listed businesses' integrated disclosures (Camilleri, 2018). Yet, the specification of specific metrics would possibly help to address the problem of information asymmetry. The universal requirements for those firms who intend adopting such metrics would probably result in the imposition of costs; which could not be justified by the benefits which would subsequently accrue (Rhodes, 2010).

MEASURING THE CORPORATIONS' ENVIRONMENTAL, SOCIAL AND GOVERNANCE PERFORMANCE

There are various ratings and reference indices that are utilized by investors to evaluate financial and SRI portfolios. Typically, the SRI indices constitute a relevant proxy as they evaluate the ESG performance of listed businesses (Le Sourd, 2011). A large number of SR contractors, analysts, and research firms are increasingly specializing in the collection of ESG information as they perform ongoing analyses of corporate behaviors (Dumas and Louche, 2016). Many of them maintain a database and use it to provide their clients with a thorough ESG analysis (including proxy advice), benchmarks and engagement strategies of corporations. They publish directories of ethical and SRI funds, as they outline their investment strategies, screening criteria, and voting policies. In a sense, these data providers support the responsible investors in their selection of funds.

SRI Indices, Ratings and Information Providers

KLD/Jantzi Global Environmental Index, Jantzi Research, Ethical Investment Research Service (Vigeo EIRIS) and Innovest (among others) analyze the corporations' socially responsible and environmentally-sound behaviors as reported in Table 1. Some of their indices (to name a few) shed light about the impact of products (e.g. resource use, waste), the production processes (e.g. logging, pesticides), or proactive corporate activities (e.g. clean energy, recycling).

Similarly, social issues are also a common category for these contractors. In the main, the SRI indices benchmark different types of firms hailing from diverse industries and sectors. They adjust their weighting for specific screening criteria as they choose which firms to include (or exclude) from their indices. One of the oldest SRI indices for CSR and Sustainability ratings is the Dow Jones Sustainability Index. The companies that are featured in the Dow Jones Indices are analyzed by the Sustainable Asset Management (SAM) Group (i.e., a Swiss asset management company). Another popular SRI index is FTSE Russell's KLD's Domini 400 Social Index (also known as the KLD400) which partners with the Financial Times on a range of issues. Similarly, the Financial Times partners with an ESG research firm (i.e., EIRES) to construct its FTSE4 Good Index series. Smaller FTSE Responsible Investment Indices include the Catholic Values Index, the Calvert Social Index, the FTSE4Good indices, and the Dow Jones family of SRI Indices, among others. The KLD400 index screens the companies' performance on a set of ESG criteria. It eliminates those companies that are involved in non-eligible industries. Impax, a specialist finance house (that focuses on the markets for cleaner or more efficient delivery of basic services of energy, water, and waste) also maintain a group of FTSE Indices that are related to environmental technologies and business activities (FTSE Environment Technology and Environmental Opportunities). The Catholic Values Index uses the US Conference of Catholic Bishops' Socially Responsible Investment Guidelines (i.e., positive screening approach) to scrutinize eligible companies (e.g., corporations with generous wage and benefit policies, or those who create environmentally beneficial technologies). This index could also exclude certain businesses trading in "irresponsible" activities. Calvert Group's Calvert Social Index examines 1,000 of the largest US companies according to their social audit of four criteria: the company's products, their impact on the environment, labor relations, and community relations. The latter "community relations" variable includes issues such as the treatment of indigenous people, provision of local credit, operations of overseas subsidiaries, and the like. The responsible companies are then featured in the Index when and if they meet Calvert's criteria. This index also maintains a target economic sector weighting scheme. Other smaller indices include; Ethibel Sustainability Index for Belgian (and other European) companies and OMX GES Ethical Index for Scandinavian companies, among others.

Generally, these SRI indices are considered as investment benchmarks. In a nutshell, SRI Indices have spawned a range of products, including index mutual funds, ETFs, and structured products (Riedl and Smeets, 2017). A wide array of SRI mutual funds regularly evaluate target companies and manage their investment portfolios. Therefore, they are expected to consider other important criteria, such as risk and return targets. For instance, iShares lists two ETFs based on the KLD Index funds, and the Domini itself offers a number of actively managed mutual funds based on both ESG and community development issues (such as impact investments). In addition, there are research and ratings vendors who also manage a series of mutual funds, including Calvert and Domini.

Table 1. Screenings of responsible investments (The author's compilation)

Positive Screens	Negative Screens
Community Investment	Alcohol
Employment / Equality	Animal Testing
Environment	Defence / Weapons
Human Rights	Gambling
Labour Relations	Tobacco
Proxy Voting	

DISCUSSION AND CONCLUSIONS

The SRI indices serve as a 'seal of approval' function for the responsible businesses that want to prove their positive impact investment credentials to their stakeholders. Currently, there are many factors that may be contributing to the growth of SRI. Firstly, one of the most important factors for the proliferation of SRI is the access to information. Today's investors are increasingly using technologies, including mobile devices and their related applications to keep them up to date on the most recent developments in business and society. Certain apps inform investors on the latest movements in the financial markets, in real-time. Notwithstanding, the SRI contractors are providing much higher quality data than ever before. As a result, all investors are in a position to make informed decisions that are based on evidence and research. Investors and analysts use "extra-financial information" to help them analyze investment decisions (GRI, 2019). This "extra-financial information" includes ESG disclosures on non-financial issues. These sources of information will encourage many businesses and enterprises to report on their responsible and sustainable practices. The companies' integrated thinking could be a precursor for their integrated reporting (Camilleri, 2018; 2017b; GRI, 2019). Business can use integrated disclosures, where they provide details on their financial as well as on their non-financial information for the benefit of prospective investors and analysts, among other stakeholders.

Secondly, the gender equality issue has inevitably led to some of the most significant developments in the financial services industry. Nowadays, there are more emancipated women who are in employment, who are gainfully occupied as they are actively contributing to the labor market. Many women are completing higher educational programs and attaining relevant qualifications including MBA programs. Very often, these women move their way up the career ladder with large organizations. They may even become members on boards of directors and assume fiduciary duties and responsibilities. Other women are becoming entrepreneurs as they start their own business. During the last decades, an increased equality in the developed economies has led to SRI's prolific growth. As a result, women are no longer the only the beneficiaries of social finance, as they are building a complete ecosystem of social investing (Maretick, 2015). "By 2020 women are expected to hold USD 72trn, 32% of the total. Most of the private wealth that changes hands in the coming decades is likely to go to women" (The Economist, 2018). This wave of wealth is set to land in the laps of female investors who have shown positive attitudes toward social investing when compared to their male counterparts. Maretick (2015) reported that half of the wealthiest women expressed an interest in social and environmental investing when compared to one-third of the wealthy men.

Thirdly, today's investors are increasingly diversifying their portfolio of financial products. The default investment is the market portfolio, which is a value-weighted portfolio of all investable securities (Trinks and Scholtens, 2017). A growing body of evidence suggests that many investors do not necessarily have to sacrifice performance when they invest in socially responsible or environmentally sustainable assets. A relevant literature review denied the contention that social screening could result in corporate underperformance (Trinks and Scholtens, 2017; Lobe and Walkshäusl, 2011; Salaber 2013). Investors have realized that strategic corporate responsibility is congruent with prosperity (Porter and Kramer, 2011; Schueth, 2003). In fact, today's major asset classes including global, international, domestic equity, balanced and fixed-income categories, also comprise top-performing socially responsible mutual funds (Riedl and Smeets, 2017). Therefore, various financial products are reflecting the investors' values and beliefs. Consequentially, the broad range of competitive socially responsible investment options have resulted in diverse, well-balanced portfolios. In the U.S. and in other western economies, top-performing SRI funds can be found in all major asset classes. More and more investors realize that they can add value to their portfolios whilst supporting social and environmental causes.

Fourthly, there are economic justifications for the existence of mutual funds in diversified portfolios. Although SRI funds are rated well above average performers no matter which ranking process one prefers to use (Schueth, 2003), other literature suggests that there are situations where the positive or negative screens did not add nor destroy the financial products' portfolio value (Auer, 2016; Trinks and Scholtens, 2017). This matter can result in having mixed investments where there are SRI products that are marketed with other financial portfolios.

Currently, the financial industry is witnessing a consumer-driven phenomenon as there is a surge in demand for social investments. This chapter mentioned a number of organizations that have developed indices to measure the organizational behaviors and their laudable practices. Very often, their metrics rely on positive or negative screens that are used to define socially responsible and sustainable investments. However, despite these developments, the balanced investors are still investing their portfolio in different industries. As a result, they may be putting their money to support controversial businesses. Perhaps, in the future, there could be alternative screening methods in addition to the extant inclusionary and exclusionary approaches. Several corporations are willingly disclosing their integrated reporting of financial and non-financial performance; as stakeholders including investors, demand a higher degree of accountability and transparency from them. As a result, a growing number of firms, are recognizing the business case for integrated thinking that incorporates financial and strategic corporate responsible behaviors. They can support the community through positive impact investments by allocating funds to reduce their externalities in society. Alternatively, they may facilitate shareholder activism and advocacy, among other actions. In sum, the responsible businesses' stakeholder engagement, as well as their sustainable investments, can help them improve their bottom lines, whilst addressing their social and community deficits.

Future Research Directions

Further research is needed to determine the investors' attitudes toward the screening of SRIs. There may be investors who still view this phenomenon under a negative lens, as positive or negative screen can have an impact on value-weighted portfolios. Therefore, future research can explore how financial services institutions are using the SRI contractors' data as they incorporate socially responsible investments in a balanced portfolio of mutual funds.

While some non-socially responsible investors may simply feel that the returns are better elsewhere, others could be strongly opposed to SRI and other related investments. Presumably, there may be instances where institutional investors could be skeptical on the companies' genuine CSR commitment and maybe dubious on their intrinsic motives behind their ESG or integrated disclosures. Most probably, they may be concerned on the corporations' greenwashing, and on how, where and when they are actually engaging in responsible activities.

REFERENCES

Aras, G., & Crowther, D. (2009). Corporate sustainability reporting: A study in disingenuity? *Journal of Business Ethics*, *87*(1), 279–288. doi:10.100710551-008-9806-0

Aras, G. D., & Crowther, D. (2007). What Level of Trust is Needed for Sustainability? *Social Responsibility Journal*, *3*(3), 60–68. doi:10.1108/17471110710835590

Auer, B. R. (2016). Do Socially Responsible Investment Policies Add or Destroy European Stock Portfolio Value? *Journal of Business Ethics*, *135*(2), 381–397. doi:10.100710551-014-2454-7

Barber, R. (1982). Pension Funds in the United States Issues of Investment and Control. *Economic and Industrial Democracy*, *3*(1), 31–73. doi:10.1177/0143831X8231004

Becchetti, L., Ciciretti, R., Dalò, A., & Herzel, S. (2015). Socially responsible and conventional investment funds: Performance comparison and the global financial crisis. *Applied Economics*, *47*(25), 2541–2562. doi:10.1080/00036846.2014.1000517

Bengtsson, E. (2008). Socially responsible investing in Scandinavia–a comparative analysis. *Sustainable Development*, *16*(3), 155–168. doi:10.1002d.360

Benijts, T. (2010). A framework for comparing socially responsible investment markets: An analysis of the Dutch and Belgian retail markets. *Business Ethics (Oxford, England)*, *19*(1), 50–63. doi:10.1111/j.1467-8608.2009.01578.x

Berry, T. C., & Junkus, J. C. (2013). Socially responsible investing: An investor perspective. *Journal of Business Ethics*, *112*(4), 707–720. doi:10.100710551-012-1567-0

Bilbao-Terol, A., Arenas-Parra, M., Cañal-Fernández, V., & Bilbao-Terol, C. (2013). Selection of socially responsible portfolios using hedonic prices. *Journal of Business Ethics*, *115*(3), 515–529. doi:10.100710551-012-1411-6

Brundtland, G. H. (1989). Global change and our common future. *Environment*, *31*(5), 16–43. doi:10.1080/00139157.1989.9928941

Bugg-Levine, A., & Emerson, J. (2011). Impact investing: Transforming how we make money while making a difference. *Innovations: Technology, Governance, Globalization*, *6*(3), 9–18. doi:10.1162/INOV_a_00077

Busch, T., Bauer, R., & Orlitzky, M. (2016). Sustainable development and financial markets: Old paths and new avenues. *Business & Society*, *55*(3), 303–329. doi:10.1177/0007650315570701

Camilleri, M. A. (2015a). Valuing stakeholder engagement and sustainability reporting. *Corporate Reputation Review*, *18*(3), 210–222. doi:10.1057/crr.2015.9

Camilleri, M. A. (2015b). Environmental, social and governance disclosures in Europe, *Sustainability Accounting. Management and Policy Journal*, *6*(2), 224–242.

Camilleri, M. A. (2017a). Measuring the corporate managers' attitudes towards ISO's social responsibility standard. *Total Quality Management & Business Excellence*, 1-13. Retrieved from https://www.tandfonline.com/doi/full/10.1080/14783363.2017.1413344

Camilleri, M. A. (2017b). The integrated reporting of financial, social and sustainability capitals: A critical review and appraisal. *International Journal of Sustainable Society*, *9*(4), 311–326. doi:10.1504/IJSSOC.2017.090523

Camilleri, M. A. (2018). Theoretical insights on integrated reporting: The inclusion of non-financial capitals in corporate disclosures. *Corporate Communications*, *23*(4), 567–581. doi:10.1108/CCIJ-01-2018-0016

Camilleri, M. A. (2019). The circular economy's closed loop and product service systems for sustainable development: A review and appraisal. *Sustainable Development*, *27*(3), 530–536. doi:10.1002d.1909

Capelle-Blancard, G., & Monjon, S. (2012). Trends in the literature on socially responsible investment: Looking for the keys under the lamppost. *Business Ethics (Oxford, England)*, *21*(3), 239–250. doi:10.1111/j.1467-8608.2012.01658.x

Carroll, A. B. (1999). Corporate social responsibility evolution of a definitional construct. *Business & Society*, *38*(3), 268–295. doi:10.1177/000765039903800303

CDFA. (2005). *Inside Out: The State of Community Development Finance*. London, UK: CDFA.

Crifo, P., & Mottis, N. (2016). Socially responsible investment in France. *Business & Society*, *55*(4), 576–593. doi:10.1177/0007650313500216

Dumas, C., & Louche, C. (2016). Collective beliefs on responsible investment. *Business & Society*, *55*(3), 427–457. doi:10.1177/0007650315575327

Durand, R. B., Koh, S., & Limkriangkrai, M. (2013a). Saints versus Sinners. Does morality matter? *Journal of International Financial Markets, Institutions and Money*, *24*(4), 166–183. doi:10.1016/j.intfin.2012.12.002

Eichholtz, P., Kok, N., & Quigley, J. M. (2010). Doing well by doing good? Green office buildings. *The American Economic Review*, *100*(5), 2492–2509. doi:10.1257/aer.100.5.2492

Emmelhainz, M. A., & Adams, R. J. (1999). The apparel industry response to "sweatshop" concerns: A review and analysis of codes of conduct. *The Journal of Supply Chain Management*, *35*(2), 51–57. doi:10.1111/j.1745-493X.1999.tb00062.x

Entine, J. (2003). The myth of social investing: A critique of its practice and consequences for corporate social performance research. *Organization & Environment*, *16*(3), 352–368. doi:10.1177/1086026603256283

Epstein, M. J. (2018). *Making sustainability work: Best practices in managing and measuring corporate social, environmental and economic impacts*. Oxford, UK: Routledge. doi:10.4324/9781351280129

EUROSIF. (2019). *SDGs for SRI Investors*. Retrieved from: http://www.eurosif.org/wp-content/uploads/2018/01/Eurosif-SDGs-brochure.pdf

Fabozzi, F. J., Ma, K. C., & Oliphant, B. J. (2008). Sin stock returns. *Journal of Portfolio Management, 35*(1), 82–94. doi:10.3905/JPM.2008.35.1.82

Freireich, J., & Fulton, K. (2009). Investing for social and environmental impact: A design for catalyzing an emerging industry. Monitor Institute.

Friedman, A. L., & Miles, S. (2001). Socially responsible investment and corporate social and environmental reporting in the UK: An exploratory study. *The British Accounting Review, 33*(4), 523–548. doi:10.1006/bare.2001.0172

Friedman, M. (2007). The social responsibility of business is to increase its profits. In *Corporate ethics and corporate governance* (pp. 173–178). Berlin, Germany: Springer. doi:10.1007/978-3-540-70818-6_14

Garriga, E., & Melé, D. (2004). Corporate social responsibility theories: Mapping the territory. *Journal of Business Ethics, 53*(1-2), 51–71. doi:10.1023/B:BUSI.0000039399.90587.34

Ghoul, W., & Karam, P. (2007). MRI and SRI mutual funds: A comparison of Christian, Islamic (morally responsible investing). and socially responsible investing (SRI) mutual funds. *Journal of Investing, 16*(2), 96–102. doi:10.3905/joi.2007.686416

Giamporcaro, S., & Gond, J. P. (2016). Calculability as politics in the construction of markets: The case of socially responsible investment in France. *Organization Studies, 37*(4), 465–495. doi:10.1177/0170840615604498

Gillan, S. L., & Starks, L. T. (2000). Corporate governance proposals and shareholder activism: The role of institutional investors. *Journal of Financial Economics, 57*(2), 275–305. doi:10.1016/S0304-405X(00)00058-1

Global Footprint Network. (2019). *Do we fit on the planet?* Retrieved from: http://www.footprintnetwork.org/en/index.php/GFN/page/world_footprint/

GRI. (2019). *Linking GRI standards and the EU directive on non-financial and diversity disclosure*. Retrieved from: https://www.globalreporting.org/standards/resource-download-center/linking-gri-standards-and-european-directive-on-non-financial-and-diversity disclosure/

Guay, T., Doh, J. P., & Sinclair, G. (2004). Non-governmental organizations, shareholder activism, and socially responsible investments: Ethical, strategic, and governance implications. *Journal of Business Ethics, 52*(1), 125–139. doi:10.1023/B:BUSI.0000033112.11461.69

Hellsten, S., & Mallin, C. (2006). Are 'ethical'or 'socially responsible'investments socially responsible? *Journal of Business Ethics, 66*(4), 393–406. doi:10.100710551-006-0001-x

Hong, H., & Kacperczyk, M. (2009). The price of sin: The effects of social norms on markets. *Journal of Financial Economics, 93*(1), 15–36. doi:10.1016/j.jfineco.2008.09.001

Humphrey, J. E., & Tan, D. T. (2014). Does it really hurt to be responsible? *Journal of Business Ethics, 122*(3), 375–386. doi:10.100710551-013-1741-z

Humphrey, J. E., Warren, G. J., & Boon, J. (2016). What is different about socially responsible funds? A holdings-based analysis. *Journal of Business Ethics, 138*(2), 263–277. doi:10.100710551-015-2583-7

Jackson, E. T. (2013). Interrogating the theory of change: Evaluating impact investing where it matters most. *Journal of Sustainable Finance and Investment, 3*(2), 95–110. doi:10.1080/20430795.2013.776257

Jackson, J. (2009). How risky are sustainable real estate projects? An evaluation of LEED and ENERGY STAR development options. *Journal of Sustainable Real Estate, 1*(1), 91–106.

Kempf, A., & Osthoff, P. (2007). The effect of socially responsible investing on portfolio performance. *European Financial Management, 13*(5), 908–922. doi:10.1111/j.1468-036X.2007.00402.x

Krumsiek, B. J. (1997). The emergence of a new era in mutual fund investing: Socially responsible investing comes of age. *Journal of Investing, 6*(4), 25–30. doi:10.3905/joi.1997.408438

Lane, M. J. (2015). *The Mission-Driven Venture: Business Solutions to the World's Most Vexing Social Problems*. Hoboken, NJ: Wiley. doi:10.1002/9781118809815

Le Sourd, V. (2011). *Performance of socially responsible investment funds against an efficient SRI index: The impact of benchmark choice when evaluating active managers*. Nice, France: EDHEC-Risk and Asset Management Research Centre.

Logue, A. C. (2009). *Socially Responsible Investing for Dummies*. Indianapolis, IN: John Wiley and Sons.

Lydenberg, S. D. (2002). Envisioning socially responsible investing. *Journal of Corporate Citizenship, 7*(7), 57–77. doi:10.9774/GLEAF.4700.2002.au.00007

Mair, J., & Milligan, K. (2012). Q and A roundtable on impact investing. *Stanford Social Innovation Review*. Retrieved from: http://ssir.org/articles/entry/qa_roundtable_on_impact_investing

Majoch, A. A., Hoepner, A. G., & Hebb, T. (2017). Sources of stakeholder salience in the responsible investment movement: Why do investors sign the principles for responsible investment? *Journal of Business Ethics, 140*(4), 723–741. doi:10.100710551-016-3057-2

Maretick, M. (2015). Women Rule: Why the Future of Social, Sustainable and Impact Investing is in Female Hands. *TriplePundit*. Retrieved from: http://www.triplepundit.com/2015/04/womenrule-future-social-sustainable-impact-investing-female-hands/#

Martí-Ballester, C. P. (2015). Investor reactions to socially responsible investment. *Management Decision, 53*(3), 571–604. doi:10.1108/MD-04-2014-0207

Matten, D., & Moon, J. (2008). Implicit and explicit CSR: A conceptual framework for a comparative understanding of corporate social responsibility. *Academy of Management Review, 33*(2), 404–424. doi:10.5465/amr.2008.31193458

McCann, L., Solomon, A., & Solomon, J. (2003). Explaining the growth in UK socially responsible investment. *Journal of General Management, 28*(4), 15–36. doi:10.1177/030630700302800402

McLaren, D. (2004). Global stakeholders: Corporate accountability and investor engagement. *Corporate Governance*, *12*(2), 191–201. doi:10.1111/j.1467-8683.2004.00360.x

Miller, A. (1992). Green Investment. In D. Owen (Ed.), *Green Reporting: Accountancy and the Challenge of the Nineties* (pp. 242–255). London, UK: Chapman and Hall.

Nilsson, J. (2009). Segmenting socially responsible mutual fund investors: The influence of financial return and social responsibility. *International Journal of Bank Marketing*, *27*(1), 5–31. doi:10.1108/02652320910928218

Ogrizek, M. (2002). The effect of corporate social responsibility on the branding of financial services. *Journal of Financial Services Marketing*, *6*(3), 215–228. doi:10.1057/palgrave.fsm.4770053

Oikonomou, I., Platanakis, E., & Sutcliffe, C. (2018). Socially responsible investment portfolios: Does the optimization process matter? *The British Accounting Review*, *50*(4), 379–401. doi:10.1016/j.bar.2017.10.003

Ooi, E., & Lajbcygier, P. (2013). Virtue remains after removing sin: Finding skill amongst socially responsible investment managers. *Journal of Business Ethics*, *113*(2), 199–224. doi:10.100710551-012-1290-x

Paul, K. (2017). The effect of business cycle, market return and momentum on financial performance of socially responsible investing mutual funds. *Social Responsibility Journal*, *13*(3), 513–528. doi:10.1108/SRJ-09-2016-0154

Pienitz, R., & Vincent, W. F. (2000). Effect of climate change relative to ozone depletion on UV exposure in subarctic lakes. *Nature*, *404*(6777), 484–487. doi:10.1038/35006616 PMID:10761913

Porter, M. E., & Kramer, M. R. (2011). The big idea: Creating shared value. *Harvard Business Review*, *89*(1), 1–12.

Rendtorff, J. D. (2009). Responsibility, Ethics and Legitimacy of Corporations. *Society and Business Review*, *4*(3), 266–268.

Renneboog, L., Ter Horst, J., & Zhang, C. (2008). Socially responsible investments: Institutional aspects, performance, and investor behaviour. *Journal of Banking & Finance*, *32*(9), 1723–1742. doi:10.1016/j.jbankfin.2007.12.039

Rhodes, M. J. (2010). Information asymmetry and socially responsible investment. *Journal of Business Ethics*, *95*(1), 145–150. doi:10.100710551-009-0343-2

Richardson, B. J. (2008). *Socially Responsible Investment Law: Regulating the Unseen Polluters*. Oxford, UK: Oxford University Press. doi:10.1093/acprof:oso/9780195333459.001.0001

Riedl, A., & Smeets, P. (2017). Why do investors hold socially responsible mutual funds? *The Journal of Finance*, *72*(6), 2505–2550. doi:10.1111/jofi.12547

Rojas, M., M'zali, B., Turcotte, M., & Merrigan, P. (2009). Bringing about changes to corporate social policy through shareholder activism: Filers, issues, targets, and success. *Business and Society Review*, *114*(2), 217–252. doi:10.1111/j.1467-8594.2009.00341.x

Salaber, J. (2013). Religion and returns in Europe. *European Journal of Political Economy*, *32*(1), 149–160. doi:10.1016/j.ejpoleco.2013.07.002

Sandberg, J. (2011). Socially responsible investment and fiduciary duty: Putting the freshfields report into perspective. *Journal of Business Ethics*, *101*(1), 143–162. doi:10.100710551-010-0714-8

Sandberg, J. (2013). (Re-) interpreting fiduciary duty to justify socially responsible investment for pension funds? *Corporate Governance*, *21*(5), 436–446. doi:10.1111/corg.12028

Schepers, D. H., & Prakash Sethi, S. (2003). Bridging the Gap Between the Promise and Performance of Socially Responsible Funds. *Business and Society Review*, *108*(1), 11–32. doi:10.1111/1467-8594.00006

Scholtens, B., & Sievänen, R. (2013). Drivers of socially responsible investing: A case study of four Nordic countries. *Journal of Business Ethics*, *115*(3), 605–616. doi:10.100710551-012-1410-7

Schueth, S. (2003). Socially responsible investing in the United States. *Journal of Business Ethics*, *43*(3), 189–194. doi:10.1023/A:1022981828869

Smith, M. P. (1996). Shareholder activism by institutional investors: Evidence from CalPERS. *The Journal of Finance*, *51*(1), 227–252. doi:10.1111/j.1540-6261.1996.tb05208.x

Sparkes, R. (2001). Ethical investment: Whose ethics, which investment? *Business Ethics (Oxford, England)*, *10*(3), 194–205. doi:10.1111/1467-8608.00233

Sparkes, R. (2017). A historical perspective on the growth of socially responsible investment. In *Responsible investment* (pp. 39–54). Oxford, UK: Routledge. doi:10.4324/9781351283441-3

Sparkes, R., & Cowton, C. J. (2004). The maturing of socially responsible investment: A review of the developing link with corporate social responsibility. *Journal of Business Ethics*, *52*(1), 45–57. doi:10.1023/B:BUSI.0000033106.43260.99

The Economist. (2018). *Women's wealth is rising*. Retrieved from: https://www.economist.com/graphic-detail/2018/03/08/womens-wealth-is-rising

Thornley, B., Wood, D., Grace, K., & Sullivant, S. (2011). Impact Investing a Framework for Policy Design and Analysis. InSight at Pacific Community Ventures and The Initiative for Responsible Investment at Harvard University, Cambridge, MA.

Trinks, P. J., & Scholtens, B. (2017). The opportunity cost of negative screening in socially responsible investing. *Journal of Business Ethics*, *140*(2), 193–208. doi:10.100710551-015-2684-3

Walker, H., & Brammer, S. (2009). Sustainable procurement in the United Kingdom public sector. *Supply Chain Management*, *14*(2), 128–137. doi:10.1108/13598540910941993

Willis, A. (2003). The role of the global reporting initiative's sustainability reporting guidelines in the social screening of investments. *Journal of Business Ethics*, *43*(3), 233–237. doi:10.1023/A:1022958618391

ADDITIONAL READING

Camilleri, M. A. (2017). *Corporate Sustainability, Social Responsibility and Environmental Management: An Introduction to Theory and Practice with Case Studies*. Cham, Switzerland: Springer. doi:10.1007/978-3-319-46849-5

Camilleri, M. A. (Ed.). (2017). *CSR 2.0 and the New Era of Corporate Citizenship*. Hershey, PA: IGI Global. doi:10.4018/978-1-5225-1842-6

KEY TERMS AND DEFINITIONS

Community Investing: This category of socially responsible investing (SRI) is related to the provision of investment capital that is intended to add value to the community at large.

Environmental,: Social, and Governance (ESG): These three non-financial dimensions measure the sustainability and ethical impacts of specific investments in businesses.

Ethical Investment: This category of SRI refers to the individuals' ethical principles and norms that can possibly influence their selection of securities investing.

Impact Investing: This category of SRI refers to the provision of investment capital to businesses, non-profit organizations, and funds with the underlying intention to generate a measurable, social or environmental impact alongside a financial return.

Investment Portfolio: This refers to a group of assets, including equity transactions, securities, and debt instruments, including; banknotes, bonds, and debentures.

Negative Screening: This form of screening involves excluding certain businesses that are not complying with specific, social norms or environmental criteria. Negative screening may exclude businesses that are involved in the production of entertainment drugs, tobacco, or gambling products.

Positive Screening: This form of screening involves selecting responsible and sustainable businesses for investment purposes. Positive screening may include businesses that sell educational material and/or essential requirements like; food, clothing, electricity, water or housing.

Socially Responsible Investing: This is the umbrella term that refers to socially-conscious, sustainable or ethical investing. Such an investment strategy will usually consider both financial return as well as the societal well-being and/or environmental sustainability.

SRI Index: This index is a capitalization-weighted index that provides exposure to those responsible businesses that have demonstrated outstanding environmental, social, and governance (ESG) ratings. It excludes other businesses whose products or services have negative impacts on society and the ecology.

Sustainability Investing: This category of SRI refers to investment capital that is directed to sustainable businesses that are protecting the natural environment by reducing and/or offsetting their externalities.

Chapter 10
Green Investment Financing Instruments

Vilma Kazlauskiene
https://orcid.org/0000-0003-0295-6543
Vytautas Magnus University, Lithuania

Aura Draksaite
Kaunas University of Technology, Lithuania

ABSTRACT

The chapter analyses the peculiarities of current green financing instruments. Rapid development of these instruments markets prompts the need to comprehend the main factors behind it, and thus the necessity to recognize opportunities to profit by the occasion. In the chapter, such green financial instruments as green bonds, green equities, and green loans are discussed. Also, private green investment promotion instruments are overviewed. Current green financial instrument market development trends are presented, and main contributing factors are provided. Furthermore, main challenges of investing and development of environmentally sustainable business practices are analyzed. Based on the analysis results, insight regarding further development of green financial markets is offered.

INTRODUCTION

Environmental sustainability issue is one of the most important issues worldwide. Attempt to create environmentally responsible environment requires a considerable amount of capital. Therefore, the need for innovative fundraising alternatives has emerged and caused the evolution of the green financial markets. Since the very beginning, new markets and financial instruments face various challenges. Even definitions of many green instruments are not unified globally or even internationally. Lack of agreement on the terms of green financing, green instruments' features often results in the lost opportunities for green project funding. Various issues of green financing were analysed by Banahan (2019), Bracking (2019), Dafermos et al. (2018), Park (2018), Tripathy (2017), Trompeter (2017) and many others.

DOI: 10.4018/978-1-7998-2193-9.ch010

Copyright © 2020, IGI Global. Copying or distributing in print or electronic forms without written permission of IGI Global is prohibited.

Significance of the issue is also attested by the number of countries, involved in an attempt to resolve the challenge of raising capital for various green projects. For example, the Paris Agreement (agreement to reduce the global warming or at least to minimize its growth rate) was signed in 2015 by 179 countries of various development levels. Issued guidelines for green investing in many countries can be followed voluntarily, but in some countries, such guidelines are already compulsory. All transnational institutions (such as World Bank, Organization for Economic Cooperation and Development, World Resources Institute, European Investment Bank and many more) also take an active role in solving problem of fundraising for the development of environmentally sustainable practices. Different green financing instruments were introduced in search of optimal way to raise the needed funds (cases of such instruments and their effect were analyzed by Dafermos et al. (2018), Yadav et al. (2016), Silva and Cortez (2016), Little et al. (2015), Heckerta and Rosan (2016) and others. And new green financial instruments are being introduced at fairly fast pace.

It might be caused by the fact, that despite many setbacks, green financing instrument markets are rapidly evolving and growing. Therefore, analysis of the main factors, contributing to this market evolution should be analyzed in order to understand (for decision-makers – to make informed decisions), what further market makers' actions could induce market growth rate or maintain it at a desired level. Also, the peculiarities of the green financial instruments themselves should be analyzed as it has a direct effect on the fundraising potential.

The goal of the chapter is to analyze main current green financing instruments, trends, causes and challenges of their market development, and potential accelerators of green financing instruments markets. Therefore the main objectives are the following: overview and analysis of green bonds and green equities attributes and market trends, overview of types and significance of green loans and budget financing instruments, presentation of private green investment promotion instruments, showcasing different types of the instruments, the role of public financing institutions in financing green investment.

The up to date literature and databases were selected to achieve the objectives mentioned above. The latest policies concerning green financing instruments are presented, while historical data is also used to demonstrate trends of the analyzed instruments.

BACKGROUND

The word "green" in nowadays economy is associated with the green growth, which in turn often means the way of economic development that is oriented towards the sustainability of the economy. Simultaneously, the term alludes to the saving or preserving the natural resources so that natural assets would be sustainable as well (OECD, 2011). Seeking green growth, green finance play an important role. There no single definition of the term „green finance" presented in scientific literature. The G20 (Green Finance Study Group) defines green finance as „...financing of investments that provide environmental benefits in the broader context of environmentally sustainable development. These environmental benefits include reductions in air, water and land pollution, reductions in greenhouse gas emissions, improved energy efficiency while utilizing existing natural resources, as well as mitigation of and adaptation to climate change and their co-benefits". Inderst et al. (2012) relate the term green finance to socially responsible investing (SRI), environmental, social, and governance investing (ESG), sustainable, long-term investing or similar concepts. The scientists of Finance Watch and Z/Yen in the Global Green Finance Index (2018) define green finance as „... any financial instrument or financial services activity – including insurance, equity, bonds, commodity, and derivatives trading, analytical or risk management tools – which results in positive change for the environment and society over the long term (sustainability)". Sachs et al. (2019) define green finance as new financial instruments (green bonds, green banks, carbon market instruments) and new policies (fiscal policy, green central banking, financial technologies), that are aimed at financing green projects. Lindenberg (2014a) defines green finance as the financing of public and private green investments in the following areas: environmental goods and services; prevention, minimization and compensation of damages to the environment and to the climate; the financing of public policies that encourage the implementation of environmental and environmental-damage mitigation or adaptation projects and initiatives; components of the financial system that deal specifically with green investments, such as the Green Climate Fund or financial instruments for green investments, including their specific legal, economic and institutional framework conditions. Green finance represents a positive shift in the global economy's transition to sustainability through the financing of public and private green investments and public policies that support green initiatives (Berensmann, Lindenberg, 2016).

Despite slight differences in the presented definitions, green finance is usually related to investments in such green projects as environment protection, renewable energy, more efficient consumption of energy, and others. The scientists who deal with green investments point out the following areas of investment: renewable energy (including bio fuels); general environmental management (waste management, air and water pollution abatement, soil remediation); climate change mitigation; combustion technologies for improved efficiency; indirect contribution (energy storage); buildings (energy efficiency); transportation. Green investments also incorporate other investment approaches such as: ESG (environmental, social and governance), SRI (sustainable responsibility investing), RI (responsible investing), SI (sustainable investing), double or triple bottom-line investing, universal ownership concept, etc. (Voica et al., 2014). These investments are significant for green growth. Green growth, in its turn, plays a vital role in the implementation of sustainable development goals. Green growth fosters economic growth and development. Our well-being depends on the resources and environmental services that are provided by natural assets. In order to stimulate green growth, investment and innovation must be catalyzed underpinning sustained growth and giving a rise to new economic opportunities. The data of the investigations carried out by World Bank, the OECD, World Resources Institute, the Global Sustainable Investment Alliance (GSIA) and some others proves that investments into green projects have been growing recently and will keep growing in the future. From 2015 to 2030 the transition to low-carbon economy will require USD 93 trillion of investment. The intensive growth of green investments is presented in different studies, e.g. the World Recourses Institute's study shows that from 2012 to 2014 green investments increased by 30% in Asia and by nearly 80% in the USA. Though Europe was the leader in investments flow, the growth was much lower than in the USA and reached less than 60%. In the EU, the need for green investments is related to the targets of Europe 2020 strategy. These targets are known as the '20-20-20' targets. Europe 2020 strategy sets three objectives for climate and energy policy to be reached by 2020: 1) to reduce GHG emissions by at least 20% compared with 1990 levels; 2) to increase the share of renewable energy in final energy consumption to 20%; 3) to move towards a 20% increase in energy efficiency.

In the analysis of green investments, an imperative role is played by financial instruments used for financing green investment projects.

THE BREAKDOWN OF GREEN INVESTMENT FINANCING INSTRUMENTS

Scientific literature, studies by European and world organizations, research centres, financial institutions all indicate that there are no universal green financing instruments that would be universal for all green growth projects. The choice of the specific instrument is determined by various factors: the type of investment, the size of a project, financing instrument source availability, state policy, financing institution's policy etc. According to Inderst et al. (2012), greenness of the financing instrument derives from the use to which they are being put – the goal of underlying assets or activities. Often the most common conventional financing instruments (e.g., loans), just because of being instruments for financing green projects, take on a new form and are called new, innovative investment instruments. Examples of such instruments are green loans, green bonds, green microcredits, green equity and others. There is no universal green financing instruments' classification presented in the literature. Lindenberg (2014a) groups green investment financing instruments into three groups: instruments that provide financing directly to projects (equity, grants, loans, credit lines); instruments that do not directly transfer money, but transfer knowledge or mitigate risk (guarantees, technical assistance); instruments that are used to raise additional private funds, which can be transferred to green projects via one of the above mentioned instruments (green bonds and structured funds). Buchner et al. (2014) present three major categories of instruments: grants, low-cost debt including concessional loans; capital instruments at commercial terms, including project-level market rate debt, project-level equity, and balance sheet financing. Researchers of the Center for International Climate and Environmental Research in Background Report on Long-term Climate Finance (2015) present these green investment financing instruments: grants, debt, risk mitigation measures, equity, carbon offsets. Del Rio and Mir-Artigues (2014) divide financing instruments for renewable electricity projects into primary and secondary. Voica et al. (2014) present two main forms of green investment: green equity and green bonds. Venugopal et al. (2012) divide financing instruments and mechanisms that encourage participation of private capital in green investment financing into two groups: public support mechanisms (policy and overacting support and project-level assistance); public financing instruments (lending, equity investment, de-risking instruments). These instruments are particularly important to attract private capital investment in case of green projects.

The analysis of scientific literature allows to identify the key green investments financing instruments. These instruments are: green bonds, green equity, green loans, and budget financing instruments.

Green Bonds

Green bond is a debt security, in many ways similar to the non-green or conventional bonds. But because of its sustainabilityoriented purpose, has some specific peculiarities, discussed further. In general, purpose of the green bonds is to provide funds for development of green projects, green economy, etc. Therefore green bonds can be considered as one of the alternatives to other lending means. Being part of securities markets, this type of investment also provides opportunity to utilize advantages of the financial markets. Various green investment aspects were analyzed by Banahan (2019), Bracking (2019), Dafermos et al. (2018), Park (2018), Monasterolo and Raberto (2018), Trompeter (2017), Martin et al. (2016), Voica et al. (2015), Lesser et al. (2016), Gonzalez et al. (2016), Markandya et al. (2015), Mathews and Kidney (2012).

Figure 1. The World Bank green bond issuance by sectors, 2008-2018 (The World Bank, 2018)

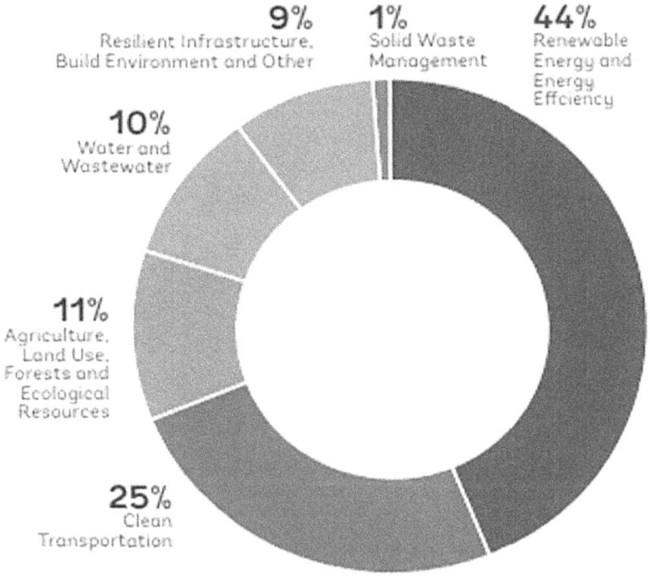

Usually, green bond is a financial instrument with fixed income, but there are cases, when green bonds were issued with zero coupon rate or floating coupon rate (for example, green bond, launched by the World Bank in 2014). Although the idea of green funding has existed since several decades ago, the green bonds market as such and with attempt to distinguish the "green" feature of the bonds, is relatively young. The start of the green market is often considered to be in the year 2007. The World Bank states that they have issued first green bonds in 2008, where the eligibility of the green project was defined (The World Bank, 2018). In 10 years from 2008 World Bank has issued almost 150 green bonds in 20 currencies, totaling in 11 billion USD in funding to support the green policy projects (The World Bank, 2018). Their green bond issuance by sectors from 2008 (the first green bond) to 2018 (30th of June) is shown in the Figure 1.

As this type of investment is relatively new, its effects on the green finance development and economic sustainability cannot be reliably verified, at least long term effects. But impact on separate green economy or green growth factors can be measured in the short run. Various aspects of the green economy and green growth attributes are analyzed by Park (2018), Monasterolo and Raberto (2018), Trompeter (2017), Barbier (2016), Ng and Tao (2016), Criscuolo et al. (2015), Yue et al. (2016), Loiseau et al. (2016), Shah et al. (2016), Vasquez-Brust et al. (2014), Caister (2013), Mathews and Kidney (2012) etc. Also various aspects of effects on the green financing and sustainability of the economy were analyzed by Bracking (2019), Dafermos et al. (2018), Tripathy (2017), Trompeter (2017), Yadav et al. (2016), Silva and Cortez (2016), Little et al. (2015), Heckerta and Rosan (2016) etc.

Since the start, green bond market is rapidly growing, especially starting with the year 2012. Global sustainable debt annual issuance from 2012 to 2018 is shown in Figure 2 (legend is stacked in the same order as the bars, green bonds shown on the bottom section). Since the first emission of the green bonds, demand and popularity, as well as the issuance of this type of bonds have grown almost exponentially and the market has been diversified by the currencies, types of issuers and instruments with different attributes. Following the successful development of green bonds market, other sustainability-oriented

Figure 2. Global sustainable debt annual issuance, 2012-2018 (BloombergNEF, 2019)

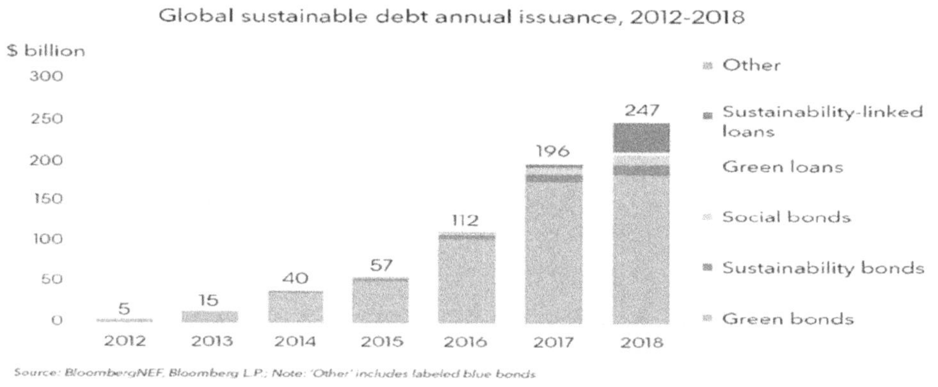

instruments were introduced. This includes sustainability bonds, social bonds, green loans, sustainability-linked loans, etc.

Green bonds, mostly associated with resolving climate change challenges, are issued to support sustainability in many different green policy areas. The term "green" itself is also mostly linked to environmental sustainability and thus, environmental responsibility. To qualify for the status of "green" instrument, in this case – green bonds, bonds must be verified by competent institution, for example by Climate Bond Standard Board (*Climate Bonds Initiative*, 2019). The latter can provide with the certification that bonds are issued for funding project, which is beneficial for the environment. Green economy includes such sustainable practices in business and infrastructure that include clean transportation, more efficient and cleaner energy production, better water usage and management, greener buildings, clean and efficient waste management and improved land usage through sustainable farming and forestry (*Green Equity Indexes*, 2019). In general, green bonds can be considered as bonds, proceeds of which contribute to any eligible green project, aiming to address environmental problems and/or challenges.

The first green bonds were issued as an innovative financial instrument to fund an immense amount of money, needed for environmental targets. For example, the Organization for Economic Cooperation and Development (OECD) in 2017 has estimated that in order to keep temperature growth within limits of two degrees, almost 7 trillion USD are needed annually until year 2030 (*Financing Climate Futures: Rethinking Infrastructure*, 2018). Non-compulsory guidelines for green bonds issuance are provided in the Green Bond Principles (GBP) (2018), which are continuously revised by the leading issuers of green bonds. Governments of separate countries can also issue country-specific guidelines for the green bond issuance. For example, the Peoples Bank of China issued guidelines in year 2015, India issued rules for green bond issuance in 2017, Brazil and Morocco issued guidelines in 2016, etc. It demonstrates relatively recent need for such guidelines. The importance of the green investment is also explicitly recognized in the G20 Sustainable Finance Synthesis Report (2018), in which the mobilization of the private capital towards green investment is encouraged. Worldwide often it is stated the objective and ambition to facilitate the further development of green bond market and foster global collaboration in green bond investments.

As mentioned, the year 2008 is often referred as the green bond market initiation year. Although sustainability aimed bonds were issued at earlier years too. For example, according to Bloomberg database (2019), green bond issuance is recorded in 1998 as well (issuance by European Bank for Reconstruction

Figure 3. The top national issuers of the green bonds, 2019 (Holbrook, 2019)

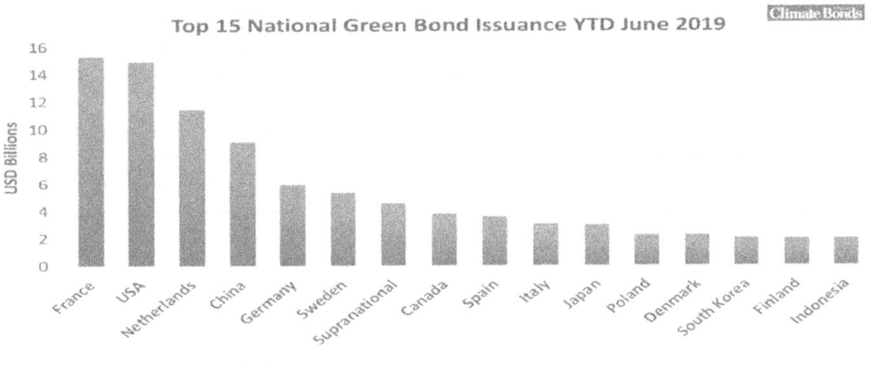

Figure 4. Green bond issuers, 2008-2018 (up to date) (BloombergNEF, 2018)

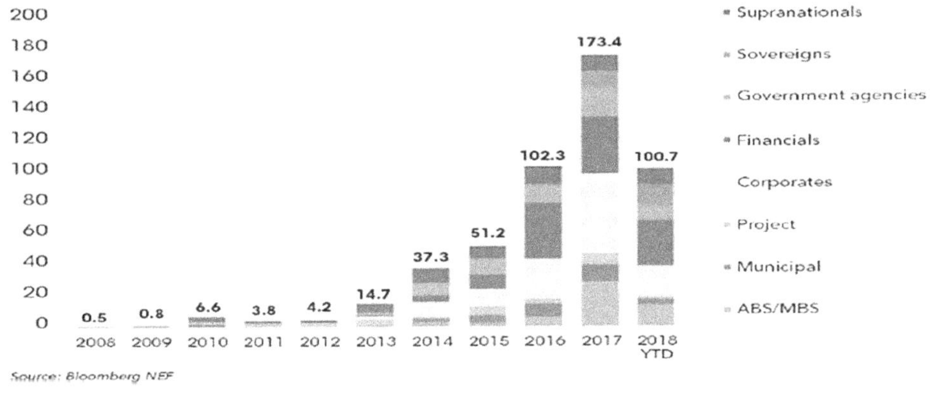

and Development (EBRD), bonds maturing on the end of 2029). It is estimated, that green bond issuance will exceed 200 billion USD in 2019 (Moody's, 2019). Currently the top national issuers of the green bonds are France, USA, and Netherlands (Figure 3).

Also, currently in the largest corporate bonds issued are at 1,9 billion USA, 1,6 billion USA, and 1,5 billion USA. And the largest sovereign green bond is at 6,7 billion USA, issued by the Netherlands (Climate Bonds Certified issuance) (Holbrook, 2019). Different types of green bond issuers are shown in Figure 4 (legend is stacked in the same order as the bars, green bonds shown on the bottom section). Corporates and financials are of increasing importance in green market development as they the issue highest amount of green bonds.

S&P Global Ratings estimate that the green bond market in 2019 may grow approximately 8% in 2019 (Whieldon, 2019). They estimate that green bond issuance maybe around 180 billion USD, which would be approximately 7.78% growth to compare it with the previous year issuance. It is expected due to increasing number of issuers, because of strong market fundamentals and increasing interest in environmental, social, and governance (ESG) movement. Holbrook (2019) states that it is estimated, that annual issuance in the year 2019 might even reach 240-250 billion USD.

Figure 5. Market share of green bonds by currency, higher than 1% (on the left) and biggest respective market shares (on the right) (data from Bloomberg, 2019)

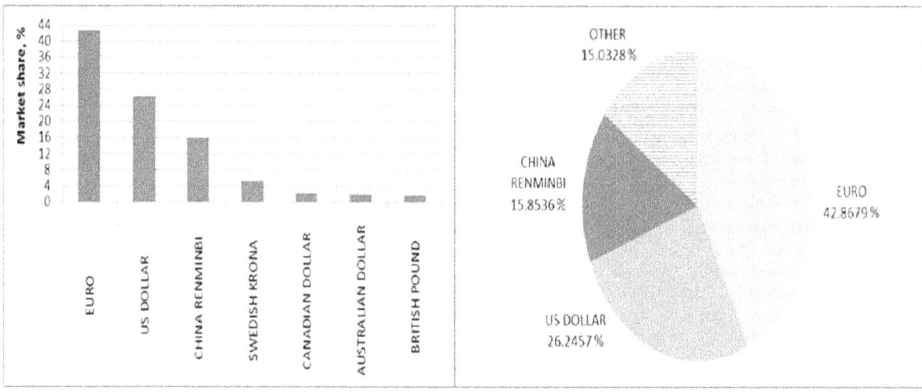

In 2018 nearly 40% of new green issuance from financial institutions were from China. But most of growth in 2018 was because of new issuers from financial institutions in Western Europe and North America. It is expected that European region will remain dominant green bond issuer, where lately proceeds of the green bonds are mainly allocated to the transportation, energy, and building sectors.

Between 2007 (starting year) and 2012 green bond issuers were mostly multilateral development banks and other public institutions. Acceleration of the green bond market growth is evident since 2013, when market was entered by the private sector.

By the amount issued in one issuance, the biggest issued amount is 0.02 trillion USD (French Republic Government Bond OATs) (Bloomberg, 2019). As of June 2019, Bloomberg database lists 258 green bonds issuers with the active securities. By the currency, biggest market shares are of bonds, issued in Euro (42.87%; second highest number of securities), US Dollars (26.25%; highest number of securities) and China's Renminbis (15.85%; fourth number of securities, Swedish krona denominated bonds being in the third place by number of securities) (Bloomberg, 2019). Market share of green bonds by currency, higher than 1% (on the left) and biggest respective market shares (on the right) are shown in Figure 5.

The appeal and popularity of the green bonds as financial investment alternative is determined by both the support of sustainability policy (or "green") ideas and performance of the bonds. The purpose of the proceeds of green bonds (towards achievement of green policy targets and in accordance with the Green Bond Framework) is often considered as a prime incentive among the pro-sustainability oriented investors.

As a financial instrument, in its essence, green bonds are not different from other bonds in terms of the bond-specific attributes. But green investments instruments are often furthermore "promoted" by introducing additional value-creating incentives for the investors. For example, tax credits or exemptions can be fairly appealing, even to compare to investment is taxable bonds.

Top 5 green bonds holders by the amount (value) held are shown in the Figure 6. Respectively, 5.68% totaled of 403 securities, 4.95% - 278 securities, 3.36% - 222 securities, 3.25% (fourth place) – 286 securities, 3.25% (fifth place) – 124 securities.

Considering green bonds as investment alternative from the yield standpoint, results of comparison with the benchmark add to useful insight towards return expectations.

Figure 6. Top five green bonds holders by the amount (value) held (data from Bloomberg, 2019)

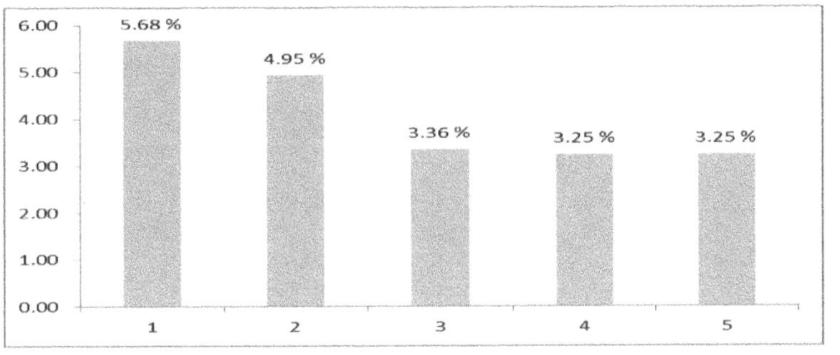

Figure 7. The Global Green Bond Total Return Index, 2013- 2019 (Bloomberg, 2019)

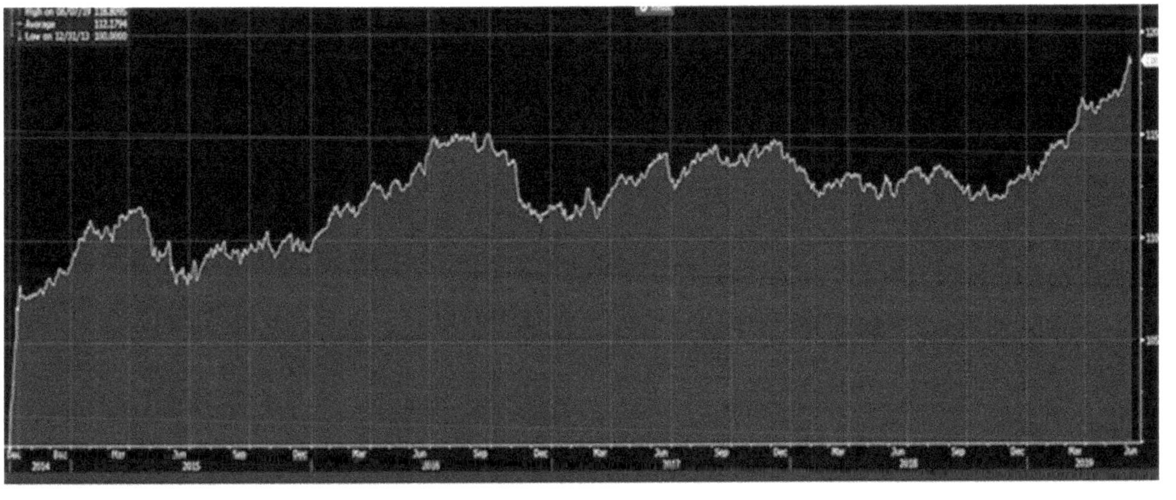

According to Bloomberg (2019) database, as of June 2019 highest coupon rate of the green bonds was 15.6%. This issuance in the domestic bond market (in Africa) aims at green infrastructure development funding and is of 15-year maturity. Issuer is an electricity generation company, interested in developing renewable energy sector (Bloomberg, 2019). Second and third highest coupon rates were 15.5% (1-year maturity) and 12.85% (2-year maturity). Both issuances are made by a private company in China. Longest maturity is 60-year green bonds with 4.496% coupon rate, issuer being in the energy sector.

Returns of Climate Awareness Bond, launched by the European Investment Bank (EIB) in 2007, were linked to an equity index. Thus the issuance was a structured product. The first fixed income green bond issuance was made by World Bank to attract the mainstream investors, willing to participate in the green bond market.

There are a lot of different indexes (for different sectors, regions, proceeds' targets, etc.), reflecting investment return expectations. For example, the Last Price of Bloomberg Barclays MSCI showing Global Green Bond Total Return Index (Index) from the end of 2013 (start of the index) to June of 2019 is shown in the Figure 7.

Figure 8. Regression between the Index and S&P500 Index, 2013- 2019 (Bloomberg, 2019)

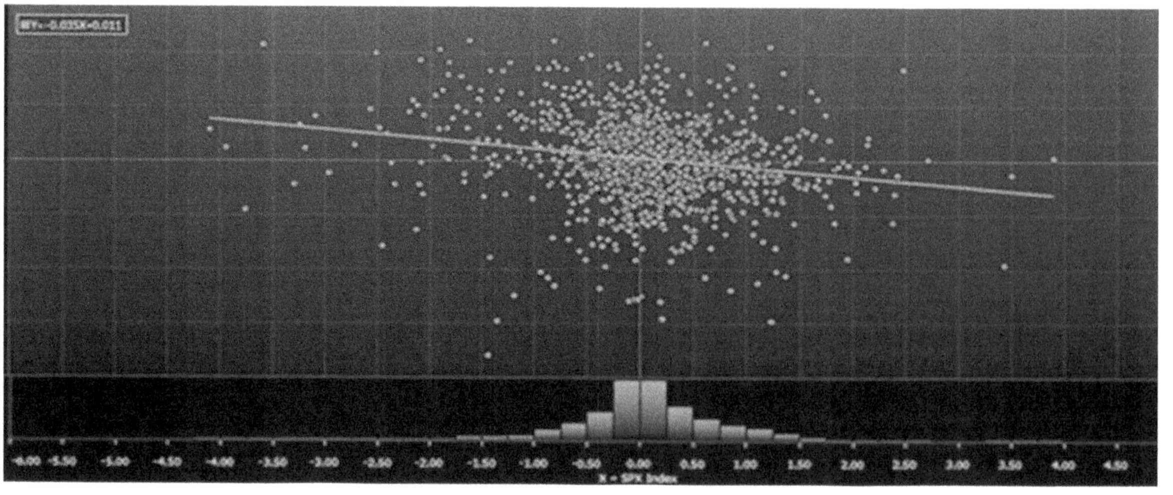

Figure 9. Volatility (spread) of the analyzed Global Green Bond Index, 2013- 2019 (Bloomberg, 2019)

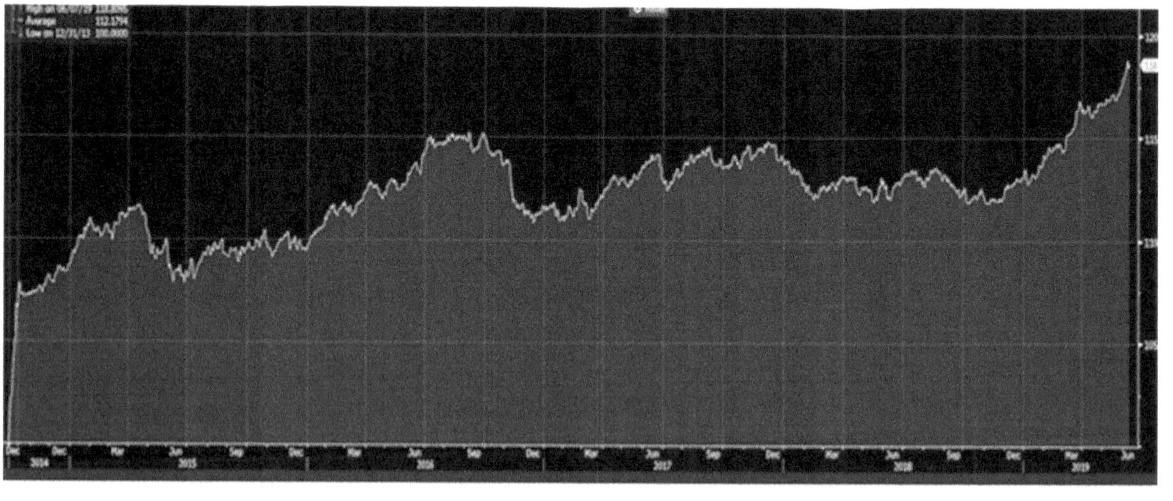

According to the Index data, the total return of the price change for the period was 9.1%. Bloomberg database also provides comprehensive, comparable analysis of the Index with any other selected Index. When compared with the S&P 500 Index and S&P Green Bonds Index (total return), highest price change during the analyzed period is of S&P 500 Index (67.13%), S&P Green Bonds Index – 16.97%. Total return is also highest in the case of S&P 500 Index.

Regression between the Index and S&P500 Index is shown in the Figure 8.

Raw beta coefficient is -0,035, alpha (intercept) coefficient 0,011, standard deviation of error 0,155, standard error of alpha 0,005, standard error of beta 0,005, number of points 1181.

Considering financial investment, volatility is one of the important factors. Volatility (spread) of the analyzed Global Green Bond Index for the same period is shown in the Figure 9.

Table 1. Sample of the analyzed indicators

Security	Price	Yield	Sprd	G-Sprd	I-Sprd	OAS	Basis	ASW	Z-Sprd
1 to 2 years									
EIBKOR 1 3/4 02/27/18	100,065	1,695	58,46	79,5	52,1	80,9	-38,7	50,8	51,5
EIB 7 3/4 03/12/18	99,767	7,903	-16,11	-12,6	40,8	-8,1	-10,9	22,4	22,9
2 to 3 years									
EIB 8 1/2 03/27/19	95,529	10,479	8,87	8,6	-98,3	-5,4	120	-97,4	-107
EIB 3 04/23/19	107,613	-0,198	50,04	48,1	16,9	47,4	-4,1	17	17,4
EIB 1 3/4 11/15/19	105,111	-0,355	32,96	31,9	-27,6	21,8	41,6	-28,1	-27,4

Also, the previous research on the volatility of green bonds showed, that green bonds tend to be less volatile than non-green bonds (Draksaite et al., 2018). In order to analyze the investment appeal, green bonds were evaluated against non-green bonds. Both selected green and non-green bonds were of the same issuer. The European Investment Bank (EIB) was selected as an issuer of both types of bonds. Considering market share, it is one of the domain issuers of green bonds. Also, analyzed bonds, issued by the EIB, are of the highest rating. The data was obtained from the EIB database, the Bloomberg database, public official statistics databases and financial markets' databases. Historical data of the period 2007-2016 was analyzed. In total, 32 green bonds and more than 200 times more non-green bonds were analyzed. Also, only fixed rate green and non-green bonds were analyzed, because of data comparability reasons.

Regression between the two types of the investment instruments was calculated, using regression equations, suggested by Eyraud et al. (2013):

$$y_{it} = a_i + \sum_{k=1}^{K} \beta^k * x_{it}^k + \varepsilon_{it}, \tag{1}$$

where y - green investment, x – the covariates, a – country-specific fixed effects.

Bond price volatility was assessed, evaluating variance. Sample of the analyzed indicators are shown in the Table 1.

Price – ask price; yield – yield to convention; Sprd - spread to benchmark; G-Sprd - interpolated spread to government curve; I-Sprd - interpolated spread to swap curve; OAS - option adjusted spread; Basis - default swap basis; ASW - asset swap spread; Z-Sprd - zero volatility spread.

Standard deviation from average and standard deviation from average difference to the sector was calculated for the analyzed data. Correlation results showed negative or positive correlation. Based on the results of these analyzes, green bond performance analysis, respective analysis of non-green bonds and the research prerequisites, it was established that green bonds tend to be less volatile to compare with non-green bonds. Also, as expected, it was established that both green and non-green bond prices have similar fluctuation trend.

Figure 10. 10-year performance of the NASDAQ OMX Green Economy Total Return Index, 2009- 2019 (Green Equity Indexes, 2019)

Green Equity

Similarly to green bonds, one of the common purpose of the green equities is to provide funds for the development of green projects. Fundamentally, equity translates into proprietary rights, therefore this type of investment could be also viewed as of higher commitment to the cause (Lindenberg, 2014b). On the other hand, it is usually obtained as a financial instrument, generating financial gain.

Both green bonds and green equity markets are growing due to rise in environmental awareness, increasing private sectors' participation in the market and worldwide support for green financing instruments. As there is green equity market, different green equity indexes are useful when evaluating the performance of this financial instrument. Some indexes are sector-specific, others include a bigger variety of equities. The S&P Global Clean Energy Index, for example, is comprised based on data from 30 companies in clean energy-related businesses. More extensive range of sectors is covered by the Nasdaq Green Economy Global Benchmark Index (QGREEN) (Green Equity Indexes, 2019). Green investing indexes of Nasdaq cover companies, working towards reducing the carbon usage.

10-year performance of the NASDAQ OMX Green Economy Total Return Index is shown in the Figure 10. This market-capitalization weighted index is a total return calculation of QGREEN. It tracks the performance of companies in different economic sectors, related to the green economy development (Green Equity Indexes, 2019).

As of June 2019 QGREEN index breakdown (left) and top 10 securities by weight (right) are shown in the Table 2.

Despite comparatively rapid development of green equity market, it is likely that investments exclusively in the green financial markets do not outperform return maximization oriented investments in any available market. One of the reasons being risk, associated with the relatively high capital costs of funded green projects, especially if the project is relatively short or funding is needed for the beginning stages of the project. To compensate shortcomings of the green investment attractiveness, additional value is often offered for the investor (for example, fiscal or monetary means, allowing higher returns on

Table 2. QGREEN index breakdown (left) and top 10 securities by weight (right), 2019.

Industry	Weight, %	Securities	Ticker	Security	Weight, %
Oil & Gas	2,53	39	CSCO	CISCO SYSTEMS INC	10,06
Basic Materials	7,18	24	NEE	NEXTERA ENERGY INC	3,91
Industrials	37,82	127	DHR	DANAHER CP	3,87
Consumer Goods	7,60	36	CNR	CANADIAN NATL RL RG	2,75
Health Care	2,43	5	IBE	IBERDROLA	2,43
Consumer Services	3,30	11	SPG	SIMON PPTY GRP INC	2,42
Telecommunications	0,00	0	AI	AIR LIQUIDE	2,31
Utilities	14,74	52	ECL	ECOLAB INC	2,16
Financials	6,10	15	DE	DEERE CO	2,16
Technology	17,93	22	TSLA	TESLA INC	2,05

Source: (Green Equity Indexes, 2019)

investments). Although there are more and more attractive attributes offered for the investors, inherent green instruments' market problems still exist. Lack of liquidity in the green financial markets, unstable political and economic environment in developing countries, where projects are implemented, high industry development costs are just some examples of such problems. To handle these challenges, various risk management means can be introduced. For example, in the researches grants, hedging means, loan guaranties, etc. are often suggested.

Green Loan

Green loan is a type of loan, which is used by financial institutions (banks, credit unions) in many countries around the world to finance the environment-friendly projects. The biggest part of loans is provided by banks. According to OECD, banks provide roughly 80 percent of green finance. For green projects financing (especially in start-up fazes of small businesses) green microfinance and green crowdfunding instruments are used (*Investing in Climate, Investing in Growth,* 2017). The purpose of green microcredits is to finance small green projects. These credits are provided by microfinance institutions (MFIs) which are alternative financial providers of green microcredits (especially in developing countries). The EU promotes microcredits to support small businesses and, at the same time, to protect the environment (Forcella and Hudon, 2016). Crowdfunding is "a collective effort by people who network and pool their money together, usually via the internet, in order to invest in and support efforts initiated by other people or organizations" (Ordanini et al., 2011). The most common types of crowdfunding are: donation-based crowdfunding, reward-based crowdfunding, and equity-based crowdfunding. In donation-based crowdfunding, there is no financial benefit to contributors or investors. In reward-based crowdfunding, individual contributors receive some form of product or service as a reward for their contribution. In the equity-based crowdfunding, contributors become part-owners of the business by trading capital for equity shares. Crowdfunding plays an important and increasingly widespread role at the start of a renewable energy project's life-cycle (Lam, Law, 2016). Many online crowdfunding platforms are specializing on financing green projects. The largest crowdfunding platforms for green projects are: Mosaic, SunFunder, EquityNet, StartSomeGood, and others. They specialize in different areas of green growth.

Budget Financing Instruments

Budget financing instruments play a significant role in financing of green investments. The main sources of public budgets for financing green growth are: revenues from taxes, revenues from resource trading, and auctioning. The main public actors of budget financing are: state actors, national and public institutions, multilateral development finance institutions. The main instruments are: grants, debt, guarantees, insurance, and others. The green projects usually are financed with regard to the state programmes. In the EU green investment financing is appointed with regard to the EU programs (e.g., Horizon 2020, LIFE), European Structural and Investment Funds (European Regional Development Fund, Cohesion Fund, European Agricultural Fund for Rural Development, European Maritime and Fisheries Fund). The funds and programmes are used for financing particular areas of green growth. The funding areas of Horizon 2020 are: energy efficiency; renewable energy; sustainable urban mobility. The LIFE programme is used to finance the environment and climate change projects. The areas of The European Structural and Investment Funds investments are: energy efficiency; renewable energy and smart grids; environment protection; low carbon economy. These programmes and funds contribute to green economy initiatives implemented by the EU. In 2014, the Council of the European Union adopted conclusions on the European Semester and the strategy Europe 2020 greening. Sustainability and resource efficiency issues were included in the strategy Europe 2020. The EU aim is to achieve, by the end of 2030 energy efficiency. It would reach 40%, the production of energy from renewable energy sources would increase to 30% and greenhouse gas emissions compared to 1990 would level down to 40%. For the period of 2014-2020, 20% of the EU budget will be allocated to climate-related action. Given the EU's objectives, it can be expected that in the coming 2021-2027 period, the focus on climate change issues will increase and this will condition more green investment funding needs. The European Commission is planning to donate 25% of the EU budget as minimum in 2021-2027. The EU, the Member States and the European Investment Bank are the biggest contributors of public climate finance to developing countries. In 2017 the total contribution made EUR20.4 billion. Besides, they are the world top providers of official development assistance (a total EUR74.4 billion in 2018).

Private Green Investment Promotion Instruments

As public budgets alone would not be able to provide the necessary financing (Lindenberg, 2014b), it is vital to attract private green investment. In scientific literature, barriers restricting private capital involvement in promoting green growth financing are as such: greater investment in green projects costs; unstable legal and economic environment; distortionary subsidies; lack of liquid debt and equity markets and others. In order to overcome these barriers, governments should seek to mobilize private green investment by creating an enabling environment for long term green investment; using public budgets and investments efficiently, also using private green investment de-risking instruments. The analysis of the literature shows that the risk is one of the most important reasons influencing lack of private green investment. Green investments typically suffer higher risk perceptions due to the dependence on public policy and, often, the relative immaturity of technologies, markets, and industries (Frisari et al., 2013).

According to scientific literature and the studies conducted by various organizations, no universal green investment risks classification has ever been provided. Frisari et al. (2013) group the risks into four categories according to their different sources and character: political, policy, and social risks; technical, physical risks; market, commercial risks; outcome risks. According to Green Investment Report (2013), presented by The World Economic Forum, private investment in green technologies faces a number of risks: political risks; macroeconomic risks; policy risks; technology and operational related risks; capacity risks. The variety of risks is determined by various factors: the amount of investment, investment area, the state in which a project is realized, etc. Certain types of risk (e.g., economic risk, industry risk, political risk) are inherent not only to green but also to conventional investments. Some risks are faced only while investing in green projects.

Mobilizing private finance at scale requires risks of green investments to be reduced to about the same levels as those faced by alternative, conventional investments (*The Green Investment Report,* 2013). Different public instruments are used for reducing the risks. Public financial instruments are designed to reduce real or perceived risk and / or to increase return on investment (Amin et al., 2014).

As promotion of private capital is most often associated with reducing investment risk or increasing benefit, the main de-risking instruments will be presented below. These instruments reduce private investment risk and encourage a more active participation in financing green investments. In scientific literature, different de-risking instruments and their classifications are presented. Micale et al. (2013) identify two main categories of de-risking instruments: policy de-risking instruments or other interventions that address underlying barriers which cause risks; financial de-risking instruments (concessional loans, grants for risk-mitigation, guarantees, insurance and public equity co-investment). Policies can also be a source of risk themselves if they change frequently and destabilize the investment environment. Financial de-risking instruments may not directly address underlying barriers but rather strategically transfer risks that private investors face to public actors such as national governments or development banks. Researchers of the Center for International Climate and Environmental Research in Background Report on Long-term Climate Finance (2015) mention two risk mitigation instruments: guarantees and insurance. Frisari et al. (2013) identify six categories of risk mitigation instruments: bilateral contracts; credit enhancement instruments; insurance; revenue support policies; direct concessional investments; indirect political/institutional support. This list includes both dedicated instruments that directly address specific risks (e.g., contracts and insurance policies), as well as broader or more diffused instruments that address multiple risks (e.g., political commitments to environmental protection). Single instruments may affect several risks simultaneously, directly, and indirectly. Researchers of the World Economic Forum in Green investment report (2013) present the following de-risking instruments: loan guarantees; insurance; foreign exchange/liquidity facilities. The most popular de-risking instruments most frequently used in practice are as follows: grants, loan guarantees, and insurance. These instruments may be used at different points in an investment program cycle to target different investors (Amin et al., 2014).

Grants are resources, intended to finance green investment. This instrument is easily applied to all kinds of projects, especially in early project development phase (Lindenberg, 2014b). Often, grants are used to cover costs during the highest risk development phase and by this provide confidence to private investors. This instrument has many pros and very few cons. It is simple to implement and manage, gives viability to a project, covers full cost of adaptation, complements other instruments, and reduces administrative costs, as no payback is required. The main drawback of this instrument is that there are no reflows and hence it is costly for public budgets. Green grants are available from a variety of organizations and government agencies. The best known organization is Global Greengrants Fund. Since its establishment in 1993, Global Greengrants Fund has granted over 12,000 grants in 168 countries, providing a total of over USD 84 million.

To promote the private green investment, **guarantees** and innovative **insurance** instruments are used. These instruments are provided by governments and financial development institutions and often are intended to decrease the political risk. Political risk guarantees are particularly useful in developing and emerging markets (*The Green Investment Report,* 2013). The World Bank Group's Multilateral Investment Guarantee Agency (MIGA) is one of the main institutions providing the guaranties that minimize political risk. Insurance is used to transfer risk from one entity to another while specializing in pooling risks together (Frisari et al., 2013). Insurance policies are very common in mitigating physical and political risks.

In order to promote private green investments (especially in case of Emerging countries), the EU organizes different initiatives and programmes. One of the most significant initiatives is the External Investment Plan (EIP), which was launched in 2017. It is designed to attract more investment, in particular from businesses and private investors, into countries near the EU and in Africa. It is expected to leverage EUR44 billion of investment through the EU input of EUR4.5 billion. It is planned to do so by using public money to lower the risk of investing in key sectors like sustainable energy or lending to small businesses. One of the part of EIP is the European Fund for Sustainable Development (EFSD). This fund includes two types of instruments: financial guarantee and blending. These instruments are used to leverage much more public and private investment in sustainable development. Blending is the use of a limited amount of public grants or non-grant resources to mobilize financing from financial institutions and the private sector for the projects that promote the development of the countries. The EU has been carrying out blended finance operations since 2007. In the content of EIP blending helps to: achieve more with less taxpayers' money while saving time; improve project sustainability, development impact, quality, and innovation; support reforms that partner countries pursue; improve cooperation between European and non-European donors and financial institutions; raise the profile of the EU development funding.

Climate change problems encourage the EU countries to initiate and finance programmes that deal with these problems, e.g., in January, 2019 the Clean Energy Finance and Investment Mobilisation (CEFIM) programme started working. It is supported financially by the government of Denmark and is aimed to attract finance and investment in renewable energy and energy efficiency in buildings in emerging economies (Latin America, South, and Southeast Asia).

Apart from de-risking instruments, public support mechanisms that promote private green investment are applied. The diversity of public support mechanisms is observed in literature. Examples of such mechanisms are the following: feed-in tariffs, renewable energy quotas, standards, tax credit programmes and repealing support for „brown" sectors (*The Green Investment Report*, 2013). These mechanisms are used to raise the private investment level by reducing the cost of capital of green growth. Some of the mechanisms and instruments are used only in specific areas, e.g. the US uses production tax credit to promote wind energy and investment tax credit to promote solar energy. Companies could use these tax credits to reduce income tax or corporate tax deductions in exchange for investing in renewable energy. These instruments and mechanisms can be used to accelerate private investment in green growth by improving the risk-reward calculus, reducing the cost of capital, providing prerequisites and enabling conditions (*Green Investment Report*, 2013). Apart from the instruments and mechanisms mentioned above, technical assistance plays a significant role. Technical support combined with finance from development banks and other lenders has helped promote market awareness among consumers, build the capacity of local institutions, train local staff, and manage local green and climate-policy development (*Green Investment Report*, 2013). It might include, market research, business planning, staff training, or the establishment of technical standards and engineering due diligence (Lindenberg, 2014b). The strength of technical assistance is that it can help to establish a successful track-record for financing or implementing green projects. The weak point of technical support is high transaction costs.

The Role of Public Financing Institutions In Financing Green Investment

An important role in leveraging private capital is performed by public financing institutions (PFIs). PFIs can provide financing (through a variety of financing instruments: debt, equity, and/or de-risking instruments) and advisory services (providing assistance to public authorities in creating favorable conditions for private sector investment). There are three levels of PFIs: multilateral, bilateral, and domestic. Multilateral institutions include global and regional multilateral development banks (MDBs) and international climate funds. Bilateral sources and intermediaries include aid agencies, bilateral development banks, export credit agencies and bilateral climate funds. Domestic sources are: national development banks, national climate funds, and national agencies.

The main PFIs are development banks. Development banks leverage finance from capital markets due to their strong credit ratings and the backing of their shareholder governments, and in turn provide financing to support development outcomes. Development banks use a range of risk mitigation instruments, mezzanine financing and syndication to attract commercial investment to low-emission infrastructure projects (*Financing Climate Futures: Rethinking Infrastructure*, 2018).

Climate funds play a very important role in financing green projects. The Green Climate Fund (GCF) is the largest, most visible, and politically most significant of the multilateral climate funds (Waslander, Vallejos, 2018). This fund plays an important role in financing the Paris Agreement and other green policy outcomes all over the developing world (Tolliver et al., 2019). The GCF started its firs commitment period in 2014. In 2018 it approved 76 projects, with a total of USD3.7 billion in GCF funding.

Most PFIs (e.g., WBG) provide financing instruments not only for green but also for other projects. The number of institutions that specialize in financing green projects is increasing. These institutions are called green banks. The advantages of green banks include offering better credit conditions for clean energy projects, the ability to aggregate small projects in order to achieve a commercially attractive scale, creation of innovative financial products, and market expansion through dissemination of information about the benefits of clean energy (Sachs et al., 2019). One of the green banks is a rapidly rising Green Investment Bank (GIB). A GIB is a publicly capitalized entity established specifically to facilitate private investment into domestic low-carbon, climate-resilient (LCR) infrastructure and other green sectors such as water and waste management (Green Investment Banks, 2017). Using innovative transaction structures, risk-reduction, transaction-enabling techniques, local and market expertise, GIBs are channeling private investment. GIBs are facilitating investment in such areas as commercial and residential energy efficiency retrofits, rooftop solar photovoltaic systems and municipal-level, energy-efficient street lighting. GIBs directly invest in LCR infrastructure using a range of instruments and funding including loans, bond-based financing, and equity. In 2017 there were 13 national and regional/local level GIB"s all around the world: in the United States, Australia, Japan, the United Kingdom, Malaysia, Switzerland and others. The maximum number of such banks was established in the United States. Most GIBs were set up in 2014. The first bank of its kind was established in the United Arab Emirates in 2006. GIB establishment is a clear proof of the fact that the state (or region) is seeking to become a leader in scaling up private low-carbon investments (Green Investment Banks, 2017). GIB plays a particularly significant role in financing green investment projects in emerging markets. By the way, as evidenced in recent

Figure 11. The structure of PFIs financing instruments (World Resources Institute, 2012)

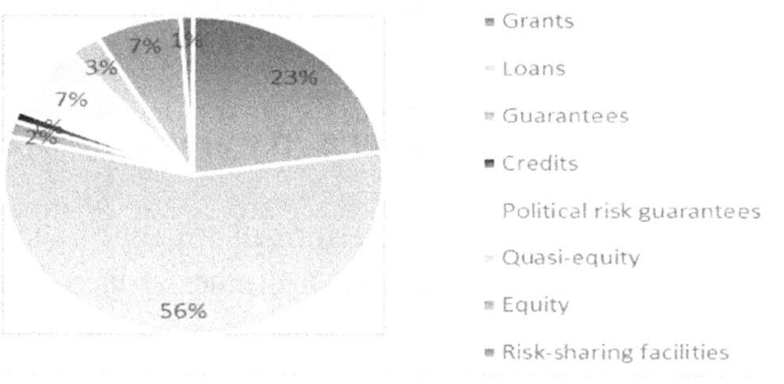

years, the green banks are already successfully leveraging private capital in many countries and proving that such investments can be profitable.

In 2012 World Resource Institute (WRI) conducted the research which aimed at to identify green investment financing instruments applied by the main public sector actors (developed banks and climate funds) from 2005 to 2011. 214 green projects were investigated. The results showed that loans and grants were applied most often (see fig.11). The most popular instrument was loans. Of all 214 projects, almost half (56 percent) were financed through this instrument. The study also sought to identify the sectors that had been granted the lions share. The results showed that the largest share of the funding was allocated to energy and mining (energy efficiency, renewable energy) project funding.

Figure 11 shows the primary financing instruments, i.e. those that make up the largest part of the institutions financing instruments. These instruments can be supplemented by secondary and, in some cases, in tertiary instruments. Institutions also use other instruments, which contribution is relatively low, but also significant. Such instruments include: currency swaps, interest rate swaps, interest rate caps and collars, commodity swaps, securitization, and others.

The examination of the practical application of financial instruments shows that there are no universal green investments financing instrument or their combinations. The quantity of instruments applied for financing the projects varies, as well as their proportions. In reality, the same instruments used by different institutions possess their peculiarities.

FUTURE RESEARCH DIRECTIONS

More in-depth analysis, encompassing more of financial instruments' attributes would reveal peculiarities of the green investing instruments more comprehensively. Also risk level adjusting analysis techniques would be beneficial for the reliability of the results.

Green financial instruments' impact or effect factor should be analyzed in more detail in the future, when enough of historical data will be available.

Further research on the innovative green instruments' usage for optimal green projects funding should be performed.

CONCLUSION

As analyzed green investing financial instruments are of rather specific features, selection of the green financial instrument should be based on the comparative analysis and maximization of estimated return or proceeds.

Green bond investment can be considered as almost the symbiosis between solving environmental sustainability problems and receiving the financial gain. The synergy between the two is often further facilitated by fiscal or monetary means, such as tax exemptions, and worldwide encouragement to develop the green bond market. Currently, investors' preference remains focused more on the financial gain, rather than social gain especially when it is evident that green bond appeal factors are mostly of the same reasoning as ones of the non-green bonds.

Nevertheless, considering green financial markets' development rate, the use of green financial instruments is of significant potential to boost the sustainability of the economy.

The green bond market is fairly diversified by issuers, currency and instruments. Investment trends are mostly defined by separate attributes of the green bonds. Therefore, considering financial gain, it is recommended to make investment decisions based on the fundamental analysis.

Green equity often faces the same challenges attracting investments as green bonds' market. In order to boost green instruments' market, risk management in green projects should be improved, liquidity of the green instrument markets ensured and stimulated, value added benefits, as well as other investment return increasing means should be introduced. It is certainly difficult and complex task, but the aspects of it should be the basis for further green instruments market development.

Rapidly evolving green finance instruments' markets contribute to increase of demand for these instruments and thus help accelerate the performance of environmentally sustainable businesses.

REFERENCES

G20 Sustainable Finance Synthesis Report. (2018). Available at: http://unepinquiry.org/wp-content/uploads/2018/11/G20_Sustainable_Finance_Synthesis Report_2018.pdf

Amin, A., Naidoo, Ch., & Whitley, Sh. (2014). Green Growth in Practice: Lessons from Country Experiences. *Mobilising investments.* Available at: http://www.ggbp.org/sites/all/themes/ggbp/uploads/Green-Growth-in-Practice-062014-Full.pdf

Banahan, C. M. (2019). The Bond Villains of Green Investment: Why an Unregulated Securities Market Needs Government To Lay Down The Law. *Vermont Law Review*, *43*(4), 841–869. Available at https://lawreview.vermontlaw.edu/wp-content/uploads/2019/06/vlaw_43n4_Banahan.pdf

Barbier, E. B. (2016). Is green growth relevant for poor economies? *Resource and Energy Economics*, *45*, 178–191. Available at https://www.sciencedirect.com/science/article/abs/pii/S0928765516301154

Berensmann, K., & Lindenberg, N. (2016). *Green finance: actors, challenges and policy recommendations. German Development Institute.* Briefing Paper 23. Available at: https://papers.ssrn.com/sol3/papers.cfm?abstract_id=2881922

Bloomberg, N. E. F. (2018). *Green Bond Issuance Exceeds $100 Billion for 3rd Year*. Available at: https://about.bnef.com/blog/green-bond-issuance-exceeds-100-billion-3rd-year/

Bloomberg, N. E. F. (2019). *Issuance of sustainable debt products surged 26% to $247 billion last year, as the market innovated to meet demand from investors*. Available at: https://about.bnef.com/blog/sustainable-debt-market-sees-record-activity-2018/

Bloomberg. (2019). *Bloomberg platform database*. Author.

Bracking, S. (2019). Financialisation, Climate Finance, and the Calculative Challenges of Managing Environmental Change. *Antipode*, *51*(3), 709–729. doi:10.1111/anti.12510

Buchner, B., Stadelmann, M., Wilkinson, J., Mazza, F., Rosenberg, A., & Abramskiehn, D. (2014). *The Global Landscape of Climate Finance*. Available at: https://www.climatefinance-developmenteffectiveness.org/sites/default/files/event/CFSDforum2015/climate/The%20Global%20Landscape%20of%20Climate%20Finance_2014.pdf

Caister, D. (2013). Buy Your Green Bonds. *Alternatives Journal (AJ) - Canada's Environmental Voice*, *39*(6), 24-29. Available at: https://www.alternativesjournal.ca/science-and-solutions/buy-your-green-bonds-exclusive-interview-footage

CICERO. (2015). *Background Report on Long-term Climate Finance*. Prepared for the German G7 Presidency 2015. Available at: http://www.g7.utoronto.ca/summit/2015elmau/2015-G7-climate-finance.pdf

Climate Bonds Initiative. (2019). *Climate Bond Standard Board*. Available at: https://www.climatebonds.net/standard/governance/board

Criscuolo, Ch., & Menon, C. (2015). Environmental policies and risk finance in the green sector: Cross-country evidence. *Energy Policy*, *83*, 38–56. Available at https://www.sciencedirect.com/science/article/pii/S0301421515001299

Dafermos, Y., Nikolaidi, M., & Galanis, G. (2018). Climate Change, Financial Stability and Monetary Policy. *Ecological Economics*, *152*, 219–234. doi:10.1016/j.ecolecon.2018.05.011

Del Rio, P., & Mir-Artigues, P. (2014). Combinations of support instruments for renewable electricity in Europe: A review. *Renewable & Sustainable Energy Reviews*, *40*, 287–295. Available at https://www.researchgate.net/publication/264981902_Combinations_of_support_instruments_for_renewable_electricity_in_Europe_A_review

Draksaite, A., Kazlauskiene, V., & Melnyk, L. (2018). The Perspective of the Green Bonds as Novel Debt Instruments in Sustainable Economy. *Consumer Behavior, Organizational Strategy and Financial Economics*, 221-230. Available at: https://www.springerprofessional.de/en/the-perspective-of-the-green-bonds-as-novel-debt-instruments-in-/15580842

Eyraud, L., Clement, B., & Wane, A. (2013). Green investment: Trends and determinants. *Energy Policy*, *60*, 852–865. Available at https://econpapers.repec.org/article/eeeenepol/v_3a60_3ay_3a2013_3ai_3ac_3ap_3a852-865.htm

Financing Climate Futures, Rethinking Infrastructure. (2018). *Policy Highlights*. Available at: https://www.oecd.org/environment/cc/climate-futures/policy-highlights-financing-climate-futures.pdf

Forcella, D., & Hudon, M. (2016). Green microfinance in Europe. *Journal of Business Ethics, 135*, 445–459. doi:10.100710551-014-2452-9

Frisari, G., Hervé-Mignucci, M., Mazza, F., & Micale, V. (2013). *Risk Gaps: A Map of Risk Mitigation Instruments for Clean Investments*. Available at: http://climatepolicyinitiative.org/wp-content/uploads/2013/01/Risk-Gaps-A-Map-of-Risk-Mitigation-Instruments-for-Clean-Investments.pdf

González Ruiza, J. D., Arboledab, C. A., & Boteroc, S. (2016). A Proposal for Green Financing as a Mechanism to Increase Private Participation in Sustainable Water Infrastructure Systems: The Colombian Case. *Procedia Engineering, 145*, 180–187. Available at https://www.sciencedirect.com/science/article/pii/S1877705816300637

Green Bond Principles. (2018). *International Capital Market Association*. Available at: https://www.icmagroup.org/green-social-and-sustainability-bonds/green-bond-principles-gbp/

Green Equity Indexes. (2019). Available at: https://business.nasdaq.com/intel/indexes/equity/green

Green Investment Banks. (2017). *OECD environment policy paper no. 6*. Available at: https://www.oecd-ilibrary.org/environment/green-investment-banks_e3c2526c-en;jsessionid=uGwV0MLx56ijonfdL-1fEvFj.ip-10-240-5-102

Heckerta, M., & Rosan, Ch. D. (2016). Developing a green infrastructure equity index to promote equity planning. *Urban Forestry & Urban Greening, 19*, 263–270. Available at https://www.sciencedirect.com/science/article/pii/S1618866715001892

Holbrook, E. (2019). *A Financial First: Green Bond Issuance Surpasses $100 Billion Mark in First Half of 2019*. Available at: https://www.environmentalleader.com/2019/06/a-financial-first-green-bond-issuance-surpasses-100-billion-mark-in-first-half-of-2019/

Inderst, G., Kaminker, Ch., & Stewart, F. (2012). *Defining and Measuring Green Investments: Implications for Institutional Investors" Asset Allocations*. OECD Working Papers on Finance, Insurance and Private Pensions, 24. OECD Publishing. Available at: https://econpapers.repec.org/paper/oecdafaad/24-en.htm

Lam, P., & Law, A. (2016). Crowdfunding for renewable and sustainable energy projects: An exploratory case study approach. *Renewable & Sustainable Energy Reviews, 60*, 11–20. Available at https://kundoc.com/pdf-crowdfunding-for-renewable-and-sustainable-energy-projects-an-exploratory-case-s.html

Lesser, K., Rößle, F., & Walkshäusl, Ch. (2016). Socially responsible, green, and faith-based investment strategies: Screening activity matters! *Finance Research Letters, 16*, 171–178. Available at https://www.sciencedirect.com/science/article/abs/pii/S1544612315001233

Lindenberg, N. (2014a). *Definition of Green Finance*. DIE. Available at: https://www.die-gdi.de/uploads/media/Lindenberg_Definition_green_finance.pdf

Lindenberg, N. (2014b). *Public Instruments to Leverage Private Capital for Green Investments in Developing Countries*. German Development Institute. Discussion Paper, 50. Available at: https://econpapers.repec.org/paper/zbwdiedps/42014.htm

Little, L. R., Hobday, A. J., Parslow, J., Davies, C. R., & Grafton, R. Q. (2015). Funding climate adaptation strategies with climate derivatives. *Climate Risk Management*, *8*, 9–15. Available at https://www.sciencedirect.com/science/article/pii/S221209631500011X

Loiseau, E., Saikku, L., Antikainen, R., Droste, N., Hansjürgens, B., Pitkanen, K., ... Thomsen, M. (2016). Green economy and related concepts: An overview. *Journal of Cleaner Production*, *139*, 361–371. Available at https://www.researchgate.net/publication/306125941_Green_economy_and_related_concepts_An_overview

Markandya, A., Antimiani, A., Costantini, V., Martini, C., Palma, A., & Tommasino, M. C. (2015). Analyzing Trade-offs in International Climate Policy Options: The Case of the Green Climate Fund. *World Development*, *74*, 93–107. Available at https://www.researchgate.net/publication/276298820_Analyzing_Trade-offs_in_International_Climate_Policy_Options_The_Case_of_the_Green_Climate_Fund

Martin, P. R., & Moser, D. V. (2016). Managers' green investment disclosures and investors' reaction. *Journal of Accounting and Economics*, *61*, 239–254. Available at https://www.sciencedirect.com/science/article/abs/pii/S0165410115000610

Mathews, J. A., & Kidney, S. (2012). Financing climate-friendly energy development through bonds. *Development Southern Africa*, *29*(2), 337–349. doi:10.1080/0376835X.2012.675702

Micale, V., Frisari, G., Herve-Mignucci, M., & Mazza, F. (2013). *The Global Landscape of Climate Finance*. CPI Report. Available at: http://indiaenvironmentportal.org.in/files/file/The-Global-Landscape-of-Climate-Finance-2013.pdf

Monasterolo, I., & Raberto, M. (2018). The EIRIN Flow-of-funds Behavioural Model of Green Fiscal Policies and Green Sovereign Bonds. *Ecological Economics*, *144*, 228–243. doi:10.1016/j.ecolecon.2017.07.029

Moody's. (2019). *Research Announcement: Moody's: Green bond market poised to hit $200 billion in 2019*. Available at: https://www.moodys.com/research/Moodys-Green-bond-market-poised-to-hit-200-billion-in--PBC_1159526

Ng, T. H., & Tao, J. Y. (2016). Bond financing for renewable energy in Asia. *Energy Policy*, *95*, 509–517. Available at https://econpapers.repec.org/bookchap/erachaptr/2014-rpr-27-11.htm

OECD. (2011). *Towards Green Growth. Green Growth Study*. OECD Publishing. Available at: https://www.oecd-ilibrary.org/environment/towards-green-growth_9789264111318-en

OECD. (2017). *Investing in Climate, Investing in Growth*. OECD Publishing. Available at: https://www.oecd-ilibrary.org/economics/investing-in-climate-investing-in-growth_9789264273528-en;jsessionid=BlBH-C0OsdlUozRja6VKedZc.ip-10-240-5-116

Ordanini, A., Miceli, L., Pizzetti, M., & Parasuraman, A. (2011). Crowdfunding: Transforming customers into investors through innovative service platforms. *Journal of Service Management*, *22*(4), 443–470. Available at https://www.researchgate.net/publication/235251062_Crowd-funding_Transforming_customers_into_investors_through_innovative_service_platforms

Park, S. K. (2018). Investors as Regulators: Green Bonds and the Governance Challenges of the Sustainable Finance Revolution. *Stanford Journal of International Law*, *54*(1), 1–47. Available at https://papers.ssrn.com/sol3/papers.cfm?abstract_id=3142887

Sachs, J. D., Woo, W. T., Yoshino, N., & Taghizadeh-Hesary, F. (2019). *Why Is Green Finance Important? ADBI Working Paper 917*. Tokyo: Asian Development Bank Institute. Available at https://www.adb.org/publications/why-green-finance-important

Shah, K. U., Arjoon, S., & Rambocas, M. (2016). Aligning Corporate Social Responsibility with Green Economy Development Pathways in Developing Countries. *Sustainable Development*, *24*, 237–253. Available at https://onlinelibrary.wiley.com/doi/abs/10.1002/sd.1625

Silva, F., & Cortez, M. C. (2016). The performance of US and European green funds in different market conditions. *Journal of Cleaner Production*, *135*, 558–566. Available at https://pubag.nal.usda.gov/catalog/5246768

S&P Green bond index. (n.d.). Available at http://us.spindices.com/indices/fixed-income/sp-green-bond-index

The World Bank. (2018). *Green Bond Impact Report 2018*. Available at: http://pubdocs.worldbank.org/en/632251542641579226/report-impact-green-bond-2018.pdf

Tolliver, C., Keeley, A., & Managi, S. (2019). Green bonds for the Paris agreement and sustainable development goals. *Environmental Research Letters*, *14*. Available at https://iopscience.iop.org/article/10.1088/1748-9326/ab1118

Tripathy, A. (2017). Translating to risk: The legibility of climate change and nature in the green bond market. *Economic Anthropology*, *4*(2), 239–250. doi:10.1002ea2.12091

Trompeter, L. (2017). Green is Good: how Green Bonds Cultivated Into Wall Street's Environmental Paradox. *Sustainable Development Law & Policy, 17*(2), 4-43. Available at: https://papers.ssrn.com/sol3/papers.cfm?abstract_id=2992926

Vazquez-Brust, D., Smith, A. M., & Sarkis, J. (2014). Managing the transition to critical green growth: The 'Green Growth State'. *Futures*, *64*, 38–50. Available at https://researchportal.port.ac.uk/portal/en/publications/managing-the-transition-to-critical-green-growth-the-green-growth-state(4b3e92f0-6ed0-4d25-871f-60f5da4d5c1c)/export.html

Voica, M. C., Panaitb, M., & Radulescu, I. (2015). Green Investments - between necessity, fiscal constraints and profit. *Procedia Economics and Finance*, *22*, 72–79. Available at https://www.sciencedirect.com/science/article/pii/S2212567115002282

Waslander, J., & Vallejos, P. Q. (2018). *Setting the stage for the green climate fund's first replenishment. Working paper*. World Resources Institute. Available at https://www.wri.org/publication/green-climate-fund-first-replenishment

Whieldon, E. (2019). *S&P Ratings forecasts moderate green bond market growth in 2019*. Available at: https://www.spglobal.com/marketintelligence/en/news-insights/trending/P9Lq4MCmw-HL6iM-RUKgEHg2

World Economic Forum. (2013). *The Green Investment Report*. Available at: http://www3.weforum.org/docs/WEF_GreenInvestment_Report_2013.pdf

Yadav, P. L., Han, S. H., & Rho, J. J. (2016). Impact of Environmental Performance on Firm Value for Sustainable Investment: Evidence from Large US Firms. *Business Strategy and the Environment*, *25*, 402–420. Available at https://onlinelibrary.wiley.com/doi/abs/10.1002/bse.1883

Yue, Sh., Yang, Y., & Hu, Y. (2016). Does Foreign Direct Investment Affect Green Growth? Evidence from China's Experience. *Sustainability*, *8*(158), 2–14. Available at https://www.researchgate.net/publication/295101572_Does_Foreign_Direct_Investment_Affect_Green_Growth_Evidence_from_China's_Experience

ADDITIONAL READING

Agliardi, E., & Agliardi, R. (2019). Financing environmentally-sustainable projects with green bonds. *Environment and Development Economics*, 1–16. doi:10.1017/S1355770X19000020

Azhgaliyeva, D., Kapsaplyamova, Z., & Low, L. (2018). Implications of fiscal and financial policies for unlocking green finance and green investment. ADBI Working Paper Series, 861. Available at: https://www.adb.org/sites/default/files/publication/445076/adbi-wp861.pdf

Kaminker, Ch., & Majowski, Ch. (2018). Green Bonds – Ecosystem, Issuance Process and Regional Perspectives Mexico Edition. Available at: http://www.emergingmarketsdialogue.org/wp-content/uploads/2018/04/GIZ-SEB-ABM_Green-Bonds_Mexico-Edition.pdf

Landberg, R., Watanabe, Ch., & Lee, H. (2018). Climate Crisis Spurs UN Call for $2.4 Trillion Fossil Fuel Shift. Available at: https://www.bloomberg.com/news/articles/2018-10-08/scientists-call-for-2-4-trillion-shift-from-coal-to-renewables

OECD. (2019). Growth, Investment and the Low-Carbon Transition. Available at: http://www.oecd.org/environment/cc/g20-climate/

The Global Green Finance Index 3 (2019). Available at: https://www.longfinance.net/programmes/financial-centre-futures/global-green-finance-index/

The Global Sustainable Investment Alliance. (2018). Global Sustainable Investment Review. Available at: http://www.gsi-alliance.org/wp-content/uploads/2019/03/GSIR_Review2018.3.28.pdf

KEY TERMS AND DEFINITIONS

De-Risking Instruments: The instruments that reduce private investment risk and encourage a more active participation in financing green investments.

Grants: Resources that are intended to finance green investment, without expecting the money to be repaid.

Green Bond: A debt security, issued to fund green or sustainability-oriented business practices, eligible for such funding.

Green Equity: Equity of the company, working to increase environmental sustainability and using raised capital for this cause.

Green Index: An index, covering companies mostly working to induce environmental sustainability.

Green Investing: Investing in coherence with the socially responsible investing, but focuses on eligible environmentally conscious business practices.

Green Loan: A type of loan, which is used by financial institutions (banks, credit unions) to finance the environmentally friendly projects.

Chapter 11
Value Creation via Corporate Social Responsibility:
The Case of Emerging Countries

Małgorzata Macuda
https://orcid.org/0000-0002-9270-2610
Poznań University of Economics and Business, Poland

Justyna Fijałkowska
University of Łódź, Poland

ABSTRACT

The concept of creating company value is constantly evolving due to globalization, changing business realities, and the widely expanded idea of corporate social responsibility (CSR). The purpose of the chapter is three-fold. Firstly, it describes CSR involvement and CSR reporting practices in emerging countries. Secondly, it presents different theories related to value creation. Thirdly, it investigates CSR value creation measurement and disclosure in emerging economies (Brazil, Chile, China, Colombia, Egypt, India, Indonesia, South Korea, Malaysia, Peru, Russia, Taiwan, Thailand, Turkey, and Vietnam). The authors conducted content analysis of all publications concerning CSR issues and value creation in emerging countries over the years 1984-2019 included in Scopus database. Among publications over the years 2014-2019, several concerned strictly CSR implications to value creation in emerging economies.

INTRODUCTION

Corporate social responsibility (CSR) and sustainable development (SD) are two notions that are increasingly researched all over the world. CSR can be understood as "the social responsibility of business that encompasses the economic, legal, ethical, and discretionary expectations that society has of organizations at a given point in time" (Carroll, 1979). CSR is generally considered as a firm's obligation to protect and improve social welfare (Staples, 2004) through various business and social actions (Sen & Bhattacharya, 2001; Turban & Greening, 1997), ensuring equitable and sustainable benefits for the

DOI: 10.4018/978-1-7998-2193-9.ch011

Copyright © 2020, IGI Global. Copying or distributing in print or electronic forms without written permission of IGI Global is prohibited.

stakeholders. The second idea – sustainable development – represents an ethical concept related to fight against poverty and protect the environment simultaneously and on a macro-level (Baumgartner & Ebner, 2010). When incorporated by the firm, it is called corporate sustainability (CS), and it contains, like the former concept, three aspects: economic, environmental, and social (Baumgartner & Ebner, 2010).

Engagement in activities leading to sustainable development has emerged as an important dimension of corporate voluntary practice worldwide (Lacy, Cooper, Hayward, & Neuberger, 2010). Almost all business decisions involve social and environmental issues; decisions about how much to pay the executives, what technologies to install in a new manufacturing facility, as well as how and when to retire old plants – all affect the firm's stakeholders and the natural environment (Montiel, 2008). They are frequently analyzed in the Western and US economies. Jamali and Karam (2016) note that CSR remains a concept dominated by Western frames, nuances, and connotations, as presented in mainstream management and business literature. Developed market economies demonstrate a growing interest in issues concerning CSR and its effects, as it is confirmed by the sizeable theoretical and empirical literature on that subject (Fijałkowska, Zyznarska-Dworczak & Garsztka, 2018; Jamali, Karam, Yin & Soundararajan, 2017). While ideas of sustainability and corporate social responsibility have a relatively long history in developed economies due to well-established values of business standards, stable socio-economic, and political conditions as well as strong legal systems, in practice, however, it is the emerging economies who are most in need of sustainable ways of conducting business (Voinea & Fratostiteanu, 2018).

Baskin (2006) claims that CSR in emerging markets (especially South Africa, Brazil, India, and parts of Eastern Europe) is more developed than commonly thought, often exceeding standards in some high-income countries/regions. Visser (2008) highlights that it is wrongly presumed that developed markets are leading players on CSR. He suggests that it is instead the developing countries, in particular emerging market economies that are spearheading the growth and progression of CSR. As it is underlined by Voinea and Fratostiteanu (2018): "Over the last few decades, emerging markets have increased their share in world GDP and have come to play a prominent and growing role in global business. Their period of impressive growth was triggered by major global advances such as economic liberalization and governance reforms and deregulation". However, still most of the existing literature on determinants of corporate sustainability is based on companies operating in developed countries (Artiach, Lee, Nelson & Walker, 2010; Bansal, 2005; Ziegler & Schröder, 2010) with little known on the determinants of corporate sustainability performance in emerging countries. Li et al. (2010) underline that "already more established in developed-country firms, CSR has become increasingly important also for firms in the developing countries". A few years later, Rosenthal (2014) again suggests that "despite the growing importance of CSR, the concept continues to be more widely used in large consumer-facing companies from developed economies. (…) Nevertheless, research has shown that there is a growing trend towards CSR activities in emerging economies". Rosenthal (2014), quoting the GTZ (2011), notices that many larger corporations from emerging economies have improved environmental and social governance compared with their developed economy peers. As conclusion, the work of Jones (1999) should be mentioned in which it is established that an institutional framework for the determinants of CSR, suggesting that institutional structure, such as socio-cultural, national economy, industry, firm, and individual, are the crucial determinants of CSR. Therefore, given the difference in people's ethical reasoning and decisions between developed and emerging countries (Ge & Thomas, 2007; Lam & Shi, 2008; Whitcomb et al., 1998), the main research question of this chapter is whether the CSR engagement, and in consequence its reporting influences the value creation in emerging countries.

The concept of creating company value is constantly evolving due to globalization, changing business realities, and accordingly, changing business models, as well as to the widely expanded idea of corporate social responsibility. Nowadays, companies are increasingly interested in the concept of CSR. Companies involved in CSR activities perceive it as a source of competitive advantage and value creation. Therefore, the CSR effectiveness should be evaluated, and its impact on the company value creation should be proved. Additionally, the effects of the measurement should be communicated in CSR reports. The following questions arise: (1) Do companies measure and report the value created via CSR engagement?, or (2) Do they only present mainly descriptive information concerning their actions and activities within CSR? Accounting as the basis of the company information system should meet the new challenges posed by the constantly changing economic reality, and indeed, the measurement of the CSR effectiveness is such a challenge in today's business conditions. The effectiveness of CSR involvement should be evaluated in order to put the theoretical knowledge concerning value creation into practice in the process of rational decision making within different dimensions of business management. The practice needs tools of CSR involvement evaluation.

The purpose of the chapter is three-fold. Firstly, it describes CSR reporting practices in emerging countries. Secondly, it presents different concepts (theories) related to value creation. Thirdly, it investigates CSR value creation measurement and disclosure in emerging economies (e.g., Brazil, Chile, China, Colombia, Indonesia, Korea, Malaysia, Peru, Russia, and Taiwan). The empirical research concerning the impact of CSR engagement on the value creation in developed countries is extensive. At the same time, the practice shows that the businesses in emerging markets have made quick strides in the field of sustainability by rapidly adopting mainstream activities. The study contributes to the literature on the importance of corporate social sustainability by examining the literature concerning empirical evidence from selected emerging countries worldwide.

CSR IN EMERGING COUNTRIES – BACKGROUND

The heterogeneous socio-economic, historical and political realities of developing countries provide impetus and a niche for unique forms of responsible business as well as tailored adaptations of globally dominant CSR practices to local contexts (Jamali & Neville, 2011; Prieto-Carron, Lund-Thomsen, Chan, Muro, & Bhushan, 2006). According to Sraders (2018), "emerging markets (or EME, for the emerging market economy) are economies of countries that are in the progress of becoming a developed country and typically are moving toward mixed or free markets. Emerging market economies often have lower per capita income than developed countries, and often have liquidity in equity markets, are instituting regulatory bodies and exchanges, and see rapid growth (…). Emerging market countries are those that are striving to become advanced countries and are generally on a more economically disciplined track to become more sophisticated – including increased fiscal transparency, focus on production, developing regulatory bodies and exchanges, and acceptance of outside investment". Around 80% of the world's economy is comprised of emerging markets – including some of the largest countries in the world, like China, India, and Russia. With the advent of globalization and its consequent quick expansion, the leading emerging market economies are an increasingly dominant force in the global economic world. Emerging economies represent the world's largest potential markets and the source of both much of the world's natural and human resources. They represent the area of leading global brands and innovations. But at the same time, they are also related to CSR and sustainability challenges.

Given the difference in people's ethical reasoning and decisions between developed and emerging countries (Ge & Thomas, 2007; Lam & Shi, 2008; Whitcomb et al., 1998) there are some specific conditions and premises, determining the unique characteristics of emerging countries that call for a socially responsible approach to be taken by companies operating in these parts of the world. Some of the countries considered "emerging economies" face and are confronted with widespread problems of poverty, human rights violations, corruption, inequalities, social injustice, and human exploitations. Therefore, it is argued that businesses operating in emerging economies have a responsibility to address some of these problems (Pachauri, 2006). For example, CSR in Africa has recently gained heightened interest generally due to high levels of poverty and inequalities, particularly among those countries in which sustainable development challenges appear most intractable (Cheruiyot & Maru, 2012; Kivuitu, Yambayamba & Fox, 2005). In such countries, CSR has gained resonance among local communities and the general public (Cheruiyot & Onsando, 2016). CSR is increasingly drawing attention in African enterprises and contexts (Cheruiyot & Maru, 2012), partially because of social legislation that is apparently less comprehensive and poorly enforceable (Cheruiyot & Onsando, 2016). CSR in Africa is still a largely misunderstood, misused and abused concept. This is partly due to its diverse conceptualization and operationalization (Cheruiyot & Onsando, 2016).

The idea of CSR takes on particular importance and has a unique resonance in the emerging market countries, which are facing various problems and challenges specific to them. CSR, maybe more than in any other region, is seen there as the commitment of businesses to sustainable economic development that improves the quality of life of an assortment of people, including employees, their families, and the local community (Aguilera-Caracuel et al., 2015). Moreover, CSR is also defined as a behavior that is connected with business ethics, meaning the obligation of the operations of a firm to social, as well as environmental concerns (Wang et al., 2015) that are of a particular significance in the less developed economies. Therefore, e.g. Mehra (2006) indicates that CSR is a perceptible, readily identifiable movement in the process of migrating from the "west to the rest" and in the latest studies it is underlined that emerging markets are nowadays particularly facing sustainability challenges due to their fast-growing pace and fuzzy or inexistent sustainability regulations (Voinea & Fratostiteanu, 2018).

As companies in emerging economies face serious social problems and operate in the ambiance of the difficult political, social, and economic situation, they are involved in CSR activities in different ways and to a diverse extent. In table 1, the main issues concerning the context of the three main emerging market's regions – Africa, Asia, and Latin America – are presented.

Welford (2004) has found that companies from emerging markets lag behind their counterparts in the mature economies with regard to CSR implementation and activities. Whilst the focus accorded to CSR in developed countries, appears to revolve around its role in facilitating greater accountability to stakeholders, particularly given the devastating consequences of corporate collapses on wider stakeholders, as well as the need for more effective corporate governance mechanisms, the focus of CSR as a means of philanthropy and charitable donations, appears to be a more predominant feature in developing countries (Jamali & Mirshak, 2007). According to Saleh, Zulkifli and Muhamad (2011), there are differences in how CSR activities are carried out in emerging countries compared to developed countries, in terms of the socio-economic and cultural contexts. They indicate the following unique characteristics of CSR in emerging markets:

Table 1. Three emerging markets' regions

Region	Countries
Africa	Africa is the second-largest continent with a population of close to 1 billion people. It is also the second fastest-growing region in the world. Economies in Africa, and especially Sub-Saharan Africa, have been growing more rapidly in recent years than at any time in modern history, for instance between 2001 and 2008, African economies grew at an increasing rate, averaging over 6% for the period and in 2010 the average economic growth rate across the continent However, eighty percent of Africans still earn US$2 a day or less. African economies reliant on the export of low value-added basic goods are subject to international market fluctuations and weak terms of trade.
Asia	Asia is a fast-growing region, demonstrating substantial economic growth since the 1980s. In particular, there has been a rising interest in investing in Asian Emerging Markets, particularly China and India. As it is underlined by Cheung, Tan, Ahn, and Zhang (2010, p. 402): "The Asian equity markets are, however, quite different from those of western countries. The Asian business community is characterized by high family ownership and a lack of transparency. The Asian equity markets are relatively more illiquid than compared to western markets. The traditional agency problem is not applicable in Asia because there is seldom a separation of management and ownership. It is common to find that the chairman of the board is also the chief executive officer in Asian listed companies. Besides, market discipline mechanisms, such as hostile takeovers, cannot function properly in Asia because of the concentrated or family ownership. This could explain why CSR has had a slow start in Asia".
Latin America	Latin America and the Caribbean have seen remarkable socio-economic progress since the beginning of the century. The macroeconomic situation of individual countries has strengthened, living standards have improved, and poverty and inequality have declined. Yet significant structural vulnerabilities remain, and new ones have emerged. Many of these are linked to countries' transition to higher income and development levels. There is a need for improving domestic capacities and adopting a new vision of international co-operation as a facilitator to support those efforts (OECD 2019 Latin America Outlook).

Source: own work

- CSR activities are less formalized in terms of CSR benchmarks, compared to developed markets.
- Formal CSR is utilized by big national and multinational corporations, and particularly those that have recognized global brands or have international status.
- CSR is mainly related to philanthropy or charity (e.g., social investment in education, sports sponsorships, and public health, and other community services, etc.).
- An economic contribution is usually assumed as a crucial and practical method for companies to create social effects (e.g., work opportunities, knowledge transfer, paying taxes, etc.).
- The motivation and involvement in CSR practices are usually related to traditional and spiritual values in emerging markets (e.g., harmonious society (*xiaokang*) in China, African humanism (*ubuntu*) in South Africa, mutual cooperation (*gotong-royong*) in ASEAN countries) (Visser, 2008).

However, contrary to Welford (2004), Baskin (2006) investigated the extent of corporate sustainability uptake in leading emerging countries, and concluded that not only there were some emerging market companies taking an active interest in corporate sustainability, but also they are among the global leaders (especially in South Africa and Brazil).

REPORTING OF CSR IN EMERGING COUNTRIES

In the mature economies, such as those of the US and Western European countries, corporate communication is often used to highlight companies' commitments to CSR (Esrock & Leichty, 1998; Hooghiemstra, 2000), enhance marketing efforts, and legitimize a given company's corporate image in the eyes of its various stakeholders (Birch & Moon, 2004; Ringov & Zollo, 2007). Disclosure on CSR has, therefore, appeared as a vital and integrated part of organizational marketing to enhance the corporate image (Chahal & Sharma, 2006). A broad viewpoint of CSR activities should be taken into account, and then reported.

The previous research confirms that there are no significant differences in the impact of traditional determinants (size, financial performance, industry, and cultural environment) of CSR reporting practices between developed or developing countries (Miras-Rodríguez, Martínez-Martínez, & Escobar-Pérez, 2018). In general, larger and more profitable companies and those which operate in environmentally sensitive industries show a greater commitment to non-financial disclosures, regardless of the cultural and environment (Miras-Rodríguez et al., 2018). Evidence of growth in the importance attributed by companies to CSR and CS, as well as to the reporting of these issues is reflected in the increasingly larger interest of companies in instruments such as CSR sustainability reporting worldwide (Lozano & Huisingh, 2011). One of the key variables for explaining the adoption of a CSR reporting practice, particularly in emerging countries, is the company's level of internationalization (Arrive & Feng, 2018; Chapple & Moonm, 2005; Araya, 2006). If companies want to operate globally, they need to meet the formal and informal requirements in all markets where they conduct their activity. Regulation is also usually an important driver of CSR disclosure particularly in the environment of emerging markets, whereas some of the studies (e.g., Baskin, 2006) confirm – is avoided by companies unless legally required. CSR engagement, as well as reporting on that is also frequently connected to the foreign direct investment (FDI) curried out by the developed countries in emerging markets. Ojo (2016) underlines the important role which political environments may play in obstructing the desired objectives of contributing positively to the economies of the host countries, where matters relating to Foreign Direct Investment are involved, and where regulations, standards, principles, and codes of conduct are not complied with.

Moreover, Visser (2008) indicates there are examples such as Indonesia, Brazil, and South Africa of how emerging markets are proving themselves highly adept at delivering the so-called triple bottom line of sustainability, namely balanced and integrated social, economic and environmental benefits. He argues it is not surprising, since in such markets these three spheres are seldom separable – economic development almost inevitably results in social upliftment and environmental improvement, and vice versa. His argument establishes that emerging markets have the necessary tools to pilot the way on CSR.

CSR IMPLICATIONS FOR VALUE CREATION

For a long time, the dominance of the shareholder view and the overwhelming emphasis on economic responsibility have been observed. According to Salvioni and Gennari (2017), these two factors have determined a different temporal orientation in the value creation of outsider and insider corporate governance systems. In their opinion, strategies oriented towards CSR are clearly aware of the responsibilities towards different stakeholders, and they adopt methods and tools of governance aimed at improving economic, social and ecological performance. At the same time, introducing these strategies does not mean that value creation for shareholders and their adequate remuneration are less important, as business decisions always require feasibility and economic convenience, but the effective and fair integration between economic and socio-environmental responsibilities enhances the close interdependence between shareholders and stakeholder view, ensuring the company's long-term competitive advantage.

Previously, the value for stakeholders was marginalized by companies. However, all groups of stakeholders (investors, customers, suppliers, managers and employees, creditors, central and local authorities, as well as society in general) care about the growth of the company's value, because they participate not only in its creation but also in its consumption (Masztalerz, 2014). Nowadays, the notion of a company's sustainable value, which occurs only when the created value is positive simultaneously for shareholders and stakeholders, is proposed (Laszlo, 2008b). As said by Salvioni and Gennari (2017), the potential for creating sustainable value stands on two pillars: (1) the quality of corporate governance decisions through an integrated approach to responsibility and (2) the ability to transfer the sustainability objectives derived from the socially responsible strategy into the behaviours of the entire organisation. Moreover, Jonikas (2013) suggests integrating CSR in the whole value creation chain (VCC). He elaborated a framework of value creation through CSR in a separate member of VCC, called shared value. Creating shared value has become, however, a buzzword in recent years, in business practice, as well as in management theory (Beschorner & Hajduk, 2017). There are different concepts (theories) concerning value creation (Fijałkowska & Macuda, 2017):

1. **Stakeholder approach** (Freeman, 1984):
   - All stakeholders, perceived widely (as any group or individual who is affected by or can affect the achievement of a company's objectives), are equally important.
   - A company should actively analyze its relationships with all stakeholders and try to understand the concerns of shareholders, employees, customers, suppliers, competitors, chartered auditors, the local community, regulators, the government, and public opinion to develop objectives and business strategies that stakeholders would support. This support is needed for the long-term success of the company. It is a never-ending task of integrating multiple relationships and multiple objectives, which influences the value creation.
2. **Value chain – value for the customer** (Porter, 1985):
   - According to this activity-based theory, the value for customers (being a source of competitive advantage in all areas of the firm's operation) is created by interrelated activities.
3. **Shareholder value** (Rappaport, 1986):
   – The idea of the shareholder value assumes that the ultimate test of business strategy, and as well the only reliable measure, is whether it creates economic value for shareholders. Taking into account a highly competitive global economy, it is not enough to stay in business, more important is to remain at the forefront of enterprises achieving success. Appropriate practical tools, able to generate the highest possible return, should be used by managers.
   – Rappaport suggested seven drivers within a business that can be managed to create value (improvements in these value drivers lead to an increase in shareholder value):

(1) a growth in sales;
(2) an increase in the operating profit margin;
(3) a reduction in the cash tax rate;
(4) a reduction in the working capital investment;
(5) a reduction in the fixed asset investment;
(6) a reduction in the weighted average cost of capital;
(7) an increase in the competitive advantage period.

4. **Triple bottom line** (Elkington, 1994):
   – A sustainable company is one that contributes to sustainable development while ensuring economic, social, and environmental benefits.
5. **Sustainable value** (Hart, 1997):
   - The ecological value constitutes the main component of sustainable value. While envisaging the development of a business strategy, three factors threatening the natural environment: population, affluence (which is a proxy for consumption), and technology, have to be taken into consideration. The firm's pursuit of sustainable development (a sustainable vision of the company) is done by product stewardship, clean technology, and preventing pollution.
   - Hart notices the existence of the direct link between the social challenges of global sustainable development and the creation of shareholder value. Building a sustainable business strategy, expressed in the concept of environmental awareness, is accompanied by shape-framing relationships with customers, suppliers, other companies, and other stakeholders.
6. **Blended value** (Emerson, 2000):
   - All enterprises have within them both a social and a financial/economic value, regardless of their legal status (for-profit or non-profit). Thus, they create blended value, which can be positive or negative.
   - This idea of the blended value refers to investments, return on investment, and the firm's value on the socially integrated capital market (Integrated Social Capital Market).
   - The creation of wealth or social changes is possible, but the problem is to create company value, which simultaneously provides economic and social benefits to investors, investees, and society. Social costs and economic should be tracked. However, the interaction and trade-off between the two do not take place in a smooth line, one operating in a directly inverse relationship to the other.
   - Emerson expects in the coming years an increasing number of funds and investment pools created with the direct intent of providing capital to investees based on both social and financial performance. Maximization of the social value, while at the same time, intending to maximize economic value to obtain an appropriate blend of social and economic value creation, will be the goal of the investment. Blended ROI will be the basis of the assessment of these investments.
7. **Sustainable shareholder value** (Hart & Milstein, 2003):
   - The company's sustainability has to be directly linked to the creation of shareholder value. Identifying strategies and practices that contribute to a more sustainable world should drive at the same time shareholder value. The key dimensions of shareholder value are the following:
     - innovation and repositioning,
     - cost and risk reduction – both within the internal dimension,
     - growth path and trajectory,

        - reputation and legitimacy – within the external dimension.
    - The enterprise needs to manage today's business while simultaneously creating tomorrow's technology and markets – realizing short-term results while also generating expectations for future growth.
    - The companies are encouraged to engage in interaction and dialogue with external stakeholders but not to create value for them. They might develop solutions to social and environmental problems for the future.
8. **Sustainable value** (Laszlo, Sherman, Whalen & Ellinson, 2005; Laszlo 2008a, 2008b, 2008c):
    - The sustainability value occurs only when it is created simultaneously for all stakeholders (shareholders and other stakeholders) – when it comprises economic, social, and environmental value. When value is transferred from stakeholders to shareholders, the stakeholders represent a risk to the future of the company. When the value is transferred from shareholders to stakeholders, the company incurs a fiduciary liability to its shareholders. In both cases, Laszlo indicates value transfer. When the value is destroyed for both sides, an unsustainable value (loss) occurs.
    - Six levels (six types of sustainability-related business projects), which can constitute a source of company value, are suggested:
        - risk mitigation and compliance-oriented management of risks,
        - process cost reduction,
        - product differentiation to meet new customers' needs for social and environmental attributes,
        - penetrating new markets and developing new businesses based on sustainability,
        - enhancing corporate reputation and image,
        - business context – changing the industry „rules of the game".
9. **Shared Value** (Porter & Kramer, 2011):
    - The concept of value creation through CSR. Shared value is defined as policies and operating practices that enhance the competitiveness of a company while simultaneously advancing the economic and social conditions in the communities in which it operates. Shared value creation focuses on identifying and expanding the connections between societal and economic progress.
    - The solution lies in the principle of shared value, which involves creating economic value in a way that also creates value for society by addressing its needs and challenges. The concept of shared value tries to focus on a tremendous opportunity to create economic value through creating social benefits. Companies can create economic value by creating societal value.
10. **Shared Value** (Jonikas, 2013):
    - The framework of value creation through CSR, considering CSR implementation might help to create shared value for few beneficiaries simultaneously.
    - The framework consists of all four types of responsibilities described by Carroll (1999): ethic, philanthropic, legal, and economic different levels of CSR activity, as well as of three major groups of beneficiaries (company, society, stakeholders) and areas of possible value creation.
    - The framework is developed from a single company viewpoint, which is the part of VCC. If the company is bounded to responsibility by legal means, the company must perform current action of CSR, independently of what value it will create. So in such case, the proposed

conceptual model could only give some indications to the company but will not influence the decision on CSR implementation. A quite similar situation is, once a company decides to take some CSR actions due to ethic or philanthropic motives. CSR actions will be taken, most likely, without more in-depth evaluations of possible to create value. But such a framework at least suggests taking a look at possible alternative CSR actions – maybe any other action could bring higher shared value. This conceptual framework is most useful for situations when CSR responsibility emerges as an outcome of economic considerations because any company in such situation wants to know costs and benefits before making any decisions on CSR action.

- Leading and following companies of VCC should be identified. Theoretical research shows that there is a much higher possibility for leading companies to benefit from CSR implementation in VCC, while following companies are forced to follow the requirements of leading a company, even if compliance with them causes more costs than benefits.
- This framework could be developed into a calculation system which would be based on CSR efforts (as input for calculation) and created exchange value (as an output). Such calculation system could be useful in at least a few ways:
- it could forecast expected value volumes if the company implements CSR activities at a certain amount (or level);
- it to implement certain CSR initiatives (costs of CSR activity versus value received by company);
- to forecast allocation of created value – to show which beneficiary receives;
- to forecast the added value in the VCC created through the implementation of CSR.

"Creating value" within the social environment of global society is the goal of corporate self-perfection, above the simple pursuit of profits (Shanahan & Seele, 2017). CSR is increasingly becoming a driver of business because it makes the business sustainable and creates value for shareholders and other stakeholders, promoting consensus concerning the corporate project. CSR is one of the business competition levers that attract consumers and investors, who are increasingly aware and willing to reward companies oriented towards the creation of sustainable value (Salvioni & Gennari 2017). According to Adamczyk (2009), a company value is created by the economic value-added (measured in terms of generated profit), the market value-added (giving a competitive advantage), the social value-added (expressing concern for employees and the local community), and the ecological value-added (reflecting the care of the environment).

Barnett and Salomon (2012) affirmed that over the last several decades researchers have sought to theorize and determine the relationship between the social performance and the financial performance of businesses, and although hundreds of empirical studies that test that relationship have been published, results have been mixed. CSR is seen as a vital approach to generate wealth and improve firm performance (Gallardo-Vazquez and Sanchez-Hernandez, 2014; Garriga and Mele, 2004). Several studies have been conducted in an attempt to link CSR with financial performance (Waddock & Graves, 1997; Russo & Fouts, 1997; Aupperle et al., 1985; Abratt & Sacks, 1988). A positive relation between CSR and financial performance was found by Griffin and Mahon (1997), Stanwick and Stanwick (1998), Margolis and Walsh (2003), Allouche and Laroche (2005), Margolis and Elfenbein (2008), Lin et al. (2009), Peloza (2009), Alafi and Hasoneh (2012), Sun and Kim (2013), Kurapatskie and Darnall (2013), and Wang et al. (2015). From this perspective, Waddock and Graves (1997) stated that the benefits to be gained from

CSR practices are greater than the costs involved. High environmental and social standards will lead to higher operating costs that translate into lower profitability, but on the other hand, strong social policies could strengthen a company's reputation and brand name, thus enhancing the firm's financial performance. Shin and Thai (2015) suggested that companies' social commitment could improve economic performance. Donaldson and Preston (1995) define CSR as a source of profits and competitive advantage, while Branco and Rodrigues (2006), McWilliams et al. (2006), and Porter and Kramer (2006) suggest integrating CSR to corporate strategy as a mean for enhancing corporate image and competitiveness. On the opposite side of the equation, other researchers (especially neoclassical economists) point out a negative impact of CSR on financial performance, concerning costs involved in CSR engagement (Chen et al., 2015; Mallin et al., 2014). In some cases, no impact of CSR practices on financial performance or a neutral relationship between the two have been observed (Lu et al., 2014). In practice, the relationship between CSR activities and financial performance is usually affected by other, more indirect factors (Saeidi et al., 2015): some variables (institutional environment, corporate reputation) or stakeholders (customers, suppliers, employees) that influence the relationship between CSR and financial performance. In this study, to construct a theoretical framework in the context of transition economies, we focus on the possible connections between CSR and financial performance from the perspectives of the customer satisfaction (a market factor) and the institutional environment (a non-market factor).

Cahan, De Villiers, Jeter, Naiker and Van Staden (2015) point out that CSR disclosure may have an impact on company value either directly or indirectly. Dhaliwal, Li, Tsang and Yang (2011) state that firms initiating CSR reporting practices can attract dedicated institutional investors, raise more equity capital, and draw greater analyst attention, which constitute a direct effect. Oppositely, Elliott, Jackson, Peecher, and White claim that CSR disclosures may indirectly affect company valuation by altering investors' perceptions of company value. Whether it is direct or indirect, Ioannou and Serafeim's (2012) findings suggest that the informativeness of CSR reporting may vary across countries depending on the strength of a country's nation-level institutions. The literature supports the value creation relevance of CSR reporting. Cahan et al. (2015) examine the valuation implications of CSR disclosures and consider how the relation between CSR disclosures and firm value varies across 21 countries. They define unexpected disclosure as incremental information disclosure. Higher disclosure is related to higher firm value. Cahan et al. (2015) relate their findings to the political influences, such as democracy, press freedom, and environmental commitments.

The literature study of the impact of CSR engagement and CSR reporting on value creation shows that the theory is in place. The next step is to analyze the empirical evidence concerning the value creation via CSR.

THE IMPACT OF CSR ON VALUE CREATION IN EMERGING MARKETS – ANALYSIS OF THE EMPIRICAL RESEARCH

Methodology

In this study, the literature review method has been adopted. In light of the increasing quantity of publication outlets, research output, and potentially conflicting findings, literature reviews serve an important function of knowledge systematization (Oll & Rommerskirchen, 2018). Attempts to synthesize research have often been achieved through narrative and qualitative integrative review (Kirca & Yaprak, 2010).

Table 2. CSR The number of publications dedicated to the value creation and CSR issues in emerging countries indexed in Scopus in 1984-2019

Year	Scopus
1984-2003	0
2004	2
2005	0
2006	2
2007	4
2008	5
2009	5
2010	2
2011	4
2012	10
2013	8
2014	16
2015	17
2016	21
2017	13
2018	20
2019	15

Source: own work

Qualitative research syntheses have offered state-of-the-art reviews on various thematic, ontological, and methodological issues (e.g., Cavusgil, Deligonul & Yaprak, 2005). Among various review approaches, a distinction between traditional (narrative) and systematic reviews is made (Rousseau et al., 2008; Tranfield et al., 2003). For the present study, the traditional (narrative) review has been followed.

The aim of this study was to collect publications concerning value creation and CSR related to emerging countries issued over the years 1984-2019 to get an approximate picture of the popularity of the concepts as the topic of research studies conducted in Asia, Africa, and Latin America. The start date of the research is set by the date of the first concept of value creation – Stakeholder approach of Freeman, and it concludes with the most recent literature. The articles for the empirical analysis have been retrieved from Scopus database (a source-neutral abstract and citation database). Scopus indexes include information concerning 24,600 active titles and 5,000 publishers, which is rigorously vetted and selected by an independent review board. Scopus resources were examined with the use of such keywords as “value creation” & “CSR” and “value creation” & “emerging countries”. The content analysis of the papers referring to the analyzed topic was conducted. Table 2 presents the results.

Within this study, 144 articles dedicated to the value creation and CSR issues in emerging countries were analyzed. According to the data presented in table 2, the number of publications on the researched topic increased over the years 2012-2019. A noticeable increase in the number of publications in Scopus occurred in 2014, 2015, 2016, and 2018, respectively. The highest number was published in 2016. In the first half of the analyzed period (1984-2003), there was no publication related to value creation and

CSR issues in emerging countries. In 2004-2011, only 24 research studies altogether were conducted and published. The largest decreases were identified in the years 2016 vs. 2017. Among all publications over the years 2014-2019, several concerned CSR implications to value creation in emerging countries strictly. Within this study, the content of the publications was analyzed from the point of view of the country that was examined, aims of the study, and findings.

Results of the Conducted Research

Within the analysis on the impact of the CSR on the value created, there were only a few articles concerning the cases of emerging countries. The empirical studies were concluded in reference to individual countries embracing Taiwan, Indonesia, Malaysia, and Colombia. There were also four studies that analyzed value creation in the groups of countries, e.g., in sub-Saharan African countries, Latin America, Asia, South America, South Africa, or comparative study referring to Brazil, Chile, China, Colombia, Malaysia, Peru, Russia, South Africa. The resume of the analysis is presented in table 3.

A positive relationship between corporate social responsibility and corporate financial performance in companies from emerging countries has been stated by almost all the articles analyzed in this research. Only according to M.M. Miralles-Quirós, J.L. Miralles-Quirós and Redondo Hernández (2019), in the emerging banking sector, the environmental and corporate governance variables have a positive and signiðcant relationship with shareholder value creation, while the social one has a negative and signiðcant correlation. In the analyzed studies, it was also proved that not only CSR activities but also reporting about CSR involvement of the company has an influence on value creation. Darus, Mad, Nejati and Yusoff (2016) found the positive relationship between the quality of CSR disclosures and value creation.

FUTURE RESEARCH DIRECTIONS

Most of the studies analyzed in this chapter while researching value creation via CSR engagement refer to the CSR disclosure in the annual reports. However, an exclusive focus on annual reports might not capture all social and environmental disclosures in the emerging countries (Bebbington & Unerman, 2008; Guthrie, Cuganesan & Ward, 2008). The future research might focused on internet releases, media communication on CSR engagement and other channels of contact with stakeholders, and refer them to value creation. More research is needed to scrutinize the observation concerning different CSR media. As concluding theoretical assumptions and analyzed practices about value creation via CSR in emerging countries, there is still much work to be done. This topic seems to be a challenge for future research.

CONCLUSION

Emerging economies are promising business markets that offer companies great opportunities. They are related to a continuous intensification of business activities and fast economic growth. However, at the same time, these are the markets that are most in need of sustainable ways of conducting business. The issues of social justice, equality, transparency, and accountability are extremely important, especially in these countries. Therefore there is a prerequisite to follow the CSR norms, standards, and values. If

Table 3. CSR implications to company value creation in emerging countries

Author	Country	Aim of the study and Findings
Lin, Hung, Chou and Lai (2019)	Taiwan	– Aim: examine the effect of CSR dimensions on the financial performance of firms in Taiwan. – As the Authors used sustainability ratings by CSRHub, they were able to cover a broader range of companies in size, geography, and industry type than those previously studied.Allocating resources to diversity, labor rights, treatment of unions, compensation, benefits, training, health, and worker safety can be beneficial to a firm's value creation.
Tarigan, Hatane, Stacia and Widjaja (2019)	Indonesia	– Aim: with a purpose to give a deep understanding relating to the manifestation of social responsibilities practices among Indonesian companies, this paper reflects the relationship of corporate social responsibility (CSR), corporate profitability (CP), value creation (VC), and good corporate governance (GCG). – Economic value added (EVA), a new method to measure the company's performance through value creation was used by the Authors. – CSR serves as a tool in assisting shareholders' value and performance.
Abugre and Anlesinya (2019)	sub-Saharan Africa	– Aim: examine the relationship between CSR and business value of multinational companies (MNCs) in sub-Saharan Africa. – CSR can positively and significantly predict business values in the multinational subsidiaries. These values include direct (economic value) and indirect (human capital value and reputational business value). – The Authors recommend MNCs operating in Africa to enhance their social investment through their CSR strategy with the aim that CSR must not be regarded as a cost center, but an investment instrument.
M.M. Miralles-Quirós, J.L. Miralles-Quirós and Redondo Hernández (2019)	Asia, South America, South Africa	– Aim: study the role of socially responsible activities on shareholder value creation in a sample of 166 commercial banks listed with CSR practices from 31 countries over the 2010-2015 period (46 from Asia, including China (21), India (8) and Russia (3); 13 from South America, including Brazil (6), Chile (3) and Colombia (10); as well as 4 from South Africa). – In emerging markets, the environmental and corporate governance variables are the ones that have a positive and signiðcant relationship with shareholder value creation, while the social one has a negative and signiðcant correlation. – Many banks that are quoted in emerging and transition markets are under pressure to manage better the risk arising from environmental liabilities. Thus, there is expected to be increasing pressure on banks that do not have environmental management systems to begin to take actions to improve the management of the environmental variable.
Brieger and De Clercq (2019)	Brazil, Chile, China, Colombia, Malaysia, Peru, Russia, South Africa	– Aim: provide a better understanding of how the interplay of individual-level resources (measured as financial, human and social capital) and culture affects entrepreneurs' propensity to adopt social value creation goals, using a sample of 12,685 entrepreneurs in 35 countries from the Global Entrepreneurship Monitor (Brazil, Chile, China, Colombia, Malaysia, Peru, Russia, South Africa). – Individual-level resources are relevant for predicting the extent to which entrepreneurs emphasize social goals for their business. In individualist cultures, higher education may be especially potent for increasing awareness about social issues. – Culture influences the way entrepreneurs allocate their resources towards social value creation. Financially wealthy and highly educated entrepreneurs in feminine cultures, compared with their counterparts in masculine cultures, are more willing to create social value.
Chung, Jung, and Young (2018)	Korea	– Aim: analysis of the effect of CSR on firm value using data from all firms listed on the Korea Exchange from 2005 to 2015 that provide corporate social responsibility information. – The results strongly support a positive relation between CSR and firm value. – In the findings, the authors suggest that every corporation should adopt corporate social responsibility as an active competitive strategy, taking the corporate condition into account.
Kelley, Hemphill and Thams (2018)	Latin America	– Aim: explore the relationship between corporate social responsibility (CSR) and corporate financial performance (CFP) from a shared value perspective. Adopting reputation as a multilevel form of value that mediates the CSR–CFP relationship, the paper explains how CSR initiatives may enhance both firm and country reputation and how the amount of shared value between the two leads to CFP. The paper discusses the moderating influences of this relationship that may vary contextually with emerging economies (Latin America). – As markets become further developed, CSR initiatives will create a higher proportion of shared reputational value between a corporation and a country.
Darus, Mad, Nejati and Yusoff (2016)	Malaysia	– An improvement in the quantity and quality of CSR disclosure among the financial institutions in Malaysia from 2008 to 2011 (three years after the introduction of CSR framework to all Malaysian Public Listed Companies) is observed (study sample includes 80 observations, comprising 20 financial institutions in Malaysia over a four-year period). – It was found that the concentration of the CSR activities among the financial institutions was towards the well-being of the community in which they operate. – Quality of CSR disclosure matters more than quantity, as disclosure quality was found to be the only significant predictor of value creation for organizations. These findings suggest that stakeholders require more non-financial information in order to evaluate the social performance of a company. – The positive link between the quality of CSR and value creation can create a bandwagon effect and encourage more firms to engage in the practice and disclosure of strategic CSR in line with their core business.
Biswas-Tortajada and Biswas (2015)	Colombia	– Aim: examine sustainable coffee production in Colombia, specifically the initiatives to create shared value. – As coffee has iconic cultural and economic significance for Colombia, the publication describes the transformation of the coffee landscape by the development of economically, socially, and environmentally viable and dedicated supply chains. Suppliers have been encouraged to shift production and quality paradigms in order to develop long-term and sustainable strategies for a higher value. – It constitutes an important lesson of corporate social responsibility and the creation of shared value for the benefit of farmers, corporations, and consumers.

Source: own work based on Biswas-Tortajada and Biswas (2015), Darus, Mad, Nejati and Yusoff (2016), Kelley, Hemphill and Thams (2018), Brieger and De Clercq (2019), M.M. Miralles-Quirós, J.L. Miralles-Quirós and Redondo Hernández (2019), Abugre and Anlesinya (2019), Tarigan, Hatane, Stacia and Widjaja (2019), Lin, Hung, Chou and Lai (2019).

the CSR concept is expected to 'take-off' or to fatherly develop in emerging markets, it cannot be taken for granted or left to accident.

CSR engagement is referred to value creation. It should be noted that different types of value might emerge (Jonicas, 2013). However, according to most researchers, only shared value creation through CSR seems to be sustainable. It's already foreseen that CSR will evolve, and value creation through CSR will change. Implementation of CSR will become more oriented towards the creation of shared value, also in emerging countries. Taking into account the findings of the analysis conducted in this chapter, it is possible to conclude that the popularity of this topic of research is still very low, however growing in the last 6 years (2014-2019). All studies demonstrate the positive impact of CSR engagement on the value of companies. Therefore, it may be concluded that CSR engagement is appreciated by the participants of the emerging markets, should be developed, and at the same time, should be the subject of future analysis and research. The international community, multinational corporations, and firms in the emerging economies all need to gain a better understanding of the importance of CSR that creates a challenge for the academic community to study on that.

In this study, the majority of analyzed empirical research shows a positive relationship between CSR engagement and value creation. However, it is worth underlining that, especially in emerging market economies, the issues of sustainable development and corporate social responsibility are crucial. Therefore, apart from the direct impact on the financial performance expectations, there should be also strong incentives for companies to adopt better sustainable strategies and practices. As a conclusion it may be agreed with the statement of Khanna and Palepu (1997) that investors may appreciate firms with more CSR practices and this argument may be particularly salient in emerging economies because firms with CSR practices, such as equal employment and environmental pollution control, signal that they have superior capabilities for filling institutional voids.

The management of business in emerging countries should be committed to CSR activities now and in the future, as it will be a prerequisite to attract and retain customers, investors, and employees and thus furtherly develop and catch up economically with other countries. CSR and sustainable activities should be consistent with long-term plans.

The main limitation of this study is the relatively small amount of papers that were subject to the analysis. However, to the best knowledge of the Authors, they cover all the sources accessible in the Scopus database. It is not excluded that there is more research on this topic in less recognized databases. In this study, only the English language papers were analyzed.

REFERENCES

Abugre, J. B., & Anlesinya, A. (2019). Corporate Social Responsibility and Business Value of Multinational Companies: Lessons from a Sub-Saharan African Environment. *Journal of African Business*.

Adamczyk, J. (2009). *Społeczna odpowiedzialność biznesu*. Warszawa: PWE.

Aguilera-Caracuel, J., Aragón-Correa, J. A., Hurtado-Torres, N. E., & Rugman, A. M. (2012). The effects of institutional distance and headquarters' financial performance on the generation of environmental standards in multinational companies. *Journal of Business Ethics*, *105*(4), 461–474. doi:10.100710551-011-0978-7

Allouche, J., & Laroche, P. (2005). A Meta-analytical Investigation of the Relationship between Corporate Social and Financial Performance. *Revue de Gestion des Ressources Humaines*, *57*, 8–41.

Araya, M. (2006). Exploring Terra Incognita: Non-financial Reporting in Latin America. *Journal of Corporate Citizenship*, *21*(21), 25–38. doi:10.9774/GLEAF.4700.2006.sp.00005

Arrive, J. T., & Feng, M. (2018). Corporate social responsibility disclosure: Evidence from BRICS nations. *Corporate Social Responsibility and Environmental Management*, *25*(5), 920–927. doi:10.1002/csr.1508

Artiach, T., Lee, D., Nelson, D., & Walker, J. (2010). The determinants of corporate sustainability performance. *Accounting and Finance*, *50*(1), 31–51. doi:10.1111/j.1467-629X.2009.00315.x

Bansal, P. (2005). Evolving sustainably: A longitudinal study of corporate sustainable development. *Strategic Management Journal*, *26*(3), 197–218. doi:10.1002mj.441

Baskin, J. (2006). Corporate responsibility in emerging markets. *Journal of Corporate Citizenship*, *24*(24), 29–47. doi:10.9774/GLEAF.4700.2006.wi.00006

Baumgartner, R. J., & Ebner, D. (2010). Corporate sustainability strategies: Sustainability profiles and maturity levels. *Sustainable Development*, *18*(2), 76–89. doi:10.1002d.447

Bebbington, J., & Unerman, J. (2008). Editorial. *Social and Environmental Accountability Journal*, *28*(1), 1–2. doi:10.1080/0969160X.2008.9651786

Beschorner, T., & Hajduk, T. (2017). Creating Shared Value. A Fundamental Critique. In J. Wieland (Ed.), Creating Shared Value – Concepts, Experience, Criticism (pp. 27–38). Springer International Publishing AG.

Birch, D., & Moon, J. (2004). Introduction: CSR in Asia. *Journal of Corporate Citizenship*, *13*(Special Issue), 18–23. doi:10.9774/GLEAF.4700.2004.sp.00004

Brieger, S. A., & De Clercq, D. (2019). Entrepreneurs' individual level resources and social value creation goals: The moderating role of cultural context. *International Journal of Entrepreneurial Behaviour & Research*, *25*(2), 193–216. doi:10.1108/IJEBR-12-2017-0503

Carroll, A. B. (1979). A three-dimensional conceptual model of corporate performance. *Academy of Management Review*, *4*(4), 497–505. doi:10.5465/amr.1979.4498296

Cavusgil, T., Deligonul, S., & Yaprak, A. (2005). International marketing as a field of study: A critical assessment of earlier development and a look forward. *Journal of International Marketing*, *13*(4), 1–27. doi:10.1509/jimk.2005.13.4.1

Chahal, H., & Sharma, R. D. (2006). Implications of corporate social responsibility on marketing performance: A conceptual framework. *Journal of Services Research*, *6*(1), 205–216.

Chapple, W., & Moon, J. (2005). Corporate social responsibility (CSR) in Asia a seven-country study of CSR web site reporting. *Business & Society*, *44*(4), 415–441. doi:10.1177/0007650305281658

Chapple, W., & Moon, J. (2007). Introduction: CSR Agendas for Asia. *Corporate Social Responsibility and Environmental Management*, *14*(3), 183–188. doi:10.1002/csr.159

Chen, E., & Gavious, I. (2015). Does CSR have different value implications for different shareholders? *Finance Research Letters*, *14*, 29–35. doi:10.1016/j.frl.2015.07.001

Cheruiyot, T. K., & Maru, L. C. (2012). Employee social responsibility practices and outcomes in Kenya's tourist hotels. *African Journal of Economic and Management Studies*, *3*(1), 23–41. doi:10.1108/20400701211197267

Cheruiyot, T. K., & Onsando, P. (2016). Corporate Social responsibility in Africa: Context, Paradoxes, Stakeholder Orientations, Contestations and Reflections. In A. Stachowicz-Stanush (Ed.), *Corporate Social Performance in the Age of Irresponsibility-Cross National Perspective*. Charlotte, NC: Information Age Publishing.

Cheung, Y. L., Tan, W., Ahn, H. J., & Zhang, Z. (2010). Does corporate social responsibility matter in Asian Emerging Markets? *Journal of Business Ethics*, *92*(3), 401–413. doi:10.100710551-009-0164-3

Chune, Y. C., Sangjun, J., & Jason, Y. (2018). CSR Activities Increase Firm Value? Evidence from the Korean Market. *Sustainability*, *10*(9), 3164. doi:10.3390u10093164

Darus, F., Mad, S., Nejati, M., & Yusoff, R. (2016). When quality matters! CSR disclosure and value creation. *International Journal of Economics and Management*, *10*(2), 285–302.

Dell'Acqua, A., Etro, L., Piva, M., & Teti, E. (2018). Investor protection and value creation in cross-border M&As by emerging economies. *Journal of International Financial Management & Accounting*, *29*(1), 83–100. doi:10.1111/jifm.12069

Dhaliwal, D. S., Li, O. Z., Tsang, A. H., & Yang, Y. G. (2011). Voluntary non-financial disclosure and the cost of equity capital: The initiation of corporate social responsibility reporting. *The Accounting Review*, *86*(1), 59–100. doi:10.2308/accr.00000005

Dicken, P. (2011). *Global shift: mapping the changing contours of world economy* (6th ed.). New York: The Guilford Press.

Elkington, J. (1994). Towards the sustainable corporation: Win-win-win business strategies for sustainable development. *California Management Review*, *36*(2), 90–100. doi:10.2307/41165746

Elliott, W. B., Jackson, K. E., Peecher, M. E., & White, B. J. (2014). The unintended effect of corporate social responsibility performance on investors' estimates of fundamental value. *The Accounting Review*, *89*(1), 275–302. doi:10.2308/accr-50577

Esrock, S., & Leichty, G. (1998). Social responsibility and corporate web pages: Self-presentation or agenda-setting? *Public Relations Review*, *24*(3), 305–319. doi:10.1016/S0363-8111(99)80142-8

Fijałkowska, J., & Macuda, M. (2017). Value Creation Disclosure in CSR Reports – Evidence from Poland. *Zeszyty Teoretyczne Rachunkowości*, *93*(149), 61–78. doi:10.5604/01.3001.0010.3189

Fijałkowska, J., Zyznarska-Dworczak, B., & Garsztka, P. (2018). Corporate Social-Environmental Performance versus Financial Performance of Banks in Central and Eastern European Countries. *Sustainability*, *10*(3), 772. doi:10.3390u10030772

Freeman, R. E. (1984). *Strategic management: a stakeholder approach*. Marshfield: Pitman Publishing.

Ge, L., & Thomas, S. (2007). A Cross-Cultural Comparison of the Deliberative Reasoning of Canadian and Chinese Accounting Students. *Journal of Business Ethics*, *82*(1), 189–211. doi:10.100710551-007-9571-5

Griffin, J. J., & Mahon, J. F. (1997). The Corporate Social Performance and Corporate Financial Performance Debate: Twenty-Five Years of Incomparable Research. *Business & Society*, *36*(1), 5–31. doi:10.1177/000765039703600102

GTZ. (2011). *Fast growth and big impacts: How Emerging Market Multinationals are advancing sustainable development*. Retrieved from www.giz.de

Guthrie, J. E., Cuganesan, S., & Ward, L. (2008). Disclosure media for social and environmental matters within the Australian food and beverage industry. *Social and Environmental Accountability Journal*, *28*(1), 33–44. doi:10.1080/0969160X.2008.9651789

Haniffa, R. M., & Cooke, T. E. (2005). The impact of culture and governance on corporate social reporting. *Journal of Accounting and Public Policy*, *24*(5), 391–430. doi:10.1016/j.jaccpubpol.2005.06.001

Hart, S. L. (1997). Beyond Greening: Strategies for a Sustainable World. *Harvard Business Review*, (January–February): 67–76.

Hart, S. L., & Milstein, M. B. (2003). Creating sustainable value. *The Academy of Management Executive*, *17*(2), 56–69.

Hassel, L., Nilsson, H., & Nyquist, S. (2005). The value relevance of environmental performance. *European Accounting Review*, *14*(1), 41–61. doi:10.1080/0963818042000279722

Hooghiemstra, R. (2000). Corporate communication and impression management: NEW perspectives why companies engage in corporate social reporting. *Journal of Business Ethics*, *27*(1/2), 55–68. doi:10.1023/A:1006400707757

Ioannou, I., & Serafeim, G. (2012). What drives corporate social performance? The role of nation-level institutions. *Journal of International Business Studies*, *43*(9), 834–864. doi:10.1057/jibs.2012.26

Jamali, D., & Karam, C. (2016). Corporate social responsibility in developing countries as an emerging field of study. *International Journal of Management Reviews*.

Jamali, D., Karam, C., Yin, J., & Soundararajan, V. (2017). CSR logics in developing countries: Translation, adaptation and stalled development. *Journal of World Business*, *52*(3), 343–359. doi:10.1016/j.jwb.2017.02.001

Jamali, D., & Neville, B. (2011). Convergence versus divergence of CSR in developing countries: An embedded multi-layered institutional lens. *Journal of Business Ethics*, *102*(4), 599–621. doi:10.100710551-011-0830-0

Jonikas, D. (2013). Conceptual framework of value creation through CSR in separate member of value creation chain. In D. Szymańska & J. Chodkowska-Miszczuk (Eds.), Bulletin of Geography. Socio-economic Series No. 21 (pp. 69–78). Toruń: Nicolaus Copernicus University Press. doi:10.2478/bog-2013-0022

Juscius, V., & Jonikas, D. (2013). Integration of CSR into Value Creation Chain: Conceptual Framework. *Inzinerine Ekonomika-Engineering Economics*, *24*(1), 63–70.

Kar, S. K., Padhi, S. K., & Samantarai, M. (2016). Disruptive innovation and economic value creation: A service sector perspective. *Indian Journal of Management*, *9*(8), 11–25.

Kelley, K. J., Hemphill, T. A., & Thams, Y. (2018). Corporate social responsibility, country reputation and corporate reputation: A perspective on the creation of shared value in emerging markets. *Multinational Business Review*.

Khanna, T., & Palepu, K. (1997). Why focused strategies may be wrong for emerging markets. *Harvard Business Review*, *75*(4), 41–51.

Kirca, A. H., & Yaprak, A. (2010). The use of meta-analysis in international business research: Its current status and suggestions for better practice. *International Business Review*, *19*(3), 306–314. doi:10.1016/j.ibusrev.2010.01.001

Lacy, P., Cooper, T., Hayward, R., & Neuberger, L. (2010). *A new era of sustainability: UN Global Compact-Accenture CEO Study 2010*. Retrieved from https://scholar.google.com/scholar_lookup?title=ANewEraofSustainability–UNGlobalCompact-AccentureCEOStudy2010&author=P.Lacy&publication_year=2010

Lam, K. C., Shi, G., & Shi, G. (2008). Factors Affecting Ethical Attitudes in Mainland China and Hong Kong. *Journal of Business Ethics*, *77*(4), 463–479. doi:10.100710551-007-9360-1

Laszlo, C. (2008a). *Firma zrównoważonego rozwoju*. Warszawa: Studio EMKA.

Laszlo C. (2008b). Wartość w zrównoważonym rozwoju. Sustainable Value. *Problemy ekorozwoju*, *3*(2), 25–29.

Laszlo, C. (2008c). *Sustainable Value: How te Wrld's Leading Companies Are Doing Well by Doing Good.* Stanford, CA: Business Books.

Laszlo, C., Sherman, D., Whalen, J., & Ellinson, J. (2005). Expanding the Value Horizon: How Stakeholders Value Contributes to Competitive Advantage. *Journal of Corporate Citizenship*, *20*(Winter), 65–76. doi:10.9774/GLEAF.4700.2005.wi.00009

Li, S., Fetscherin, M., Alon, I., & Lattemann, C. (2010). *Corporate Social Responsibility in Emerging Markets The Importance of the Governance Environment*. Academic Press.

Li, W., & Zhang, R. (2010). Corporate Social Responsibility, Ownership Structure, and Political Interference: Evidence from China. *Journal of Business Ethics*, *96*(4), 631–645. doi:10.100710551-010-0488-z

Lin, L., Hung, P.-H., Chou, D.-W., & Lai, C. W. (2019). Financial performance and corporate social responsibility: Empirical evidence from Taiwan. *Asia Pacific Management Review*, *24*(1), 61–71. doi:10.1016/j.apmrv.2018.07.001

Lourenço, I. C., & Branco, M. C. (2013). Determinants of corporate sustainability performance in emerging markets: The Brazilian case. *Journal of Cleaner Production*, *57*, 134–141. doi:10.1016/j.jclepro.2013.06.013

Lozano, R., & Huisingh, D. (2011). Inter-linking issues and dimensions in sustainability reporting. *Journal of Cleaner Production*, *19*(2–3), 99–107. doi:10.1016/j.jclepro.2010.01.004

Margolis, J. D., & Walsh, J. P. (2003). Misery Loves Companies: Rethinking Social Initiatives by Business. *Administrative Science Quarterly*, *48*(2), 268–305. doi:10.2307/3556659

Masztalerz M. (2014). Wartość dla interesariuszy w zrównoważonym przedsiębiorstwie. *Studia Oeconomica Posnaniensia, 8*(269), 66–77.

Mehra, M. (2006). Turning Point: Corporate Social Responsibility in Emerging Economies. *Journal of Corporate Citizenship: Corporate Social Responsibility in Emerging Economies*, *24*(Special Issue), 20–22. doi:10.9774/GLEAF.4700.2006.wi.00004

Miralles-Quirós, M. M., Miralles-Quirós, J. L., & Hernández, J. R. (2019). ESG performance and shareholder value creation in the banking industry: International differences. *Sustainability*, *11*(5), 1404. doi:10.3390u11051404

Miras-Rodríguez, M., Martínez-Martínez, D., & Escobar-Pérez, B. (2018). Which corporate governance mechanisms drive CSR disclosure practices in emerging countries? *Sustainability*, *11*(1), 61. doi:10.3390u11010061

Montiel, I. (2008). Corporate social responsibility and corporate sustainability: Separate pasts, common futures. *Organization & Environment*, *21*(3), 245–269. doi:10.1177/1086026608321329

Muller, A., & Kolk, A. (2010). Extrinsic and intrinsic drivers of corporate social performance: Evidence from foreign and domestic firms in Mexico. *Journal of Management Studies*, *47*(1), 1–26. doi:10.1111/j.1467-6486.2009.00855.x

Ojo, M. (2016). Corporate Social Responsibility and Foreign Direct Investment: Engaging Innovation, Auditors, and Stakeholders in Corporate Social Responsibility. In M. Ojo (Ed.), *Analyzing the Relationship between Corporate Social Responsibility and Foreign Direct Investment* (pp. 49–63). Hershey, PA: IGI Global. doi:10.4018/978-1-5225-0305-7.ch005

Oliveira, J. (2006). Introduction. *Journal of Corporate Citizenship: Corporate Citizenship in Latin America: New Challenges for Business*, *21*(Special Issue), 17–20.

Oll, J., & Rommerskirchen, S. (2018). What's wrong with integrated reporting? A systematic review. *Sustainability Management Forum, 26*(1–4), 19–34.

Pachauri, R. K. (2006). CSR in new dimensions. *The Economic Times*.

Peloza, J. (2009). The Challenge of Measuring Financial Impacts From Investments in Corporate Social Performance. *Journal of Management*, *35*(6), 1518–1541. doi:10.1177/0149206309335188

Porter, M. (1985). *Competitive Advantage: Creating and Sustaining Superior Performance*. New York: The Free Press.

Porter, M., & Kramer, M. R. (2011). Creating shared value. *Harvard Business Review*, *89*(1/2), 62–77.

Prieto-Carron, M., Lund-Thomsen, P., Chan, A., Muro, A., & Bhushan, C. (2006). Critical perspectives on CSR and development: What we know, what we don't know, and what we need to know. *International Affairs*, *82*(5), 977–987. doi:10.1111/j.1468-2346.2006.00581.x

Rappaport, A. (1986). *Creating Shareholder Value*. New York: Free Press.

Ray, S., & Ray Chaudhuri, B. (2018). Business Group Affiliation and Corporate Sustainability Strategies of Firms: An Investigation of Firms in India. *Journal of Business Ethics*, *153*(4), 955–976. doi:10.100710551-018-3917-z

Ringov, D., & Zollo, M. (2007). The impact of national culture on corporate social performance. *Corporate Governance*, *7*(4), 476–485. doi:10.1108/14720700710820551

Rosenthal, N. (2014). Corporate Social Responsibility in Emerging Markets: Getting it right the first time? *Clarmondial*. Retrieved June 18, 2019, from Clarmondial website: https://www.clarmondial.com/corporate-social-responsibility-in-emerging-markets-getting-it-right-the-first-time/

Rousseau, D. M., Manning, J., & Denyer, D. (2008). Evidence in management and organizational science: Assembling the field's full weight of scientific knowledge through syntheses. *The Academy of Management Annals*, *2*(1), 475–515. doi:10.5465/19416520802211651

Saleh, M., Zulkifli, N., & Muhamad, R. (2011). Looking for evidence of the relationship between corporate social responsibility and corporate financial performance in an emerging market. *Asia-Pacific Journal of Business Administration*, *3*(2), 165–190. doi:10.1108/17574321111169849

Salvioni, D. M., & Gennari, F. (2017). CSR, Sustainable Value Creation and Shareholder Relations. Cham: Symphonya. *Emerging Issues in Management*, *1*, 36–49.

Sardana, D., Bamiatzi, V., & Zhu, Y. (2019). Decoding the Process of Social Value Creation by Chinese and Indian Social Entrepreneurs: Contributory Factors and Contextual Embeddedness. *Management and Organization Review*, *15*(2), 269–306. doi:10.1017/mor.2019.21

Sen, S., & Bhattacharya, C. B. (2001). Does doing good always lead to doing better? Consumer reactions to corporate social responsibility. *JMR, Journal of Marketing Research*, *38*(2), 225–243. doi:10.1509/jmkr.38.2.225.18838

Shanahan, F., & Seele, P. (2017). Creating Shared Value. Looking at Shared Value Through an Aristotelian Lens. In J. Wieland (Ed.), Creating Shared Value – Concepts, Experience, Criticism (pp. 141–151). Cham: Springer International Publishing AG.

Sinkin, C., Wright, C. J., & Burnett, R. D. (2008). Eco-efficiency and firm value. *Journal of Accounting and Public Policy*, *27*(2), 167–176. doi:10.1016/j.jaccpubpol.2008.01.003

Spitzeck, H., & Chapman, S. (2012). Creating shared value as a differentiation strategy – the example of BASF in Brazil. *Corporate Governance*, *12*(4), 499–513. doi:10.1108/14720701211267838

Sraders, A. (2018). What Are Emerging Markets? Characteristics and List in 2019. *TheStreet*. Retrieved from https://www.thestreet.com/markets/emerging-markets/what-are-emerging-markets-14819803

Stanley, T. D. (2001). Wheat from chaff: Meta-analysis as quantitative literature review. *The Journal of Economic Perspectives*, *15*(3), 131–150. doi:10.1257/jep.15.3.131

Staples, C. (2004). What does corporate social responsibility mean for charitable fundraising in the UK? *International Journal of Nonprofit and Voluntary Sector Marketing*, *9*(2), 154–158. doi:10.1002/nvsm.242

Tarigan, J., Hatane, S. E., Stacia, L., & Widjaja, D. C. (2019). Corporate social responsibility policies and value creation: Does corporate governance and profitability mediate that relationship? *Investment Management and Financial Innovations*, *16*(2), 270–280. doi:10.21511/imfi.16(2).2019.23

Tranfield, D., Denyer, D., & Smart, P. (2003). Towards a methodology for developing evidence-informed management knowledge by means of systematic review. *British Journal of Management*, *14*(3), 207–222. doi:10.1111/1467-8551.00375

Turban, D., & Greening, D. (1997). Corporate social performance and organizational attractiveness to prospective employees. *Academy of Management Journal*, *40*(3), 658–672.

Visser, W. (2008). Corporate Social Responsibility in Developing Countries. In A. Crane, A. McWilliams, D. Matten, J. Moon, & D. Siegel (Eds.), The Oxford Handbook of Corporate Social Responsibility (pp. 473-479). Oxford, UK: Oxford University Press.

Voinea, C., & Fratostiteanu, C. (2018). *Corporate Social Responsibility in Emerging Economies. Reality and Illusion*. New York: Routledge. doi:10.4324/9781315112411

Wang, Q., Dou, J., & Jia, S. (2015). A meta-analytic review of corporate social responsibility and corporate financial performance: The moderating effect of contextual factors. *Business & Society*, *1*, 1–39.

Whitcomb, L. L., Erdener, C. B., & Li, C. (1998). Business Ethical Values in China and the U.S. *Journal of Business Ethics*, *17*(8), 839–852. doi:10.1023/A:1005793424492

Ziegler, A., & Schröder, M. (2010). What determines the inclusion in a sustainability stock index?: A panel data analysis for european firms. *Ecological Economics*, *69*(4), 848–856. doi:10.1016/j.ecolecon.2009.10.009

Zu, L., & Song, L. (2009). Determinants of managerial values on corporate social responsibility: Evidence from China. *Journal of Business Ethics*, *88*(S1), 105–117. doi:10.100710551-008-9828-7

ADDITIONAL READING

Bouten, L., Everaert, P., Van Liedekerke, L., De Moor, L., & Christiaens, J. (2011). Corporate social responsibility reporting: A comprehensive picture? *Accounting Forum*, *35*(3), 187–204. doi:10.1016/j.accfor.2011.06.007

Henderson, D. (2004). *The Role of Business in the Modern World*. London: Institute of Economic Affairs.

Leal Filho, W., Idowu, S. O., & Louche, C. (2010). *Innovative CSR: From Risk Management to Value Creation*. Sheffield, UK: Routledge.

World Growth. (2011). *Corporate Social Responsibility. How Global Business is Getting it Wrong in Emerging Markets. A World Growth Report*. Arlington: World Growth.

KEY TERMS AND DEFINITIONS

Corporate Social Responsibility: (CSR): A concept whereby companies integrate social and environmental concerns in their business operations and interactions with their stakeholders.

CSR Report: A report published by a company or organization about the economic, environmental, and social impacts caused by its everyday activities.

Shareholder: An individual, group, or organization that owns one or more shares in a company, and in whose name the share certificate is issued.

Stakeholder: Any person, organization, social group, or society at large that has a stake (vital interest) in the business, which can include ownership and property interests, legal interests and obligations, and moral rights.

Sustainable Development: Development that meets the needs of the present, without compromising the ability of future, generations to meet their own needs.

Sustainable Value: The ability to provide value that sustains the organization and the context within which it exists, that integrates the economic, environmental and social dimension of sustainability.

Value Creation: The performance of actions that increase the worth of goods, services or even a business. Many business operators now focus on value creation both in the context of creating better value for customers purchasing its products and services, as well as for shareholders in the business who want to see their stake appreciate in value.

Chapter 12
"It Fits My Business": Corporate Social Responsibility Activities of Companies on the Route to Gain Competitive Advantage

Burak Çapraz
https://orcid.org/0000-0002-4631-2080
Ege University, Turkey

ABSTRACT

For many years, companies have tried to keep the public as close partners. In this bilateral relationship, financial gains of the companies have raised public views on the distribution of these gains. Likewise, regulations and standards determined by supranational institutions such as the United Nations forced companies to give higher priority on CSR activities. The primary purpose of this research is to explain the relation between CSR activities and the preferability of these activities among companies. Summative content analysis is conducted on data collected from the websites of the top 100 companies in the Turkish BIST 100 Stock Index. Findings show that CSR activity choices differ among industries, and these choices unveil related and unrelated differentiation in CSR activities.

INTRODUCTION

Since the 1950s, what corporate social responsibility (CSR) is and how CSR should be considered as a management tool is progressively being debated among scholars. These debates have given birth to various definitions and different views on CSR. From a broader perspective, it can easily be seen that applications of CSR head for a continuum in which corporate benefits stand on one side and public benefits on another side. Even if it is the benefit of the public or the firm, CSR activities are known to influence different stakeholders. Thus, CSR can be considered as a tool to gain competitive advantage. Whatever the direction of CSR is, in its life cycle, a firm faces the problem of ensuring profit sustainability. Higher budget need and the difficulty of predicting the financial return of CSR activities make CSR a contradictory topic about the real gains from CSR activities. Financial gains that do not meet

DOI: 10.4018/978-1-7998-2193-9.ch012

Copyright © 2020, IGI Global. Copying or distributing in print or electronic forms without written permission of IGI Global is prohibited.

expectations on CSR investments may cause senior management teams to have a more skeptical view about CSR activities. It is difficult to reveal the real impact of CSR on the financial performance of firms. Thus, determining the gains from the CSR activities cannot exactly be measured, which means it is not very sufficient to explain how firms can gain competitive advantage through CSR activities. But the effect of CSR on reputation (Smith, 2007; El-Garaihy et al., 2014; Saeidi et al., 2015), brand (Melo and Galan, 2011; Hsu, 2012), financial performance (Surroca et al., 2010), etc. support its effect on competitive advantage. The importance companies give to CSR activities in developing countries may dissociate negatively when compared to developed countries. This situation may cause the expectations of the enterprises operating in the markets of developing countries to be more oriented towards financial gains in terms of CSR activities.

Studies in the USA, such as Cochran and Wood (1984, p. 43) states there is weak evidence of a positive correlation between CSR and financial performance. In another study, Nelling and Webb (2009, p. 201) have found almost no correlation between corporate social responsibility and financial performance (ROI, Stock Return, Sales, Assets, Financial Leverage) in USA.

In emerging financial market examples, Yang et al. (2010, p. 409) found almost no correlation between return on assets and previous corporate social performance of firms. Tang et al. (2012, p. 1288) in their study found ROA (return on assets) has a low positive relationship with CSR. In another Taiwanese study, Huang and Lien's (2012, p. 268) findings show that CSR dimensions are positively correlated with financial performance. Findings from Cheung et al. (2010, p. 408) in Vietnamese companies only show evidence on a negative very low correlation between corporate social responsibility score and current asset ratio. Rodrigez-Fernandez (2016, p. 138) pays attention that most of the findings on CSR-Financial performance relation is generally positive, but the results are not shown homogeneity.

This situation creates an environment in which the significant part of CSR activities of firms in developing countries is expected to have an impact on the financial results of the enterprises and indirectly it is aimed to gain competitive advantage against their rivals. Porter and Kramer (2006, p. 83) point out how corporate social agenda can mitigate harm by reinforcing corporate strategy. Also, Weber (2008, p. 250) in her CSR impact model argues the effect of CSR on competitiveness with the moderating effect of monetary and non-monetary benefits.

This book chapter focuses on how CSR preferences of enterprises are formed to gain competitive advantage through CSR activities and how CSR preferences and company demographics are formed. In addition, it has been tried to put forward how CSR activities that are considered being more innocent on industry basis and related CSR activities which may be considered providing excavations to the enterprise and how they are separated. In this context, CSR activities of the companies operating in the BIST 100 Stock Index of Turkey are analyzed. BIST 100 index has been selected as it represents the most valuable 100 Turkish companies that can carry out the most comprehensive CSR activities in this country market.

DEFINING CSR

The social pressure of public on firms to share their incomes with their stakeholders goes back to very old days. Ever since businessmen are always considered as the best interest group of the public when a donation is needed. This social pressure on businessmen has evolved the idea of social responsibility, and with the increase in the number of corporations transformed this idea to corporate social responsibility.

The first definitions of CSR were focused on the responsibility of businessmen and companies. One definition from 1950s is stated by Bowen in 1953 (Bowen, 2013, p. 6). It shows that businessmen should act desirable in terms of the objectives and values of our society. Thus the society as a stakeholder is commonly seen as the key figure in terms of social responsibility. While 1950s is a decade the post-war effect on searching for prosperity was highly felt by public, entrepreneurs and enterprises became a part in social responsibility (Chalmers, 1959, p. 20).

After the 1960s, corporate social responsibility is affected by profit-based views. Heald (1961, p. 139) states the confusion on social responsibility, and the traditional belief of profit-focused management approach started debate on the business thought. The main idea was that a business should be profitable to make CSR. Scholars such as Friedman (1970) also have crucial ideas on this perspective. What he names "fundamentally subversive doctrine" focuses on increasing profits by using and engaging its resources in profit-related activities. This argument proposes a vision on CSR as we could not consider it as a tool for business without gaining an outcome. Hence, it is the shareholders, not stakeholders, which should be considered as the priority by top management teams. Schneider and Scherer (2015, p. 310) point out the importance of maximizing corporate value. But executives may act without taking consideration of stakeholders which might be unfair, undemocratic and abusing trust. This act is defined as Friedman's paradigm (Mulligan, 1986, p. 266).

In the 1970s with the involvement of the Iron Law of Responsibility, responsible behavior is integrated as a dimension of CSR. When society's expectations are not covered by those who have power, they will lose this social power as The Iron Law of Responsibility states. The iron law is based on an analytical prediction (Davis, 1973, p. 314). The expectation is social responsibilities should be balanced with social power. If the responsible behavior does not occur as the society expects, the business will lose power.

With the increasing attention on stakeholder theory, the relationship between stakeholders and CSR is also studied (Jamali, 2008; Russo and Perrini, 2010; O'Riordan and Fairbass, 2014). In this context, agency problem is one crucial topic in which management scholars focus on the moral choices of managers in CSR (McWilliams and Siegel, 2001a, p. 505). Today, CSR is used by firms as a tool to increase organizational visibility. Brammer and Millington (2006, p. 8) state that it's not organizations that are themselves which are visible. Corporate actions such as CSR enable them to be visible. Thus, the strategic selection of actions by organizations become vital in order to have more long-lasting effects.

There is still debate on the definition of CSR. The main reason of this debate is based on the different perspectives on CSR. A commonly shared definition defined by European Commission (2001, p. 7) in The Green Paper states CSR is "a concept whereby companies integrate social and environmental concerns in their business operations and in their interaction with their stakeholders on a voluntary basis". Even though social and environmental issues are defined in the roots of CSR, according to the ISO 26000 Standard, CSR also includes organizational governance, labor practices, fair operating practices, and consumer issues. Thus CSR should be studied from a broader perspective, and this need to understand CSR from different views has evolved different models on CSR. The International Organization for Standardization (ISO) also has a definition of CSR (Leonard and McAdam, 2003) that focus on benefits of people, communities and society in terms of economic, social and environmental issues.

Regarding these definitions, research in this book chapter is based on stakeholder theory, where firms are practicing unique CSR activities to their related stakeholders. Some of these activities are found related and unrelated to their core business. Thus, the profit-focused management approach is taken into consideration as well as responsibility approach in which CSR activities in most unrelated terms are held with social needs.

Table 1. Dimensions in four selected models on CSR

Author (year)	Model	Dimensions
Carroll (1979)	Four Components of CSR	Economic responsibilities, legal responsibilities, ethical responsibilities, discretionary responsibilities
Jones (1991)	CSR Approaches	obstructionist, defensive, accommodative and proactive
Quazi and O'Brian (2000)	Responsibility & CSR Action	narrow responsibility; wide responsibility; benefits gained from CSR; cost of CSR
Mostovicz et al. (2009)	Four Views on CSR	Long term view; wide view; macro view; micro view

MODELS ON CSR

Besides the efforts on creating a definition of CSR, it is also one of the most important aims of CSR studies to define how CSR interacts with other constraints. This effort has given birth to many models on CSR. One very familiar model belongs to Carroll (1979). In this model, he defined four components for CSR which are economic responsibilities, legal responsibilities, ethical responsibilities, discretionary responsibilities where he states CSR is an outcome of responsibilities. In this sense, firms have to be dealing with external pressures forcing themselves to be holding CSR such as legal responsibilities. But on another sense, they may feel themselves to be creating CSR activities from their discretionary and ethical responsibilities. This categorization of CSR give a hierarchical understanding of CSR activities firms have to deal with.

One another model is Jones' (1991) "Approaches to Social Responsibility". The model briefly defines four approaches in social responsibility: obstructionist, defensive, accommodative, and proactive. Jones (1991) defines the obstructionist approach as the approach that social responsibility is retrojected in which unethical behaviors can be seen. The defensive approach supports putting effort into social responsibility when there are controversy forces (esp. legal forces) which enforces the organization to put effort into it. In the accommodative approach, usually, pressure can be seen from stakeholders that force the organization to show social responsibility. And proactive approach supports to be proactive with the stakeholders' needs to make the right actions. Jones' model in terms of a continuum from being profitable to be a good citizen shows similar mentality with Carroll's model. Where Jones' model differs is the "obstructionist approach", which could be related with economic responsibilities but also can include obstructionist efforts that would gain benefits to the firm itself.

In their two axes model, Quazi and O'Brian (2000, p. 35) focus on the responsibility and CSR action. The two extreme sides of the responsibility axis are narrow responsibility (based more on profit maximization) and wide responsibility (broader context of CSR including philanthropy). And, the second axis focuses on the consequences of CSR. On one side, benefits gained from CSR and on the other side the cost of CSR are considered. Based on these two axes, they define four different views on CSR. The classical view focuses on profit maximization with no real benefit from CSR action. With profit maximization socio-economic view focus on relationship enhancing with the stakeholders. Modern view with a broader perspective on CSR aims to have enjoyed from CSR actions while philanthropic view supports participation in CSR activities even there is a cost to pay for the company.

In another model, Mostovicz et al. (2009) explain the different views on CSR from their perspective. According to them, four basic views are based on the social view and organizational view of the firm.

"Long Term View" is the view that companies both focus on extrinsic and intrinsic issues based on sustainability. The organization is responsible for all of its actions through its life. "Wide View" focuses more on the social view (extrinsic) than the organization itself. Here to build a competitive reputation is an important part that also intends to increase. In the "Macro View" perspective, moral obligation to society is in front, and in "Micro View" has a perspective to minimize both social and organizational views on CSR. Micro View focuses on keeping the organization operating.

All four models (Table 1) in their root focus on two ends of a continuum that are behaving philanthropic or focusing on benefits. Firms that find CSR as a tool on both sides of this continuum tries to match their strategic goals with CSR strategies. Through CSR activities, firms will try to find their ways to meet CSR strategies.

CSR STRATEGIES & CSR ACTIVITIES

Debates on defining CSR strategies, tools, and activities are very limited. A recent study by Ligeti and Oravecz, 2009, p. 139) states CSR is treated as a separate activity. But Russo and Tencati (2009, p. 341) claim CSR strategies as tools and activities focus on responsible behavior. They also see CSR strategies, tools, and activities as intertwined concepts in CSR literature. Another important question is how CSR strategies differ among firms. There are not many studies found in management literature, but again according to Russo and Tencati (2009), CSR strategies of large-sized enterprises do not differ from SME's.

In gaining competitive advantage, CSR and competitiveness relation is built on image, reputation, identity, and branding by Vilanova et al. (2009). Thus reputation and image have a different priority in CSR strategies. In recent years, the relation of reputation with CSR has been discussed by Pérez (2015), Minor and Morgan (2011), and Dupire and M'Zali (2018). The importance of reputation and image as CSR strategy can be seen in the usage of tools in maintaining legitimacy and avoiding bad publicity (Runhaar and Lafferty, 2009, p. 479).

From selected studies, CSR strategies defined in the literature are as follows:

- Environmental management (Perrini et al., 2007; Russo and Tencati, 2009),
- Employment (Perrini et al., 2007; Russo and Tencati, 2009; UN Global Compact; Santos, 2011),
- Supply chain (Perrini et al., 2007; Russo and Tencati, 2009),
- Local community (Perrini et al., 2007; Russo and Tencati, 2009),
- Community volunteering (Perrini et al., 2007; Russo and Tencati, 2009),
- Controlling and reporting (Perrini et al., 2007),
- Human rights (UN Global Compact),
- Labor conditions (UN Global Compact),
- Anti-corruption (UN Global Compact),
- Clients management (Santos, 2011),
- Product/ Service Utilization (Santos, 2011),
- Sponsorships and donations (Santos, 2011).

Even though companies do not commonly use these strategies, most of them are in search for the best strategies or tools that will enable them to reach their proposed target in terms of CSR. Russo and Tencati (2009, p. 341) point out SMEs need for a search for the best method of integrating CSR. But the truth lies more on replication of these strategies. One important factor here could be the financial strength of SMEs. Not all SME's would be in the same CSR view. This difference forces them to make satisfactory decisions on CSR strategy selection. While an enormous proportion of the SME's is related to family firms, the decisions on CSR is usually related to the family's view. Thus, powerful members' decisions could become more dominant than the CSR committee. In this perspective, family effect on CSR decisions in SME's should be understood with empirical studies. One another issue could be the talented workforce enabling better CSR strategies and tools in action. As a management topic, CSR itself is a topic that companies need experts to solve CSR issues. An obvious issue about financial strength here comes out again. Recruiting a talented workforce also has a cost for the companies. While the effect on CSR is not always enabling companies to measure the amount of gain in intangible assets such as reputation, the suspicious look on the investment-profit expectancy becomes a contradictory issue for the owners and executives of the SME's.

Even so, CSR activities are increasingly taking place among companies. The question is, while there are so many constraints affecting CSR, why companies still insist on keep going with CSR strategies. Common debate on CSR is if activities named as CSR should be considered or not. McWilliams and Siegel (2001b, p. 117) state CSR should be "going beyond the law". It means not anything based on legal issues should be called CSR. There is also a conflict in defining CSR activities and CSR strategies. As previously mentioned, CSR activities and CSR strategies are mostly intertwined. The reason is that activities could transform to a strategy. A firm can be involved in activities about environment such as environmental protection training, recycling company products, etc. When the focus of these activities show a specific area and the firm re-builds, its CSR activities in this area, these activities serve to a specific strategy such as an environmental strategy. Previous studies on CSR show rising of CSR activities are especially affected from ethics, philanthropy, social power, financial expectations, legal obligations, shareholder value, and local public concerns which are related with the dimensions defined in models on CSR.

Ethics

As ethical considerations of B2B and B2C customers are rising, companies are trying to find ways to fill the gaps they have in ethical behavior. It's not only the company itself who is in charge of ethical behavior but also through the supply chain, and interest groups could also be considered as determinators in the value chain. Thus, being part of the value chain encumber the parties a collective ethical responsibility. McWilliams and Siegel (2001b, p. 117) point stakeholders as pressure groups on CSR, including customers and suppliers. We expect organizations to behave ethically. Some argue that long-lasting relationships are also based on ethics. But some argues about productive and advantageous economic relationships (Jones, 1995, p. 416).

In some occasions, stakeholders question ethical considered behaviors of companies which also can get a negative reaction from the public. A company that behaves ethically may feel secure in front of the public. But when an unethical behavior appears by another firm in the supply chain, the negative consequences may also affect the main firm. Thus, the expectancy of the public transforms into a mentality as the company is responsible for its behaviors, and it is also responsible from other companies that it is interacting. This responsibility understanding addresses social standards in the supply chain and gave birth to organizations such as Fair Label Association and United Kingdom's Ethical Trading Initiative (Doane, 2005, p. 24). Based on the ethical components of CSR defined by Carroll (1991, p.

41), an organization should behave consistent with societal mores and ethical norms and should respect evolving norms in society.

Philanthropy

Businessmen are already the best interest group of the public when a donation is a need. The mentally of rich gives the poor has put businessmen in the first place when talking about philanthropy. But what is standing behind root in public image? For decades, philanthropy is one of the best tools to meet with new people, have better social power, and increase trustworthiness in trade. Thus, people themselves were much more keen to show interest in taking part in these kinds of events. Today, not much has changed. When we look at philanthropy, we still see the people's names more than their companies. Classifying actions as philanthropy is sometimes a contradiction. Carroll (1991, p. 41) states voluntary activities, charitable activities and assisting arts as examples of philanthropy.

Organizations are also trying to increase their organizational visibility by using different tools such as CSR, philanthropy, promotional activities, etc. Brammer and Millington (2006, p. 8) state it is not organizations it is issued that are themselves which are visible. Thus, the selection of philanthropic actions by organizations may vary according to this idea. So one question for organizations should be if CSR activities are selected as more long-lasting issues like schools, hospitals, etc.

Philanthropy is also a very common tool for networking. Building new relationships with new firms is usually a contradictory decision. The effort to build these relations needs time and has cost. When time is a pendulum swing, and there is no tolerance for losing time, accelerators are needed in building relations. One very good example of these accelerators is philanthropic actions? Navarro (1988, p. 65) points out that profit maximization is an important motive for driving contributions. When philanthropic actions generate profit for the companies, the will to make more contributions is expected to be higher. Evidence shows that this proposition is contradictory. Campbell et al. (1999, p. 379) found no significant difference in corporate giving with the business field and size of the company. But in another study Udayasankar (2008) found a U-shaped relationship between firm size and CSR participation in which middle-sized companies are the ones where CSR participation is the lowest. So what effects the philanthropic action lies in different reasons. In one thought from Campbell et al. (1999, p. 379) attributes this to the altruistic view of companies, where Podnar and Golob (2007, p. 334) state ethical-philanthropic CSR has the strongest influence on the readiness to support CSR.

Social Power

The Iron Law of Responsibility is one very much talked rule in CSR studies. According to this law, when society's expectations are not covered by those who have power, they will start to lose this social power. Davis (1973, p. 314) explains that the law is based on an analytical prediction. The expectation is social responsibilities balanced with social power. Nelling and Webb (2009, p. 198) suggest that good social performance with managerial practice may lead to strong financial performance. In this case, another question on CSR is if companies are also involved in the CSR process to keep the balance in the Law of Responsibility.

Power is an important variable in relations with society. Garriga and Mele (2004, p. 52) points to the importance of power both in relationships and responsibilities. Power can also be considered a variable related to reputation. The more a company has power, the more it is expected to have a better reputation in the eye of its stakeholders. But one thing should not be forgotten. Power could be acquired hard, but it's not hard to lose it. Davis (1960, p. 73) warns organizations to be careful about their CSR strategies. He states that "the avoidance of social responsibility leads to a gradual erosion of social power". This assumption should take companies to think about their CSR bundle. A sharp reduction in CSR budgets and applications may harm these organizations.

Financial Expectations

One another aim of CSR activities is to be successful in terms of financial gains. McWilliams and Siegel (2000) explain that the results of previous studies on CSR and financial performance are conflicting with one another. Where some studies have findings that show a positive relation, some show negative and some are neutral. Thus, there is not a definite consensus on the financial outcomes of CSR. But McWilliams and Siegel (2000, p. 605) point out the importance of CSR's effect on creating new product categories as a financial gain.

It's also obvious that CSR activities need to be financed. So another important question is if we're expecting a financial gain what will be so could be called "return on CSR investment". One defined strategy, CSR engagement strategy, focuses on creating commercial outputs by CSR related activities (Tang et al., 2012, p. 1275). With the effect of social media and digitalization, CSR outcomes are more quickly shared with stakeholders.

Expectations of financial gains can also shatter within the changes in financial markets. Cochran and Wood (1984, p. 45) explain the differences in some findings of financial outcomes in different studies. They point out the fact that when financial markets are showing the characteristics of "Bear Market" the outcomes as financial gains will also change. Because of fluctuations in commodity and financial markets, organizations can change their CSR engagement strategy and so their investments in CSR. This change decision enforces organizations to understand the effects of CSR applications on organizational outcomes better. However, it is difficult to evaluate this effect. The measurement problem of corporate social performance and financial performance is pointed out in the literature (Waddock and Graves, 1997, p. 304). Alexander and Buchholz (1978, p. 485) found no significant relationship between social responsibility and stock market performance. The relationship between CSR and financial performance is also contradictory. McGuire et al. (1988, p. 869) suggest that maybe it should be considered as financial performance effects CSR.

In this study, financial expectations are not taken into consideration. Collected data in research is not thought to give an address to the question of the relationship of CSR activities with financial performance. But from a different perspective, one another issue, market value and its relationship with CSR activities variation is questioned. It could be seen that some companies choose to be in CSR activities which are related to their business. Peloza (2006) points out the insurance value of CSR. CSR activities can also be used as insurance to financial performance when unexpected events occur. He defines effort & commitment, promotion of positive CSR, and relationship to core business as three variables which affect the ability of CSR as insurance. But as insurance, another research question focuses on the relation of CSR activity with the core business.

Legal Obligations

Even CSR activities might be seen as philanthropic activities, they occur at the organizational level. It means that any philanthropic activity can cause ethical and legal problems in the eye of the government. In the risk of exploiting public and tax abuse, it is a need for government to stand in CSR activities as a regulatory body. There are even examples of philanthropy in which not only the company itself is the donator but also makes people make donations. The auditing of these activities if they really are used in public benefit these regulatory bodies are in action. Thus governments with their legitimacy and the power to correct market inefficiencies (Kitzmueller and Shimshack, 2012, p. 54). Porter and Kramer (2006, p. 82) point out the effect of strong regulatory standards and their effect on consumer and competitive companies' protection from exploitation.

"Government is often considered as the regulatory other of CSR" (Vallentin and Murillo, 2011, p. 826). The government could be the regulatory body that mandates. But the focus of government on CSR should not be considered only as a regulatory force. Direct and indirect support of governments is also influential in the increase of CSR activities in countries. Škare and Golje (2014, p. 562) claims countries that strongly support CSR achieve higher growth rates. Government involving in CSR enlarges into a wider perspective on being in networks which is far beyond regulatory issues (Vallentin and Murillo, 2011, p. 826).

Besides government involvement, it is also the public that determines the CSR standard. Stakeholders effect CSR strategies, and even these stakeholder groups may decrease the quality and qualification of CSR activities. If a country or a region do not have high standards of CSR with a low level of public pressure, MNE's may define their CSR strategy to meet these lower standards (Muller, 2006, p. 189). This situation may arise a conflict inside MNEs as not having a global CSR standard. And of course, it could be expected that in terms of reputation these companies may have a differing reputation across countries.

Briefly, when CSR and its legal components are thought Carroll (1991, p. 40) states it is important for companies to pay attention to government and law, legal obligations, and regulations. Carroll (1991, p. 40) also takes attention to being a law-abiding corporate citizen. Hamann (2006, p. 181) shows the state is the key factor that shape corporate citizenship in developing countries. He points it to the reason why government enforcement is often constrained. In the end, even government and the state have an effect on CSR activities or not, the mentality of corporations should be transformed into a perspective from "corporate social responsibility" to "corporate social integration" (Porter and Kramer, 2006, p. 90).

Shareholder Value

When the return on investment could not be measured properly, it is usually hard to let decision-makers to invest. So the CSR investments are one type of these, that is hard to evaluate the gain. In order to invest in CSR, top executives are making decisions on behalf of shareholders. But there is one problem to convince the shareholders. Cost-benefit analysis is important in terms of social cost curve and a social benefit curve (Husted and Salazar, 2006, p. 77). Jensen (2002) in this sense has proposed enlightened value maximization that means long-term value maximization by trying to find value for a company's targets. The expectations of shareholders may vary. Especially because of financial concerns some shareholders may not approve the budget on CSR activities. Barnea and Rubin (2010, p. 72) state that affiliated shareholders may confer benefits but not the non-affiliated ones. They also state the firm's policy step forward, which can create conflict between shareholders.

Marginal investors who are short-term investors making trade may not have a very intense relationship with the firms. But long-term investors are getting married to the firm, which increases both sides dependence on each other. According to Chen and Gavious (2015, p. 29), marginal investors value a firm's commitment to social responsibility positively. But they also found that CSR do not attract long-term investors. This finding shows that CSR is perceived as beneficial to shareholders in the short term rather than the long term.

Local Public Concerns

Public opinion on the company is important within the exchanges of firms with its stakeholders. Basically, reputation is one constraint. CSR can have positive effects on employees' motivation and morale that will increase commitment and increase efficiency (Branco and Rodrigues, 2006, p. 121). In this way, the organizational resources will progress, and the company would have better financial performance. One major problem in this process is how to communicate CSR. According to the study of Jamali and Mirshak (2007, p. 255), most of the companies fail in the communication of outcomes and impacts of their CSR programs which they call "Silent CSR". Another risk is the CSR effect on top executives more than the company. In many CSR cases, the face of the company takes the benefit of communication. Businessmen and executives can use social power in their own right (Davis, 1960, p. 69). Seifert et al. (2003, p. 196) state the philanthropic actions may enhance CEO prestige. Because of these concerns, the quality and qualification of CSR may vary by time.

CSR STUDIES IN TURKEY

Although CSR activities have been held for many years, CSR is still a new and emerging topic in Turkey. Studies of Ararat (2008) and Selvi et al. (2010) are found to be the highest cited studies published in International Journals. In both international and local published studies, the dissemination of knowledge on CSR in Turkey is limited but emerging. Some of these studies are case studies (Eren-Erdoğmuş et al., 2014; Çoknaz et al., 2016; Omur et al., 2012) while most of them focus on field research. Studies published in international journals and books show results as follow.

In their study, Ozdora-Aksak and Atakan-Duman (2016, p. 238) focused on the influence of isomorphism mechanisms on the adoption of CSR initiatives in BIST-30 index companies. Their study shows in CSR activities B2B companies focus more on their core business while B2C companies focus on more philanthropic activities. However, companies that work in both B2B and B2C have an equal distribution of core business focused and discretionary CSR activities (Ozdora-Aksak and Atakan-Duman, 2016, p. 249). In an interview-based study of Robertson (2009, p. 630), CSR is commonly seen as philanthropy in Turkey.

In a country comparison study, Golob et al. (2018, p. 437) found the most frequently mentioned activities in Turkey are providing employment opportunities, support for education, and contribution to the national economy.

NGOs and their relationship in CSR activities is also a specific research field. Balaban et al. (2012) researched CSR activities of firms and NGO Relations and found that holdings have their own foundations (as NGO) regarding CSR activities. In another study on NGO's Iyigun (2013, p. 165) found legal responsibility have positive relationships with both ethical responsibility and philanthropy in terms of NGO members' perception.

Some studies in Turkey focus on specific industries. Construction companies are aware of the increasing importance of CSR (Ulutaş Duman et al., 2016, p. 218). Kılıç (2016, p. 560) found in his study on 25 banks, CSR disclosure, has highest correlation with level of environment and energy disclosure (0.930; $p<0.01$) and level of community involvement disclosure (0.887; $p<0.01$). In another study on companies in Manufacturing Index (XUSIN) of Istanbul Stock Exchange (BIST), Karasioğlu and Demirel-Arici (2012, p. 455) found a positive relationship between corporate social responsibility and corporate financial performance.

METHODOLOGY

Sample and Data

To test the hypothesis, CSR data is driven from the Istanbul Stock Exchange BIST-100 Index Companies. BIST-100 index consists of the top 100 companies in Turkey. The reason while these companies are chosen is that while CSR including philanthropy is linked with companies market value, researcher expectancy is the highest to see the most advanced CSR activities in this scope of companies. In this context, company websites are used to gather CSR data. This data is coded for each firm, and data is grouped in a certain logic. In these 100 companies, while two companies' data is aggregated data as subsidiaries of the same group, the group company is taken into consideration. In this regard, the data pool consists of 99 companies from BIST 100 Index. Data is collected between April 12 and September 26, 2018.

Research Methodology

In the study, summative content analysis as qualitative content analysis is conducted. Keywords as CSR sub-activities are identified during data analysis, and classified in categories of CSR activities. Qualitative content analysis is defined as a research method for the subjective interpretation of the content of text data through the systematic classification process of coding and identifying themes or patterns (Hsieh and Shannon, 2005).

Empirical Results

Data collected as CSR sub-activities are coded and grouped in 34 CSR activity groups. In the distribution of these CSR activities, education, sports, environment, culture, and arts, afforestation, disabled people, health and women as CSR activities are found as the most preferred activities for the companies. On the common end, products with social messages, support on TV programs, refugees, elders, superstructures and open visits are seen as the least preferred CSR activities (Figure 1).

Distribution of the CSR activities according to industries show that the same eight CSR activities with changing rank are found as a cluster in the industries (Figure 2).

Figure 1. Distribution of CSR activities % in BIST 100 Companies

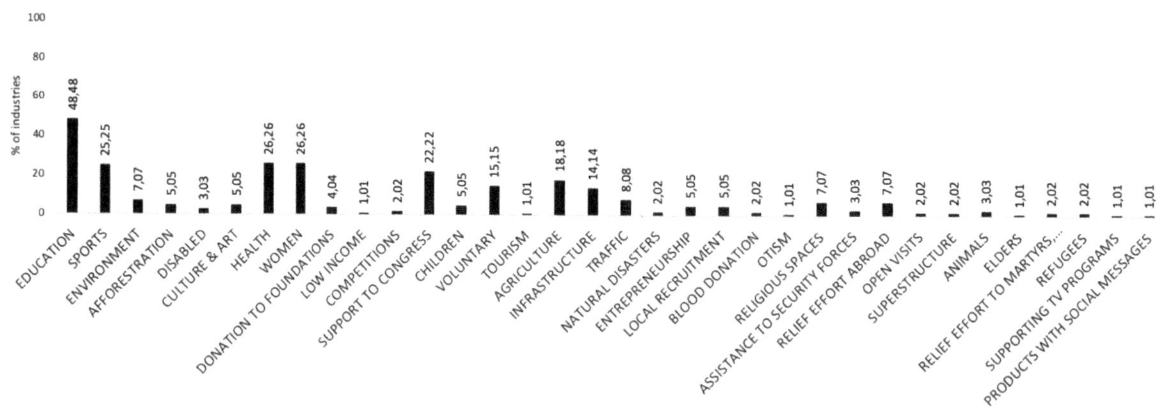

Figure 2. Industry Based Distribution of CSR Activities % in BIST 100 Companies

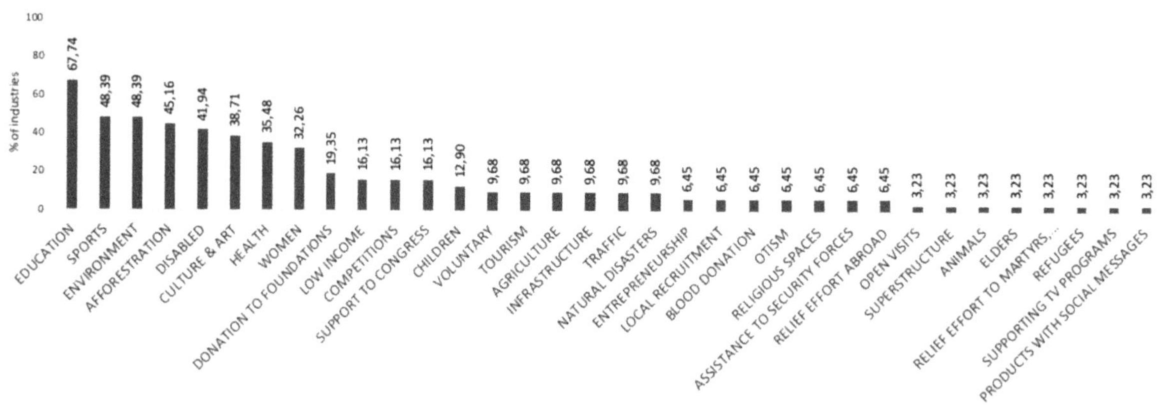

Another finding is that CSR activities differ among industries. Figure 3 shows the distribution of the top eight CSR activities among industries. As it can be seen, finance, energy, food & beverage, and holdings are the industries that these top 8 CSR activities perform.

The first hypothesis of the research is based on the assumption that CSR activities are used with some other specific CSR activities.

H1: CSR activities have a relationship with other CSR activities.

One of the research questions is if there is a relationship between CSR activities. Correlation table between CSR activities in companies (Table 2) show there is a correlation between "open visits" and "blood donation" ($r=0,703$; $p<0,01$); "infrastructure" and "low income" ($r=0,609$; $p<0,01$); "infrastructure" and "assistance to security forces" ($r=0,623$; $p<0,01$), "tourism" and "elders" ($r=0,571$; $p<0,01$); "natural disasters" and "refugees" ($r=0,571$; $p<0,01$), "support to congress and events" and "relief effort abroad" ($r=0,521$; $p<0,01$).

Figure 3. Distribution of Top 8 CSR Activities by Industries

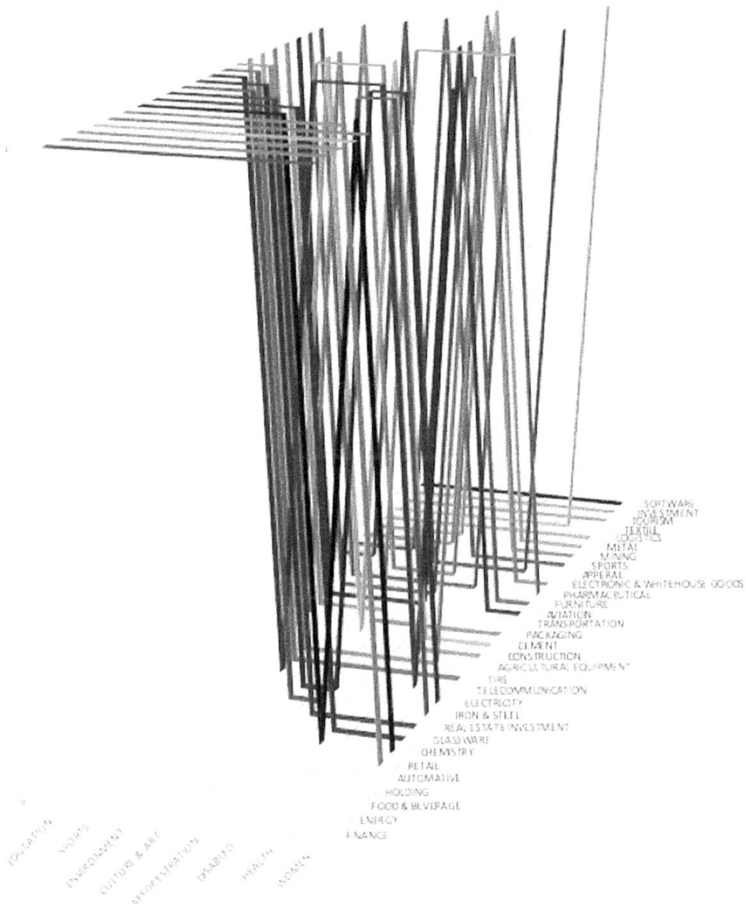

Correlation analysis is also made for industry averages. Selected outcomes are; there is a high correlation between "elders" and "voluntary actions" (r=0,929; p<0,01); "elders" and "entrepreneurship" (r=0,925; p<0,01); moderate correlation between "culture & art" and "entrepreneurship" (r=0,746; p<0,01); "culture & art" and "voluntary" (r=0,836; p<0,01); "culture & art" and "tourism" (r=0,697; p<0,01); "voluntary" and "entrepreneurship" (r=0,850; p<0,01); "education" and "health" (r=0,515; p<0,05); "education" and "afforestation" (r=0,575; p<0,05). In correlation analysis, it is commonly seen that the CSR action choice of the companies are mostly related with one another (ex. CSR on agriculture as well as CSR on health) (Table 3).

H2: CSR activities have relation with company demographics

It is also questioned if there is a correlation between the companies' between company demographics (number of employees, market value, industry) and CSR activities (Table 4). Low correlation is found between "culture& art" and "market value" (r=0,460, p<0,01), "CSR on disabled people" and "Market value" (r=0,433; p<0,01)

Table 2. Correlation - CSR Activities (BIST 100 Companies)*

	Blood Donation	Low Income Groups	Elders	Refugees	Assistance To Security Forces	Relief Effort Abroad
Voluntary	-0,033	-0,068	**,438****	-0,023	-0,033	-0,033
Tourism	-0,025	-0,052	**,571****	-0,018	-0,025	-0,025
Open Visits	**,703****	-0,03	-0,01	-0,01	-0,015	-0,015
Infrastructure		**,609****	-0,023	-0,023	**,623****	**,295****
Low Income Groups			-0,03	-0,03	**,484****	**,221***
Competitions			**,438****	-0,023	**,295****	**,295****
Children			**,438****	-0,023	-0,033	-0,033
Support To Congress				-0,028	**,240***	**,521****
Relief Effort To Martyrs, Veterans & Their Relatives				-0,015	**,490****	**,490****
Religious Spaces				-0,015	-0,021	-0,021
Natural Disasters				**,571****	-0,025	-0,025
Assistance To Security Forces						**,490****

**. Correlation is significant at the 0.01 level (2-tailed)
*. Correlation is significant at the 0.05 level (2-tailed)

H3: CSR actions differ in industries

Mean value for CSR action's variety is taken into consideration. According to the findings shown in figure 4, figure 5, figure 6, and figure 7, CSR actions vary in industries.

Education, as the most popular CSR activity, has the greatest variety of use in the finance and energy industries. An interesting finding in terms of CSR activity variety is that the finance and construction industries have the highest rates. In terms of the competitive environment, especially for banks in the finance industry, one of the main targets is the increase in the number of clients. In long-term targets to attract the public and potential clients in long-term educational and cultural CSR activities are commonly used. Training programs for different age groups, scholarships, and training programs for professionals are the most common activities under educational CSR activities.

Another finding from the study is that most industries choose only a limited number of CSR activities among the eight most preferred CSR activities. Focused differentiation is seen in the selection of CSR strategies. Sports as CSR activities is most varied in the food & beverage industry, and CSR activities for women are more varied in textile, apparel, tourism industries with holding companies. Researchers assumption is for the consumption of food and beverages are mostly linked with sports activities; thus, the interest target group for these companies may force them to focus on these type of CSR activities. As decision-makers in families and consumption rate in apparel and textile industries, CSR activities for women might be a strategic decision for long-term sustainability in these companies' competitive positions. On the CSR activities for disabled people, electronic & white house goods manufacturers, transportation and telecommunication companies are taking the lead. Especially on mobility (transportation & telecommunication) importance for this consumer group and the easiness of life inside the house (electronic & white house goods manufacturers) might force these companies to show such an

Table 3. Correlation- CSR Activities' proportion inside industry average rates

	Education	Culture & Art	Entrepreneurship	Voluntary	Tourism	Agriculture	Sports	Local Recruitment	Open Visits	Blood Donation	Infrastructure	Health	Superstructure	Women	Low Income Groups	Competitions	Autism	Donation to Foundations	Support to Congress	Relief Effort to Martyrs, Veterans and Their Relatives	Religious Spaces
Entrepreneurship	0,25	,746**																			
Voluntary	0,30	,836**	,850**																		
Tourism	0,19	,697**	0,36	,600*																	
Sports	0,45	0,33	0,17	0,13	,502*	0,35															
Local Recruitment	0,37	0,41	0,14	0,18	0,33	-0,17	,500*														
Open Visits	0,48	-0,11	-0,09	-0,09	-0,12	,574*	0,08	-0,10													
Afforestation	,575*	,516*	0,48	0,42	0,36	0,40	0,14	-0,02	0,37	-0,06											
Health	,515*	0,15	0,07	0,10	0,49	,546*	,780**	0,40	0,31	0,33	0,43										
Superstructure	0,48	-0,11	-0,09	-0,09	-0,12	,574*	0,08	-0,10	1,000**	,515*	-0,11	0,31									
Women	0,30	,503*	0,27	0,20	,620*	0,21	,646**	,667**	-0,18	-0,26	-0,18	,533*	-0,18								
Low Income Groups	0,05	-0,41	-0,11	-0,17	-0,24	-0,09	0,26	-0,07	-0,13	0,36	,880**	0,40	-0,13	-0,23							
Competitions	0,34	0,07	0,26	0,28	0,14	-0,28	0,49	0,33	-0,16	0,30	,882**	,532*	-0,16	0,11	,770**						
Children	0,06	,630**	,743**	,591*	,573*	0,35	0,34	0,07	-0,14	-0,20	-0,24	0,32	-0,14	0,44	-0,02	0,07					
Autism	0,21	0,35	0,29	0,29	0,06	-0,16	-0,32	-0,13	-0,09	-0,13	-0,15	-0,26	-0,09	-0,15	-0,18	-0,07					
Elders	0,19	,724**	,925**	,929**	0,43	-0,12	0,02	-0,10	-0,07	-0,10	-0,11	-0,02	-0,07	0,06	-0,13	0,19	0,34				
Donation to Foundations	0,43	-0,01	0,19	0,20	-0,03	0,35	0,26	-0,17	,741**	,877**	0,21	0,35	,741**	-0,23	0,16	0,21	-0,01				
Traffic	0,37	0,41	0,14	0,18	0,33	-0,17	,500*	1,000**	-0,10	-0,14	0,01	0,40	-0,10	,667**	-0,07	0,33	-0,13	-0,17			
Support to Congress	0,12	0,27	0,33	0,33	-0,01	-0,08	-0,03	-0,25	0,17	0,39	0,04	-0,14	0,17	-0,32	-0,03	0,08	,650**	0,49			
Relief Effort to Martyrs, Veterans and their Relatives	-0,03	-0,28	-0,09	-0,09	-0,12	-0,12	0,30	-0,10	-0,07	,821**	,550*	0,17	-0,07	-0,18	,506*	0,46	-0,09	,527*	0,34		
Religious Spaces	-0,02	-0,26	-0,12	-0,12	-0,17	-0,16	0,09	-0,13	-0,09	-0,13	,682**	0,19	-0,09	-0,24	,624**	,560*	-0,12	-0,16	0,01	-0,09	
Assistance to Security Forces	0,10	-0,40	-0,13	-0,13	-0,18	-0,17	0,26	-0,14	-0,10	0,43	,979**	0,37	-0,10	-0,26	,908**	,832**	-0,13	0,23	0,07	,565*	,701**
Relief Effort Abroad	-0,22	-0,24	-0,13	-0,12	-0,17	-0,16	0,28	-0,14	-0,09	,685**	0,44	0,02	-0,09	-0,25	0,39	0,33	-0,13	0,41	,518*	,860**	0,09
Supporting Tv Programs	0,48	-0,11	-0,09	-0,09	-0,12	,574*	0,08	-0,10	1,000**	,515*	-0,11	0,31	1,000**	-0,18	-0,13	-0,16	-0,09	,741**	0,17	-0,07	-0,09

**. Correlation is significant at the 0.01 level (2-tailed)

*. Correlation is significant at the 0.05 level (2-tailed)

Table 4. Correlation- CSR Activities & Company Demographics

	Number of employees	Market value	Industry
Education	0,029	,213*	-0,161
Culture & Art	,331**	,460**	-,288**
Entrepreneurship	0,074	,283**	-,298**
Voluntary	0,073	,389**	-,202*
Sports	,309**	,313**	-0,18
Environment	-0,001	0,028	-,289**
Blood Donation	-0,02	,209*	-0,063
Infrastructure	-0,077	0,069	-,234*
Disabled	,294**	,433**	-0,09
Competitions	-0,031	-0,007	-,208*
Autism	0,115	,231*	-0,096
Natural Disasters	,298**	,207*	0,085
Refugees	0,071	,222*	0,142

**. Correlation is significant at the 0.01 level (2-tailed)

*. Correlation is significant at the 0.05 level (2-tailed)

Figure 4. Mean values of CSR action's variety in education, culture, and arts

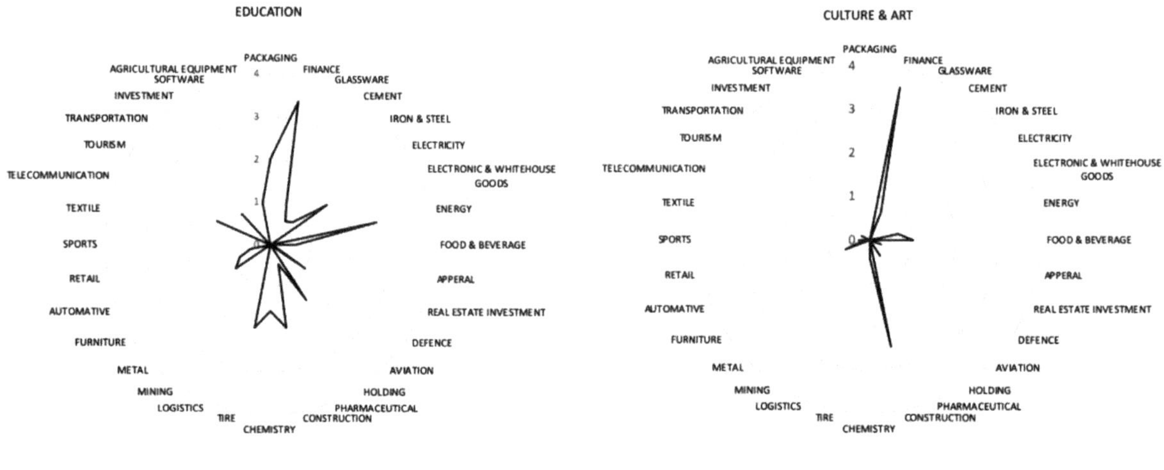

Figure 5. Mean values of CSR action's variety in environment, afforestation

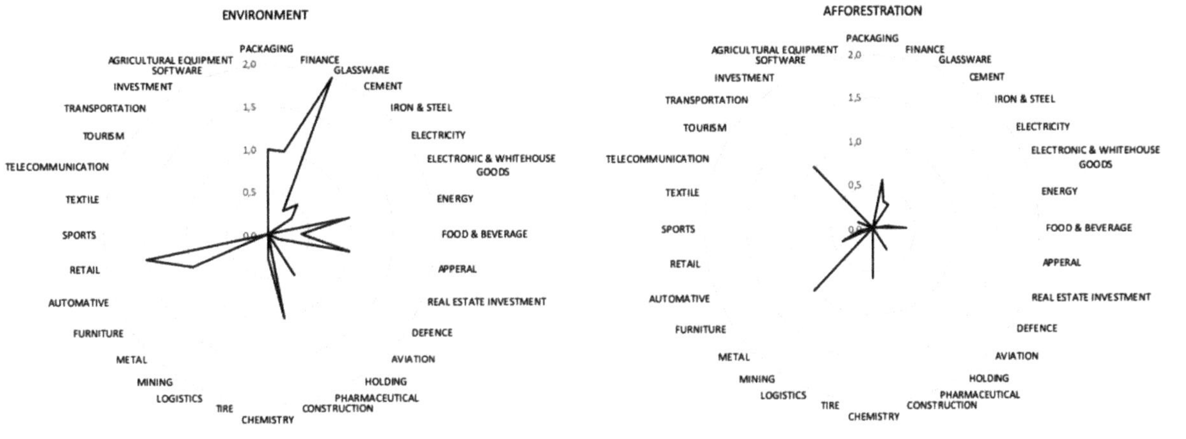

Figure 6. Mean values of CSR action's variety in sports, disabled people

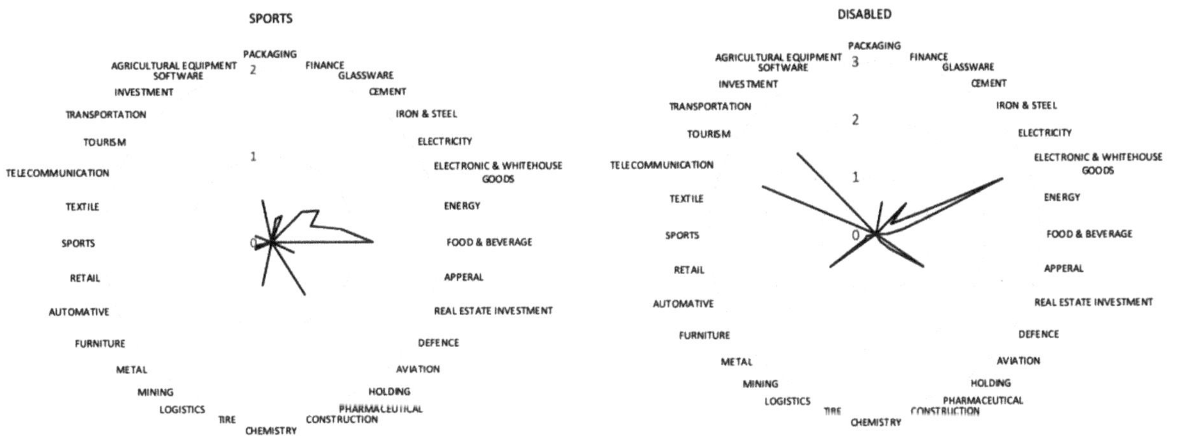

Figure 7. Mean values of CSR action's variety in health, women

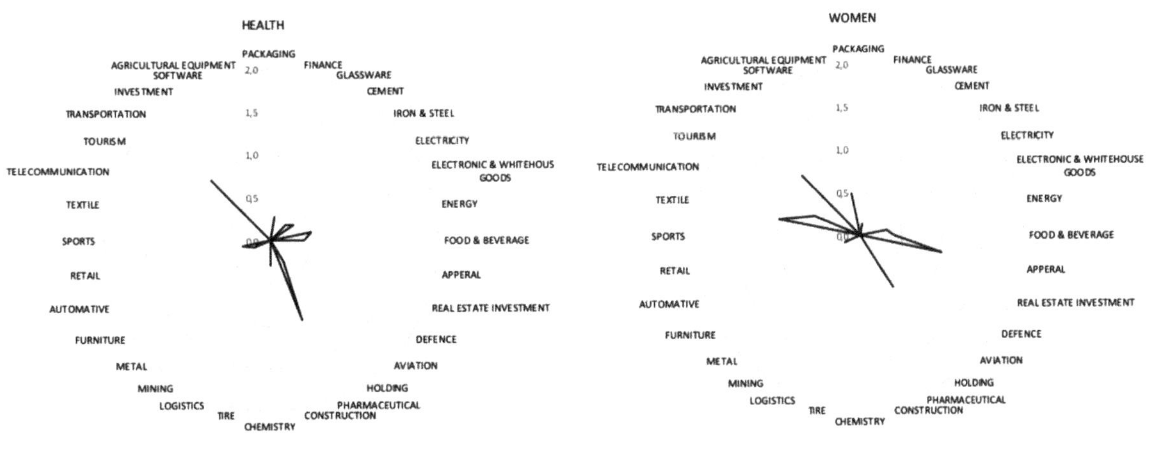

Figure 8. Mean values of related and unrelated CSR action's (education and culture) variety in industry

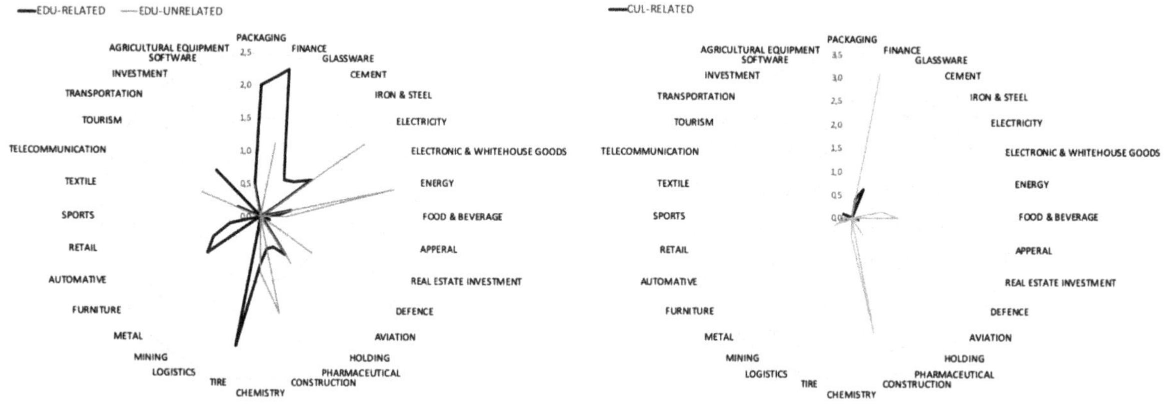

Figure 9. Mean values of related and unrelated CSR action's (afforestation and health) variety in industry

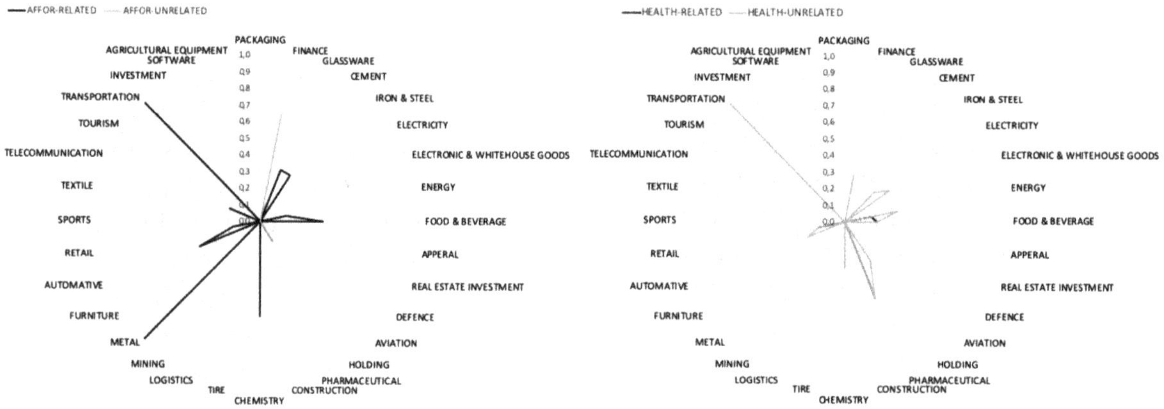

Figure 10. Mean values of related and unrelated CSR action's (sports and environment) variety in industry

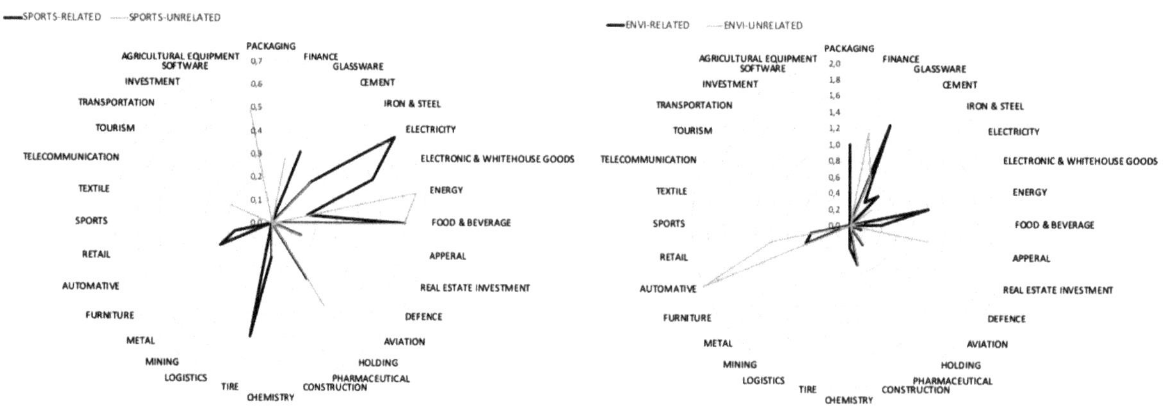

Figure 11. Mean values of related and unrelated CSR action's (disabled people and women) variety in industry

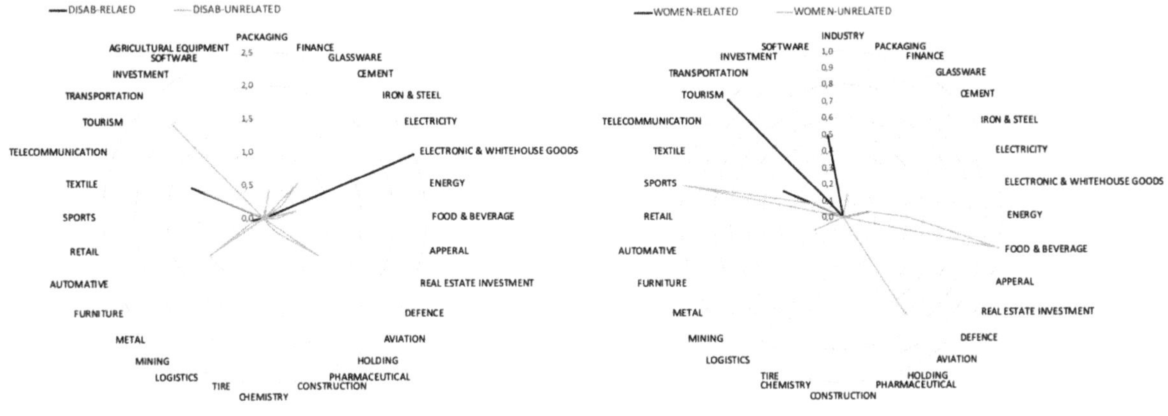

approach. The reason why these companies choose a focused differentiation strategy in CSR activities should be explored.

H4: Related and unrelated CSR actions vary in industries.

It is also tried to be defined in the CSR strategies if related and unrelated actions differ. In this regard, the mean value of each CSR action for industries is calculated. For the top 8 CSR activities, it is found that CSR activities on culture & arts, disabled people and health topics are mostly unrelated CSR strategies. Even these strategies are unrelated to the reason why companies hold on these strategies should be understood. On the other hand, culture, environment, afforestation, and sports-related CSR activities are mostly related to the industries (Figure 8, Figure 9, Figure 10, Figure 11).

FUTURE RESEARCH DIRECTIONS

Although numerous research has been conducted on CSR, still some topics should be discussed more broadly. How CSR activities differ among industries in different countries is one important topic. Cross-country comparisons are needed within the standpoint of industries. In addition, research on explaining the effect of CSR actions on the strategic goals and targets of companies is a need. In this sense, a deeper understanding from the companies' perspective is needed. Some earlier studies have concentrated on the measurement of CSR performance. But, more empirical study is needed to figure out how companies benefit from CSR.

CONCLUSION

It is commonly seen that as a connection between companies and public, CSR activities regardless of budget are used as a tool by many companies. The amount of budget spent on socially responsible investing funds by large-scaled companies is growing (Doane, 2005, p. 24). As a philanthropic approach, companies might be trying to satisfy the needs of the public. Thus CSR activities conducted and CSR strategies held by the companies could be unrelated to their core business. But in the opposite perspective, CSR activities can be used as a tool to improve a company's reputation, financial performance, and shareholder value. Through all these efforts, while CSR is mostly an intangible topic, it is always a question mark what is earned as output for CSR activities that are held by the company. This chapter through the research outputs tries to enlighten the strategic view on CSR. It is obvious that both related and unrelated CSR activities are held by the companies. So in a strategic sense companies use related and unrelated diversification as a strategy. For future studies, the decision making and selection process of CSR strategy is an important topic. Mainly there is not enough study on the driving forces of CSR in the context of decision-making process.

REFERENCES

Alexander, G. J., & Buchholz, R. A. (1978). Corporate social responsibility and stock market performance. *Academy of Management Journal*, *21*(3), 479–486.

Ararat, M. (2008). A development perspective for "corporate social responsibility": Case of Turkey. *Corporate Governance: The International Journal of Business in Society*, *8*(3), 271–285. doi:10.1108/14720700810879169

Balaban, Ö., Cicioğlu, F., & Okutan, E. (2012). A Survey aimed at role and importance of nongovernmental organizations in the corporate social responsibility (CSR). *Procedia: Social and Behavioral Sciences*, *58*, 1174–1182. doi:10.1016/j.sbspro.2012.09.1099

Barnea, A., & Rubin, A. (2010). Corporate social responsibility as a conflict between shareholders. *Journal of Business Ethics*, *97*(1), 71–86. doi:10.100710551-010-0496-z

Bowen, H. R. (2013). *Social responsibilities of the businessman*. University of Iowa Press. doi:10.2307/j.ctt20q1w8f

Brammer, S., & Millington, A. (2006). Firm size, organizational visibility and corporate philanthropy: An empirical analysis. *Business Ethics (Oxford, England)*, *15*(1), 6–18. doi:10.1111/j.1467-8608.2006.00424.x

Branco, M. C., & Rodrigues, L. L. (2006). Corporate social responsibility and resource-based perspectives. *Journal of Business Ethics*, *69*(2), 111–132. doi:10.100710551-006-9071-z

Campbell, L., Gulas, C. S., & Gruca, T. S. (1999). Corporate giving behavior and decision-maker social consciousness. *Journal of Business Ethics*, *19*(4), 375–383. doi:10.1023/A:1006080417909

Carroll, A. B. (1979). A three dimensional conceptual model of corporate social performance. *Academy of Management Review*, *4*(4), 497–505. doi:10.5465/amr.1979.4498296

Carroll, A. B. (1991). The pyramid of corporate social responsibility: Toward the moral management of organizational stakeholders. *Business Horizons, 34*(4), 39–48. doi:10.1016/0007-6813(91)90005-G

Chalmers, D. M. (1959). The muckrakers and the growth of corporate power: A study in constructive journalism. *American Journal of Economics and Sociology, 18*(3), 295–311. doi:10.1111/j.1536-7150.1959.tb00326.x

Chen, E., & Gavious, I. (2015). Does CSR have different value implications for different shareholders? *Finance Research Letters, 14*, 29–35. doi:10.1016/j.frl.2015.07.001

Cheung, Y. L., Tan, W., Ahn, H. J., & Zhang, Z. (2010). Does corporate social responsibility matter in Asian emerging markets? *Journal of Business Ethics, 92*(3), 401–413. doi:10.100710551-009-0164-3

Cochran, P. L., & Wood, R. A. (1984). Corporate social responsibility and financial performance. *Academy of Management Journal, 27*, 42–56.

Çoknaz, D., Sönmezoğlu, U., Eskicioğlu, Y., & Pehlivan, M. (2016). Corporate social responsibility and sports clubs: A case from Turkey. *International Journal of Sport Management, Recreation and Tourism, 22*, 26–43. doi:10.5199/ijsmart-1791-874X-22b

Davis, K. (1960). Can business afford to ignore social responsibilities? *California Management Review, 2*(3), 70–76. doi:10.2307/41166246

Davis, K. (1973). The case for and against business assumption of social responsibilities. *Academy of Management Journal, 16*(2), 312–322.

Doane, D. (2005). The myth of CSR. *Stanford Social Innovation Review, 3*(3), 22–29.

Dupire, M., & M'Zali, B. (2018). CSR strategies in response to competitive pressures. *Journal of Business Ethics, 148*(3), 603–623. doi:10.100710551-015-2981-x

El-Garaihy, W. H., Mobarak, A. K. M., & Albahussain, S. A. (2014). Measuring the impact of corporate social responsibility practices on competitive advantage: A mediation role of reputation and customer satisfaction. *International Journal of Business and Management, 9*(5), 109–124. doi:10.5539/ijbm.v9n5p109

Eren-Erdoğmuş, İ., Çobanoğlu, E., & Öğüt, B. (2014). Success in philanthropic corporate social responsibility: The case of Turkey. In A. Yüksel Mermod & S. O. Idowu (Eds.), *Corporate social responsibility in the global business world* (pp. 271–286). Berlin: Springer. doi:10.1007/978-3-642-37620-7_16

European Commission (2001): *Green Paper, Promoting a European framework for Corporate Social Responsibility*. COM(2001) 366/1.

Friedman, M. (1970). A Friedman doctrine: The social responsibility of business is to increase its profits. *The New York Times Magazine, 13*(1970), 32-33.

Garriga, E., & Melé, D. (2004). Corporate social responsibility theories: Mapping the territory. *Journal of Business Ethics, 53*(1-2), 51–71. doi:10.1023/B:BUSI.0000039399.90587.34

Golob, U., Turkel, S., Kronegger, L., & Uzunoglu, E. (2018). Uncovering CSR meaning networks: A cross-national comparison of Turkey and Slovenia. *Public Relations Review*, *44*(4), 433–443. doi:10.1016/j.pubrev.2018.05.003

Hamann, R. (2006). Can business make decisive contributions to development? Towards a research agenda on corporate citizenship and beyond. *Development Southern Africa*, *23*(2), 175–195. doi:10.1080/03768350600707587

Heald, M. (1961). Business thought in the twenties: Social responsibility. *American Quarterly*, *13*(2), 126–139. doi:10.2307/2710548

Hsieh, H. F., & Shannon, S. E. (2005). Three approaches to qualitative content analysis. *Qualitative Health Research*, *15*(9), 1277–1288. doi:10.1177/1049732305276687 PMID:16204405

Hsu, K. T. (2012). The advertising effects of corporate social responsibility on corporate reputation and brand equity: Evidence from the life insurance industry in Taiwan. *Journal of Business Ethics*, *109*(2), 189–201. doi:10.100710551-011-1118-0

Huang, C. F., & Lien, H. C. (2012). An empirical analysis of the influences of corporate social responsibility on organizational performance of Taiwan's construction industry: Using corporate image as a mediator. *Construction Management and Economics*, *30*(4), 263–275. doi:10.1080/01446193.2012.668620

Husted, B. W., & de Jesus Salazar, J. (2006). Taking Friedman seriously: Maximizing profits and social performance. *Journal of Management Studies*, *43*(1), 75–91. doi:10.1111/j.1467-6486.2006.00583.x

Iyigün, N. Ö. (2013). A research on the corporate social responsibility perception: An evidence from Turkey. *International Journal of Business and Social Science*, *4*(12).

Jamali, D. (2008). A stakeholder approach to corporate social responsibility: A fresh perspective into theory and practice. *Journal of Business Ethics*, *82*(1), 213–231. doi:10.100710551-007-9572-4

Jamali, D., & Mirshak, R. (2007). Corporate social responsibility (CSR): Theory and practice in a developing country context. *Journal of Business Ethics*, *72*(3), 243–262. doi:10.100710551-006-9168-4

Jensen, M. C. (2002). Value maximization, stakeholder theory, and the corporate objective function. *Business Ethics Quarterly*, *12*(2), 235–256. doi:10.2307/3857812

Jones, G. (1991). *Organizational Theory Design & Change*. Pearson Prentice Hall.

Jones, T. M. (1995). Instrumental stakeholder theory: A synthesis of ethics and economics. *Academy of Management Review*, *20*(2), 404–437. doi:10.5465/amr.1995.9507312924

Karasioğlu, F., & Arıcı, N. D. (2012). The relationship between corporate social responsibility and corporate financial performance: Evidence from Turkey. *Economic and Environmental Studies*, *12*(4), 443–457.

Kılıç, M. (2016). Online corporate social responsibility (CSR) disclosure in the banking industry: Evidence from Turkey. *International Journal of Bank Marketing*, *34*(4), 550–569. doi:10.1108/IJBM-04-2015-0060

Kitzmueller, M., & Shimshack, J. (2012). Economic perspectives on corporate social responsibility. *Journal of Economic Literature*, *50*(1), 51–84. doi:10.1257/jel.50.1.51

Leonard, D., & McAdam, R. (2003). Corporate social responsibility. *Quality Progress*, *36*(10), 27–32.

Ligeti, G., & Oravecz, Á. (2009). CSR communication of corporate enterprises in Hungary. *Journal of Business Ethics*, *84*(2), 137–149. doi:10.100710551-008-9678-3

McGuire, J. B., Sundgren, A., & Schneeweis, T. (1988). Corporate social responsibility and firm financial performance. *Academy of Management Journal*, *31*(4), 854–872.

McWilliams, A., & Siegel, D. (2000). Corporate social responsibility and financial performance: Correlation or misspecification? *Strategic Management Journal*, *21*(5), 603–609. doi:10.1002/(SICI)1097-0266(200005)21:5<603::AID-SMJ101>3.0.CO;2-3

McWilliams, A., & Siegel, D. (2001a). Profit maximizing corporate social responsibility. *Academy of Management Review*, *26*(4), 504–505.

McWilliams, A., & Siegel, D. (2001b). Corporate social responsibility: A theory of the firm perspective. *Academy of Management Review*, *26*(1), 117–127. doi:10.5465/amr.2001.4011987

Melo, T., & Galan, J. I. (2011). Effects of corporate social responsibility on brand value. *Journal of Brand Management*, *18*(6), 423–437. doi:10.1057/bm.2010.54

Minor, D., & Morgan, J. (2011). CSR as reputation insurance: Primum non nocere. *California Management Review*, *53*(3), 40–59. doi:10.1525/cmr.2011.53.3.40

Mostovicz, I., Kakabadse, N., & Kakabadse, A. (2009). CSR: The role of leadership in driving ethical outcomes. *Corporate Governance: The International Journal of Business in Society*, *9*(4), 448–460. doi:10.1108/14720700910984990

Muller, A. (2006). Global versus local CSR strategies. *European Management Journal*, *24*(2-3), 189–198. doi:10.1016/j.emj.2006.03.008

Mulligan, T. (1986). A critique of Milton Friedman's essay 'the social responsibility of business is to increase its profits'. *Journal of Business Ethics*, *5*(4), 265–269. doi:10.1007/BF00383091

Navarro, P. (1988). Why do corporations give to charity? *The Journal of Business*, *61*(1), 65–93. doi:10.1086/296420

Nelling, E., & Webb, E. (2009). Corporate social responsibility and financial performance: The "virtuous circle" revisited. *Review of Quantitative Finance and Accounting*, *32*(2), 197–209. doi:10.100711156-008-0090-y

O'Riordan, L., & Fairbrass, J. (2014). Managing CSR stakeholder engagement: A new conceptual framework. *Journal of Business Ethics*, *125*(1), 121–145. doi:10.100710551-013-1913-x

Omur, G. A., Tunc, A. O., & Caliskan, E. N. (2012). Corporate social and environmental responsibility in the service sector: A case study from Turkey. *International Journal of Business and Management Studies*, *4*(1), 11–20.

Ozdora-Aksak, E., & Atakan-Duman, S. (2016). Gaining legitimacy through CSR: An analysis of Turkey's 30 largest corporations. *Business Ethics (Oxford, England)*, *25*(3), 238–257. doi:10.1111/beer.12114

Peloza, J. (2006). Using corporate social responsibility as insurance for financial performance. *California Management Review*, *48*(2), 52–72. doi:10.2307/41166338

Pérez, A. (2015). Corporate reputation and CSR reporting to stakeholders: Gaps in the literature and future lines of research. *Corporate Communications*, *20*(1), 11–29. doi:10.1108/CCIJ-01-2014-0003

Perrini, F., Russo, A., & Tencati, A. (2007). CSR strategies of SMEs and large firms. Evidence from Italy. *Journal of Business Ethics*, *74*(3), 285–300. doi:10.100710551-006-9235-x

Podnar, K., & Golob, U. (2007). CSR expectations: The focus of corporate marketing. *Corporate Communications*, *12*(4), 326–340. doi:10.1108/13563280710832498

Porter, M. E., & Kramer, M. R. (2006). The link between competitive advantage and corporate social responsibility. *Harvard Business Review*, *84*(12), 78–92. PMID:17183795

Quazi, A. M., & O'Brien, D. (2000). An empirical test of a cross-national model of corporate social responsibility. *Journal of Business Ethics*, *25*(1), 33–51. doi:10.1023/A:1006305111122

Robertson, D. C. (2009). Corporate social responsibility and different stages of economic development: Singapore, Turkey, and Ethiopia. *Journal of Business Ethics*, *88*(4), 617–633. doi:10.100710551-009-0311-x

Rodriguez-Fernandez, M. (2016). Social responsibility and financial performance: The role of good corporate governance. *BRQ Business Research Quarterly*, *19*(2), 137–151. doi:10.1016/j.brq.2015.08.001

Runhaar, H., & Lafferty, H. (2009). Governing corporate social responsibility: An assessment of the contribution of the UN Global Compact to CSR strategies in the telecommunications industry. *Journal of Business Ethics*, *84*(4), 479–495. doi:10.100710551-008-9720-5

Russo, A., & Perrini, F. (2010). Investigating stakeholder theory and social capital: CSR in large firms and SMEs. *Journal of Business Ethics*, *91*(2), 207–221. doi:10.100710551-009-0079-z

Russo, A., & Tencati, A. (2009). Formal vs. informal CSR strategies: Evidence from Italian micro, small, medium-sized, and large firms. *Journal of Business Ethics*, *85*(2), 339–353. doi:10.100710551-008-9736-x

Saeidi, S. P., Sofian, S., Saeidi, P., Saeidi, S. P., & Saaeidi, S. A. (2015). How does corporate social responsibility contribute to firm financial performance? The mediating role of competitive advantage, reputation, and customer satisfaction. *Journal of Business Research*, *68*(2), 341–350. doi:10.1016/j.jbusres.2014.06.024

Santos, M. (2011). CSR in SMEs: Strategies, practices, motivations and obstacles. *Social Responsibility Journal*, *7*(3), 490–508. doi:10.1108/17471111111154581

Schneider, A., & Scherer, A. G. (2015). Corporate governance in a risk society. *Journal of Business Ethics*, *126*(2), 309–323. doi:10.100710551-013-1943-4

Seifert, B., Morris, S. A., & Bartkus, B. R. (2003). Comparing big givers and small givers: Financial correlates of corporate philanthropy. *Journal of Business Ethics*, *45*(3), 195–211. doi:10.1023/A:1024199411807

Selvi, Y., Wagner, E., & Türel, A. (2010). Corporate social responsibility in the time of financial crisis: Evidence from Turkey. *Annales Universitatis Apulensis-Series Oeconomica*, *12*(1), 281–290.

Škare, M., & Golja, T. (2014). The impact of government CSR supporting policies on economic growth. *Journal of Policy Modeling*, *36*(3), 562–577. doi:10.1016/j.jpolmod.2014.01.008

Smith, A. D. (2007). Making the case for the competitive advantage of corporate social responsibility. *Business Strategy Series*, *8*(3), 186–195. doi:10.1108/17515630710684187

Surroca, J., Tribó, J. A., & Waddock, S. (2010). Corporate responsibility and financial performance: The role of intangible resources. *Strategic Management Journal*, *31*(5), 463–490. doi:10.1002mj.820

Tang, Z., Hull, C. E., & Rothenberg, S. (2012). How corporate social responsibility engagement strategy moderates the CSR–financial performance relationship. *Journal of Management Studies*, *49*(7), 1274–1303. doi:10.1111/j.1467-6486.2012.01068.x

Udayasankar, K. (2008). Corporate social responsibility and firm size. *Journal of Business Ethics*, *83*(2), 167–175. doi:10.100710551-007-9609-8

Ulutaş Duman, D., Giritli, H., & McDermott, P. (2016). Corporate social responsibility in construction industry: A comparative study between UK and Turkey. *Built Environment Project and Asset Management*, *6*(2), 218–231. doi:10.1108/BEPAM-08-2014-0039

UN Global Compact. (n.d.). *The ten principles of the UN global compact*. Retrieved from: https://www.unglobalcompact.org/ what-is-gc/mission/principles

Vallentin, S., & Murillo, D. (2012). Governmentality and the politics of CSR. *Organization*, *19*(6), 825–843. doi:10.1177/1350508411426183

Vilanova, M., Lozano, J. M., & Arenas, D. (2009). Exploring the nature of the relationship between CSR and competitiveness. *Journal of Business Ethics*, *87*(1), 57–69. doi:10.100710551-008-9812-2

Waddock, S. A., & Graves, S. B. (1997). The corporate social performance–financial performance link. *Strategic Management Journal*, *18*(4), 303–319. doi:10.1002/(SICI)1097-0266(199704)18:4<303::AID-SMJ869>3.0.CO;2-G

Weber, M. (2008). The business case for corporate social responsibility: A company-level measurement approach for CSR. *European Management Journal*, *26*(4), 247–261. doi:10.1016/j.emj.2008.01.006

Yang, F. J., Lin, C. W., & Chang, Y. N. (2010). The linkage between corporate social performance and corporate financial performance. *African Journal of Business Management*, *4*(4), 406–413.

ADDITIONAL READING

Banerjee, S. B. (2008). Corporate social responsibility: The good, the bad and the ugly. *Critical Sociology*, *34*(1), 51–79. doi:10.1177/0896920507084623

Carroll, A. B. (1999). Corporate social responsibility: Evolution of a definitional construct. *Business & Society*, *38*(3), 268–295. doi:10.1177/000765039903800303

Carroll, A. B., & Shabana, K. M. (2010). The business case for corporate social responsibility: A review of concepts, research and practice. *International Journal of Management Reviews*, *12*(1), 85–105. doi:10.1111/j.1468-2370.2009.00275.x

Dahlsrud, A. (2008). How corporate social responsibility is defined: An analysis of 37 definitions. *Corporate Social Responsibility and Environmental Management*, *15*(1), 1–13. doi:10.1002/csr.132

Matten, D., & Moon, J. (2008). "Implicit" and "explicit" CSR: A conceptual framework for a comparative understanding of corporate social responsibility. *Academy of Management Review*, *33*(2), 404–424. doi:10.5465/amr.2008.31193458

McWilliams, A., & Siegel, D. (2000). Corporate social responsibility and financial performance: Correlation or misspecification? *Strategic Management Journal*, *21*(5), 603–609. doi:10.1002/(SICI)1097-0266(200005)21:5<603::AID-SMJ101>3.0.CO;2-3

Visser, W. (2011). *The age of responsibility: CSR 2.0 and the new DNA of business*. John Wiley & Sons.

Visser, W., & Tolhurst, N. (2017). *The world guide to CSR: A country-by-country analysis of corporate sustainability and responsibility*. Routledge. doi:10.4324/9781351278928

Zimmerli, W. C., Richter, K., & Holzinger, M. (2007). *Corporate ethics and corporate governance*. Springer. doi:10.1007/978-3-540-70818-6

KEY TERMS AND DEFINITIONS

Corporate Value: Creating value by responding the expectations of stakeholders.
CSR Activity: Activities that are carried out for corporate social responsibility.
Intangible Asset: Assets that are not physically perceived.
Marginal Investor: Investors that search for short-term gains by trading stocks.
Philanthropy: Organizing activities to raise the economic and social standards of others.
Profit-Focused Management: Management approach considering financial gains in priority.
Reputation: Being valuable, respected, and familiar in the eyes of the audience.

Chapter 13
Corporate Social Responsibility in Emerging Economies:
A Study With Special Reference to India

Ayesha Khatun
Mittal School of Business, Lovely Professional University, India

Sajad Nabi Dar
School of Humanities, Lovely Professional University, India

ABSTRACT

India, a developing and the second largest populated country in the world after China, is characterized by many burning issues like unemployment, low literacy, lack of modern medical facilities mainly in rural areas, lack of connectivity of the rural areas with the mainland cities, and the like. Although government has been working on all these issues and has been very much successful, it is not possible for the government alone to solve all the issues in such a vast populated country in a desired period of time. Amidst such situation, it is the corporate sector that can play a bigger role in the development of the society through its CSR initiatives. This chapter attempts to study corporate social responsibility, its role and issues in a developing country with special reference to India. The findings show that lack of understanding, inadequately trained personnel, lack of proper policy making, lack of participation of the local people, and so on affects the reach and effectiveness of CSR programs in India.

INTRODUCTION

Corporate Social Responsibility (CSR) can be defined as a concept whereby companies integrate social and environmental concerns in their operations and in their interaction with their stakeholders on a voluntary basis (CEC, 2001). It is defined as instances where a firm goes beyond the firm's interest and legal compliances to engage in activities that are able to advance social good (Hah, 2014). CSR is best put into practice when it helps meet the expectations of a firm's stakeholders. This implies that CSR must have a business perspective without being obsessed with profits. To make CSR sustainable,

DOI: 10.4018/978-1-7998-2193-9.ch013

Copyright © 2020, IGI Global. Copying or distributing in print or electronic forms without written permission of IGI Global is prohibited.

it is necessary to keep the business interest of the company uppermost in mind. If this is not done, then CSR programs will run so long as the top executive is personally involved in them and wither away when something more gripping comes around and grabs the leader's attention. CSR is too important an undertaking to be left to anyone's personal whims and fancies, nor should it be seen as something that is done as an afterthought once profits have been made. CSR is an aspect of everyday business and executives would do well to see it that way (Gupta, 2005). All over the world, Corporate Social Responsibility has become more and more popular in the business community particularly since the implementation of globalization, liberalization, and privatization worldwide.Although CSR has been in practice since long back, but the emerging business culture of profit and competition has made this CSR requirement more prominent as this marginalizes more and more the social welfare issues such as health, education, and social security of the vulnerable sections of the society into merely a peripheral pursuit. CSR is the continuing commitment by a business house to contribute to the socio-economic development, while developing the quality of life of the workforce and their families as well as the local community and society at large.

According to the World Business Council for Sustainable Development, Corporate Social Responsibility represents a company's devotion to contributing to the sustainability of economic development, in cooperation with the unemployed, their families, the local communities and the society in general, towards the goal of improving the quality of their lives. The term "corporate social responsibility" came into common use in the late 1960s and early 1970s after many multinational corporations formed the term stakeholder, meaning those on whom an organization's activities have an impact. It was used to describe corporate owners beyond shareholders.

CSR is about the active participation of public, private, and non-profit sectors. However, effective management of corporate responsibility requires not only the participation of business but also the engagement of civil society and the encouragement of government. India is a country of magnificent contradictions. The country is widely inflicted with baffling economic disparity among urban, semi-urban, and rural populace. Market-based economic practice has further widened the scope of inequalities in the country. Given that, Government of India along with the active civil society participation has tried to create a sense of business ethics and responsibility among the corporate both legally and ideologically. There are a good number of studies available on CSR but studies on issues and challenges of CSR in emerging economies is relatively less. The objective of this chapter is to discuss the issues and challenges associated with CSR in emerging economies with special reverence to India.

CORPORATE SOCIAL RESPONSIBILITY

Business depends on society for the needed inputs like money, men, and skills. Business also depends on society for a market where products may be sold. Thus, business depends on society for existence, sustenance, and encouragement. Being so much dependent, companies has definite responsibility towards society (Bhatia, 2006). Today, CSR reiterates the notion that the development is not the exclusive responsibility of the government. Business too has a legitimate and responsible role to play, with safety, health and environment protection high on its corporate agenda (Priya & Ajoy, 2013).

CSR means the obligation of business enterprises to make decisions and follow lines of action which are desirable in terms of the objectives and values of society (Bhatia, 2006). The core idea of the CSR concept is that the business sector should play a deeper role in society than only producing goods and making profits, meaning that business sector should go beyond its profit-oriented commercial activities and increase the well being of the community and thereby making the world a better place (Timane & Tale, 2012; Shastri & Singh, 2012).

The authors discussed this with the help of two different aspects viz., positive and negative. On the negative side, the local communities have tremendous power with respect to zoning regulations, the prohibition of certain businesses, and use of tax policy to let business know if it is welcome or not. On the positive side, the local community provides the infrastructure that makes business possible. In fact, the local community is a legitimate stakeholder of the company. As a legitimate stakeholder, the corporation has duties to the local community (Bowie & Werhane, 2005).

A corporate enterprise has been recognized as a person by law. It should also be recognized as a person in society. A corporate takes birth and grows in response to needs and labors of various stake holders-entrepreneurs, managers, workers, local community, society, buyer, supplier and of course the state. Healthy survival and development depends on adequate nurturing by all these stakeholders. The concept of social responsibility should therefore, include the whole spectrum of stakeholders (Seth, 2012). A company is considered an entity distinct from its member. Therefore, it is an artificial person in the eyes of law, and like a distinct person, a corporate, or a company is also expected to fulfill its social obligations. CSR is a form of social responsibility of a company towards society at large. Corporate take a lot from society in the form of resources for carrying out its functions and earning profits;hence it should also be able to return to society some of the benefits reaped. Companies in India have been proactive in taking up CSR initiatives and integrating them into their business processes (Bhola & Sukhija, 2012).

The society and local community is the resource pool from which any organization gets its man power and also to say "the license to operate." The society is the entity to which an organization owes its existence. The organization exists in society because of the inputs received from it– material, and human and ultimately sells its products and services to it. Any organization, henceforth, must pay its due in various ways to this important constituency (Bhaskar, 2010).

Similar opinion has been expressed by Gautam and Anju in their article by explaining that the broad rationale for a new set of ethics for corporate decision making, which clearly constructs and uphold an organization's social responsibility, arises from the fact that a business enterprise derives several benefits from society, which must, therefore, require the enterprise to provide returns to society as well. This therefore, clearly establishes the stake of a business organization in the good health and wealth of a society of which it is a part. More importantly, in this age of widespread communication and growing emphasize on transparency, the managers should help their company in development of CSR management and reporting framework. The more the concept of CSR is fostered and integrated into the business process, the easier it will be to benefit from alternative thinking and perhaps handle the occasional problems that for certain will occur in the organization (Gautam & Anju, 2010).

In the global economy, consumers are becoming more and more educated and informed and hence becoming much more demanding in terms of securing development goals. In the global context, sustainable development guidelines are being defined in order to establish a balance between the goals of economic development on the one side and social development on the other, while taking considerations of the need to improve and protect the environment. Corporate ethics have become the supreme demand in all business undertakings, from the boardrooms of the world's biggest firm to the classrooms in business schools and colleges the world over. Ethical considerations and demands for preserving the environment will have an even greater future influence on the demand for companies' products and services (Dordevic, 2008).

DRIVERS OF CSR

Baxi and Prasad (2005) described that the process, form, and content of globalization, privatization and liberalization created pressures on companies to perform according to internationally compatible trade practices. CSR is recognized as the vital backbone of the business. The following factors are taken into consideration for understanding the importance of CSR:

1. Globalization and the associated growth in competition;
2. Increased size and influence of companies;
3. Retrenchment or repositioning of government and its roles;
4. War for talent; companies competing for expertise;
5. Growth of global civil society activism;
6. Increased importance of intangible assets.

CSR AND EMERGING ECONOMIES

One aspect of globalization that has become particularly salient in recent years is the rise of emerging economies. Sometimes referred to as BRICs for Brazil, Russia, India, and China, they can be defined as countries that show both rapid economic development and that had adopted government policies geared towards economic liberation. Emerging economies can be classified into two groups: newly industrialized countries in Asia, Latin America, and Africa on the one hand and transition economies of the former Soviet Union and China on the other hand. An emerging economy is a national economy on a progression towards becoming an advanced economy. An emerging economy provides opportunities for foreign investments and enjoys a low to mid-level per capita income. Emerging economies can be classified in two groups: Newly industrialized countries in Asia, Latin America, and Africa on the one hand and transition economies of the former Soviet Union and China on the other hand (Lutz Preuss, 2011).

It was Drucker's (1954) work on social responsibility and the responsibility of management, which first made inroads into the discussion for the public good. Drucker is credited with giving birth to social responsibility theory. Social responsibility theorists directed managers to ensure that the corporation would not undermine social believes and cohesion of a society. It was clearly stated that managers should consider the needs of the public when creating strategies for organizational growth. Organizations were admonished to consider societal needs as well as corporate self-interest (Fider, 2012). For multinational corporations operating in emerging markets, the first growing wealth represents a tremendous opportunities. At the same time, these emerging markets also present a huge challenge to MNCs due to underdeveloped institutional environment, weak public governance, widespread bribery and corruption, lack of regulatory legislations and rules, public transparency, and respect for human beings (JayaKumar, 2013).

Corporate social responsibility is attracting increasing scholarly interest among researchers who study multinational enterprises. The growing attention of CSR research had been focused primarily on the major emerging economies like Brazil, Russia, India, Indonesia, and China. In Asia, CSR research is particularly focused on India and China but research on ethics and CSR is still very wek in other regions of such as South and South East Asia. The literature on CSR in emerging countries can be grouped along two main themes. One the one hand, scholars have stressed that in broad term CSR is hardly a new idea for most emerging countries. Evidence is emerging that emerging economy firms are setting CSR priorities that are different from those in industrializednations. On the other hand, scholars have pointed to the significant isomorphic pressures that compel emerging country firms to engage with the CSR agenda. It is through mechanisms like supply arrangements and the requirements of financial markets that emerging countries have become exposed to CSR. Conceptually these two perspectives on international differences in CSR and sustainability reporting can be captured through the tension between neo-institutionalism and national business system: based explanation of developments in modern capitalism. Neo-institutionalisms stress that organizations need to maintain legitimacy within their societal context and therefore are subject to a range of mimetic, coercive and normative pressures. Such pressures lead to the global convergence of a managerial practice-CSR- once it become recognized as "best practice" or as part of societal expectations regarding the company's conduct towards it stakeholders.

CORPORATE SOCIAL RESPONSIBILITY PRACTICES & ISSUES

CSR in a globalized industrial world is about making the business investment and the community promise sustainability for the company and for the communities they operate in, its people, and the environment. It demands responsible governance based on principles of leadership, integrity, respect, commitment, and relationships (Das & Halder, 2011). Accordingly, the firms must now focus their attention on both increasing its bottom line and being a good corporate citizen (D'Amato, Henderson, & Florence, 2009).

However, firms strategically engage in profit-maximizing CSR. The specific attributes of business and types of CSR activities that make it more likely that "socially responsible" actions actually contribute to profit maximization. The article concludes that high profile CSR activities, e.g., voluntary efforts to reduce pollution or to improve working conditions for employees, etc. are more likely undertaken when such activities can be more easily integrated into a firm's differentiation strategy (Hernandez, Murillo, & Martinek, 2009).

In 2003, People were more likely to purchase brands over generics when they felt that the retailer is 'Socially responsible.' People are more likely to buy more and pay more for brands they consider socially responsible. CSR is key tool to develop and sustain differential brand names and bolster competitive advantage and achieve higher profitability (Girod & Michaell, 2003). Firms can contribute to their own wealth and to overall societal wealth by considering the effect they have on the world at large when making decisions. There is a close link between responsible business and good business. Investors and financial markets have begun to see that CSR activities that integrate broader societal concerns into business strategy and performance are evidence of good management (Hohnen, 2007).

However, it is also said that CSR is a hypocritical window dressing. Companies undertake CSR activities for marketing purposes. Such as Visa is creating a new market in the developing world by closely aligning with social causes with it's overarching corporate strategies. According to Eric Orts, for companies to take CSR seriously, it has to be integrated into the DNA of the enterprise, and it has to be expressed through the kinds of jobs they provide, the kind of products they make and how they use the resources (Why companies can no longer afford ..., 2012).

Though it is said that large firms are more committed to Corporate Social (Chang, Oh, Jung, & Lee, 2012) CSR is much better understood by SMEs and is well connected to their communities and understand the value of relationships built over time (Webb, 2011). Other evidences suggest that small or local companies usually have a less developed community strategy and less concern for social and environmental dimensions of their operations. Again, it is true that one company on its own cannot make a very large difference and hence collective action is required (Skjaerseth, Tangen, Swanson, Christiansen, Moe, & Lunde, 2004).

CSR does vary considerably among countries, but that is not explained by the development stage but by factors in the respective national business systems. The study also concludes that multinational companies are more likely to adopt CSR than those operating solely in their home country but that the profile of their CSR tends to reflect the profile of the country of operation rather than the country of origin (Chapple & Moon, 2005). Coca-cola is committed to sustainable business practices, and as such, it has developed a comprehensive CSR program permeating every aspect of its business and has a range of community-based projects covering education, health care, and the environment. However, the main project is its portable drinking water program (Disilva, 2010).

Impact, not input, is true measure of the project's worth. Impact means the effect or influence of an outcome. Thus, if the objective of CSR efforts is to provide schooling to all children in a particular village, then one obvious outcome would be the percentage increase in high school graduates in that village. On the other hand, the real impact could be enhanced economic wellbeing of families in that village (Pereira, 2013).

The relationship between country-specific characteristics and corporate participation in CSR is very significant. Country specific factors like economic condition (GDP per capita, employment rate), Political system (degree of political freedom), cultural aspects (power distance, individualism, masculinity, uncertainty avoidance), and regions have an influence on Corporate participation in CSR(Choi, 2012). From the above discussion of CSR as a concept and its various issues we can delineate some of its objectives and points of focus. According to Behringer and Szegedi (2016), the focal points of CSR based on various definitions are as follows:

a) Focus on environment and social relationships; CSR focuses on environment and social relationships as corporations operate in the environment and society in an integrated form.
b) Focus on stakeholders' approach; Companies' make an effort to take into account the interests of shareholders and other stakeholders as all the participants concerned have in the responsible behavior of Cos. The term corporate responsibility has been in use instead of corporate social responsibility as it reflects a broader approach.
c) Focus on ethical behavior; CSR not only takes into account the impact of corporations on the communities concerned, but it also stresses the need for ethical behavior which respects the interests and values of these communities. Some researchers consider CSR and ethics as synonyms. Several experts think that CSR is the expression of business ethics in corporate practice.
d) Focus on volunteering; having acknowledged their responsibilities companies then decide to assume them on a voluntary basis. Volunteering reflects their commitments and provides them and the communities involved with opportunities to apply the most favorable instruments.

CORPORATE SOCIAL RESPONSIBILITY IN INDIA

CSR developed in India long back though it was known by a different name. It assumed greater importance in 21st century. There is a trend in the corporate sector of promoting environment friendliness, social accountability, emphasizing employees' safety, human rights promotion and health care in the organization and the community around areas of operation. Tata, ITC, Birla, Reliance, etc. in India are directly engaged in social responsibility in various fields, from innovation in agriculture to education, to saving the environment (Enock & Basavaraji, 2013).

India's CSR performance of public sector enterprises has ranked some of the best in Asia. For instance, Coal India Ltd. invested USD 67.5 million in 2010-2011 on social and environmental causes. NALCO contributed USD 3.23 million for development work in Odisha's Koraput district as part of its CSR.However, though few companies have been practicing CSR for decades, CSR in India is still in the budding stage. A lack of understanding, inadequately trained personnel, coverage, policy, etc. adds to the reach and effectiveness of CSR program. A large number of companies are undertaking these activities superficially and promoting the activities in media. Corporate should integrate CSR with organization's values to make it easy and fulfill the real objectives (Berad, 2011).

Social responsibility is regarded as an important business issue of Indian Companies irrespective of size, sector, business goal, location of the company, because Indian companies are realizing that without socio-economic development of the local communities, there can be no stability and sustainability for doing business so as to compete with the global market (Praghan & Ranjan, 2010).

The concept of CSR has undergone a sea change from meeting marketing needs to Millennium Development Goals (MDG) for national and International development. The study in Indian Context concluded that TATA steel Limited's CSR activities implicitly follow the Millennium Development Goals of the UN as a developmental tool for Jharkhand. These CSR activities, which are well structured following the MDG's, act like tools for development and try to feel the developmental gaps of the government (Ghosh & Chakraborti, 2010).

Dalmia Bharat Group Foundation is committed to carry forward the seven-decade legacy of Dalmia Bharat Group in corporate citizenship and philanthropy by enabling socio-economic transformation in the communities. Social responsibility and commitment to sustainable development are high priority with Dalmia Bharat Group foundation working to fulfill the aspiration of its donor companies within the Dalmia Bharat group, and serving the interest of the communities in the targeted areas (DalmiaGroup, 2011-12).

ONGC has a budget of 500 Cr. a year, as it is committed to spend 2% of its net profit in CSR activities. The company uses its budget for several social and community development activities such as education, skill development etc. NTPC is also aligning its CSR activities to the government's development program, such as Nirmal Bharat Abhiyan. The company plans to build community and individual toilets around its existing power stations (Jayaswa & Singhl, 2013).

Study on CSR program of GMR industry evidently brought rural characteristics of the people like lower levels of literacy, agricultural-based labor and marginalized earnings and inadequacy of resources. GMR Foundation launched a series of CSR projects in the surrounding villages affected by the GMR sugar Industries. Need identification, an important dimension of effective CSR implementation is suffering due to poor participation of people, and to bridge gap, monitoring, and evaluation tools is really needed, which is ensured through field visit to have firsthand information by GMR staff (Prasad & Kumar, 2011).

It is known that 2% of the net profit has been made mandatory for CSR activities in India since 2013,but there exist lots of challenges and confusions in this like whether 2% generated from India or from global operation, can companies find financial equivalent of volunteering hours as part of their CSR spend or not etc. The study ends with the conclusion that CSR teams in most companies are headed by people with corporate communication or HR background. These teams are usually small and get little time to update themselves with social, environmental and economics canvas of India. Sadly, the activity does not reach the really backward areawhich calls for a separate CSR department in corporations (Bapat, 2013).

FUTURE RESEARCH DIRECTIONS

As it has been found from the study that most of the CSR initiatives undertaken by firms are having short term or temporary developmental impact on society the future research can be directed towards studying the various CSR initiatives undertaken by firms operating in different industries to find out the best CSR practices sector-wise in emerging countries. The CSR practices which have long term developmental impacts on society should be appreciated by all means to encourage the firms to contribute towards nation building.

Moreover, as it was found that poor participation of the stakeholders, particularly the local people resulted in low quality CSR activities, the stakeholders' engagements in CSR can form another area of future CSR study in India.

DISCUSSION AND CONCLUSION

In order to build the best possible relation with both consumers and the local community, companies should incorporate best practices of CSR into their business concepts. CSR though not new to business houses but it gained its ultimate momentum during recent years and has become as important as any other factors which have an impact on business like working capital, share market, etc. Government in India is also playing a vital role in facilitating the formulation and implementation of CSR. However, the recent decision of the Govt. of India regarding CSR spend of 2% from profit after tax is not clear to many corporations as they are confused regarding financial equivalent of volunteering hours offered by their employees and many more which should be made clear.

In practice the majority of companies' CSR takes the form of charitable activities like blood donations, one-time money or equipments donationsto civil organizations, participation in community events, supporting voluntary initiatives by employees. Some other companies focus on increasing operational effectiveness in the focus of CSR, where they try to achieve benefits for society within an existing business model. Examples are-initiatives that reduce consumption of resources or reduce the amount of waste or emissions, resulting in lower costs. Other examples are investment in improving working conditions for employees, providing health care, providing training or education facility (Ranjan, Chase & Karim, 2015).

However, it is recommended for companies in developing countries like India to undertake CSR activities which are of long term benefit to the people, society and environment at large, for instance, setting up schools in backward areas, providing continuous scholarship for higher education to a selected number of students, building up hospitals, constructions of roads, market places and the like.

The government should also work on creating more and more awareness on corporate social responsibility, as well as individual social responsibility and these topics, should also be included in the curriculum of not only business education but general education too. Moreover, the general public should be taught to be more participative about the CSR activities by different corporations in their locality, as is evidenced from GMR case that low participation of local people negatively affects CSR activities. Moreover, the corporations should develop core competency and adopt adequate institutional safeguards to ensure an appropriate framework for CSR implementation.

REFERENCES

Bapat, S. (2013). *Challenges of the 2% CSR paradigm*. Forbs India Magazine.

Baxi, C. V., & Prasad, A. (2005). *Corporate Social Responsibility: Concepts and Cases-the Indian Experiences*. New Delhi: Excel Publishing.

Berad, N. R. (2011). CSR: Issues and Challenges in India. *International Conference on Technology and Business Management*, 101-108.

Bhaskar, S. P. (2010). CSR in an Indian Public sector organization. A case study of Bharat petroleum Corporation Ltd. *Journal of Human Values*, *16*(2), 143–156. doi:10.1177/097168581001600202

Bhatia, S. K. (2006). Corporate Social Responsibility. In *Business Ethics & Managerial Values* (pp. 143–145). New Delhi: Deep & Deep Publications Pvt. Ltd.

Bhola, S., & Sukhija, A. (2012, November). *India-CSR Boom for social upliftment*. Retrieved from Mondaq: www.mondaq.com

Bowie, N. E., & Werhane, P. H. (2005). Corporate Social Responsibility. In *Management Ethics* (pp. 99–115). Blackwell Publishing.

CEC. (2001). *Green Paper Promoting a European frame for corporate social responsibility*. Commission of the European communities. Retrived from httpp://eur-aex.europa.eu/LexUriServ/LexUriUerv.do?uri=CMO:2001:0366:FIN:EN:PDF

Chang, Y. K., Oh, W. Y., Jung, J. C., & Lee, J. Y. (2012). Firm Size and Corporate Social Performance. *Journal of Leadership & Organizational Studies*, *19*(4), 486–500. doi:10.1177/1548051812455239

Chapple, W., & Moon, J. (2005). CSR in Asia. *Business & Society*, *44*(4), 415–441. doi:10.1177/0007650305281658

Choi, Y. J. (2012). Does Country Matter in Corporate Participation in CSR. *IPE Journal of Management*, *2*(2), 1–15.

D'Amato, A., Henderson, S., & Florence, S. (2009). *CSR and Sustainable Business*. CCL Press.

DalmiaGroup. (2011-12). *CSR Report 2011-12*. Dalmia Group.

Das, B. K., & Halder, P. P. (2011). CSR initiatives of Oil: A case study of ONGC. *Management Convergence, 2*(2), 75-85.

Disilva, J. (2010). *CSR Case Studies:Coco-cola. Global Compact Network.*

Dordevic, S. (2008). The role of CSR in contemporary business. *Megatrend Review, 5*(1).

Enock, O. N., & Basavaraji, D. K. (2013). CSR of TATA Company and ITC Company: A comparative study. *International Journal of Business and Management Tomorrow*, *3*(3).

Fider, E. A. (2012, Feb 28). Corporate Social Responsibility, Competitive Advantage and Profitability: A Study of Telecommunications Provider in an Emerging Economy. *Corporate Social Responsibility, Competitive Advantage and Profitability*. ProQuest.

Gautam, R., & Anju, S. (2010). CSR Practices in India: A Study of top 500 companies. *International Journal of Global Business and Management Research.*

Ghosh, A., & Chakraborti, C. (2010). CSR: A developmental tool for India. *IUP Journal of Corporate Governance*, *IX*(4), 40–56.

Girod, S., & Michaell, B. (2003). Branding in European retailing: A corporate social responsibility perspective. *European Retail Digest*, 1-6.

Gupta, D. (2005). Corporate Responsibility. In C. V. Baxi & A. Prasad (Eds.), *Corporate Social Responsibility: Concepts and Cases* (pp. 21–27). New Delhi: Excel Books.

Hernandez, R., Murillo, & Martinek, C. J. (2009). CSR can be profitable. *The Regional Economist.*

Hohnen, P. (2007). *CSR – An implementation Guide for Business.* Retrived from http://www.iisd.org/pdf/2007/csr_guide.pdf

Jaya Kumar, T. (2013, October-December). MNC CSR in Emerging Economic conflect zones - A Case study of HULs North East Operations in India. *Vikalpa*, *38*(4), 69–82. doi:10.1177/0256090920130405

Jayaswa, R., & Singhl, S. C. (2013). *ONGC, NTPC among energy companies thinking out of the box on CSR*. New Delhi, India: Economic Times.

Karoley Behringer, K. S. (2016). The Role of Corporate Social Responsibility in Achieving Sustainable Development-Theoritical Approach. *European Scientific Journal*, *12*(22), 10–25. doi:10.19044/esj.2016.v12n22p10

Kasturi Ranjan, L. C. (2015). The Truth About CSR. *Harvard Business Review*, *93*(1), 40–49.

Kristin Hah, S. F. (2014). Multinational Enterprise Subsideries and their CSR: A Conceptual Frame Work of the Management of CSR in Smaller Emerginig Economies. *Journal of Business Ethics*, *121*, 125–136.

Lutz Preuss, R. B. (2011). CSR priorities of emerging economy firms:Is Russia shape of BRIC? *Corporate Governance*, *11*(4), 371–385. doi:10.1108/14720701111159226

Pereira, A. (2013). *CSR: Impact, not input, is true measure of project's worth.* New Delhi, India: Economic Times.

Prasad, B. A., & Kumar, P. R. (2011). Monitoring and Evaluation of CSR interventions. A study of CSR programs in GMR industries. *SMS Varanasi*, *VII*(2), 79–84.

Priya, M. S., & Ajoy, A. (2013). A comparative study on CSR Practices of HPCL and IOCL. *Abhinav-International Monthly Refereed Journal of Research in Management and Technology*, *II*, 109–117.

Seth, P. N. (2012). *CSR World.* Retrieved from http://www.csrworld.net

Shastri, R. K., & Singh, A. (2012). An Empirical Study on CSR Practices of selected Indian PSU's. *National Conference on Emerging Challenges for Sustainable Business*, 441-459.

SkjaersethJ. B.TangenK.SwansonP.ChristiansenA. C.MoeA.LundeL. (2004). Retrieved from http://www.fni.no/doc&pdf/FNI-R0704.pdf

Timane, R., & Tale, T. (2012). A study on CSR in India. *International Journal of Research in IT and Management*, *2*(12).

Visser, W. (2008). Corporate Social Responsibility in Developing Countries. In *The Oxford Handbook of Corporate Social Responsibility*. Oxford University Press.

Webb, T. (2011). *The CSR/Sustainability Business. Case for SMEs*. Ethical Corporation.

Why companies can no longer afford to ignore their social responsibilities. (2012). *Time Business and Money*.

ADDITIONAL READING

Freeman, R. E. (1984). Strategic Management, A Stakeholder Approach. Boston, MA: Pitman Publishing.

Srivastava, H., & Venkateshwaran, S. (2000). *The Business of Social Responsibility*. Bangalore: Books for Change.

KEY TERMS AND DEFINITIONS

CSR: A continuing commitment of the corporations to contribute to the socio-economic development, while developing the quality of life of the workforce and their families as well as the local community and the society at large.

Emerging Economy: Economy which is on a progression towards becoming an advanced economy. It provides opportunities for foreign investments and enjoys a low to mid-level per capita income.

Chapter 14
Mandatory Corporate Social Responsibility and After That?
An Analysis From India

Remya Lathabhavan
https://orcid.org/0000-0002-4666-4748
VIT University, India

ABSTRACT

India became the first country in the world to have a mandatory CSR contribution legislation in 2014. This mandate every qualifying company must spend at least 2% of its average net profit on CSR activities. This chapter analyses these following aspects of CSR. First, it describes Sustainable Development, CSR, and its relevance across the world. Second, it explores the prevailing CSR models and models used in India. Third, it discusses the importance of CSR in India, mandatory CSR, and its provisions. Fourth, it analyses the response of Indian corporates on SDGs in terms of their contribution. Fifth, it analyses existing Socially Responsible Investing strategies in India and their scope. Finally, it analyses the current scenario after mandatory CSR, considering the CSR contributions from different corporates. Such discussion is essential for a country like India, an emerging economy with diverse groups with non-aligned social, cultural, economic, and environmental backgrounds.

INTRODUCTION

The introduction of mandatory Corporate Social Responsibility (CSR) in 2014 in India marked the country as a pioneer in enacting such a legal obligation that holds tremendous social and environmental potential. According to Section 135 of the Companies Act,2013, the threshold limits for applicability of the CSR to a Company are (a) net worth of the company is Rs 500 crore (USD 7 crore) or more; (b) turnover of the company is Rs 1000 crore (USD 14 crore) or more; (c) net profit of the company is Rs 5 crore (USD 7 lakhs) or more. According to the CSR Rules, the provisions of CSR are not only applicable to Indian companies but also branch and project offices of foreign companies in India. Every

DOI: 10.4018/978-1-7998-2193-9.ch014

Copyright © 2020, IGI Global. Copying or distributing in print or electronic forms without written permission of IGI Global is prohibited.

qualifying company must spend at least 2% of its average net profit for the immediately preceding three financial years on CSR activities.

The idea of corporate social responsibility, i.e., businesses bearing a responsibility to society and a broader set of stakeholders beyond its shareholders, gained importance in the 1960s. Since then, attention to corporate social responsibility has been increasing in both academic and practitioners around the world. Over the last few decades, academicians have paid considerable attention to CSR, as can be seen in its prevalence in management literature.

It is encouraging to note that companies have become active in engaging in CSR activities. The driving force behind this has been an upsurge in environmentally sensitive consumers who are demanding sustainable and more environmentally friendly products and services. According to Van Beurden and Gössling (2008), CSR deals with the uncertainties in the social contexts of the dynamic, global, and technological business arena of today. According to Carroll (1979), CSR is the social responsibility of a business and encompasses the economic, legal, ethical, and discretionary expectations that society has of organizations at any time

This chapter analyses the following aspects of CSR. First, it describes Sustainable Development and CSR and its relevance across the world. Second, it explores the prevailing CSR models and models used in India. Third, it discusses the importance of CSR in India, mandatory CSR, and its provisions. Fourth, it analyses the response of Indian corporates on SDGs in terms of their contribution to water, renewable energy, waste - plastic, e-waste and community waste, and data privacy. Fifth, it analyses existing Socially Responsible Investing strategies in India and its scope in the future. Finally, the chapter explains the current scenario after mandatory CSR, considering CSR contributions from different companies.

METHOD

The key aspects to be covered in this chapter are Sustainable Development and CSR, CSR models, CSR provisions in India, response of Indian corporates to SDGs, and of CSR activities after it was made mandatory. Towards this, a critical review of relevant literature was conducted. The literature search included a computerized search on available accessible materials on CSR, published reports of various institutions and media reports.

SUSTAINABLE DEVELOPMENT AND ITS RELEVANCE

The subject of sustainable development (SD) has become popular as a result of the impacts of industrial development in the world (Nixon, Burns & Jazayeri, 2011). Issues such as climate change, exhaustion of natural resources, and growth in inequality have become increasingly important with industrial development (Montiel, 2008). It has led people and institutions to be proactive in SD.

The first recorded discussion on Sustainable Development appears in the report of the World Commission on Environment and Development (WCED), a body created by the UN General Assembly in 1983. Gro Brundtland was headed this Commission, then prime minister of Norway and later head of the World Health Organization. The Commission's 1987 report, often referred to as the Brundtland Commission Report defined "sustainable development" as development that "meets the needs of the present without compromising the ability of future generations to meet their own needs."

Sustainable development has three dimensions: economic, environmental, and social (Lueg & Radlach, 2016). These are frequently referred to as the triple bottom line and are used to gauge the success of a particular developmental program or project. It is critical that each component be given equal attention in order to ensure a sustainable outcome. This balance becomes obvious when each component is examined individually.

1. The economic approach: Maximize income while maintaining constant or increasing stock of capital.
2. The ecological approach: Maintain the resilience and robustness of biological and physical systems.
3. The socio-cultural approach: Maintain the stability of social and cultural systems.

Various terms are used to point to SD, e.g., sustainability, sustainable business, and corporate social responsibility (CSR).

CORPORATE SOCIAL RESPONSIBILITY

The idea of Corporate Social Responsibility arose in the 1960s, and since then, attention on CSR has been increasing among researchers and practitioners around the world (Wang, Tong, Takeuchi & George, 2016). Governments, activists, and media have increasingly held companies accountable for the social consequences of their activities, and as a result, CSR has emerged as an inescapable priority for businesses across the world (Porter & Kramer, 2006).

Over the last few decades, CSR has received considerable attention among academicians as seen in the surge of research reports in management literature in this area (Nejati & Ghasemi, 2012). This interest has been driven by the drastic increase in environmentally sensitive consumers who are demanding sustainable and environmentally friendly products and services from corporate organizations (Saeidi, Sofian, Saeidi, Saeidi & Saaeidi, 2015).

The definition of CSR has been varied in academic researches considering the vast scope and aspects of the area (Van Marrewijk, 2003). It has been difficult to come up with a simple definition that encompasses the entire scope and all the aspects of this topic. Considering holistic aspects, CSR has been defined as the social responsibilities of businesses, which includes the economic, legal, ethical, and discretionary expectations that society has of organizations at any time (Carroll, 1979). According to Van Beurden and Gössling (2008), CSR answers the uncertainties that business corporations face in the dynamic, global, and technological business arena of today.

Approaches Of CSR

Various approaches have driven the evolution of CSR and have been based on varying responses to the question – to whom is an organization accountable? (Van Marrewijk, 2003). Thus, the approaches towards CSR have been from the perspectives of the shareholder, stakeholder, society, and philanthropy.

The shareholder approach says the social responsibility of business is to increase profit (Quazi & O'brien, 2000). In other words, a business would participate in CSR only to the extent to which the activity contributes to the company's commercial aim, through the creation of long-term value for the shareholders of the firm (Ben Youssef, Leicht, Pellicelli & Kitchen, 2018). The stakeholder approach, on the other hand, posits that organizations are accountable to stakeholders. Achievements of organizations need to balance their interests of stakeholders (Harrison & Freeman, 1999). In the societal approach of CSR, companies are responsible to society as a whole, must serve society constructively, and cater to the satisfaction of the community (Ellerup Nielsen & Thomsen, 2007). It is considered the broader view of CSR. The philanthropic approach appears to be a response to changing circumstances and new corporate challenges (Palazzo & Richter, 2005). It requires organizations to rethink their positions and act in terms of the complex societal context.

CSR Models

Many models have evolved, considering these approaches, to strategically implement various CSR practices. These models deal with formulation, implementation, and other aspects of CSR.

The various models of CSR are:

1. Ackerman's Model,
2. The Pyramid model,
3. The Intersecting Circles Model,
4. The Concentric Circles Model,
5. 3C-SR Model.

Ackerman's Model

Ackerman's model is a pioneer among the CSR models. The model was developed much before the idea of modeling CSR activities according to the priorities, liabilities, and responsibilities was formulated. Rather than a model, it can be considered as a strategy for the implementation of CSR activities. Ackerman's model was designed in three phases (Bauer & Ackerman, 1976). The first phase was about the high-level managers recognizing a social problem, the second phase was an extensive study of the problem and finding solutions by hiring experts, and the last phase was implementation of the proposed solutions.

The Pyramid Model

This model was propounded by Carroll. It defines the individual responsibilities and obligations in different fields and comprises four aspects (Carroll, 1991). The pyramid is arranged in decreasing order of priorities viz. economic responsibilities, legal responsibilities, ethical responsibilities, and philanthropic responsibilities.

The pyramid model argues against the widely accepted separation thesis, which states that businesses cannot focus on both social and financial concerns at the same time. It arranges the different fields of responsibilities and obligations without integrating them in any manner. The model agrees that business aims to gain maximum profit staying within the limits of legal and ethical boundaries.

The Intersecting Circles Model

Schwartz and Carroll (2003) proposed the intersecting circles model. The model integrates three aspects- economic, legal, and moral. According to this model, although a business aims to make a profit,

Figure 1.

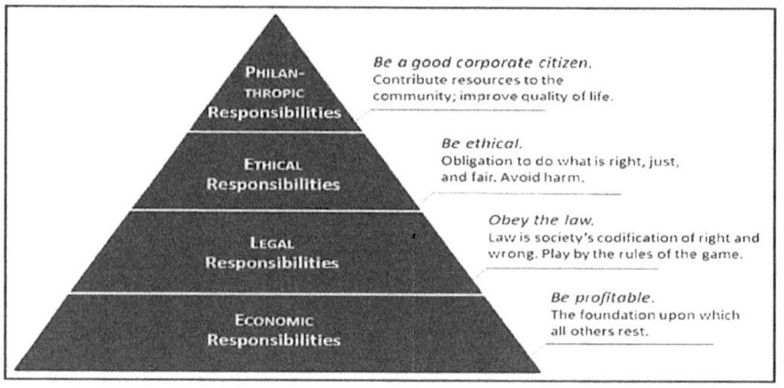

Figure 2.

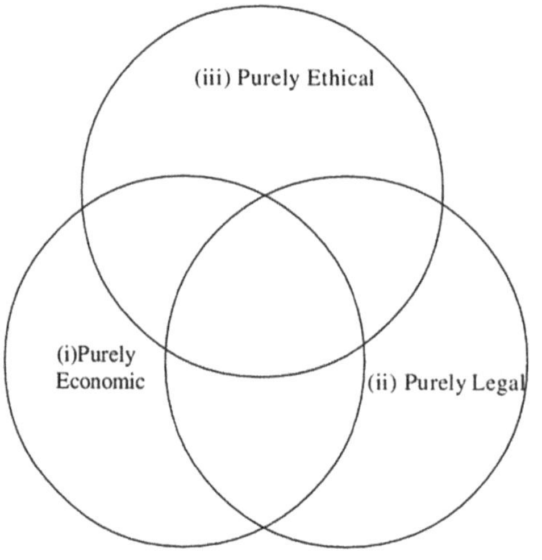

it is a social creation, and the society must be willing to support and endure it in order for it to survive and thrive. Such support from the society can only be earned through the responsibilities and obligations it fulfills. The model can be used to establish CSR profiles for different entities like individuals, corporations, stakeholders, industries, and nations. The model is flexible as one has the advantage of interpreting it as required.

The Concentric Circles Model

The concentric circles model of CSR has been adopted from a statement issued in 1971 by the Committee for Economic Development. The model includes economic, legal, ethical, and philanthropic aspects of CSR. It posits that corporations must adopt a more human view toward their functions in society.

This model has a wider scope of economic responsibilities, which consists of: wealth generation to improve the standard of living and to provide goods and services to people to meet their requirements.

Figure 3.

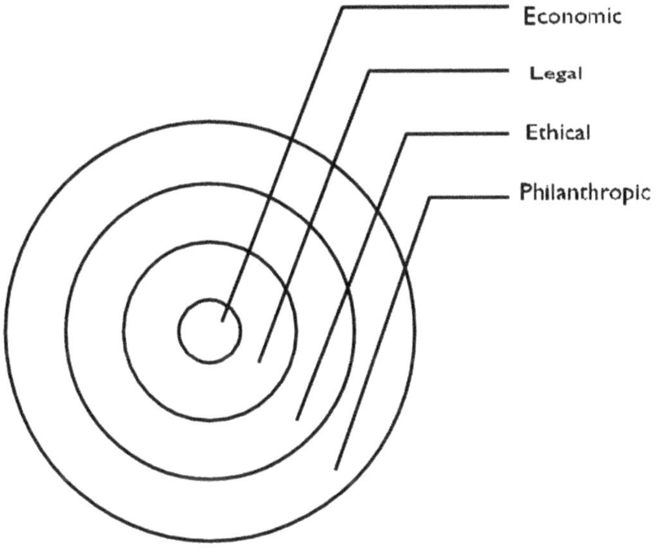

It also includes selling goods and services at fair prices, providing employment and fair wages and eliminating poverty in a holistic manner.

3C-SR Model

This model was developed by John Meehan, Karon Meehan, and Adam Richards (Meehan, Meehan, & Richards, 2006). The components of the model are ethical and social commitments, connections with partners in the value network, and consistency of behavior over time to build trust. The last two elements, i.e. connections and consistency, refer to space and time dimensions of the model and are inter-related.

THE INDIAN MODELS OF CSR

The two models viz. ethical model and statist model are Indian models in CSR. The ethical model was developed based on Mahatma Gandhi's notions of trusteeship, whereby the owners of properties are considered volunteer managers to societal wealth. Such concepts of trusteeship induced Indian corporates to commit to social development (Kanji & Agrawal, 2016). The statist model evolved after India's independence and establishment of a socialist and mixed economy framework in which both public sector and private sector co-existed.

India And CSR

While CSR is relevant for business for all societies, it is particularly essential for developing countries and emerging economies. Hence in a country like India, characterized by limited resources that are expected to meet the ever growing aspirations and diversity of a pluralistic society, the process of sustainable development becomes challenging, and hence the CSR activities become significant. Considering

Figure 4.

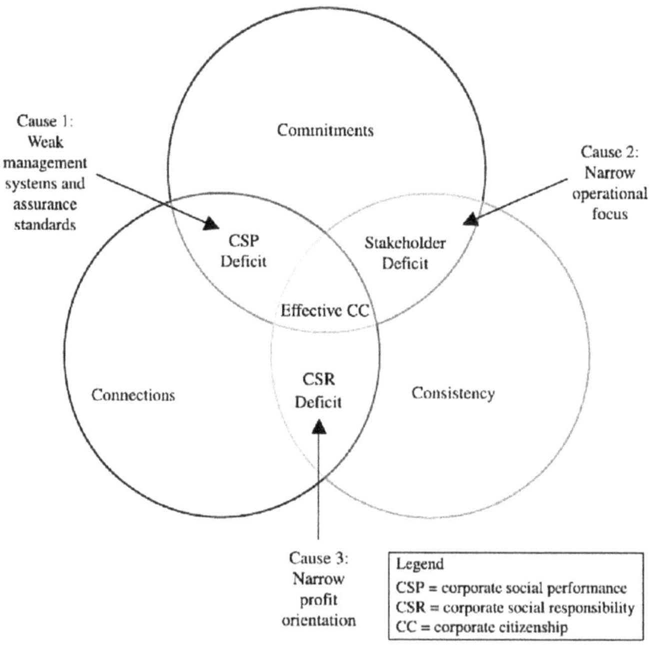

the evolution of CSR activities in India, it can be divided into four stages. The first stage is the pre-independence practice of charity that manifested the concept of CSR. The businessmen, industrialists, and philanthropists performed actions of charity with strong religious sentiments. The next stage was the post-independence advocation of the Gandhian philosophy of trusteeship. It advocated the role of Public Sector Undertakings as essential elements in fulfilling the development agenda. The third stage was the post-1991, i.e., Post globalization era, which allowed the entry of global players which enhanced competition in the market. Global standards of CSR motivated the global players to respond to the needs of society, increase brand value, and acquire customer satisfaction. And the final stage is the post-2000 phase characterized by global information sharing, which allowed the Indian government to incorporate practices that made India the first country to mandate CSR.

Mandatory CSR In India

In 2014, India introduced a mandatory CSR contribution in Section 135 of the Companies Act, 2013. According to Section 135 of the Companies Act, 2013, the threshold limits for applicability of the CSR to a Company are (a) net worth of the company is Rs 500 crore (USD 7 crore) or more; (b) turnover of the company is Rs 1000 crore (USD 14 crore) or more; (c) net profit of the company is Rs 5 crore (USD 7 lakhs) or more. Every qualifying company requires spending of at least 2% of its average net profit for the immediately preceding three financial years on CSR activities.

Further, the qualifying company is required to constitute a committee (CSR Committee) of the Board of Directors (Board) consisting of three or more directors, of which one director must be an independent director. The CSR Committee would formulate and recommend to the Board, a policy indicative of the activities to be undertaken (CSR Policy); recommend the amount of expenditure to be incurred on the activities referred and monitor the CSR Policy of the company from time to time.

The Board of every company would, after taking into account the recommendations made by the Corporate Social Responsibility Committee, approve the Corporate Social Responsibility Policy for the company. This Committee disclose contents of such Policy in its report and also place it on the company's website, if any, in such manner as may be prescribed. It would also ensure that the company undertakes the activities that are included in the Corporate Social Responsibility Policy of the company. The company would also ensure that every fiscal year, at least two percent of the average net profits of the company made during the three immediately preceding financial years, is spent on CSR activities, performed in the local area and areas around its location. The board is required to provide reasons in case of failure of the company is spending this amount on CSR activities.

The mandatory CSR also prescribe different avenues in which a firm can contribute. This list is provided on Schedule VII of the Act. Accordingly, companies have the following CSR options:

(i) eradicating hunger, poverty, and malnutrition, promoting preventive health care and hygiene care including contribution to the Swach Bharat Kosh set-up by the Central Government for the promotion of sanitation and making available, safe drinking water;
(ii) promoting education, including special education and employment enhancing vocation skills especially among children, women, elderly, and the differently-abled and livelihood enhancement projects;
(iii) promoting gender equality, empowering women, setting up homes and hostels for women and orphans; setting up nursing homes, daycare centers and such other facilities for senior citizens and measures for reducing inequalities faced by socially and economically backward groups;
(iv) ensuring environmental sustainability, ecological balance, protection of flora and fauna, animal welfare, agroforestry, conservation of natural resources and maintaining quality of soil, air, and water including contribution to the Clean Ganga Fund set-up by the Central Government for the promotion of sanitation;
(v) protection of national heritage, art, and culture including restoration of buildings and sites of historical importance and works of art; setting up public libraries; promotion and development of traditional arts, and handicrafts;
(vi) measures for the benefit of armed forces veterans, war widows, and their dependents;
(vii) training to promote rural sports, nationally recognized sports, paralympic sports, and Olympic sports;
(viii) contribution to the Prime Minister's National Relief Fund or any other fund set up by the Central Government for socio-economic development and relief and welfare of the Scheduled Castes, the Scheduled Tribes, other backward classes, minorities, and women;
(ix) contributions or funds provided to technology incubators located within academic institutions, which are approved by the Central Government;
(x) rural development projects;
(xi) slum area development.

SUSTAINABLE DEVELOPMENT GOALS

The Sustainable Development Goals are a collection of 17 global goals set by the United Nations General Assembly in 2015 for the year 2030. They have the potential to provide a framework for mobilizing companies to invest in sustainable development in an ongoing and scalable way, while also pursuing their business interests. Indian companies have started focusing on these areas.

The Sustainable Development Goals are:

Goal 1: End poverty in all its forms everywhere

Poverty eradication can only be done through a universal social protection system. Such systems should be able to safeguard all individuals throughout their life. It also requires focused measures to reduce vulnerability to disasters and geographic regions prone to disasters in each country. (Sustainable Development Goals Report, 2018).

Goal 2: End Hunger, achieve food security and improved nutrition and promote sustainable agriculture

World hunger is on the rise again. The reasons for this are conflicts, droughts, and disasters linked to climate change.

Goal 3:Ensure healthy and promote well-being for all at all ages

Although there are improvements in health aspects now compared to the past, there remain problems such as premature death and preventable diseases. Overcoming such problems requires concerted and focused efforts.

Goal 4: Ensure inclusive and equitable quality education and promote life long learning opportunities for all

About 58% of children and adolescents around the world do not meet the minimum proficiency standards in reading and mathematics. Focused efforts are needed to improve the quality of education with more investment in education infrastructure.

Goal 5: Achieve gender equality and empower all women and girls

Gender inequality continues despite considerable efforts worldwide to end it, and women in many countries continue to be denied fundamental rights and opportunities. Some efforts have borne results, such as the reduction in child marriages in Southern Asia by 40% between 2000 and 2017.

Goal 6: Ensure availability and sustainable management of water and sanitation for all

Water scarcity, floods, and lack of proper wastewater management along with lack of access to safely managed water supplies and sanitation water supplies hinder social and economic development.

Goal 7: Ensure access to affordable, reliable, sustainable and modern energy for all

Recent progress in electrification, especially in the Least Developed Countries, help to ensure access to affordable, reliable, and modern energy.

Goal 8: Promote sustained, inclusive and sustainable economic growth, full and productive employment and decent work for all

Although labor productivity has increased, more focussed efforts are required to increase employment opportunities, especially for young people.

Goal 9: Built resilient infrastructure, promote inclusive and sustainable industrialisation and foster innovation

With intensive and focussed efforts, global carbon intensity decreased by 19% between 2000 and 2015. Efficient use of technologies and international trade are essential for achieving inclusive and sustainable industrialization.

Goal 10: Reduce inequality within and among countries

There have been many efforts to reduce income inequality. However, more programs are required to minimize growing disparities within and among countries.

Goal 11:Make cities and human settlements inclusive, safe, resilient and sustainable

The main challenge faced by many cities around the world is managing rapid urbanization. It includes adequate housing to support the growing population and reducing vulnerability to disasters.

Goal 12: Ensure sustainable consumption and production pattern

108 countries around the world have national policies on sustainable consumption and production. 93% of the world's 250 largest companies are now reporting on sustainability.

Goal 13: Take urgent action to compact climate change and its impacts

Majority countries have ratified the Paris Agreement and provided Nationally Determined Contributions (NDCs).

Goal 14: Conserve and sustainably use the oceans, seas and marine resources for sustainable development

Effective strategies must be drawn to combat the adverse effects of overfishing, growing ocean acidification, and worsening coastal eutrophication.

Goal 15: Protect, restore and promote sustainable use of terrestrial ecosystems, sustainable manage forests, combat desertification, and halt and reverse land degradation and halt biodiversity loss

Land degradation is a severe threat in all countries. Protection of the forest and terrestrial ecosystem is on the rise, and this has slowed down rates of deforestation.

Goal 16: Promote peaceful and inclusive societies for sustainable development, provide access to justice for all and build effective, accountable and inclusive institutions at all levels

Armed conflict or other forms of violence occur within societies and at the domestic level. However, there is progress being made in regulations to promote public access to information, and in strengthening institutions upholding human rights at the national level.

Goal 17: Strengthen the means of implementation and revitalize the Global Partnership for Sustainable Development

This goal seeks to strengthen global partnerships to support and achieve the targets of SDGs. It brings together national governments, international communities, civilian society, private sectors, and others.

SDG AND CSR - ROLE OF CORPORATES

Corporate involvement in the Millennium Development Goals was focused on poorer countries. SDGs, on the other hand, are universal, cover almost all sectors, and are signed by all countries (Hopkins, 2016). Business and industry act as drivers of socio-economic progress. CSR is now an important corporate function that spreads the awareness of how corporate activity must be managed to ensure profitable sustainability (Hopkins, 2017). CSR is seen as a vital element of SDG's performance (Stawicka, 2017). For the first time in history, the corporate sector has the opportunity to design SDGs along with stakeholders (Scheyvens, Banks, & Hughes, 2016). In Goal 12.6, the corporates are encouraged to adopt responsible practices and sustainable impact reports, and in Goal 17, they are required to participate with governments and civil society for attainment of SDGs. Hence each organization must integrate corporate values, governance, and strategy and pursue CSR at the sectoral level to achieve SDGs (BSDC, 2017).

SDG AND INDIAN CORPORATES

Indian companies have made remarkable contributions towards the goal attainment of SDGs. The steps are taken and current initiatives in the areas of renewable energy, water, waste management, and data privacy are described below.

Renewable Energy

There is increased interest among companies in utilizing renewable energy. Statistics show that there was a 3-18% increase in the use of renewable energy in the IT sector in 2016-2017 over 2015-2016. In the automotive industry, this increase was about 4-18%, and in healthcare, it was 2-14% (Futurescape, 2018).

Water

India faces water issues either in the form of shortage or contamination. Companies being large scale consumers can contribute significantly to such problems. Hence, with the support of Government policies, Indian companies have come up with programs to not only manage water in their operations but also to benefit all stakeholders. With increasing implementation of water treatment units in daily activities more companies have started meeting Zero Liquid Discharge standards compared to previous years. 15% of companies have taken up rainwater harvesting projects by building rainwater harvesting structures (like dams, farm ponds, ring wells), increasing groundwater levels, strengthening existing water structures, developing watersheds, and recharging groundwater (Futurescape, 2018).

Waste Management

Waste management is divided into plastic waste management, e-waste management, and community waste management. Companies have adopted the following programs for plastic management through the life cycle at various levels:

a) In operations – reducing material consumption, reuse of plastic packing, increasing recycled content in packaging and utilizing bio-based packaging material;
b) At the consumer level – a collection of consumer waste and building awareness among consumers on waste management;
c) waste management – co-processing and recycling.

For e-waste management, after revision in e-waste management rules, there is a noticeable increase in the number of companies that have reported responsible e-waste management.

For community waste management, companies have undertaken initiatives to manage both solid waste and wastewater. Most of these initiatives focus on solid waste with wastewater management being reported by only a few companies. The most commonly followed practices in community solid waste management have been creating awareness and undertaking cleanliness drives. Companies organize cleanliness drives at pilgrimages, public transport hubs, and other tourist areas. They set up kiosks to collect waste and create awareness among the public.

Data Privacy

In India, data privacy/protection is governed by The Information Technology Act, 2000 and Information Technology Rules, 2011. The Act applies to the protection of sensitive personal information as defined in it. Additionally, financial institutions that are regulated by RBI are required to maintain data privacy, unless consented otherwise by the customer. Separately, Indian companies with securities issued/listed in stock exchanges outside India or with operations outside of India, are required to comply with data privacy regulations of those countries. As a result, most companies with multinational operations or with securities listed on stock exchanges outside India have Information security policy/cybersecurity policies (Futurescape, 2018).

SOCIALLY RESPONSIBLE INVESTING STRATEGIES IN INDIA

Socially Responsible Investing (SRI) is an investment process that integrates social and environmental concerns with investment decisions (Berry & Junkus, 2013). SRI is accepted and practiced globally. SRIs allow the investor to identify and invest in a company that meets specific standards of CSR (Tripathi & Bhandari, 2015). The motive for investment in socially responsible companies varies among different investors. It can be ethical considerations, interest in advantageous return profiles, as a response to legal and regulatory constraints or for improving their reputation by exhibiting their concern for the environment (Tripathi & Bhandari, 2015).

The concept of SRI has received attention in recent years due to the growing concern for CSR. Problems such as global financial crisis, global warming, environmental degradation, major corporate frauds, negligence on social concerns from business and awareness about society among the people, etc. have led to the rapid acceptance of CSR. It has paved the way for relevance of Environmental, Social and Governance (ESG) issues in investment decision making and has consequently led to SRI. Some avoid businesses that are connected to alcohol, tobacco, fast food, gambling, pornography, weapons, contraception/abortifacients/abortion, fossil fuel production, and the military.

India is considered the cradle of SRI because of the large size of its demography, and unfulfilled demands of social and economic services. India is one of the most vibrant emerging economies in the world and the rise of the entrepreneurial eco-system has allowed SRI to get wide recognition.

In 2012, the Securities Exchange Board of India (SEBI) enacted the Alternative Investments Funds (AIF), which included 'social venture funds'. AIFs are funds that have been established in India for pooling capital from domestic and foreign investors for investing in pre-decided social impact policies. Although SRIs have been prevalent in India in different forms for a long time, they were formally recognized only under AIF regulations. Under AIF regulation, a social venture fund is defined as "an alternative investment fund that invests primarily in securities or units of social ventures and which satisfies social performance norms laid down by the fund and whose investors may agree to receive restricted or muted returns". These SRIs predominantly invest in sustainable and innovative business models.

According to the Indian Impact Investors council, 'more than 30 impact funds have invested in social enterprises in India'.. While socially responsible investing is still not as big as traditional investing in India, it is a rapidly growing market. Social investing in India has helped provide basic needs such as housing and education to the poor.

Although SRIs are in a nascent stage in India, it is expected to gain momentum in the near future. Stakeholders have become more diligent and are looking to integrate ESG aspects of businesses in their mainstream investment strategies. The current strategies are Government-controlled funds, mutual funds, and ETFs, separately managed accounts, shareholder advocacy, community investing, etc.

In India, the S&P BSE index has three indices in the sustainability space.

1. S&P BSE 100 ESG Index: This index is designed to measure securities that meet sustainability investing criteria on ESG aspects while maintaining a risk and performance profile similar to the S&P BSE 100.
2. S&P BSE CARBONEX: This index is designed to measure the performance of companies within the S&P BSE 100 based on their commitment to mitigating risks arising from climate change.
3. S&P BSE GREENEX: This index is designed to measure the performance of the top 25 "green" companies in the S&P BSE 100 in terms of greenhouse gas emissions.

CONTRIBUTION TRENDS IN INDIA AFTER MANDATORY CSR

The following section analyses the CSR survey conducted on top 100 (N100) listed companies as per the market capital, and these companies are required to comply with the requirements of the act (KPMG, 2018).

The survey shows that 99 of 100 companies have their CSR policy in a public domain that is readily accessible to the public. Disclosing the details regarding the mode of implementation of CSR is a mandatory requirement of the Act. Ninety three companies disclosed their mode of implementation in CSR policy in 2016-2017, compared to 88 in 2014-2015. The Act mandates that the surplus arising from CSR projects shall not form a company's business profit. 75% of the companies disclosed the details around the treatment of surplus arising from the CSR projects.

As per the Act, eligible companies are mandated to form a CSR committee. Survey shows that all 100 companies currently have a CSR committee as compared to 90 in 2014-2015.

Companies have to mandatorily disclose the details regarding the board-level committees, including the CSR committee. Ninety one companies have published disclosed these details compare to the 77 companies in 2014-2015. It is interesting to note that seven companies had five or more CSR committee meetings during 2017-2018, a welcome trend that is not mandated by the Act. 60% of companies have reported details regarding the outreach or people impacted, although it is not mandated by the Act. Over 55% of the companies have disclosed the involvement of employees as volunteers for the implementation of the CSR projects during the current year.

As per the Act, N100 companies are required to spend INR 7410 crore (USD 104 crore). Against the prescribed CSR amount, companies have committed INR 7715 crore (USD 108 crore). Twenty two companies have invested a higher CSR budget outlay than the others. Regarding the overhead expenditure defined in Schedule VII, overhead expenditure towards education continues to be the highest at 37% and increased by over 30% as compared to the previous year. The overhead expenditure towards health and environment-related CSR activities has reduced compared to the previous year, i.e., 2015-2016. The project overhead expenditure has remained static in case of rural developmental projects.

The Act mandates the provision of reason if 2% CSR amount has not been spent. More than 50% of companies stated 'scaling up projects or exploring opportunities' and 16% of companies have proposed long term projects. About 10% of companies blamed the approval processes or reported a delay in implementation.

A total of 1895 CSR projects were implemented during the year of 2016-2017. Among this, 967 projects were executed through an implementing agency with an expenditure of INR 1314 crore (USD 18 crore), highest among all modes of implementation. Other modes are directly by the company and through their foundation. 484 projects were executed directly by the companies and 108 through their foundation. Companies with more women representation had more programs aimed at reducing inequality as a part of CSR contribution.

Service sector companies have seen the highest increase (168%) in their prescribed 2% amount during the current year, followed by Telecom (164%), Pharmaceuticals (158%), and IT Consulting & Software (153%).

DISCUSSIONS AND RECOMMENDATIONS

The primary aim of the chapter is to understand the different aspects of CSR in the Indian context. Each aspect was analyzed in terms of literature in these areas.

The first aspect considered was sustainable development and its relevance in the world. The concept of sustainable development has attracted increasing attention over the last two decades. One of the most prominent definitions was given by the World Commission on Environment and Development that view a development as sustainable when it "meets the needs of the present without compromising the ability of future generations to meet their own needs". The basic aim of sustainable development is to balance the environmental, social, and economic dimensions of doing business. Various terms are used synonymously for similar concepts, e.g., sustainability, sustainable business, and corporate (social) responsibility. The earlier section of this chapter provided an in-depth review of related research articles and reports. It brought out various definitions of sustainable development and approaches.

The second part of the chapter dealt with prevailing CSR models. It described various models including Ackerman's Model and Carroll's model (1991), Intersecting Circles Model, The Concentric Circles Model, and 3C-SR Model, etc. It also discussed models used in India, such as ethical model and statist model.

The third part of this chapter discussed the nature and outcomes of a mandatory CSR implemented in India. In 2014, India introduced mandatory CSR contribution in Section 135 of the Companies Act, 2013. The provisions and subsections related to the mandatory CSR contribution were discussed. According to Section 135 of the Companies Act, 2013, the threshold limits for applicability of the CSR to a Company are (a) net worth of the company is Rs 500 crore or more; (b) turnover of the company is Rs 1000 crore or more; (c) net profit of the company is Rs 5 crore or more. Every qualifying company requires spending at least 2% of its average net profit for the immediately preceding three financial years on CSR activities.

Further, the qualifying company is also expected to constitute a committee (CSR Committee) of the Board of Directors (Board) consisting of three or more directors. The CSR Committee would formulate and recommend to the Board, a policy that indicates the activities to be undertaken (CSR Policy), recommend the amount of money to be spent on the activities proposed and monitor the CSR Policy of the company. The Board is also required to take into account the recommendations made by the CSR Committee and approve the CSR Policy of the company. This chapter also described the various avenues on which a firm can contribute, as listed on Schedule VII of the Act.

The chapter then analyzed the response of Indian firms towards SDGs. This is based on the reports on the contribution of the companies in the areas of renewable energy, water, waste - plastic, e-waste and community waste, and data privacy. The statistical data from the reports were taken for analysis. From the data and the analysis, it is evident that Indian firms are increasing their knowledge and awareness on environmental issues and have shown interest in alleviating some common socio-cultural and environmental problems.

The fifth aspect considered in this chapter was Socially Responsible Investing strategies in India and their scope. SRI is any investment strategy that considers both financial returns and social/environmental impacts. Recently, it has also become known as "sustainable investing" or "responsible investing". There is also a subset of SRI known as "impact investing", devoted to the conscious creation of social impact through investment. In general, socially responsible investors encourage corporate practices that promote environmental stewardship, consumer protection, human rights, and diversity. Although still nascent, investors and stakeholders have shown much interest in SRI.

Finally, the paper analyzed the Corporate Social Responsibility contribution trends in India through reports of surveys conducted by reputed financial and auditing institutions in India. The analysis shows that the mandatory CSR was an eye-opener to all the stakeholders as well as for the common man. The stakeholders include businesses, corporates, customers, employees and all related to the business. There has been significant CSR contribution by companies after mandatory CSR. There has been a gradual increase in contribution through the years, and this increased participation of companies. Although the Act mandated investment of only 2% of the profit on CSR activities, many companies are contributing much more in this area.

The practical implications of the study need a concern for discussion since India being an emerging economy with diverse groups in social, cultural, economic and environmental backgrounds. This study would help practitioners, policymakers, and governments in analyzing the trends in response to the CSR policy and would help in the formulation of strategies based on these trends.

FUTURE RESEARCH DIRECTIONS

This chapter would also provide the launchpad for future research in this area. Future studies can focus more on empirical aspects to get more clarity on the concept. The studies can further look upon the perceptions of employees, employers, and society as such. More comparative studies among the nations, economies, etc. will provide a better way to explore the concept in depth. More factors can be considered for analyzing the relationship with CSR aspects.

CONCLUSION

India, a vibrant emerging economy, became the first country to make CSR contribution mandatory among companies. Our analyses show that CSR activities have been successful since the implementation of mandatory CSR. Organizations have started channelizing their profit for social and environmental progress. CSR initiatives can potentially lead to growth in social, economic, environmental and cultural areas in a developing country like India. This, in turn, can lead to a holistic approach to the industry, not only in the country but also for the rest of the world.

REFERENCES

Bauer, R. A., & Ackerman, R. W. (1976). *Corporate social responsiveness: the modern dilemma*. Reston, VA: Reston Publishing.

Ben Youssef, K., Leicht, T., Pellicelli, M., & Kitchen, P. J. (2018). The importance of corporate social responsibility (CSR) for branding and business success in small and medium-sized enterprises (SME) in a business-to-distributor (B2D) context. *Journal of Strategic Marketing*, *26*(8), 723–739. doi:10.1080/0965254X.2017.1384038

Berry, T. C., & Junkus, J. C. (2013). Socially responsible investing: An investor perspective. *Journal of Business Ethics*, *112*(4), 707–720. doi:10.100710551-012-1567-0

BSDC (Business and Sustainable Development Commission). (2017). *Better Business, Better World*. Retrieved from http://report.businesscommission.org

Carroll, A. B. (1979). A three Dimensional model of corporate performance. *Academy of Management Review*, *4*(4), 497–505. doi:10.5465/amr.1979.4498296

Carroll, A. B. (1991). The pyramid of corporate social responsibility: Toward the moral management of organizational stakeholders. *Business Horizons*, *34*(4), 39–48. doi:10.1016/0007-6813(91)90005-G

Ellerup Nielsen, A., & Thomsen, C. (2007). Reporting CSR–what and how to say it? *Corporate Communications*, *12*(1), 25–40. doi:10.1108/13563280710723732

Futurescape. (2018). *India's top companies for sustainability and CSR, 2018*. Author.

Harrison, J. S., & Freeman, R. E. (1999). Stakeholders, social responsibility, and performance: Empirical evidence and theoretical perspectives. *Academy of Management Journal*, *42*(5), 479–485.

Hopkins, M. (2016). *Corporate social responsibility (CSR) and the United Nations sustainable development goals (SDG): The role of the private sector*. CSR Finance Institute.

Hopkins, M. (2017). CSR and international development. In *CSR and Sustainability* (pp. 88–108). Routledge. doi:10.4324/9781351284646-3

Kanji, R., & Agrawal, R. (2016). Models of corporate social responsibility: Comparison, evolution and convergence. *IIM Kozhikode Society & Management Review*, *5*(2), 141–155. doi:10.1177/2277975216634478

KPMG. (2018). *India's CSR reporting survey 2018*. Retrieved from https://assets.kpmg/content/dam/kpmg/in/pdf/2019/01/India_CSR_Reporting_Survey_2018.pdf

Lueg, R., & Radlach, R. (2016). Managing sustainable development with management control systems: A literature review. *European Management Journal*, *34*(2), 158–171. doi:10.1016/j.emj.2015.11.005

Meehan, J., Meehan, K., & Richards, A. (2006). Corporate social responsibility: The 3C-SR model. *International Journal of Social Economics*, *33*(5/6), 386–398. doi:10.1108/03068290610660661

Montiel, I. (2008). Corporate social responsibility and corporate sustainability: Separate pasts, common futures. *Organization & Environment*, *21*(3), 245–269. doi:10.1177/1086026608321329

Nejati, M., & Ghasemi, S. (2012). Corporate social responsibility in Iran from the perspective of employees. *Social Responsibility Journal*, *8*(4), 578–588. doi:10.1108/17471111211272552

Nixon, B., Burns, J., & Jazayeri, M. (2011). The role of management accounting in new product design and development decisions. *CIMA Research Executive Summary Series*, *9*(1), 1–7.

Palazzo, G., & Richter, U. (2005). CSR business as usual? The case of the tobacco industry. *Journal of Business Ethics*, *61*(4), 387–401. doi:10.100710551-005-7444-3

Porter, M. E., & Kramer, M. R. (2006). The link between competitive advantage and corporate social responsibility. *Harvard Business Review*, *84*(12), 78–92. PMID:17183795

Quazi, A. M., & O'brien, D. (2000). An empirical test of a cross-national model of corporate social responsibility. *Journal of Business Ethics*, *25*(1), 33–51. doi:10.1023/A:1006305111122

Saeidi, S. P., Sofian, S., Saeidi, P., Saeidi, S. P., & Saaeidi, S. A. (2015). How does corporate social responsibility contribute to firm financial performance? The mediating role of competitive advantage, reputation, and customer satisfaction. *Journal of Business Research*, *68*(2), 341–350. doi:10.1016/j.jbusres.2014.06.024

Scheyvens, R., Banks, G., & Hughes, E. (2016). The private sector and the SDGs: The need to move beyond 'business as usual'. *Sustainable Development*, *24*(6), 371–382. doi:10.1002d.1623

Schwartz, M. S., & Carroll, A. B. (2003). Corporate social responsibility: A three-domain approach. *Business Ethics Quarterly*, *13*(4), 503–530. doi:10.5840/beq200313435

Stawicka, E. (2017). Sustainable development and the business context of CSR benefits on the Polish market. *Acta Scientiarum Polonorum. Oeconomia*, *16*(3).

Sustainable Development Goals Report. (2018). Retrieved from https://unstats.un.org/sdgs/report/2018/overview/

Tripathi, V., & Bhandari, V. (2015). Socially responsible stocks: A boon for investors in India. *Journal of Advances in Management Research*, *12*(2), 209–225. doi:10.1108/JAMR-03-2014-0021

Van Marrewijk, M. (2003). Concepts and definitions of CSR and corporate sustainability: Between agency and communion. *Journal of Business Ethics*, *44*(2-3), 95–105. doi:10.1023/A:1023331212247

Wang, H., Tong, L., Takeuchi, R., & George, G. (2016). Corporate social responsibility: An overview and new research directions. *Thematic issue on corporate social responsibility*, 534-544.

ADDITIONAL READING

Crane, A., Matten, D., & Spence, L. (Eds.). (2019). *Corporate social responsibility: Readings and cases in a global context*. Routledge. doi:10.4324/9780429294273

Lütge, C. (2019). The Honorable Merchant and the Corporate Social Responsibility Movement. In *The Honorable Merchant–Between Modesty and Risk-Taking* (pp. 19–28). Cham: Springer. doi:10.1007/978-3-030-04351-3_2

Morsing, M., & Spence, L. J. (2019). Corporate social responsibility (CSR) communication and small and medium sized enterprises: The governmentality dilemma of explicit and implicit CSR communication. *Human Relations*, 1–28.

Swathi, P. S. (2019). A Study On The Role Of Directors In The Realm Of Corporate Social Responsibility To Ensure Society's Sustainability–An Analysis Of Companies Act, 2013–An Indian Perspective. *International Journal on Recent Trends in Business and Tourism*, *3*(2), 77–84.

KEY TERMS AND DEFINITIONS

Companies Act, 2013: Companies Act 2013 is an Act of the Parliament of India which regulates incorporation of a company, responsibilities of a company, directors, dissolution of a company.

Corporate Social Responsibility: It is a business self-regulation that aims to contribute to societal goals of a philanthropic, activist, or charitable nature or by engage in or support volunteering or ethically oriented practices.

Sustainable Development Goals: The Sustainable Development Goals (SDGs), also known as the Global Goals, were adopted by all United Nations Member States in 2015 as a universal call to action to end poverty, protect the planet and ensure that all people enjoy peace and prosperity by 2030.

Compilation of References

Aaker, D. (1991). Brand equity. *La gestione de lvalore della marca.*

Abdirahman, Z. Z., Sauvée, L., & Shiri, G. (2014). Analyzing network effects of Corporate Social Responsibility implementation in food small and medium enterprises. *Journal on Chain and Network Science, 14*(2), 103–115. doi:10.3920/JCNS2014.x005

Abugre, J. B., & Anlesinya, A. (2019). Corporate Social Responsibility and Business Value of Multinational Companies: Lessons from a Sub-Saharan African Environment. *Journal of African Business.*

Adamczyk, J. (2009). *Społeczna odpowiedzialność biznesu.* Warszawa: PWE.

Aguilera-Caracuel, J., Aragón-Correa, J. A., Hurtado-Torres, N. E., & Rugman, A. M. (2012). The effects of institutional distance and headquarters' financial performance on the generation of environmental standards in multinational companies. *Journal of Business Ethics, 105*(4), 461–474. doi:10.100710551-011-0978-7

Ahmad, M. (2008, Jan. 24). Global CEOs at World Economic Forum cite sovereign wealth funds as the new power broker. *BI-ME.*

Ahmed, F. (2012, November 25). At least 117 killed in fire at Bangladeshi clothing factory. *CNN.* Retrieved April 8, 2019, from: https://edition.cnn.com/2012/11/25/world/asia/bangladesh-factory-fire/

Alessio, R. (2003). Responsabilidade social dasempresas no Brasil: Reprodução de posturas ou novosrumos? *Revista Virtual Textos&Contextos, 2*(2), 1–10.

Alexander, G. J., & Buchholz, R. A. (1978). Corporate social responsibility and stock market performance. *Academy of Management Journal, 21*(3), 479–486.

Allchin, J., & Kazmin, A. (2013, April 25). Scores dead in Bangladeshi garment factory collapse. *Financial Times.* Retrieved April 9, 2019, from: https://www.ft.com/content/bf534db4-acbe-11e2-b27f-00144feabdc0

Allouche, J., & Laroche, P. (2005). A Meta-analytical Investigation of the Relationship between Corporate Social and Financial Performance. *Revue de Gestion des Ressources Humaines, 57,* 8–41.

Al-mulali, U., Fereidouni, H. G., & Lee, J. Y. (2014). Electricity Consumption from Renewable and Non-renewable Sources and Economic Growth: Evidence from Latin American countries. *Renewable & Sustainable Energy Reviews, 30,* 290–298. doi:10.1016/j.rser.2013.10.006

Al-mulali, U., Fereidouni, H. G., Lee, J. Y., & Sab, C. N. B. C. (2013). Examining the Bi-directional Long Run Relationship between Renewable Energy Consumption and GDP Growth. *Renewable & Sustainable Energy Reviews, 22,* 209–222. doi:10.1016/j.rser.2013.02.005

Amadeo, K. (2014). *World's largest economy.* Academic Press.

Amin, A., Naidoo, Ch., & Whitley, Sh. (2014). Green Growth in Practice: Lessons from Country Experiences. *Mobilising investments*. Available at: http://www.ggbp.org/sites/all/themes/ggbp/uploads/Green-Growth-in-Practice-062014-Full.pdf

Aminia, M., & Bienstock, C. C. (2014). Corporate sustainability: An integrative definition and framework to evaluate corporate practice and guide academic research. *Journal of Cleaner Production*, *76*, 12–19. doi:10.1016/j.jclepro.2014.02.016

Amri, F. (2016). The Relationship amongst Energy Consumption, Foreign Direct Investment and Output in Developed and Developing Countries. *Renewable & Sustainable Energy Reviews*, *64*, 694–702. doi:10.1016/j.rser.2016.06.065

Andreini, D., Pedeliento, G., & Signori, S. (2014). CSR and service quality in nonprofit organizations: The case of a performing arts association. *International Journal of Nonprofit and Voluntary Sector Marketing*, *19*(2), 127–142. doi:10.1002/nvsm.1488

Andriof, J., Waddock, S., Husted, B., & Rahman, S. (2002). Unfolding Stakeholder Thinking: Theory, Responsibility and Engagement. (S. Andriof, J., Waddock, Eds.). Abingdon, UK: Routledge.

Anggraini, C., Kriyantono, R., & Wulandari, M. P. (2018). Corporate Social Responsibility (CSR): An Opportunity for the Poverty Alleviation. *Advanced Science Letters*, *24*(12), 9341–9344. doi:10.1166/asl.2018.12269

Apergis, N., & Payne, J. E. (2010a). Renewable Energy Consumption and Economic Growth: Evidence from a Panel of OECD Countries. *Energy Policy*, *38*(1), 656–660. doi:10.1016/j.enpol.2009.09.002

Apergis, N., & Payne, J. E. (2010b). Renewable Energy Consumption and Growth in Eurasia. *Energy Economics*, *32*(6), 1392–1397. doi:10.1016/j.eneco.2010.06.001

Apergis, N., & Payne, J. E. (2011a). Renewable and Non-renewable Electricity Consumption–growth Nexus: Evidence from Emerging Market Economies. *Applied Energy*, *88*(12), 5226–5230. doi:10.1016/j.apenergy.2011.06.041

Apergis, N., & Payne, J. E. (2011b). The Renewable Energy Consumption–Growth nexus in Central America. *Applied Energy*, *88*(1), 343–347. doi:10.1016/j.apenergy.2010.07.013

Apergis, N., & Payne, J. E. (2012). Renewable and Non-renewable Energy Consumption-Growth Nexus: Evidence from a Panel Error Correction Model. *Energy Economics*, *34*(3), 733–738. doi:10.1016/j.eneco.2011.04.007

Apollo Alliance. (2008). *Green-Collar Jobs in America's Cities, United States*. Retrieved October 23, 2019, from: https://www.cows.org/_data/documents/1165.pdf

Ararat, M. (2008). A development perspective for "corporate social responsibility": Case of Turkey. *Corporate Governance: The International Journal of Business in Society*, *8*(3), 271–285. doi:10.1108/14720700810879169

Aras, G. D., & Crowther, D. (2007). What Level of Trust is Needed for Sustainability? *Social Responsibility Journal*, *3*(3), 60–68. doi:10.1108/17471110710835590

Aras, G., & Crowther, D. (2009). Corporate sustainability reporting: A study in disingenuity? *Journal of Business Ethics*, *87*(1), 279–288. doi:10.100710551-008-9806-0

Araya, M. (2006). Exploring Terra Incognita: Non-financial Reporting in Latin America. *Journal of Corporate Citizenship*, *21*(21), 25–38. doi:10.9774/GLEAF.4700.2006.sp.00005

Arrive, J. T., & Feng, M. (2018). Corporate social responsibility disclosure: Evidence from BRICS nations. *Corporate Social Responsibility and Environmental Management*, *25*(5), 920–927. doi:10.1002/csr.1508

Artiach, T., Lee, D., Nelson, D., & Walker, J. (2010). The determinants of corporate sustainability performance. *Accounting and Finance*, *50*(1), 31–51. doi:10.1111/j.1467-629X.2009.00315.x

Ashley, P. A. (2002). *Ética e responsabilidade social nosnegócios*. São Paulo: Saraiva.

Ashton, D., & Sung, J. (1994). *The State, Economic Development and Skill Formation: A New Asian Model?* CLMS Working Paper No 3. Retrieved from https://www.researchgate.net/publication/242641461_The_State_Economic_Development_and_Skill_Formation_A_New_East_Asian_Model

Ashton, D., & Green, F. (1996). *Education, Training and the Global Economy* (1st ed.). Cheltenham, UK: Edward Elgar.

Asifa, M., Searcy, C., Zutshi, A., & Fisscher, O. A. M. (2013). An integrated management systems approach to corporate social responsibility. *Journal of Cleaner Production*, *56*, 7–17. doi:10.1016/j.jclepro.2011.10.034

Auer, B. R. (2016). Do Socially Responsible Investment Policies Add or Destroy European Stock Portfolio Value? *Journal of Business Ethics*, *135*(2), 381–397. doi:10.100710551-014-2454-7

Backman, J. (1975). *Social responsibility and accountability* (1st ed.). New York: New York University Press.

Bagire, V. A., Tusiime, I., Nalweyiso, G., & Kakooza, J. B. (2011). Contextual environment and stakeholder perception of corporate social responsibility practices in Uganda. *Corporate Social Responsibility and Environmental Management*, *18*(2), 102–109. doi:10.1002/csr.252

Bajaj, V. (2012, November 25). Fatal Fire in Bangladesh Highlights the Dangers Facing Garment Workers. *The New York Times*. Retrieved April 8, 2019, from: https://www.nytimes.com/2012/11/26/world/asia/bangladesh-fire-kills-more-than-100-and-injures-many.html?_r=0

Bakardjieva, R. (2009). Corporate social responsibility of the firms in Bulgaria. *Economic Studies, 2*, 33-63.

Bakardjieva, R. (2019). *Corporate responsibility through application of international social standards - challenges and European dimensions*. Plovdiv, Bulgaria: Talent Academic Publishing House at the University of agribusiness and rural development.

Bakardjieva, R. (2012). Corporate social responsibility standards. *Economic Studies*, *2*, 149–160.

Bakardjieva, R. (2016). Sustainable development and corporate social responsibility: Linking goals to standards. *Journal of Innovations and Sustainability*, *2*(4), 23–35.

Balaban, Ö., Cicioğlu, F., & Okutan, E. (2012). A Survey aimed at role and importance of nongovernmental organizations in the corporate social responsibility (CSR). *Procedia: Social and Behavioral Sciences*, *58*, 1174–1182. doi:10.1016/j.sbspro.2012.09.1099

Balashova, E. (2009). Problems and prospects of small business development in Russia. *Siberian Trade and Economic Journal,* (9), 3-5.

Banahan, C. M. (2019). The Bond Villains of Green Investment: Why an Unregulated Securities Market Needs Government To Lay Down The Law. *Vermont Law Review*, *43*(4), 841–869. Available at https://lawreview.vermontlaw.edu/wp-content/uploads/2019/06/vlaw_43n4_Banahan.pdf

Banerjee, S. (2014). A Critical Perspective on Corporate Social Responsibility. *Critical Perspectives on International Business*, *10*(1/2), 84–95. doi:10.1108/cpoib-06-2013-0021

Bansal, P., & Corley, K. (2011). From the editors: The coming of age for qualitative research: Embracing the diversity of qualitative methods. The Academy of Management Journal, 54(2), 233-237.

Bansal, P. (2005). Evolving sustainably: A longitudinal study of corporate sustainable development. *Strategic Management Journal*, *26*(3), 197–218. doi:10.1002mj.441

Bapat, S. (2013). *Challenges of the 2% CSR paradigm.* Forbs India Magazine.

Barber, R. (1982). Pension Funds in the United States Issues of Investment and Control. *Economic and Industrial Democracy, 3*(1), 31–73. doi:10.1177/0143831X8231004

Barbier, E. B. (2016). Is green growth relevant for poor economies? *Resource and Energy Economics, 45*, 178–191. Available at https://www.sciencedirect.com/science/article/abs/pii/S0928765516301154

Barbier, E. B., & Markandya, A. (1989). *A Blueprint for a Green Economy.* London: Routledge.

Barnea, A., & Rubin, A. (2010). Corporate social responsibility as a conflict between shareholders. *Journal of Business Ethics, 97*(1), 71–86. doi:10.100710551-010-0496-z

Barney, J. (1991). Firm resources and sustained competitive advantage. *Journal of Management, 17*(1), 99–120. doi:10.1177/014920639101700108

Baskin, J. (2006). Corporate Responsibility in Emerging Markets. *Journal of Corporate Citizenship, 24,* 29–47.

Baskin, J. (2006). Corporate responsibility in emerging markets. *Journal of Corporate Citizenship, 24*(24), 29–47. doi:10.9774/GLEAF.4700.2006.wi.00006

Bass, A. E., & Milosevic, I. (2018). The ethnographic method in CSR research: The role and importance of methodological fit. *Business & Society, 57*(1), 174–215. doi:10.1177/0007650316648666

Bataeva, B. S. (2010). Directions of formation of the Russian model of corporate responsibility. News of St. Petersburg State University, (5), 67-72.

Bauer, R. A., & Ackerman, R. W. (1976). *Corporate social responsiveness: the modern dilemma.* Reston, VA: Reston Publishing.

Baumback, C. M. (1988). *How to organize and operate a small business.* Prentice Hall.

Baumgartner, R. J., & Ebner, D. (2010). Corporate sustainability strategies: Sustainability profiles and maturity levels. *Sustainable Development, 18*(2), 76–89. doi:10.1002d.447

Baxi, C. V., & Prasad, A. (2005). *Corporate Social Responsibility: Concepts and Cases-the Indian Experiences.* New Delhi: Excel Publishing.

Bazerman, M. H., & Chugh, D. (2005). Bounded awareness: Focusing failures in negotiation. In L. Thompson (Ed.), *Frontiers of Social Psychology: Negotiation* (pp. 7–26). New York, NY: Psychological Press.

Bazerman, M. H., Gino, F., Shu, L. L., & Tsay, C.-J. (2011). Joint evaluation as a real-world tool for managing emotional assessment of morality. *Emotion Review, 3*(3), 290–292. doi:10.1177/1754073911402370

Bazerman, M. H., & Moore, D. (2009). *Judgment in managerial decision making.* Hoboken: Wiley.

Bazerman, M. H., & Tenbrunsel, A. E. (2011). *Blind spots: Why we fail to do what's right and what to do about it.* Princeton, NJ: Princeton University Press. doi:10.1515/9781400837991

Bebbington, J., & Unerman, J. (2008). Editorial. *Social and Environmental Accountability Journal, 28*(1), 1–2. doi:10.1080/0969160X.2008.9651786

Becchetti, L., Ciciretti, R., Dalò, A., & Herzel, S. (2015). Socially responsible and conventional investment funds: Performance comparison and the global financial crisis. *Applied Economics, 47*(25), 2541–2562. doi:10.1080/00036846.2014.1000517

Beck, U. (1998). Wie wird Demokratie im Zeitalter der Globalisierung möglich? In U. Beck (Ed.), *Politik der Globalisierung* (pp. 7–67). Frankfurt am Main: Suhrkamp.

Bekefi, T. (2006). *Business as a partner in tackling micronutrient deficiency: Lessons in multisector partnership. Report of the Corporate Responsibility Initiative.* Cambridge, MA: Harvard University Press.

Bélaïd, F., & Youssef, M. (2017). Environmental Degradation, Renewable and Non-renewable Electricity Consumption, and Economic Growth: Assessing the evidence from Algeria. *Energy Policy*, *102*, 277–287. doi:10.1016/j.enpol.2016.12.012

Ben Youssef, K., Leicht, T., Pellicelli, M., & Kitchen, P. J. (2018). The importance of corporate social responsibility (CSR) for branding and business success in small and medium-sized enterprises (SME) in a business-to-distributor (B2D) context. *Journal of Strategic Marketing*, *26*(8), 723–739. doi:10.1080/0965254X.2017.1384038

Bengtsson, E. (2008). Socially responsible investing in Scandinavia–a comparative analysis. *Sustainable Development*, *16*(3), 155–168. doi:10.1002d.360

Benijts, T. (2010). A framework for comparing socially responsible investment markets: An analysis of the Dutch and Belgian retail markets. *Business Ethics (Oxford, England)*, *19*(1), 50–63. doi:10.1111/j.1467-8608.2009.01578.x

Berad, N. R. (2011). CSR: Issues and Challenges in India. *International Conference on Technology and Business Management*, 101-108.

Berensmann, K., & Lindenberg, N. (2016). *Green finance: actors, challenges and policy recommendations. German Development Institute.* Briefing Paper 23. Available at: https://papers.ssrn.com/sol3/papers.cfm?abstract_id=2881922

Bergman, D., & Rashid, M. (2012, November 25). Bangladesh factory fire kills 111 garment workers. *The Telegraph.* Retrieved April 8, 2019, from: https://www.telegraph.co.uk/news/worldnews/asia/bangladesh/9701826/Bangladesh-factory-fire-kills-111-garment-workers.html

Berry, T. C., & Junkus, J. C. (2013). Socially responsible investing: An investor perspective. *Journal of Business Ethics*, *112*(4), 707–720. doi:10.100710551-012-1567-0

Berthon, P., Pitt, L., Plangger, K., & Shapiro, D. (2012). Marketing meets Web 2.0, social media, and creative consumers: Implications for international marketing strategy. *Business Horizons*, *55*(3), 261–271. doi:10.1016/j.bushor.2012.01.007

Beschorner, T., & Hajduk, T. (2017). Creating Shared Value. A Fundamental Critique. In J. Wieland (Ed.), Creating Shared Value – Concepts, Experience, Criticism (pp. 27–38). Springer International Publishing AG.

Bhaskar, S. P. (2010). CSR in an Indian Public sector organization. A case study of Bharat petroleum Corporation Ltd. *Journal of Human Values*, *16*(2), 143–156. doi:10.1177/097168581001600202

Bhatia, S. K. (2006). Corporate Social Responsibility. In *Business Ethics & Managerial Values* (pp. 143–145). New Delhi: Deep & Deep Publications Pvt. Ltd.

Bhattacharya, M., Churchill, S. A., & Paramati, S. R. (2017). The Dynamic Impact of Renewable Energy and Institutions on Economic Output and CO_2 Eemissions across Regions. *Renewable Energy*, *111*, 157–167. doi:10.1016/j.renene.2017.03.102

Bhola, S., & Sukhija, A. (2012, November). *India-CSR Boom for social upliftment.* Retrieved from Mondaq: www.mondaq.com

Bilbao-Terol, A., Arenas-Parra, M., Cañal-Fernández, V., & Bilbao-Terol, C. (2013). Selection of socially responsible portfolios using hedonic prices. *Journal of Business Ethics*, *115*(3), 515–529. doi:10.100710551-012-1411-6

Birch, D., & Moon, J. (2004). Introduction: CSR in Asia. *Journal of Corporate Citizenship, 13*(Special Issue), 18–23. doi:10.9774/GLEAF.4700.2004.sp.00004

Blagov, Y. E. (2010). *Corporate social responsibility: the evolution of the concept. Graduate School of Management.-SPb.* Publishing House of the Graduate School of Management.

Blagoycheva, H. (2016). *Corporate Social Responsibility Between the Profit and Social Welfare. International scientific and practical conference "Economics, management, law: realities and perspectives", April 29, 2016.* Retrieved from http://conferencii.com/files/archive/2016-04.pdf

Blagoycheva, H. (2018). The Involvement of the Public Sector in Corporate Social Responsibility – the Changing Reality. *International Journal of Economic Research, 15*(1), 119–131.

Blagoycheva, H., Andreeva, A., & Yolova, G. (2019). Obligation and Responsibility of Employers to Provide Health and Safety at Work – Principles, Current Regulation and Prospects. *Economic Studies, 28*(2), 115–137.

Blair, D., & Bergman, D. (2013, May 3). Bangladesh: Rana Plaza architect says building was never meant for factories. *The Telegraph.* Retrieved April 8, 2019, from: https://www.telegraph.co.uk/news/worldnews/asia/bangladesh/10036546/Bangladesh-Rana-Plaza-architect-says-building-was-never-meant-for-factories.html

Blodgett, M. S., Hoitash, R. I., & Markelevich, A. (2014). Sustaining the financial value of global CSR: Reconciling corporate and stakeholder interests in a less regulated environment. *Business and Society Review, 119*(1), 195–124. doi:10.1111/basr.12026

Bloomberg, N. E. F. (2018). *Green Bond Issuance Exceeds $100 Billion for 3rd Year.* Available at: https://about.bnef.com/blog/green-bond-issuance-exceeds-100-billion-3rd-year/

Bloomberg, N. E. F. (2019). *Issuance of sustainable debt products surged 26% to $247 billion last year, as the market innovated to meet demand from investors.* Available at: https://about.bnef.com/blog/sustainable-debt-market-sees-record-activity-2018/

Bloomberg. (2019). *Bloomberg platform database.* Author.

Bobrova, O. S., & Kovaleva, A. S. (2015a). How to do it? Russian businessmen about business: happiness and responsibility, innovative activity. *Russian Business, 16*(16), 2313-2498

Bobrova, O. S., & Kovaleva, A. S. (2015b). How to do it? Russian businessmen on business (according to the results of the survey of 2014): goals and motives. *Russian Business, 16*(15)б 2599-2618

Bocken, N. M. P., Short, S. W., Rana, P., & Evans, S. (2014). A literature and practice review to develop sustainable business model archetypes. *Journal of Cleaner Production, 65*, 42–56. doi:10.1016/j.jclepro.2013.11.039

Boon, E. K., & Ababio, F. (2009, May). Corporate social responsibility in Ghana: Lessons from the mining sector. *IAIIA09 Conference Proceedings, Impact Assessment and Human Well-Being.*

Boursorama. (2013). *L'AFG et le FIR donnent une nouvelle définition à l'ISR.* Retrieved from https://www.boursorama.com/bourse/actualites/l-afg-et-le-fir-donnent-une-nouvelle-definition-a-l-isr-7b9a4fd7c8cf2466e003dfc0e21a4d46

Bowen, A., & Kuralbayeva, K. (2015). Looking for Green Jobs: the Impact of Green Growth on Employment. *Global Green Growth Institute.* Retrieved October 23, 2019, from: http://www.lse.ac.uk/GranthamInstitute/wp-content/uploads/2015/03/Looking-for-green-jobs_the-impact-of-green-growth-on-employment.pdf

Bowen, H. (1953). *Social Responsibilities of the Businessman.* New York: Harper.

Bowen, H. R. (1953). *The Social Responsibility of the Businessman* (1st ed.). New York: Harper.

Bowen, H. R. (2013). *Social responsibilities of the businessman.* University of Iowa Press. doi:10.2307/j.ctt20q1w8f

Bowie, N. E., & Werhane, P. H. (2005). Corporate Social Responsibility. In *Management Ethics* (pp. 99–115). Blackwell Publishing.

Bowman, E. H., & Haire, M. (1975). A Strategic Posture toward Corporate Social Responsibility. *California Management Review, 18*(2), 49–58. doi:10.2307/41164638

Bracking, S. (2019). Financialisation, Climate Finance, and the Calculative Challenges of Managing Environmental Change. *Antipode, 51*(3), 709–729. doi:10.1111/anti.12510

Brammer, S., & Millington, A. (2006). Firm size, organizational visibility and corporate philanthropy: An empirical analysis. *Business Ethics (Oxford, England), 15*(1), 6–18. doi:10.1111/j.1467-8608.2006.00424.x

Branco, M. C., & Rodrigues, L. L. (2006). Corporate social responsibility and resource-based perspectives. *Journal of Business Ethics, 69*(2), 111–132. doi:10.100710551-006-9071-z

Brekke, K., & Nyborg, K. (2008). Attracting responsible employees: Green production as labor market screening. *Resource and Energy Economics, 30*(4), 509–526. doi:10.1016/j.reseneeco.2008.05.001

Brieger, S. A., & De Clercq, D. (2019). Entrepreneurs' individual-level resources and social value creation goals: The moderating role of cultural context. *International Journal of Entrepreneurial Behaviour & Research, 25*(2), 193–216. doi:10.1108/IJEBR-12-2017-0503

Brini, R., Amara, M., & Jemmali, H. (2017). Renewable energy consumption, International trade, oil price and economic growth inter-linkages: The case of Tunisia. *Renewable & Sustainable Energy Reviews, 76*, 620–627. doi:10.1016/j.rser.2017.03.067

Brundtland, G. H. (1989). Global change and our common future. *Environment, 31*(5), 16–43. doi:10.1080/00139157.1989.9928941

Bruyn, S. T. (1987). *The field of social investment.* Cambridge, MA: Cambridge University Press. doi:10.1017/CBO9780511570872

Brynjolfsson, E., Hitt, L. M., & Kim, H. H. (2011). Strength in numbers: How does data-driven decision making affect firm performance? *SSRN Electronic Journal, 1.* doi:10.2139srn.1819486

Brynjolfsson, E., & Mcafee, A. (2011). *Race against the machine: how the digital revolution is accelerating innovation, driving productivity, and irreversibly transforming employment and the economy.* Lexington: Digital Frontier Press.

BSDC (Business and Sustainable Development Commission). (2017). *Better Business, Better World.* Retrieved from http://report.businesscommission.org

Buchner, B., Stadelmann, M., Wilkinson, J., Mazza, F., Rosenberg, A., & Abramskiehn, D. (2014). *The Global Landscape of Climate Finance.* Available at: https://www.climatefinance-developmenteffectiveness.org/sites/default/files/event/CFSDforum2015/climate/The%20Global%20Landscape%20of%20Climate%20Finance_2014.pdf

Bugai, I. A., Akishina, M. L., & Fannenshtil', A. A. (2014). The level of social responsibility of the rural business and its impact on the development of rural areas. *Journal of the Altai State Agrarian University, 12*(122), 143–148.

Bugai, I. A., Akishina, M. L., & Fannenshtil', A. A. (2015). Impact of corporate social responsibility of rural business on rural employment and development of rural areas. *Journal of the Altai State Agrarian University, 6*(128), 156–161.

Bugg-Levine, A., & Emerson, J. (2011). Impact investing: Transforming how we make money while making a difference. *Innovations: Technology, Governance, Globalization, 6*(3), 9–18. doi:10.1162/INOV_a_00077

Bulgarian association of CSR specialists. (2018, December 7). *Corporate responsibility experts have set up their own professional organization.* Retrieved from http://www.bcause.bg/razvitie-na-sredata/news-sredata/449-ekspertite-po-korporativna-otgovornost-s%C5%ADzdadokha-svoyata-profesionalna organizatsiya.html

Bulgarian business leaders forum. (2019). *CSR in Bulgaria*. Retrieved from http://www.bblf.bg/content/30/CSR+in+Bulgaria

Bulgarian NGO's Information Portal. (2019, February 20). *The first specialized survey on the state of corporate social responsibility in Bulgaria*. Retrieved from https://www.ngobg.info

Burns, N., & Grove, S. K. (1997). Selecting a research design. *The Practice of Nursing Research: Conduct, Critique, &. Utilization*, *3*, 249–291.

Busch, T., Bauer, R., & Orlitzky, M. (2016). Sustainable development and financial markets: Old paths and new avenues. *Business & Society*, *55*(3), 303–329. doi:10.1177/0007650315570701

Caister, D. (2013). Buy Your Green Bonds. *Alternatives Journal (AJ) - Canada's Environmental Voice*, *39*(6), 24-29. Available at: https://www.alternativesjournal.ca/science-and-solutions/buy-your-green-bonds-exclusive-interview-footage

Camilleri, M. A. (2017a). Measuring the corporate managers' attitudes towards ISO's social responsibility standard. *Total Quality Management & Business Excellence*, 1-13. Retrieved from https://www.tandfonline.com/doi/full/10.1080/14783363.2017.1413344

Camilleri, M. A. (2015a). Valuing stakeholder engagement and sustainability reporting. *Corporate Reputation Review*, *18*(3), 210–222. doi:10.1057/crr.2015.9

Camilleri, M. A. (2015b). Environmental, social and governance disclosures in Europe, *Sustainability Accounting. Management and Policy Journal*, *6*(2), 224–242.

Camilleri, M. A. (2017). Socially Responsible and Sustainable Investing. In *Corporate Sustainability, Social Responsibility and Environmental Management* (pp. 61–77). Cham: Springer International Publishing. doi:10.1007/978-3-319-46849-5_4

Camilleri, M. A. (2017b). The integrated reporting of financial, social and sustainability capitals: A critical review and appraisal. *International Journal of Sustainable Society*, *9*(4), 311–326. doi:10.1504/IJSSOC.2017.090523

Camilleri, M. A. (2018). Theoretical insights on integrated reporting: The inclusion of non-financial capitals in corporate disclosures. *Corporate Communications*, *23*(4), 567–581. doi:10.1108/CCIJ-01-2018-0016

Camilleri, M. A. (2019). The circular economy's closed loop and product service systems for sustainable development: A review and appraisal. *Sustainable Development*, *27*(3), 530–536. doi:10.1002d.1909

Campbell, L., Gulas, C. S., & Gruca, T. S. (1999). Corporate giving behavior and decision-maker social consciousness. *Journal of Business Ethics*, *19*(4), 375–383. doi:10.1023/A:1006080417909

Can, H., & Korkmaz, Ö. (2019). The Relationship between Renewable Energy Consumption and Economic Growth: The Case of Bulgaria. *International Journal of Energy Sector Management.*, *13*(3), 573–589. doi:10.1108/IJESM-11-2017-0005

Capelle-Blancard, G., & Monjon, S. (2012). Trends in the literature on socially responsible investment: Looking for the keys under the lamppost. *Business Ethics (Oxford, England)*, *21*(3), 239–250. doi:10.1111/j.1467-8608.2012.01658.x

Carroll, A. B. (1979). A Three-Dimensional Conceptual Model of Corporate Performance. *Academy of Management Review*, *4*(4), 497–505. doi:10.5465/amr.1979.4498296

Carroll, A. B. (1991). The Pyramid of Corporate Social Responsibility: Toward the Moral Management of Organizational Stakeholders. *Business Horizons*, *34*(4), 39–48. doi:10.1016/0007-6813(91)90005-G

Carroll, A. B. (1999). Corporate Social Responsibility: Evolution of a definitional construct. *Business & Society*, *38*(3), 268–295. doi:10.1177/000765039903800303

Carroll, A. B. (2000). Ethical Challenges for Business in the New Millennium: Corporate Social Responsibility and Models of Management Morality. *Business Ethics Quarterly*, *10*(1), 33–42. doi:10.2307/3857692

Carroll, A. B. (2004). Managing ethically with global stakeholders: A present and future challenge. *The Academy of Management Perspectives*, *18*(2), 114–120. doi:10.5465/ame.2004.13836269

Carroll, A. B., & Shabana, K. M. (2010). The Business Case for Corporate Social Responsibility: A Review of Concepts, Research and Practice. *International Journal of Management Reviews*, *12*(1), 85–105. doi:10.1111/j.1468-2370.2009.00275.x

Cassel, D. (2001). Human Rights and Business Responsibilities in the Global Marketplace. *Business Ethics Quarterly*, *11*(2), 261–274. doi:10.2307/3857749

Cavusgil, T., Deligonul, S., & Yaprak, A. (2005). International marketing as a field of study: A critical assessment of earlier development and a look forward. *Journal of International Marketing*, *13*(4), 1–27. doi:10.1509/jimk.2005.13.4.1

CDFA. (2005). *Inside Out: The State of Community Development Finance*. London, UK: CDFA.

CEC. (2001). *Green Paper Promoting a European frame for corporate social responsibility*. Commission of the European communities. Retrived from httpp://eur-aex.europa.eu/LexUriServ/LexUriUerv.do?uri=CMO:2001:0366:FIN:EN:PDF

Cecere, G., & Mazzanti, M. (2015). *Green Jobs, Innovation and Environmentally Oriented Strategies in European SMEs* (No. 2115). SEEDS, Sustainability Environmental Economics and Dynamics Studies. Retrieved October 23, 2019, https://ideas.repec.org/p/srt/wpaper/2115.html

Chahal, H., & Sharma, R. D. (2006). Implications of corporate social responsibility on marketing performance: A conceptual framework. *Journal of Services Research*, *6*(1), 205–216.

Chalmers, D. M. (1959). The muckrakers and the growth of corporate power: A study in constructive journalism. *American Journal of Economics and Sociology*, *18*(3), 295–311. doi:10.1111/j.1536-7150.1959.tb00326.x

Chang, Y. K., Oh, W. Y., Jung, J. C., & Lee, J. Y. (2012). Firm Size and Corporate Social Performance. *Journal of Leadership & Organizational Studies*, *19*(4), 486–500. doi:10.1177/1548051812455239

Chan, K. C., Fung, H.-G., & Yau, J. (2010). Business ethics research: A global perspective. *Journal of Business Ethics*, *95*(1), 39–53. doi:10.100710551-009-0346-z

Chapple, W., & Moon, J. (2005). Corporate social responsibility (CSR) in Asia a seven-country study of CSR web site reporting. *Business & Society*, *44*(4), 415–441. doi:10.1177/0007650305281658

Chapple, W., & Moon, J. (2007). Introduction: CSR Agendas for Asia. *Corporate Social Responsibility and Environmental Management*, *14*(3), 183–188. doi:10.1002/csr.159

Chege, E. S. (2013). *Corporate Social Responsibility and Competitive Advantage of Commercial Banks in Kenya. A Research Project*. School of Business University of Nairobi-Kenya.

Chen, E., & Gavious, I. (2015). Does CSR have different value implications for different shareholders? *Finance Research Letters*, *14*, 29–35. doi:10.1016/j.frl.2015.07.001

Chen-Yu, J., Cho, S., & Kincade, D. (2016). Brand perception and brand repurchase intent in online apparel shopping: An examination of brand experience, image congruence, brand affect, and brand trust. *Journal of Global Fashion Marketing*, *7*(1), 30–44. doi:10.1080/20932685.2015.1110042

Cheruiyot, T. K., & Maru, L. C. (2012). Employee social responsibility practices and outcomes in Kenya's tourist hotels. *African Journal of Economic and Management Studies*, *3*(1), 23–41. doi:10.1108/20400701211197267

Cheruiyot, T. K., & Onsando, P. (2016). Corporate Social responsibility in Africa: Context, Paradoxes, Stakeholder Orientations, Contestations and Reflections. In A. Stachowicz-Stanush (Ed.), *Corporate Social Performance in the Age of Irresponsibility-Cross National Perspective*. Charlotte, NC: Information Age Publishing.

Cheung, Y. L., Tan, W., Ahn, H. J., & Zhang, Z. (2010). Does corporate social responsibility matter in Asian Emerging Markets? *Journal of Business Ethics*, *92*(3), 401–413. doi:10.100710551-009-0164-3

China Daily. (2010). *China-Africa trade volume set to hit new record high*. Retrieved from: http://www.chinadaily.com.cn/china/2010–10/14/content_11412120.htm

Chirikova, A. (2006). Business as a subject of social policy in modern Russia. *Society and Economy*, (9): 100–119.

Chirikova, A. (2007). Interaction of Government and business in the implementation of social policy: Regional projection. *Independent Institute for Social Policy*, *152*, 90.

Choi, Y. J. (2012). Does Country Matter in Corporate Participation in CSR. *IPE Journal of Management*, *2*(2), 1–15.

Chrisman, J. J., & Archer, R. W. (1984). Small business social responsibility: Some perceptions and insights. *American Journal of Small Business*, *9*(2), 46–58. doi:10.1177/104225878400900206

Chua, A. (2003). *World on fire: How exporting free market democracy breeds ethnic hatred and global instability*. New York: Anchor.

Chune, Y. C., Sangjun, J., & Jason, Y. (2018). CSR Activities Increase Firm Value? Evidence from the Korean Market. *Sustainability*, *10*(9), 3164. doi:10.3390u10093164

CICERO. (2015). *Background Report on Long-term Climate Finance*. Prepared for the German G7 Presidency 2015. Available at: http://www.g7.utoronto.ca/summit/2015elmau/2015-G7-climate-finance.pdf

CISCO. (2015). *White Paper: Launching a Generation of Global Problem Solvers*. Retrieved May 28, 2019, from: https://www.cisco.com/c/dam/assets/csr/pdf/Global-Problem-Solver-whitepaper.pdf

Civil Code of the Russian Federation. (2017). Retrieved from http://www.consultant.ru/document/cons_doc_LAW_5142/

Clarkson, M. E. (1995). A stakeholder frameswork for analyzing and evaluating corporate social performance. *Academy of Management Review*, *20*(1), 92–117. doi:10.5465/amr.1995.9503271994

Climate Bonds Initiative. (2019). *Climate Bond Standard Board*. Available at: https://www.climatebonds.net/standard/governance/board

Cochran, P. L. (2007). The evolution of corporate social responsibility. *Business Horizons*, *50*(6), 449–454. doi:10.1016/j.bushor.2007.06.004

Cochran, P. L., & Wood, R. A. (1984). Corporate social responsibility and financial performance. *Academy of Management Journal*, *27*, 42–56.

Cognizant. (2015). *Elevating the Digital Employee Experience*. Retrieved May 19, 2019, from: https://www.cognizant.com/whitepapers/Elevating-the-Digital-Employee-Experience.pdf

Çoknaz, D., Sönmezoğlu, U., Eskicioğlu, Y., & Pehlivan, M. (2016). Corporate social responsibility and sports clubs: A case from Turkey. *International Journal of Sport Management, Recreation and Tourism*, *22*, 26–43. doi:10.5199/ijsmart-1791-874X-22b

Coles, T., Fenclova, E., & Dinan, C. (2013). Tourism and corporate social responsibility: A critical review and research agenda. *Tourism Management Perspectives*, *6*, 122–141. doi:10.1016/j.tmp.2013.02.001

Commission of the European Communities. (2002). *Corporate Social Responsibility: A business contribution to Sustainable Development*. Retrieved from https://ec.europa.eu/europeaid/sites/devco/files/communication-corporate-social-responsibility-sustainable-development-com2002347-20020702_en.pdf

Cooper, C., & Schlegelmilch, B. (1993). Key issues in ethical investment: Business ethics: A European approach. Prentice Hall, NJ: Hemel Hempstead.

Cosic, M. (2016, January 25). Unlimited annual leave: is it good HR or good PR? *The Guardian*. Retrieved May 9, 2019, from: https://www.theguardian.com/sustainable-business/2016/jan/25/unlimited-annual-leave-is-it-good-hr-or-good-pr

Council of Ministers Portal for public consultations (2009, November 25). *Corporate social responsibility strategy of the Republic of Bulgaria 2009-2013*. Retrieved from https://www.strategy.bg/StrategicDocuments/View.aspx?lang=bg-BG&Id=600

Crane, A., Matten, D., & Moon, D. (2004). Stakeholder as citizens? Rethinking rights, participation and democracy. *Journal of Business Ethics*, *53*(1/2), 107–122. doi:10.1023/B:BUSI.0000039403.96150.b6

Crifo, P., & Mottis, N. (2016). Socially responsible investment in France. *Business & Society*, *55*(4), 576–593. doi:10.1177/0007650313500216

Criscuolo, Ch., & Menon, C. (2015). Environmental policies and risk finance in the green sector: Cross-country evidence. *Energy Policy*, *83*, 38–56. Available at https://www.sciencedirect.com/science/article/pii/S0301421515001299

Crook, T. R., Todd, S. Y., Combs, J. G., Woehr, D. J., & Ketchen, D. J. (2011). Does human capital matter? A meta-analysis of the relationship between human capital and firm performance. *The Journal of Applied Psychology*, *96*(3), 443–456. doi:10.1037/a0022147 PMID:21244126

CSR advice box. (2018). *State of CSR in Bulgaria. Annual Review, 2018*. Retrieved from https://www.csrab.com/en/products/state-of-csr-in-bulgaria-2018.html

CSR Bulgaria. (2019). *Social responsibility*. Retrieved from https://csr.bg/social-responsibility?start=20

Cuesta de la, G. M. & Valor, C. (2007). Fostering corporate social responsibility through public initiative: From the EU to the Spanish case. *Journal of Business Ethics*, *55*(3), 275–293.

Curtis, S., & Bradly, A. P. (2012). Corporate Social Responsibility and Poverty Alleviation: A Conceptual Framework. Academy of Management Proceedings, 2012(1), 10406. doi:10.5465/AMBPP.2012.10406abstract

D'Amato, A., Henderson, S., & Florence, S. (2009). *CSR and Sustainable Business*. CCL Press.

Dafermos, Y., Nikolaidi, M., & Galanis, G. (2018). Climate Change, Financial Stability and Monetary Policy. *Ecological Economics*, *152*, 219–234. doi:10.1016/j.ecolecon.2018.05.011

DalmiaGroup. (2011-12). *CSR Report 2011-12*. Dalmia Group.

Dartey-Baah, K., & Amponsah-Tawiah, K. (2011). Exploring the limits of western corporate social responsibility theories in Africa. *International Journal of Business and Social Science*, *2*(18), 126–137.

Dartey-Baah, K., Amponsah-Tawiah, K., & Agbeibor, V. (2015). Corporate social responsibility in Ghana's national development. *Africa Today*, *62*(2), 71–92. doi:10.2979/africatoday.62.2.71

Darus, F., Mad, S., Nejati, M., & Yusoff, R. (2016). When quality matters! CSR disclosure and value creation. *International Journal of Economics and Management, 10*(2), 285–302.

Das, B. K., & Halder, P. P. (2011). CSR initiatives of Oil: A case study of ONGC. *Management Convergence, 2*(2), 75-85.

Davis, K. (1960). Can Business Afford to Ignore Social Responsibilities? *California Management Review, 2*(3), 70–76. doi:10.2307/41166246

Davis, K. (1973). The case for and against business assumption of social responsibilities. *Academy of Management Journal, 16*(2), 312–322.

Davis, K. (1973). The Case for and Against Business Assumption of Social Responsibilities. *Academy of Management Journal, 16*(2), 312–322. doi:10.2307/255331

Davis, K., & Blomstrom, R. (1966). *Business and its environment* (1st ed.). New York: McGraw-Hill Book Company.

Davis, K., & Blomstrom, R. (1975). *Business and society: Environment and responsibility* (3rd ed.). New York: McGraw-Hill Book Company.

De Silva, S., & Amerasinghe, F. (2004). *Corporate social responsibility: Issues, problems and challenges.* Colombo: Lake House.

Debrah, Y. A., & Ofori, G. (2006). Human resource development of professionals in an emerging economy: The case of the Tanzanian construction industry. *International Journal of Human Resource Management, 17*(3), 440–463. doi:10.1080/09585190500521425

Degryse, C. (2016). *Digitalisation of the economy and its impact on labour markets.* Working Paper 2016.02, European Trade Union Institute. Retrieved May 27, 2019, from:https://www.etui.org/Publications2/Working-Papers/Digitalisation-of-the-economy-and-its-impact-on-labour-markets

Del Rio, P., & Mir-Artigues, P. (2014). Combinations of support instruments for renewable electricity in Europe: A review. *Renewable & Sustainable Energy Reviews, 40*, 287–295. Available at https://www.researchgate.net/publication/264981902_Combinations_of_support_instruments_for_renewable_electricity_in_Europe_A_review

Dell'Acqua, A., Etro, L., Piva, M., & Teti, E. (2018). Investor protection and value creation in cross-border M&As by emerging economies. *Journal of International Financial Management & Accounting, 29*(1), 83–100. doi:10.1111/jifm.12069

Denzin, N. K., & Lincoln, Y. (2000). *Qualitative research* (2nd ed.). Sage.

Department for International Development. (2004a). Achieving the Millennium Development Goals: The Middle-Income Countries. London: Academic Press.

Department for International Development. (2004b). *Department for International Development: Departmental Report 2004.* Retrieved from https://publications.parliament.uk/pa/cm200304/cmselect/cmintdev/749/749.pdf

Detomasi, D. A. (2007). The political roots of corporate social responsibility. *Journal of Business Ethics, 82*(4), 807–819. doi:10.100710551-007-9594-y

Devnath, A., & Srivastava, M. (2013, April 25). 'Suddenly the Floor Wasn't There,' Factory Survivor Says. *Bloomberg Business.* Retrieved April 8, 2019, from: https://www.bloomberg.com/news/articles/2013-04-25/-suddenly-the-floor-wasn-t-there-factory-survivor-says

Dhaliwal, D. S., Li, O. Z., Tsang, A. H., & Yang, Y. G. (2011). Voluntary non-financial disclosure and the cost of equity capital: The initiation of corporate social responsibility reporting. *The Accounting Review, 86*(1), 59–100. doi:10.2308/accr.00000005

Dhaliwal, D., Zhen Li, O., Tsang, A., & Yang, Y. G. (2014). Corporate social responsibility disclosure and the cost of equity capital: The roles of stakeholder orientation and financial transparency. *Journal of Accounting and Public Policy*, *33*(4), 328–355. doi:10.1016/j.jaccpubpol.2014.04.006

Dicken, P. (2011). *Global shift: mapping the changing contours of world economy* (6th ed.). New York: The Guilford Press.

DiGabriele, M. (2019). Corporate Social Responsibility as a Tool for Poverty Reduction. In J. DiGabriele, J., Goyal, A., Joshi, M., Miguez, J., Neumann, & N., Ojo (Eds.), Corporate Social Responsibility (pp. 1463–1470). IGI Global. doi:10.4018/978-1-5225-6192-7.ch077

Dimitrov, M., Keremedchiev, S., Chipev, P., Bakardjieva, R., Daskalov, V., & Ivanova, N. (2014). *Corporate governance for XXI century: consolidation of standards for good corporate governance in Bulgaria*. Sofia: Academic Press.

Disilva, J. (2010). *CSR Case Studies:Coco-cola. Global Compact Network.*

Doane, D. (2005). The myth of CSR. *Stanford Social Innovation Review*, *3*(3), 22–29.

Donaldson, T., & Preston, L. (1995). The Stakeholder Theory of the Corporation: Concepts, Evidence and Implications. *Academy of Management Review*, *20*(1), 65–91. doi:10.5465/amr.1995.9503271992

Dordevic, S. (2008). The role of CSR in contemporary business. *Megatrend Review*, *5*(1).

Draksaite, A., Kazlauskiene, V., & Melnyk, L. (2018). The Perspective of the Green Bonds as Novel Debt Instruments in Sustainable Economy. *Consumer Behavior, Organizational Strategy and Financial Economics*, 221-230. Available at: https://www.springerprofessional.de/en/the-perspective-of-the-green-bonds-as-novel-debt-instruments-in-/15580842

Dumas, C., & Louche, C. (2016). Collective beliefs on responsible investment. *Business & Society*, *55*(3), 427–457. doi:10.1177/0007650315575327

Dupire, M., & M'Zali, B. (2018). CSR strategies in response to competitive pressures. *Journal of Business Ethics*, *148*(3), 603–623. doi:10.100710551-015-2981-x

Durand, R. B., Koh, S., & Limkriangkrai, M. (2013a). Saints versus Sinners. Does morality matter? *Journal of International Financial Markets, Institutions and Money*, *24*(4), 166–183. doi:10.1016/j.intfin.2012.12.002

Du, S., Bhattacharya, C. B., & Sen, S. (2007). Reaping relational rewards from corporate social responsibility: The role of competitive positioning. *International Journal of Research in Marketing*, *24*(3), 224–241. doi:10.1016/j.ijresmar.2007.01.001

Dzhindzholiia, O. (2011). Social responsibility of small business (Sotsial'naia otvetstvennost' malogo predprinimatel'stva). *News of Volgograd State Technical University*, *4*(11), 99–103.

EaP GREEN. (2015). *Greening Economies in the EU's Eastern Partnership Countries*. EaP GREEN.

EaP GREEN. (2015). *Promoting better environmental performance of SMEs*. EaP GREEN.

EaP GREEN. (2016). *Measuring the Green Transformation of the Economy: A Guide for EU Eastern Partnership Countries*. Paris: EaP GREEN.

EaP GREEN. (2017). *Greening Economies in the EU Eastern Neighbourhood. From Commitment to Results*. EaP GREEN.

Eichholtz, P., Kok, N., & Quigley, J. M. (2010). Doing well by doing good? Green office buildings. *The American Economic Review*, *100*(5), 2492–2509. doi:10.1257/aer.100.5.2492

El-Garaihy, W. H., Mobarak, A. K. M., & Albahussain, S. A. (2014). Measuring the impact of corporate social responsibility practices on competitive advantage: A mediation role of reputation and customer satisfaction. *International Journal of Business and Management*, *9*(5), 109–124. doi:10.5539/ijbm.v9n5p109

Elkington, J. (1994). Towards the sustainable corporation: Win-win-win business strategies for sustainable development. *California Management Review*, *36*(2), 90–100. doi:10.2307/41165746

Elkington, J. (1998). *Cannibals with forks: The triple bottom line of 21st century business.* New Society.

Ellerup Nielsen, A., & Thomsen, C. (2007). Reporting CSR–what and how to say it? *Corporate Communications*, *12*(1), 25–40. doi:10.1108/13563280710723732

Elliott, W. B., Jackson, K. E., Peecher, M. E., & White, B. J. (2014). The unintended effect of corporate social responsibility performance on investors' estimates of fundamental value. *The Accounting Review*, *89*(1), 275–302. doi:10.2308/accr-50577

Emmelhainz, M. A., & Adams, R. J. (1999). The apparel industry response to "sweatshop" concerns: A review and analysis of codes of conduct. *The Journal of Supply Chain Management*, *35*(2), 51–57. doi:10.1111/j.1745-493X.1999.tb00062.x

Engsig, H. (2011). *CSR communication – stakeholder information, response or involvement?* (Master thesis). Aarhus School of Business, Aarhus University.

Enock, O. N., & Basavaraji, D. K. (2013). CSR of TATA Company and ITC Company: A comparative study. *International Journal of Business and Management Tomorrow*, *3*(3).

Entine, J. (2003). The myth of social investing: A critique of its practice and consequences for corporate social performance research. *Organization & Environment*, *16*(3), 352–368. doi:10.1177/1086026603256283

Environment EuropeAid. (2009). Opportunities and options for promoting a green economy in the eastern partnership countries. *Beneficiaries 2009 – LOT 6: Environment EuropeAid.*

Epstein, M. J. (2018). *Making sustainability work: Best practices in managing and measuring corporate social, environmental and economic impacts*. Oxford, UK: Routledge. doi:10.4324/9781351280129

Eren-Erdoğmuş, İ., Çobanoğlu, E., & Öğüt, B. (2014). Success in philanthropic corporate social responsibility: The case of Turkey. In A. Yüksel Mermod & S. O. Idowu (Eds.), *Corporate social responsibility in the global business world* (pp. 271–286). Berlin: Springer. doi:10.1007/978-3-642-37620-7_16

ESPN. (2017). *Access to social protection for people working on non-standard contracts and as self-employed in Europe: A study of national policies*. Brussels: European Commission.

Esrock, S., & Leichty, G. (1998). Social responsibility and corporate web pages: Self-presentation or agenda-setting? *Public Relations Review*, *24*(3), 305–319. doi:10.1016/S0363-8111(99)80142-8

Ethical Consumer. (2015, May 29). *Boycott Amazon*. Retrieved May 14, 2019, from: https://www.ethicalconsumer.org/ethicalcampaigns/boycott-amazon

EUROFOUND. (2018). *Non-standard forms of employment: Recent trends and future prospects*. Dublin: Eurofound.

European Commission (2001): *Green Paper, Promoting a European framework for Corporate Social Responsibility*. COM(2001) 366/1.

European Commission. (2014). *Fact Sheet Data cPPP*. Retrieved June 22, 2019, from: https://ec.europa.eu/research/industrial_technologies/pdf/factsheet-cppp_en.pdf

European Commission. (2017a). *A concept paper on digitisation, employability and inclusiveness. The role of Europe, DG Communications Networks, Content &Technology (CONNECT).* The Publications Office of the European Union.

European Commission. (2017b). *Enter the Data Economy. EU Policies for a Thriving Data Ecosystem. EPSC Strategic Notes 21.* European Political Strategy Centre.

European Union. External Action. (2014) *Armenia Development Strategy for 2014-2025.* Annex To RA Government Decree # 442 - N on 27th of March, 2014. European Union. External Action.

EUROSIF. (2019). *SDGs for SRI Investors.* Retrieved from: http://www.eurosif.org/wp-content/uploads/2018/01/Eurosif-SDGs-brochure.pdf

Evan, W., & Freeman, R. (1988). A stakeholder theory of the modern corporation: Kantian capitalism. In T. Beauchamp & N. Bowie (Eds.), *Ethical theory and business* (pp. 75–93). Englewood Cliffs, NJ: Prentice Hall.

Eyraud, L., Clement, B., & Wane, A. (2013). Green investment: Trends and determinants. *Energy Policy*, *60*, 852–865. Available at https://econpapers.repec.org/article/eeeenepol/v_3a60_3ay_3a2013_3ai_3ac_3ap_3a852-865.htm

Fabozzi, F. J., Ma, K. C., & Oliphant, B. J. (2008). Sin stock returns. *Journal of Portfolio Management*, *35*(1), 82–94. doi:10.3905/JPM.2008.35.1.82

Fang, Y. (2011). Economic Welfare Impacts from Renewable Energy Consumption: The China Experience. *Renewable & Sustainable Energy Reviews*, *15*(9), 5120–5128. doi:10.1016/j.rser.2011.07.044

Federal Law of Russian Federation #209-FZ of July 24th, 2007. (n.d.). *About the Development of small and medium entrepreneurship in the Russian Federation.* ConsultantPlus. Retrieved from http://www.consultant.ru/cons/cgi/online.cgi?from=329368-0&rnd=B886EF15343A8F61310B2D8B220AD267&req=doc&base=LAW&n=330792&REFDOC=329368&REFBASE=LAW#1xnmj9vjs0q

Federal Tax Service. (2019). *The unified register of subjects of small and medium business.* ConsultantPlus. Retrieved from http://www.consultant.ru/document/cons_doc_LAW_34447/

Fider, E. A. (2012, Feb 28). Corporate Social Responsibility, Competitive Advantage and Profitability: A Study of Telecommunications Provider in an Emerging Economy. *Corporate Social Responsibility, Competitive Advantage and Profitability.* ProQuest.

Fijałkowska, J., & Macuda, M. (2017). Value Creation Disclosure in CSR Reports – Evidence from Poland. *Zeszyty Teoretyczne Rachunkowości*, *93*(149), 61–78. doi:10.5604/01.3001.0010.3189

Fijałkowska, J., Zyznarska-Dworczak, B., & Garsztka, P. (2018). Corporate Social-Environmental Performance versus Financial Performance of Banks in Central and Eastern European Countries. *Sustainability*, *10*(3), 772. doi:10.3390u10030772

Financing Climate Futures, Rethinking Infrastructure. (2018). *Policy Highlights.* Available at: https://www.oecd.org/environment/cc/climate-futures/policy-highlights-financing-climate-futures.pdf

Fitch, H. G. (1976). Achieving Corporate Social Responsibility. *Academy of Management Review*, *1*(1), 38–46. doi:10.5465/amr.1976.4408754

Fitzgerald, N., & Cormack, M. (2007). *The role of business in society: An agenda for action.* Retrieved from the internet at Frankel, T. (1984). Decision making for social investing. In D. M. McGill (Ed.), *Social Investing* (pp. 131–162). Homewood, IL: Irwin.

Font, X., Garay, L., & Jones, S. (2014). Sustainability motivations and practices in small tourism enterprises in European protected areas. *Journal of Cleaner Production*, *137*, 1439–1448. doi:10.1016/j.jclepro.2014.01.071

Forcella, D., & Hudon, M. (2016). Green microfinance in Europe. *Journal of Business Ethics, 135*, 445–459. doi:10.100710551-014-2452-9

Ford, M. (2015). *Rise of the robots: technology and the threat of a jobless future*. New York: Basic Books.

Fox, T. (2005). *Small and medium-sized enterprises (SMEs) and corporate social responsibility: a discussion paper. International Institute for Environment and Development*. London: IIED.

Frederick, W. C. (2006). *Corporation, Be Good! The story of Corporate Social Responsibility*. Indianapolis, IN: Dog Ear Publishing.

Freeman, R. E. (1984). *Strategic Management. A Stakeholder Approach*. Boston: Pitman.

Freeman, R. E. (1984). *Strategic management: a stakeholder approach*. Marshfield: Pitman Publishing.

Freeman, R. E. (1994). The politics of stakeholder theory: Some future directions. *Business Ethics Quarterly, 4*(4), 409–421. doi:10.2307/3857340

Freeman, R., Wicks, A., & Parmar, B. (2004). Stakeholder Theory and "The Corporate Objective Revisited". *Organization Science, 15*(3), 364–369. doi:10.1287/orsc.1040.0066

Freireich, J., & Fulton, K. (2009). Investing for social and environmental impact: A design for catalyzing an emerging industry. Monitor Institute.

Friedman, M. (1970). A Friedman doctrine: The social responsibility of business is to increase its profits. *The New York Times Magazine, 13*(1970), 32-33.

Friedman, M. (1970). The Social Responsibility of Business is to Increase its Profits. *The New York Times Magazine, 13*(9), 6. Retrieved from http://umich.edu/~thecore/doc/Friedman.pdf

Friedman, M. (1970, September 13), The Social Responsibility of Business is to Increase its Profits. *The New York Times Magazine*. Retrieved April 21, 2019, from: http://umich.edu/~thecore/doc/Friedman.pdf

Friedman, A. L., & Miles, S. (2001). Socially responsible investment and corporate social and environmental reporting in the UK: An exploratory study. *The British Accounting Review, 33*(4), 523–548. doi:10.1006/bare.2001.0172

Friedman, M. (2007). The social responsibility of business is to increase its profits. In *Corporate ethics and corporate governance* (pp. 173–178). Berlin, Germany: Springer. doi:10.1007/978-3-540-70818-6_14

Frisari, G., Hervé-Mignucci, M., Mazza, F., & Micale, V. (2013). *Risk Gaps: A Map of Risk Mitigation Instruments for Clean Investments*. Available at: http://climatepolicyinitiative.org/wp-content/uploads/2013/01/Risk-Gaps-A-Map-of-Risk-Mitigation-Instruments-for-Clean-Investments.pdf

Frynas, J. (2000). *Oil in Nigeria: Conflict and Litigation between Oil Companies and Village Communities* (1st ed.). Hamburg, Germany: LIT Verlag Münster.

Fullerton, J. (2018, January 7). Suicide at Chinese iPhone factory reignites concern over working conditions, *The Telegraph*. Retrieved April 9, 2019, from: https://www.telegraph.co.uk/news/2018/01/07/suicide-chinese-iphone-factory-reignites-concern-working-conditions/

Futurescape. (2018). *India's top companies for sustainability and CSR, 2018*. Author.

G20 Sustainable Finance Synthesis Report. (2018). Available at: http://unepinquiry.org/wp-content/uploads/2018/11/G20_Sustainable_Finance_Synthesis_Report_2018.pdf

Galbreath, J. (2011). Sustainable development in business: a strategic view. In Theory and Practice of Corporate Social Responsibility (pp. 89–105). London: Springer-Verlag Berlin Heidelberg. doi:10.1007/978-3-642-16461-3_6

Ganuza, J.-J. (2012). *Corporate Social Responsibility and Social Welfare. How to Promote Socially Responsible Business Strategies*. Barcelona: Centre de Recerca en Economia Internacional. Retrieved May 14, 2019, from: http://www.crei.cat/wp-content/uploads/opuscles/120321092822_ENG_30_ANG.pdf

García de Leaniz, P. M., & Gómez-López, R. (2019). Responsible Management in the CSR 2.0 Era. In Corporate Social Responsibility (pp. 231–248). IGI Global. doi:10.4018/978-1-5225-6192-7.ch013

Garriga, E., & Melé, D. (2004). Corporate Social Responsibility Theories: Mapping the Territory. *Journal of Business Ethics*, *53*(1/2), 51–71. doi:10.1023/B:BUSI.0000039399.90587.34

Gautam, R., & Anju, S. (2010). CSR Practices in India: A Study of top 500 companies. *International Journal of Global Business and Management Research.*

Ge, L., & Thomas, S. (2007). A Cross-Cultural Comparison of the Deliberative Reasoning of Canadian and Chinese Accounting Students. *Journal of Business Ethics*, *82*(1), 189–211. doi:10.100710551-007-9571-5

Ghosh, A., & Chakraborti, C. (2010). CSR: A developmental tool for India. *IUP Journal of Corporate Governance*, *IX*(4), 40–56.

Ghoul, W., & Karam, P. (2007). MRI and SRI Mutual Funds. *Journal of Investing*, *16*(2), 96–102. doi:10.3905/joi.2007.686416

Giamporcaro, S., & Gond, J. P. (2016). Calculability as politics in the construction of markets: The case of socially responsible investment in France. *Organization Studies*, *37*(4), 465–495. doi:10.1177/0170840615604498

Gillan, S. L., & Starks, L. T. (2000). Corporate governance proposals and shareholder activism: The role of institutional investors. *Journal of Financial Economics*, *57*(2), 275–305. doi:10.1016/S0304-405X(00)00058-1

Gino, F., & Margolis, J. (2011). Bringing ethics into focus: How regulatory focus and risk preferences influence (un)ethical behavior. *Organizational Behavior and Human Decision Processes*, *115*(2), 145–156. doi:10.1016/j.obhdp.2011.01.006

Gino, F., Schweitzer, M., Mead, N., & Ariely, D. (2011). Unable to resist temptation: How self-control depletion promotes unethical behavior. *Organizational Behavior and Human Decision Processes*, *115*(2), 191–203. doi:10.1016/j.obhdp.2011.03.001

Girod, S., & Michaell, B. (2003). Branding in European retailing: A corporate social responsibility perspective. *European Retail Digest*, 1-6.

Global Footprint Network. (2019). *Do we fit on the planet?* Retrieved from: http://www.footprintnetwork.org/en/index.php/GFN/page/world_footprint/

Göbbels, M. (2002). Reframing Corporate Social Responsibility: The contemporary conception of a fuzzy notion. Journal of Business Ethics, 44, 95-105.

Golob, U., Turkel, S., Kronegger, L., & Uzunoglu, E. (2018). Uncovering CSR meaning networks: A cross-national comparison of Turkey and Slovenia. *Public Relations Review*, *44*(4), 433–443. doi:10.1016/j.pubrev.2018.05.003

González Ruiza, J. D., Arboledab, C. A., & Boteroc, S. (2016). A Proposal for Green Financing as a Mechanism to Increase Private Participation in Sustainable Water Infrastructure Systems: The Colombian Case. *Procedia Engineering*, *145*, 180–187. Available at https://www.sciencedirect.com/science/article/pii/S1877705816300637

Gramser, S. (2016). *Developing CSR and CSR communication: Brazilian and Dutch consumers' attitude towards CSR (communication) through different communication channels*. Radboud University.

Granger, C. (1969). Investigating Causal Relations by Econometric Models and Cross-spectral Methods. *Econometrica*, *37*(3), 424–438. doi:10.2307/1912791

Greater Kansas City Community Foundation. (2010). *Pyramid of Corporate Social Responsibility*. Retrieved from https://www.growyourgiving.org/giving-blog/pyramid-corporate-social-responsibility

Green Bond Principles. (2018). *International Capital Market Association*. Available at: https://www.icmagroup.org/green-social-and-sustainability-bonds/green-bond-principles-gbp/

Green Equity Indexes. (2019). Available at: https://business.nasdaq.com/intel/indexes/equity/green

Green Investment Banks. (2017). *OECD environment policy paper no. 6*. Available at: https://www.oecd-ilibrary.org/environment/green-investment-banks_e3c2526c-en;jsessionid=uGwV0MLx56ijonfdL-1fEvFj.ip-10-240-5-102

Greenspan, A. (2007). *The age of turbulence: Adventures in a new world*. New York, NY: Penguin.

GRI. (2019). *Linking GRI standards and the EU directive on non-financial and diversity disclosure*. Retrieved from: https://www.globalreporting.org/standards/resource-download-center/linking-gri-standards-and-european-directive-on-non-financial-and-diversity disclosure/

Griffin, J. J., & Mahon, J. F. (1997). The Corporate Social Performance and Corporate Financial Performance Debate: Twenty-Five Years of Incomparable Research. *Business & Society*, *36*(1), 5–31. doi:10.1177/000765039703600102

Grigore, G., Molesworth, M., & Watkins, R. D. (2017). Responsibility in the Digital Economy. In *Corporate Social Responsibility Post-Financial Crisis* (pp. 41-62). London: Palgrave MacMillan. Retrieved April 5, 2019, from: http://link.springer.com/chapter/10.1007%2F978-3-319-40096-9_3

GTZ. (2011). *Fast growth and big impacts: How Emerging Market Multinationals are advancing sustainable development*. Retrieved from www.giz.de

Guay, T., Doh, J. P., & Sinclair, G. (2004). Non-governmental organizations, shareholder activism, and socially responsible investments: Ethical, strategic, and governance implications. *Journal of Business Ethics*, *52*(1), 125–139. doi:10.1023/B:BUSI.0000033112.11461.69

Guo, L., Hsu, S.-H., Holton, A., & Jeong, S. H. (2012). A case study of the Foxconn suicides: An international perspective to framing the sweatshop issue. *The International Communication Gazette*, *74*(5), 484–503. doi:10.1177/1748048512445155

Gupta, D. (2005). Corporate Responsibility. In C. V. Baxi & A. Prasad (Eds.), *Corporate Social Responsibility: Concepts and Cases* (pp. 21–27). New Delhi: Excel Books.

Guthrie, J. E., Cuganesan, S., & Ward, L. (2008). Disclosure media for social and environmental matters within the Australian food and beverage industry. *Social and Environmental Accountability Journal*, *28*(1), 33–44. doi:10.1080/0969160X.2008.9651789

Hack, L., Kenyon, A. J., & Wood, E. (2014). A critical Corporate Social Responsibility (CSR) timeline: How should it be understood now? *International Journal of Management Cases*, *16*(4), 46–55. Retrieved from http://connection.ebscohost.com/c/articles/97489531/critical-corporate-social-responsibility-csr-timeline-how-should-be-understood-now

Hamann, R. (2006). Can business make decisive contributions to development? Towards a research agenda on corporate citizenship and beyond. *Development Southern Africa*, *23*(2), 175–195. doi:10.1080/03768350600707587

Hamidu, A. A., Haron, M., & Amran, A. (2016). Exploring the Drivers and Nature of Corporate Social Responsibility Practice from an African Perspective. *International Review of Management and Marketing*, *6*(4), 696–703.

Hammann, E. M., Habisch, A., & Pechlaner, H. (2009). Values that create value: Socially responsible business practices in SMEs–empirical evidence from German companies. *Business Ethics (Oxford, England)*, *18*(1), 37–51. doi:10.1111/j.1467-8608.2009.01547.x

Haniffa, R. M., & Cooke, T. E. (2005). The impact of culture and governance on corporate social reporting. *Journal of Accounting and Public Policy*, *24*(5), 391–430. doi:10.1016/j.jaccpubpol.2005.06.001

Hannam, P. (2008). *The Challenges Facing Green Job Growth*. Retrieved October 23, 2019, from https://www.greenbiz.com/news/2008/09/21/challenges-facing-green-job-growth

Hanzaee, K. H., & Sadeghian, M. (2014). The impact of corporate social responsibility on customer satisfaction and corporate reputation in automotive industry: Evidence from Iran. *Journal of Islamic Marketing*, *5*(1), 125–143. doi:10.1108/JIMA-05-2013-0033

Harris, F., & de Chernatony, L. (2001). Corporate branding and corporate brand performance. *European Journal of Marketing*, *35*(3/4), 441–456. doi:10.1108/03090560110382101

Harrison, J. S., & Freeman, R. E. (1999). Stakeholders, social responsibility, and performance: Empirical evidence and theoretical perspectives. *Academy of Management Journal*, *42*(5), 479–485.

Hart, S. L. (1997). Beyond Greening: Strategies for a Sustainable World. *Harvard Business Review*, (January–February): 67–76.

Hart, S. L., & Milstein, M. B. (2003). Creating sustainable value. *The Academy of Management Executive*, *17*(2), 56–69.

Hassel, L., Nilsson, H., & Nyquist, S. (2005). The value relevance of environmental performance. *European Accounting Review*, *14*(1), 41–61. doi:10.1080/0963818042000279722

Heald, M. (1961). Business thought in the twenties: Social responsibility. *American Quarterly*, *13*(2), 126–139. doi:10.2307/2710548

Heckerta, M., & Rosan, Ch. D. (2016). Developing a green infrastructure equity index to promote equity planning. *Urban Forestry & Urban Greening*, *19*, 263–270. Available at https://www.sciencedirect.com/science/article/pii/S1618866715001892

Hellsten, S., & Mallin, C. (2006). Are 'ethical'or 'socially responsible'investments socially responsible? *Journal of Business Ethics*, *66*(4), 393–406. doi:10.100710551-006-0001-x

Henderson, D. (2001). *Misguided Virtue: False Notions of Corporate Social Responsibility* (1st ed.). Oxford, UK: New Zealand Business Roundtable. Retrieved from http://www.iea.org.uk/sites/default/files/publications/files/upldbook126pdf.pdf

Hernandez, R., Murillo, & Martinck, C. J. (2009). CSR can be profitable. *The Regional Economist.*

Herzberg, F., Mausner, B., & Snyderman, B. (1959). *The Motivation to Work* (2nd ed.). John Wiley and Sons.

Hohnen, P. (2007). *CSR – An implementation Guide for Business*. Retrived from http://www.iisd.org/pdf/2007/csr_guide.pdf

Holbrook, E. (2019). *A Financial First: Green Bond Issuance Surpasses $100 Billion Mark in First Half of 2019.* Available at: https://www.environmentalleader.com/2019/06/a-financial-first-green-bond-issuance-surpasses-100-billion-mark-in-first-half-of-2019/

Homburg, C., Stierl, M., & Bornemann, T. (2013). Corporate social responsibility in business-to-business markets: How organizational customers account for supplier corporate social responsibility engagement. *Journal of Marketing, 77*(6), 54–72. doi:10.1509/jm.12.0089

Hong, H., & Kacperczyk, M. (2009). The price of sin: The effects of social norms on markets. *Journal of Financial Economics, 93*(1), 15–36. doi:10.1016/j.jfineco.2008.09.001

Hooghiemstra, R. (2000). Corporate communication and impression management: NEW perspectives why companies engage in corporate social reporting. *Journal of Business Ethics, 27*(1/2), 55–68. doi:10.1023/A:1006400707757

Hopkins, T. (2015, April 23). Reliving the Rana Plaza factory collapse: a history of cities in 50 buildings, day 22. *The Guardian*. Retrieved April 8, 2019, from: https://www.theguardian.com/cities/2015/apr/23/rana-plaza-factory-collapse-history-cities-50-buildings

Hopkins, M. (2016). *Corporate social responsibility (CSR) and the United Nations sustainable development goals (SDG): The role of the private sector*. CSR Finance Institute.

Hopkins, M. (2017). CSR and international development. In *CSR and Sustainability* (pp. 88–108). Routledge. doi:10.4324/9781351284646-3

Horberg, E. J., Oveis, C., & Keltner, D. (2011). Emotions as moral amplifiers: An appraisal tendency approach to the influences of distinct emotions upon moral judgment. *Emotion Review, 3*(3), 237–244. doi:10.1177/1754073911402384

Hsieh, H. F., & Shannon, S. E. (2005). Three approaches to qualitative content analysis. *Qualitative Health Research, 15*(9), 1277–1288. doi:10.1177/1049732305276687 PMID:16204405

Hsu, K. T. (2012). The advertising effects of corporate social responsibility on corporate reputation and brand equity: Evidence from the life insurance industry in Taiwan. *Journal of Business Ethics, 109*(2), 189–201. doi:10.100710551-011-1118-0

Huang, C. F., & Lien, H. C. (2012). An empirical analysis of the influences of corporate social responsibility on organizational performance of Taiwan's construction industry: Using corporate image as a mediator. *Construction Management and Economics, 30*(4), 263–275. doi:10.1080/01446193.2012.668620

Humphrey, J. E., & Tan, D. T. (2014). Does it really hurt to be responsible? *Journal of Business Ethics, 122*(3), 375–386. doi:10.100710551-013-1741-z

Humphrey, J. E., Warren, G. J., & Boon, J. (2016). What is different about socially responsible funds? A holdings-based analysis. *Journal of Business Ethics, 138*(2), 263–277. doi:10.100710551-015-2583-7

Husted, B. W., & Allen, D. B. (2001, August). Toward a model of corporate social strategy formulation. *Proceedings of the Social Issues in Management Division at Academy of Management Conference*, 1-35.

Husted, B. W., & de Jesus Salazar, J. (2006). Taking Friedman seriously: Maximizing profits and social performance. *Journal of Management Studies, 43*(1), 75–91. doi:10.1111/j.1467-6486.2006.00583.x

Huws, U. (2014). *Labor in the Digital Economy: The Cybertariat Comes of Age*. NYU Press.

Iadov, V. A. (2003). *Strategy of sociological research*. Moscow: Akademkniga, Dobrosvet.

ICC. (2011). *10 Conditions for a Transition toward a Green Economy*. ICC.

Idowu, S. O. (2012). Corporate social responsibility: A capitalist ideology? *International Journal of Social Entrepreneurship and Innovation, 1*(3), 239–254. doi:10.1504/IJSEI.2012.047628

IFAD. (2018). *Investing in Rural People. Republic of Armenia Country Strategic Opportunities Programme 2018-2024.* IFAD.

IFC. (2010). *Energy Efficiency: A New Resource for Sustainable Growth (Researching energy efficiency practices in Armenia, Azerbaijan, Belarus, Georgia, Russia and Ukraine).* IFC.

ILO. (2017). *Tripartite Declaration of Principles concerning Multinational Enterprises and Social Policy.* Retrieved from https://www.ilo.org/wcmsp5/groups/public/---ed_emp/---emp_ent/---multi/documents/publication/wcms_094386.pdf

Inderst, G., Kaminker, Ch., & Stewart, F. (2012). *Defining and Measuring Green Investments: Implications for Institutional Investors" Asset Allocations.* OECD Working Papers on Finance, Insurance and Private Pensions, 24. OECD Publishing. Available at: https://econpapers.repec.org/paper/oecdafaad/24-en.htm

International Chamber of Commerce. (2012). *Green Economy Roadmap – a Guide for Business, Policymakers and Society.* Retrieved October 23, 2019, from https://iccwbo.org/content/uploads/sites/3/2012/08/Green-Economy-Roadmap-a-guide-for-business_-policy-makers-and-society.pdf

Ioannou, I., & Serafeim, G. (2012). What drives corporate social performance? The role of nation-level institutions. *Journal of International Business Studies, 43*(9), 834–864. doi:10.1057/jibs.2012.26

Irani, L. (2015). *Justice for 'data janitors', Public Books, 15 January 2015.* Retrieved April 28, 2019, from: http://www.publicbooks.org/nonfiction/justice-for-data-janitors

Isaksson, L., Kiessling, T., & Harvey, M. (2014). Corporate social responsibility: Why bother? *Organizational Dynamics, 43*(1), 64–72. doi:10.1016/j.orgdyn.2013.10.008

Ito, K. (2017). CO_2 Emissions, Renewable and Non-renewable Energy Consumption, and Economic Growth: Evidence from Panel Data for Developing Countries. *International Economics, 151*, 1-6. Retrieved October 23, 2019, from: https://ideas.repec.org/a/eee/inteco/v151y2017icp1-6.html

Ivashina, M. M. (2016). Peculiarities of realization of corporate social activity in small and medium business of Russia. *Journal of Saratov State Social and Economic University, 4*(63), 32–34.

Iyigün, N. O. (2013). A research on the corporate social responsibility perception: An evidence from Turkey. *International Journal of Business and Social Science, 4*(12).

Jackson, E. T. (2013). Interrogating the theory of change: Evaluating impact investing where it matters most. *Journal of Sustainable Finance and Investment, 3*(2), 95–110. doi:10.1080/20430795.2013.776257

Jackson, J. (2009). How risky are sustainable real estate projects? An evaluation of LEED and ENERGY STAR development options. *Journal of Sustainable Real Estate, 1*(1), 91–106.

Jamali, D. (2008). A stakeholder approach to corporate social responsibility: A fresh perspective into theory and practice. *Journal of Business Ethics, 82*(1), 213–231. doi:10.100710551-007-9572-4

Jamali, D., & Karam, C. (2016). Corporate social responsibility in developing countries as an emerging field of study. *International Journal of Management Reviews.*

Jamali, D., Karam, C., Yin, J., & Soundararajan, V. (2017). CSR logics in developing countries: Translation, adaptation and stalled development. *Journal of World Business, 52*(3), 343–359. doi:10.1016/j.jwb.2017.02.001

Jamali, D., Lund-Thomsen, P., & Jeppesen, S. (2017). SMEs and CSR in developing countries. *Business & Society, 56*(1), 11–22. doi:10.1177/0007650315571258

Jamali, D., & Mirshak, R. (2007). Corporate social responsibility (CSR): Theory and practice in a developing country context. *Journal of Business Ethics*, *72*(3), 243–262. doi:10.100710551-006-9168-4

Jamali, D., & Neville, B. (2011). Convergence versus divergence of CSR in developing countries: An embedded multi-layered institutional lens. *Journal of Business Ethics*, *102*(4), 599–621. doi:10.100710551-011-0830-0

Jaya Kumar, T. (2013, October-December). MNC CSR in Emerging Economic conflect zones - A Case study of HULs North East Operations in India. *Vikalpa*, *38*(4), 69–82. doi:10.1177/0256090920130405

Jayaswa, R., & Singhl, S. C. (2013). *ONGC, NTPC among energy companies thinking out of the box on CSR*. New Delhi, India: Economic Times.

Jayne, M. R., & Skerratt, G. (2003). Socially responsible investment in the UK? Criteria that are used to evaluate suitability. *Corporate Social Responsibility and Environmental Management*, *10*(1), 1–11. doi:10.1002/csr.25

Jebli, M. B., & Youssef, S. B. (2015). Output, Renewable and Non-renewable Energy Consumption and International Trade: Evidence from a Panel of 69 Countries. *Renewable Energy*, *83*, 799–808. doi:10.1016/j.renene.2015.04.061

Jenkins, H. (2004). A critique of conventional CSR theory: An SME perspective. *Journal of General Management*, *29*(4), 37–57. doi:10.1177/030630700402900403

Jenkins, R. (2005). Globalization, Corporate Social Responsibility and poverty. *International Affairs*, *81*(3), 525–540. doi:10.1111/j.1468-2346.2005.00467.x

Jensen, M. C. (2002). Value maximization, stakeholder theory, and the corporate objective function. *Business Ethics Quarterly*, *12*(2), 235–256. doi:10.2307/3857812

Jeong, H. J., Paek, H.-J., & Lee, M. (2013). Corporate social responsibility effects on social network sites. *Journal of Business Research*, *66*(10), 1889–1895. doi:10.1016/j.jbusres.2013.02.010

Jones, G. (1991). *Organizational Theory Design & Change*. Pearson Prentice Hall.

Jones, I., & Pollitt, M. (1998). *The role of business ethics in economic performance*. London: Macmillan. doi:10.1057/9780230379794

Jones, T. M. (1995). Instrumental stakeholder theory: A synthesis of ethics and economics. *Academy of Management Review*, *20*(2), 404–437. doi:10.5465/amr.1995.9507312924

Jonikas, D. (2013). Conceptual framework of value creation through CSR in separate member of value creation chain. In D. Szymańska & J. Chodkowska-Miszczuk (Eds.), Bulletin of Geography. Socio-economic Series No. 21 (pp. 69–78). Toruń: Nicolaus Copernicus University Press. doi:10.2478/bog-2013-0022

Juscius, V., & Jonikas, D. (2013). Integration of CSR into Value Creation Chain: Conceptual Framework. *Inzinerine Ekonomika-Engineering Economics*, *24*(1), 63–70.

Kahia, M., Aïssa, M. S. B., & Charfeddine, L. (2016). Impact of renewable and non-renewable energy consumption on economic growth: New evidence from the MENA Net Oil Exporting Countries (NOECs). *Energy*, *116*, 102–115. doi:10.1016/j.energy.2016.07.126

Kalnitskaya, P., Gentile, M., & Rohen, D. (2012). Peculiarities of realization of corporate social activity in small and medium business of Russia. *International Business Leaders Forum*.

Kanji, R., & Agrawal, R. (2016). Models of corporate social responsibility: Comparison, evolution and convergence. *IIM Kozhikode Society & Management Review*, *5*(2), 141–155. doi:10.1177/2277975216634478

Kanungo, R. N., & Mendonca, M. (2001). Ethical leadership and governance in organizations: A preamble. *Canadian Journal of Administrative Sciences*, *18*(4), 241–243. doi:10.1111/j.1936-4490.2001.tb00259.x

Karasioğlu, F., & Arıcı, N. D. (2012). The relationship between corporate social responsibility and corporate financial performance: Evidence from Turkey. *Economic and Environmental Studies*, *12*(4), 443–457.

Karoley Behringer, K. S. (2016). The Role of Corporate Social Responsibility in Achieving Sustainable Development-Theoritical Approach. *European Scientific Journal*, *12*(22), 10–25. doi:10.19044/esj.2016.v12n22p10

Kar, S. K., Padhi, S. K., & Samantarai, M. (2016). Disruptive innovation and economic value creation: A service sector perspective. *Indian Journal of Management*, *9*(8), 11–25.

Kasturi Ranjan, L. C. (2015). The Truth About CSR. *Harvard Business Review*, *93*(1), 40–49.

Kelley, K. J., Hemphill, T. A., & Thams, Y. (2018). Corporate social responsibility, country reputation and corporate reputation: A perspective on the creation of shared value in emerging markets. *Multinational Business Review*.

Kemper, J., Schilke, O., Reimann, M., Wang, X., & Brettel, M. (2013). Competition-motivated corporate social responsibility. *Journal of Business Research*, *66*(10), 1954–1963. doi:10.1016/j.jbusres.2013.02.018

Kempf, A., & Osthoff, P. (2007). The effect of socially responsible investing on portfolio performance. *European Financial Management*, *13*(5), 908–922. doi:10.1111/j.1468-036X.2007.00402.x

Kervyn, N., Fiske, S. T., & Malone, C. (2012). Brands as intentional agents framework: How perceived intentions and ability can map brand perception. *Journal of Consumer Psychology: The Official Journal of the Society for Consumer Psychology*, *22*(2), 166–176. doi:10.1016/j.jcps.2011.09.006 PMID:24403815

Kettl, D. F. (2006). *The global public management revolution*. Washington, DC: The Brookings Institution.

Khan, K. (2012, November 25). Garment factory blaze kills 109 in Bangladesh. *JakartaGlobe*. Retrieved August 28, 2019, from: https://www.webcitation.org/6CRR29lSi?url=http://www.thejakartaglobe.com/afp/garment-factory-blaze-kills-109-in-bangladesh/558153

Khanna, T., & Palepu, K. (1997). Why focused strategies may be wrong for emerging markets. *Harvard Business Review*, *75*(4), 41–51.

Kılıç, M. (2016). Online corporate social responsibility (CSR) disclosure in the banking industry: Evidence from Turkey. *International Journal of Bank Marketing*, *34*(4), 550–569. doi:10.1108/IJBM-04-2015-0060

Kirca, A. H., & Yaprak, A. (2010). The use of meta-analysis in international business research: Its current status and suggestions for better practice. *International Business Review*, *19*(3), 306–314. doi:10.1016/j.ibusrev.2010.01.001

Kitzmueller, M., & Shimshack, J. (2012). Economic perspectives on corporate social responsibility. *Journal of Economic Literature*, *50*(1), 51–84. doi:10.1257/jel.50.1.51

Knaut, A. (2017). How CSR Should Understand Digitalization. In T. Osburg & C. Lohrmann (Eds.), *Sustainability in a Digital World. New Opportunities Through New Technologies* (pp. 249–256). Springer International Publishing AG. doi:10.1007/978-3-319-54603-2_21

Kolk, A., & van Tulder, R. (2006). Poverty alleviation as business strategy? Evaluating commitments of frontrunner Multinational Corporations. *World Development*, *34*(5), 789–801. doi:10.1016/j.worlddev.2005.10.005

Korschun, D., & Du, S. (2013). How virtual corporate social responsibility dialogs generate value: A framework and propositions. *Journal of Business Research*, *66*(9), 1494–1504. doi:10.1016/j.jbusres.2012.09.011

Kotler, P. K., Keller, K. L., & Jha, A. M. (2013). *Marketing Management A South Asian Perspective. Creating Brand Equity* (14th ed.). Pearson.

Kotler, P., & Lee, N. (2005). Best of breed: When it comes to gaining a market edge while supporting a social cause, "corporate social marketing" leads the pack. *Social Marketing Quarterly*, *11*(3-4), 91–103. doi:10.1080/15245000500414480

Kotler, Ph., & Lee, N. (2005). *Corporate social responsibility: doing the most good for your company and your cause.* Hoboken, NJ: John Wiley & Sons, Inc.

KPMG. (2018). *India's CSR reporting survey 2018*. Retrieved from https://assets.kpmg/content/dam/kpmg/in/pdf/2019/01/India_CSR_Reporting_Survey_2018.pdf

Kraus, P., & Brtitzelmaier, B. (2012). A literature review on corporate social responsibility: Definitions, theories and recent empirical research. *International Journal of Management Cases*, *14*(4), 273–287. doi:10.5848/APBJ.2012.00105

Krejcie, R. V., & Morgan, D. W. (1970). Determining sample size for research activities. *Educational and Psychological Measurement*, *30*(3), 607–610. doi:10.1177/001316447003000308

Kristin Hah, S. F. (2014). Multinational Enterprise Subsideries and their CSR: A Conceptual Frame Work of the Management of CSR in Smaller Emerginig Economies. *Journal of Business Ethics*, *121*, 125–136.

Krumsiek, B. J. (1997). The emergence of a new era in mutual fund investing: Socially responsible investing comes of age. *Journal of Investing*, *6*(4), 25–30. doi:10.3905/joi.1997.408438

Lacy, P., Cooper, T., Hayward, R., & Neuberger, L. (2010). *A new era of sustainability: UN Global Compact-Accenture CEO Study 2010.* Retrieved from https://scholar.google.com/scholar_lookup?title=ANewEraofSustainability–UNGlobalCompact-AccentureCEOStudy2010&author=P.Lacy&publication_year=2010

Lahrich, I. (2018). *Human Rights: Yesterday and today*. Retrieved from https://www.academia.edu/19694864/Human_Rights_General_overview

Lai, C. S., Chiu, C. J., Yang, C. F., & Pai, D. C. (2010). The Effects of Corporate Social Responsibility on Brand Performance: The Mediating Effect of Industrial Brand Equity and Corporate Reputation. *Journal of Business Ethics*, *95*(3), 457–469. doi:10.100710551-010-0433-1

Lam, K. C., Shi, G., & Shi, G. (2008). Factors Affecting Ethical Attitudes in Mainland China and Hong Kong. *Journal of Business Ethics*, *77*(4), 463–479. doi:10.100710551-007-9360-1

Lam, P., & Law, A. (2016). Crowdfunding for renewable and sustainable energy projects: An exploratory case study approach. *Renewable & Sustainable Energy Reviews*, *60*, 11–20. Available at https://kundoc.com/pdf-crowdfunding-for-renewable-and-sustainable-energy-projects-an-exploratory-case-s.html

Lane, M. J. (2015). *The Mission-Driven Venture: Business Solutions to the World's Most Vexing Social Problems*. Hoboken, NJ: Wiley. doi:10.1002/9781118809815

Lanfranchi, L. & Pekovic. S. (2012). *How Green is My Firm? Workers' Attitudes towards Job, Job Involvement and Effort in Environmentally-Related Firms*. Document du Travail 160, Centre d'Etudes de L'Emploi.

Laszlo C. (2008b). Wartość w zrównoważonym rozwoju. Sustainable Value. *Problemy ekorozwoju, 3*(2), 25–29.

Laszlo, C. (2008a). *Firma zrównoważonego rozwoju*. Warszawa: Studio EMKA.

Laszlo, C. (2008c). *Sustainable Value: How te Wrld's Leading Companies Are Doing Well by Doing Good.* Stanford, CA: Business Books.

Laszlo, C., Sherman, D., Whalen, J., & Ellinson, J. (2005). Expanding the Value Horizon: How Stakeholders Value Contributes to Competitive Advantage. *Journal of Corporate Citizenship*, *20*(Winter), 65–76. doi:10.9774/GLEAF.4700.2005.wi.00009

Le Sourd, V. (2011). *Performance of socially responsible investment funds against an efficient SRI index: The impact of benchmark choice when evaluating active managers.* Nice, France: EDHEC-Risk and Asset Management Research Centre.

Lea, R. (2002). Corporate social responsibility: Institute of Directors (IoD) member opinion survey. IoD.

Lee, C. C., & Chiu, Y. B. (2011). Oil prices, nuclear energy consumption, and economic growth: New evidence using a heterogeneous panel analysis. *Energy Policy*, *39*(4), 2111–2120. doi:10.1016/j.enpol.2011.02.002

Leonard, D., & McAdam, R. (2003). Corporate social responsibility. *Quality Progress*, *36*(10), 27–32.

Lesser, K., Rößle, F., & Walkshäusl, Ch. (2016). Socially responsible, green, and faith-based investment strategies: Screening activity matters! *Finance Research Letters*, *16*, 171–178. Available at https://www.sciencedirect.com/science/article/abs/pii/S1544612315001233

Levitt, T. (1958, Sept.). The dangers of Social Responsibility. *Harvard Business Review*, 41-50.

Levitt, T. (1983). The globalization of markets. *Harvard Business Review*, *61*, 2–11.

Li, S., Fetscherin, M., Alon, I., & Lattemann, C. (2010). *Corporate Social Responsibility in Emerging Markets The Importance of the Governance Environment*. Academic Press.

Ligeti, G., & Oravecz, Á. (2009). CSR communication of corporate enterprises in Hungary. *Journal of Business Ethics*, *84*(2), 137–149. doi:10.100710551-008-9678-3

Lin, B., & Moubarak, M. (2014). Renewable energy consumption–economic growth nexus for China. *Renewable & Sustainable Energy Reviews*, *40*, 111–117. doi:10.1016/j.rser.2014.07.128

Lindenberg, N. (2014a). *Definition of Green Finance*. DIE. Available at: https://www.die-gdi.de/uploads/media/Lindenberg_Definition_green_finance.pdf

Lindenberg, N. (2014b). *Public Instruments to Leverage Private Capital for Green Investments in Developing Countries.* German Development Institute. Discussion Paper, 50. Available at: https://econpapers.repec.org/paper/zbwdiedps/42014.htm

Lindgreen, A., Swaen, V., & Campbell, T. T. (2009). Corporate social responsibility practices in developing and transitional countries: Botswana and Malawi. *Journal of Business Ethics*, *90*(S3), 429–440. doi:10.100710551-010-0415-3

Lin, L., Hung, P.-H., Chou, D.-W., & Lai, C. W. (2019). Financial performance and corporate social responsibility: Empirical evidence from Taiwan. *Asia Pacific Management Review*, *24*(1), 61–71. doi:10.1016/j.apmrv.2018.07.001

Linsley, P. M., & Slack, R. E. (2013). Crisis management and an ethic of care: The case of Northern Rock Bank. *Journal of Business Ethics*, *113*(2), 285–295. doi:10.100710551-012-1304-8

Little, K. (2008). *Socially responsible investing: Put your money where your values are.* New York, NY: Penguin.

Little, L. R., Hobday, A. J., Parslow, J., Davies, C. R., & Grafton, R. Q. (2015). Funding climate adaptation strategies with climate derivatives. *Climate Risk Management*, *8*, 9–15. Available at https://www.sciencedirect.com/science/article/pii/S221209631500011X

Livesey, S. (2002). The discourse of the middle ground: Citizen Shell commits to sustainable development. *Management Communication Quarterly*, *15*(3), 313–349. doi:10.1177/0893318902153001

Li, W., & Zhang, R. (2010). Corporate Social Responsibility, Ownership Structure, and Political Interference: Evidence from China. *Journal of Business Ethics*, *96*(4), 631–645. doi:10.100710551-010-0488-z

Locke, J. (1988). *Two Treatises of Government* (P. Laslett, Ed.). Cambridge, UK: Cambridge University Press. doi:10.1017/CBO9780511810268

Locke, K. (2001). Grounded theory in management research. *Sage (Atlanta, Ga.)*.

Logue, A. C. (2009). *Socially Responsible Investing for Dummies*. Indianapolis, IN: John Wiley and Sons.

Loiseau, E., Saikku, L., Antikainen, R., Droste, N., Hansjürgens, B., Pitkanen, K., ... Thomsen, M. (2016). Green economy and related concepts: An overview. *Journal of Cleaner Production*, *139*, 361–371. Available at https://www.researchgate.net/publication/306125941_Green_economy_and_related_concepts_An_overview

López-Morales, J. S., & Ortega-Ridaura, I. (2019). Internationalization, Corporate Social Responsibility, and Poverty Alleviation. In Corporate Social Responsibility: Concepts, Methodologies, Tools, and Applications (pp. 1276–1298). IGI Global. doi:10.4018/978-1-5225-6192-7.ch067

Lourenço, I. C., & Branco, M. C. (2013). Determinants of corporate sustainability performance in emerging markets: The Brazilian case. *Journal of Cleaner Production*, *57*, 134–141. doi:10.1016/j.jclepro.2013.06.013

Low, M. P. (2016). Corporate Social Responsibility and the Evolution of Internal Corporate Social Responsibility in 21st Century. *Asian Journal of Social Sciences and Management Studies*, *3*(1), 56–74. doi:10.20448/journal.500/2016.3.1/500.1.56.74

Lozano, R., & Huisingh, D. (2011). Inter-linking issues and dimensions in sustainability reporting. *Journal of Cleaner Production*, *19*(2–3), 99–107. doi:10.1016/j.jclepro.2010.01.004

Lueg, R., & Radlach, R. (2016). Managing sustainable development with management control systems: A literature review. *European Management Journal*, *34*(2), 158–171. doi:10.1016/j.emj.2015.11.005

Lutz Preuss, R. B. (2011). CSR priorities of emerging economy firms:Is Russia shape of BRIC? *Corporate Governance*, *11*(4), 371–385. doi:10.1108/14720701111159226

Lydenberg, S. D. (2002). Envisioning socially responsible investing. *Journal of Corporate Citizenship*, *7*(7), 57–77. doi:10.9774/GLEAF.4700.2002.au.00007

Maas, S., & Reniers, G. (2014). Development of a CSR model for practice: Connecting five inherent areas of sustainable business. *Journal of Cleaner Production*, *64*, 104–114. doi:10.1016/j.jclepro.2013.07.039

Maciek, E. (2013). Principles of social responsibility in small and medium business. *Skhid,* (5), 65-70.

Ma, F., & Hanna, M. A. (1999). Biodiesel production: A review. *Bioresource Technology*, *70*(1), 1–15. doi:10.1016/S0960-8524(99)00025-5

Mahon, J. F. (2002). Corporate reputation: Research agenda using strategy and stakeholder literature. *Business & Society*, *41*(4), 415–445. doi:10.1177/0007650302238776

Maignan, I., & Ferrell, O. C. (2000). Measuring corporate citizenship in two countries: The case of the United States and France. *Journal of Business Ethics*, *23*(3), 283–297. doi:10.1023/A:1006262325211

Mair, J., & Milligan, K. (2012). Q and A roundtable on impact investing. *Stanford Social Innovation Review.* Retrieved from: http://ssir.org/articles/entry/qa_roundtable_on_impact_investing

Ma, J. (2012). A study on the models for corporate social responsibility of small and medium enterprises. *Physics Procedia*, *25*, 435–442. doi:10.1016/j.phpro.2012.03.108

Majoch, A. A., Hoepner, A. G., & Hebb, T. (2017). Sources of stakeholder salience in the responsible investment movement: Why do investors sign the principles for responsible investment? *Journal of Business Ethics*, *140*(4), 723–741. doi:10.100710551-016-3057-2

Maretick, M. (2015). Women Rule: Why the Future of Social, Sustainable and Impact Investing is in Female Hands. *TriplePundit*. Retrieved from: http://www.triplepundit.com/2015/04/womenrule-future-social-sustainable-impact-investing-female-hands/#

Margolis, J. D., & Walsh, J. P. (2003). Misery Loves Companies: Rethinking Social Initiatives by Business. *Administrative Science Quarterly*, *48*(2), 268–305. doi:10.2307/3556659

Markandya, A., Antimiani, A., Costantini, V., Martini, C., Palma, A., & Tommasino, M. C. (2015). Analyzing Trade-offs in International Climate Policy Options: The Case of the Green Climate Fund. *World Development*, *74*, 93–107. Available at https://www.researchgate.net/publication/276298820_Analyzing_Trade-offs_in_International_Climate_Policy_Options_The_Case_of_the_Green_Climate_Fund

Marrewijk, M. (2003). Concepts and Definitions of CSR and Corporate Sustainability. *Journal of Business Ethics*, *44*(2), 95–105. doi:10.1023/A:1023331212247

Martí-Ballester, C. P. (2015). Investor reactions to socially responsible investment. *Management Decision*, *53*(3), 571–604. doi:10.1108/MD-04-2014-0207

Martinez-Fernandez, C., Hinojosa, C., & Miranda, G. (2010). *Greening Jobs and Skills: Labour Market Implications of Addressing Climate Change*. OECD. Retrieved October 23, 2019, from: www.oecd.org/dataoecd/54/43/44683169.pdf?contentId=44683170

Martin, P. R., & Moser, D. V. (2016). Managers' green investment disclosures and investors' reaction. *Journal of Accounting and Economics*, *61*, 239–254. Available at https://www.sciencedirect.com/science/article/abs/pii/S0165410115000610

Massoud, J. A., Daily, B. F., & Willi, A. (2019). How do Argentine SMEs define CSR? Cases in educational social development. *World Journal of Entrepreneurship, Management and Sustainable Development*. doi:10.1108/WJEMSD-10-2018-0090

Masztalerz M. (2014). Wartość dla interesariuszy w zrównoważonym przedsiębiorstwie. *Studia Oeconomica Posnaniensia, 8*(269), 66–77.

Mathews, J. A., & Kidney, S. (2012). Financing climate-friendly energy development through bonds. *Development Southern Africa*, *29*(2), 337–349. doi:10.1080/0376835X.2012.675702

Matten, D., & Crane, A. (2005). Corporate Citizenship: Toward an Extended Theoretical Conceptualization. *Academy of Management Review*, *30*(1), 166–179. doi:10.5465/amr.2005.15281448

Matten, D., & Moon, J. (2008). "Implicit" and "explicit" CSR: A conceptual framework for a comparative understanding of Corporate Social Responsibility. *Academy of Management Review*, *33*(2), 402–424. doi:10.5465/amr.2008.31193458

McCann, L., Solomon, A., & Solomon, J. (2003). Explaining the growth in UK socially responsible investment. *Journal of General Management*, *28*(4), 15–36. doi:10.1177/030630700302800402

McCarthy, D. J., Puffer, S. M., Dunlap, D. R., & Jaeger, A. M. (2012). A Stakeholder Approach to the Ethicality of BRIC-firm Managers' Use of Favors. *Journal of Business Ethics*, *109*(1), 27–38. doi:10.100710551-012-1377-4

McGuire, J. B., Sundgren, A., & Schneeweis, T. (1988). Corporate social responsibility and firm financial performance. *Academy of Management Journal*, *31*(4), 854–872.

McLaren, D. (2004). Global Stakeholders: Corporate accountability and investor engagement. *Corporate Governance*, *12*(2), 191–201. doi:10.1111/j.1467-8683.2004.00360.x

McWilliams, A. (2000). *Corporate social responsibility*. Wiley Encyclopedia of Management.

McWilliams, A., & Siegel, D. (2000). Corporate social responsibility and financial performance: Correlation or misspecification? *Strategic Management Journal*, *21*(5), 603–609. doi:10.1002/(SICI)1097-0266(200005)21:5<603::AID-SMJ101>3.0.CO;2-3

McWilliams, A., & Siegel, D. (2001a). Profit maximizing corporate social responsibility. *Academy of Management Review*, *26*(4), 504–505.

McWilliams, A., & Siegel, D. (2001b). Corporate social responsibility: A theory of the firm perspective. *Academy of Management Review*, *26*(1), 117–127. doi:10.5465/amr.2001.4011987

Meehan, J., Meehan, K., & Richards, A. (2006). Corporate social responsibility: The 3C-SR model. *International Journal of Social Economics*, *33*(5/6), 386–398. doi:10.1108/03068290610660661

Mehra, M. (2006). Turning Point: Corporate Social Responsibility in Emerging Economies. *Journal of Corporate Citizenship: Corporate Social Responsibility in Emerging Economies*, *24*(Special Issue), 20–22. doi:10.9774/GLEAF.4700.2006.wi.00004

Melo, T., & Galan, J. I. (2011). Effects of corporate social responsibility on brand value. *Journal of Brand Management*, *18*(6), 423–437. doi:10.1057/bm.2010.54

Menguc, B., & Ozanne, L. K. (2005). Challenges of the "green imperative": A natural resource-based approach to the environmental orientation–business performance relationship. *Journal of Business Research*, *58*(4), 430–438. doi:10.1016/j.jbusres.2003.09.002

Meridian Group International. (2006). *CSR in Africa: Internet Research Study*. Extending Service Delivery Project. Retrieved from: http://www.esdproj.org/site/DocServer/CSR_in_Africa_06_FINAL.pdf

Micale, V., Frisari, G., Herve-Mignucci, M., & Mazza, F. (2013). *The Global Landscape of Climate Finance*. CPI Report. Available at: http://indiaenvironmentportal.org.in/files/file/The-Global-Landscape-of-Climate-Finance-2013.pdf

Micklethwait, J., & Wooldridge, A. (2003). *A future perfect: The challenge and promise of globalization*. New York, NY: Crown Business Press.

Mihailenko, O. (2007). Social responsibility as corporate value of the company. *Journal of Saratov State Social and Economic University*, (18), 13-15.

Miles, J. R. (2019, February 27). Corporate social responsibility 2.0, The Bold plan to transform society. *BOLD Business*. Retrieved June 18, 2019, from: https://www.boldbusiness.com/digital/corporate-social-responsibility-2-0-bold-plan-transform-society/

Miller, A. (1992). Green Investment. In D. Owen (Ed.), *Green Reporting: Accountancy and the Challenge of the Nineties* (pp. 242–255). London, UK: Chapman and Hall.

Minor, D., & Morgan, J. (2011). CSR as reputation insurance: Primum non nocere. *California Management Review*, *53*(3), 40–59. doi:10.1525/cmr.2011.53.3.40

Miralles-Quirós, M. M., Miralles-Quirós, J. L., & Hernández, J. R. (2019). ESG performance and shareholder value creation in the banking industry: International differences. *Sustainability*, *11*(5), 1404. doi:10.3390u11051404

Miras-Rodríguez, M., Martínez-Martínez, D., & Escobar-Pérez, B. (2018). Which corporate governance mechanisms drive CSR disclosure practices in emerging countries? *Sustainability*, *11*(1), 61. doi:10.3390u11010061

Mitchell, R., Agle, B., & Wood, D. (1997). Toward a Theory of Stakeholders Identification and Salience: Defining the Principle of who and what Really Counts. *Academy of Management Review*, *22*(4), 853–886. doi:10.5465/amr.1997.9711022105

Miteva, A., Stoyanova, Z., Harizanova, H., Peicheva, M., Doichinova, J., & Kanchev, I. (2014). Green Jobs-tool of Ecologisation of Bulgarian Economy. . doi:10.5937/ekoPolj1502369S

Mohr, L. A., Webb, D. J., & Harris, K. E. (2001). Do consumers expect companies to be socially responsible? The impact of corporate social responsibility on buying behavior. *The Journal of Consumer Affairs*, *35*(1), 45–72. doi:10.1111/j.1745-6606.2001.tb00102.x

Monasterolo, I., & Raberto, M. (2018). The EIRIN Flow-of-funds Behavioural Model of Green Fiscal Policies and Green Sovereign Bonds. *Ecological Economics*, *144*, 228–243. doi:10.1016/j.ecolecon.2017.07.029

Montiel, I. (2008). Corporate social responsibility and corporate sustainability: Separate pasts, common futures. *Organization & Environment*, *21*(3), 245–269. doi:10.1177/1086026608321329

Moody's. (2019). *Research Announcement: Moody's: Green bond market poised to hit $200 billion in 2019*. Available at: https://www.moodys.com/research/Moodys-Green-bond-market-poised-to-hit-200-billion-in--PBC_1159526

Moon, J., Crane, A., & Matten, D. (2003). Can corporations be citizens? Corporate citizenship as a metaphor for business participation in society. *Research Paper Series of ICCSR*, *4*, 2-17.

Moon, H., & Parc, J. (2019). Shifting Corporate Social Responsibility to Corporate Social Opportunity through Creating Shared Value. *Strategic Change*, *28*(2), 115–122. doi:10.1002/jsc.2252

Morsing, M., & Schultz, M. (2006). Corporate social responsibility communication: Stakeholder information, response and involvement strategies. *Business Ethics a European Review*, *15*(4), 324–338. doi:10.1111/j.1467-8608.2006.00460.x

Morsy, L., & Rothstein, R. (2015). *Parents' non-standard work schedules make adequate childrearing difficult, Issue Brief 400*. Washington, DC: Economic Policy Institute. Retrieved June 30, 2019, from: http://www.epi.org/files/pdf/88777.pdf

Mostovicz, I., Kakabadse, N., & Kakabadse, A. (2009). CSR: The role of leadership in driving ethical outcomes. *Corporate Governance: The International Journal of Business in Society*, *9*(4), 448–460. doi:10.1108/14720700910984990

Muller, A. (2006). Global versus local CSR strategies. *European Management Journal*, *24*(2-3), 189–198. doi:10.1016/j.emj.2006.03.008

Muller, A., & Kolk, A. (2010). Extrinsic and intrinsic drivers of corporate social performance: Evidence from foreign and domestic firms in Mexico. *Journal of Management Studies*, *47*(1), 1–26. doi:10.1111/j.1467-6486.2009.00855.x

Mulligan, T. (1986). A critique of Milton Friedman's essay 'the social responsibility of business is to increase its profits'. *Journal of Business Ethics*, *5*(4), 265–269. doi:10.1007/BF00383091

Naseri, S. F., Motamedi, S., & Ahmadian, M. (2016). Study of mediated consumption effect of renewable energy on economic growth of OECD countries. *Procedia Economics and Finance*, *36*, 502–509. doi:10.1016/S2212-5671(16)30068-5

Navarro, P. (1988). Why do corporations give to charity? *The Journal of Business*, *61*(1), 65–93. doi:10.1086/296420

Nejati, M., & Ghasemi, S. (2012). Corporate social responsibility in Iran from the perspective of employees. *Social Responsibility Journal*, *8*(4), 578–588. doi:10.1108/17471111211272552

Nelling, E., & Webb, E. (2009). Corporate social responsibility and financial performance: The "virtuous circle" revisited. *Review of Quantitative Finance and Accounting*, *32*(2), 197–209. doi:10.100711156-008-0090-y

Nelson, J. (2004). *Leadership, accountability and partnership: Critical trends and issues in corporate social responsibility. Report of the Corporate Responsibility Initiative*. Cambridge, MA: Harvard University.

Netflix. Fortune 500. (n.d.). Retrieved June 3, 2019, from: https://fortune.com/fortune500/netflix/

Neverov, A. V., & Davydenkova, E. S. (2016). Social responsibility of small and medium business organizations in Russia. *Journal of the Voronezh University of Friendship of Peoples. Series. Sociology*, (1), 130–140.

Ng, T. H., & Tao, J. Y. (2016). Bond financing for renewable energy in Asia. *Energy Policy*, *95*, 509–517. Available at https://econpapers.repec.org/bookchap/erachaptr/2014-rpr-27-11.htm

Nikitina, Y. (2015). Innovative Behavioral Models as a Method for a Social System Adaptation in the Unstable External Environment. *Procedia: Social and Behavioral Sciences*, *166*, 135–141. doi:10.1016/j.sbspro.2014.12.498

Nikolova, N., & Yordanova, I. (2014). Corporate social responsibility as a mechanism for the integration of economic, social and ecological goals of the organization. *Proceedings of the Closing conference under the project "System of qualification and career development of the university teachers", Vasil Levski National Military University – Veliko Tarnovo, Bulgaria*, 219-229.

Nikolova, N., Todorova, I., & Nenova, N. (2014). Corporate social responsibility as a strategic priority in the competitive behavior of the company. Scientific works "MathTech 2014", Bishop Konstantin Preslavski University of Shumen, 1, 333-340.

Nilsson, J. (2009). Segmenting socially responsible mutual fund investors: The influence of financial return and social responsibility. *International Journal of Bank Marketing*, *27*(1), 5–31. doi:10.1108/02652320910928218

Nixon, B., Burns, J., & Jazayeri, M. (2011). The role of management accounting in new product design and development decisions. *CIMA Research Executive Summary Series*, *9*(1), 1–7.

Nyborg, K. (2014). Do responsible employers attract responsible employees? *IZA World of Labor*, *17*. doi:10.15185/izawol.17

O'Riordan, L., & Fairbrass, J. (2014). Managing CSR stakeholder engagement: A new conceptual framework. *Journal of Business Ethics*, *125*(1), 121–145. doi:10.100710551-013-1913-x

Öberseder, M., Schlegelmilch, B. B., & Murphy, P. E. (2013). CSR practices and consumer perceptions. *Journal of Business Research*, *66*(10), 1839–1851. doi:10.1016/j.jbusres.2013.02.005

OECD. (2002). *OECD For Economic Small and Medium Sized Enterprise Outlook*. Paris: OECD.

OECD. (2011). *Environmental Governance in Context of Green Growth in EECCA: Main Policy Conclusions. ENV/EPOC/EAP (2011)3*. OECD.

OECD. (2011). *Green Growth Strategy Synthesis Report (Note by the Secretary General). C (2011)29/Rev1*. OECD.

OECD. (2011). *Monitoring Progress towards Green Growth OECD Indicators, OECD working document C (2011)30*. OECD.

OECD. (2011). *Towards Green Growth. Green Growth Study*. OECD Publishing. Available at: https://www.oecd-ilibrary.org/environment/towards-green-growth_9789264111318-en

OECD. (2015). *Creating Incentives for Greener Products: A Policy Manual for Eastern Partnership Countries*. OECD.

OECD. (2017). *Investing in Climate, Investing in Growth.* OECD Publishing. Available at: https://www.oecd-ilibrary.org/economics/investing-in-climate-investing-in-growth_9789264273528-en;jsessionid=BlBH-C0OsdlUozRja6VKedZc.ip-10-240-5-116

Ofori, D. F., & Hinson, R. E. (2007). Corporate social responsibility (CSR) perspectives of leading firms in Ghana. *Corporate Governance: The International Journal Of Business In Society*, *7*(2), 178–193. doi:10.1108/14720700710739813

Ogrizek, M. (2002). The effect of corporate social responsibility on the branding of financial services. *Journal of Financial Services Marketing*, *6*(3), 215–228. doi:10.1057/palgrave.fsm.4770053

Oikonomou, I., Platanakis, E., & Sutcliffe, C. (2018). Socially responsible investment portfolios: Does the optimization process matter? *The British Accounting Review*, *50*(4), 379–401. doi:10.1016/j.bar.2017.10.003

Ojo, M. (2016). Corporate Social Responsibility and Foreign Direct Investment: Engaging Innovation, Auditors, and Stakeholders in Corporate Social Responsibility. In M. Ojo (Ed.), *Analyzing the Relationship between Corporate Social Responsibility and Foreign Direct Investment* (pp. 49–63). Hershey, PA: IGI Global. doi:10.4018/978-1-5225-0305-7.ch005

Oliveira, J. (2006). Introduction. *Journal of Corporate Citizenship: Corporate Citizenship in Latin America: New Challenges for Business*, *21*(Special Issue), 17–20.

Oll, J., & Rommerskirchen, S. (2018). What's wrong with integrated reporting? A systematic review. *Sustainability Management Forum, 26*(1–4), 19–34.

Omur, G. A., Tunc, A. O., & Caliskan, E. N. (2012). Corporate social and environmental responsibility in the service sector: A case study from Turkey. *International Journal of Business and Management Studies*, *4*(1), 11–20.

Ooi, E., & Lajbcygier, P. (2013). Virtue remains after removing sin: Finding skill amongst socially responsible investment managers. *Journal of Business Ethics*, *113*(2), 199–224. doi:10.100710551-012-1290-x

Ordanini, A., Miceli, L., Pizzetti, M., & Parasuraman, A. (2011). Crowdfunding: Transforming customers into investors through innovative service platforms. *Journal of Service Management*, *22*(4), 443–470. Available at https://www.researchgate.net/publication/235251062_Crowd-funding_Transforming_customers_into_investors_through_innovative_service_platforms

Orsato, R. J., Garcia, A., Mendes-Da-Silva, W., Simonetti, R., & Monzoni, M. (2015). Sustainability indexes: Why join in? A study of the 'Corporate Sustainability Index (ISE)' in Brazil. *Journal of Cleaner Production*, *96*, 161–170. doi:10.1016/j.jclepro.2014.10.071

Ostrom, E. (2009). The Sveriges Riksbank Prize in Economic Sciences in Memory of Alfred Nobel Laureate 2009 speech.

Ozdora-Aksak, E., & Atakan-Duman, S. (2016). Gaining legitimacy through CSR: An analysis of Turkey's 30 largest corporations. *Business Ethics (Oxford, England)*, *25*(3), 238–257. doi:10.1111/beer.12114

Pachauri, R. K. (2006). CSR in new dimensions. *The Economic Times*.

Palazzo, G., & Richter, U. (2005). CSR business as usual? The case of the tobacco industry. *Journal of Business Ethics*, *61*(4), 387–401. doi:10.100710551-005-7444-3

Palidda, S. (Ed.). (2016). *Governance of Security and Ignored Insecurities in Contemporary Europe*. New York: Routledge. doi:10.4324/9781315585482

Pandey, S. K., & Wright, B. E. (2006). Connecting the dots in public management: Political environment, organizational goal ambiguity and public manager's role ambiguity. *Journal of Public Administration: Research and Theory*, *16*(4), 511–532. doi:10.1093/jopart/muj006

Pao, H. T., & Fu, H. C. (2013). Renewable energy, non-renewable energy and economic growth in Brazil. *Renewable & Sustainable Energy Reviews*, *25*, 381–392. doi:10.1016/j.rser.2013.05.004

Paramati, S. R., Mo, D., & Gupta, R. (2017). The effects of stock market growth and renewable energy use on CO_2 emissions: Evidence from G20 countries. *Energy Economics*, *66*, 360–371. doi:10.1016/j.eneco.2017.06.025

Park, J., Lee, H., & Kim, C. (2014). Corporate social responsibilities, consumer trust and corporate reputation: South Korean consumers' perspectives. *Journal of Business Research*, *67*(3), 295–302. doi:10.1016/j.jbusres.2013.05.016

Park, S. K. (2018). Investors as Regulators: Green Bonds and the Governance Challenges of the Sustainable Finance Revolution. *Stanford Journal of International Law*, *54*(1), 1–47. Available at https://papers.ssrn.com/sol3/papers.cfm?abstract_id=3142887

Pash, C. (2018, August 28). Unlimited leave is working so well, some companies are offering it fully paid. *The Sidney Morning Herald*. Retrieved May 14, 2019, from: https://www.smh.com.au/business/companies/unlimited-leave-is-working-so-well-some-companies-are-offering-it-fully-paid-20180828-p500ah.html

Passemard, M., & Calantone, K. (2000). *Competitive Advantage: Creating and Sustaining Superior Performance by Michael E.* Academic Press.

Paul, K. (2017). The effect of business cycle, market return and momentum on financial performance of socially responsible investing mutual funds. *Social Responsibility Journal*, *13*(3), 513–528. doi:10.1108/SRJ-09-2016-0154

Peloza, J. (2006). Using corporate social responsibility as insurance for financial performance. *California Management Review*, *48*(2), 52–72. doi:10.2307/41166338

Peloza, J. (2009). The Challenge of Measuring Financial Impacts From Investments in Corporate Social Performance. *Journal of Management*, *35*(6), 1518–1541. doi:10.1177/0149206309335188

Peregudov, S., & Semenenko, I. S. (2008). *Corporate Citizenship: Concepts, world practice and Russian realities*. Moscow: Progress Tradition.

Pereira, A. (2013). *CSR: Impact, not input, is true measure of project's worth*. New Delhi, India: Economic Times.

Pérez, A. (2015). Corporate reputation and CSR reporting to stakeholders: Gaps in the literature and future lines of research. *Corporate Communications*, *20*(1), 11–29. doi:10.1108/CCIJ-01-2014-0003

Perrini, F., Russo, A., & Tencati, A. (2007). CSR strategies of SMEs and large firms. Evidence from Italy. *Journal of Business Ethics*, *74*(3), 285–300. doi:10.100710551-006-9235-x

PES. (2017). *Workers' rights and social progress in the digital economy*. Retrieved May 30, 2019, from: http://www.pervencheberes.fr/wp-content/uploads/2017/09/digital-economy-brochure-web-version-002.pdf

Petrov, D. (2018). Blockchain Technology - A Bank Lending (R)evolution: The Case of Syndicated Loans. In *New Challenges of Economic and Business Development. Productivity and Economic Growth: Proceedings*. University of Latvia. Retrieved June 14, 2019, from: https://www.bvef.lu.lv/fileadmin/user_upload/lu_portal/projekti/bvef/konferences/evf_conf2018/Proceedings_2018.pdf

Petrunin, I. I., & Borisov, V. K. (2010). *Business ethics*. Moscow: Prospekt.

Phillpott, S. (2018). The 13 Most Philanthropic Companies in the World. Dublin: Academic Press.

Pienitz, R., & Vincent, W. F. (2000). Effect of climate change relative to ozone depletion on UV exposure in subarctic lakes. *Nature*, *404*(6777), 484–487. doi:10.1038/35006616 PMID:10761913

Pimpa, N. (2013). Poverty Alleviation: Corporate Social Responsibility Approaches by Multinational Corporations in Lao PDR and Thailand. *Journal of Business and Policy Research, 8*(1), 60–77. Retrieved from https://www.researchgate.net/publication/231537882_Poverty_Alleviation_CSR_Approaches_by_Multinational_Corporations_in_Lao_PDR_and_Thailand

Pimpa, N., Fry, S., & Gekara, V. (2012). MNCs and poverty alleviation: Approaches and challenges in Lao PDR and Thailand. In *Proceedings of the Academy of Management Annual Meeting 2012* (pp. 1–37). Boston: Academy of Management. doi:10.5465/AMBPP.2012.11068abstract

Pink, D. (2010, Aug 14). Netflix lets its staff take as much holiday as they want, whenever they want – and it works. *The Telegraph*. Retrieved June 12, 2019, from: https://www.telegraph.co.uk/finance/newsbysector/mediatechnologyandtelecoms/7945719/Netflix-lets-its-staff-take-as-much-holiday-as-they-want-whenever-they-want-and-it-works.html

Pletnev, D. A., & Nicolaeva, E. V. (2016). The success of small and medium-sized businesses in Russia and the social responsibility of its leaders. *Journal of Chelyabinsk State University, 6*(388), 128-138.

Plumer, B. (2015, September 23). Volkswagen's appalling clean diesel scandal, explained. *Vox*. Retrieved June 18, 2019, from: http://www.vox.com/2015/9/21/9365667/volkswagen-clean-diesel-recallpassenger-cars

Podnar, K., & Golob, U. (2007). CSR expectations: The focus of corporate marketing. *Corporate Communications, 12*(4), 326–340. doi:10.1108/13563280710832498

Pohludka, M., & Stverkova, H. (2019). The Best Practice of CRM Implementation for Small- and Medium-Sized Enterprises. *Administrative Sciences, 9*(22). doi:10.3390/admsci9010022

Pop, O., Dina, G. C., & Martin, C. (2011). Promoting the corporate social responsibility for a green economy and innovative jobs. *Procedia: Social and Behavioral Sciences, 15*, 1020–1023. doi:10.1016/j.sbspro.2011.03.232

Porter, M. (1985). *Competitive Advantage: Creating and Sustaining Superior Performance*. New York: The Free Press.

Porter, M. E., & Kramer, M. R. (2006). Strategy and society: The link between corporate social responsibility and competitive advantage. *Harvard Business Review, 84*(12), 78–92. PMID:17183795

Porter, M. E., & Kramer, M. R. (2006). The link between competitive advantage and corporate social responsibility. *Harvard Business Review, 84*(12), 78–92. PMID:17183795

Porter, M. E., & Kramer, M. R. (2011). The big idea: Creating shared value. *Harvard Business Review, 89*(1), 1–12.

Porter, M. F. (1980). An algorithm for suffix stripping. *Program, 14*(3), 130–137. doi:10.1108/eb046814

Porter, M., & Kramer, M. (2003). The Competitive Advantage of Corporate Philanthropy. *Harvard Business Review, 80*(12), 1–16. Retrieved from https://www.sharedvalue.org/sites/default/files/resource-files/Competitive_Advantage.pdf PMID:12510538

Porter, M., & Kramer, M. R. (2011). Creating shared value. *Harvard Business Review, 89*(1/2), 62–77.

Porter, T., & Miles, P. (2013). CSR Longevity: Evidence from long-term practices in large corporations. *Corporate Reputation Review, 16*(4), 313–340. doi:10.1057/crr.2013.17

Potts, T. (2010). The Natural Advantage of Regions: Linking Sustainability, Innovation, and Regional Development in Australia. *Journal of Cleaner Production, 18*(8), 713–725. doi:10.1016/j.jclepro.2010.01.008

Prahalad, C. K., & Hammond, A. (2003). *Serving the world's poor profitably. Harvard Business Review on Corporate Responsibility*. Cambridge, MA: Harvard Business School.

Prasad, B. A., & Kumar, P. R. (2011). Monitoring and Evaluation of CSR interventions. A study of CSR programs in GMR industries. *SMS Varanasi*, *VII*(2), 79–84.

Preston, L. E., & Post, J. E. (1975). Private management and public policy: The principle of public responsibility (1st ed.). Englewood Cliffs, NJ: Prentice- Hall.

Prieto-Carrón, M., Lund-Thomsen, P., Chan, A., Muro, A., & Bhushan, C. (2006). Critical perspectives on CSR and development: What we know, what we don't know, and what we need to know. *International Affairs*, *82*(5), 977–987. doi:10.1111/j.1468-2346.2006.00581.x

Priya, M. S., & Ajoy, A. (2013). A comparative study on CSR Practices of HPCL and IOCL. *Abhinav-International Monthly Refereed Journal of Research in Management and Technology*, *II*, 109–117.

Puaschunder, J. M. (2010). *On Corporate and Financial Social Responsibility* (Unpublished Dissertation). Faculty of Psychology, Department of General and Basic Psychology, University of Vienna.

Puaschunder, J. M. (2015c). Trust and reciprocity drive common goods allocation norms. In *Proceedings of the Cambridge Business & Economics Conference*. Cambridge, UK: Cambridge University.

Puaschunder, J. M. (2018a). Climate Wealth of Nations. In *Proceedings of the 11th International Research Association for Interdisciplinary Studies (RAIS) Conference on Social Sciences*. Academic Press.

Puaschunder, J. M. (2018g). The history of ethical, environmental, social and governance-oriented investments as a key to sustainable prosperity in the finance world. In Corporate Social Responsibility, Ethics and Sustainable Prosperity, (pp. 359-388), Heidelberg: Springer.

Puaschunder, J. M. (Ed.). (forthcoming b). Intergenerational Governance and Leadership in the Corporate World. Idea Group, Inc.

Puaschunder, J. M., & Schwarz, G. (2012). *The future is now: How joint decision making curbs hyperbolic discounting but blurs social responsibility in the intergenerational equity public policy domain*. Harvard University Situationist Law and Mind Sciences Working Paper.

Puaschunder, J.M. (2011). *Intergenerational equity as a natural behavioral law*. Library of Congress United States of America Copyright Office Copyright Catalogue TXu001743422/2011-03-08.

Puaschunder, J.M. (2017b). Ethical, environmental, social and governance-oriented investments. *Archives of Business Research, 5*(8), 151-159.

Puaschunder, J.M. (forthcoming a). *Governance and Climate Justice: Global South and Developing Nations*. Cham: Switzerland: Springer International & Nature, New York, New York: Palgrave Macmillan.

Puaschunder, J.M. (forthcoming c). Long-term investments. *Encyclopedia of the UN Sustainable Development Goals: Partnerships for the Goals*.

Puaschunder, J.M. (forthcoming d). When investors care about causes: Learning from political divestiture during Apartheid and the Sudan crisis for the transition to renewable energy via green bonds. Academic Press.

Puaschunder, J.M. (forthcoming e). On Corporate and Financial Social Responsibility. Cambridge, UK: Cambridge Scholars Publishing.

Puaschunder, J. M. (2015a). On the social representations of intergenerational equity. *Oxford Journal of Finance and Risk Perspectives*, *4*(4), 78–99.

Puaschunder, J. M. (2015b). The call for global responsible intergenerational leadership in the corporate world: The quest of an integration of intergenerational equity in contemporary Corporate Social Responsibility (CSR) models. In *Proceedings of the 2015 6th International Conference of the Association of Global Management Studies at* Alfred Lerner Hall of Columbia University. New York: The Association of Global Management Studies. 10.2139srn.2591032

Puaschunder, J. M. (2016a). Global responsible intergenerational leadership: The quest of an integration of intergenerational equity in Corporate Social Responsibility (CSR) models. *Annals in Social Responsibility*, *2*(1), 1–12. doi:10.1108/ASR-10-2015-0016

Puaschunder, J. M. (2016b). On eternal equity in the fin-de-millénaire. *Journal of Leadership, Accountability and Ethics*, *13*(2), 11–24.

Puaschunder, J. M. (2016c). On eternal equity in the fin-de-millénaire: Rethinking capitalism for intergenerational justice. *Journal of Leadership, Accountability and Ethics*, *13*(2), 11–24.

Puaschunder, J. M. (2016d). On the emergence, current state and future perspectives of Socially Responsible Investment (SRI). *Consilience: The Columbia University Journal of Sustainable Development*, *16*(1), 38–63.

Puaschunder, J. M. (2016e). The call for global responsible inter-generational leadership: The quest of an integration of inter-generational equity in Corporate Social Responsibility (CSR) models. In D. Jamali (Ed.), *Comparative Perspectives on Global Corporate Social Responsibility* (pp. 276–289). Hershey, PA: IGI Global Advances in Business Strategy and Competitive Advantage Book Series.

Puaschunder, J. M. (2016f). The call for global responsible inter-generational leadership: The quest of an integration of inter-generational equity in Corporate Social Responsibility (CSR) models. In *Natural Resources Management: Concepts, Methodologies, Tools, and Applications. Information Resource Management Association*. Hershey, PA: IGI Publishing.

Puaschunder, J. M. (2017a). Ethical decision making under social uncertainty: An introduction to Überethicality. *Sustainable Production and Consumption*, *12*, 78–89. doi:10.1016/j.spc.2017.05.005

Puaschunder, J. M. (2017c). Financing climate justice through climate change bonds. *Oxford Journal of Finance and Risk Perspectives*, *6*(3), 1–10.

Puaschunder, J. M. (2017d). Intergenerational leadership: Coordinating common goods and economic stability. *Journal of Applied Business and Economics*, *19*(11/12), 65–78.

Puaschunder, J. M. (2017e). Krisenrobuste Alternativen. *Global Investor*, *3*(5), 69.

Puaschunder, J. M. (2017f). Mapping Climate Justice in the 21st Century. *Agriculture Research and Technology*, *10*(5), 1–3.

Puaschunder, J. M. (2017g). Mapping Climate in the 21st Century. *Development*, *59*(3), 211–216.

Puaschunder, J. M. (2017h). Socio-psychological motives of socially responsible investors. *Global Corporate Governance: Advances in Financial Economics*, *19*, 209–247.

Puaschunder, J. M. (2017i). The climatorial imperative. *Agriculture Research and Technology*, *7*(4), 1–2.

Puaschunder, J. M. (2017j). We – today's and tomorrow's – people of the United World: Rethinking capitalism for intergenerational justice in the fin-de-millénaire. *Corporate Governance and Sustainability Review*, *1*(2), 30–35. doi:10.22495/cgsrv1i2p4

Puaschunder, J. M. (2018b). *Corporate Social Responsibility and Opportunities for Sustainable Financial Success*. Hershey, PA: IGI Publishing.

Puaschunder, J. M. (2018c). Intergenerational leadership: An extension of contemporary corporate social responsibility models. *Corporate Governance & Organizational Behavior Review*, *2*(1), 7–17. doi:10.22495/cgobr_v2_i1_p1

Puaschunder, J. M. (2018d). *Intergenerational responsibility in the 21st century*. Wilmington, DE: Vernon Art and Science.

Puaschunder, J. M. (2018e). Nachhaltigkeit und Investment: Psychologische Aspekte von nachhaltigkeitsorientiertem Investitionsverhalten. In C. T. Schmitt & E. Bamberg (Eds.), *Psychologie und Nachhaltigkeit: Konzeptionelle Grundlagen, Anwendungsbeispiele und Zukunftsperspektiven* (pp. 127–134). Wiesbaden: Springer. doi:10.1007/978-3-658-19965-4_11

Puaschunder, J. M. (2018f). Socio-psychological motives of Socially Responsible Investments (SRI). In S. Boubaker, D. Cumming, & D. K. Nguyen (Eds.), *Research Handbook of Investing in the Triple Bottom Line: Finance, Society and the Environment* (pp. 447–472). London: Edward Elgar. doi:10.4337/9781788110006.00029

Quazi, A. M., & O'Brien, D. (2000). An empirical test of a cross-national model of corporate social responsibility. *Journal of Business Ethics*, *25*(1), 33–51. doi:10.1023/A:1006305111122

Rappaport, A. (1986). *Creating Shareholder Value*. New York: Free Press.

Ray, S., & Ray Chaudhuri, B. (2018). Business Group Affiliation and Corporate Sustainability Strategies of Firms: An Investigation of Firms in India. *Journal of Business Ethics*, *153*(4), 955–976. doi:10.100710551-018-3917-z

RBC. (2019). *Rosstat for the first time revealed the share of small and medium-sized businesses in the economy*. Retrieved from https://www.rbc.ru/economics/05/02/2019/5c5948c59a794758389cfdf7

Reggiani, T. (2008). *Recensione a Muhammad Yunus - "Un mondo senza povertà."* Retrieved from https://mpra.ub.uni-muenchen.de/14974/1/MPRA_paper_14974.pdf

Rendtorff, J. D. (2009). Responsibility, Ethics and Legitimacy of Corporations. *Society and Business Review*, *4*(3), 266–268.

Renneboog, L., Ter Horst, J., & Zhang, C. (2008). Socially responsible investments: Institutional aspects, performance, and investor behaviour. *Journal of Banking & Finance*, *32*(9), 1723–1742. doi:10.1016/j.jbankfin.2007.12.039

Rhodes, M. J. (2010). Information asymmetry and socially responsible investment. *Journal of Business Ethics*, *95*(1), 145–150. doi:10.100710551-009-0343-2

Richardson, B. J. (2008). *Socially Responsible Investment Law: Regulating the Unseen Polluters*. Oxford, UK: Oxford University Press. doi:10.1093/acprof:oso/9780195333459.001.0001

Riedl, A., & Smeets, P. (2017). Why do investors hold socially responsible mutual funds? *The Journal of Finance*, *72*(6), 2505–2550. doi:10.1111/jofi.12547

Ringov, D., & Zollo, M. (2007). The impact of national culture on corporate social performance. *Corporate Governance*, *7*(4), 476–485. doi:10.1108/14720700710820551

Riordan, C., Gatewood, R., & Bill, J. (1997). Corporate image: Employee reactions and implications for managing corporate social performance. *Journal of Business Ethics*, *16*(4), 401–412. doi:10.1023/A:1017989205184

Roberts, A. S. (2010). *Disciplined democracies: Global capitalism and the new architecture of government*. Oxford, UK: Oxford University Press. doi:10.1093/acprof:oso/9780195374988.001.0001

Robertson, D. C. (2009). Corporate social responsibility and different stages of economic development: Singapore, Turkey, and Ethiopia. *Journal of Business Ethics*, *88*(4), 617–633. doi:10.100710551-009-0311-x

Rodionova, M. E. (2011). Corporate behavior in business community views. *Higher Education in Russia,* (6), 140-143.

Rodriguez-Fernandez, M. (2016). Social responsibility and financial performance: The role of good corporate governance. *BRQ Business Research Quarterly*, *19*(2), 137–151. doi:10.1016/j.brq.2015.08.001

Rodriguez, P., Siegel, D., Hillman, A., & Eden, L. (2006). Three lenses on the multinational enterprise: Politics, corruption, and corporate social responsibi. *Journal of International Business Studies*, *37*(6), 733–746. doi:10.1057/palgrave.jibs.8400229

Rojas, M., M'zali, B., Turcotte, M., & Merrigan, P. (2009). Bringing about changes to corporate social policy through shareholder activism: Filers, issues, targets, and success. *Business and Society Review*, *114*(2), 217–252. doi:10.1111/j.1467-8594.2009.00341.x

Roscoe, A. (2015, July 8). The Digital Future of Corporate Responsibility. *Stanford Social Innovation Review*. Retrieved June 10, 2019, from: https://ssir.org/articles/entry/the_digital_future_of_corporate_responsibility

Rosen, B. N., Sandler, D. M., & Shani, D. (1991). Social issues and socially responsibility investment behavior: Preliminary empirical investigation. *The Journal of Consumer Affairs*, *25*(2), 221–234. doi:10.1111/j.1745-6606.1991.tb00003.x

Rosenthal, N. (2014). Corporate Social Responsibility in Emerging Markets: Getting it right the first time? *Clarmondial*. Retrieved June 18, 2019, from Clarmondial website: https://www.clarmondial.com/corporate-social-responsibility-in-emerging-markets-getting-it-right-the-first-time/

Rothkopf, D. (2008). *Superclass: The global power elite and the world they are making*. New York, NY: Farrar, Straus & Giroux.

Rousseau, D. M., Manning, J., & Denyer, D. (2008). Evidence in management and organizational science: Assembling the field's full weight of scientific knowledge through syntheses. *The Academy of Management Annals*, *2*(1), 475–515. doi:10.5465/19416520802211651

Runhaar, H., & Lafferty, H. (2009). Governing corporate social responsibility: An assessment of the contribution of the UN Global Compact to CSR strategies in the telecommunications industry. *Journal of Business Ethics*, *84*(4), 479–495. doi:10.100710551-008-9720-5

Russian Association of Business Ethics. (2019). *RBEN*. Retrieved from https://rben.ru/

Russian National Standard. (n.d.). *GOST R ISO 26000-2012 Guidance for Social Responsibility*. URL: http://protect.gost.ru/v.aspx

Russo, A., & Perrini, F. (2010). Investigating stakeholder theory and social capital: CSR in large firms and SMEs. *Journal of Business Ethics*, *91*(2), 207–221. doi:10.100710551-009-0079-z

Russo, A., & Tencati, A. (2009). Formal vs. informal CSR strategies: Evidence from Italian micro, small, medium-sized, and large firms. *Journal of Business Ethics*, *85*(2), 339–353. doi:10.100710551-008-9736-x

S&P Green bond index. (n.d.). Available at http://us.spindices.com/indices/fixed-income/sp-green-bond-index

Sabir, S., Hamza, S. M., Arshad, M. U., Sajid, M., & Tahir, S. (2015). Causality Relationship among Foreign Direct Investment, Gross Domestic Product and Exports for Pakistan. *European Journal of Business and Management*, *7*(13), 76–82. Retrieved from http://citeseerx.ist.psu.edu/viewdoc/download?doi=10.1.1.734.8343&rep=rep1&type=pdf

Sachs, J. D., Woo, W. T., Yoshino, N., & Taghizadeh-Hesary, F. (2019). *Why Is Green Finance Important? ADBI Working Paper 917*. Tokyo: Asian Development Bank Institute. Available at https://www.adb.org/publications/why-green-finance-important

Saeed, M. M., & Arshad, F. (2012). Corporate social responsibility as a source of competitive advantage: The mediating role of social capital and reputational capital. *Journal of Database Marketing & Customer Strategy Management*, *19*(4), 219–232. doi:10.1057/dbm.2012.19

Saeidi, S. P., Sofian, S., Saeidi, P., Saeidi, S. P., & Saaeidi, S. A. (2015). How does corporate social responsibility contribute to firm financial performance? The mediating role of competitive advantage, reputation, and customer satisfaction. *Journal of Business Research*, *68*(2), 341–350. doi:10.1016/j.jbusres.2014.06.024

Saidi, K., & Mbarek, M. B. (2016). Nuclear energy, renewable energy, CO_2 emissions, and economic growth for nine developed countries: Evidence from panel Granger causality tests. *Progress in Nuclear Energy*, *88*, 364–374. doi:10.1016/j.pnucene.2016.01.018

Salaber, J. (2013). Religion and returns in Europe. *European Journal of Political Economy*, *32*(1), 149–160. doi:10.1016/j.ejpoleco.2013.07.002

Saleh, M., Zulkifli, N., & Muhamad, R. (2011). Looking for evidence of the relationship between corporate social responsibility and corporate financial performance in an emerging market. *Asia-Pacific Journal of Business Administration*, *3*(2), 165–190. doi:10.1108/17574321111169849

Salvioni, D. M., & Gennari, F. (2017). CSR, Sustainable Value Creation and Shareholder Relations. Cham: Symphonya. *Emerging Issues in Management*, *1*, 36–49.

Sandberg, J. (2011). Socially responsible investment and fiduciary duty: Putting the freshfields report into perspective. *Journal of Business Ethics*, *101*(1), 143–162. doi:10.100710551-010-0714-8

Sandberg, J. (2013). (Re-) interpreting fiduciary duty to justify socially responsible investment for pension funds? *Corporate Governance*, *21*(5), 436–446. doi:10.1111/corg.12028

Santos, M. (2011). CSR in SMEs: Strategies, practices, motivations and obstacles. *Social Responsibility Journal*, *7*(3), 490–508. doi:10.1108/17471111111154581

Sardana, D., Bamiatzi, V., & Zhu, Y. (2019). Decoding the Process of Social Value Creation by Chinese and Indian Social Entrepreneurs: Contributory Factors and Contextual Embeddedness. *Management and Organization Review*, *15*(2), 269–306. doi:10.1017/mor.2019.21

Savicheva, E. Y. (2010). Models of social responsibility of small business in Russia. *Problems of Modern Economy*, *36*(4), 164–167.

Schepers, D. H., & Prakash Sethi, S. (2003). Bridging the Gap Between the Promise and Performance of Socially Responsible Funds. *Business and Society Review*, *108*(1), 11–32. doi:10.1111/1467-8594.00006

Scheyvens, R., Banks, G., & Hughes, E. (2016). The Private Sector and the SDGs: The Need to Move Beyond 'Business as Usual.'. *Sustainable Development*, *24*(6), 371–382. doi:10.1002d.1623

Schneider, A., & Scherer, A. G. (2015). Corporate governance in a risk society. *Journal of Business Ethics*, *126*(2), 309–323. doi:10.100710551-013-1943-4

Scholte, J. A. (2000). *Globalization: A critical introduction*. Basingstoke, UK: Palgrave.

Scholtens, B., & Sievänen, R. (2013). Drivers of socially responsible investing: A case study of four Nordic countries. *Journal of Business Ethics*, *115*(3), 605–616. doi:10.100710551-012-1410-7

Schueth, S. (2003). Socially responsible investing in the United States. *Journal of Business Ethics*, *43*(3), 189–194. doi:10.1023/A:1022981828869

Schwartz, M. S., & Carroll, A. B. (2003). Corporate social responsibility: A three-domain approach. *Business Ethics Quarterly*, *13*(4), 503–530. doi:10.5840/beq200313435

Sebri, M., & Ben-Salha, O. (2014). On the causal dynamics between economic growth, renewable energy consumption, CO_2 emissions and trade openness: Fresh evidence from BRICS countries. *Renewable & Sustainable Energy Reviews*, *39*, 14–23. doi:10.1016/j.rser.2014.07.033

Seifert, B., Morris, S. A., & Bartkus, B. R. (2003). Comparing big givers and small givers: Financial correlates of corporate philanthropy. *Journal of Business Ethics*, *45*(3), 195–211. doi:10.1023/A:1024199411807

Selvi, Y., Wagner, E., & Türel, A. (2010). Corporate social responsibility in the time of financial crisis: Evidence from Turkey. *Annales Universitatis Apulensis-Series Oeconomica*, *12*(1), 281–290.

Sen, S., & Bhattacharya, C. B. (2001). Does doing good always lead to doing better? Consumer reactions to corporate social responsibility. *JMR, Journal of Marketing Research*, *38*(2), 225–243. doi:10.1509/jmkr.38.2.225.18838

Serafimova, D. (2017). CSR and Sustainable Development – Two Concepts with Different Beginnings and a Common Future. *Journal of Emerging Trends in Marketing and Management*, *I*(1), 77–87. Retrieved from https://ideas.repec.org/a/aes/jetimm/v1y2017i1p77-87.html

Seth, P. N. (2012). *CSR World*. Retrieved from http://www.csrworld.net

Sethi, S. P. (1975). Dimensions of Corporate Social Performance: An Analytical Framework. *California Management Review*, *17*(3), 58–64. doi:10.2307/41162149

Shahbaz, M., Loganathan, N., Zeshan, M., & Zaman, K. (2015). Does renewable energy consumption add in economic growth? An application of auto-regressive distributed lag model in Pakistan. *Renewable & Sustainable Energy Reviews*, *44*, 576–585. doi:10.1016/j.rser.2015.01.017

Shah, K. U., Arjoon, S., & Rambocas, M. (2016). Aligning Corporate Social Responsibility with Green Economy Development Pathways in Developing Countries. *Sustainable Development*, *24*, 237–253. Available at https://onlinelibrary.wiley.com/doi/abs/10.1002/sd.1625

Shanahan, F., & Seele, P. (2017). Creating Shared Value. Looking at Shared Value Through an Aristotelian Lens. In J. Wieland (Ed.), Creating Shared Value – Concepts, Experience, Criticism (pp. 141–151). Cham: Springer International Publishing AG.

Sharma, A., & Sanjeev, M. A. (2019). Can Creating Shared Value Supersede Corporate Social Responsibility. In *International Conference on Creating a Sustainable Business: Managerial Implications and Challenges (ICSBMC-12)* (pp. 37–41). Jaipur, India: Academic Press.

Shastri, R. K., & Singh, A. (2012). An Empirical Study on CSR Practices of selected Indian PSU's. *National Conference on Emerging Challenges for Sustainable Business*, 441-459.

Shell International Petroleum Company. (2001). *People, planet and profits. The Shell Report 2001*. Retrieved from http://www.bcsd.org.tw/2010/images/doc/301/002/002_3/SHELL REPORT_2001.PDF

Shteinberg, I. E. (2009). *Quality methods. Field Sociological Research*. St. Petersburg: Aleteia.

Shu, L. L., & Bazerman, M. H. (2011). *Cognitive barriers to environmental action: Problems and solutions. In Oxford Handbook of Business and the Environment*. Oxford, UK: Oxford University Press. doi:10.1093/oxfordhb/9780199584451.003.0009

Sichler, R. (2006). *Autonomie in der Arbeitswelt: Psychologie und Beruf*. Göttingen: Vandenhoeck & Ruprecht.

Silva, F., & Cortez, M. C. (2016). The performance of US and European green funds in different market conditions. *Journal of Cleaner Production*, *135*, 558–566. Available at https://pubag.nal.usda.gov/catalog/5246768

Sinkin, C., Wright, C. J., & Burnett, R. D. (2008). Eco-efficiency and firm value. *Journal of Accounting and Public Policy*, *27*(2), 167–176. doi:10.1016/j.jaccpubpol.2008.01.003

Sizova, I. L., & Chilipenok, Y. Y. (2017). Social responsibility within labour relations among the employers in small and medium businesses. *Zhurnal Issledovanii Sotsial'noi Politiki*, *15*(1), 67–80. doi:10.17323/1727-0634-2017-15-1-67-80

Skare, M., & Golja, T. (2014). The impact of government CSR supporting policies on economic growth. *Journal of Policy Modeling*, *36*(3), 562–577. doi:10.1016/j.jpolmod.2014.01.008

SkjaersethJ. B.TangenK.SwansonP.ChristiansenA. C.MoeA.LundeL. (2004). Retrieved from http://www.fni.no/doc&pdf/FNI-R0704.pdf

Smith, A. (1776). *The wealth of nations* (5th ed.). New York: Bantam Dell.

Smith, A. (1976). *An inquiry into the nature and causes of the wealth of nations*. Oxford, UK: Clarendon. (Original work published 1776)

Smith, A. D. (2007). Making the case for the competitive advantage of corporate social responsibility. *Business Strategy Series*, *8*(3), 186–195. doi:10.1108/17515630710684187

Smithers, R. (2013, April 29). Benetton admits link with firm in collapsed Bangladesh building. *The Guardian*. Retrieved June 3, 2019, from: https://www.theguardian.com/world/2013/apr/29/benetton-link-collapsed-building-bangladesh

Smith, M. P. (1996). Shareholder activism by institutional investors: Evidence from CalPERS. *The Journal of Finance*, *51*(1), 227–252. doi:10.1111/j.1540-6261.1996.tb05208.x

Snider, J., Hill, R. P., & Martin, D. (2003). Corporate Social Responsibility in the 21st Century: A View from the World's Most Successful Firms. *Journal of Business Ethics*, *48*(2), 175–187. doi:10.1023/B:BUSI.0000004606.29523.db

Soppe, A. (2016). New Financial Ethics A Normative Approach. New York: Routledge. doi:10.4324/9781315462578

Sparkes, R. (2001). Ethical investment: Whose ethics, which investment? *Business Ethics (Oxford, England)*, *10*(3), 194–205. doi:10.1111/1467-8608.00233

Sparkes, R. (2002). *Socially responsible investment: A global revolution*. Wiley.

Sparkes, R. (2017). A historical perspective on the growth of socially responsible investment. In *Responsible investment* (pp. 39–54). Oxford, UK: Routledge. doi:10.4324/9781351283441-3

Sparkes, R., & Cowton, C. J. (2004). The maturing of socially responsible investment: A review of the developing link with corporate social responsibility. *Journal of Business Ethics*, *52*(1), 45–57. doi:10.1023/B:BUSI.0000033106.43260.99

Spence, L. J., & Lozano, J. F. (2000). Communicating about ethics with small firms: Experiences from the UK and Spain. *Journal of Business Ethics*, *27*(1), 43–53. doi:10.1023/A:1006417425446

Spence, L., Schmidpeter, R., & Habisch, A. (2003). Assessing social capital: Small and medium sized enterprises in Germany. *Journal of Business Ethics*, *47*(1), 17–29. doi:10.1023/A:1026284727037

Spencer, R. (2018). CSR for Sustainable Development and Poverty Reduction? Critical Perspectives from the Anthropology of Development. In Disciplining the Undisciplined? Perspectives from Business, Society and Politics on Responsible Citizenship, Corporate Social Responsibility and Sustainability (pp. 73–87). Springer International Publishing. doi:10.1007/978-3-319-71449-3_5

Spitzeck, H., & Chapman, S. (2012). Creating shared value as a differentiation strategy – the example of BASF in Brazil. *Corporate Governance*, *12*(4), 499–513. doi:10.1108/14720701211267838

Sraders, A. (2018). What Are Emerging Markets? Characteristics and List in 2019. *TheStreet*. Retrieved from https://www.thestreet.com/markets/emerging-markets/what-are-emerging-markets-14819803

Stanley, T. D. (2001). Wheat from chaff: Meta-analysis as quantitative literature review. *The Journal of Economic Perspectives*, *15*(3), 131–150. doi:10.1257/jep.15.3.131

Staples, C. (2004). What does corporate social responsibility mean for charitable fundraising in the UK? *International Journal of Nonprofit and Voluntary Sector Marketing*, *9*(2), 154–158. doi:10.1002/nvsm.242

Statman, M. (2000). Socially Responsible Mutual Funds (corrected). *Financial Analysts Journal*, *56*(3), 30–39. doi:10.2469/faj.v56.n3.2358

Stawicka, E. (2017). Sustainable development and the business context of CSR benefits on the Polish market. *Acta Scientiarum Polonorum. Oeconomia*, *16*(3).

Stefanova, M., & Toms, J. (2014). *Corporate social responsibility and communications for sustainable development of business*. Sofia, Bulgaria: Siela.

Stohl, C., Michael, E., Scott, B., & Woo, D. (2015). Social Media Policies: Implications for Contemporary Notions of Corporate Social Responsibility. *Journal of Business Ethics*, *14*(3), 413–436. doi:10.100710551-015-2743-9

Storchevoy, M. (2018). Business Ethics: Normative, Positive, and Practical. In *Business Ethics as a Science: Methodology and Implications* (pp. 71–95). Cham: Springer International Publishing. doi:10.1007/978-3-319-68861-9_3

Stovall, O. S., Neill, J. D., & Perkins, D. (2004). Corporate governance, internal decision making, and the invisible hand. *Journal of Business Ethics*, *51*(2), 221–227. doi:10.1023/B:BUSI.0000033615.22269.e3

Subramaniam, V. (2013). *Poverty : A Corporate Creation and Ratio Controls for Eradication*. Retrieved from https://mpra.ub.uni-muenchen.de/75234/1/MPRA_paper_75234.pdf

Surroca, J., Tribó, J. A., & Waddock, S. (2010). Corporate responsibility and financial performance: The role of intangible resources. *Strategic Management Journal*, *31*(5), 463–490. doi:10.1002mj.820

Sustainable Development Goals Report. (2018). Retrieved from https://unstats.un.org/sdgs/report/2018/overview/

Tang, Z., Hull, C. E., & Rothenberg, S. (2012). How corporate social responsibility engagement strategy moderates the CSR–financial performance relationship. *Journal of Management Studies*, *49*(7), 1274–1303. doi:10.1111/j.1467-6486.2012.01068.x

Tarigan, J., Hatane, S. E., Stacia, L., & Widjaja, D. C. (2019). Corporate social responsibility policies and value creation: Does corporate governance and profitability mediate that relationship? *Investment Management and Financial Innovations*, *16*(2), 270–280. doi:10.21511/imfi.16(2).2019.23

Tenbrunsel, A. E., & Messick, D. M. (2004). Ethical fading: The role of self-deception in unethical behavior. *Social Justice Research*, *17*(2), 223–236. doi:10.1023/B:SORE.0000027411.35832.53

The Economist. (2018). *Women's wealth is rising*. Retrieved from: https://www.economist.com/graphic-detail/2018/03/08/womens-wealth-is-rising

The Russian Government. (2016). *Approval of the Strategy for the Development of Small and Medium-sized Enterprises until 2030*. Retrieved from http://government.ru/docs/23354/

The World Bank. (2018). *Green Bond Impact Report 2018.* Available at: http://pubdocs.worldbank.org/en/632251542641579226/report-impact-green-bond-2018.pdf

Thornley, B., Wood, D., Grace, K., & Sullivant, S. (2011). Impact Investing a Framework for Policy Design and Analysis. InSight at Pacific Community Ventures and The Initiative for Responsible Investment at Harvard University, Cambridge, MA.

Timane, R., & Tale, T. (2012). A study on CSR in India. *International Journal of Research in IT and Management, 2*(12).

Tolliver, C., Keeley, A., & Managi, S. (2019). Green bonds for the Paris agreement and sustainable development goals. *Environmental Research Letters, 14.* Available at https://iopscience.iop.org/article/10.1088/1748-9326/ab1118

Tranfield, D., Denyer, D., & Smart, P. (2003). Towards a methodology for developing evidence-informed management knowledge by means of systematic review. *British Journal of Management, 14*(3), 207–222. doi:10.1111/1467-8551.00375

Treviño, L. K., den Nieuwenboer, N. A., & Kish-Gephart, J. J. (2014). (Un) ethical behavior in organizations. *Annual Review of Psychology, 65*(1), 635–660. doi:10.1146/annurev-psych-113011-143745 PMID:23834354

Treviño, L. K., den Nieuwenboer, N. A., Kreiner, G. E., & Bishop, D. G. (2014). Legitimating the legitimate: A grounded theory study of legitimacy work among Ethics and Compliance Officers. *Organizational Behavior and Human Decision Processes, 123*(2), 186–205. doi:10.1016/j.obhdp.2013.10.009

Treviño, L. K., Hartman, L. P., & Brown, M. (2000). Moral Person and Moral Manager: How Executives Develop a Reputation for Ethical Leadership. *California Management Review, 42*(4), 128–142. doi:10.2307/41166057

Trevino, L. K., & Nelson, K. A. (2004). *Managing business ethics: Straight talk about how to do right.* Hoboken, NJ: Wiley.

Treviño, L. K., Weaver, G. R., Gibson, D. G., & Toffler, B. L. (1999). Managing ethics and legal compliance: What works and what hurts. *California Management Review, 41*(2), 131–151. doi:10.2307/41165990

Trinks, P. J., & Scholtens, B. (2017). The opportunity cost of negative screening in socially responsible investing. *Journal of Business Ethics, 140*(2), 193–208. doi:10.100710551-015-2684-3

Tripathi, V., & Bhandari, V. (2015). Socially responsible stocks: A boon for investors in India. *Journal of Advances in Management Research, 12*(2), 209–225. doi:10.1108/JAMR-03-2014-0021

Tripathy, A. (2017). Translating to risk: The legibility of climate change and nature in the green bond market. *Economic Anthropology, 4*(2), 239–250. doi:10.1002ea2.12091

Trompeter, L. (2017). Green is Good: how Green Bonds Cultivated Into Wall Street's Environmental Paradox. *Sustainable Development Law & Policy, 17*(2), 4-43. Available at: https://papers.ssrn.com/sol3/papers.cfm?abstract_id=2992926

Tsay, Ch.-J., Shu, L. L., & Bazerman, M. (2011). Naiveté and cynicism in negotiations and other competitive contexts. *The Academy of Management Annals, 5*(1), 495–518. doi:10.5465/19416520.2011.587283

Turban, D., & Greening, D. (1997). Corporate social performance and organizational attractiveness to prospective employees. *Academy of Management Journal, 40*(3), 658–672.

Türkel, S., & Akan, A. (2015). Corporate Social Responsibility (CSR) Communication: A Turkish Industry Example. In *Integrated Communications in the Postmodern Era* (pp. 151–174). Palgrave Macmillan. doi:10.1057/9781137388551_7

Turkin, S. (2007). *How to be good: make your business socially responsible.* Moscow: Alpina Pablisher.

Tversky, A., & Kahneman, D. (1974). Judgment under uncertainty: Heuristics and biases. *Science, 185*(4157), 1124–1131. doi:10.1126cience.185.4157.1124 PMID:17835457

U.S. Bureau of Labor Statistics. (2018a). *Employment Situation Summary*. United States Department of Labor. Retrieved January 27, 2019, from: https://www.bls.gov/news.release/empsit.nr0.htm

U.S. Bureau of Labor Statistics. (2018b). *Job Openings and Labor Turnover Survey Highlights*. Retrieved January 27, 2019, from: https://www.bls.gov/web/jolts/jlt_labstatgraphs.pdf

Udayasankar, K. (2008). Corporate social responsibility and firm size. *Journal of Business Ethics*, *83*(2), 167–175. doi:10.100710551-007-9609-8

Ulutaş Duman, D., Giritli, H., & McDermott, P. (2016). Corporate social responsibility in construction industry: A comparative study between UK and Turkey. *Built Environment Project and Asset Management*, *6*(2), 218–231. doi:10.1108/BEPAM-08-2014-0039

UN Global Compact. (n.d.). *The ten principles of the UN global compact*. Retrieved from: https://www.unglobalcompact.org/ what-is-gc/mission/principles

UNEMG. (2011). *Working towards a Balanced and Inclusive Green Economy*. UNEMG.

UNEP. (2008). *Green Jobs: Towards decent work in a sustainable, low carbon world*. UNEP.

UNEP. (2011). *Towards a Green Economy: Pathways to Sustainable Development and Poverty Eradication – Synthesis for Policy Makers*. UNEP.

UNEP. (2015). *Sustainable Consumption and Production Policies and Initiatives in Eastern Europe and the Caucasus: Review of Progress and Way Forward*. Geneva: UNEP.

United Nations Armenia Office. (2012). *"RIO+20" National Assessment Report*. United Nations Armenia Office.

United Nations. (2015). *United Nations Sustainable Development Summit 2015*. Retrieved from https://sustainabledevelopment.un.org/post2015/summit

United Nations. (2018). *United Nations Global Compact*. Retrieved from https://www.unglobalcompact.org/

United Nations. (2019). *Goal 17: Revitalize the global partnership for sustainable development*. Retrieved from https://www.un.org/sustainabledevelopment/globalpartnerships/

USAID. (2007). *National Program on Energy Saving and Renewable Energy of Republic of Armenia*. USAID.

Valenduc, G., & Vendramin, P. (2016). *Work in the digital economy: sorting the old from the new*. Working Paper 2016.03 Brussels: ETUI. Retrieved June 17, 2019, from: http://ftu-namur.org/fichiers/Work_in_the_digital_economy-ETUI2016-3-EN.pdf

Vallentin, S., & Murillo, D. (2012). Governmentality and the politics of CSR. *Organization*, *19*(6), 825–843. doi:10.1177/1350508411426183

Vasilescu, R., Barna, C., Epure, M., & Baicu, C. (2010). Developing university social responsibility: A model for the challenges of the new civil society. *Procedia: Social and Behavioral Sciences*, *2*(2), 4177–4182. doi:10.1016/j.sbspro.2010.03.660

Vazquez-Brust, D., Smith, A. M., & Sarkis, J. (2014). Managing the transition to critical green growth: The 'Green Growth State'. *Futures*, *64*, 38–50. Available at https://researchportal.port.ac.uk/portal/en/publications/managing-the-transition-to-critical-green-growth-the-green-growth-state(4b3e92f0-6ed0-4d25-871f-60f5da4d5c1c)/export.html

Vilanova, M., Lozano, J. M., & Arenas, D. (2009). Exploring the nature of the relationship between CSR and competitiveness. *Journal of Business Ethics*, *87*(1), 57–69. doi:10.100710551-008-9812-2

Viola, I., Ruggeri, F, & Rotondo, G. (2013) Corporate social responsibility and green economy in the agri-food business. *Quality - Access to Success, 14*(1), 151-156.

Visser, W. (2008). Corporate Social Responsibility in Developing Countries. In A. Crane, A. McWilliams, D. Matten, J. Moon, & D. Siegel (Eds.), The Oxford Handbook of Corporate Social Responsibility (pp. 473-479). Oxford, UK: Oxford University Press.

Visser, W. (2006). Revisiting Carroll's CSR pyramid: An African perspective. In M. Huniche & E. R. Pedersen (Eds.), *Corporate citizenship in developing countries: New partnership perspectives* (pp. 29–56). Gylling, Denmark: Narayana Press.

Visser, W. (2007). Revisiting Carroll's CSR pyramid. In A. Crane & D. Matten (Eds.), *An African Perspective*. Nottingham, UK: The University of Nottingham.

Visser, W. (2008). Corporate social responsibility in developing countries. In *The Oxford Handbook of Corporate Social Responsibility*. Oxford University Press.

Visser, W. (2008). Corporate Social Responsibility in Developing Countries. In *The Oxford Handbook of Corporate Social Responsibility*. Oxford University Press.

Vitell, S. J., Dickerson, E. B., & Festervand, T. A. (2000). Ethical problems, conflicts and beliefs of small business professionals. *Journal of Business Ethics, 28*(1), 15–24. doi:10.1023/A:1006217129077

Vives, A. (2004). The Role of Multilateral Development Institutions in Fostering Corporate Social Responsibility. *Development, 47*(3), 45–52. doi:10.1057/palgrave.development.1100065

Vives, A. (2006). Social and environmental responsibility in small and medium enterprises in Latin America. *Journal of Corporate Citizenship, 2006*(21), 39–50. doi:10.9774/GLEAF.4700.2006.sp.00006

Voica, M. C., Panaitb, M., & Radulescu, I. (2015). Green Investments - between necessity, fiscal constraints and profit. *Procedia Economics and Finance, 22*, 72–79. Available at https://www.sciencedirect.com/science/article/pii/S2212567115002282

Voinea, C., & Fratostiteanu, C. (2018). *Corporate Social Responsibility in Emerging Economies. Reality and Illusion*. New York: Routledge. doi:10.4324/9781315112411

Vyakarnam, S., Bailey, A., Myers, A., & Burnett, D. (1997). Towards an understanding of ethical behaviour in small firms. *Journal of Business Ethics, 16*(15), 1625–1636. doi:10.1023/A:1022452502299

Waddock, S. A., Bodwell, C., & Graves, S. B. (2002). Responsibility: The new business imperative. *The Academy of Management Perspectives, 16*(2), 132–148. doi:10.5465/ame.2002.7173581

Waddock, S. A., & Graves, S. B. (1997). The corporate social performance–financial performance link. *Strategic Management Journal, 18*(4), 303–319. doi:10.1002/(SICI)1097-0266(199704)18:4<303::AID-SMJ869>3.0.CO;2-G

Waldman, D. A., De Luque, M. S., Washburn, N., House, R. J., Adetoun, B., Barrasa, A., ... Debbarma, S. (2006). Cultural and leadership predictors of corporate social responsibility values of top management: A GLOBE study of 15 countries. *Journal of International Business Studies, 37*(6), 823–837. doi:10.1057/palgrave.jibs.8400230

Walker, H., & Brammer, S. (2009). Sustainable procurement in the United Kingdom public sector. *Supply Chain Management, 14*(2), 128–137. doi:10.1108/13598540910941993

Walker, M., Aubrey, K., & Vincent, J. (2010). Communicating Socially Responsible Initiatives: An Analysis of U.S. Professional Teams. *Sport Marketing Quarterly, 19*(4), 187–195.

Walsh, G., & Bartikowski, B. (2013). Exploring corporate ability and social responsibility associations as antecedents of customer satisfaction cross-culturally. *Journal of Business Research*, *66*(8), 989–995. doi:10.1016/j.jbusres.2011.12.022

Walton, C. (1967). *Corporate Social Responsibilities* (1st ed.). Belmont, CA: Wadsworth Publishing Company.

Walwei, U. (2016). *Digitalization and structural labour market problems: The case of Germany*. ILO Research Paper No. 17. Retrieved May 12, 2019, from: https://www.ilo.org/wcmsp5/groups/public/---dgreports/---inst/documents/publication/wcms_522355.pdf

Wang, H., Tong, L., Takeuchi, R., & George, G. (2016). Corporate social responsibility: An overview and new research directions. *Thematic issue on corporate social responsibility*, 534-544.

Wang, H., & Qian, C. (2011). Corporate Philanthropy and Corporate Financial Performance: The Roles of Stakeholder Response and Political Access. *Academy of Management Journal*, *54*(6), 1159–1181. doi:10.5465/amj.2009.0548

Wang, Q., Dou, J., & Jia, S. (2015). A meta-analytic review of corporate social responsibility and corporate financial performance: The moderating effect of contextual factors. *Business & Society*, *1*, 1–39.

Warhurst, A. (2001). Corporate Citizenship and Corporate Social Investment. *Journal of Corporate Citizenship*, *2001*(1), 57–73. doi:10.9774/GLEAF.4700.2001.sp.00008

Waslander, J., & Vallejos, P. Q. (2018). *Setting the stage for the green climate fund's first replenishment. Working paper*. World Resources Institute. Available at https://www.wri.org/publication/green-climate-fund-first-replenishment

Webb, T. (2011). *The CSR/Sustainability Business. Case for SMEs*. Ethical Corporation.

Weber, M. (2008). The business case for corporate social responsibility: A company-level measurement approach for CSR. *European Management Journal*, *26*(4), 247–261. doi:10.1016/j.emj.2008.01.006

Welford, R., & Frost, S. (2006). Corporate social responsibility in Asian supply chains. *Corporate Social Responsibility and Environmental Management*, *13*(3), 166–176. doi:10.1002/csr.121

Werther, W. B., & Chandler, D. (2006). *Strategic corporate social responsibility: Stakeholders in a global environment*. Thousand Oaks, CA: Sage.

Werther, W. B. Jr, & Chandler, D. (2005). Strategic corporate social responsibility as global brand insurance. *Business Horizons*, *48*(4), 317–324. doi:10.1016/j.bushor.2004.11.009

Whieldon, E. (2019). *S&P Ratings forecasts moderate green bond market growth in 2019*. Available at: https://www.spglobal.com/marketintelligence/en/news-insights/trending/P9Lq4MCmw-HL6iMRUKgEHg2

Whitcomb, L. L., Erdener, C. B., & Li, C. (1998). Business Ethical Values in China and the U.S. *Journal of Business Ethics*, *17*(8), 839–852. doi:10.1023/A:1005793424492

Why companies can no longer afford to ignore their social responsibilities. (2012). *Time Business and Money*.

Williams, G. (2005). *Are socially responsible investors different from conventional investors? A comparison across six countries*. Unpublished working paper, University of Bath.

Willis, A. (2003). The role of the global reporting initiative's sustainability reporting guidelines in the social screening of investments. *Journal of Business Ethics*, *43*(3), 233–237. doi:10.1023/A:1022958618391

Windsor, D. (2013). Corporate social responsibility and irresponsibility: A positive theory approach. *Journal of Business Research*, *66*(10), 1937–1944. doi:10.1016/j.jbusres.2013.02.016

Wolde-Rufael, Y. (2010). Bounds test approach to cointegration and causality between nuclear energy consumption and economic growth in India. *Energy Policy*, *38*(1), 52–58. doi:10.1016/j.enpol.2009.08.053

Wolde-Rufael, Y., & Menyah, K. (2010). Nuclear energy consumption and economic growth in nine developed countries. *Energy Economics*, *32*(3), 550–556. doi:10.1016/j.eneco.2010.01.004

Wolff, M. (2002). Response to "Confronting the critics.". *New Academy Review*, *1*, 230–237.

Workplace Research Centre. (2007). *Skills and Sustainable Business Development*. A report to the NSW Board of Vocational Education and Training, University of Sydney.

World Economic Forum. (2013). *The Green Investment Report*. Available at: http://www3.weforum.org/docs/WEF_Green-Investment_Report_2013.pdf

Yadav, P. L., Han, S. H., & Rho, J. J. (2016). Impact of Environmental Performance on Firm Value for Sustainable Investment: Evidence from Large US Firms. *Business Strategy and the Environment*, *25*, 402–420. Available at https://onlinelibrary.wiley.com/doi/abs/10.1002/bse.1883

Yang, F. J., Lin, C. W., & Chang, Y. N. (2010). The linkage between corporate social performance and corporate financial performance. *African Journal of Business Management*, *4*(4), 406–413.

Yaniv, E., & Farkas, F. (2005). The impact of person-organization fit on the corporate brand perception of employees and of customers. *Journal of Change Management*, *5*(4), 447–461. doi:10.1080/14697010500372600

Yoo, S. H., & Ku, S. J. (2009). Causal relationship between nuclear energy consumption and economic growth: A multi-country analysis. *Energy Policy*, *37*(5), 1905–1913. doi:10.1016/j.enpol.2009.01.012

Yue, Sh., Yang, Y., & Hu, Y. (2016). Does Foreign Direct Investment Affect Green Growth? Evidence from China's Experience. *Sustainability*, *8*(158), 2–14. Available at https://www.researchgate.net/publication/295101572_Does_Foreign_Direct_Investment_Affect_Green_Growth_Evidence_from_China's_Experience

Zahariev, E. (2013). *Challenges before the industrial management: priorities and solutions*. Plovdiv, Bulgaria: Talent Academic Publishing House at the University of Agribusiness and Rural Development.

Zahariev, E., & Arabska, E. (2015). Corporate social responsibility and organic production business model – sustainability performance, consumer trust and motivation. *Proceedings of IV International scientific conference Clımate Change, Economıc Development, Envıronment and People Conference (CCEDEP) under the subtopic Regional development of Central and Eastern European countries, 7-9 October 2014, UARD – Plovdiv, 2*, 285-296.

Zhang, D., Jiang, Q., Ma, X., & Li, B. (2014). Drivers for food risk management and corporate social responsibility; a case of Chinese food companies. *Journal of Cleaner Production*, *66*, 520–527. doi:10.1016/j.jclepro.2013.11.075

Ziegler, A., & Schröder, M. (2010). What determines the inclusion in a sustainability stock index?: A panel data analysis for european firms. *Ecological Economics*, *69*(4), 848–856. doi:10.1016/j.ecolecon.2009.10.009

Zu, L., & Song, L. (2009). Determinants of managerial values on corporate social responsibility: Evidence from China. *Journal of Business Ethics*, *88*(S1), 105–117. doi:10.100710551-008-9828-7

About the Contributors

Anetta Kuna-Marszałek has Ph.D., is an associate professor, the Head at the Department of International Trade in Institute of Economics, University of Łódź (Poland). Her primary research interests focus on various aspects of contemporary economics, including research on corporate social responsibility, green economy, internationalization of business activities, foreign direct investment and the interlinks between trade liberalization and environmental policies. She is an author and co-author of over 80 papers, chapters and articles including the award-winning books about (1) Poland's outward foreign direct investments and (2) anti-dumping investigations as an instrument of contingent protection. She participated in several research projects, including projects co-financed by the EU and the National Science Centre. She is a member to several prestigious international organizations.

Agnieszka Kłysik-Uryszek holds a Ph.D. degree in economics. She works as an assistant professor in the Department of International Trade, Institute of Economics, University of Łódź (Poland). From the very beginning of an academic career, her interests focused on different aspects of the process of internationalization of companies: organizational, strategic, marketing and financial. She has been involved in several research projects (of which 3 were financed by EU Funds and National Science Center) which resulted in more than 40 publications (books, chapters, and articles). She is a member of Eurasia Business and Economics Society. Her professional experience include also a position of Editorial Secretary of Acta Universitatis Lodziensis Folia Oeconomica (2009 – 2012) and Dean's Plenipotentiary responsible for managing the EU programme of international internships for students - Leonardo (2004-2008). Additionally, she actively cooperates with business entities helping companies to analyze their strategic position and prepare their international development strategies.

* * *

Gagik Aghajanyan is the head Chair of Environmental Economy at Armenian State University of Economics (ASUE). Having PhD in Economics, he continued his lifelong learning in University of Catalonia (Spain), also getting Master's degree in "Management of food security program". He has got several certificates on «Food Balances as a Policy Analysis and Decision Making Tool» within the framework of the EC / FAO Decision Making Improvement Program for 2010-2012; «Agricultural Policy for Rural Economic Development and Food Security and Poverty Reduction in the Eastern Region of the European Neighborhood Policy» within the framework of the European Neighborhood Policy Eastern Partnership for Information Systems Decision Making Process. His interests' area also include education quality assurance. He also worked as quality assurance specialist at ASUE. He is an author of more than 25 publications in the area of food security, ecological problems, nutrition improvement, sustainable development, climate change management, social protection. He is actively participating in different environmental initiatives, tries to promote environmental thinking and the essence of environmental education, to promote ecological upbringing and culture, to harmonize the interactions of man, society and the natural environment with the development of a fully developed person. He is actively participating in the discussion of state policy on ecological education.

Susanna Aghajanyan is an assistant professor at the chair of International Economic Relations at Armenian State University of Economics (ASUE). She has got PhD in World Economy. She has participated in United Nations-DESA Symposium "Mainstreaming Sector Policies into Integrated National Sustainable Development Planning: Enhancing Sustainable Tourism, Urbanization, Resource Efficiency, Biodiversity and Environmental protection", as well as Eurhodip 23rd conference "Tourism education: on the road to new destinations" Her main area of interests include international economic relations, the activity of transnational corporation, competitiveness integration and globalization, global economic problems, as well as tourism markets and hospitality. She has more than 10 scientific publications She has about 15 year experience in managing pharmaceutical company. Susanna is actively participating in international exchange programs and had lectures in many European universities.

George Kofi Amoako, BSc (Hons, KNUST); MBA (Marketing, UG); PhD (LondonMet) Chartered Marketer-CIM-UK Profile George Kofi Amoako, is a senior lecturer and head of department at Marketing Department of Central Business School, Central University in Accra Ghana, an academic and a practising Chartered Marketer (CIM_UK) with specialization in Branding, CSR and Strategic Marketing. He was educated in Kwame Nkrumah University of Science and Technology in Kumasi Ghana and at the University of Ghana and the London School of Marketing (UK). He obtained his PhD at London Metropolitan University UK. He has considerable research, teaching, consulting and practise experience in the application of Marketing Theory and principles to everyday marketing challenges and management and Organisational issues. He is a Chartered Marketer with The Chartered Institute of Marketing-UK. He has consulted for Public Sector and Private organisations both in Ghana and UK. George has published extensively in internationally peer-reviewed academic journals and presented many papers at international conferences

Ekaterina Arabska, Assoc. Prof. Ekaterina Arabska, Ph.D. is working on the issues of sustainable development in its different aspects - economic, ecological and social, incl. studies on the development of the concept of CSR and its implementation in Bulgaria. Her educational and scientific background is in the field of human resources management, labor market and social policy, project management, vocational training and higher education management, sustainable business models. She is the author of more than 250 research papers presented and published in international conferences and journals. Vice-rector of University of agribusiness and rural development, Plovdiv, Bulgaria. Member of non-profit organizations working in the field of science and education, editorial boards of scientific journals and organizational and scientific committees of international scientific and practical conferences.

Bela Bataeva is a Professor at the Department of Corporate Finance and Corporate Governance of the Finance University under the Government of Russian Federation, Moscow, Russia. B. Bataeva received her Ph.D degree in Economics from the Finance University under the Government of Russian Federation in 2010. Her research interests cover corporate governance, corporate social responsibility (CSR) and corporate values of modern businesses, with over 170 published monographs, working papers and articles. Professor Bataeva is the chief editor of the scientific journal «Discussion» supported by the Higher Attestation Commission of the Ministry of Education of the Russian Federation; she is also a member of the Russian Association of Independent Directors, National Association of Directors, European Network of the Association of Business Ethics and CSR, Russian Business Ethics Network etc. Professor Bataeva serves as an independent director in several boards of Russian public companies.

Hristina Vilhelm Blagoycheva received her MS in University of Economics – Varna, Varna, Bulgaria in 1991. In 1997 she was hired as assistant at Finance Department, University of Economics – Varna. Since 2007 she gets Ph.D. degree. Since 2011 she is Associated professor. Since 2019 she is Dean of the Faculty of Finance and Accounting, University of Economics – Varna. She writes and presents on issues of social security, corporate social responsibility and social innovations. She is an author of 84 publications in Bulgaria and abroad with more than 100 citations of her publications.

Mark Anthony Camilleri is an Associate Professor in the Department of Corporate Communication at the University of Malta. He successfully finalised his full-time PhD (Management) at the University of Edinburgh in Scotland - where he was also nominated for his "Excellence in Teaching". Dr Camilleri is a member in the Global Reporting Initiative (GRI)'s Stakeholder Council, where he is representing the European civil society organisations. He is a scientific expert in research for the Ministero dell' Istruzione, dell' Universita e della Ricerca (in Italy) and a reviewer for the Austrian Science Fund (FWF). He is an editorial board member in a number of journals and conference committees. He is a frequent speaker at the Academy of Marketing Science (USA), Academy of Management (USA) and in the British Academy of Management annual gatherings.

Hamit Can has a Ph.D. from the Department of Programming and Computer Technologies at Technical University of Sofia (Sofia, Bulgaria). He completed his master's degree in Economics, from the Namık Kemal University (Tekirdağ, Turkey). His research interests include Artificial Intelligence, Programming Languages, Energy Economics. He has many articles in prestigious journals.

Burak Çapraz is an associate professor of management in the Department of Business Administration at Ege University, İzmir Turkey. He is also a member of Quality Commission of Ege University and acting as advisor for Human Resources Coordinatorship of Ege University. His research interest focus on OD & Strategy (Inter-organizational Linkages, Strategic HR, Innovation Management). His teaching areas are Strategic Management and Human Resources Management. He has also consultancy experience on strategic planning, human resources information systems, digitalization of HR, and risk management.

Liudmila Cheglakova is an Associate Professor of the Department of Human Resources Management at the School of Business Administration of the Faculty of Business and Management at the National Research University "Higher School of Economics", Moscow, Russia. In 2006 L. Cheglakova received her doctoral degree in social sciences from the Saratov State Technical University, Saratov, Russia. Her research interests include business ethics, sustainability, corporate social responsibility (CSR), specifically individual, organizational and environmental factors for ethical decision-making process; corporate culture and values, employee engagement, industrial relations, manufacturing management. Liudmila Cheglakova combines activities in academic and research areas with a consulting practice, which allows her to interact directly with Russian businesses from different industries and scale of operations.

Sajad Nabi Dar is an Assistant Professor, in the Department of Geography, Lovely Professional University, Jalandhar-Punjab (India) for last 1 year. He completed his PhD and M.Phil from the Department of Geography, University of Kashmir-J and K (India). The author has published one book and a number of research papers in national and international journals of repute.

Kwasi Dartey-Baah is the Head of the Department of Organisation & Human Resource Management, University of Ghana Business School. He holds a PhD in Leadership and Human Resource Development from Trinity College, USA and Canterbury University, United Kingdom and a Civil Engineering Degree from Imperial College, London. He has significant experience in industry and academia. He serves on numerous committees in the University of Ghana. He's an assessor for National Accreditation Board, Ghana and serves on the Grievance Review Committee of Ghana's Fair Wages and Salaries Commission. He reviews for reputable international journals and has published extensively in Leadership, CSR and Oil & Gas.

Aura Draksaite is an Associate Professor in the School of Economics and Business at Kaunas University of Technology, a member of Sustainable Economics research group. She obtained her Ph. D. degree in Economics at Kaunas University of Technology in 2013. Her main research interests are in Sustainable Finance, Financial Technology Innovations, and Investment Strategies.

Justyna Fijałkowska is an associate professor at the University of Lodz and the University of Social Sciences in Lodz, Poland as well as at Clark University Worcester USA, branch campus in Lodz and Warsaw. She received her PhD in Management. Her scientific interests include: CSR, integrated reporting, intellectual capital, intangibles, accountability of universities. She is an author and co-author of several scientific publications in the area of CSR, IR, intangibles, accountability, harmonization, and standardization of accounting, published in international refereed journals, national journals, chapters in collective works published in Polish, English, and Portuguese. She is a member of the European Accounting Association and Le Réseau Universitaire des Pays du Groupe de Vysegrad (PGV Research Network).

Vilma Kazlauskiene is an Associate Professor in the department of Finance at Vytautas Magnus University. She obtained her Ph.D. degree in Economics at Kaunas University of Technology in 2005. She has coauthored over 20 publications. She is interested in Sustainable Finance, Green Investment, Cost-Benefit Analysis of Public Investment Projects.

Ayesha Khatun is an Assistant Professor in the Dept. of Management, Mittal School of Business, Lovely Professional University, Punjab (India). The author completed her masters in Management Science and pursued PhD on Knowledge Management from Assam University, Silchar (India). She has 5 years of teaching experience and has number of book chapters and research papers published to her credit.

Remya Lathabhavan is an Senior Assistant Professor at Department of Technology Management of VIT University, Vellore, India. Her research interests include Glass Ceiling, Human Resource Management and Career Progression. She (co-)authored many publications in peer reviewed journals.

Małgorzata Macuda, PhD, is an Assistant Professor in the Department of Managerial Accounting at the Poznań University of Economics and Business. Her PhD thesis received the 2nd degree award in the competition of the Scientific Council of the Accountants Association in Poland for the best habilitation, doctoral and master theses in accounting. Her research interests include: financial accounting, cost accounting, operational and strategic management accounting, corporate social responsibility and hospital accounting. She is an author and a co-author of c.a. 40 scientific publications (monographies, articles, conference papers). She is a member of European Accounting Association (EAA), International Association for Accounting Education & Research (IAAER) and Association Internationale des Economistes de Langue Française (AIELF). In 2016-2017 she was a secretary of the international journal La Revue Internationale des Economistes de Langue Française (RIELF).

Olga Melitonyan is an Associate Professor of the Department of General and Strategic Management at the School of Business Administration of the Faculty of Business and Management at the National Research University "Higher School of Economics", Moscow, Russia. O. Melitonyan received her Ph. D. degree in Economics in 2005 from the State University of Management, Moscow, Russia. For a number of years Olga Melitonyan worked as a Deputy Head of the Corporate Governance Center at the National Research University "Higher School of Economics" which was created in the framework of a joint educational initiative in the field of corporate governance by the Schulich School of Business, York University, Toronto, Canada, and NRU "Higher School of Economics". At the moment, Olga Melitonyan acts successfully as a lecturer, a researcher and a business consultant. Her research interests include corporate governance, corporate strategy, corporate social responsibility, corporations in public policy, change management.

Daniela Minkovska is Assoc. Prof. PhD in the professional research field of Communication and computer technologies and Vice dean of Faculty of Computer Systems and Technologies at Technical University of Sofia (Sofia, Bulgaria). She has Ph.D. degree in the specialty "Automation of non-material's sphere (medicine, education, science, administration)" in the field of modeling and automation of the learning process – e-learning systems. She has 34 years of experience in educational sector. Her main research interests are in the field of Programming Languages, Information Systems, Methodologies and Technologies for E-learning, Systems for Assessment in the Education, Multimedia Technologies, Multimedia in Education, Virtual Reality and Cloud Computing. She has experience in many scientific projects including Erasmus+ projects.

Cornelia Philipova is assistance at the Finance department in the University of Economics – Varna, Bulgaria. Since 25th October 2017 she is also PhD candidate at the same department. The topic of her dissertation is related to government expenditures for social assistance and poverty in Bulgaria. Her general scientific interests are in the fields: Public Finances, Insurance and Social Security, EU Finances, Social Assistance and Social Welfare. She is co-author of three textbooks, a chapter, four articles and fifteen scientific papers.

Julia M. Puaschunder is educated as a behavioral economist with doctorates in Social and Economic Sciences and Natural Sciences, and Master's degrees in Business, Public Administration and Philosophy/ Psychology as well as training in Global Political Economy and Finance, Julia Margarete Puaschunder has over 15 years of experience in applied social sciences empirical research in the international arena. Before starting a Prize Fellowship in the Inter-University Consortium of New York at The New School with placements at Columbia University and Princeton University, she held several postdoctoral positions at Harvard University and the Vienna University of Economics and Business. She has published numerous books and journal articles, and was awarded the 2018 Albert Nelson Marquis Lifetime Achievement Award. She has also been included in the '2018 Marquis Who's Who in America and in the World', and is an official listee of the '2019 Marquis Who's Who in the World' among the top 3% of professionals around the globe.

Index

Purchase Print, E-Book, or Print + E-Book

IGI Global's reference books are available in three unique pricing formats:
Print Only, E-Book Only, or Print + E-Book.
Shipping fees may apply.

www.igi-global.com

Recommended Reference Books

ISBN: 978-1-5225-6201-6
© 2019; 341 pp.
List Price: $345

ISBN: 978-1-5225-7262-6
© 2019; 360 pp.
List Price: $215

ISBN: 978-1-5225-8003-4
© 2019; 216 pp.
List Price: $205

ISBN: 978-1-5225-5763-0
© 2019; 304 pp.
List Price: $205

ISBN: 978-1-5225-6980-0
© 2019; 325 pp.
List Price: $235

ISBN: 978-1-5225-7808-6
© 2019; 397 pp.
List Price: $215

Do you want to stay current on the latest research trends, product announcements, news and special offers?
Join IGI Global's mailing list today and start enjoying exclusive perks sent only to IGI Global members.
Add your name to the list at **www.igi-global.com/newsletters.**

Publisher of Peer-Reviewed, Timely, and Innovative Academic Research

IGI Global
DISSEMINATOR OF KNOWLEDGE

www.igi-global.com | Sign up at www.igi-global.com/newsletters | facebook.com/igiglobal | twitter.com/igiglobal | linkedin.com/igiglobal

Ensure Quality Research is Introduced to the Academic Community

Become an IGI Global Reviewer for Authored Book Projects

The overall success of an authored book project is dependent on quality and timely reviews.

In this competitive age of scholarly publishing, constructive and timely feedback significantly expedites the turnaround time of manuscripts from submission to acceptance, allowing the publication and discovery of forward-thinking research at a much more expeditious rate. Several IGI Global authored book projects are currently seeking highly-qualified experts in the field to fill vacancies on their respective editorial review boards:

Applications and Inquiries may be sent to:
development@igi-global.com

Applicants must have a doctorate (or an equivalent degree) as well as publishing and reviewing experience. Reviewers are asked to complete the open-ended evaluation questions with as much detail as possible in a timely, collegial, and constructive manner. All reviewers' tenures run for one-year terms on the editorial review boards and are expected to complete at least three reviews per term. Upon successful completion of this term, reviewers can be considered for an additional term.

If you have a colleague that may be interested in this opportunity,
we encourage you to share this information with them.

IGI Global Proudly Partners With eContent Pro International

Receive a 25% Discount on all Editorial Services

Editorial Services

IGI Global expects all final manuscripts submitted for publication to be in their final form. This means they must be reviewed, revised, and professionally copy edited prior to their final submission. Not only does this support with accelerating the publication process, but it also ensures that the highest quality scholarly work can be disseminated.

English Language Copy Editing

Let eContent Pro International's expert copy editors perform edits on your manuscript to resolve spelling, punctuaion, grammar, syntax, flow, formatting issues and more.

Scientific and Scholarly Editing

Allow colleagues in your research area to examine the content of your manuscript and provide you with valuable feedback and suggestions before submission.

Figure, Table, Chart & Equation Conversions

Do you have poor quality figures? Do you need visual elements in your manuscript created or converted? A design expert can help!

Translation

Need your documjent translated into English? eContent Pro International's expert translators are fluent in English and more than 40 different languages.

Hear What Your Colleagues are Saying About Editorial Services Supported by IGI Global

"The service was very fast, very thorough, and very helpful in ensuring our chapter meets the criteria and requirements of the book's editors. I was quite impressed and happy with your service."

– Prof. Tom Brinthaupt,
Middle Tennessee State University, USA

"I found the work actually spectacular. The editing, formatting, and other checks were very thorough. The turnaround time was great as well. I will definitely use eContent Pro in the future."

– Nickanor Amwata, Lecturer,
University of Kurdistan Hawler, Iraq

"I was impressed that it was done timely, and wherever the content was not clear for the reader, the paper was improved with better readability for the audience."

– Prof. James Chilembwe,
Mzuzu University, Malawi

Email: customerservice@econtentpro.com

www.igi-global.com/editorial-service-partners

IGI Global
DISSEMINATOR OF KNOWLEDGE
www.igi-global.com

Celebrating Over 30 Years of Scholarly Knowledge Creation & Dissemination

InfoSci®-Books

A Database of Over 5,300+ Reference Books Containing Over 100,000+ Chapters Focusing on Emerging Research

GAIN ACCESS TO **THOUSANDS** OF REFERENCE BOOKS AT **A FRACTION** OF THEIR INDIVIDUAL LIST **PRICE**.

InfoSci®-Books Database

The **InfoSci®-Books** database is a collection of over 5,300+ IGI Global single and multi-volume reference books, handbooks of research, and encyclopedias, encompassing groundbreaking research from prominent experts worldwide that span over 350+ topics in 11 core subject areas including business, computer science, education, science and engineering, social sciences and more.

Open Access Fee Waiver (Offset Model) Initiative

For any library that invests in IGI Global's InfoSci-Journals and/or InfoSci-Books databases, IGI Global will match the library's investment with a fund of equal value to go toward **subsidizing the OA article processing charges (APCs) for their students, faculty, and staff** at that institution when their work is submitted and accepted under OA into an IGI Global journal.*

INFOSCI® PLATFORM FEATURES

- No DRM
- No Set-Up or Maintenance Fees
- A Guarantee of No More Than a 5% Annual Increase
- Full-Text HTML and PDF Viewing Options
- Downloadable MARC Records
- Unlimited Simultaneous Access
- COUNTER 5 Compliant Reports
- Formatted Citations With Ability to Export to RefWorks and EasyBib
- No Embargo of Content (Research is Available Months in Advance of the Print Release)

**The fund will be offered on an annual basis and expire at the end of the subscription period. The fund would renew as the subscription is renewed for each year thereafter. The open access fees will be waived after the student, faculty, or staff's paper has been vetted and accepted into an IGI Global journal and the fund can only be used toward publishing OA in an IGI Global journal. Libraries in developing countries will have the match on their investment doubled.*

To Learn More or To Purchase This Database:
www.igi-global.com/infosci-books
eresources@igi-global.com • Toll Free: 1-866-342-6657 ext. 100 • Phone: 717-533-8845 x100

IGI Global
DISSEMINATOR OF KNOWLEDGE
www.igi-global.com

IGI Global
DISSEMINATOR OF KNOWLEDGE
www.igi-global.com

Publisher of Peer-Reviewed, Timely, and Innovative Academic Research Since 1988

IGI Global's Transformative Open Access (OA) Model: How to Turn Your University Library's Database Acquisitions Into a Source of OA Funding

In response to the OA movement and well in advance of Plan S, IGI Global, early last year, unveiled their OA Fee Waiver (Offset Model) Initiative.

Under this initiative, librarians who invest in IGI Global's InfoSci-Books (5,300+ reference books) and/or InfoSci-Journals (185+ scholarly journals) databases will be able to subsidize their patron's OA article processing charges (APC) when their work is submitted and accepted (after the peer review process) into an IGI Global journal.*

How Does it Work?

1. When a library subscribes or perpetually purchases IGI Global's InfoSci-Databases including InfoSci-Books (5,300+ e-books), InfoSci-Journals (185+ e-journals), and/or their discipline/subject-focused subsets, IGI Global will match the library's investment with a fund of equal value to go toward subsidizing the OA article processing charges (APCs) for their patrons.

   Researchers: Be sure to recommend the InfoSci-Books and InfoSci-Journals to take advantage of this initiative.
2. When a student, faculty, or staff member submits a paper and it is accepted (following the peer review) into one of IGI Global's 185+ scholarly journals, the author will have the option to have their paper published under a traditional publishing model or as OA.
3. When the author chooses to have their paper published under OA, IGI Global will notify them of the OA Fee Waiver (Offset Model) Initiative. If the author decides they would like to take advantage of this initiative, IGI Global will deduct the US$ 1,500 APC from the created fund.
4. This fund will be offered on an annual basis and will renew as the subscription is renewed for each year thereafter. IGI Global will manage the fund and award the APC waivers unless the librarian has a preference as to how the funds should be managed.

Hear From the Experts on This Initiative:

"I'm very happy to have been able to make one of my recent research contributions, 'Visualizing the Social Media Conversations of a National Information Technology Professional Association' featured in the *International Journal of Human Capital and Information Technology Professionals*, freely available along with having access to the valuable resources found within IGI Global's InfoSci-Journals database."

– **Prof. Stuart Palmer**, Deakin University, Australia

For More Information, Visit: www.igi-global.com/publish/contributor-resources/open-access or contact IGI Global's Database Team at eresources@igi-global.com.

Are You Ready to Publish Your Research?

IGI Global
DISSEMINATOR OF KNOWLEDGE

IGI Global offers book authorship and editorship opportunities across 11 subject areas, including business, computer science, education, science and engineering, social sciences, and more!

Benefits of Publishing with IGI Global:

- Free one-on-one editorial and promotional support.
- Expedited publishing timelines that can take your book from start to finish in less than one (1) year.
- Choose from a variety of formats including: Edited and Authored References, Handbooks of Research, Encyclopedias, and Research Insights.
- Utilize IGI Global's eEditorial Discovery® submission system in support of conducting the submission and blind review process.
- IGI Global maintains a strict adherence to ethical practices due in part to our full membership with the Committee on Publication Ethics (COPE).
- Indexing potential in prestigious indices such as Scopus®, Web of Science™, PsycINFO®, and ERIC – Education Resources Information Center.
- Ability to connect your ORCID iD to your IGI Global publications.
- Earn royalties on your publication as well as receive complimentary copies and exclusive discounts.

Get Started Today by Contacting the Acquisitions Department at:

acquisition@igi-global.com

www.igi-global.com/infosci-ondemand

InfoSci®-OnDemand

Continuously updated with new material on a weekly basis, InfoSci®-OnDemand offers the ability to search through thousands of quality full-text research papers. Users can narrow each search by identifying key topic areas of interest, then display a complete listing of relevant papers, and purchase materials specific to their research needs.

Comprehensive Service

- Over 125,000+ journal articles, book chapters, and case studies.
- All content is downloadable in PDF and HTML format and can be stored locally for future use.

No Subscription Fees

- One time fee of $37.50 per PDF download.

Instant Access

- Receive a download link immediately after order completion!

"It really provides an excellent entry into the research literature of the field. It presents a manageable number of highly relevant sources on topics of interest to a wide range of researchers. The sources are scholarly, but also accessible to 'practitioners'."

- Lisa Stimatz, MLS, University of North Carolina at Chapel Hill, USA

"It is an excellent and well designed database which will facilitate research, publication, and teaching. It is a very useful tool to have."

- George Ditsa, PhD, University of Wollongong, Australia

"I have accessed the database and find it to be a valuable tool to the IT/IS community. I found valuable articles meeting my search criteria 95% of the time."

- Prof. Lynda Louis, Xavier University of Louisiana, USA

Recommended for use by researchers who wish to immediately download PDFs of individual chapters or articles.

www.igi-global.com/e-resources/infosci-ondemand

IGI Global
DISSEMINATOR OF KNOWLEDGE
www.igi-global.com

www.ingramcontent.com/pod-product-compliance
Lightning Source LLC
LaVergne TN
LVHW060413300926
849162LV00006B/1417